CW01065219

ANTIQUARIES

Antiquaries

The Discovery of the Past in Eighteenth-Century Britain

Rosemary Sweet

Hambledon and London
London and New York

Hambledon and London

102 Gloucester Avenue
London, NW1 8HX

175 Fifth Avenue
New York, NY 10010
USA

First Published 2004

ISBN 1 85285 309 3

A description of this book is available from the
British Library and from the Library of Congress.

Typeset by Carnegie Publishing, Lancaster,
and printed in Great Britain by Cambridge University Press

Distributed in the United States and Canada
exclusively by Palgrave Macmillan,
A division of St Martin's Press.

Contents

Illustrations

Between Pages 74 and 75

Between Pages 138 and 139

Between Pages 234 and 235

Text Illustrations

For JPMS and MVS

Acknowledgements

In writing this book I have benefited from the knowledge and expertise of many scholars. Foremost amongst these has been Julian Pooley, whose enthusiasm for eighteenth-century antiquaries matches my own and who has been unfailingly generous in fielding queries and offering suggestions. Michael Honeybone kindly allowed me to read and use unpublished papers. Hannah Barker, Peter Borsay, Elaine Chalus, Paul Elliott, Joanna Innes, Paul Langford, Susan Skedd and David Wykes provided advice, assistance and encouragement during the period of research and writing. I began this book whilst still a junior research fellow at St John's College Oxford and I would like to thank the fellows for supporting the early stages of my research. Most of the research and writing has been completed whilst teaching in the Department of Economic and Social History at the University of Leicester, now the School of Historical Studies. The support of colleagues in the School during my time at Leicester has been a great strength in both academic and personal terms, and in particular I must pay tribute to the sanity, patience and friendship of Jo Story and Robert Colls. If this book is too antiquarian, it is not their fault. I am also grateful for the generous hospitality – provided on numerous occasions – of family and friends in Edinburgh, Oxford, Cambridge and London. Elizabeth Stone read the proofs promptly and meticulously. Finally, I must thank my editors at Hambledon, Tony Morris and Martin Sheppard. Tony's enthusiasm at the onset encouraged me to embark upon the project; Martin's efficiency and exemplary attention to detail brought it to fruition.

I am grateful to the Special Collections Librarian and the Society of Antiquaries of London for permission to reproduce the illustrations and to Sir Robert Clerk of Penicuik for permission to quote from family papers. I would also like to thank the staff at the many archives and libraries who have allowed me to use their collections and have assisted me with my research. These include the staff at the Manuscripts Reading Room and the Rare Books Room of the British Library; the Bodleian Library, Oxford; the Rare Books Room at Cambridge University Library; the Parker Library, Corpus Christi College, Cambridge; Enfield Local Studies Library; the Gentlemen's Society of Spalding; Lambeth Palace Library; the University of

Leicester Special Collections; Chetham's Library, Manchester; John Rylands Library, Manchester; the National Library of Scotland; Bernard Nurse and Adrian Jones at the Society of Antiquaries of London; St John's College Library, Oxford; the Huntington Library, San Marino, California; Colchester Record Office; Leicester, Leicestershire and Rutland Record Office; Norfolk and Norwich Record Office; National Archives of Scotland; Surrey History Centre; Warwickshire Record Office and West Suffolk Record Office. I would like to thank the Faculty of Social Sciences at the University of Leicester and the British Academy for grants towards travel expenses which made the necessary research trips possible. This book was only completed because I was able to enjoy a year's study leave, for which I must thank the University of Leicester, and in particular my colleagues in the School of Historical Studies, and the Arts and Humanities Research Board for the award of a grant under their Research Leave Scheme.

Illustration Acknowledgements

The author and publishers are most grateful to the following for permission to reproduce illustrations: Julian Pooley, plates 3, 6–9, 11–13 and page 315; the Society of Antiquaries, plates 2, 4, 5, 16, 17, 20–22, 24, 25, 28, 29, 35 and pages xvii, 85, 123, 193, 239; Special Collections, University of Leicester, plates 14, 15, 19, 23, 26, 27, 30–34, 36, 37 and pages 7, 50, 169, 281. Plate 10 comes from a private collection.

Introduction

Antiquaries are an easy target for those wishing to display the superiority of their literary or critical faculties. The pejorative overtones of the word 'antiquarian' have a long history which dates back to the seventeenth century. John Earle identified the type in *Micro-Cosmographie*, first published in 1628:

> Hee is one that hath that unnaturall disease to bee enamour'd of old age, and wrinckles, and loves all things (as Dutchmen doe Cheese) the better for being mouldy and worme-eaten. He is of our Religion, because wee say it is most ancient; and yet a broken Statue would almost make him an Idolater. A great admirer hee is of the rust of old Monuments, and reades onely those characters, where time hath eaten out the letters. Hee will goe you forty miles to see a Saint's Well, or a ruin'd Abbey: and if there be but a Crosse or stone footstoole in the way, hee'l be considering it so long, till he forget his journey.[1]

Earle's satirical caricature of antiquarianism, presented as both ridiculous and futile, proved instantly recognisable and equally durable. A succession of literary wits built upon this stereotype of the scholar with an unnatural and unhealthy obsession with the past; a person whose judgement and critical faculties were severely compromised; whose pedantry submerged the lessons of history in a morass of detail; and whose credulous enthusiasm allowed him to be duped by every forgery and to be transfixed by even the most banal and bathetic remains of the past. Earle's character re-emerges in Ned Ward's *London Spy*, in satires such as James Bramston's *Man of Taste* and Alexander Pope's *Memoirs of Martinus Scriblerus*. Samuel Foote drew upon the familiar caricature in his plays *Taste* and *The Nabob*. Sir Walter Scott then provided the definitive image of antiquarian eccentricity in his eponymous novel, *The Antiquary*.[2] Since then it has often proved difficult to penetrate beyond the image of Jonathan Oldbuck, inhabiting a chaotic study, crammed full of objects of dubious authenticity, festooned with cobwebs. In the later eighteenth century, it has been said, 'we really see the emergence of the antiquary as Sir Walter Scott saw him; Jonathan Oldbuck who eagerly identified Roman camps from hearsay rather than fieldwork, collectors of curios and old armour, uncritical and credulous, and ignorant of the essential disciplines of their scholarship'.[3]

Harsh words and unjust ones; but antiquaries should not be regarded as the eighteenth-century equivalent of stamp collectors or devotees of Civil War re-enactments. Nor were they a backward-looking minority, immersed in laborious obfuscation, out of touch with the main trends of historical and political thought. Rather, they were important actors in that explosion of print and ideas, that thirst for knowledge and understanding which some have called the British Enlightenment.[4] In their self-declared belief that their researches contributed to dissipate the gloom of religion and enlarge the mind, they adopted the spirit of the Enlightenment and contributed to its mission.[5] A belief in progress and improvement was not necessarily predicated upon a denial of the value of the past, and antiquarianism had as much to contribute to the Whiggish project of charting the rise of a polite and commercial society as it had to give to the consolidation of a Tory ideology based upon nostalgic conservatism. There was no simple dichotomy between the enlightened world of conjectural history and the tedious pedantry of antiquarianism. To examine the figures who made up the antiquarian community of the eighteenth century is to consider how a large proportion of those who comprised the social and intellectual elite of this period understood the past, its interpretation and its meaning for contemporary life. Investigating the activities and writings of eighteenth-century antiquaries reveals a constant interaction between past and present, in which antiquarian knowledge informed the culture and identities of the modern world, and in which the intellectual agenda of a polite and commercial society dictated the directions to be taken by antiquarian research. Even their mistakes and misapprehensions are illuminating, if we seek to use them as a point of access from which to understand the limitations of historical knowledge and the intellectual parameters within which they worked.

'The proper business of an Antiquary', declared William Borlase, 'is to collect what is dispersed, more fully to unfold what is already discovered, to examine controverted points, to settle what is doubtful, and by the authority of Monuments and Histories, to throw light upon the manners, Arts, Languages, Policy and Religion of past Ages.'[6] Borlase's summary of the antiquary's business might strike the reader today as very much akin to current conceptions of the work of a historian. Indeed, the antiquary of the eighteenth century probably had more in common with the professional historian of the twenty-first century, in terms of methodology, approach to sources and the struggle to reconcile erudition with style, than did the authors of the grand narratives of national history such as Rapin, Hume or Robertson, who generally provide the starting point for discussions of historical thought and attitudes to the past in this period. The scholarly attention devoted to eighteenth-century antiquaries, by contrast, has seldom reflected their contributions to historical methodology or the construction of a national past, or their role in establishing any disciplines apart from that of archaeology.[7] Modern scholarship tends to cherrypick the most outstanding scholars, such as Thomas Madox or William Stukeley, in order to accommodate them into a grand narrative of the rise of history or of the emergence of archaeology, whilst ignoring the work of other antiquaries whose researches fit less neatly with the requirements of our teleological frameworks. This modern perspective has had the effect of distorting the intellectual world in which such scholars operated, obscuring the fact that they were writing for and responding to a wider antiquarian community. These men identified themselves as antiquaries – not as archaeologists or historians – and viewed their own work as a contribution to *antiquarian* scholarship. The tendency to pigeonhole antiquaries as amateurs and eccentrics risks isolating their interests and activities from the broader intellectual trends of the eighteenth century and belittles the intellectual status of antiquarianism as a discipline.

Antiquaries were fired by a love of the past. Time and again we find them confessing their love of antiquity, their excitement at the discovery of some ancient manuscript or their delight in deciphering an inscription. They were energetic researchers, travelling the countryside to excavate barrows, draw churches or transcribe manuscripts, recording their observations and their reading as they did so. They made copious collections of coins and antiquities and coerced their female relatives into making sketches or transcribing documents. They wrote to each other endlessly, exchanging information, making extracts, describing local antiquities, debating points of etymology or history. They carried their debates into the coffee houses and literary societies of provincial and metropolitan society; they published their findings and their opinions in periodicals, pamphlets and weighty tomes. They used their knowledge thus acquired in the law, in politics and in the church; it informed their sense of identity at both a local and a national level; and it gave them a sense of purpose, a sense of patriotism and a sense of pride. They took immense satisfaction in their achievements and were confident that they had made a significant contribution to the learned world. An informed knowledge of the past was a key element of the literary culture of the time. It was, as one antiquary remarked, an 'antiquarian' age.[8]

It is important not to fall into the trap of assuming that all that the antiquaries achieved was to provide the dross of raw materials from which historians proper could refine the narrative of history. One cannot account for the changes in historical knowledge, methodology and interpretation between the early modern period and the nineteenth century without recognising the enormous importance of 'antiquarian' research. The nineteenth-century emphasis upon empiricism and documentation arose directly out of antiquarian methods. Leopold von Ranke's hope that rigorous research would establish 'wie es eigentlich gewesen war' was anticipated in the writings of many antiquaries, who were similarly confident that the systematic collection of antiquities would enable them to reconstruct the 'shipwreck of time'. The emancipation of history, and the study of the past more broadly defined, from the imperatives of religious interpretation and political controversy owed not a little to the endeavours of the antiquaries. Their perception of the past can, of course, be shown to have been coloured by their religious or political affiliations, but there was nevertheless a strong resistance within the antiquarian tradition to the idea that antiquities should be subordinated to the elaboration of some ulterior argument. In their abhorrence of system and theory, and in their emphasis upon allowing the antiquities to 'speak for themselves', they foreshadowed many aspects of the modern pursuit of historical objectivity.

The antiquaries also showed how evidence could be derived from non-literary sources through a process of comparison and classification. Artefacts excavated from barrows, ancient buildings and even the landscape – as well as manuscripts – could be made to yield up the secrets of the past. Antiquaries such as Thomas Madox showed how history could be extracted and written from such dry materials as the records of the exchequer or the charters of towns. William Stukeley, for all his fascination with Druids, set standards of archaeological fieldwork that were unsurpassed for years to come. He was not, however, a lone figure. There were many other antiquaries who similarly learnt how to read the evidence of landscape or to use the science of stratigraphy to recover antiquity. Antiquaries such as Charles Lyttelton and Richard Gough played a pivotal role in establishing the systematic study of architectural history, and in their re-evaluation of the Gothic style of architecture contributed to the development of a historicist approach to the past. John Carter's emotive journalism in the pages of periodicals such as the *Gentleman's Magazine* introduced the study of Gothic architecture to a broad readership for the first time and helped to generate a consciousness of the architectural heritage of the middle ages and the importance of its preservation. The Gothic Revival of the nineteenth century owed more to these antiquaries than to Horace Walpole. The antiquary's fascination with the objects of everyday life – as well as the trappings of power and authority – was key to the emergence of a form of historical inquiry which concentrated upon social organisation and its cultural forms. The engraver and antiquary Joseph Strutt revealed the rich potential of illuminated manuscripts for the study of medieval history, and in his

Francis Grose, 'Antiquaries Peeping into Boadicea's Night Urn'. (*Society of Antiquaries*)

illustrated histories of manners and customs, sports and pastimes effectively composed the first social history of the English people.

It was with domestic antiquities – not those of Greece or Rome – with which these antiquaries were primarily concerned, and it was in the discovery and recording of the national pasts of England, Scotland, Wales and Ireland that some of their most important contributions were made. For many people in the eighteenth century their active engagement with national history lay not so much in reading a volume of Rapin or Hume, but in the pursuit of local history and antiquities. Given the popularity of local and family history today, this should come as no surprise to us. Scores of antiquaries across the country were engaged in pursuing the history and antiquities of their localities, recording the physical appearance of their church, tracing out Roman roads, collecting hoards of coins or excavating barrows. Much of this work survives today in unpublished form in local record offices or in private hands. Its historical value now is twofold; such documents offer a unique record of churches which have since been lost, landscapes which have disappeared or antiquities which have been destroyed, but they also bear witness to the commanding presence of the past in the lives of eighteenth-century Britons. The greatest monument to this local activity is in the local historical and topographical works that proliferated during the eighteenth century.

The starting point for all antiquaries was Edmund Gibson's revision of William Camden's *Britannia*, still a staple work of reference today. *Britannia* collated the historical evidence for the early history of the British Isles, and described and recorded the antiquities to be found county by county. Gibson revised it once more in 1722; Richard Gough embarked upon a third wholesale revision and retranslation published in 1789, which was expanded again in 1806. By now Camden's single volume had become a sprawling, rambling assemblage of material filling four hefty tomes. The overblown proportions of *Britannia* reflect the level of industry in the study of local antiquities – druidical, Roman, Saxon or Gothic – across the country.

This was the great age of the county history, and there were few English counties which were not the subject of a multi-volume history by the end of the reign of George III. Works such as John Nichols's *History and Antiquities of Leicestershire*, Philip Morant's *History and Antiquities of Essex* or John Hutchins's *History and Antiquities of Dorset* are impressive testimony to the labours of scores of private scholars who contributed their efforts to something that they found not only inherently interesting, but also perceived to be a public good. Although it is easy to fault the scholarship now, the labour of compilation and accuracy of observation which they represent are still a valuable resource. Moreover, they were highly regarded in their own time. Britain, and in particular England, led the rest of Europe in this respect, and it was a matter of pride to British antiquaries that no other country in Europe could boast such richness of antiquarian description.

It must be acknowledged that the antiquaries of the early modern period have been better served than their eighteenth-century successors. Important studies of historical and antiquarian culture in the sixteenth and seventeenth centuries have demonstrated how English antiquarianism followed a distinctive path within Europe.[9] Although John Leland and William Camden were undoubtedly heavily influenced by the continental traditions of Renaissance humanism, with its emphasis on philology and textual criticism, they laid the foundations for a different approach which was based upon topography, fieldwork and genealogical studies. By the end of the seventeenth century the native (and at this time it was still largely English) antiquarian tradition could boast two main strengths. The first was the topographical regional study. This combined the observation of landscape and archaeological fieldwork with the detailed record of heraldry, genealogies and the descent of property, best represented in a county history such as Sir William Dugdale's *Antiquities of Warwickshire.* The other strength lay in the study of medieval texts and documents, where there were outstanding contributions to research into legal antiquities and political antiquarianism. Scholars such as Sir Robert Cotton, Sir Henry Spelman or John Selden investigated the origins of parliament and the early foundations of common law, whilst Anglican churchmen, who sought to defend the established church by reference to historical precedent, led a recovery of Anglo-Saxon language and literature.[10] The dynamic interaction of politics, religion, antiquarianism and history in the seventeenth century was ably delineated by D. C. Douglas in *English Scholars*, a seminal work which has informed all the subsequent literature, and to which this study, like many others, is deeply indebted.[11] Nor has the topographical dimension to antiquarianism wanted attention; through the vigour of antiquarian studies amongst the county gentry, historians have been able to explore the dominant ideologies of politics, religion and familial loyalty amongst the landed elite of seventeenth-century Britain.[12]

What unites many of the more recent studies of antiquarianism in the seventeenth century is the emphasis which has been placed on understanding antiquarianism as a response to the religious and political conflicts of the day, and the efforts to contextualise the ways in which the early modern antiquaries approached the study of the past within the broader cultural and intellectual patterns of the seventeenth century. The antiquaries of the eighteenth century, by contrast, have generally been sidelined, as historians have concentrated on the authors of the better-known national histories.

The antiquaries' interest in the material artefacts of the past has meant that most academic interest has been generated by archaeologists, whose priority has been more to establish the origins of modern archaeological practice than to place the antiquaries within a wider historical culture. If we are to appreciate fully the place of history in the eighteenth century, particularly in terms of its practice and reception beyond a handful of scholars from the literary and intellectual elite, we have to take the antiquaries and their publications seriously. This book is an attempt to do just that.

The first chapter will focus upon the development of antiquarian scholarship and its place in the intellectual culture of the eighteenth century. There was a fatal internal tension within antiquarianism: on the one hand, it was the 'handmaid to history', but, on the other, it saw itself as a science and prided itself on an empirical rigour that was anathema to history. The tension was never resolved, but the legacy of antiquarianism in its two main offspring – history and archaeology – is very apparent. Chapter 2 considers the social identity of the antiquary and examines the networks and societies through which antiquarian activity was organised. Few antiquaries engaged in their studies to the exclusion of all else and it is important to understand how the study of antiquities dovetailed with their literary, scientific or theological interests, or complemented their professional activities. The real strength of antiquarianism in the eighteenth century lay with these networks of antiquaries located throughout provincial Britain and Ireland, but it is impossible to deny the importance of the Society of Antiquaries of London, which dominates the discussion in Chapter 3. The Society of Antiquaries was one of the leading learned societies of its day, and at its peak had a membership which exceeded that even of the Royal Society. Its importance lay less in the activities which it undertook than in the institutional presence and identity which it gave to the discipline and to its members. Chapters 4 to 7 take a roughly chronological approach, surveying the ways in which antiquaries approached the study of different periods of British history, from the ancient Britons to the medieval period. It should be acknowledged here that there is little direct discussion of antiquaries' approach to the period after 1500. This does not betoken a lack of interest on their part; on the contrary the sixteenth and seventeenth centuries were the focus of much discussion for both antiquaries and historians. They collected manuscripts, tradesmen's tokens and early printed books as eagerly as they amassed the coins and inscriptions of more remote periods. The subject is in fact one which deserves a separate study, but it is also one which in some senses was qualitatively different from other aspects of antiquarian activity. The propinquity of the recent past rendered it more familiar; it did not make the same interpretative demands upon the antiquary, it did not offer the same challenge of discovery nor could it exercise a comparable imaginative hold.

The intention throughout had been less to concentrate on the achievements of any particular antiquary, than to set their researches and their publications in a broader context, relating them to the political, religious and literary contexts in which the antiquaries were working. Throughout these chapters contrasts are drawn between the differing approaches of antiquaries in England, Wales, Scotland and Ireland, it being one of the major themes of this work that antiquarian activity was directed by the imperative of establishing a national past. The final two chapters take a different thematic approach: Chapter 8 builds on the preceding discussion of medieval antiquities to consider the contribution of the eighteenth-century antiquarian movement to the development of the concept of a national heritage and the importance of preserving the records of the nation's past. This issue of preservation arose most forcefully in eighteenth-century attitudes to Gothic architecture and in the debates over restoration and preservation many of the issues which continue to confront the heritage movement today were raised for the first time. For the concept of a national heritage to carry any plausibility it has to be able to be shown that antiquarianism had penetrated beyond the circle of educated gentlemen and had reached a wider readership.

The final chapter considers some of the ways in which antiquarianism succeeded in reaching a non-specialist readership. Antiquarianism had started the century as a pursuit dominated by the landed elite. By the end of the century that position had been comprehensively challenged. Antiquarianism was still important to the ruling orders in legitimating their dominant position in society and upholding the social order, but other constituencies had appropriated the genre and diversified the subject matter. William Camden had written of restoring Britain to antiquities and antiquity to Britain. By the nineteenth century it was a matter of restoring antiquities to the people and the people to antiquity.

1

The Rise of the Antiquary

The first antiquary has traditionally been identified as Marcus Terrentius Varro, whose *Antiquitates rerum humanarum et divinarum* comprised a historical encyclopaedia of people, places, dates and events pertaining to the history of Rome. Varro provided a model for the antiquaries of the Renaissance era, which guided their attempts to recover the history and antiquities of ancient Rome. The first antiquaries were concerned primarily with artefacts of the written word, examining the evidence of coins, manuscripts and inscriptions and subjecting them to philological analysis to retrieve new material about the past which the narrative accounts did not supply. At this point the contrast between the antiquary and the historian was reasonably clear. For Renaissance humanists, history properly understood concerned only the events of classical antiquity; it was composed in a narrative form and raised matters of philosophy and ethics. The events subsequent to the fall of Rome, by contrast, were the stuff of chronicles – an inferior form of literature which lacked the intellectual profundity of classical history. The period preceding the testimony of the classical authorities was too uncertain to merit consideration as history and those who studied it could not draw upon the literary texts from which historical narratives were composed.[1] In this way, the antiquary might also study the non-Roman history of his own country, even if, like William Camden, what he actually wrote was an historical narrative rather than a random collection of facts.[2] The distinction between historian and antiquary was thus always more complicated than a simple opposition between narrative and description.

In the seventeenth century the epistemological distance between the students of non-classical and classical worlds began to diminish. Historians began to draw heavily on the evidence of coins or inscriptions in writing the history of the ancient world and primary documentation became increasingly important as the basis for narratives of more recent times.[3] The religious controversists of the latter part of the seventeenth century relied upon historical evidence to substantiate their respective positions. Empiricism was the basis of historical truth and historical truth was the means by which orthodoxy was maintained or challenged. Religious histories of the late seventeenth century were replete with evidence cited from manuscripts and other authorities. Some of the earliest histories to utilise a significant element of documentary evidence to corroborate a narrative were the religious histories written to defend an ideological position, such as Gilbert Burnet's *History of the Reformation* or the propaganda in defence of the Anglican establishment produced by White Kennett and Edmund Gibson, who were themselves amongst the foremost antiquarian scholars of their day.[4] At the same time Pyrrhonist scepticism challenged historians and antiquaries to distinguish between reliable and unreliable forms of evidence. The literary materials upon which the historian conventionally depended were easily shown to be suspect; the testimony of coins, inscriptions or statues, however, could not be forged or tampered with in the same way. The value of a history could now be judged by the quantity of public documents, inscriptions and coins examined by the historian.[5] The historian used the evidence of the antiquary, and the antiquary depended upon the historical narrative of the historian to provide the framework according to which the artefacts of the past could be interpreted: they were natural partners, a fact to which their frequent titular pairing is sufficient testimony. During the eighteenth century historical narrative and antiquarian discourse continued to converge, most conspicuously in Edward Gibbon's *The Decline and Fall of the Roman Empire.* Gibbon combined the erudition of classical antiquaries and the researches of the Parisian Académie des Belles Lettres et Inscriptions with the philosophical insights and literary elegance of classical history composition. Less attention has been paid, however, to the changes which took place within the traditions of domestic antiquarian and historical discourse, and the responses of those who were engaged on rather less monumental projects.[6]

For all that the historian and the antiquary shared a common interest in the past, and were increasingly occupying the same territory by the eighteenth century, the contrast between the two was an important one, which both sides of the partnership would duly emphasise as occasion demanded. Both disciplines involved the study of the past and both made similar claims for the utility of their subject; but, whilst the antiquary would freely acknowledge his studies to be a contribution to historical learning and accepted the subordinate role of his discipline, historians were much more likely to attempt to preserve a lofty distance from antiquaries. The historian was naturally affiliated to the man of letters or the philosopher, whilst the pull on the antiquary was stronger from the camp of the natural historians.

History occupied a place of much higher regard than did mere antiquities, in the same way that art in the classical style occupied a place of infinitely greater esteem than did the depiction of everyday life, with its minute realisation of quotidian details. The historian looked down upon the antiquary in the same way that Reynolds dismissed the genre art of the Dutch Republic. The value of history and its literary status went unquestioned. In the hands of its greatest practitioners it was the noblest form of literature. In the early eighteenth century attitudes to history writing in Britain were largely derivative of those of continental Renaissance humanism.[7] The respect with which the classical historians were held made it hard for any eighteenth-century practitioner to rank with Livy or Thucydides. Indeed their aim was to emulate them in the eloquence of their rhetoric. The Ciceronian dictum that history only dealt with those things worthy of recollection – what would now be considered as high politics – was still largely unchallenged in the early eighteenth century.[8] Henry Bolingbroke's *Letters on the Study and Use of History*, written in the 1730s but not published until 1752, represented a commentary and amplification of that very theme. The purpose of history was not so much to discover the past as to use it as a vehicle to improve the present. 'An application to any study that tends neither directly nor indirectly to make us better men and better citizens, is at best but a specious and ingenious sort of idleness.'[9] Bolingbroke took up the argument of Tacitus and Seneca that the value of history was primarily didactic: it was 'philosophy teaching by example'. Abstract principles were more deeply felt when witnessed through the narrative of human action. The search for historical truth was not so much a search for factual information but for the truth of human character and the motives governing men's behaviour. History hinged upon the manner of telling rather than on precise scholarship. Ancient learning was challenged, however, by the achievements of modern science and scholarship in the Battle of the Books, which divided the scholarly community of Europe at the end of the seventeenth century. Historians were firmly on the side of the Ancients in this conflict: the mere collation of disconnected facts could not challenge the literary elegance or the rhetorical power of the Ancients. The antiquaries, despite the age of their subject matter, were in the camp of the Moderns. Whilst the two camps were united in admiration of the remnants of classical antiquity, antiquaries nevertheless proceeded upon the assumption that the collection of antiquities could yield up new truths.

The Battle of the Books had been fought and largely lost by the Ancients by the start of the eighteenth century. Although its echoes continued to reverberate throughout the period, the models according to which history was written underwent significant change. The second half of the eighteenth century was the era of 'philosophical history', famously associated with Voltaire and his *Essai sur les moeurs*, but also characterised by the histories of David Hume or William Robertson, influencing to a greater or lesser extent the majority of narrative histories of Britain which were published in the second half of the century. Philosophical history eschewed the providentialist view of history, which saw the narrative of the past as the unfolding of a divine plan. It also rejected the type of history which was written around the actions of a single protagonist or which was narrowly concerned with the dissection of the politics of a single country. This was typically a story of human society which took a cosmopolitan perspective, elucidating the general laws of historical development common to all societies. It was written on a grand scale, with little need for the minute detail or accuracy upon which the antiquary might pride himself. Voltaire, as Edward Gibbon remarked, was not the man to turn over 'musty monkish writers' to instruct himself. The ambition was not simply to record great deeds but to develop a more reflective understanding of the operation of society and its political forms, and the relationship between commerce, economy and political order. History was seen as the product of a relationship of cause and effect, and in order to understand the operation of history it was necessary to understand both the workings of the economy and the beliefs and passions which were the springs of human action.[10]

A knowledge of history was essential to the education of any polite gentleman. The antiquary's supposedly omnivorous consumption of every morsel of the past, however, detracted from the regard with which the study of antiquities was held and made it vulnerable to ridicule in print and graphic satire.[11] Antiquaries were widely assumed to be obsessed with minutiae, with the recovery of particular facts and insignificant events; details which could have no bearing upon the grand narrative and indeed served to detract from it. They ventured into periods about which little was known, cobbling together disparate pieces of information with flights of imaginative speculation and false etymology based on 'fantastical similitude of sounds'. The antiquary was caught up in a morass of facts and points of technical proof, whereas the gentleman aspired to the lofty overview, unencumbered by an excess of specialist knowledge or undigested information. The necessity of studying charters, opined the author of a *New Method of Studying History*, extended only to a limited number of people: they were useless to gentlemen who wanted only general historical knowledge.[12] Too much learning and too obsessive an attention to detail constituted pedantry, and a pedant, as Joseph Addison reminded the readers of the *Spectator*, was a very indifferent companion.[13] Pedantry betokened an unguarded enthusiasm, an obsessive interest with antiquities which went against the carefully cultivated moderation and restraint which befitted the true gentleman. The objects too with which the antiquary was supposed to busy himself were easily ridiculed. Addison mocked the gentlemen who 'value themselves upon being critics in Rust'. It was a science built upon 'unconcerning parts of knowledge' and on 'mean materials'.[14] Rather than studying objects of artistic merit or beauty, which would in turn hone and refine his own taste and might be construed as an encouragement to the arts, the antiquary preferred tarnished medals, broken pottery or illegible manuscripts. If the conduct of the Saxons and the Danes was so unedifying for a man of taste such as the Scottish virtuoso, Sir John Clerk of Penicuik, there was commensurately little benefit to be derived from considering their monuments, which were crude, ugly and a perversion of nature. Clerk could never bring himself to study the runic crosses of the north of England. They were, he informed Samuel Gale, a reproach to the artificers of the time. 'Such clumsy monuments as these, I am sure, can never communicate to us any instruction.'[15]

The compass within which the antiquaries conducted their researches was also at issue. Histories were conventionally narratives written of statesmen or of nations; of politics and of war. Much antiquarian literature concerned either a specific locality – a town, a parish or a county – or a single type of object or institution, be it a system of land tenure or a collection of inscriptions. Such a narrow scope did not yield so readily lessons of broader application; the antiquary was condemned to the sidelines. Nothing that he produced could have any significant bearing on the greater truths taught by history. Locality was equated with antiquarianism; and antiquarianism thereby acquired the reputation of parochialism and trivia. An interest in particularities seemed to betoken a narrowness of thought and illiberality in outlook: 'Had his education been superior', it was remarked of the Suffolk antiquary Isaac Gillingwater, 'perhaps he would not have descended to the minutiae which he records.'[16] Histories of counties contained 'only materials of a circumscribed and particular nature',[17] and the histories of towns were simply extensions of monkish chronicles. 'I apprehend the history of any very remarkable ancient city, or peculiar county in *Britain*, is enough to exercise the genius of the ablest historian or antiquary', wrote Francis Drake. 'And yet I am well aware that the history of any particular place, or local history, meets with no such encouragement from the world as the more general historians are honoured with.'[18] The success of John Whitaker's *History of Manchester* was due at least in part to the fact that, as he pointed out in the preface, the reader need not expect only the 'private and uninteresting history of a single town', but would be presented with whatever served to illustrate the antiquities of the kingdom or county and which had a bearing upon the interests of Manchester.[19]

The gulf between antiquary and historian was deepened further by contrasting modes of presentation. The antiquary might draw up tables, transcribe documents or illustrate coins, but these facts, complained the critics, were unrelieved by any kind of reflection. There would be no sustained narrative, and the result was 'dry' and deeply unappealing to all but those who had a specialist knowledge of the subject. Antiquaries were not renowned for their literary elegance. As the antiquary William Stukeley admitted, writers on antiquities generally 'find more difficulty, in so handling the matter, as to render it agreeable to the reader, than in most other subjects'.[20] A 'laconic style' expressive of the matter was deemed preferable to 'flights of eloquence'.[21] Foote Gower promised that his projected history of Cheshire would provide a narrative to be read with pleasure, rather than an antiquarian dictionary to be consulted occasionally, but his correspondent, Richard Gough, was not convinced. He was, he admitted, too much the 'sourheaded antiquary' to approve of such a mode of proceeding.[22] Furthermore, the very appearance of an antiquarian publication could be deeply unprepossessing, with its dry recital of charters or pedigrees and abstruse etymological derivations. These were problems which were often exacerbated by the need to cut costs on volumes for which there would be limited sales, by using small typefaces, narrow margins and few illustrations.

The contrasting attitudes of antiquaries and historians to the footnote encapsulates their respective differences. The lengthy footnote was an indispensable part of the antiquary's scholarship, but to the classically trained historian it represented an unwanted interruption to the narrative flow. The footnote threatened to detract from the force of the argument, it distracted the eye, and represented an excess of erudition over taste. In the opinion of Charles James Fox, 'all which an historian wished to say, should be introduced as part of a continued narration'.[23] After David Hume's drubbing at the hands of Horace Walpole for failing to include any notes at all in the first volume of his *History of England*, most historians, Charles James Fox excepted, acknowledged their desirability. But this raised the further issue of where such notes should be positioned. Historians such as Hume or William Robertson, striving for narrative coherence and textual integrity, inserted them at the end of a chapter. Antiquaries, who had no such qualms about interrupting the narrative flow or disrupting the appearance of the page, placed them at the bottom, beneath the text. John Whitaker's decision to put the notes at the end of each chapter of the *History of Manchester* signalled that his was not a volume to be positioned exclusively within the antiquarian genre, but aroused some hostile comment amongst his antiquarian peers. 'His method of sequestering his Notes at too great distance from the Text is shockingly unpardonable', pronounced Richard Gough.[24] Gough objected to the separation between statement and the evidential proof by which it could be verified, which was the hallmark of the antiquary.

'History Preserving the Monuments of Antiquity', frontispiece from Francis Grose, *The Antiquities of England and Wales*, 4 vols (1772–76). (*Special Collections, University of Leicester*)

At the root of many of the points of difference between the antiquary and the historian was the opposition between gentlemanly learning and scholarship, which was manifest in both the pursuit of science and of antiquities. For all that antiquarianism was the handmaid to history, in many ways the discipline enjoyed a more equal relationship with natural history and the realm of science; and, like science, the study of antiquities was often perceived to be at odds with the gentlemanly ideal.[25] The relationship between the antiquary and the natural historian had always been a close one, and the seventeenth-century tradition of the virtuoso was perpetuated in the careers of many of the natural historians and antiquaries of the eighteenth century, of whom Sir Joseph Banks was perhaps the best example.[26] They inhabited a world where disciplinary divisions had not been firmly marked out and educated gentlemen could take an interest in any branch of learning. The two sciences of natural history and antiquities explicated both the past and the present using the same method of inquiry. Even Richard Gough, arguably the most single-minded antiquary of his day, was also a fellow of the Royal Society. He attended its meetings and took an informed interest in the plans of his friend Michael Tyson for a botanical history of Cambridgeshire. Dual membership, denoted by the initials FRSAS, was commonplace and election to one society generally followed rapidly upon election to the other.[27] Intellectually these individuals were able to move smoothly from the observation of antiquities to the observation of natural phenomena, whilst physically, due to the careful timing of meetings, they were able to progress from the meeting room of the Royal Society to that of the Antiquaries on the same evening. The publication of *Philosophical Transactions* and from 1770 *Archaeologia*, not to mention the frequent correspondence on matters antiquarian and natural historical in the pages of the *Gentleman's Magazine*, facilitated communication on both sides, and was further encouraged in private correspondence and in the proceedings of provincial societies such as the Gentlemen's Society of Spalding.[28]

Whether or not the individual practitioner combined an interest in science and antiquities, the methodology and language of natural history and scientific inquiry coloured that of antiquarianism. Antiquaries proceeded upon the Baconian assumption that antiquities were the fragments of the historical shipwreck of time, and that if sufficient were collected some progress could be made towards recovering the shape of that wreck.

> Antiquities, or remnants of history, are when industrious persons, by an exact and scrupulous diligence and observations, out of monuments, names, words, proverbs, traditions, private records and evidences, fragments of stories, passages

of books, that concern not story, and the like, preserve and recover somewhat from the deluge of time.[29]

Both naturalist and antiquary had to work hard to counter the common supposition that the virtuoso collected objects with no discrimination, and with no higher purpose of intellectual enlightenment in mind. To their critics, both naturalist and antiquary wasted time in petty speculation rather than striving towards the improvement of society with the increase of true knowledge. That much was true of their seventeenth-century forebears, it was allowed, but in the eighteenth century most antiquaries struggled to distance themselves from the undiscriminating collections which had graced (or cluttered) the cabinets of curiosities of the past. The emphasis for both was therefore necessarily upon the rigorous and systematic collection of any kind of data, and upon empirical observation from which the demonstration of truth would follow. At the heart of the antiquarian discipline was the need to compile, compare and contrast. Only then could any pattern be discerned, or any kind of truths established. If nature was to be understood by the collection and classification of plants and animals, antiquities could be made to yield up the facts of history by similarly systematic compilation. 'All *true* conclusions of Science', pronounced the president of the Society of Antiquaries in 1784, 'must depend upon the collection of a *variety* of facts; and upon comparing *very many* remains and appearances of things, one with another.'[30] Late eighteenth-century antiquaries ridiculed the virtuoso's collection of coins, arranged according to metal or size rather than as a historical sequence.[31]

The remarkably eclectic range of subject matter which comprised antiquarian studies, and which provoked such frequent ridicule, represented a further legacy of the seventeenth-century virtuoso's approach to collecting, one which encompassed both natural and man-made curiosities and antiquities. 'I intend not to meddle with the *pedigrees* or *descents* either of *families* or *lands*', Robert Plot had reassured readers of his natural history of Staffordshire. Rather he would 'chiefly apply myself to *things*; and amongst these too, only such as are very remote from the present *Age*: such as ancient *Medalls, Ways, Lows, Pavements, Urns, Monuments* of *Stone Fortifications*, &c whether of the ancient *Britans, Romans, Saxons, Danes* or *Normans*. Which being all made and fashioned out of *Natural* things, may as well be brought under a *Natural History* as any thing of *Art*.'[32] The artefacts with which the antiquary was conventionally interested were typically coins, manuscripts and monumental inscriptions, but most antiquaries extended their interests much more broadly. Natural history merged into antiquarianism in the study of fossils and skeletal remains, or in the excavation of barrows and the observation of soil strata. Stone arrowheads and axe heads were grouped alongside the fossils and other curiosities dug out of the ground in the collector's cabinet. Shells and fossils, remarked Robert Hooke, were 'the Medals, Urnes or Monuments of Nature'. A century later John Walker, professor of chemistry in late eighteenth-century Edinburgh, referred to fossils and other artefacts as the physical and historical monuments by which he could establish the earth's age.[33] The composition of Roman roads offered clues as to the patterns of trade and analysis of the rocks at Stonehenge would indicate from which part of Britain they had originated. The porosity of a Roman brick was of interest to the scientist looking at ways to improve current building materials, but it was also an object of curiosity to the antiquary who saw it as another indication of the highly sophisticated technology of the Romans.[34]

In the late seventeenth and early eighteenth century the Royal Society had been the natural forum in which antiquaries reported their findings in a public context, even under the resolutely mathematical presidency of Sir Isaac Newton. The *Philosophical Transactions* are peppered with papers on Roman roads, Roman coins, the excavation of barrows, and even points of etymology. Roughly 0.6 per cent of papers appearing in *Philosophical Transactions* during the 1720s dealt with antiquarian matters. By the 1740s, under the broader church established during the presidency of Sir Hans Sloane, the proportion had reached 7.0 per cent, falling to 6.4 per cent in 1750s and 5.3 per cent in the 1760s. Thereafter there was a significant drop to 2.4 per cent.[35] The peak coincided with a period of considerable upheaval within the Society of Antiquaries when it was feared by some that Martin Folkes (at that time president of both societies) and his 'cabal' were intent on amalgamating the antiquaries with the senior society. Factional politics within the respective societies aside, this disciplinary overlap in publications offers further confirmation of the perceived compatibility between the interests of the two societies.[36]

Antiquaries themselves did not draw hard and fast boundaries between the societies' respective spheres of inquiry. William Stukeley read the first part of his dissertation on the coins of Carausius before the Royal Society and the second part before the Society of Antiquaries.[37] The Derbyshire antiquary Samuel Pegge published papers on Roman pigs of lead in *Philosophical Transactions, Archaeologia* and the *Gentleman's Magazine*.[38] A recently disinterred body in 1772 provoked some dispute between the two societies as to which one it more properly belonged. The Society of Antiquaries, asserted Gough, should claim property in everything found in the ruins of an abbey and the fellows of the Royal Society were trying to encroach too far on the antiquaries' environs.[39] Sir John Pringle's suggestion in 1776 that the excavation of Silbury Barrow in Wiltshire should be funded by one of the learned societies was passed from the Royal Society (of which he was president) to the Society of Antiquaries (of which he was also a member), as being more suited to their interests (although the real reason was undoubtedly the reluctance of either society to contribute towards the cost of excavations).[40] London was in fact unusual in supporting two learned societies of this kind. In Edinburgh the Philosophical Society provided the forum for any kind of learned discussion whether scientific or historical, until 1780 when the earl of Buchan launched the Scottish Society of Antiquaries.[41] In Ireland a separate society for the discussion of antiquities lasted only a few years between 1780 and 1784, and for the most part antiquities were discussed alongside science, natural history, theology and literature in gatherings such as the Royal Irish Academy or the Dublin Society. In the provinces local associations such as the Gentlemen's Society of Spalding, William Stukeley's Brazenose Society and the literary and philosophical societies founded in the later eighteenth century met for the encouragement of the liberal sciences and polite literature. Papers on Roman roads, Saxon barrows and monumental inscriptions sat alongside meteorological observations, botanical notes or treatises on electrical experimentation.

By mid century the traditional virtuoso approach to natural history and antiquities was looked down upon. Both antiquary and natural historian could see the shortcomings in such an indiscriminate mode of proceeding. In both branches of inquiry comparisons were drawn between the more rigorous approach of their own day and the less discerning habits of the past. Richard Gough remarked of the Yorkshire historian Ralph Thoresby (d. 1723), whose private museum was widely regarded as the finest of his day, that his 'credulity and want of judgment in collecting his curiosities must be charged on the infancy of those pursuits in the age he lived in'.[42] At the same time, antiquaries were also establishing a clearer distance between themselves and 'men of taste' – such as Horace Walpole – who valued antiquities on the basis of their aesthetic excellence. By the late eighteenth century it was becoming increasingly clear that connoisseurship was inimical to the antiquarian project. The antiquarian reaction was brought into sharp relief in the late 1780s when the alterations under way at Salisbury Cathedral were debated within the Society of Antiquaries. The architect had proposed to alter the Hungerford Chapel and whitewash over the painted ceilings, arguing that these were poor specimens of art and architecture. That, replied the antiquary John Milner, was no reason at all for the Society of Antiquaries to disregard them. The antiquary's role was not simply to gaze upon and admire beauty but rather to trace the history of the arts themselves in order that he might be able to draw useful inferences and gain insights into the transaction of past ages.[43] The sciences too were becoming considerably more specialised as the scientific professions became more defined: the Linnaean Society for botany was founded in 1788; the Royal Institution for the study of mineralogy in 1799; the Royal Geological Society in 1807; and the Society for the Promotion of Animal Chemistry in 1809.[44] In Edinburgh medical science was developing its own agenda of research in societies which existed independently of those of a more general nature.[45] Some of the ties between antiquities and natural history were weakening. They were not, however, broken, and amongst the amateurs who comprised the majority of members of both the Royal and the Antiquarian Societies, as well as the provincial societies, there continued to be a considerable degree of overlap and reciprocity of exchange in information and interest.[46]

Antiquaries and natural historians moved in similar circles, were governed by the same epistemological models, belonged to the same culture of inquiry, and in addition, habitually conducted their research within the same regional framework. The parish or county was the obvious unit within which to record and describe both natural history and antiquities. By the end of the seventeenth century there was a well-established tradition of natural historical and topographical literature to match the antiquarian studies, best represented in Robert Plot's histories of Staffordshire and Oxfordshire and John Aubrey's collections for the natural history of Wiltshire.[47] Both antiquarian and natural historical inquiries depended heavily on the printed questionnaire which was circulated in advance amongst the gentlemen and clergy who were resident in the area to be surveyed. These sets of queries, which preceded almost every topographical survey from the 1670s onwards, are revealing of the essential conformity of the agenda of both antiquary and natural historian.[48] The project initiated by the Society of Antiquaries to collect information on the counties in 1754 was as much about the current as the historical state of the nation. It was the brainchild of James Theobald, himself one of those antiquaries who enjoyed dual membership with the Royal Society. The list of queries drawn up on that occasion subsequently provided the model for Sir John Sinclair's wide-ranging inquiry, *The Statistical Account of Scotland*, launched in 1792, which included amidst a wealth of economic and demographic information, a section devoted to itemising the variety of antiquities in each area. The nation could only be known through its geography and its history; its monuments and antiquities were there to be counted and recorded like houses, crops and customs duties.[49] The patriotic imperative of political economy, which lay behind so much topographical literature, pressed the necessity of becoming fully acquainted with both the human and economic resources and the history and antiquities of the nation in order to maximise its potential and to enhance its reputation.

Amongst both scholarly communities excessive speculation and theorisation was frowned upon; the emphasis was upon reporting and describing. It has been remarked of the Royal Society that, 'Direct reporting of experiences (natural historical or experimental) untarnished by theoretical considerations or generalisations came to be seen as the duty of the Fellow and (in some areas) within the capacity of all.' The comment could equally apply to the expectations governing antiquarian scholarship.[50] Fieldwork, rather than recounting from hearsay, was fundamental to both. As Richard Gough instructed the aspiring antiquary:

> Whoever sits down to compile the history and antiquities of a county or a town, should confirm the evidence he collects from books and manuscripts by inspection of places described. The face of the country, and the monuments remaining on it, are as interesting as the progress of descents or revolutions of property.[51]

Antiquaries were judged by the accuracy of their observations. Arguments had to be supported with evidential proof. Proper referencing and citation of authorities was crucial to both disciplines – hence the importance of footnotes, whatever the objections on the grounds of taste. The numismatist William Clarke compared the use of the quotations, references and footnotes which supported the structure of an argument to the buttresses of a Gothic building: 'not beautiful, but useful; though they look heavy, and throw a shade within, the whole could not be so well supported without them'.[52] Richard Gough advised Samuel Rudder, who was undertaking a revision of Sir Robert Atkyns history of Gloucestershire (a work notably deficient in references), that 'Works of this kind [county histories] are not like sermons in which the author may interweave texts of scripture without naming chapter or verse. Every article from record should bring its voucher with it.'[53]

The most important underlying principle of antiquarianism was that antiquities could confirm and illustrate the facts of history, and occasionally provide information on matters upon which the historical record was silent. Antiquaries, however, were convinced of the intrinsic value and importance of their subject and were adept at defending their cause, in the process of which they developed the basis of a rationale for their methodology. The arguments which were adduced, particularly in the earlier eighteenth century, were heavily influenced by contemporary continental scholarship. By the later eighteenth century, however, British antiquaries had developed a stronger sense of their own tradition and owed less to continental models, which indeed they often held to have been surpassed. Traditionally the importance of antiquities was rehearsed with reference to the value of coins and medals, these being the commonest relics of antiquity and objects that a gentleman might include in his cabinet of curiosities.[54]

By the end of the seventeenth century there was a well-established genre of literature, including works such as John Evelyn's *Numismata*, which guided the would-be virtuoso in collecting coins and showed him how a cabinet of coins complemented the study of history.[55] In the eighteenth century one of the most widely cited discussions was Joseph Addison's *Dialogue upon the Usefulness of Ancient Medals.* For all the satire which he directed against the arcane interests of the pedantic antiquary, Addison's work included a typical summary of the value of numismatic and medallic antiquities for the historian and the man of letters. They were a valuable supplement to texts: an image could convey information much more rapidly and immediately than could be done through words. 'Not to be tedious', explained Addison, 'one might make a magazine for all sorts of antiquities, that would show a man in an afternoon more than he could learn out of books in a twelve month'; they illustrated customs such as sacrifices and triumphs, matters upon which written sources were largely silent. They could be used to corroborate or to confirm texts and to reconcile differences. 'In this case a cabinet of Medals is a body of history.'[56] The bulk of the pamphlet, however, was devoted to the affinity between coins and medals and poetry, and their value for illustrating poetic metaphors, rather than developing the theme of their potential use as sources of historical information. In the preface to *Britannia romana*, the Oxford antiquary John Pointer reproduced a number of well-worn arguments: a cabinet of coins was not so much a treatise of money as a treatise of knowledge; it was the embodiment of the truest history in epitome; it would confirm passages of history which were true, settle those which were ambiguous and record those passages which have been omitted.[57] Antiquaries were particularly conscious that coins, inscriptions and other monumental evidence had stronger claims to authenticity than written texts, which were more easily forged, and were frequently generated in partisan circumstances. The political and religious conflicts of the seventeenth century had highlighted how history could be written, rewritten and distorted for political ends. Antiquaries considered that artefacts offered a stronger foundation of truth. 'If there is any faith in civil history,' wrote John Strange, 'it is surely in that part of it which is grounded on the real monuments of antiquity, which speak for themselves, *dum tacent, clamant*, and are neither offered to us through the medium of prejudice or party.'[58]

Artefacts and antiquities were incorruptible – as long as the antiquary was faithful in their reproduction or description. The antiquary's reputation for pedantry could be a reflection of a diseased mind, but attention to detail underpinned the factual accuracy upon which the antiquary's claims to possession of an irrefragable truth were based. The Oxford antiquary and non-juror Thomas Hearne, who undertook the publication of some of the most important texts of medieval history during the early eighteenth century, fully appreciated the importance of accuracy as the essence of the antiquarian project, 'it being a principle with me not to alter MSS even where better and more proper Readings are very plain and obvious'. Fidelity to the original represented the only means of recovering the truth of the past, and if their studies could not lay claim to establishing the truth, they were valueless. Hearne's laboriousness and partisan politics, as well as his humble origins, made him the object of condescension from later antiquaries, but they had to acknowledge, however grudgingly, that his insistence upon accuracy in reproducing the originals was the only defence against the penetrating criticisms of the sceptics. The study of antiquities provided a foundation of truth, hence, argued John Pinkerton, the 'vast utility' of studying medals was clear, 'because it serves as a basis to the most important of all human sciences'.[59]

The study of antiquities, however, was always more than simply the collection of coins and medals. Whilst antiquaries in Britain and Scotland had been inspired by the insights of Spanheim on numismatics and Graevius and Gronovius on inscriptions, they had also absorbed the lessons of Maffei, Mabillon and Montfaucon in the study of palaeography and diplomatic. The manuscripts and documents to be found in archives, libraries and private collections were a rich mine of information which could only be exploited through the efforts of the antiquary. 'To them historians are particularly indebted for the elucidation of numberless important facts', wrote Thomas Astle.[60] Manuscripts and charters were the surest proof of history and numbers of antiquaries devoted themselves to collecting and transcribing charters and other documents generated by the administrative and ecclesiastical institutions of the state. State recognition of this was demonstrated in 1694 when Thomas Rymer was employed by the committee chaired by Lord Somers to compile a collection of state records pertaining to England's foreign relations. This became the *Foedera*, which eventually became better known in the abridged form of *Acta regia*.[61] The material published in the *Foedera* was used to considerable effect by Rapin de Thoyras in his history of England, and many other historians subsequent to him.[62] The antiquary who demonstrated most successfully how the raw materials of state records and charters could be deployed in terms of constructing a history was, however, Thomas Madox. Despite holding the position of Historiographer Royal, Madox deserves to be remembered as an antiquary rather than as a historian. He was one of the earliest members of the Society of Antiquaries and regarded his work primarily as a contribution to the study of antiquities, although he also referred to it in terms of writing history.[63] His subject matter of legal antiquities, charters and public records was inherently antiquarian as was his methodology, which he lucidly expounded through the prefaces to his various publication. 'The first part of my business', he wrote, 'was to make as full a collection from Records as I could, of Materials relating to the Subject.' He went on to explain that, 'I used for the most part to write down, in the draught of this Book, the respective Records or testimonies, first of all ... and from Them formed my history or account of things; connecting and applying them afterwards, as the case would admit.' It was only when antiquaries applied themselves to the documents – the bare rolls and membranes – that historical learning could be improved.[64]

Madox's recommendations were quickly endorsed in William Nicolson's second edition of *English Historical Library* (1714), a publication which, despite its title, was addressed as much to the antiquary as the historian. Nicolson's concern was to encourage and promote the composition of a complete history of England, which, as an antiquary, he fully appreciated would need to draw heavily on antiquarian research. The *English Historical Library* was intended, therefore, to alert the potential student of history to the range of sources available, in both printed and manuscript form, and the existing literature on the subject Subsequent volumes covered the materials for Scottish and Irish history. The *Library*, proved to be a staple work of antiquarian reference, but it was effectively a statement of how antiquarian scholarship could be used to construct a much fuller and more comprehensive general history. Nicolson's own research interests were concentrated upon Saxon antiquities, and he used the *Library* as a platform from which to make strenuous representations for the study of Saxon antiquities and the writing of Saxon history, as well as promoting a strongly Whiggish, pro-Hanoverian perspective on the past.[65] He also devoted the final third of the book to enumerating the range and variety of institutional records which would need to be studied preparatory to such a history, taking particular notice of the work already done by Madox.[66] As any reader might swiftly note, however, he failed to make any concrete suggestions as to how such a narrative history might successfully be written.[67]

Madox, by contrast, laid a greater emphasis upon the importance of connecting and digesting such materials as he had already collected into a proper discourse. If a man desired to improve historical knowledge, 'Let him collect as great a Treasure as he can of records and Authenticks, Let him connect them and digest them into Historical Discourse, Let him explain, compare and illustrate them with Candour and Judgement, Let him use them for Proofs and Testimonies to support what he writes. He will do a thing useful to the Publick, if out of them he can extract True history ... it will be more for the service of Learning, to write a little in this way, than to lay before the Publick a huge mass of miscellaneous uncemented Collections.' He also stressed the need to be rigorous in citing the proper authorities, and in giving references in the original language; the testimonies couched in the margin were, he argued, the most valuable part of a history. An account drawn from authentic memorials in this way would not reflect private opinions preconceived in the author's own mind but would reflect historical truth, untouched by the political agenda of the present day.[68]

Whilst Madox's insights into the development of the financial institutions of the crown and the evolution of chartered boroughs represent landmarks in historical scholarship in their own right, what is of interest here is the articulation of a methodology to which antiquaries throughout the century aspired, even if they fell short of achieving it, being rather more likely to produce the uncemented collections from which Madox sought to distance himself. From a modern perspective, it is easy to hail Madox as a precocious exponent of a new mode of history writing, one based upon original sources and their interpretation, and to distinguish him from the uncritical compilers of antiquarian collections. His ambition, however, was 'to form this History, in such a manner, that it may be a Pattern for the *Antiquaries* to follow'. The programme which he laid out, to digest and elucidate, was one which antiquaries kept very much to the fore when they engaged in any theoretical discussion of their discipline. It continued to differentiate their own pursuit from that of 'history' proper, which continued, largely, to depend more on the manner of telling than upon rigorous historical documentation.

These two issues – the need to digest and to interpret antiquities rather than to amass and admire, and the importance of providing the correct kind of scholarly apparatus – were repeatedly rehearsed by antiquaries throughout the eighteenth century. Richard Gough's introduction to the first volume of the published transactions of the Society of Antiquaries, *Archaeologia* (1770), made bold claims for the importance of antiquarianism to the study of history in terms which were highly reminiscent of Madox. 'The arrangement and the proper use of facts is history', he began. Even the most indistinct collection had the merit of supplying materials to those who had the 'sagacity or leisure' to extract from them 'whatever may answer useful purposes'.[69] Only by applying experimental reasoning and comparison to collections of antiquities could any approximation of knowledge be arrived at, argued another antiquary. 'To make cumbrous collections of numberless particulars, merely because they are fragments; and to admire them merely as they are antique, is not the spirit of antient learning, but the mere doating of superannuation.'[70] Such behaviour amounted to no more than a superstitious veneration for relics. Antiquaries were aware of their vulnerability on this point. Publications such as the periodical the *Antiquarian Repertory* warned would-be antiquaries against making collections which had no other merit than that of being old, rather than being illustrative of any point of history.[71] Mindless pedantry was attacked by the more critically astute antiquaries not only because it exposed both themselves and the discipline to ridicule and contempt, but also because it obscured the real value of antiquarianism in furnishing historical truths.[72]

Many, of course, lacked the 'sagacity and leisure' which Richard Gough recommended to bring their studies to a proper fruition. The libraries and record offices of the nation provide ample evidence of an overabundance of the latter and a deficit of the former qualities amongst many of those engaged in antiquarian researches. Such collections could be of little value in illuminating history or determining controversies. 'Chappelle [sic] is tedious and bewildered in a heap of collections [on Devonshire] from which he knows not how to disentangle himself', reported Jeremiah Milles to Richard Gough.[73] Chapple was not alone. The sheer volume of materials which antiquarian enthusiasts were prone to collect in their 'excess' of zeal frequently proved to be overwhelming. Sir Peter Thompson collected materials for the history of Poole, but, as he confessed to Browne Willis, 'I own I have a great many materials for a History of this Town; but the putting them into a Method for the Public is too arduous a task for me to think on.'[74] William Cole, a key figure in the antiquarian network and inexhaustible mine of information to his brother antiquaries, never published anything more substantial than a few brief pamphlets. His collections were extensive but repetitive, and were hardly arranged in the 'luminous order and regular system' which was recommended. Numerous collections like his, particularly in the field of local and topographical history, remained unpublished. Correspondingly, many antiquarian histories which did reach the public domain represented an editorial synthesis of a variety of unfinished collections, rather than the unassisted efforts of a single author. It was White Kennett, commenting on the number of still-born antiquarian projects of the seventeenth century, who identified the fatal tendency in antiquaries to amass a superabundance of materials. 'It is this has made more Antiquaries fail of their proposed attempts, than any other sort of writers.'[75]

The antiquary strove also to maintain a position of studied objectivity, which precluded the imposition of opinions, reflections or a preconceived agenda – which could be turned into an additional justification for failing to introduce any high degree of order upon the materials. Sambrooke Russell, a Leicestershire antiquary, maintained that he aimed at 'truth and actual information'. Rather than mixing narrative with his own reflections, he claimed to offer a simple statement of fact that would allow readers to draw any conclusions for themselves.[76] Antiquaries, however, had to accept that such Olympian detachment might not be widely welcomed or understood. Readers accustomed to the less interpretatively demanding format of narrative history did not always appreciate the methodological principles which inhibited the author from imposing a narrative form upon his collections, or wish to draw the conclusions themselves. The *Analytical Review* was disappointed in John Brand's *History of Newcastle* (1789). The author, noted the reviewer, had collected together all that had the most distant connection with the history and antiquities of the town, 'But still the work is not a history.' Brand had not provided a general and connected account of the subject, he had simply brought together all the materials and arranged them thematically, leaving the reader to form his own interpretation.[77] Antiquarian compilers therefore often forestalled criticism by presenting their work as 'Collections Towards'. Their materials thus presented to the public would, they hoped, inspire someone else more able than themselves to produce the final historical synthesis. Such disingenuous humility, however, was received with scepticism: 'what kind of stimulus will the miscarriage of one writer give another to undertake a work on the same subject?'[78] Yet not all readers were put off by these disconnected treatises. Richard Gough's assessment of Brand's history written for the *Gentleman's Magazine* glowed with satisfaction, highlighting the gap which still existed between the antiquary, whose primary concern was with the evidence, and the historian, who was expected to spurn the particular in favour of the general. Gough was no advocate for obfuscating detail, disconnected facts or rambling disquisitions, but he was very wary of the dangers inherent in drawing generalisations, which he associated with a theoretical or conjectural approach. The phrase 'must have been' cropped up with telling frequency as antiquaries and historians 'supposed' events to have taken place, or 'presumed' a state of affairs in the more obscure periods of the nation's history. Whilst some antiquaries might find themselves overwhelmed with material, the very paucity of the information which survived on other topics made such arguments based upon analogy and conjecture powerfully attractive.

In order to rise above a dry recitation of disconnected facts which could be of little interest to the reader, some element of conjecture in piecing the elements together was essential; the issue then was one of balance and one which provoked widely differing opinions. It was exactly this problem which

Henry Rowlands confronted in writing of the early British history of Anglesey. As he explained in the preface to *Mona antiqua* in 1723, he had never been able to see any reason why 'an Hypothetical Discourse' or a 'Conjectural Way of accounting', when performed with 'Caution and due Regard to peculiar Circumstances', should not be as applicable to the writing of a history of a place as it was allowed to be in writing of natural history.[79] Almost all antiquaries and natural historians resorted to conjecture in framing an argument. Of those who used it to excess, one of the worst offenders was John Whitaker, the historian of Manchester. Whitaker tellingly chose to describe antiquarianism as the 'younger Sister of History, less sedate and more fanciful'.[80] His antiquarian publications, as will subsequently appear, certainly merited the adjective fanciful, and showed little of the caution counselled by Rowlands. Fellow antiquaries were bemused: William Cole reported to Horace Walpole, after the publication of the second volume of the *History of Manchester*, that Whitaker was rumoured to have lost his reason.[81] Such notoriety did not, however, prevent his history becoming one of the most widely read of antiquarian publications, and one of the few works on British antiquities to be cited by Edward Gibbon in *The Decline and Fall*.[82] Whitaker was also possessed of an extraordinary ability to pull the mote from his brother antiquary's eye, whilst ignoring the beam in his own. His own criticisms of the local antiquary Thomas Percival might just as easily have been applied against him. Percival had

> a Wild way of asserting, without mentioning Proofs; has a wilder of supposing, without advancing Reasons: he asserts without Argument, and imagines without Warrant; by which Means the Multiplicity of Roman Stations is easy, and the Fate obvious. And had he been left to the Guidance of his own untutored Genius, he wou'd have stock'd Lancashire with an infinite Variety of Stations.[83]

As an antiquary and historian of Manchester, however, Whitaker was equally vulnerable to charges of making assertions without proof and constructing wild suppositions. His critics pointed to his reliance on the phrase 'must have' when lacking any other kind of authority and his failure to cite the sources for the colourful circumstantial detail with which he furnished his narrative. He manipulated etymology in an attempt to establish the 'British' origins of the Manchester area, tracing words from Welsh even when there were much more plausible Saxon or French derivations. Furthermore, he allowed his political preconceptions to colour his account; reputable antiquarian sources were cited where it suited the argument, but, 'when some new Whim is to be prov'd or lugg'd into Day', he resorted to the infinite opportunities offered by the 'dark and towering smoke of Ossian' and the supposed practices of the Scottish Highlanders.[84]

Richard Gough, who had little time for Whitaker, remarked that he 'out-stukelied' Stukeley.[85] William Stukeley, possibly the most famous of English antiquaries both today and in his own time, was renowned for his groundbreaking surveys of the stone circles at Stonehenge and Avebury, and also for the unorthodox conclusions upon druidical religion and ancient British civilisation which he drew from his fieldwork.[86] Whitaker himself professed to find Stukeley's methodology suspect, although he did allow that his extravagances 'should be considered as the occasionally wild colouring of that ray of genius, which has not yet been too frequently the portion of our English antiquarians'.[87] Whitaker aside, most antiquaries regarded Stukeley's 'rays of genius' as representative of the worst extremes of speculative antiquarianism. 'I never admired Stukeley,' Thomas Pennant confided to George Ashby, 'he appeared to me to have too much fancy ever to be faithful.'[88] Robert Masters, a Cambridge antiquary, objected not only to his conjectures but also to his tendency to alter his evidence to fit his theory: 'he is not only positive above measure, but capricious and fanciful withall, and is likewise deficient in one of the essentials of an Antiquarian, *accuracy*'.[89] Modern commentators focusing upon Stukeley's invention of a monotheistic druidical civilisation have bemoaned the fatal compromising of his fieldwork by such metaphysical speculation.[90] For his contemporaries, however, it was not so much the thesis of druidical civilisation which attracted their derision as his method in presenting his arguments. Belief in the *prisca theologica*, the ancient connection between eastern learning and ancient British civilisation, was not in itself particularly controversial.[91] Stukeley's method seemed to his critics to be first construct a theory, that is the descent of the Druids from the Patriarch Abraham, and then to fit to it whatever evidence came to hand, be it stone circles, brass celts for cutting the Druids' favourite mistletoe, or coins depicting ancient British chariots of eastern origin. He did not cite authorities, he was too doctrinaire in his approach, and he proceeded too often upon inadequate evidence. In one of his later publications, *The Medallic History of Carausius* (1757), he went so far as to acknowledge that some might find the publication 'fanciful', but swiftly countered such objections on the basis that his extensive knowledge and depth of experience enabled him to 'see much farther into the necessary chain' which connected the disparate elements of antiquity (the coins) placed before the reader.[92] Such arguments failed to impress readers such as Richard Gough. In one of his earliest forays into print, Gough cut his critical teeth pulling Stukeley's tendentious reasoning to pieces, railing against the hypothetical approach which Stukeley embodied. Gough drew on the eighteenth-century Englishman's abhorrence of overarching systems and theories, labelling it the 'systematic Fatality of the Age'. Antiquaries of all people, he wrote, should be most averse to 'substituting Fancy and Invention to that Fiction and Obscurity they labour to banish'.[93] Stukeley had deliberately suppressed words such as 'conjecture' or 'suppose', converting contested issues to indisputable certainty. Sources which did not substantiate his argument were ignored or misread; other points were made without any corroborating evidence.

On a lesser scale many other antiquaries committed similar offences. The conflicting theories regarding the course of Roman roads through Britain and the modern location of the stations of the Antonine Itinerary are a case in point. Camulodunum, for example, was variously proved to have been located at Colchester, Maldon in Essex and Camerton in Somerset by different antiquaries over the course of the century, all of whom selected their evidence and deduced their etymologies in order to establish their rival claims. Given the paucity of material with which antiquaries were often working, it was easy to fall into the trap of *a priori* reasoning. Foote Gower mercilessly demonstrated how John Hutchins's etymologies in the *History and Antiquities of Dorset* descended into tautological reasoning. First, he said, Hutchins fancied a particular use or origin for his antiquity; then he hunted after a meaning for its name; and when he discovered the meaning he reasoned from this arbitrary supposition to prove the use to which the antiquity was applied.[94] Similarly, the temptation to fit antiquities to whatever fragments of knowledge had already been established was always powerful. Even at the end of the eighteenth century antiquities were still generally regarded as being primarily *illustrative* to a fact or truth derived from a textual source. All antiquities had therefore to be matched to some other externally derived fact in order to acquire meaning. 'Given a date and a name, and a man of leisure and letters will, almost instantly, create a piece of history or chronology, seemingly regular and consistent; and this by mean of conjectures, by straining passages and combining the most heterogeneous, and by various other arts of literary pharmacy.'[95] But the problems inherent in such an approach were becoming increasingly apparent and in the second half of the century antiquaries were beginning to see the need to move beyond the textual straitjacket which had dominated their discipline up to that point. Thus, in 1780 James Douglas commented somewhat caustically on the attempts of earlier antiquaries to accommodate finds of Roman antiquities to the evidence of the classical texts: the seventeenth-century antiquaries William Somner and John Battely were accused of being 'theoretical and speculative' rather than 'practical' antiquaries. He astutely recognised how ingenious antiquaries would manipulate their finds to fit with the relevant text and let a 'specious appearance' of things take on the status of incontrovertible truth.[96] Douglas himself boasted that he never allowed himself to assume a position on the basis of conjecture. When deductions were made, he stipulated, they should be founded on a scrupulous comparison of fact. Antiquities, in his memorable phrase, were the alembic rather than the dreg of history.[97]

The extremes represented by Stukeley's fantasies and the austerity of Douglas or Gough do not tell the whole story. There were others within the Society of Antiquaries who were more sympathetic to the kind of approach associated with Stukeley, and who are representative of an alternative strain of antiquarian thought which was more responsive to current trends in what would now be called historical sociology. Thomas Pownall, the former governor of Massachusetts Bay and South Carolina and a fellow of the Royal Society, was also a keen antiquary, and one who diverged from the strictly empirical approach advocated by Gough or Douglas. Whilst he agreed on the importance of detailed and accurate fieldwork, and the need to digest and interpret the collected remains of antiquity, he was much more open to the idea of using what he called a philosophical method to elicit historical 'truth'. Pownall was readier than most to embrace the uncertainties of historical and antiquarian investigation which the Pyrrhonists of the early eighteenth century had raised, and which had never been entirely laid to rest. Pownall's contribution to antiquarianism has fared less well historically than his career as a colonial governor and politician. However, through a series of papers published in *Archaeologia* and in two further treatises on the subject of antiquarianism, he went some way towards articulating an alternative approach to the study of antiquities.[98]

Pownall was strongly influenced by the stadialist theory of historical development, which by the 1770s had achieved a fairly general acceptance.[99] He was also receptive to the anthropological accounts of primitive societies with which he was already familiar from America and which were currently being brought back from exploration of the South Seas. The apparent simplicity of these societies seemed to match the hypothetical early stages of civilisation posited by the philosophers, thereby awarding empirical credence to such interpretations and opening up possibilities for the construction of models of ancient British society drawn from analogies with these primitive people.[100] This was clearly of enormous importance to the fact-starved students of ancient British history. The recognition that human society assumed comparable characteristics in its various stages of development, irrespective of its ultimate racial origins, represented a significant conceptual advance; up to that point the assumption had been that any similarity between primitive monuments discovered in various parts of the world must mean that they were the remains of the same people. This diffusionist principle of a single origin forced antiquaries to infer complex and ultimately implausible patterns of migration and cultural transmission – a mode of reasoning which had not died out by the end of the eighteenth century, but which was coming under increasing attack from the theorists of polygenesis.[101]

Pownall did not use these theories of social evolution – as did many – simply as window-dressing, to give a flourish of fashionable rhetoric to content otherwise unrelieved by any philosophical reflection. He took a more rigorous approach which attempted to locate antiquities within the framework of the progressive, stadial development of human society. Building on the widely accepted theory of a universal element to human nature, he argued that a model or set of principles could be built up on the basis of extant evidence. This model could then be applied by analogy to any other society and could be used to explain even the most isolated fragment of antiquity. Just as an artist who was well acquainted with architecture could identify any building from a fragment, a 'philosophic' antiquary who had studied the different systems of society would be able to tell precisely what kind of society any piece of antiquity belonged to. One of Pownall's earliest essays, entitled 'A Description of the Sepulchral Monument at New Grange, near Drogheda', originally read before the Society of Antiquaries in 1770, was published three years later in the second volume of *Archaeologia.*[102] He began with a comparison of barrows throughout Europe, from Tartary to Ireland, encompassing in the process Homeric descriptions of ancient Greek burial practices. Asserting a fundamental similarity in the burial practices of early peoples, he proceeded to draw conclusions about the Irish monument on the basis of Scandinavian evidence. He then outlined a model of 'successive changes of forms' by which human society had lived. Woodland inhabitants who followed a hunter gatherer existence were succeeded by settled landworkers. This, he argued, constituted a great revolution, as the landworker, wherever he was, displaced the scattered woodland inhabitants. This revolution, however, had taken place at different times in different parts of Europe; thus the woodland Celts, who were the earliest inhabitants of Europe and the British Isles, were subjected to a succession of different races, Phoenicians, Teutons, Phrygians and Vics, who inhabited these regions under 'different modes of life'.[103] Proceeding upon such a theoretical premise, Pownall suggested, would enable the antiquary to identify remote antiquities about which little else was known. In another essay, published in a later volume of *Archaeologia*, he discussed a collection of vases which had been found on the Mosquito shore in South America. In this essay he attempted to relate the vases to the different stages in the development of society on the basis of their ornamentation. In the second stage of civilisation man had progressed beyond mere functionality in the production of artefacts and had begun to give expression to his 'conceited imagination' in the use of 'barbarous and deformed ornamentation'. In the next stage man began to refine his design and base it more closely upon the original; taste then led to beauty and to the full flowering of the human genius. The vases, he suggested, had left nature but not yet reached the status of art, and could therefore be presumed to come from the middle stage of civilisation.[104]

Pownall's attempts to build up a theoretical model clearly implied that the period of history prior to the Roman Conquest was not one undifferentiated continuum, as had often been assumed, but covered a period of remarkable changes, with a variety of civilisations and cultures to which antiquities bore witness. He rationalised his approach in greater depth in two pamphlets devoted to a discussion of the value of antiquarian studies.[105] Amassing facts was not, he acknowledged, in itself a useful task, and sometimes too little was known to be able to make any kind of sense of such scattered remains. He was, however, adamant that there was always a 'system' or 'golden chain' which held together all things in nature. The elucidation of this system would enable the antiquary to restore antiquity from the collected fragments. In the first treatise, he defended the use of philosophical etymology. It was, he argued, an essential desiderata of the study of antiquities and in many cases explained the customs, policy and deeds of ancient societies, and even elucidated the geography and chronology of those countries.[106] This approach clearly shows the influence of enlightenment thinkers such as Lord Monboddo, author of *Of the Origin and Progress of Language* (1773–92), 'The more I study language', he told the Danish antiquary Grimr Thorkelin, 'the more I am convinced that it is not only the most curious Art, of the most difficult Inventions, of all those invented by Man, but I am further persuaded that it is by Language chiefly, that we can discover the Origin of Nations and their Migration from one Country to another.'[107] In 1795 Pownall went further and explicitly advocated the use of what he called 'experimental inductive theorems' as a means of searching out the truth.[108] In what might seem an almost postmodernist take on the pursuit of the past, he made the provocative argument that the difference between romance, which was how he chose to describe his treatise, and history was unimportant. Romances could convey historical truths equally as well as 'history' proper. Any antiquarian work was composed of fragments which had once been part of a system, but that system had been lost; only conjecture could enable the antiquary to reconnect them and to recover the system. Pownall did not pretend to have found out a single 'truth', nor did he demand his readers' belief, but he did suggest that truths 'veiled in the fable of romance' might actually be more productive of real knowledge than the rigorous, but ultimately sterile, empiricism advocated by other antiquaries.[109]

Some welcomed Pownall's attempts to impose an organising principle or 'system' upon the study of antiquities, but not everyone was convinced by his arguments.[110] Edward Ledwich launched himself against the 'groundless hypothesis of historical romance' in a discussion of druidical antiquities, and he clearly had Pownall within his sights, as well as the 'orientalists' amongst the Irish antiquaries such as Charles Vallancey and Sylvester O'-Halloran.[111] 'Events', he observed, 'have been settled; history ascertained and manners described that never existed beyond the author's imagination.'[112] Ledwich's use of the word 'romance' was deliberately loaded; it was the stock dismissal for any history deemed to be incorrect or ill-founded. With some justice Pownall pointed out that his own papers had only ever been presented as conjecture rather than conclusive reasoning; he had always pointed out where fact and theory diverged. Relations between himself and the Society of Antiquaries, however, grew increasingly strained.[113] By the time that the seventh volume of *Archaeologia* was published in 1785 Pownall was withdrawing with defensive dignity: 'I find my ideas of the *mode of the Study of Antiquities*, and of the use to be made of it, to differ so much from those of gentlemen who aim at, and profess, celebrity in this branch of Literature, that I shall never engage myself further than to amuse myself and a few friends.'[114]

Pownall's writings also show a well-developed sense of how antiquities themselves could contribute to history, not just in terms of corroborating facts, but in opening up new areas of inquiry and facilitating a much more immediate apprehension of the past. The contribution of antiquities to the study of 'manners and customs' was a hackneyed commonplace, being adaptable to the defence of anything relating to the past. Even in the seventeenth century it was acknowledged that antiquities served this purpose. The difference in the eighteenth century was that 'manners and customs' no longer existed in such a peripheral, incidental relationship to historical studies. The philosophical historians of the Scottish Enlightenment had elevated the description of the manners and customs of a particular age from simply a matter of curiosity – a digression from the main narrative – to an issue of central importance. Paul-Henri Mallet, whose *Introduction à l'histoire de Dannemarc* was translated for an English readership by Thomas Percy, spoke for a generation of historians and antiquaries when he challenged the dominance of battles, sieges, intrigues and confusions, the tyranny of facts and dates in the conventional narratives of history. History, he argued, should rather give a picture of the opinions, customs and inclinations of a people.[115] Such features were representative of the relative civilisation, the social organisation or the state of religious belief of the society under consideration, as William Robertson demonstrated in the thematic essay, 'A View of the Progress of Society in the Middle Ages', which prefaced the more traditional narrative account of the reign of the Emperor Charles V.[116] Increasingly, matters of private experience and local concern were no longer deemed unsuitable subjects for the historian's attention. In keeping with the rise of sentiment, and its emphasis upon personal empathy and 'sensibility', the incidents of private life assumed a new importance and took their place alongside affairs of a more public nature. Other literary genres underwent a similar process of reorientation; even the lives of ordinary individuals became the object of public interest as their obituaries began to fill the pages of periodicals in place of the theophrastan homages to heroes and statesmen.[117] Private affairs, it was argued, affected the reader more powerfully; they were therefore not only more arresting in their interest for the reader, but also more effective in conveying the truths and didactic weight of history.[118]

Antiquaries were able to draw strength from these epistemological changes. The local and limited scope within which many antiquarian studies were conducted could now be presented as a positive advantage. It allowed a more personal and intense response to the narrative of history: 'the distresses of an individual, told with some particular domestic circumstances, will operate stronger than the account of a battle which may involve thousands in misery and woe', argued the author of a history of Hull.[119] History written upon a narrower scale with examples drawn from common life was also more useful, being more accessible to all ranks in society.[120] 'The proper Study of Mankind', the earl of Buchan informed the Scottish Society of Antiquaries, 'is Man & that Study is Antiquarian.' It was only by examining the foibles and weaknesses of the individual, characteristics which could not sully the page of a history, that a person could be truly known.[121] Similarly the antiquary's obsession with the artefact could be turned to a strength in the context of eighteenth-century sentimentalism which placed a new value upon history and its evocative power to conjure up images of bygone eras. The tangible physicality of the object offered a sensory point of contact with the past, which no amount of descriptive eloquence could replicate. Antiquaries drew upon the language of sentiment to exploit the capacity of the monument or ruin to move the beholder and impress more powerfully upon him than could mere words the places and presences of history. In the opinion of Thomas Burgess, 'the Antiquary forgets the painfulness of minute enquiry in the pleasure of observing the features of the times more strongly and characteristically marked in these partial and peculiar representations'.[122]

'Mine are subjects rejected by the historian to the end of each reign', wrote Richard Gough in his study of monumental effigies, 'it is a picture of private mixed with public life'. There is no doubt, however, that he considered that these 'private' matters in *Sepulchral Monuments* were of considerable historical significance in exploring 'national manners and modes'. 'It is not a History of England', he explained, nor was it an account of great events, great personages, great characters good or bad. In 1786 Gough could be reasonably confident that few of his readers, accustomed by now to a 'sentimental' view of history, would miss the self-deprecating irony in such a statement.[123] For all his abjuration of theoretical models, Gough was nevertheless responsive to the transformations which had taken place in the approach to the study of the past over the previous half century. He pointed out the difference in method between his own mode of proceeding and that of Bernard de Montfaucon, whose *Monumens de la monarchie françoise* had been a major inspiration for his own volume. Montfaucon, as a good antiquary, had described and illustrated the tombs, effigies and monuments of the French monarchy and aristocracy, assigned their dates and detailed the history of their proprietors.[124] He had not, however, exploited their potential for yielding material on bygone manners and customs. Nor had he begun to formulate comparisons between monuments, let alone draw any conclusions from the evidence. Montfaucon was interested in antiquities solely as specimens, rather than as a means to understanding the society in which they were produced.[125]

Again we may turn to Thomas Pownall to see how the study of antiquities could build upon this historiographical shift. 'The Antiquary sets before our eyes, and puts into our hands, in a way that the historian does not, every component part and whole frame of the acting system.' Antiquities brought the antiquary into a closer contact with those who had inhabited the past, 'he makes the reader live as it were in the times, and through the scenes he describes'. Classical history had failed to answer many questions as to how previous societies had been organised. The information which an antiquary amassed – in terms of coins, building materials, weapons, ships – often raised questions, about, for example, the financing of the Roman state or the construction of triremes, that would lead to a better understanding of how society worked. The antiquary and the historian would thereby be able to arrive at more informed insights upon the relative merits and competency of historical characters on the basis on the resources available to them, and what they had managed to achieve within the parameters of their circumstances.[126] In the early eighteenth century Joseph Addison had treated the antiquary's delight in recondite knowledge with ironic satire, showing how a study of coins and medals could establish historical truths of momentous importance, such as which was the first Roman emperor to use stirrups. By the end of the century the irony had lost its edge, and both antiquaries and historians would have appreciated this as a crucial piece of information, with its implications for the military advantage exercised by the Roman army as it expanded its imperial conquests.[127]

At the same time that Pownall was articulating his ideas, another antiquary, Edward King, gave some thought to the value of studying antiquities as a means of deepening historical empathy or understanding. Antiquaries made a highly significant contribution to the development of the historicist approach to the past that has been taken to be a defining characteristic of modern historiography. As will be shown, antiquaries were becoming increasingly sensitive to the necessity of divesting themselves of anachronistically conceived expectations in studying the antiquities of former ages.[128] The antiquary, steeped as he was in the past, was particularly sensitive to the specious facility with which the historian could misinterpret the past to fit his own agenda. Without a careful consideration of antiquities, the historian was in danger of making proleptic assumptions. 'Our ideas', warned Edward King, 'are apt to be contracted by the constant contemplation of the manners of the age in which we ourselves live.'[129] The very obscurity of antiquities could provide a useful function in bringing home the otherness of the past.[130] Meticulous measurements, exact plans and careful comparisons of buildings were the essential elements of the antiquary's business, for it was only by these means that the antiquary could hope to apprehend the original ideas of the architects, and as a consequence also the 'ideas corresponding to the circumstances of the times in which they lived'.[131]

King's reputation has not weathered well. This is due not least to his somewhat unorthodox theology which combined an explosive mixture of eschatology, virulent anti-Catholicism and a vigorous assertion of the compatibility of scientific truth with revealed religion. Yet his antiquarian publications, which had chiefly to do with architectural antiquities culminating in his four-volume study of castle architecture, *Munimenta antiqua*, were held in considerably more esteem by his fellow antiquaries. His speech on resigning the presidency of the Society of Antiquaries is an unusual credo of what one man at least considered the role of the Society of Antiquaries to be, and his own understanding of what the study of antiquities should entail.[132] King tried to identify a middle way between the empirical strengths of Gough's approach and the need for some selectivity and interpretation, without condoning either the 'dull unanimated pursuits' of those who searched through the rubble of past ages to no apparently useful end, or the 'fastidious, pert conceit' of those who were too refined to look upon anything but the most elegant remnants of classical antiquity. The purpose of their studies was, he concluded, to bring truth to light and to develop the true history of man.[133]

Interpretation, contrary to the caricatures, was therefore inherent to the antiquarian project. Around thirty years after King was making his speech, the anonymous author of the prospectus for a county history of Yorkshire in 1816 commented explicitly upon how the reorientation of interest towards ancient manners, which he saw as characterising antiquarian research, was proof of 'the superior intelligence and curiosity' of the modern age. In former times it had been sufficient for the antiquary simply to give a view of ruins, to name the founder and date of foundation, and to summarise the extent of the property. This was the body, not the soul of monastic history. It told the reader nothing about the monastic lifestyle or their faith. These, however, could be recovered through inference and deduction – a task which the author ascribed not to the historian, but to the antiquary.[134] Antiquaries had shown the historians the necessity of writing a new kind of history. The historian, argued the Gloucestershire antiquary Thomas Fosbroke, was a philosopher who confounded all periods and situations and universalised all qualities. The antiquary, by contrast, knew from a study of the material evidence that such conclusions were unfounded. 'In short, the judicious study of antiquities is the first basis for soundly philosophizing that the world can afford, and its professors alone can be critics of past ages and accurate instructors of the present.'[135]

2

People

'A mere antiquarian', pronounced Samuel Johnson, 'is a rugged being.'[1] Memorable though his characterisation has proved to be, it is of little use in further elucidating the peculiar quality or motives of those who undertook antiquarian studies. Antiquaries were the butt of satire – as were lawyers, clergy or writers – and equally as difficult to define as a generic type. Much though the antiquary was ridiculed and lampooned, the very power of the satire derived from the ubiquity of the character in contemporary culture. For all the associations with eccentricity and pedantry there was an element of the antiquary in many gentlemen, and also women. As the editors of the *Antiquarian Repertory* put it, every man was '"*Quoad hoc*" an Antiquarian'.[2] Indeed, the commercial success of publications with an antiquarian element to them in the later eighteenth century is tangible evidence of the undisputed place which a knowledge of history and antiquities held amongst the reading public. A large part of the appeal of antiquarianism certainly resided in the perceived importance of the historical information which could be acquired, but it was also an activity which endowed the individual with a social role and a perspective from which to view both the past and the present. Antiquarianism represented a frame of mind and a way of life.

The gentleman's penchant for the collection of classical antiquities from Rome and Greece is easily explicable on the grounds of aesthetic values and conspicuous display.[3] Engaging in the study of domestic antiquities was in itself a mark of social status, even if it did not offer quite the same opportunities for the flaunting of taste and the exercise of social superiority as going on the Grand Tour. To have the resources of time and leisure to take up the study of antiquities indicated wealth and education, and the rhetoric of benefiting the public good which was harnessed to the antiquarian endeavour confirmed its reputation as a suitable gentlemanly pursuit.[4] Antiquaries would decry the execrable taste of those who destroyed the Gothic ornaments of a church or pillaged the barrows for building materials, but the regret was always tinged with the satisfaction bred of perceived pre-eminence, as the antiquary demonstrated his own superior taste and learning. Proposals for subscription made a selling point of the limited size of the print run, and promised no more would be published than subscribed for: cheaper volumes would only diminish the prestige attached to them, and devalue the social cachet associated with antiquities themselves. For these reasons antiquarianism was largely the preserve of the social elites, although their domination was by no means exclusive. The study of antiquities was a 'lucubration' of the gentleman's leisure hours; it structured the employment of his time, and did so in a pleasing manner that could plausibly be presented as being in some measure disinterested.

The reasons antiquaries proffered for taking up the subject themselves were generally articulated in proposals for publication and appeals for subscription, addressed to the public, or in the preface to the volume itself. They were therefore part of a complex process of self-presentation to the reading public. Elaborate expressions of disinterest and modesty were made to construct the persona of the modest man of sense and virtue. By contrast, the correspondence of antiquaries – with a few notable exceptions – was less likely to have been penned with a view to publication than their prefatory disclaimers; it might therefore be assumed to be have been less disingenuous. It was, however, still structured around epistolary conventions and rules of expression. The extent to which we can take on trust apparently revelatory comments upon an individual's motivation is impossible to assess, but such professions do at least indicate what social conventions dictated would be acceptable – or plausible. There were a number of formulaic utterances to which antiquaries resorted. At the most personal level was the confession of a consuming personal fascination with the past, often originating in a pivotal childhood experience. William Stukeley described how he was captivated by ancient coins as a young boy in Stamford; Browne Willis acquired his love of Gothic architecture as a schoolboy in the precincts of Westminster Abbey; whilst Thomas Hearne's father brought him up to ramble through the Oxfordshire countryside in search of Roman antiquities.[5] As a child Thomas Martin was reported to have spent his leisure hours busily employed in searching amongst and contemplating the ruins of his native town of Thetford.[6] Richard Warner, clergyman, antiquary and man of letters, looked back upon his childhood as a schoolboy at Christ Church, Dorset, where surrounded by ancient buildings, he first began to experience a new curiosity, 'a spirit of research after things *that had been*' and excavated the barrows in the area, hoping to find the 'gory bed' of an Ossianic hero.[7]

A persistent theme which runs through every antiquary's credo was an empathetic relationship with the historical past. Stebbing Shaw wrote of the 'exquisite pleasure' which was mixed with the toils of the antiquary, 'which none but those engaged in the pursuit can know or feel'. He delighted in revivifying the features of the dead, and the arts and manners of former times.[8] Antiquaries took particular delight in the sense of historical distance or 'historicity' of the past. For some, the very obscurity of the subject matter posed an intellectual challenge in which anyone might take pleasure; as John Hodgson acknowledged to his fellow Novocastrian antiquaries, 'we love to make the little candle of our intellect extend its light as far as possible'.[9] The insignificant remnants of daily life, the detritus of the past that was scorned by the connoisseur and deemed to be below the dignity of history, created an evocative sense of former ages that particularly appealed to the sentimental ethos of the later eighteenth century. The antiquary's materials were primarily artefacts; tangible objects which represented a physical contact with the past, transcending the passage of time. In viewing, possessing or holding an object, the antiquary was transported back through history; he could relive past scenes in his imagination; he could restore the historical edifice from the fragments of time.[10] Those who studied antiquities stressed the universal elements of its attraction. The pursuit of truth embodied in antiquarian pursuits – as opposed to the partial expression of politics or religion to which the writing of history was so often reduced – must, it was said, appeal to any educated mind. Those who could not see beyond an immediate practical application for the study of antiquities were guilty of being unable to look beyond mere utilitarianism: 'To think of confining our studies to what may be deemed mere necessary truths is to expose ourselves to the danger of shortly becoming ignorant of those truths themselves.'[11] Mankind possessed a natural curiosity to know what had happened in earlier times and antiquaries were fond of repeating to each other the words of Addison's Mr Spectator, who found himself an antiquary despite himself.

> I have heard one of the greatest geniuses this age has produced, who had been trained up in all the polite Studies of Antiquity, assure me, upon his being obliged to search into several rolls and records, that notwithstanding such an employment was at first very dry and irksome to him, he at last took an incredible pleasure in it, and preferred it even to the reading of Virgil or Cicero.[12]

The study of antiquities could therefore appeal to the 'pleasures of the imagination' in which every gentleman of taste should take delight – an important point, given that Johnson's rugged antiquary, with his preoccupation with 'bare matters of fact', was often assumed to be excluded from such imaginative exercises.[13] The language of associationism lent itself well to expressing the effect of antiquities upon the individual's imagination and sensibilities in terms of emotional intensity. 'I wish you joy of your tesselated pavement', wrote Lord Dacre to Philip Morant, 'I know you will value it and step upon it with more pleasure than on finest Persian Carpet: as it raises ... up in your imagination Proconsuls, Generals &c in all their Glory, who have been dead and gone above these sixteen hundred year.'[14] Bryan Fausset of Kent wrote of how he longed to dig up the barrows in the vicinity of Kingston Down, where he was a curate, because of his conviction that it was the very spot where Julius Caesar met with and defeated the British tribes.[15] John Skinner, the Somerset antiquary, recorded his excited anticipation upon approaching the Roman camp of Housesteads: it would be a great satisfaction, he wrote, to walk over the ground selected by that powerful people for their principal station.[16] Women too could share in these personal transports of antiquarian delight. Mrs Charles Stothard, wife of the engraver Charles Stothard, and from a family of artists and antiquaries herself, described her visit to the excavations at Woodchester in August 1814. 'It seemed as if all I had read of Roman times ... was confirmed and brought before my view', she told her mother, 'I fancied I could, in imagination, conjure up Caesars, Ciceros, and Pompeys, to fill the vacant apartments.'[17] Greater familiarity with the events of the Roman history, and the influence of classical literature upon the eighteenth-century construction of self, no doubt accounted for the fact that the Romans featured most prominently in these antiquarian flights of fancy.

Such private and imaginative exercises of the fancy did not lend themselves to the rhetoric of virtue and the public good, but the study of antiquities could be represented in a variety of ways as contributing to higher ends of social stability, political virtue, religious piety and national honour, as well as intellectual satisfaction and general entertainment. The study of indigenous antiquities was closely related to a clearer articulation of national history and national origins, giving a historical legitimacy to the emergence of an increasingly powerful and confident fiscal military state. The patriotic and public spirited flavour which permeates much of the language of antiquarian literature reflects the conviction on the part of those involved of the importance of their undertaking and illuminates the historical cast of mind which still dominated religious, political and legal debate. Such language is also indicative of the rhetorical requirements of those engaged upon antiquarianism to present their activities in terms of the public good, the promotion of which defined their own place in the social order as gentlemen. The pompous assertions of high-minded altruism combined with heavy-handed self-deprecation, which figured in many prefatory remarks and dedications, were themselves generated in response to the popular counter-image of the antiquary, who fetishised the past in an excess of antiquarian pedantry and redundancy.

In the dedicatory preface addressed to Lord Somers in *The History and Antiquities of the Exchequer*, Thomas Madox posed the rhetorical question, 'Of what use are these old antiquated things?' His response was that history comprised affairs both ancient and modern and that the modern could not be understood or separated from the ancient. The study of history was therefore inseparable from the study of antiquities. The close partnership between antiquarian and historical literature allowed the antiquary to share much of the language of the historian who defended the utility of history in terms of its didactic and patriotic value. Madox stressed that a knowledge of antiquities and history encouraged veneration for the institutions which were the object of inquiry and was therefore conducive to political stability. It would 'cure that Levity and Desire of Innovation to which Unquiet and Injudicious men are commonly enclined'.[18] Age and antiquity were held naturally to inspire respect and veneration; custom and precedent formed the basis of common law and thereby underpinned the social order. In such a society there was automatically generated a space for antiquities and antiquarian scholarship, even amongst those who professed no active interest. Humfrey Wanley's draft constitution for the Society of Antiquaries drawn up in 1707 resonates with the conflicts and upheavals of the last century and expressed the hope that the society would be

> a School where in the antient Constitution, Laws and Customs of this Kingdom will be best learn'd and usefully declar'd and mentioned in Parliament; whereby ma[n]y innovations and troublesome Debates may be prevented; as we have seen great Quarels have arisen thro' the Inexperience of Person in our Antiquities and ancient Constitution, which by the Authority of such a Society would have died in their very birth.[19]

Wanley's co-worker in the Bodleian, the non-juror and Jacobite Thomas Hearne, was equally convinced of the political and religious significance of his undertakings. The past exercised an all-consuming fascination upon his imagination, but his choice of subject matter and his entire antiquarian agenda was circumscribed by his unwavering commitment to the traditions of divine right kingship and the non-jurors. His publication of medieval texts was premised upon the need to preserve such manuscripts for future generations, but also to make them more widely available, so that the gentry, the natural ruling elite, would arrive at a better understanding of national history, and by extension a right understanding of the religious and political order.[20] Many of Thomas Hearne's most faithful subscribers to his publications came from non-juring clergy and county gentry of nostalgic, if not politically active, Jacobite tendencies. A refusal to take the oaths and a yearning affection for the Old Pretender were not, however, indispensable prerequisites for undertaking antiquarian studies, and as the century progressed the ideological commitment which antiquarianism often implied became much less easy to define. Throughout the eighteenth century, however, a considerable part of the appeal of antiquarianism was the refuge it offered from the uncertainties of contemporary life and its promise of stability and even resistance to further change. At the end of the century, at a time when the religious and political order appeared uniquely imperilled by events in France, the Somerset antiquary and parson, John Collinson, explained that the county history, with its quota of genealogies, charters, and local rights and privileges, 'has often proved a considerable barrier against the violence of despotism on the one hand, and the inconsiderate rage of popular fury on the other'.[21]

Samuel Johnson famously suggested that a man who had not been to Italy was always conscious of an inferiority, but the gentleman who had not had the opportunity for travel abroad could make a positive virtue of this insularity. Students of domestic antiquities exploited in full measure the capital of patriotic virtue that was their due in staying at home to study the monuments of the nation's past, rather than travelling abroad to seek out the ruins of some foreign antique land. A recurring theme in eighteenth-century topographical literature dwelt upon the desirability of encouraging travel within Britain and promoting the study of British antiquities, rather than seeking them out abroad.[22] Foreigners, claimed John Warburton, greatly blamed the English for sending their children to travel aboard before they knew anything of their own country. William Borlase made almost exactly the same observation as he pressed the case for his own study of the antiquities of Cornwall. English travellers, he pronounced, were too little acquainted with their own country.[23] William Camden was cast as a national hero by the eighteenth-century antiquaries – in the words of William Nicolson, he was the 'immortal Camden' and the 'sun whereat our modern Writers have all lighted their little Torches'. The debt of modern antiquaries to Camden was that of the poets of ancient Greece to Homer.[24] In this spirit, antiquaries were encouraged to record and preserve the memory of the monuments of history before their disappearance from the face of the nation. Such actions were firmly grounded in a patriotic agenda because antiquities cast light upon history, and a nation's history was its identity. A glorious past was something to be proud of. 'There is no greater Argument', asserted White Kennett, 'why the Antiquities of England should be more and more illustrated than this: to correct the mistakes and reconcile the contradictions of foreign Writers.'[25]

The geographical unit within which the gentleman antiquary was most likely to work and with which he would identify himself was the county history. The county history, which demonstrated the historical longevity of the gentry class, was the natural medium through which the legitimacy of the place of the landed gentry in society could be asserted. The 'county community', once a leading actor upon the historical stage of the Civil War, has been reduced in counter-revisionist studies to something of a bit-part player. The full blown thesis of the inward looking, endogamous county cannot be resurrected for the seventeenth century and is even less plausible for the eighteenth, when ease of transport eroded distance and the growth of communications and print culture encouraged the articulation of a national consciousness. The gentry of eighteenth-century England were regularly at London, often for extended periods, and were identified by their politics or their fashionable connections rather than their county of origin. The county continued, however, to operate in a meaningful way on a number of levels, administratively and politically and imaginatively, and the counties themselves were understood to be the building blocks of the nation in both its ancient and modern state. The county was the major locus of local administration for England, if not Scotland, and all those who held any kind of public office, as JP or above, held that office by virtue of possession of land in a county, and their authority was predicated upon the reality of that county. The conduct of county business was a significant part of the persona of the public life of the propertied Englishman, and it drew on a strong sense of public responsibility which was reinforced by the expansion of county administration in the hands of the justices of the peace during the eighteenth century.[26] Similarly, the favoured organisational model in the eighteenth century, whether for improving agriculture, prosecuting crime, reforming morals or educating the poor, was the county society.[27] Association then, reinforced the cohesion of the county elite, whilst politics, although frequently divisive, was similarly conducted within a county framework, drawing on a rhetoric of local patriotism. Even whilst regional differences were being eroded by swifter communications and the dissemination of a common metropolitan culture, the county identity was gaining in strength in other contexts.

There was therefore a strong sense of county feeling amongst the landed elite; this manifested itself in the county history, celebrating the historical continuity of the county from Anglo-Saxon times and, most importantly, the place of the landed elite within that unit. For all that druidical rocks or Roman roads were carefully identified and notable barrows or fine Gothic buildings were described, the substantive part of almost every county history was devoted to manorial histories: the descent of property, the genealogies of families and the illustrations of their seats. 'As for Dr Todd's *History of Cumberland*', one antiquary commented ruefully to Roger Gale, 'there are severall good remarks and observations in it upon the Roman remains in Cumberland and Westmoreland, but he has intermixt the affairs of the countrey familys and antiquities of churches with the Scottish incursions with a design to engage the gentry and clergy here to come into subscriptions.'[28] The security of tenure which these antiquarian publications celebrated deserved to be recorded not least because it was this stability which provided the key to the progress of civilisation which antiquaries demonstrated in other spheres. The history of property, declared the short-lived periodical, *The Topographer*, was the most important aspect of antiquarian study.[29] More pragmatically, at a time when property rights had to be proved by title, the record of the descent of property represented not simply an obsession with detail, but had a very practical application; county histories could be, and indeed were, used in courts of law as evidence of title to land, and this was counted not the least amongst their uses.[30] County histories took the place of heraldic books of visitation which had fallen into abeyance in the eighteenth century and were little regarded by the law.[31] John Watson, reflecting that the reputation of antiquarian publications such as his own *History and Antiquities of the Parish of Halifax* had somewhat improved in recent years, suggested that this might be attributed to the public's being better satisfied of their utility, since they had, he claimed, been read in the highest courts of justice.[32] It was Domesday Book's importance as a record of private property which accounted for the inclusion of a transcript in almost every major county history of the eighteenth century. Social mobility and the rapid transfer of property in a buoyant property market created a fear of instability amongst those who placed their faith in the unbroken transmission of property and saw the rise of new families within a county as an indicator of a dangerous degree of social change. County histories brought a permanency to the descent of families and property which might otherwise have been lost.[33]

The county history was a celebration of the power and wealth of the landed elite and as such necessarily emphasised this element to the cost of other subjects: hence the impressive bulk of the volumes, the dominance of pedigrees and the profusion of plates of country seats. County histories were a sop to family pride, aimed at those who liked nothing better than to see their family's name ranked amongst those of the other noble personages of the county and it was the natural point of reference for any who wished to discover an account of illustrious men.[34] One antiquary found that his own appeal for materials had led simply to endless requests for information on points of family history from those who sought to see themselves recognised amongst the names of the county elite.[35] The market for large antiquarian books was never extensive, and particularly so for volumes which dealt, as county histories did, with a particular locality. The antiquary had to appeal to the vanity of the gentry and their family pride, in the hope that they would purchase it. 'There is some satisfaction', wrote John Hutchins hopefully, 'in a gentleman's knowing the particular history of his own family, and being able to point out through what hands his several lands and tenements have passed, and whether they were acquired by purchase, grant, or inheritance.'[36] Natural filial respect for one's ancestors was gratified by seeing their names preserved for posterity on the printed page, whilst their brave and generous actions acted as both a stimulus to virtue and reproach to the degeneracy of modern times. The shame of failing to live up to the historic reputation of one's family, it was hoped, would deter current generations from committing base or unworthy actions.[37] For all the interest in Roman roads or Saxon coins evinced by British, and particularly English antiquaries, it should not be forgotten that a huge proportion of antiquarian activity had always revolved around what was essentially genealogical material.[38] Such matters were meat and drink to antiquaries, who may or may not have noted down the presence of zig-zag ornamentation around an archway, or the tracery of the pointed windows, but would almost certainly have recorded the tombs and the epitaphs within. This is what lay behind the collection of 'church notes': the epitaphs and monumental inscriptions; the funeral escutcheons; the heraldic blazons ornamenting the stained glass windows. With the decline of heraldic visitations, 'gentlemen', Samuel Pegge told George Ashby, 'do well to take care of their own Genealogies'.[39] Even genealogies could be made to serve a broader social purpose, giving a visible presence to those invisible bonds of deference that bound society together: as Edward Hasted explained, 'relationship of family extended, by the preservation of pedigrees, promotes a chain of society and good will that often affords assistance and support to every link of it'.[40]

How much of such genealogical material it was advisable to include in a county history was always a nice point. Too much detail deterred the casual reader, was expensive to produce, and risked high levels of inaccuracy in reproducing the minutiae.[41] The omission of such genealogical content, however, raised the hazard of offending prospective purchasers who bought the volumes less in the spirit of scholarly antiquarianism than out of a desire to see their family's name and honour duly recorded for posterity. The right to bear arms and the genealogies which supported this privilege was, as Ralph Bigland reminded his readers, a form of property in itself.[42] Philip Morant was praised by Charles Gray,[43] for his 'pains and labour in preserving the history of our families and estates', but he came in for some sharp criticism from other antiquaries, notably Richard Gough, for his failure to include a complete account of the epitaphs and monumental inscriptions.[44] But this was exactly what Morant's patron and mentor in the project, Lord Dacre of Belhouse, had commanded of him. He had repeatedly instructed Morant on the importance of avoiding minute detail or trifling and inconsiderable matter and persons, advising him, 'Especially not to give the Epitaphs indiscriminately at length: but only those of considerable persons.' Nathaniel Salmon (who had published nineteen numbers of a history of Essex) had been guilty of including far too much trivial matter, which could only lower the dignity of the history.[45] The 'trivial' by definition comprehended all such details as did not relate specifically to Dacre's tiny elite of great families.

Richard Gough's ire, on the other hand, seems to have been provoked by what he saw as a misuse of Salmon's materials and a suspicion that Morant had been cutting corners; in his opinion, epitaphs and inscriptions were to be recorded systematically and accurately, or not at all. He could not share Dacre's view of a county history as being essentially the genealogical record of the most eminent families. Hence his oft-quoted outburst from the preface to *Anecdotes of British Topography*, in which he poured coruscating criticism upon the content of most such county histories:

> Incorrect pedigrees, futile etymologies, verbose disquisitions, crowds of epitaphs, lists of landholders, and such farrago, thrown together without method, unanimated by reflections and delivered in the most uncouth and horrid style, make the bulk of our county histories.[46]

Gough belonged to a generation of antiquaries in the second half of the century who regarded the traditional emphasis upon genealogy and heraldry as outdated and restrictive. He saw John Hutchins's *History and Antiquities of Dorset* through the press, and even revised it for a second edition, but all the while he was acutely aware of the very old-fashioned format that Hutchins had adopted, with its primary focus upon families and the descent of property. The county history of the late eighteenth century was expected to serve a much broader range of interests. The agenda of queries to be addressed had expanded significantly, reflecting the considerable advances in knowledge which had been made since the early eighteenth century, whether in the appreciation of medieval architecture or in mapping the remains of Roman Britain. Moreover, if the county historian was to continue to lay claim to the spirit of patriotism and service to the public, it was no longer enough simply to preserve the records of family and property. As a reviewer of Edward Hasted's *History and Topographical Survey of Kent* put it, there was 'not much taste for the history of … mere landholders, or … mere squires: something more is necessary to obtain for them the record of a printed volume'.[47] The fortunes of the nation were no longer reducible to the interests of a small landed elite, but were dependent upon the state of commerce, manufactures and agriculture. Compilers of county histories had to take cognisance of the vast increase of information available in the public domain, whether from agricultural surveys, statistics on trade and industry or inquiries into charitable relief and the state of the poor. The reading public had become accustomed to acquiring such information from the many published tours, from Daniel Defoe's to Arthur Young's. The consequence was that not only did a county history at the end of the century run to many more volumes than its predecessors – John Nichols's *History and Antiquities of Leicestershire* eventually stretched to eight volumes – but its content was expected to range through 'Geology, Mineralogy, Natural History, Agriculture, Manufactures, Commerce, with the Manners, Customs, and Language, so far as they are peculiar and characteristic'.[48] The reaction against a form of antiquarianism which served only the interests of the elite, espoused by antiquaries with an interest in the history of the common people such as William Hutton or Joseph Ritson, developed in parallel with a growing appreciation from within the antiquarian movement itself that it was incumbent upon the antiquary to comprehend a broader range of material.[49] Now more than ever, the county history was a work of editorial compilation, rather than the unassisted efforts of a single individual.

To explain the support for county histories simply in terms of the gratification of personal and family sentiment would be both reductionist and deficient. Yet there was clearly a sense in which the gentry of eighteenth-century England identified with the county as an entity; their sense of personal honour was ineluctably tied to the honour and reputation of the county. The respect which Thomas Tanner had for Francis Blomefield, and his 'Love to Norfolk and any design which may go for the Credit of that County', induced him to agree to what he had refused many others, that Blomefield should dedicate his history of Norfolk to him.[50] Lord Dacre congratulated Philip Morant on the honour which he would bring to the county of Essex.[51] It was a blot on the reputation of a county such as Bedfordshire, by contrast, that no history had ever been published.[52] Committees of county gentlemen were often established to promote the completion of the county history: although these gentlemen might have no particular interest in antiquities for their own part, they still perceived it as incumbent upon them to support such projects. There was therefore a penumbra to antiquarianism into which many were drawn, who had only a passing interest, but who accepted the importance of such projects. In some cases the initiative for a county history lay with the gentlemen themselves. Samuel Pegge was approached to write the history and antiquities of 'one of the principal counties in England'.[53] William Hamper hoped to persuade his fellow members of the grand jury to employ John Britton to revise Dugdale's *History of Warwickshire.*[54] In Northampton, a committee of thirteen gentlemen, headed by Sir Thomas Cave (also an active promoter of Leicestershire history) was formed in order to see through the publication of the history of Northamptonshire – a volume which had had a chequered history up to that point. Begun and left incomplete by John Bridges, the history was then handed over by the committee to Benjamin Buckler of All Souls College, Oxford in 1755. Buckler promptly reneged on his engagement, and it was passed on to Peter Whalley, a schoolmaster with literary leanings, who eventually brought the project to completion over a thirty year period. John Hutchins's history of Dorset passed through fewer hands, but was equally a product of concerted activity amongst the county gentry. Sir Peter Thompson paid for the transcription of material in London on his behalf and organised a subscription of over £100 amongst the county gentry to pay for a curate who would cover Hutchins's parochial responsibilities whilst he travelled the county collecting materials.[55] As Hutchins's health declined towards the end of his life he suffered the further blow of seeing his home go up in flames. The chances of his completing the history, on which he had been working since the 1730s, seemed increasingly remote. A committee of gentlemen was therefore established to promote subscriptions and support the publication.[56] The gentlemen of Leicestershire subscribed additional sums in order to ensure that the history of Leicestershire, which would so much enhance the honour of their county, would in fact be published, despite the disastrous fire which had taken place at Nichols's printing press in 1808.[57] This emphasis on the honour to the county is a recurrent theme in correspondence concerning the promotion or publication of county histories into the nineteenth century, and showed little sign of dilution.[58] If nothing else, the financial exigencies of publishing a history breathed new life into a rhetoric of county patriotism. The level of involvement of the county elite is a reminder that identities operated at a local, regional and national level and were constructed through a sense of history, tradition and continuity. Even at the end of the eighteenth century, when the growth of the London Season, metropolitan culture and a national press had done much to loosen the ties of the gentry to the locality, the county still operated as a powerful 'imagined community' amongst the landed elite of England.[59]

The county tradition and the county history, however, were definitively English phenomena. One of the interesting cultural differences between England and Scotland that emerges when examining Richard Gough's attempts to update the sections on Scotland in Camden's *Britannia* was the English inability to comprehend the vagueness surrounding the county unit in Scotland. As he pointed out, the county unit was not one that Scottish antiquaries were accustomed to employ, and there was no Scottish equivalent to the English published chorographical tradition which went back even beyond Camden to William Lambarde's *Perambulation of Kent* (1576). The sense of county identity was in fact so weak that when George Paton was pressed by Richard Gough for clarification on the matter of county boundaries for the purposes of revising Camden's *Britannia*, he was hard put to find anyone who could pronounce authoritatively upon this point. With great diffidence, he tried to persuade Gough to remedy the confusion of Camden's original: 'you have so interwoven places in different shires that do not properly belong to them', he told Gough, 'that I am at a very great Loss how to derange your Plan'.[60] The largest collections of antiquarian material were made by Walter Macfarlane and, to the extent that they were antiquarian, were primarily genealogical in their scope, and remained largely unpublished. During the eighteenth century the only Scottish 'county histories' to appear in the public domain were those of Sir Robert Sibbald, a history of the province of Moray (therefore not strictly speaking a county history) and histories of Stirlingshire and Renfrewshire.[61] Scotland had never experienced a comparable pattern of county government to that of England – there had been no Saxon rationalisation of local government nor was the system of political representation based upon a county unit. The county had no place in the Scottish myth of the ancient constitution, nor did gentlemen conceive of their relationship to the state or the locality in terms of the county unit. The importance of the clan and kinship networks in the Highlands, however, was proportionately greater. The clan was the focus of local loyalties and identities. Scottish antiquarian traditions were rooted in kinship networks and genealogy rather than territorial boundaries and the descent of property. This in turn may help to account for the relative paucity of antiquarian and topographical publications in Scotland. The lower density of population and smaller propertied class to purchase such volumes were obvious impediments, but political considerations would also have checked the publication of works with a genealogical emphasis, which might also fall under suspicion for maintaining Jacobite networks.[62]

In Wales there was an indigenous tradition of topographical literature, albeit one which was rather weaker than in England. 'Very little pains have been taken by natives or neighbours to illustrate the history or antiquities of this part of the island', observed Richard Gough.[63] William Nicolson did not even bother to devote a separate section to Welsh antiquities in the *English Historical Library*; such chorographical and antiquarian collections as there were in the early modern period remained unpublished.[64]

In the eighteenth century antiquarianism in Wales tended to be focused upon the revival of the Celtic language and the bardic heritage rather than the topographical survey of antiquities. It was only towards the end of the century, under the stimulus of English tourism and the influence of antiquaries such as Sir Richard Colt Hoare, that a series of county histories was written.[65] Enthusiasm for the Celtic revival and the recovery of bardic traditions, however, has also been interpreted as integral to the efforts of a 'new' gentry to establish their own antiquity in the period after 1760; it was an act of legitimisation, whereby they appropriated the traditions of hospitality, bards and music through their own antiquarian activities.[66] 'Antiquity and Welsh culture', remarks one commentator, 'became social and political assets under George III – and the new gentry assumed it with enthusiasm'.[67] The position in Ireland was different again, and Richard Gough's attitude to Irish antiquities was even more brusque. This was partly because he had never visited the country and was therefore even less familiar with it and had fewer contacts upon whom to call for information on antiquarian matters.[68] County studies did exist, but as in Scotland the county unit did not have the same administrative and historical presence, nor did it provide a basis for local identity.[69] The Irish gentry who might have patronised such works were less numerous and less wealthy than their English counterparts. From the perspective of the native, Irish majority the county was an imposition and instrument of English colonisation; in no way did it command the powerful rhetorical and representational force which it held in England. A limited number of county histories were written but the important stimulus to topography came from the government-sponsored initiative of Statistical Surveys published in the early nineteenth century.

Antiquarianism depended upon the active support of the gentry; but the most active antiquaries came from the ranks of the lesser gentry and those who merged with the professional classes, rather than from the great landowners and the aristocracy. Wealthy proprietors who were also active antiquaries as opposed to simply exercising patronage, such as Sir Richard Colt Hoare or Stukeley's patron the earl of Pembroke, were the exception rather than the rule. Amongst the gentry certain types were more likely to follow up antiquities than were others. Legal experience was an obvious advantage, for example, and amongst the members of the Society of Antiquaries there was a heavy preponderance of gentlemen listed as belonging to one or other of the Inns of Court.[70] Whilst this does not necessarily indicate that the individual in question was actively following a legal career, it did imply some legal training and familiarity with legal documents. Moreover, there were considerably more who practised as lawyers without being attached to the Inns. Since the seventeenth century the study of legal antiquities had represented one of the strengths of the English antiquarian tradition. The legacy of Sir Henry Spelman, Sir John Selden, Sir Robert Cotton and the other luminaries of the common law tradition lived on throughout the eighteenth century, and legal antiquities continued to represent an important branch of historical research amongst English and Scottish antiquaries. The most famous of all eighteenth-century lawyers, Sir William Blackstone, belonged to the London society, and was intermittently an active member. In Scotland, the lawyers Lord Hailes and Lord Kames were amongst the most highly regarded antiquaries of their time. The legal elite aside, lawyers conventionally operated with a very broad brief, undertaking a diverse range of responsibilities for their clients, managing estates, presiding at local courts and acting as trustees for charities and local statutory bodies. This kind of experience could be extremely valuable in a much broader range of antiquarian activities and is particularly well exemplified, and documented, in the career of William Bray.

William Bray (1736–1832), a solicitor from Surrey, is best known for his contribution to the *History and Antiquities of Surrey* and his *Sketch of a Tour in Derbyshire and Yorkshire* (1777); he was also treasurer of the Society of Antiquaries from 1803, having been elected a fellow in 1771. Bray is an outstanding example of an antiquary who combined his legal practice and other professional duties with his antiquarian interests. His own consciousness that his professional training had prepared him to undertake the work is expressed in the preface to the second volume of the history of Surrey. Here he commented on the need for 'industry in searching for records and papers, patience in examining them and accuracy and extracting them'. His antiquarian curiosity was undoubtedly stimulated by the access to deeds, estate records and other family papers that he enjoyed as legal adviser to many of the landed families of Surrey. Early in his career, in 1761, he had been appointed to the Board of Green Cloth, which oversaw the domestic affairs of the royal household, through the patronage of another Surrey family, the Evelyns of Wotton. Whilst requiring him to live in London in Great Russell Street, it also facilitated his access to record depositories in London and an entrée to the Exchequer Office, the Rolls Chapel, the Tower and the other depositories of state records. Bray appears, from the evidence of his diaries, to have begun collecting material relating to Surrey history and antiquities in the 1760s. He was also making transcriptions from manuscripts at the British Museum for Philip Morant in 1767. Even before his election to the Society of Antiquaries in 1771 he was already moving within social circles which included a number of the leading members of the society. Sir Joseph Ayloffe, Michael Lort, Thomas Astle, John Topham and Andrew Coltée Ducarel all numbered amongst his regular dining companions. Bray could hardly have selected his social circle more felicitously with a view to securing access to documents of antiquarian interest. Ayloffe was employed at the state paper office, as were Thomas Astle, and in later years John Topham. Michael Lort was librarian at Lambeth, succeeding Andrew Coltée Ducarel; another of Bray's close friends was Richard Penneck, rector of Abinger in Surrey, and a deputy keeper of the British Museum.

Bray's first publication, *A Sketch of a Tour in Derbyshire and Yorkshire* (1777), was a typical example of the burgeoning genre of travel literature, but one with a marked antiquarian emphasis – which not all readers found to their taste.[71] Bray's most important contribution to antiquarianism, however, did not begin until around 1800 when John Nichols and Richard Gough persuaded him to undertake the completion and publication of Owen Manning's history of Surrey. Manning had lost his sight towards the end of his life and badly needed assistance in bringing the project to completion; he died shortly after Bray was recruited to the project in 1801. The project that Bray inherited was not inconsiderable; Bray's preface to the second volume, in its carefully phrased understatement, reveals the enormity of the task that still awaited him. Manning had made 'very extensive' collections, but they consisted of 'notes put down as they occurred'. Bray found that it was necessary in most instances to go back to the original records himself, as well as searching out new materials.[72] But armed with his extensive knowledge of Surrey families and their estates, his familiarity with the records of the Tower, the Exchequer Office, the Augmentations Office, Chapter House at Westminster, Lambeth Palace Library and the British Museum, Bray was admirably placed to undertake the task. His diaries, which noted simply his activities on a daily basis rather than being a record of self-examination and introspection, show how successfully he was able to integrate his own interests with his professional duties.

Spare time in London was invariably filled with research at one or other of the record repositories. He moved from Great Russell Street, where his legal practice was based, to the British Museum and then to meetings of the Board of Green Cloth or one of the charities for which he acted as trustee. During the dead period of high summer he was able to devote concentrated bursts of activity to compiling materials. In the course of a four week period over August and September 1803, for example, he spent seven days at the Exchequer Office, two days at the Tower and additional days at the Rolls Chapel, as well as consulting Rogers Ruding the numismatist and vicar of Malden in Surrey upon matters pertaining to the history of coinage.[73] When visiting clients and friends in Surrey, such as the Molyneuxs of Losely or the Westons of Sutton, he took advantage of his position to request the chance to examine family documents. This was an undoubted advantage given that a number of antiquaries were wont to bemoan the difficulties they encountered in gaining access to materials and family records. The gentry were frequently exhorted by antiquaries to be liberal in communicating material from their family papers, it having been 'justly complained of in other counties, that papers of the utmost consequence to their histories, have, with an useless precaution, been timidly withholden from public inspection'.[74] Without a personal introduction it could be extremely problematic, not least because the issues of property which these papers documented could be so sensitive. The position of trust which Bray clearly enjoyed amongst his clients and fellow gentry must undoubtedly have mitigated anxieties surrounding titles to property and facilitated his access – unlike the Norfolk parson Francis Blomefield, who experienced considerable difficulties in collecting material from the local gentry due to his comparatively lowly social status.[75] In his capacity as steward to numerous manors, Bray had also to attend frequent sessions of the manorial courts, but used this opportunity to visit the local churches and make church notes. He claimed with some pride in the preface to have personally visited every church in the county. Vicars such as Mr Diggle of Esher were happy to allow him to inspect their registers and to 'break open' the parish chest to lend him other records and papers.[76]

Bray's professional familiarity in dealing with the type of documents which were the bread and butter of antiquarian studies was an obvious advantage, but other professionals who occupied similar positions of trust and social standing could equally exploit it to antiquarian ends. Doctors, surgeons and physicians were more commonly associated with natural history, but, for those with an interest in antiquities, the wide social acquaintance with families of wealth which their profession inevitably entailed provided similar opportunities for the collection of materials as those enjoyed by William Bray. Richard Wilkes, it was said, was able to collect his materials towards a history of Staffordshire by gaining access to the papers of families whom he visited in his capacity as a physician.[77] The Bristol surgeon William Barrett, author of *The History and Antiquities of Bristol* (1789), similarly remarked that his profession had gained him admittance to many families from whom he procured important manuscript records.[78]

Traditionally, antiquaries had been closely connected with the Heralds College or the College of Arms as it became known in the eighteenth century. William Camden, William Dugdale and Elias Ashmole, who numbered amongst the leading antiquaries of the previous century, had all been heralds. Despite the declining institutional importance of the College of

Arms in the eighteenth century, a close relationship continued to exist between the antiquarian movement and the heralds, signified by the fact that the first president of the Society in 1717 was Peter le Neve, Norroy King at Arms.[79] Heralds were the closest approximation that there was to professional antiquaries, given that their business lay in validating the right to bear arms and in tracing lines of familial descent. Whether they became heralds in order to indulge their interest in antiquarian matters or whether the interest developed as a result of their occupation is difficult to determine. The office of herald could be awarded in recognition of merit, as was evidently the case for Somerset Herald, John Charles Brooke, but was also a sinecure in the gift of the Earl Marshal and therefore attracted unlikely candidates for office such as Sir John Vanbrugh who occupied the post of Clarenceux Herald in the early eighteenth century.[80] The office of herald created the circumstances in which a young man such as Brooke, who had developed an obsessive interest in genealogy and heraldry from an early age, could indulge his interests for pecuniary reward. That is not to say that he was solely interested in pedigrees; he developed much broader antiquarian interests than those necessitated by the remit of his employment and became one of Gough's most valued correspondents, particularly with reference to the topographical antiquities of Yorkshire.[81] Most heralds specialised in heraldry and genealogy, as one would expect, but Peter le Neve, Francis Grose, John Warburton, John Charles Brooke and the precocious John Ives all made notable contributions in topographical antiquarianism, whilst Ralph Bigland's work on genealogy and parish records was of considerable methodological importance.[82]

The same congruence of professional occupation and antiquarian interests is evident in the careers of those employed in the various libraries, museums and archives of the metropolis and its growing administration. Such figures were always well represented in the Society of Antiquaries. Given their residence in London and their access to many of the major collections upon which antiquaries routinely based their inquiries, their presence is hardly surprising, and was indeed desirable for other members of the Society of Antiquaries, who relied upon their good offices in order to secure information as to the holdings in the various offices and for arranging for the collation or transcription of documents. Of the early members of the society, Humfrey Wanley was the librarian to the earl of Oxford, George Holmes was deputy keeper of the records in the Tower (a position which he used to accomplish many favours on behalf of his fellow antiquaries), whilst Thomas Madox enjoyed the position of Historiographer Royal. Sir Joseph Ayloffe, Thomas Astle and John Topham, all leading figures in the society during the second half of the century, enjoyed careers in the State Paper

Office and Samuel Ayscough, Richard Penneck and Francis Douce were keepers at the British Museum. Once again, it is not always possible to determine whether the position of record keeper or archivist was sought in order to satisfy antiquarian leanings, or whether the individual concerned became an antiquary by virtue of his occupation.

The most numerous occupational grouping amongst the antiquaries, however, consisted of the clergymen, predominantly of the Church of England, but also numbering non-conformists and Roman Catholics. Clergymen represented between 10 and 15 per cent of the members of the Society of Antiquaries during the eighteenth century, and they included some of the most active members.[83] Two of the presidents, Charles Lyttelton and Jeremiah Milles, were churchmen, as were the secretaries William Norris, Thomas Wrighte and John Brand. The prolixity of provincial members, who seldom attended the London society, such as Samuel Pegge of Derbyshire and Samuel Denne of Kent (the self-styled working bees of the society), provided a steady stream of papers for the society's entertainment. Between them Pegge (d. 1797) and Denne (d. 1799) accounted for sixty-four of just over 400 attributed papers published in *Archaeologia* between 1770 and 1796. Overall roughly one third of the papers published in this period were contributed by clergymen. A similar proportion of the county histories and the urban histories published between 1700 and 1820 were produced by the clerical profession.[84] Away from the metropolis, with its high concentration of parliamentarians, lawyers, doctors and other professionals, the clergy were even more important in sustaining antiquarian and literary societies. In the Gentlemen's Society of Spalding they numbered nearly a quarter of the total membership between 1712 and 1760 – the largest of any single occupational category. The clergy were even more dominant at Spalding's sister society in Peterborough, where the influence of the cathedral close upon the town's intellectual and cultural life loomed large.[85]

The clergy were in many ways the best placed and best prepared of all occupational categories to take up such studies. A large number were the product of an education at Oxford or Cambridge. Although the study of antiquities was never a part of the formal university curriculum, the narrow basis of the examined curricula in both Universities should not be taken as representing the sum of intellectual activity. Interests ranged more broadly and the ready availability of manuscripts, coins and other collections in the Public Library at Cambridge, the Bodleian at Oxford, and the individual college libraries provided a natural stimulus to antiquarian activity.[86] The Ashmolean at Oxford was more concerned with natural historical specimens in this period, but also housed within its collections coins and other notable

Francis Peck. (*Special Collections, University of Leicester*)

antiquities, such as the Alfred Jewel. In Cambridge, Trinity College held an important corpus of Romano-British antiquities, including the Cottonian collection of inscriptions from the Roman Wall (presented in 1759) and the Battely collection from Richborough and Reculver. Roger Gale had also given the college his father's collections of manuscripts.[87] Other Cambridge colleges held significant coin collections.[88] Corpus Christi, or Benet College as it was then known, maintained a tradition of antiquarian study which went back to Archbishop Parker, producing such eighteenth-century antiquaries as William Cole, William Colman, Richard Gough, Robert Masters, Nathaniel Salmon, William Stukeley and Michael Tyson, of whom all but Gough were clergymen. Tyson was pleased to tell Gough that William Colman, the master of Benet College, was seeking membership of the Society of Antiquaries. 'We may hope that, under his future guidance, a new generation may rise up, fit and able to serve our holy Mother *Antiquity*.'[89] The significance of this critical mass of antiquarian-minded fellows at Oxford and Cambridge is immediately apparent from the subscription lists for antiquarian publications, many of which emanated from the university presses, and which were dominated by college libraries and fellows.[90]

Beyond the sphere of the universities, the parish priest was an indispensable element in the eighteenth-century drive to amass information. He was a mediating figure between centre and locality and essential in the network of communication that supported the construction of the eighteenth-century state. Ideologies of political obedience and social deference were inculcated through the pulpit and the use of fast days. Information on the political economy of the nation was derived from the responses of clergy to questionnaires circulated throughout the country, seen most notably in Sir John Sinclair's survey of Scotland. The swelling volume of topographical and antiquarian knowledge upon which a sense of nationhood could be constructed was also dependent upon the responses of the clergy to the questionnaires which inevitably preceded the compilation of local antiquarian projects. Such queries were generally addressed to the gentlemen, nobility and clergy, but the most conscientious responses invariably came from the clergy. Most clergy would have had intermittent experience of responding to such requests for information in the course of their normal duties from having had to fill in archidiaconal and episcopal visitation returns, which demanded information of a similar nature to that required by antiquaries and natural historians. Question number seven of Bishop Wake's visitation articles for the diocese of Lincoln in 1706, for example, asked whether there were 'any Monuments of Note in your Parish Church or Chappell? Or what other antiquities do you know of within your Parish?'[91] John Nichols relied heavily on the clergy of Leicestershire in assisting him in compiling information and correcting the text to the history of Leicestershire, and Sir Richard Colt Hoare exerted his considerable personal influence in encouraging all the clergy of the county of Wiltshire to collect any antiquities in their several parishes towards his own history of that county.[92] As an appeal for information on local history and antiquities placed in the *Morning Post* expressed it, 'Who is there, generally speaking, better qualified by education, than the clergy generally living on the spot? Who have more leisure? Or who can be better than they informed, being by education themselves esteemed gentlemen?'[93]

From the perspective of ecclesiastical antiquities, the clergy had a professional interest. The impetus for the study of Saxon antiquities drew much of its strength from the need to show, in the words of George Hickes, 'the faith and other chief doctrines of the English-Saxon Church to be the same with ours, and perfectly answer that never ending question: where was your Church before Luther?'[94] Ecclesiastical antiquities were never the monopoly of churchmen, but nevertheless continued to engage the attention of the clergy throughout the century. Whilst some, such as Henry Rowlands or William Stukeley, concerned themselves with establishing evidence for the monotheistic beliefs of their British ancestors, others were more concerned with the physical fabric of the church. The interest in architectural antiquities which gathered in strength over the course of the century not unnaturally engaged the attention of many clerical antiquaries, given their professional familiarity with the ecclesiastical architecture under discussion and their responsibility for the maintenance of the church fabric. Moreover, as monuments to the faith of former ages and the continuity of the Christian tradition, the clergy might be expected to entertain a particular interest in the study of such architectural antiquities. At the end of the century events in Europe conspired to present the preservation of ecclesiastical antiquities as a matter of national importance, and the conservative rhetoric of Church and King fuelled the production of both sermons and antiquarian literature by the clergy.[95] Amongst the leading authorities on architectural antiquities in the late eighteenth and early nineteenth centuries James Bentham, William Gunn, Thomas Kerrich, John Milner, John Haggitt, Robert Darly Waddilove and Richard Yates were all clergymen.[96] Concern at the damage inflicted upon the church fabric by neglect, clumsy repair and misjudged improvement may be found with increasing frequency in archidiaconal returns by the early nineteenth century. This enhanced awareness of the physical fabric of the church was to a large extent a by-product of the antiquarian movement and a more informed appreciation of architectural antiquities.[97] Thomas Rickman, author of *An Attempt to Discriminate the Styles of English Architecture* (1817), often regarded as one of the defining works of the Gothic revival, saw the clergy as his most important target audience. His motive, he wrote, was 'to afford the guardians of our ecclesiastical edifices such clear discriminative remarks on the buildings now existing, as may enable them to judge with considerable accuracy of the restorations necessary to be made'.[98] By the 1830s it was being recommended that basic instruction upon architectural antiquities should be provided within the university curriculum. The architectural societies which were to spring up in Oxford and Cambridge in the 1830s on the back of the High Church Movement drew on well-established traditions of clerical interest in ecclesiastical architecture.[99]

More prosaically, the reason why many clergymen were the best respondents to parochial inquiries or took up the study of antiquities themselves was that it provided them with some kind of intellectual stimulation – this being the same reason that other clergymen, most famously Gilbert White, took up natural history. But even White, it should be noted, also recorded the local antiquities in the midst of his botanical and ornithological observations. Educated gentlemen who found themselves isolated in rural communities and with time on their hands turned to the study of antiquities as a means of occupying their mind profitably. Stranded in Cornwall, with no other intellectual company and little in the way of books, William Borlase found himself 'obliged to amuse myself with such remarkables as were within my reach'.[100] He used the lure of antiquities to attract visitors to his Cornish parish, promising Charles Lyttelton the attractions of not only a fire in the bedroom and specially ordered Pyrmont water, but whole days employed in searching out monuments and antiquities.[101] For a character such as John Skinner, the rector of Camerton in Somerset, his study of Roman antiquities, which centred upon a determination to prove his own living of Camerton to have been the Camulodunum of the Romans, became something of an obsession. His correspondence with antiquaries such as James Douglas, Aylmer Bourke Lambert and Sir Richard Colt Hoare enabled him to inhabit an alternative world removed from the problems of insubordination and fast-encroaching Methodism amongst his parishioners, as well as allowing him relief from personal grief after the loss of his wife and daughter. It was a form of escapism which 'turned my attention to other objects than the people around me, whose bad conduct only vexed and irritated my mind'.[102]

The correspondence of clerical antiquaries clearly demonstrates that the subject of antiquities provided them with an identity and brought them into a corresponding society of like-minded individuals, even if unable (or ineligible) to attend meetings of the Society of Antiquaries in person. Complaints about the anti-intellectualism and torpidity of life in the eighteenth-century country parish are rife in the correspondence of the clergy. They looked to communication with others to break down their sense of isolation and to alleviate the boredom of a rural living. Clergymen such as Benjamin Ray in the Lincolnshire fogs and fens,[103] and Bryan Faussett, Samuel Denne or Samuel Pegge, all deep in rural Kent, eagerly awaited the receipt of letters which brought them news of publications and fellow acquaintances amongst the antiquarian brethren, as well as information on antiquities or answers to obscure points of etymological inquiry.[104] They pressed their London correspondents for news as to who had been present at the meetings, who had attended the anniversary dinner, who had been elected to the society's offices – or when the next volume of *Archaeologia* was due to be published. Antiquarianism was the means by which they maintained a presence in the Republic of Letters.

The study of antiquities was also a means by which an aspirant clergyman might hope to make a name for himself by venturing into print. For clergymen answerable to a bishop such as Edmund Gibson, an interest in antiquities could present itself as a strategy for attracting preferment. Philip Morant's interest in historical and antiquarian matters developed early in his career; it is likely that he was drawn to historical study irrespective of any difference that it might make to his chances of preferment, but he rapidly realised that such intellectual pursuits could be a means of gaining the notice and the interest of patrons. One of his earliest mentors had been Philip Falle, whom he had assisted in his revision of his *Account of the Isle of Jersey*.[105] Falle had contributed material on Jersey to Edmund Gibson's 1695 edition of *Britannia*, and it would appear to have been through Falle that Morant was drawn to the attention of Gibson, who was by that time bishop of London. Morant was ordained priest by Gibson in 1724 and served as curate in the parish of Great Waltham, in Gibson's diocese between 1722 and 1732.[106] His vicar at Great Waltham was Nicholas Tindal, the translator and continuator of Rapin's *History of England*, who was also working on collections for a history of Essex.[107] Morant assisted Tindal in both these enterprises during his curacy and for much of the 1730s. Through Tindal, he was initiated into a network of Essex antiquaries, which included in addition to Tindal, John Booth, Anthony Holbrook, William Holman, John Ouseley and Nathaniel Salmon.[108] By 1732 Morant was angling for a living of his own, and Falle wrote to him in encouragement; he emphasised how his historical and antiquarian interests stood him in good stead, assuring him that, 'You are in as good a way as I have known any young Clergyman to be'. Various minor appointments followed and in 1737 Gibson was sufficiently impressed by Morant to offer him the living of St Mary's Colchester;[109] Morant had aspirations to a living in London, but in the short term was sufficiently grateful for this sign of episcopal favour to offer Gibson a gift of two knitted waistcoats.[110] He was not, however, greatly enamoured of Colchester; the town was undergoing a period of economic downturn and due to a slump in the cloth industry, poverty and unemployment were high. There was a strong Dissenting presence, which Morant, as a staunch defender of the established church, found offensive. The politics of the town were deeply divided, and as he soon discovered, the corporation was rendered virtually redundant by the factional manoeuvrings of the different parties. Gibson somewhat breezily advised him to keep himself clear of all 'party work' and to make it clear that his business was religion not politics. Morant promised that he would do his best, and that rather than being involved in politics, he would study hard, which would both distract him from his troubles and also serve to endear him to a bishop who clearly set store upon scholarly leanings in his clergy. The plan of study he came up with was to compile a history of the town of Colchester – his previous exposure to the history and antiquities of the county under Tindal cannot have been insignificant in influencing this decision. Gibson was gratifyingly pleased by Morant's project, writing that he hoped that it might be 'an agreeable entertainment for Morant's vacant hours'. Morant wrote to Gibson regularly, outlining the structure of the book and keeping him informed of the progress that he was making (and also reminding him of his continued presence in Colchester and desire to be transferred elsewhere).[111] The finished volume was ultimately dedicated to Gibson, 'the author's most munificent Patron and generous Benefactor' although the hoped for presentation to another living was never made.[112]

Conversely, once a bishopric or a comparable position of social and financial security had been achieved, many clerical antiquaries ceased their publications; the responsibilities of office no doubt served to inhibit their researches, but there was no longer the same motivation to publish in order to make a name or to forge valuable social connections. Gibson, Tanner, Nicolson and Thomas Percy all produced their most notable antiquarian work before being elevated to the episcopacy. Charles Lyttelton as bishop of Carlisle continued to hold office as president of the Society of Antiquaries; nothing that he wrote, however, was published during his lifetime. The papers for which he is now chiefly remembered were published posthumously in *Archaeologia.* Had not fortune rewarded the clerical partnership of Thomas Bennett with the bishopric of Cloyne and Thomas Leman with great affluence, it was said, the results of their joint labours in tracing the Roman roads through England might have been completed and published.[113] Such individuals were able to use their influence and patronage, however, to encourage the study of antiquities within their own diocese, as we have seen in the case of Morant and his patron Gibson or in William Nicolson's promotion of a history of Northumbria.

A professional interest may be assumed to have predisposed certain churchmen to the pursuit of antiquities but there were other more pragmatic reasons why they should have concerned themselves with such matters. The *Antiquarian Repertory* stated, with considerable baldness, that for a clergyman to be able to manage his own property, or that of any church over which he might preside, an insight into the 'Monastic History and Terms' was absolutely necessary. Most cogently, the right of clergy to tithes, and the scope for improving them, which was often contested in the eighteenth century, depended upon historical proof, which could only be secured by antiquarian research.[114] Although Robert Atkyns was a layman, as a devout churchman he expressed the hope that his account of religious houses, churches, impropriations and tithes would be of 'good use to the Clergy in securing their right to tithes'.[115] William Stukeley, as vicar of All Saints Stamford, argued that the study of parochial antiquities was a duty incumbent upon clergymen: 'both tis a matter of curiosity and as of real use: and admirable means of preserving the rights of a Living'.[116] It is clear that in many cases the principal force directing clergy towards antiquarian studies was the need to ascertain their rights to tithes and other privileges – to which end they had to search through all the old records to establish their title. Andrew Coltée Ducarel published his *Repertory of the Endowments of the Vicarages in the Diocese of Canterbury* (first published in 1763 and reprinted in 1782) in the hope that it would solve the problem of disputed tithes without the clergy having to resort to law, and Edward Hasted's *History of Kent* was certainly widely used for similar purposes.[117] Hasted's son, a clergyman also named Edward, drew upon his father's collections and expertise in order to force his own rector to pay him vicarial tithes.[118]

Antiquities were therefore important in sustaining not only the church's ecclesiological claims, but also in buttressing its position within society as a landowner. In this respect clerical antiquaries had much in common with the landed gentry. A concern with property, its descent and its preservation was the key to much of the antiquarian activity during this period and a crucial factor in understanding the practical utility as well as the romantic appeal of antiquarian studies for the social elite of eighteenth-century Britain. In tracing the history of property in this way antiquaries were offering a practical response to the theoretical histories of the law and property emanating from Scotland, which similarly highlighted property as the essential stimulus to the progress of civilisation. 'Industry', wrote Lord Kames, 'depends on property; and a much greater blessing depends on it, which is the gratification of the most dignified natural affections.' The conclusion was clear; without property there would be no civil society and men would remain savages for ever.[119]

Pretensions to antiquarian learning from those below the rank of gentleman or man of property were frequently derided, for to accept their worth would have been to open up the possibility that antiquarianism was not inseparable from gentlemanly status: gentlemen would therefore no longer be able to regard their antiquarian interests as self-evident proof of their own gentility. William Nicolson had set a pattern in his cutting put down of Abel Wantner, a parish clerk who had made collections towards the history of Gloucester, whom he charged with meddling in matters beyond his sphere.[120] Thomas Gent, the printer and bookseller who published on the antiquities of York, Hull and Ripon, observed in his memoirs that he had had 'several admirers, who were surprised to think that a person so obscure as I was generally deemed, should have the courage to venture on so noble a design'.[121] Fellows of the Society of Antiquaries frequently professed astonishment when they found evidence of antiquarian learning amongst tradesmen or craftsmen. The Bristol surgeon William Barrett was, according to John Whitaker, 'a more respectable man' than he had apprehended, whilst at Dorchester he had been surprised to find that the parish clerk, a joiner, had a 'wonderful genius for antiquities' and had collected some six or seven hundred Roman coins.[122] Daines Barrington presented a paper on archery to the Society of Antiquaries, offering for their perusal a manuscript treatise on its history 'which though compiled by a saddler at Manchester, contains some particulars which may deserve attention'.[123] Even James Essex, who was the companion of Gough and Tyson on many of their antiquarian tours, had been nominated for membership of the Society of Antiquaries by them, and upon whom they relied for detailed architectural knowledge, was snubbed by Gough and Tyson in their correspondence; his style, complained Tyson, was too verbose and tedious and he strayed into areas (of history) about which he knows nothing.[124] They were projecting onto Essex those very qualities of prolixity and pedantry which fashionable satire directed at the impolite antiquary. Antiquaries laid great store on the learning they had acquired as gentlemen; it was this that justified their claims to superiority. If others below them could acquire similar expertise, it immediately began to undermine the stability of the social hierarchy.

As these several examples indicate, however, there was a long and honourable tradition of antiquaries who came from relatively humble backgrounds which should not be discounted and which always existed as a minor theme alongside the dominant story of genteel participation. John Stow, a member of the original sixteenth-century society, had been a tailor;

his origins in trade inspired others to follow his example. William Camden, the inspiration for all British antiquaries, was scarcely of exalted social origins, being a schoolmaster at Westminster. Thomas Hearne, the son of a parish clerk was one of a number of antiquaries in the early eighteenth century whose background and interests led them to identify with Stow.[125] Amongst the founding members of the Society of Antiquaries, Humphrey Wanley was the son of a draper and John Bagford was a shoemaker. The tradition continued throughout the eighteenth century, and if anything became more marked as the opportunities for autodidactism and the acquisition of the printed literature became greater.

Familiarity with antiquities could also be acquired by those working with them in a visual context, as the number of artists and engravers specialising in antiquarian subjects demonstrates. There was a clear pattern of draughtsmen and engravers who were drawn to antiquarian subject matter and who developed an expertise in the subject in their own right. George Vertue, engraver to the Society of Antiquaries, was also one of its most stalwart members, and it was his collections that provided the basis for much of Walpole's *Anecdotes of Painting*.[126] Valentine Green, another engraver, the author of a study of Worcester Cathedral and a history of the city itself, was similarly a member of the Society of Antiquaries.[127] Joseph Strutt, whose publications on Saxon and medieval antiquities were amongst the most popular antiquarian works of the day, had originally cherished ambitions to become a history painter (he was a recipient of a gold medal from the Royal Academy in 1770). Early on in his career he was drawn into engraving antiquarian subjects for Foote Gower, Richard Gough's correspondent, and found himself increasingly drawn to the manuscripts upon which he based his engravings.[128] Strutt published in order to make a living: he had hopes, he wrote, that the *Regal and Ecclesiastical Antiquities* would make a tolerable profit and furthermore that it would be a means of 'introducing' him to the world.[129] Predictably, he was never nominated for membership of the Society of Antiquaries, and was given dismissive treatment by Gough, who could not allow that he had 'judgment' or 'light' enough to be considered an antiquary.[130] Commenting upon his works in *British Topography* (1780), Gough delivered a damning and prejudiced list of his shortcomings, concluding with his failure to secure sufficient credit as an antiquary before embarking upon such a work.[131] Strutt was, in fact, a more interesting and intelligent antiquary than many of those who graced the meeting room in Somerset House. His lack of formal training and comparatively limited reading meant that he was forced to concentrate on the visual aspects of the material, which he studied to far greater effect than did many gentlemen antiquaries, who could see no further than their own formulaic descriptions.

By the late eighteenth century it had become viable for an artist or engraver to specialise in the depiction of Gothic antiquities, catering for the public appetite for picturesque scenes. Thomas Hearne, Jacob Schnebbelie, John Peller Malcolm, J. T. Smith and Charles Stothard exploited this market, whilst also laying claim to a measure of antiquarian expertise.[132] Stothard, who specialised in depicting monumental antiquities, went so far as to rank his own work above that of Gough for its accuracy and interpretation.[133]

The architect, artist and antiquary John Carter also falls into this category. Carter was not so much an architect as an architectural draughtsman. Coming from a family of sculptors and craftsmen, he served his articles under a surveyor and builder in the West End, and worked largely as a draughtsman and 'improver'. Early on in his career he established his preference for the Gothic style of architecture; not only was it the native architectural idiom, but it employed much greater emotional power than the rigid formalities of classicism.[134] 'Discovered' by Michael Lort in 1780, he was employed by Lort, Gough, Walpole, Sir Henry Englefield and Sir Richard Colt Hoare amongst others, as well as being appointed draughtsman to the Society of Antiquaries in 1784. He was eventually elected a fellow in 1795 – a decision which many fellows came to repent of only two years later. The president, the earl of Leicester, publicly expressed his regret that, by voting to make a *servant* of the society a member, he had given him an opportunity to dictate to his masters.[135] Carter enjoyed little success as an architect, but his professional status allowed him to assert a superior, practical knowledge of architectural antiquities over those who had only ever made a superficial study of them, through observation and sketching or reading theoretical literature. These were mere amateurs; they lacked the expertise and practical experience fully to understand the structures which they purported to describe. Carter's outspoken claims for his own professional superiority over the gentlemen amateurs of the Society of Antiquaries met with a chilly response. Facts, dates and historical research, riposted the champion of the deceased Whittington (who had seen fit to challenge Carter's assertion of the Englishness of the Gothic arch), were the province of the 'amateur' rather than the 'architect', whose professional occupation gave him no proficiency in such matters. Carter was striking out for the autonomy of the architectural profession, but he was also attempting to dismantle the notion that only the gentleman amateur, the scion of the landed elite, could claim to be an antiquary and a custodian of the nation's antiquities. Amateurs such as Whittington had, in his view, shown their unfitness in their renegade preference for continental influences; his allegiances, thought Carter, lay with France. The guardianship of the nation's antiquities would lie safer with people such as himself.[136] Carter, who deliberately set himself in opposition to those who were traditionally associated with the study of antiquities, was in this respect typical of a growing number of antiquaries who came from more humble social origins, and who were determined to claim the study of history and antiquities for a much more inclusive definition of the public.[137]

Antiquarianism was not class neutral, but it did provide a language within which people from very different backgrounds could communicate and exchange information. It was sustained by a complex system of exchange, with relationships both of equality and deference, in which there was often a clear disparity of wealth and status between the correspondents. Such differences could open up opportunities by which an individual could hope to improve his prospects by forging contacts with those of a higher social status, who might be able to use their influence within and beyond the antiquarian circle on his behalf. Philip Morant, whose ecclesiastical career has already been considered, clearly exploited the common interest of leading clerics in antiquarian matters to further his own career. Alexander Gordon, author of *Itinerarium septentrionale*, was something of a career antiquary, who used his own interest and expertise in Roman antiquities as a means of attracting the patronage of Sir John Clerk of Penicuik. In return for Clerk's interest on his behalf, he richly fulfilled his own obligations, building up his reputation in South Britain as the British Maecenas. Without Gordon's constant eulogies, Clerk's reputation outside Edinburgh would have been much dimmer.[138]

Disparities in social background also occasioned careful negotiation. George Ballard, the staymaker's apprentice, whose self-taught skill in Anglo-Saxon endeared him to Charles Lyttelton, conducted a lengthy correspondence which evinces mutual respect and affection. It was nevertheless one in which Ballard's inferiority of birth and education was never forgotten. Ballard need have no apprehensions that the learned world would condemn him for the faults of his education, Lyttelton assured him. Rather, the position of clerk at Magdalen College, Oxford, for which Ballard was being encouraged to apply, was one which many less learned men than he had filled and from which 'nothing is expected in a Literary way'.[139] Lyttelton expressly encouraged him to apply on another occasion for the position of librarian at the Cottonian, for which Ballard felt himself socially ill-qualified. Few people, Lyttelton observed, consult the library, and those that do were antiquaries or English historians and would require only specialist assistance, 'so from that point of view you are very well qualified'. The implication being that, whilst an epistolary relationship which was purely concerned with antiquarian matters would not embarrass either Ballard or Lyttelton, in a position where a higher degree of social interaction was required – as was necessary on the part of the keeper of the British Museum who had to show round the numerous polite and fashionable visitors – Ballard's misgivings concerning his humble status and inferior education would have been well founded. Whilst Ballard was in a relationship of clientage to Lyttelton, and not seeking a position or literary reputation inappropriate to his education and birth, it was possible for a discussion of antiquities to be conducted by letter, eliding many of the social differences between the correspondents, who simply shared a common identity as antiquaries.

Ballard and Lyttelton were fellow members of an antiquarian Republic of Letters; this 'republic' gave them a sense of identity and belonging which transcended differences of geography and social background and provided a context for their own endeavours, as a contribution to a wider good.[140] 'Should anything occurr to me in relation to Hereford', Smart Lethieullier promised a fellow antiquary, 'I will not fail of acquainting Mr Walwyn with it, for I think we ought mutually to assist in these Kinds of Enquiries.' Thomas Pennant voiced similar sentiments of antiquarian solidarity, declaring to Richard Gough that he subscribed to the publications of all brother antiquaries, good and bad.[141] Gough himself exploited this sense of community to the full in calling upon correspondents who were completely unknown to him for their assistance in illustrating 'our national Antiquities'.[142] Smart Lethieullier also spoke of the 'real pleasure' to be gained from pleasing gentlemen by exchanging curiosities and information. By participating in such exchanges the antiquary was engaging in an affirmation of his own taste; and by flattering the learning and discernment of his correspondent he was indirectly laying claim to such approbation for himself.[143] It was this flourishing network of exchange and correspondence, as much as the Society of Antiquaries itself, which sustained the antiquarian enterprise. It facilitated the study of antiquities by encouraging the free exchange of artefacts, manuscripts and books, the performance of services (such as making transcriptions, identifying references) and the opportunity to exercise patronage by which the recipient was assisted and the credit and reputation of the patron was enhanced. But to work effectively it had to be based upon the assumption of moral integrity on both sides and a shared view that all those involved were gentlemen, or would at least observe a gentlemanly code, since the fundamental principles of the network were those of exchange and reciprocity of obligation.

Gough's epistolary relationship with George Paton illustrates the complex networks of communication which arose and exemplifies the subtle balance of power in relationships within the Republic of Letters. In 1771 Gough had visited Scotland and thereafter corresponded frequently with Paton, to whom he had been introduced by a letter of recommendation from William

Cuming. Cuming was a Dorset doctor, interested in natural history and numismatics, with whom Gough was dealing over the publication of John Hutchins's *History and Antiquities of Dorset.* Gough, wrote Cuming, was a 'Gentleman whom I never saw but with whose Character I am well aquainted [sic] & with whom I have been for some time past engaged in a Correspondence'. Cuming wished to do him 'an acceptable piece of Service' in recommending him to his own acquaintances in Edinburgh.[144] Once Gough had returned to London, he and Paton exchanged gifts (publications which they were each unable to obtain in their respective cities). This demonstrated that both of them were gentlemen (although Paton earned a mere £60 a year) and established a position of mutual trust which would provide the basis for future exchanges of information or antiquities. During the thirty years over which their correspondence extended the two men never saw each other again, but Paton became the main channel through which Gough obtained any information upon antiquarian affairs in Scotland. Paton was his broker for dealing with other Scottish antiquaries, writing to others of his acquaintance on Gough's behalf. Lord Hailes, for example, communicated with Gough through Paton rather than in person, even to the point of using Paton as a conduit for the exchange of their respective publications. Paton performed innumerable services for Gough; he kept him fully informed on the publishing world in Edinburgh and Scotland as a whole, and what was taking place in antiquities and topography in general. He attempted to answer all Gough's ceaseless queries and to correct the equally numerous errors in *British Topography* and *Britannia.* He also hunted out books and manuscripts for Gough and arranged for them to be sent to London. In return Gough kept him up to date with London news and sent him the latest sale catalogues, publications and news of what was going on at the Society of Antiquaries. He also provided him with advice on antiquarian matters and publications. The relationship was one of mutual assistance but demanded heavy investments of time, effort and even money from Paton to secure the information Gough required.

Paton was, however, of extremely limited means, whereas Gough enjoyed a substantial private fortune, estates and an enormous library. Paton's learning in antiquarian matters, his contacts with the Edinburgh literati, and the carefully arranged exchanges of gifts and information meant that this difference in social position was kept firmly in the background. Their letters were addressed in terms of mutual respect. Gough was scrupulous in paying for any books Paton had acquired for him on his account, 'it is but common justice he said', and was clearly wary of Paton being put to additional expense on his behalf. Paton had traced a map of Fife for Gough and had not let him know the price – he must do so, wrote Gough, or he would be forced to suspend inquiries. Gough frequently sent Paton gifts – the Windsor Print published by the Society of Antiquaries, for example – but when he did so he was always sure to emphasise in the same letter the obligations he owed to Paton for the information which the latter had procured for him.[145] Gough's generosity and his emphasis upon Paton's efforts on his behalf were a means of ensuring that the fiction of a system of reciprocal exchange was maintained – and that Paton carried on executing his requests. Only occasionally did Paton's financial problems upset the delicate calibration of the relationship. Towards the end of his life, aged seventy-nine, Paton was struggling on a fixed stipend, faced rapidly rising living costs and the loss of his savings due to his banker's bankruptcy. He was forced to try to reap some of the benefits of patronage which he had presumably hoped his efforts on behalf of Gough would eventually yield. He wrote requesting him to use his contacts in government to secure an increase in his stipend. Gough was unable to do so, but sent him a £10 bank note.[146] Their correspondence petered out and Paton died in 1807. Increasing age on both sides was clearly a factor, but so too was the fact that Paton had been forced to break the reciprocity of exchange between gentlemen in the Republic of Letters.

For Gough, Paton's correspondence was invaluable in that it kept him abreast of antiquarian scholarship in Scotland; he was effectively Gough's agent there. From Paton's perspective Gough was one of a number of English gentlemen with whom he was engaged in correspondence and for whom he performed similar services.[147] He operated a kind of information exchange, bridging the cultural divide between English and Scottish antiquaries. Thomas Pennant, Thomas Percy and Joseph Ritson numbered amongst the other Englishmen who applied to him for information. For his part, Paton channelled the material from his own network of Scottish correspondents scattered across Scotland to his English contacts. In return, he secured material for his own collections whilst the advantages of counting such people amongst his literary acquaintance could only enhance his own reputation.

John Nichols occupied a similar position to Gough in the antiquarian world as a focal point in a network of antiquaries; he lacked Gough's expertise in scholarship, but, as the main antiquarian publisher and the editor of the *Gentleman's Magazine*, he was a highly regarded source of information, advice and patronage. He attracted numerous letters from individuals who offered him their services – in providing drawings of antiquities, pieces for publication, or who requested his assistance in getting their own works published. The artist John Peller Malcolm, whom Nichols employed on many antiquarian commissions, had recurrent financial problems and was frequently reduced to writing to Nichols, begging the loan of money. In return, rather than assurances that he would pay Nichols back, he promised to put ever increasing numbers of drawings at his disposal for use in the *Gentleman's Magazine*. Drawings of antiquities thus became a kind of currency. Malcolm was not without pretensions to being an antiquary himself, and his *Londinium redivivum*, planned as a continuation to Pennant's *Account of London*, demonstrated a far from superficial acquaintance with antiquities. His correspondence with Nichols, however, was not as a fellow member of the Republic of Letters but as a financial dependent.[148]

The literary exchange of the Republic of Letters operated more or less smoothly between Gough and Paton, but the mechanism often showed signs of stress in other relationships. Gough was, for example, extremely put out by the reluctance of his Scottish correspondents to fall in with his expectations. To Paton he was gracious, but with regard to other Scotsmen he fumed with indignation at their laconic response to his inquiries. 'I cannot sufficiently praise your generous mind', he told Paton, but, 'were your Countrymen possest of the like Industry and Readiness of Communication it would be happy for the Public.'[149] Thomas Pennant similarly grumbled about the 'incivil silence' of John Brand, secretary to the Society of Antiquaries – Brand had failed to reply to an inquiry he had made for over six months. William Cole complained that Gough himself was 'one of the rudest mortals I ever corresponded with'. Cole's irritation arose from Gough's failure to acknowledge the receipt of several painstaking pages of observations which he had sent him: he felt slighted.[150] One point upon which all British antiquaries united was in condemning the conduct of the Danish antiquary Grimr Thorkelin, who had flouted all the conventions of the free exchange of information within the Republic of Letters. Thorkelin was cagily shy of communicating his thoughts, declining to assist in deciphering runic inscriptions. He carried off all his sketches back to Denmark, where finally he and his fellow Danes insisted upon publishing in Danish, rather than Latin, thus closing their communications to the rest of Europe. 'I am humbly of the opinion', wrote Paton, 'his conduct is ungratefull and deserving some public Censure, being a kind of Robbery.'[151] According to Thomas Pennant, Richard Gough was also guilty of bending the unspoken rules. Pennant declined to lend Gough a manuscript: 'Mr Gough applied to me for the loan of it which I was sorry for as I thought myself obliged to deny him for the reason I gave you.' Pennant's implication was that Gough would use the manuscript for his own purposes without due acknowledgement. Manuscripts, as Pennant pointed out in another letter, were private property. He asked Paton to check one of his own maps against that of Colonel (later Major General) Roy's unpublished survey warning him that,

'I would by no means have anything taken from him by stealth as it is a private property and even unpublished. I would be dishonourable to think of it.' Pennant had further cause to complain about Gough, later suspecting him of 'anonymous treacherous abuse in a Magazine'. Anonymous abuse breached the codes of gentlemanly conduct and Pennant therefore 'dropt his correspondence'.[152] Paton's role as intermediary consequently became even more important in ensuring the passage of information between these two touchy individuals.

Pennant's tone of righteous indignation in dealing with Gough appears more than a little disingenuous. Pennant himself was pretty unscrupulous in his use of Paton and his other Scottish informants, notably George Low and Charles Cordiner, as sources of information, maps and drawings. He was a prolific producer of tours, which combined natural historical and antiquarian observations. In order to maintain his rate of publication he relied heavily on the information of others, supplied in response to queries which he sent out in advance of his journey, and lengthier descriptions which he procured from local specialists. He liked also to think of himself as one who encouraged and sponsored the efforts of others, but on his own terms. He expected recognition and deference in return and resented it when what he considered to be his due was denied him. William Smellie, the secretary to the Scottish Society of Antiquaries, another naturalist cum antiquary, used this relationship to their mutual advantage. Smellie published a translation of Buffon, in which Pennant had given him some assistance. When it came to publication Smellie attributed the index to Pennant, thereby securing to himself credibility and status in the eyes of the literary world. In return for this 'gift' of allowing his name to be associated with Smellie's work, Pennant expected a complete set of plates. As he explained to George Paton, 'I know my name will be an advantage, so may expect the gratification of my wish'.[153] Others showed less compunction and Pennant claimed that he was deserted by people who should have adhered to him through common gratitude. The greatest betrayal in the nexus of this gift economy arose over George Low, upon whom both Gough and Pennant relied for information about the antiquities and natural history of the Orkneys. Low's manuscript, which went missing for a number of years in transit between Paton, Gough, Pennant and Low, was the source of contention. Pennant suspected Gough of keeping it and using it for his own purposes: he spoke of it as the property of Low, but showed that he considered himself to have an interest in 'what was formed at my instigation and my expence' according to the rules of patronage and exchange. The two men squabbled over access to its contents and also over who should best promote its publication. Low considered himself betrayed. On seeing

Pennant's *Arctic Zoology* he wrote in great indignation to Paton, the intermediary in all his dealings with Pennant and Gough, complaining that Pennant, and to a lesser extent Gough, had gutted his manuscript, leaving him nothing worth publishing on his own account: 'But stay, what is to be published? Is it not all published already! One has taken a leg, another an arm, some a toe, some a finger, and MR PENNANT THE VERY HEART'S BLOOD OUT OF IT.'[154] Pennant's relationship with Charles Cordiner was rather less troubled, and Cordiner always professed himself extremely grateful for the assistance Pennant had rendered him, whilst Pennant certainly made use of Cordiner's notes and drawings and promoted the publication of *Antiquities and Scenery of the North of Scotland in a Series of Letters to Thomas Pennant Esqr* (1790); a publication which shed not a little lustre upon Pennant's reputation and was replete with fulsome expressions of gratitude from Cordiner.[155]

Low's fury over what he perceived to be Pennant's misuse of his manuscript highlights a major source of tension within the antiquarian network. Manuscripts and letters were circulated between individuals like books; antiquaries would make copies or extracts and add them to their own collections. Manuscript collections were often sold along with the library of a deceased antiquary, thereby passing into the ownership of another antiquary. It then became unclear to whom precisely the content belonged. Thomas Carte, author of a history of Great Britain, broke the rules by printing extracts from letters, to which his correspondent, James Phillips, had not given his consent. 'With such Antiquaries', Philipps warned Samuel Pegge, 'it is dangerous to correspond.'[156] Others antiquaries, such as Thomas Tanner and William Cole, were simply reluctant to lend their materials, despite being keenly aware that this marked them out from their fellow antiquaries; it was a major concession on Cole's part to lend one of his volumes of manuscripts to Gough.[157] Cole was, however, very free with his information when questioned upon specific points.

The unwritten codes also dictated that information or objects should not be exchanged for financial gain; herein lay part of the reason for the contempt which gentlemen antiquaries felt for those booksellers and others who sought to make a profit from writing about antiquities. In 1735 Beaupré Bell informed Francis Blomefield, with great distaste, of a painter he had come across in a trip to King's Lynn, who was making collections of corporation records, epitaphs and armorial bearings in the church windows. The painter, however, would not lend his collections without a substantial gratuity.[158] Heralds, who derived their livelihood from antiquarian researches, could find themselves in an anomalous position when their professional practice conflicted with the expectations of the antiquarian fraternity. The Somerset Herald John Charles Brooke had counselled Treadway Nash, who was struggling to complete the history of Worcestershire, that 'the more pedigrees you enrich your work with, the better it will sell'.[159] Such advice was not wholly disinterested, given that Brooke, who was described by one of his colleagues as a 'well-regulated oeconomist', had a large professional practice. He later offered his services correcting pedigrees and heraldry on Nash's behalf.[160] Nash was furious when Brooke demanded payment of £100 for work which he had already completed on Nash's behalf. Gough, to whom Nash complained, and who was on good terms with Brooke, confessed that he was taken aback by the latter's demand – he would have been surprised had Brooke asked half the amount, and had 'never understood' the rule by which gentlemen in public office 'professed themselves to be governed'.[161]

John Hodgson, the Northumberland clergyman and antiquary, by contrast could not bring himself to exploit his collections for financial gain, despite his impecunious status. He declined to sell a cache of coins he had discovered, preferring to give them away. 'I could not', he explained, 'do violence to my antiquarian feelings by making a traffic of them.'[162] Similar sentiments dictated the actions of Rogers Ruding, vicar of Malden in Surrey. Ruding, a numismatist and author of *Annals of the Coinage of Britain* (1818) published by Nichols, also contributed to the *History of Leicestershire*. When he found himself in financial difficulties he professed that he would prefer to sell his library rather than borrow money. Fortunately, Nichols, to whom he had explained his dilemma, took the hint and offered assistance, without Ruding having to demean himself by asking for a loan.[163] Walter Mounsey, another clergyman enlisted on the Leicestershire project, underwent acute embarrassment when he found that his own financial circumstances prevented him from carrying out the commissions which Nichols had requested from him; the costs of visiting the various parishes which were beyond walking distance were too much for him to bear. He was forced to request a subsidy from Nichols, but was insistent that he would only take so much as would cover the immediate expenses incurred; any surplus he attempted to return.[164]

The antiquarian network and the ties of obligation and deference were fully activated when it came to the event of publication: 'I desire to be one of your subscribers', Francis Peck told Francis Blomefield, 'conditionally that you take one of my Antiquities of Stamford in lieu of yours.'[165] Few antiquarian works could anticipate a large market; they therefore had either to be paid for by the author himself or published by subscription. Publication for profit – which was an unlikely proposition in any case – was the mark of a tradesman, not a gentleman. The true antiquary undertook publication for the honour of his country rather than private emolument. Thus arose the convention of protesting in the preface that the volume in question was being placed before the public at the instigation of friends, rather than for financial gain, or for reasons of personal vanity. Such protests wore thin, as William Borlase remarked to Smart Lethieullier on his forthcoming account of Cornish antiquities: 'I must not trouble you with the common Cant of being sett on by the importunity of friends. If that were ever so true tis an argument I would never use, for tis us'd much oftener than believ'd.'[166] Gentlemen of private means, such as Richard Gough, preferred to publish at their own expense as it negated the necessity of soliciting for subscriptions, which as independent gentlemen they were reluctant to do. Sanderson Miller and Smart Letheiullier both declined publishing their collections, on architectural antiquities and sepulchral monuments respectively, as the cost was too much for them to bear personally and they did not wish to raise a subscription. One might also observe that it saved them from the irksome necessity of putting their collections into some kind of order. Edward Hasted contributed to his own financial ruin by shouldering the costs of publishing the *History of Kent* himself, but he was adamant that he would not sell the history to the booksellers. Rather, he would rely on the support of the gentry of the county: 'he thinks this a compliment due to them, and the only desirable method he can take of making this history public'.[167] It is easy to see why so many gentlemen were glad to be able to publish in *Archaeologia*, which cost them nothing over and above their membership fees, and for which they received offprints which they could distribute to their friends. As Horace Walpole caustically observed, 'The vanity of figuring in these repositories will make many persons contribute their MSS.'[168]

John Oliphant, a Scottish engraver of antiquities, fell foul of such conventions. When George Chalmers discovered that Oliphant intended publishing his engravings of the 'perishing ruins of grandeur' in St Andrews for gain, with a view to cornering the market in North British antiquities, he was seized with outrage at this breach of the antiquarian ethos. 'This is mean!' Were it *his* concern, avowed Chalmers, he would engrave them all and publish them as one. 'If successful I gain profit and honour. If not I gain honour alone, and brand the indifference and meanness of spirit.'[169] For many this was not an option, and securing patronage to promote the subscription was essential. Clergymen could draw upon their fraternal obligations to each other as men of the cloth: Rogers Ruding appealed to John Hodgson for assistance in securing subscriptions for his numismatic history in the north of England, because he had no acquaintance of his own in the area. 'I am conscious that I, a perfect stranger to you, ought not to trouble you with all this', he apologised, 'but the difficulty which, in times like these, a country clergyman meets with in getting an expensive work through the press, must plead my excuse.'[170] Richard Gough, with his reputation and established networks through which he could extract favours, was extremely well placed to promote any work which he chose, and Paton and others were frequently pressed to secure subscribers for yet another work in which Gough had interested himself. Francis Drake acknowledged the assistance of John Hylton of Hylton Castle in Yorkshire in securing subscriptions for *Eboracum* (1736), claiming that he could never bring himself to solicit them in person.[171] The fact that Hylton secured so many, and of such high social standing, speaks eloquently of the networks of patronage and obligation which were exercised on Drake's behalf. The recipient could also be expected to acknowledge the benefaction of his patron – as evidenced in the sycophantic dedications with which antiquarian works were often prefaced.

The Republic of Letters was not, of course, exclusively populated by men, but with respect to antiquities the representation of women was conspicuous by its absence.[172] The collection and study of antiquities was highly gendered. Antiquarianism was a 'manly' pursuit, encouraging masculine qualities, whether it was through identification with the political virtue and patriotism of ancient Rome or the military glory and contempt for death evinced by the Goths. Women were encouraged to collect specimens of natural history such as shells or fossils, with notable collections being amassed, for example, by the duchess of Portland or Sir Joseph Banks's sister, Sarah.[173] They were also directed towards reading history for its improving moral qualities and entertainment, it being considered by many moralists a preferable alternative to the pernicious influence of novels. Antiquities and antiquarianism, however, were regarded by men as being definitively masculine occupations. As far as the female sex was concerned, the brightly coloured tesserae of Roman mosaics were a source for tapestry designs and cushion covers rather than pieces in the jigsaw puzzle of Roman Britain. Ladies, opined George Lipscombe, would find reading county histories insuperably irksome and disagreeable. 'Don't laugh at me', Charles Bertram pleaded with William Stukeley, when he told him of how he had read the introduction to Stukeley's *Medallic History of Carausius* to his mother.[174] If there were few histories by women written in this period, there were even fewer antiquarian publications.

The Society of Antiquaries published two communications from aristocratic women in *Archaeologia*, and a few topographical pieces made their appearance in the early nineteenth century.[175] The only woman to publish anything of any significance upon an antiquarian subject during the eighteenth century was Elizabeth Elstob the Saxonist, who was praised for her profound learning and 'masculine abilities'.[176] Amongst the enormous correspondence of John Nichols in his capacity as Mr Urban of the *Gentlemen's Magazine* it is extremely rare to find any from women upon the subject of antiquities. Instead we find Anna Clarke writing to him with coy excitement, describing a penny of James I which she had discovered 'corroded by time' in the 'bosom of our mother earth' whilst amusing herself in her 'Liliputian garden'. Nichols's reply tactfully informed her that the length of her letter rendered it unsuitable for publication – it would make the discovery of too much consequence. The coin, he assured her, was not a rare one, probably worth only one penny. Miss Clarke's coquettish affectation in 'trying her skill' at antiquarian research reflects the assumption that the subject of antiquities was not one to which women were suited, or in which they could be likely to excel.[177]

One antiquary, George Ballard, author of a memoir upon the 'learned ladies' of Britain, did not share the view that women were by their nature unsuited to intellectual pursuits.[178] 'I hear of several Persons', he complained to Charles Lyttelton, 'who are pleased to perstringe me and my illustrious Train of Learned and worthy Ladies, & who have assurance enough to affirm that Women were never intended or design'd to be made acquainted with the Arts & Sciences, that 'tis a thing quite out of their Sphere'.[179] Ballard was the more vehement in his protestations given that he had taught his own sister, Elizabeth, Anglo-Saxon and had been corresponding with one of the learned ladies herself, Elizabeth Elstob, over the last ten years. Following the death of her brother, the Saxonist William Elstob, she was forced to abandon her books and manuscripts and eke out a living as a schoolmistress near Evesham, which left her with neither the tools nor the energy for pursuing her antiquarian studies. As she explained to Ballard, 'when my School is done, my little ones leave me incapable of either reading, writing or thinking, for their noise is not out of my head till I fall asleep, which is often too late'.[180] Ballard tried, with only partial success, to revive her interest in Saxon antiquities. He sent her pieces to translate and lent her books and manuscripts; he sought her advice on points of Saxon literature and pressed her for information on the early Saxonists. Elstob was eventually found a position with the duchess of Portland, who as the daughter of Edward Harley, earl of Oxford, and a woman of considerable education herself, was pleased to employ her as governess for her children. Elstob found herself in much greater comfort and contented, but contributed no more to the world of antiquarian learning; it was as if the struggle of trying to participate in what was essentially a masculine domain was too much effort in old age. Ballard's *Memoirs*, meanwhile, failed to convince others that women had anything of value to add to the Republic of Letters. 'I find very few of them stand in a higher Rank as Authors than Poetasters and Translators', confided Charles Lyttelton to Thomas Birch upon reading the volume.[181]

Women were excluded from antiquarian pursuits on several counts. In the first place, they were disadvantaged by their education. The ability to read Latin and a familiarity with the classical sources was a desirable, if not essential prerequisite. Whilst a reading knowledge of Latin was not uncommon amongst educated eighteenth-century women, it was comparatively uncommon and Greek, of course, was even rarer. Women's presumed preoccupation with the family, the personal and the trivial, it was argued, made them unfit to write history. Even with respect to *reading* history, its suitability for female consumption was not uncontested.[182] Early modern assumptions that history should be read primarily as a means for improvement and instruction rather than for entertainment were gradually broken down in the eighteenth century, however, and the rise of a genre of history increasingly preoccupied with the private and the personal evidently offered greater scope for feminine consumption.[183] With respect to classical history, the bedrock upon which the study of Romano-British antiquities was built, however, the majority of women clearly remained at a disadvantage, lacking the easy familiarity with Tacitus and Caesar which was the product of a gentleman's education.

The study of charters, legal documents and chronicles was likewise beyond the normal range of feminine activity. Women would have been handicapped by the same problem of language in dealing with medieval documents written largely in Latin, even if in a barbarous style. The familiarity with documents that many men gained in the course of managing an estate or in a legal capacity was denied most women, and the nature of the 'public' affairs with which such charters so often dealt was not within the conventionally defined sphere of appropriate feminine interest. Property and its rights, the conceptual prop of so much antiquarian literature, did not define the female identity as it did the masculine. Lady Elizabeth Hastings, who spent a whole afternoon between prayers and supper perusing some ancient court rolls and charters with Ralph Thoresby in order to understand them the more fully, was the exception that proved the rule.[184] The fieldwork which comprised such an important element of antiquarian research was equally problematic for ladies: if Latin rarely featured as a part of female education, surveying and mathematics were even less likely to be taught.[185] Ladies could not ride out to visit a church or a barrow unaccompanied with the same ease as a man, and the public records in the depositories in London or in the libraries of Oxford and Cambridge were closed to them, except as visitors. Although they might (and frequently did) visit the collections at the Ashmolean, or view the exhibits in the British Museum, it was highly unusual for women ever to work with the materials held there. When Dorothy Richardson, daughter of the antiquary Richard Richardson, visited the British Museum under the guidance of Dr Solander in 1775 she inspected Magna Carta and other manuscripts in the Harleian collection, complaining that even two visits were far from sufficient to view all the treasures; she does not appear to have used the reading room on her own account, however.[186] During the eighteenth century only the historian Catherine Macaulay is recorded to have entered the masculine space of the reading room.[187]

William Cole noted in his diary that one of his neighbours in the parish, Mrs Barton, was enjoying Ducarel's *Anglo Norman Antiquities*;[188] anecdotal evidence aside, however, it is extremely difficult to assess the extent to which women were readers of antiquarian literature, or what sort of publications they favoured. Subscription lists offer some suggestive hints, but subscribing to a book was as much a statement of patronage as it was an indication of intent to read. The earl of Burlington's wife, his mother, and two of his daughters subscribed to Francis Drake's *Eboracum*, for example, but we should be wary of taking this as indicative of a common familial fascination with the Roman origins of York. Rather, it savours more of a statement of Burlington's patronage and his own decision to involve his female dependants in its display. In total twenty-seven of Drake's 541 subscribers were women (5 per cent). This was rather more than for Alexander Gordon's similarly romanising *Itinerarium septentrionale* which numbered four (aristocratic) women out of 224 (3.1 per cent). Typically, most women subscribers to antiquarian works were aristocratic or from the gentry, representing the more genteel element of the subscription as a whole. For them the act of subscription was a function of their social status and the networks of patronage in which they were involved rather than an expression of interest in a particular volume.[189] At the other end of the market, Thomas Gent, the York printer, numbered eight women out of 128 subscribers (6.25 per cent) to his history of Ripon and eighteen out of 175 for his history of York (10.3 per cent). These were both books in which the antiquarian element was less erudite and which were offered as much as a guide to the town as an account of its antiquities. By the end of the century, when more popular works with an antiquarian element were becoming increasingly common, the numbers of women subscribers of middling status also appears to have increased – although this may simply reflect a global change across subscriptions to books of all genres. Sixteen out of sixty-three local historical and antiquarian publications issued between 1700 and 1820 had subscription lists in which 10 per cent or more of the subscribers were women. Only one subscription list, that for Henry Swinden's *History of Great Yarmouth* (1772), included no women at all. Some of these female subscribers were evidently family members or booksellers, but even discounting these, there was a consistent feminine presence upon the lists. The commercial publications of the late eighteenth and early nineteenth century were evidently aimed at both male and female readers. The dictates of the market ensured that antiquarian information would be presented in a form which would appeal to both ladies and gentlemen, and the more fashionable the place under discussion, the greater the likelihood of finding female names upon the list. It is, of course, another matter entirely to establish whether such women ever opened the book and cut the pages once it resided upon the bookshelf or the reading table.[190]

Women have, however, been shown to have been very much involved in what has been termed the 'social circulation of the past'; they contributed to the dissemination, if not the construction, of historical knowledge, through editing historical miscellanies, making extracts and compilations, writing translations and completing biographical works.[191] The interest of women in genealogy, as the passers on of tradition and family history, is manifest in anecdotal evidence of their reading of antiquarian works and collection of antiquities.[192] The close interest in family history and traditions, however, typified the uncritical collection of material from which the scientific antiquary tried to distance himself. When Horace Walpole chose to make derisive comments upon the Society of Antiquaries he referred to Charles Lyttelton, the president, as 'Goody Carlisle', and described *Archaeologia* as 'Old Women's Logic'. The fellows of the society, he reckoned, were 'the midwives of superannuated miscarriages'. Satires and jibes directed against antiquaries referred to their supposedly gullible compilation of stories and oral tradition as the material of old wives' tales.[193] 'As for old women's stories and vulgar traditions', observed William Cole, 'commend me to Mr Grose's *Antiquities of England and Wales.*'[194]

The concept of 'social circulation' of historical knowledge is, however, a valuable one, and it is largely in this auxiliary role that we find women participating in antiquarian activities. Almost all women who displayed an interest in antiquarian matters had a close relative – in Elizabeth Elstob's case her brother, but for others it was a father or husband – from whom they acquired training and familiarity in the subject, or who encouraged them to pursue antiquities as assistants to their own projects. Wives and daughters were enlisted as scribes and amanuenses, taking notes at dictation, transcribing documents and making drawings. Mrs Archdall is said to have 'rendered valuable assistance' to her husband the Irish antiquary Mervyn

Archdall in deciphering collections which he had inherited written in shorthand and cipher.[195] Philip Morant's daughter, Anna Maria, acted in a secretarial capacity for her father. His own letters referred to their collating Maitland's history of London with the surveys of Stowe and Styrpe together. Morant also acknowledged her assistance with the history of Archbishop Hutton, which he largely wrote on behalf of Andrew Coltée Ducarel. Miss Morant had made her own collection of coins, and as her father informed Ducarel, wished to give him an Acquitaine coin from her collection.[196] Miss Morant eventually married the antiquary Thomas Astle and it is tempting to suppose that part of the attraction lay in a mutual interest in antiquities, as well as her handsome dowry. History does not record whether she continued her role as antiquarian helpmate within marriage. Ducarel, however, looked for no such sympathy from his own wife: he had planned to bring her on a trip to Colchester to visit Morant and the antiquities, but abandoned it, 'considering she was no antiquary'.[197] James Essex's daughter Miliscent was his companion and assistant on all his expeditions[198] and Edward King thanked his niece Ann Copson for the drawings which she executed for *Munimenta antiqua*; they could, he claimed, be classed amongst the most accurate in all four volumes.[199] William Cunnington, whose excavations upon Salisbury Plain were some of the most systematic and detailed to be completed in the early nineteenth century, similarly depended upon his daughter to act as excavation secretary.[200] Cunnington's friend and associate in Wiltshire antiquities William Coxe, was not to be outdone and informed Cunnington that his wife 'tho' she does not understand Greek, is extremely fond of County Histories.'[201]

William Stukeley was another who evidently took pleasure in sharing his antiquarian interests with his female relatives, although this might be taken as a further sign of his personal eccentricity. The Society of Roman Knights, which he was instrumental in establishing, specifically allowed for the membership of ladies in its constitution, and included both the duchess of Hertford and Stukeley's future wife, Frances Williamson, who took the name of the pro-Roman British queen, Cartimandua.[202] Antiquarianism, he suggested to Alexander Gordon, was not a disadvantage in attracting the ladies; young foolish girls would not be interested, but women of sense were.[203] Stukeley's second wife, Elizabeth, sister of the antiquaries Roger and Samuel Gale, does not appear to have shared the antiquarian interests of her male relatives, but Stukeley's daughter, Anna, evidently gained considerable knowledge of antiquities, presumably from having assisted her father, not least in making drawings of his coins and other artefacts. Stukeley's friend William Warburton wrote to him in 1732, asking after her progress with Montfaucon, observing that 'in another year she will make

1. The Sanctuary at Avebury, from William Stukeley, *Abury: A Temple of the British Druids* (1743).

2. Humfrey Wanley by I. Hill (1711). (*Society of Antiquaries*)

3. The Rev. Samuel Pegge, LL.D. (*Julian Pooley*)

4. G. Cruikshank, *The Society of Antiquaries* (1812). (*Society of Antiquaries*)

5. Francis Grose, 'A Fat and Lean Antiquarian'. (*Society of Antiquaries*)

6. The Rev. Treadway Russell Nash. (*Julian Pooley*)

7. John Charles Brooke. (*Julian Pooley*)

8. Andrew Coltée Ducarel. (*Julian Pooley*)

9. The Rev. Michael Lort. (*Julian Pooley*)

10. Richard Gough. (*Private Collection*)

11. George Allan and William Hutchinson. (*Julian Pooley*)

12. Sir Richard Colt Hoare. (*Julian Pooley*)

13. John Britton. (*Julian Pooley*)

a better Antiquary than [Francis] Peck'.[204] Warburton's prediction was not without foundation. In 1758 Anna wrote to her father as a married woman, describing a visit to the White Horse in Berkshire and commented how the appearance of the horse was 'very much in the scheme of the Brittish horses on the reverse of their coins'.[205] Significantly, the scenes with which Stukeley illustrated *Itinerarium curiosum* show women as well as men inspecting the ruins and monuments of antiquity.

Rather than being seen as a statement of his own belief in the power of antiquities to attract women, Stukeley's inclusion of female staffage in his drawings could equally be taken as straightforward observation. Women, like men, enjoyed the experience of travel, even if they were more restricted in the opportunities to undertake it. The travel journals of women such as Celia Fiennes and Mrs Lybbe Powys demonstrate that educated women were equally alert to the historical associations of the places that they visited and took a keen interest in informing themselves about the antiquities. Women who had the opportunity to gain access to antiquarian literature through their male relatives could engage with the antiquarian construction of place and landscape.

Dorothy Richardson (b. 1748) came from a family with a tradition of antiquarian interests and had access to a library that was evidently well stocked with antiquarian volumes, from which she was able to build up considerable expertise and discernment in antiquarian matters.[206] This was brought to bear in the many tours she undertook over a forty year period; her first recorded journey being made at the age of twelve in 1761, the last in 1801. Richardson did not travel alone, although her travelling companions are seldom referred to, and we have no way of judging the extent to which they shared her antiquarian interests or informed her comments. She was a meticulous observer and took particular delight in recording antiquities; the brief notes which she made on the spot would be expanded upon subsequently with information gleaned from a range of other antiquarian sources. These ranged from Camden's *Britannia* to the papers published in *Archaeologia*, although she evidently also travelled with shorter guides such as West's *Tour to the Lakes* or Gilpin's various picturesque tours. It appears that she was literate in Latin: she translated, for example, epitaphs upon tomb stones and frequently referred to sources, such as Dugdale's *Monasticon anglicanum*, which did not provide translations for the charters cited. She also carefully copied the Saxon place-names given by Camden in *Britannia* when discussing etymology, but displayed no other signs of competence in Anglo-Saxon. The diaries show how she read and interpreted these texts to construct her own antiquarian record of the places she visited. On Fountains Abbey and its foundation, she referred herself to Camden, Speed, Burton and Dugdale. On another occasion she expressed her frustration at being unable to reconcile the different accounts she found in Dugdale, Burton and Grose on Bolton Abbey – she would, she wrote, leave it to 'better Antiquarians' to resolve the differences.[207] The use of the term suggests that she identified herself in her own mind as a member of the antiquarian community. Her growing self-confidence in matters of antiquity is demonstrated on the occasions when she ventured to correct or dissent from the sources to which she referred for information. Horsley, she wrote, was wrong to attribute the camp at Fairsfield to the Romans – it was quite different in shape to Roman castramentations, but was, she thought, perhaps the largest and most perfect camp in the kingdom, although so little noticed by other antiquarians. She included a sketch, complete with dimensions, stepped out for her by a male companion.[208] Richardson made full use of the family's library, but also subscribed to antiquarian publications herself: E. W. Stillingfleet, for example, wrote to her on behalf of the artist William Fowler, requesting her patronage for his engravings of Roman mosaic pavements and referring to her superior knowledge of antiquarian researches.[209] She never ventured to publish anything of an antiquarian nature on her own account. Her sole publication (conforming to the model of female facility in family history) was a memoir of her grandfather Richard Richardson MD, written for Nichols's *Illustrations of Literature.* Wider recognition of her expertise in antiquarian matters, however, never amounted to more than the footnote in which the antiquary T. D. Whitaker acknowledged her importance as a source of information for his *History of Craven.*[210]

Richardson was unusual, but not unique, in her evident enthusiasm for antiquarian literature and her deft ability to evaluate, criticise and synthesise her reading. Few other examples of such direct engagement in matters of antiquity survive. The contribution of Mrs Catherine Downes to the second volume of *Vetusta monumenta*, however, proves an interesting exception and gives further evidence that the readership for works on antiquities was by no means exclusively male. On 10 March 1788 the Society of Antiquaries received a letter giving a description of Roman pavements and antiquities discovered near Warminster in Dorset by a Mrs Catherine Downes. Mrs Downes submitted her offering as a sketch of the pavements, with an accompanying explanation as to how and when they had been found, and a suitably modest account of her own role in their preservation. She had learnt of the existence of the original fragment of pavement discovered through a report in the *Salisbury Journal*; on her own initiative she had sought permission to dig for further antiquities, the sketches of which she presented to the society. She was clearly a woman who shared Dorothy

Richardson's curiosity and enterprise, but it was necessary to play down her own role and competence Only the fact that she was persuaded by others that these were finds of some importance about which the society should be informed had convinced her of the need to trouble them with her sketches. Mrs Downes did not have a deep familiarity with the Latin texts by which to interpret her finds – she could not invoke passages from Caesar or Tacitus, but underneath the feminine deference and modesty were some shrewd and astute observations on the antiquities and the field archaeology of the site at which they had been found. She was clearly familiar with the language and practice of antiquarianism. She knew what orders to give for digging, how to describe the finds, and how to interpret the evidence of coins, mosaics, entrenchments and barrows.[211]

As antiquarianism became more concerned with matters of private life, with manners and customs, and was framed in language which drew upon the empathetic response demanded by philosophical history, the subject matter of antiquarian literature was obviously rendered more approachable for women. The 'cross-over' between literature and antiquarianism in the Celtic revival, for example, generated a genre which was readily consumed by women, and one to which they could even contribute, the most notable example being Charlotte Brooke, whose translations of Irish Gaelic verse were widely acclaimed. The countess of Moira, one of only two women to have papers published in *Archaeologia*, contributed essays on ancient Irish dress, based upon the discovery of a body of what she took to be an ancient Irish chieftain upon the Moira estate. The translator of La Curne de Sainte-Palaye's treatise on medieval chivalry, which stimulated much of the subsequent antiquarian inquiry into the subject, was a woman, Susan Dobson.[212] The aesthetic response to ruins and monuments demanded by the picturesque, rather than an emphasis on their commemorative function, opened the way for women to participate in an appreciation of 'Gothic' architecture, an area in which they could exercise considerable discrimination. Dorothy Richardson displayed a precocious attention to architectural detail. In her first tour, written aged twelve, she noted the elegant Gothic temple designed by Mr (Horace) Walpole in the park of Wentworth Castle (which was, she remarked, too much ornamented to look handsome, being built in the French taste). Extensive reading sharpened her observation; she made detailed architectural analyses of the façades of houses.[213] Her command of vocabulary to describe medieval buildings was less adequate, and she relied heavily on Francis Grose's *Antiquities of England and Wales*, but nevertheless she had a keen eye for picking up the inappropriate combination of classical with Gothic and the superficiality of modern improvements done in the 'Gothic taste'. Lord Byron had defaced Newsted Abbey, 'a most noble Gothick Ruin', she complained, by walling up one of the 'Grand Gothic Windows' and replacing it with a little sash, painted green.[214] Arthur Young's strictures upon the error of tidying up ruins expressed in his *Six Months Tour in the North of England* informed her account of Studley Royal and the 'improvements' carried out by Sir John Aislabie; and, anticipating William Gilpin, she found fault with the positioning of the trunk of a woman, said by Aislabie to be Anne Bullen, upon a Roman mosaic in the abbey. 'This', she observed, 'has a very bad effect, & seems to have no connection with the place.'[215]

The popularisation of antiquarianism opened the subject up to the participation of women and a wider range of people from the middle classes who did not have the wealth and education of the gentlemanly elite.[216] The London Society of Antiquaries was not, by the end of the century, representative of those who cherished an interest in antiquities across the country as a whole. Fashion, as well as scholarship – some would have argued instead of – encouraged people to join. More typical was the mix of clergymen, lawyers, schoolmasters and booksellers to be found in provincial gatherings such as those in Newcastle, Spalding or Perth.[217] Antiquarianism had never been exclusively the preserve of the gentry, but its emphasis on property and the legitimisation of the social order had necessarily rendered it particularly attractive to those who occupied a position at the apex of society, or who had a vested interest in the preservation of the social order, irrespective of the fact that education, money and leisure were all but essential if the study of antiquities was to be pursued to any high degree. For those who, like Richard Gough, pursued antiquarianism with a whole-hearted dedication, it was an all-consuming interest, even obsession, which structured his politics, his friendships and his life. There were numerous others, however, for whom antiquities represented one of many interests and who pursued the subject alongside a professional career, scientific inquiry or an appreciation of the arts. The study of antiquities held a particular appeal to those of a conservative disposition: the solace of the past which had soothed the outright Toryism of an earlier generation of antiquaries was, by the end of the century, placating the anxiety of a generation whose sense of alienation was provoked by changes to the economic and social order as well as threats to the religious and political establishment. Its empirical certainties offered a welcome refuge for those who took fright at the sophistry and scepticism of modern philosophy. Antiquarianism catered also to a vague and wistful longing for the past which constituted the substratum to romantic yearnings and incipient nationalism, and as such captured the imagination of individuals from very different backgrounds. It was not, however, the preserve of backward-looking Tory loyalists or romantic nationalists. Antiquarianism, as its proponents frequently stressed, had very practical applications and could be made to serve the interests of the present. It could represent a nostalgic sanctuary of bygone stability and certainty for those who feared the advent of change, but equally the illustration of the past demonstrated the progress of the present and the undoubted superiority of the modern age over the backwardness of former times, and as such was perfectly in tune with a Whiggish view of improvement and modernity.

3

Antiquarian Societies

In 1693 William Nicolson wrote in one of many letters upon antiquarian topics to the Yorkshire antiquary Ralph Thoresby, 'I wish we had in this kingdom, as they have in Sweden, a society for the collecting and preserving antiquities. This would do something for us. But as long as particular men engage in burdens beyond their strength we have millions of great matters attempted, and nothing performed to any purpose.'[1] A year later, he reiterated the need for a society through which history and antiquities could be cultivated, and again pointed to the example set by the other European nations such as France, Italy and Sweden. 'And why should not we have the like in England?', he asked. 'We have the best stock of true remains of antiquity of any nation, perhaps, in Europe; and yet our histories hitherto have been most lazily written.'[2] Nicolson would have to wait another thirteen years before the society of antiquaries of which he dreamed would begin to materialise. The first meeting of what would eventually become the Society of Antiquaries of London would not be held until the end of 1707.

Antiquarianism, like natural history, was always described as a collaborative project, which depended on the communication of information and discoveries in order to recover and illustrate the knowledge of the past. Association, in the form of learned societies, was therefore crucial to the success of the antiquarian enterprise. The Society of Antiquaries, and the Royal Society, together with numerous provincial societies, were part of a network of criss-crossing lines of communication, which extended across Europe, and even into India and the Americas. They were the institutional embodiment of the Republic of Letters. Members corresponded with each other within a particular society; societies engaged in the reciprocal exchange of minutes and transactions, and through the purchase of publications (often beyond the means of individual members) they offered their members the opportunity to participate in the wider world of learning. Indeed, the library facility proved in many cases to be their most enduring and valuable feature. The social intercourse and mutual improvement that they encouraged were key to the cultivation of politeness, the ideal which lay at the heart of eighteenth-century constructions of gentlemanly identity.

Of all these associations, the Society of Antiquaries of London maintained the greatest influence in the eighteenth century. It exerted a centripetal force, drawing on correspondents from all parts of the British Isles, particularly after the publication of its proceedings in *Archaeologia* commenced in 1770. Its active members were, unsurprisingly, drawn predominantly from the metropolitan elite, but a number of the most regular contributors scarcely ventured to London. In terms of the subject matter, the papers presented showed an eclectic range, with no particular trend towards a London bias. Members travelled the country in the summer recess on antiquarian tours or returned to their country seats where they gathered information, and entered into correspondence with local antiquaries which they subsequently shared with their fellows. The emphasis upon locality in antiquarian research and literature always tempered the extent to which the London society could shape the nature of antiquarian research on a national basis.

Addison and Steele's fictional club created in the pages of *The Spectator* provided an example of friendly discourse, free of political or religious controversy, taking place in the convivial environment of the coffee house where all met on equal terms. Coffee houses and taverns were the backdrop to a lively ferment of ideas and information exchange in which literary and learned societies flourished alongside the stock jobbers and insurance agents.[3] Discussions on matters antiquarian also took place there: Thomas Tanner writing from Norwich in 1701 promised Peter le Neve something 'out of our Will book and institutions' for discussion amongst a small coterie meeting at the Bull Head.[4] In broader terms, clubs and societies were the basis of eighteenth-century cultural, political, philanthropic and even economic activity; thus the eighteenth century is often depicted as being a golden age of clubs and societies. But, as the recent authoritative study of the phenomenon has demonstrated, for all their ubiquity and popularity, comparatively few clubs and societies were successful in the long run. Almost all experienced problems in sustaining interest and membership over a prolonged period; the problem was particularly acute for those which had pretensions to anything more than sociability and conviviality.[5] The mixed fortunes and erratic achievements of the eighteenth-century antiquarian societies are as much a reflection upon the practical problems of sustaining a learned society for a period of more than a few years as an indication of the extent to which antiquarian studies were pursued with any degree of seriousness in eighteenth-century Britain.

Eighteenth-century antiquaries attached considerable importance to the fact that the origins of their society could be traced back to the late sixteenth century, when the circle of scholars and antiquaries around Sir Henry Spelman, Sir Robert Cotton and William Camden used to meet informally to discuss antiquarian matters. In 1614 James I had taken a 'mislike' to the society, fearing that it would encroach too far upon matters of state, and the antiquaries decided to meet no more. The legacy of this society had little tangible reality in terms of publications or collections, but it had a much more important inspirational influence upon eighteenth-century antiquaries, particularly as it linked the antiquaries to the foundation of the Cottonian Library, always one of the most important resources for students of English history.[6] Eighteenth-century attempts to establish continuity in the form of an 'underground' society maintained through scholars such as Sir William Dugdale proved impossible to substantiate – the chasm between the middle of King James I's reign and 1718, complained George North who was attempting to write the society's history, could not be filled up.[7] His efforts demonstrate the all-consuming interest in establishing genealogies and the antiquity of origins, but this ambition also suggests that the antiquaries were searching for some means by which to assert their superiority over the Royal Society, which was otherwise indisputably the older, and more renowned society.

At the turn of the eighteenth century the leading society for discussion of scientific and also literary matters was certainly the Royal Society, which received its charter in 1662. Antiquities had always been a part of their proceedings but this broad-minded approach was discouraged from 1703 under the presidency of Sir Isaac Newton. Despite his interest in biblical chronology and synchronic theology, Newton was adamant that the Royal Society should not concern itself with literary matters. Whereas previously papers on antiquarian topics – Roman coins, pavements, barrows – had found a place in the pages of the *Philosophical Transactions*, it now became much harder to introduce such matters into the society's proceedings. Tellingly, in the agenda of priorities for the Royal Society drawn up in 1718, antiquities occupied an ignominious position at the bottom, under husbandry, gardening and planting.[8] The decision to form a separate society dedicated to the study of antiquities must be at least partially attributed to Newton's pressure upon the Royal Society to adopt a more rigorously scientific stance. Most other learned societies in Britain and further afield did not observe a similar distinction.

The eighteenth-century Society of Antiquaries was established upon the assumption that the cultivation of history and antiquities was essential to the construction of national honour. But it was also conceived as part of a chain of communicating societies in the European Republic of Letters. English scholars studying Saxon and Norse antiquities had greatly benefited from communication with their counterparts in Scandinavia. Numismatists looked to the scholarship of continental scholars such as Spanheim and

Grutus for inspiration, whilst students of palaeography acknowledged their debt to Mabillon, Maffei and Montfaucon. Amongst English antiquaries there was a strong sense of a need to establish an institutional identity which would place them alongside the Académie des Belles Lettres in France and the scholars of Uppsala who served the Swedish king, as the comments of William Nicolson quoted above show.[9] Royal patronage of the kind exercised by Louis XIV was clearly not to be expected in Britain's mixed constitution, but neither could an absolutist regime be allowed to exhibit superiority in any branch of learning or the polite arts, which were supposed to flourish with liberty. National rivalry, as much as international cooperation and collaboration, was an important stimulus.

At 6.00 p. m. on 5 December 1707, at a tavern on the Strand named the Bear, a small group of three men met to discuss matters of antiquity. This meeting was to prove the genesis of the Society of Antiquaries of London. The three present were Humfrey Wanley, John Talman and John Bagford. They represented a curious combination of interests and backgrounds. Wanley was librarian to the earl of Oxford, a Saxonist, palaeographer and non-juror. Talman was an artist and engraver, and a Catholic, whilst Bagford was a shoemaker and a collector of old ballads. New members were gradually admitted over the following weeks – Peter le Neve, George Holmes, Thomas Madox, John Battesley, William Elstob and Henry Hare (later Lord Coleraine). A number of those involved in the revisions to Camden's *Britannia* – that stimulus to all sorts of antiquarian endeavour – such as Thomas Tanner and the brothers Roger and Samuel Gale were also enlisted in subsequent weeks. The ten years between the first founding in 1707 and the more formal basis upon which the society was established in 1717 are somewhat hazy and poorly recorded. What is clear, however, is that there were regular meetings of a group of a dozen or so like-minded individuals, who gathered at one or other of the London taverns on a weekly basis. Regular minutes for the society date from 1717, by which time it was meeting at the Mitre Tavern in Fleet Street. Twenty-three members were present at this meeting, six of them from the original coterie which had gathered around Wanley. By the end of the year a formal constitution had been established, committing the society to the encouragement of learning, rather than simply good fellowship. The study of antiquities was pronounced to be a 'considerable part of Good Literature' and no less curious than useful and the aims of the society were declared to be to render a knowledge of antiquities more universal, to communicate private knowledge and to collect and print accounts of any monument which might illustrate the history of 'Bryttish antiquitys'. Collaboration, free communication and a common spirit of patriotism constituted the rationale upon which the society was established.[10]

William Stukeley's frontispiece to the minutes of the Society of Antiquaries. (*Society of Antiquaries*)

Early meetings were full of hopeful promise. Humfrey Wanley had drawn up a highly ambitious agenda of research to be undertaken, identifying texts to be edited and antiquities to be illustrated. A decision was taken to embark upon the publication of a complete table of English coinage as the preliminary step towards realising this plan. This early flush of enthusiasm, however, was quickly dissipated, and within ten years of its official foundation the society's future was looking uncertain. In 1726 a number of the key founding figures, including Wanley, had died. Societies such as this, which existed upon an informal footing, with no regularised constitution, or even a permanent meeting place, were heavily dependent upon the character of a few individuals for their vitality and success, and without the dynamic input of such regular attenders it was hard to maintain any momentum. The late 1720s proved a difficult period of transition as the members sought to establish a fresh basis upon which to operate. Roger Gale complained to Sir John Clerk of the 'narrow bottom' to the society and the languid character of the meetings which lacked sufficient material to make them interesting.[11] Aristocratic support was canvassed and it was hoped that the earls of Hertford and Winchelsea, who had been elected in 1724, would lend their support more actively. Unlike the Royal Society, representatives of the nobility had been conspicuously absent from the founding members, although Wanley's close links with the earl of Oxford had, until the latter's dismissal from government in 1708, held out the promise of aristocratic support. The advantage of attracting the earl of Hertford or Winchelsea lay in enhancing the social profile of the society, gaining greater public recognition and in opening the door to potential sources of patronage and government funding. But such a socially elevated membership created its own problems. Great lengths were taken to find a meeting place which was within the limited budget of the society, but which members of the nobility and episcopacy would also be willing to attend. Taverns were cheap, costing only the matter of an annual payment to the inn's servants. Private rooms were more exclusive but considerably more expensive. In the event the move to more socially elevated surroundings did not prove any more effective in attracting members to meetings than had the more convivial setting of the tavern. A brief sojourn in rooms in Gray's Inn was terminated in 1729 and the society went back to meeting in the Mitre Tavern.

Up until mid century the society continued as a small, ad hoc gathering with few resources. Its membership was capped at one hundred (later increased to 120 in 1746) and its income was correspondingly limited. It had no permanent meeting place, and its collection of books, prints and antiquities was still small. Its public profile was low-key, and amounted to little more than the occasional publication of prints. The ambitious programme, which Wanley had drawn up to impress his patron, was largely a dead letter, and the plans for publishing the table of English coinage recurrently stalled. It was very much the poor sister of the Royal Society, which already had a membership of 131 in 1700 and a European profile through the publication of its papers in *Philosophical Transactions* – it also enjoyed royal patronage and was considerably richer in resources. The Antiquaries' minutes kept by the secretary Alexander Gordon during the 1730s recorded on a number of occasions that that there were insufficient members present to be quorate, or even that none had attended the meeting. The society lacked firm leadership; the aristocratic patrons, whose notice was so important in endowing any society with social cachet, were reluctant to attend. Roger Gale's gloomy prognostications would have appeared to have been justified. It has to be allowed that the influence and achievements of the society to mid century were rather more limited than might have been warranted by the aspiration of its founders.

A key point in the development of the society came with a bequest in 1749 from one of the earliest members, Lord Coleraine, of his collection of drawings and engravings. His generosity, however, created problems. Because the society was not a chartered body, it could not hold property by law. The bequest was therefore invalid. This prompted a number of the society's members to press for incorporation, not least because they themselves envisaged making similar bequests.[12] Incorporation would establish the society upon a sounder and more permanent footing, and allow it to own property, as the Royal Society did, which in turn, it was argued, would better enable it to promote the causes for which it had been established.[13] It was hardly a novel proposition; indeed, Wanley appears to have anticipated petitioning for incorporation in 1708, only to be deterred by the dismissal of his patron, Edward Harley, from office.[14] There was stiff opposition to these proposals, however. The simplest grounds for objection was that of cost. Acquiring a charter was not a cheap business. Members were worried that the society's limited resources would be squandered on lawyers' fees, and that their membership dues would increase in proportion. And to what end? Suspicious glances were cast towards the Royal Society and those individuals who enjoyed dual membership, not the least of whom was Martin Folkes, who at the time, uniquely in the history of both societies, enjoyed a dual presidency.[15] Sceptics pronounced that it was a plot to subordinate the Antiquaries to the Royal Society and that incorporation would ultimately lead to the end of an independent existence.[16] This was not entirely improbable; under Sir Hans Sloane and Martin Folkes the Royal Society had moved away from the rigorous Newtonian emphasis upon astronomy and mathematics to espouse a much more eclectic approach, one which was much more accommodating towards antiquities. Neither society at the time could be said to be in a flourishing condition, and there were some who genuinely believed that a pooling of resources and talent would be a more effective means of furthering the ends of both, rather than 'dividing the languishing streams of literature'.[17] Few other places, it was noted, distinguished antiquities from other forms of inquiry in this way.

Extreme opinions were expressed. 'I am sorry for the dissentions amongst our brethren', wrote Francis Drake to Stukeley, 'strange that this new charter, which surely was designed as a stronger cement, to bind them faster together, should make them so loose & ungovernable.' George North was deeply suspicious of the plans; he identified a 'cabal' of members from the Royal Society who 'projected' the scheme of incorporation, 'out of resentment to a society that has subsisted several years with at least an equal degree of reputation'. Their method, he claimed, was obvious. The plan was to go ahead with incorporation, which would be so expensive as to bankrupt the society, with the result that it would be forced to amalgamate with the its wealthier sister society – that, or the membership fees would be raised to such a level that he would no longer be able to afford it.[18] Despite these reservations on the part of certain members, plans for incorporation went ahead, and ultimately cost the society £346 12*s.* 6*d.*[19] Contrary to George North's pessimistic predictions, the society did not sink beneath the heavy burden of expenditure, although it did prove necessary to increase both the number of members and the admission fees to cover the costs which had been incurred. Not all fellows subscribed to North's conspiracy theory, and it was welcomed by others, even those who were not a part of the Royal Society cabal, as a means of bringing greater stability to the fluctuating fortunes and peripatetic existence of the society, as well as enhancing its public reputation and credit.[20] Viewed in historical perspective, incorporation was not such an unusual step to take. At the time few other societies had gone to the expense of acquiring a charter, but it soon became standard practice for any society that sought to establish itself on a permanent basis. The act of incorporation provided a kind of institutional permanency and a public identity, which enabled a society to carry on through periods of apathy or low attendance.[21]

Incorporation meant that the society now had a formal constitution, complete with officers (a president, vice presidents, director, treasurer and secretary) and a council whose meetings were held distinct from the general meeting of the society. Prior to incorporation there had been various attempts to regularise the way in which the society conducted its affairs, particularly with respect to taking the minutes and collecting arrears of subscriptions from the members, but both record keeping and accounts were haphazard. As a result of gaining the charter concerted efforts were made to place the conduct of the society's business on a firmer footing, appropriate to its status as a public body, but much of this was simply the rhetoric of modernisation. As Roger Gale pointed out somewhat tersely, nothing was suggested but what had been the usual custom of old and which had simply fallen into abeyance.[22]

The Antiquaries had always compared their efforts to those of the Royal Society, the Académie des Belles Lettres et Inscriptions and the other learned societies of Europe. Now that they too were incorporated, the comparisons were made with renewed emphasis and they decided to apply to France for a copy of the plan followed by the Académie des Belles Lettres. A sharp uptake in the number of foreign honorary members to the society is also noticeable in the years following incorporation as the society sought to extend its continental links. The first honorary foreign member had been Celsius, elected in 1735; he was one of only seven *sodales honarii* elected in the years up to 1751. In the following decade thirty-one honorary fellows were elected to the society, with a peak in 1761 when nine were added, setting a pattern of foreign correspondence which was followed for the rest of the century. In 1754 the antiquaries also made representations to be included in the plan for a new building which would house both the British Museum and the Royal Society. The plan never went further than a sketch in outline, but it is indicative of the antiquaries' determination to be seen at the centre of the world of learning and intellectual improvement in London and the Republic of Letters.[23]

Incorporation had also subtly changed the way in which the fellows viewed their place in society more broadly conceived. As the petition for incorporation explained, the study of antiquities had 'ever been esteemed highly Commendable and Usefull, not only to inform the Minds of Men, but also to encite them to Noble and Virtuous Actions'.[24] The minutes of the society during the 1750s suggest genuine attempts to realise the potential of the society in its new incarnation as a public body and to secure more widespread recognition within the world of learning.[25] The practical implementation of such schemes, however, proved rather more difficult to achieve. The mixed fortunes which attended all such schemes also highlight how a handful of individuals were able to dominate the proceedings and use the society as a platform for forwarding their own favoured projects.

Two of those who had been foremost in the plans for incorporation had been James Theobald and Philip Carteret Webb, the latter being the lawyer who had actually carried out the transactions on behalf of the society.[26] Theobald was an energetic individual who soon produced a plan for the society to issue a questionnaire, which members would distribute during the recess when they left London for the country, 'to obtain materials for compiling a compleat History as well of the Antiquities as natural Production in the Several parts of the nation'. Each gentleman was expected to compile the account of his own parish, and to distribute the queries to neighbouring gentlemen and clergy to fill in. The proposals were printed for distribution by members of the society, and also appeared in the pages of the *Gentleman's Magazine* which was already becoming established as an important medium of communication for antiquarian subjects. It was not entirely clear how the resulting information would be collated once the questionnaires were returned to the society. It transpired that this never posed a problem, however, as the scheme did not meet with quite the enthusiastic reception that he had anticipated. By the end of the year no-one had responded to Theobald's plan. A handful of parochial surveys trickled in over the following years, but it was hardly the comprehensive survey of the nation's antiquities for which he had hoped.[27] Other projects were no more successful. Henry Baker suggested that the society should keep a memoranda book or chronological register in which to record 'remarkable events'. What Baker had in mind was less a chronicle of political occurrences than a record of the enormous changes and improvements which were taking place in transport, building, manufactures and sciences.[28] This attempt to broaden the society's horizons met with even fewer responses than Theobald's project. In fact, Theobald was the only member to respond.[29] The collection of useful and instructive material which Baker had hoped would reflect honour upon the society and inform the antiquaries of the future failed to materialise. Despite the attempts of Baker and Theobald to energise the society and coordinate its undertakings, members did not respond well to such directed activity. The pair achieved rather more success in the context of the Royal Society of Arts, where, with the Cornish antiquary William Borlase, they were instrumental in establishing the county surveys.[30]

Sir John Sinclair's success in eliciting responses to his general survey of Scotland during the 1790s, a project initiated by himself alone, provides an interesting contrast to the repeated failure of the Society of Antiquaries to coordinate even a table of coinage. It also contrasts with the earl of Buchan's failure to get a similar project off the ground less than ten years earlier under the auspices of the newly founded Scottish Society of Antiquaries. Buchan had intended to conduct a parochial survey of Scotland, in collaboration with the Society of Antiquaries of Perth which was founded four years after the Edinburgh Society in 1784. Despite Buchan's powers of oratory, his proposals resulted, if anything, in even fewer responses than had those of the London society.[31] Sir John, however, had a number of advantages on his side, the most important of which was that he was able to address the clergy at the General Assembly, and impress upon them the importance of responding to the questionnaire. Moreover, he commanded considerable personal influence amongst the clergy of Scotland, due not least to the fact that he had secured a very significant grant of £2000 from the king for the Society for the Benefit of the Sons of the Clergy. Sinclair persuaded the clergy that answering his queries would be in their best interests, as any profits from the work would further swell the funds. As a wealthy landowner and an MP he also had the resources and the influence to carry off such a project, and, crucially in view of the amount of correspondence involved, was able to take advantage of the parliamentary privilege of free franking for much of the project. Working with him was his own secretarial and editorial team. He was able to proceed unhampered by a need to secure the agreement or active support of other people to his plans, nor did he have to engage in negotiations for the financing of the survey, all of which were factors that tended to cast the enterprises of the Society of Antiquaries awry.[32]

The attempts of Philip Carteret Webb to promote the publication of Domesday Book met with a rather better response, even if publication was ultimately delayed until 1783. Webb, who had been responsible for securing the charter in 1751, also had a clear vision of what he expected the society to achieve. Having been one of the major actors in driving through the decision for incorporation, he clearly felt that it was incumbent upon the society to undertake some project which would vindicate its claims to erudition and public service. If incorporation had brought the Antiquaries into closer alignment with the Royal Society, it was all the more important to establish the credentials of the Antiquaries as a body of public utility, which could advise the government on matters of importance – as the Royal Society did in drafting instructions for voyages of scientific discovery, undertaking a comparison of weights and measures or performing geophysical surveying.[33] The Royal Society also received government funding to undertake projects, which enabled it to take a more proactive role. Such considerations cannot have been far from the minds of individuals such as Webb, one of those who enjoyed membership of both societies. To this end, like Theobald and Baker, he took it upon himself to galvanise the fellows into greater activity. The society should follow the example set by other learned bodies abroad, he suggested, and during the summer recess members should collect and write up interesting materials which could then be presented at meetings over the coming year.[34] Another of his hobby horses was promoting the study of palaeography and medieval manuscripts. He produced various facsimiles of different hands which he hoped would assist members in deciphering manuscripts and in ascertaining their age.[35] His major project, however, was the publication of Domesday Book. He first raised the possibility of this at the end of 1755, and by 1756 he had prepared his *Short Account of Some Particulars Concerning Domesday Book*, which he circulated amongst the fellowship. Through the society he appealed for information on the whereabouts of copies, transcriptions and extracts of Domesday dispersed through England. He soon had reports from over a dozen other members about copies of Domesday Book of which they had information in their vicinity. It was easier, perhaps, for antiquaries to respond to a specific inquiry about one volume, Domesday Book, whose importance was undisputed, than to formulate answers to a long and open-ended set of inquiries such as those found in Theobald's questionnaire.[36]

Some antiquaries published their papers in *Philosophical Transactions*, but it was self-evident that if the Antiquaries were to establish a separate identity as a learned society and build up their reputation in the Republic of Letters it would be necessary to bring their transactions before a wider public.[37] Publication of papers had been mooted at several points since the official foundation in 1717, but nothing had been achieved except for the publication of prints. The only publishing project on which any progress had been made was the table of English coinage. Even this plan, however, fell victim to a triumph of individualist over corporate behaviour. Martin Folkes claimed that he would himself publish a table of coinage from his own collections and the society conceded to his request to have the use of such materials as had already been drawn up. Folkes died with the project uncompleted, and the society had to purchase back his collections in 1754. The table was eventually completed for publication in 1763.[38] Incorporation eased some of the legal problems inherent in publication, as one of the obstacles in the early days of the society had been the fact that it had no legal right of securing to itself the copyright of anything it published. Plans were therefore made to publish not just the papers but also a history of the society's foundation and proceedings, and to 'shew the World they have neither wanted Diligence in their Researches, Success in their Discussions nor Liberality in their Communications'.[39] A committee to review the past papers and to recommend those suitable for publication was established in June 1753. It reported back with a list of eligible papers in January 1754, but executive action was repeatedly stalled until the end of the 1760s.[40] Meanwhile the publication of papers came to be seen as essential to the *raison d'être* of the society, as a means of fulfilling its claims for broader public responsibility. John Ward, who like Theobald and Baker was also a member of the Royal Society and a trustee of the British Museum to boot, sternly informed the society that it was their duty as a public body. The public would expect many new discoveries and improvements in matters relating to British history and antiquities from a society such as theirs, particularly now that it was legally incorporated and under royal patronage.[41] Just as private gentlemen were frequently exhorted to place their collections in public repositories, rather than keeping them in personal custody where they could benefit none but the owner, it behove the Society of Antiquaries to be less illiberal in sharing its knowledge.[42]

The broader horizons of the society consequent upon incorporation were also apparent in the subject matter discussed at meetings. Although it was ostensibly established for the study of native antiquities, it had never maintained this stance to the exclusion of any other sort of antiquity. During the 1730s, for example, there had been a notable burst of enthusiasm for Egyptian antiquities, and there was always a strong current of interest in the classical antiquities of Greece and Rome, which the foundation of the Society of Dilettanti in 1732 did nothing to diminish.[43] To a far greater extent than in the Society of Antiquaries, the scholarly agenda of the Dilettanti was subordinated to its social functions. A considerable part of its activities, however, lay in the encouragement of British art, through the provision of classical exemplars, rather than in antiquarian research *per se*.[44] The Dilettanti typified the approach of connoisseurship – the quest for *virtù* from which a number of the Antiquaries deliberately attempted to distance themselves. In the 1750s the Grand Tour was still essentially confined to the nobility; members of the aristocracy aside, few of the fellows of the Society of Antiquaries had travelled to Italy, except for those who had done so as artists or tutors.[45] The interests of collectors such as Lyde Brown and Thomas Hollis, however, should not be discounted, and by 1760 there was a discernible shift in the subject matter of papers presented at meetings away from the eclectic mix of coins, charters, drawings of churches and parochial surveys towards classical topics. For a number of years from the late 1750s through the 1760s Lyde Brown's name appears with great frequency in the minutes of the society, as he presented drawings of antiquities, or the antiquities themselves which had been procured for him from Italy. It was the influence of Lyde Brown and Thomas Hollis, witnessed in their signatures to the testimonials, that secured the election of such individuals as Thomas Jenkins, Brown's chief agent in Rome, James Stuart or Allan Ramsay, and artists such as Piranesi and Richard Wilson who specialised in depicting the classical antique.[46] These testimonials referred not only to the candidate's contribution to scholarship, but also to past and future services rendered to English travellers in Italy. Throughout the winter season of excavation in Rome, Jenkins sent the Society regular reports of the latest discoveries, often accompanied by drawings or prints of choice antiquities. It would be wrong, however, to attribute the classicising trend within the society solely to the influence of Grand Tourists: there was a general interest and enthusiasm which the findings at Herculaneum had done much to arouse. The first reports from the excavations were entering the public domain, generating great excitement amongst antiquaries across Europe.[47] Throughout the 1750s the society received accounts of the excavations from the Neapolitan antiquaries who were frequently elected as honorary members.[48]

The reputation of the Society of Antiquaries was certainly more firmly established by the 1760s. It seemed to offer to an enthusiast such as the young Richard Gough a means by which antiquarian research could be encouraged and promoted. Information and expertise could be shared, topics of inquiry identified, assistance with publication offered. Gough's own preliminary work, a digest of antiquarian and topographical literature, *Anecdotes of British Topography* (1768), had indicated to him how much antiquarian activity there was, and how much more work there was to be done. In 1767 he was elected to the society with high expectations of what might be achieved and for the remainder of the century his was one of the most powerful voices within it. Gough's relationship with the society was a troubled one, however, which brings into sharp relief the paradoxical basis upon which this and other societies like it existed. In order to succeed they needed to attract the social elite, men of fashion and money who brought with them patronage and influence, but in order to achieve the ends for which they were founded it was necessary to maintain a scholarly ethos which often conflicted with the rather more superficial interests of the members which it had been necessary to attract.[49] A year after his election, Gough was writing to his friend Foote Gower in tones of disillusion and disappointment. The society, he found, was not the kind of antiquarian hothouse which he had hoped for. He ridiculed the way in which his fellow members gaped over non-descript items presented for their inspection – you would have been ashamed to number yourself amongst them he told Gower. When the president Charles Lyttelton died in 1768, Gough was in despair; he feared that the fortunes of the society would deteriorate further and that it would hasten along the path of fashion rather than inquiry. It was, he repeatedly told Gower, too taken up with *virtù* than with genuine antiquarian researches.[50] The evidence of the minute books gives some substance to Gough's recriminations; attendance levels at meetings had dropped despite the fact that membership had been increased to 180;[51] the attempts to write a history of the society floundered and plans for publishing the papers were continually stalled. The burst of enthusiasm and new ideas which had characterised the years immediately following incorporation had already fizzled out and the impetus for activity seemed lost.

Lyttelton's successor as president was his nephew Jeremiah Milles, who had already filled another position left vacant by his uncle as dean of Exeter. Milles did not, perhaps, have the antiquarian acumen of Lyttelton, but he was at least committed to the study of British antiquities as well as having the requisite connections of birth and education which were necessary for a president of the society. Between them Lyttelton, Milles and Gough launched the publication of *Archaeologia*, which first appeared in 1770 and continued to be issued at roughly two yearly intervals until the early nineteenth century, with a brief interruption following Gough's resignation in 1797. The history of the society, which had been so long awaited, was finally completed by Gough as an introductory essay to the first volume. In deciding what papers to publish the committee concentrated upon those tending towards illustrating domestic antiquities, in the spirit of their foundation and charter, despite the fact that many meetings were largely taken up with the discussion of antiquities excavated in Rome and the environs of Naples, or in the exegesis of numismatic inscriptions. Publication was undoubtedly a significant step towards securing the society's wider reputation and greatly facilitated correspondence with other societies in Europe, with whom volumes of transactions could now be exchanged.[52] It also contributed to the 'imagined community' of antiquaries which existed across Britain, binding the provincial antiquaries who were unable to attend meetings more closely to the London society. John Whitaker welcomed the long-awaited publication of the first volume in the pages of his *History of Manchester*. It was, he told his readers, a rich resource in itself, but of still greater significance were its future consequences. 'It now forms a valuable and respectable repository for the effusions of the antiquarian genius. It will peculiarly stimulate the ingenious and sensible, both in and out of the society, to remit their disquisitions to it.'[53] The publication of *Archaeologia* rejuvenated expectations that the society would be able to consolidate and digest the scattered researches of its members. Through its pages, enthused John Watson, another provincial member, 'discoveries may be made to flow together as to one common centre, and such a Fund be at last acquired, as may give to Britain what the immortal Camden in vain attempted, a compleat Account of its Antiquities'.[54] There is indeed a discernible shift in emphasis away from metropolitan contributions in the society's minute books in the years following 1770s, as an increasing number of communications originated from provincial members who raised points of discussion from papers which they had read in *Archaeologia*.

Gough, who as director of the society was ultimately responsible for editing the volume, did not find it an entirely straightforward procedure. Antiquaries could be vain, captious and quick to take offence, and Gough's somewhat brusque manner did not lend itself to soothing ruffled feathers. On being informed that his paper on Irish antiquities was too long for inclusion in the forthcoming volume, Thomas Pownall demanded its return and declared that he would 'no longer incumber the learned works of the Society'. Thomas Percy, meanwhile, took offence at the council's decision to publish Samuel Pegge's criticisms of his *Reliques of Antient Poetry*. Jeremiah Milles had to intervene on this and a number of other occasions, as fellows complained about the way in which their papers had been treated. 'I find it no small undertaking', he informed Gough, 'to reconcile the little misunderstandings and Jealousies that arise amongst our members.'[55] For his part, Gough repeatedly bemoaned the poor quality of the papers presented for publication in his correspondence with his close friends. Whitaker's hopeful prophecy was not, in his opinion, borne out. 'I past Thursday and Friday last in town,' he told Michael Tyson, '& looking into the Antiq. Soc. had the mortification to find scarce a dozen persons droning over a dull paper of Antiquaries long since departed about R[oman] antiquities in the North detailed in Horsley or other printed books.'[56] 'We are cruelly deficient in papers', he told William Cole the following year, hoping that Cole himself would contribute something for *Archaeologia*.[57] He struggled with the pettiness of the contributors and the indifference of other members of the council, who failed to respond to the suggestions he put to them for enhancing the society's publications.[58] His own conception of what antiquarianism should involve meant that he was constantly at odds with the rather more miscellaneous approach which many of his fellow antiquaries employed, for whom the society operated less as a forum for the investigation of antiquities, than for the presentation of a paper on any subject upon which they were interested. Governor Pownall, he remarked acidly to George Ashby, would extend the plan of the society to take in every historical trace of human existence.[59] Viewing the list of papers due to be published in the fifth volume of *Archaeologia*, which included essays on poisonous snakes in Ireland and patriarchal customs and manners, he feared that the antiquarian principles of the society were in danger of becoming obscured.[60]

Gough's disillusionment grew steadily through the 1770s as he witnessed the society's reluctance to sponsor any engravings except a series of large historical prints. The first, the 'Field of the Cloth of Gold', published in 1775, was taken from a scene decorating the Royal Apartments at Windsor; its size was 31 by 53 inches and it had cost more than £440 pounds to complete, including 200 guineas paid to James Basire, who had spent over two years engraving the drawing. By 1775 only 144 copies had been sold realising £264 8s; there was thus a shortfall of £176.[61] The Cowdray Print, published in 1778, was a copy of one of the grand historical scenes in the great parlour at Cowdray, Sussex. It depicted the repulse of the French attack upon Portsmouth. Public interest would, it was hoped, be stimulated by the preparations currently being made to repel another feared French invasion.[62] The costs involved were similarly heavy and its dimensions, at 72 by 23 inches slightly bigger; so large was it that it had to be etched on two separate plates.[63] A third print, the embarkation of Henry VIII for Calais, taken again from a painting at Windsor Castle, was put in hand in 1779. Basire's bill was only a little less expensive at 170 guineas, and the print was published in 1781.[64] All the engravings were large undertakings, but the first was of such gargantuan proportions that specially manufactured paper had to be commissioned.[65]

Taken together they represented an extravagant gesture and certainly raised the profile of the Society of Antiquaries in fostering history painting and subjects of national historical importance, rather than sponsoring engravings of coins or buildings which held less immediate resonance for those to whom antiquities were an unfamiliar subject. In choosing to illustrate these historical scenes the society was showing itself in tune with the vogue for history painting which currently dominated the Royal Academy, where two medals for paintings illustrating scenes of national history were awarded annually.[66] Jeremiah Milles tactfully made much of this common purpose in the speech he gave on moving into the new apartments at Somerset House where the two societies were now neighbours.[67] Scenes from history were believed to encourage patriotism, and, as imperial and domestic crisis loomed at the end of the 1770s, this held considerable appeal. As Horace Walpole observed, in such times 'men are apt to inquire how great their ancestors have been; and when a kingdom is past doing anything, the few, that are studious, look into the memorials of past time'. The sheer size and richness of the prints undoubtedly caused a stir amongst the wider public and seen as a public relations exercise the series of historical prints was at least partially successful. Lord Hardwick wrote to the society in February 1779 to commend them on their 'laudable and spirited Views' in publishing the prints and specifically mentioned 'the high Opinion they stood in with the Publick upon Account thereof'. They would, he hoped, undertake more engravings of the same kind from the historical paintings at Windsor or the great parlour at Cowdray.[68] The venture, therefore, pleased many fellows, including members of the aristocracy who otherwise generally held themselves aloof; it also brought the society to the attention of the king. Impressive though the prints were, money as a consequence was extremely scarce during the 1770s and 1780s. In 1775 both Jeremiah Milles and Michael Lort warned Gough that the society's finances were badly strained and that it could ill afford to undertake any other engravings.[69] The decision to go ahead with the Cowdray print only three years later therefore particularly annoyed him. As he explained in a letter to George Ashby, the council had, in effect, been forced into commissioning the engraving because 'a person not then a member' had spent one hundred pounds on a drawing of it, on the assumption that the society would reimburse him.[70] Significantly, there were no publications of *Vetusta monumenta* during this period. Gough gave public expression to his frustration at this 'ill advised venture' in the preface to *British Topography* in 1780. The society, he fumed, had given the public two or three pieces of English history but had neglected the earlier (medieval) periods and the country still lacked anything comparable to Montfaucon's *Monumens de la monarchie françoise*.[71]

The plans to move to Somerset House elicited further condemnation of what Gough saw as ill-conceived expenditure. He had little time for most of the membership, which by this time had expanded to 180 members, and Milles's presidency, for which he had once entertained such high hopes, was a disappointment. In his frustration he drafted a letter of resignation, replete with his bitter disappointment at the society's failure to live up to his own expectations of what such a body should achieve. The society, he wrote, was his 'Hobby horse' whose interests he had promoted with the utmost zeal, but he was compelled to withdraw as he saw it decline 'from its Meridian Glory'. The communications were no longer original, the president neglected to attend, councils were not called, members did not pay their subscriptions. Such revenues as existed were lavished upon engravings to satisfy the whim of a private clique, whilst more important publications were neglected. To crown it all, the society was on the point of removing to magnificent new apartments where they might cut a great figure, but where their chief ornament, the library, was in danger of being hidden away.[72]

In the event he did not resign, reserving that ultimate expression of displeasure until the furore over James Wyatt's candidature in 1797, but his attendance at council meetings became increasingly erratic. Either Milles had dissuaded him, or he thought better of it; his temper, as his friends were well aware, was quick to flare up.[73] Gough's assessment of the society's recent fortunes reflected his own high expectations of antiquarian scholarship and his suspicion of anything that savoured of dilettantism or fashionable superficiality. It was the removal to Somerset House which really provoked Gough's fury, as the costs involved detracted from what he perceived as the true ends for which the society had been established. He applied exactly the same standards to the society as he applied to the antiquarian publications he reviewed in the pages of the *Gentleman's Magazine*. Whether the society had ever enjoyed the putative 'Meridian Glory' to which Gough referred in his letter is a moot point – securing attendance at meetings and papers of a consistent quality, as we have seen, had presented problems throughout the eighteenth century. The range and quality of papers in the 1770s and 1780s was certainly no worse, if not better, than at earlier points of the society's history.

Gough was, however, in something of a minority in his opposition to the direction the society was taking. The plans to move to Somerset House had first been broached in 1775 when it was announced to the council that there were plans to take down Somerset House and to erect new buildings for public offices. The Royal Academy was reported to have already been assigned chambers; it was also noted that the Royal Society had been allocated rooms in the building. Whatever the Royal Society did, the Antiquaries had to match. They could not afford to let the larger society overshadow them or assume a position of greater public visibility and importance. A petition to the king for similar apartments was consequently drawn up by Sir Joseph Ayloffe in 1776. Meanwhile, Sir William Chambers, architect of the new building, was swiftly elected to membership and Brownlow North, the bishop of Worcester and a fellow of the society, was deputed to negotiate with his brother, the prime minister; he was soon to report back that the king was graciously pleased to order that the society be accommodated in the new apartments.[74] As Gough predicted, the move did involve considerable additional expenses. It would be necessary, Milles informed Gough, to furnish the new rooms 'in a manner correspondent to that of the Royal Society and suitable to the Royal munificence'. Furthermore, the society would now be lodged in apartments which were open to visitors and spectators, 'and not to have proper conveniences and decorations, will disgrace our name'.[75] In addition to furniture, special arrangements had to be made for maintaining the new accommodation, with the appointment of a housekeeper and a messenger-cum-porter, incurring wages of forty pounds a year. The rooms of the Antiquarian Society were much more richly furnished than those of the Royal Society, so Michael Lort informed George Ashby, with silver-plated candlesticks, ink-stands and snuff dishes, and the most magnificent chandeliers. 'I tremble for my pocket', he added dryly.[76]

The demands of the move did at least necessitate some reorganisation of the society's affairs. An inventory was taken of all the prints, engravings, copper plates and other items that the society had amassed; the library was recatalogued and books rebound where necessary; the finances were overhauled and firmer action was to be taken against defaulters. The procedural innovations and the investment in the public persona of the society were continued under Edward King's short-lived presidency in 1784. King was, it must be said, a better administrator than antiquary; in fact he was the ultimate bureaucrat. Forms and ceremonies, he informed the society in his speech of resignation, are undoubtedly trifling things in themselves, but 'as connected with, and conducting, and arranging, the management of all the affairs of life, they are perhaps of more real utility to the world than even the greatest abilities, or the most consummate knowledge'.[77] It was King who introduced the practice of having two secretaries 'to expedite business', and who attempted to tighten up the financial procedures for the society. Accounts were audited more rigorously and members now had to sign to receive their copies of *Archaeologia* or *Vetusta monumenta.* Lists of those in arrears were displayed permanently upon the table in the meeting room. He also took the significant step of appointing a draughtsman to the society in order to ensure that all antiquities presented at meetings were correctly recorded. Like Gough, he appreciated the importance of the visual record as a historical source.

Cumulatively, the move to Somerset House, the publication of *Archaeologia*, the increase in the size of the membership, as well as the more general broadening of interest in matters of antiquity and national history, had the effect of endowing the society in the last decades of the century with a stronger institutional presence. Nevertheless, it felt the want of a public role comparable to that of the Royal Society and was further hampered by the limited powers of patronage at its disposal. Nor had it even been possible to secure agreement amongst its own members as to what this role should be or even what subjects lay properly within its sphere. The reputation of the society beyond the confines of Somerset House was a mixed one. The traditional jibes at antiquaries were a literary stock in trade, drawing on a long tradition of ridiculing the virtuoso which went back to the seventeenth century.[78] In 1772 Samuel Foote had breathed new life into the hackneyed caricatures in his comedy, *The Nabob.* Satirising the social pretensions of a vulgar parvenu newly returned to London enriched with East India wealth, the play had the eponymous nabob seeking membership of the Society of Antiquaries as part of his campaign to establish himself within the *bon ton* of London society. Horace Walpole relished Foote's satire of what he termed the society's 'nonsensical discussions', but nevertheless used the success of the play as the excuse to terminate his membership. 'They are welcome to say anything of my writings,' he explained to Cole, 'but that they are the works of a Fellow of so foolish a Society.'[79] Francis Grose, himself a fellow of the society since 1757, played up the image of pedantry and exploited its comic and commercial potential in printed word and image, giving further circulation to the popular caricature of the antiquary.[80] Grose was not alone in his ability to see the ridiculous side to antiquarianism, but whereas he responded by embracing the caricature, others reacted by trying to formulate a more coherent programme for what they as individuals and the society as a body should set out to achieve. Edward King had offered one vision of the society's role and function in his speech of resignation, delivered in a flight of rhetoric more suited to the pulpit than the gathering of a learned society. The principal pursuits of the society, he declared, should be 'to bring *truth* to light; to devellop [sic] the true history of man; to show the gradual progress of the world from darkness and ignorance to light and perfection, through succeeding ages ... and to ascertain the overruling hand of Providence in the whole progressive work'. Stirring stuff, but it hardly constituted an agenda for future activity.[81] The following year more serious criticisms were levelled against the society that went considerably further than the usual jibes at the esoteric and trivial aspects of its activities.

The polemical antiquary and man of letters John Pinkerton, writing as Philhistor, took the society to task in the pages of the *Gentleman's Magazine* for its failure to fulfil any kind of public role, comparing its activities unfavourably with the record of comparable societies in other European countries. The society, he argued, was composed of respectable men, but its transactions published in *Archaeologia* lacked any kind of profundity. They were but fugitive papers: 'The Society consists chiefly of men of fortune, exists at the expence of its members; and was not intended to serve the publick, but merely for an innocent and laudable amusement to the members themselves.'[82] Pinkerton called for a body which was more focused and disciplined in its activities; what was needed, he suggested, was an Academy of National History which would publish illustrations of the national historical monuments, promote research and engage in writings on national history. Medals, he suggested, should be awarded for the best dissertation upon a given historical subject, as was the practice in the Society for the Encouragement of Arts and Manufactures and in the continental academies. He even argued that the government should take the unprecedented measure of confining the society to the study of history alone by the terms of its charter and allot it a revenue which would allow it to publish original writers 'in an elegant manner'.[83]

What Pinkerton was suggesting was a society much more akin to the academies established by royal fiat in France or Denmark than a modern vision of state-sponsored history. His manifesto would not have appealed to most antiquaries, who would have resisted the concept of state directives in the matter of what they should research,[84] but his argument, that the society could and should play an important role in promoting the study of history and the preservation of national antiquities, would have struck a chord with Richard Gough at least. In 1785 Michael Lort offered Thomas Percy, by then bishop of Drogher, some advice on establishing a new antiquarian society in Ireland.[85] Drawing on his experience of the London society, Lort recommended that the membership should be limited – in the London society, he explained, the policy was too open, and anyone who applied was admitted. He also advised Percy to draw up a set of subjects and topics of inquiry for members to investigate – a measure which clearly anticipated Pinkerton's cry to arms in the *Gentleman's Magazine*.[86] There was, therefore, a minority at least, who had a vision of a dynamic society, that would do more in the way of coordinating research, promoting publication and establishing national history upon a sounder footing. The reality of the society in which they found themselves, however, precluded their dreams from being realised. The society was unable to act effectively as a body to promote the illustration of national history and antiquities, however much its members might wish to do so as individuals.[87]

The failure of common purpose in the proceedings of the society reflected upon the lack of unity amongst the antiquaries as a body. The fellowship was a heterogeneous mix, and became more so as numbers expanded. By the end of the eighteenth century it included some of the leading political, ecclesiastical, legal and intellectual luminaries of the day. There were many competing interests and, like any body of that size, it was afflicted by factionalism. The Antiquaries liked to pride themselves that their dissensions were nothing like as divisive as those of the Royal Society, but there was nevertheless scope for considerable disagreement, which proved a powerful obstacle to any kind of activity that involved the commitment of time or money on the part of the members. The matter of the charter and Richard Rawlinson's split with the society had been followed by a relatively quiet period, but in the 1770s and 1780s, as the society became more ambitious in its publications and pretensions, the scope for disagreement opened up again. Gough's reservations over the publication of the historical prints have already been mentioned. Rising membership fees provoked unhappiness from the country members who considered that the society was being managed in the interests of a metropolitan elite. Edward King's brief presidency had given rise to the first contested election for the presidency in the society's history in which he lost out to Lord de Ferrars, subsequently earl of Leicester. 'King seems to have a Party', Hayman Rooke told Samuel Pegge, 'which I am sorry for, being fearful lest the restlessness of such Party should cause a lasting, & not only a temporal Disease in the Society.'[88] Rooke's anxieties were not, in the short term at least, fulfilled. The contest was in reality more of a reflection upon Edward King's personal ambitions than factional manoeuvrings upon the council.

The relationship with the Royal Society, which had been so contentious in the negotiations for the charter, continued to be a somewhat delicate matter. Given that at any one point a third or more of the members also belonged to the Royal Society, and given also the extent of common intellectual ground between the two societies the interests of both societies were always going to be closely combined. The very proximity of the relationship made antiquaries the more conscious of a need both to preserve a separate identity and to match the Royal Society at every instance. Thus the move to Somerset House was not just a question of practical convenience for the hundred or so members who enjoyed dual membership at that point, and who could now move effortlessly from one meeting to the other without the inconvenience of leaving the building, but also one of competition. The cohabitation was not without its difficulties, and petty rivalries, expressed in territorial disputes over the common stairway and entrance hall and the provision of a porter, were a frequent occurrence. The Antiquaries' old fear that the Royal Society might seek to take their own society over never died away, and acquired a new cogency during the forty-two year period in which Sir Joseph Banks was president of the Royal Society. Banks was typical of the kind of polymathic individual who shaped the English Enlightenment before the period of disciplinary segregation and increasing specialisation. Just as many antiquaries had interests in natural history, Banks too could claim that 'general antiquities has been always with me a favorite pursuit of Relaxation'. He was elected to both the Royal and the Antiquarian Societies in 1766 and moved easily between the two worlds, even if his primary interests lay in botany and natural history.[89] Any chance to excavate a barrow was seized upon with alacrity, and, when in Lincolnshire at the family estates, he worked upon his collections for the history and antiquities of Lincolnshire.[90]

The Banksian hegemony in the Royal Society was challenged by those led by the mathematician Samuel Horsley, who alleged that Banks had interfered with elections to the council and the fellowship of the Royal Society. Horsley demanded a more rigorously mathematical approach in the conduct of the Royal Society in place of the rule of the virtuosi, which encouraged a much broader range of subjects.[91] Much of Banks's support within the Royal Society derived from those members who like him belonged also to the Antiquaries. 'If my friends of the Antiquarian Society support me', he told Thomas Astle when standing for election as President of the Royal Society, 'I have not the least doubt of succeeding in a very creditable manner.'[92] Banks was never an officer of the Society of Antiquaries but he was elected twice to the council. Normally this did not constitute a problem or conflict of interest; rather, Banks could, for example, direct papers which he thought more proper to the Antiquaries their way. It is very noticeable, for example, that during the 1780s increasing numbers of papers published in *Archaeologia* bore a dedication to Sir Joseph Banks, who was willing to use his considerable influence to promote the study of antiquities. Samuel Lysons's excavations at Woodchester, for example, were greatly facilitated by Banks's intervention in securing equipment and military labour to undertake the task. Much to Lysons's delight, Banks later arranged for him to exhibit the drawings of the mosaics to the royal family.[93] The fact that Banks commanded such enormous patronage in the cultural world, however, inevitably meant that a coterie of Banksites gathered around him and, given that at least a third of the members had first-hand knowledge of the dissensions in the Royal Society, there was always a lingering suspicion that the divisions would spill over into the realm of the Antiquaries as well and that Banks would try to bring the other society more effectively under his sway. It was the latter point which created tensions at the end of the 1790s and into the nineteenth century.

In 1797 the architect James Wyatt, responsible for alterations at the cathedrals of Salisbury, Lichfield, Hereford and Durham was elected to the society – despite the vehement protests of a minority led by John Carter, Richard Gough and Sir Henry Englefield who objected to what they regarded as his vandalism of the medieval fabric.[94] Gough resigned in protest and withdrew almost all contact with the society, as Samuel Pegge the younger shrewdly pointed out due to 'some Offences, old and new, that he has taken'.[95] Banks was always going to be a supporter of Wyatt, however, given the fact that Wyatt was the king's surveyor general, and with effect from 1797, surveyor to Somerset House.[96] From then on, any changes to be made to the accommodation of the Royal and Antiquarian Societies, as well as the Royal Academy, would have to win the approval of and be executed under Wyatt's direction. Wyatt's supporters knew where their best interests lay. It was Banks who called for Carter's expulsion, and his party of 'anti-Gothicists' included Samuel Lysons, Thomas Astle and John Topham. It took some time for the ill-feeling generated by the controversy to die down and the veracity of Carter's allegations was still being debated with some heat through the summer of 1799.[97] Carter's commissions were gradually dropped; he turned increasingly to journalism in the *Gentleman's Magazine*, whilst A. C. Pugin and Richard Smirke were employed by the society to complete the engravings of St David's Cathedral and St Stephen's Chapel.[98] Nevertheless Carter continued to appear regularly at meetings, where he presented papers and aired his grievances against Samuel Lysons (who took over from Richard Gough as director), and the other Banksites within the society.

When the president, the earl of Leicester signalled his intention of resigning in 1799, a year after these ructions had taken place, this seemed to Banks to present an opportunity to secure the election of someone amenable to his own influence, such as the botanist Lord Lewisham, and the chance to defeat those such as Sir Henry Englefield who had supported Carter in the Wyatt débâcle. Plans were laid to elect Lewisham but were thrown into confusion by a change of heart on the part of Leicester who resolved to stay in office. Banks and his party were reluctant to give up on Lewisham and the presidency was contested in 1799.[99] Leicester prevailed with a majority of fifty-six.[100] The fact that Lewisham had no pretensions to being anything but a botanist, combined with the knowledge that his chief supporter was Sir Joseph Banks (or Magog Banks as they referred to him in correspondence), seemed to Richard Gough and his correspondent Samuel Denne to herald another attempt to subsume the Antiquaries within the Royal Society, and to reduce their society to being part of the Banksian empire of knowledge.[101] Joseph Farington's diaries, detailing the long drawn out campaign of meetings between Lysons and Banks and the endless canvassing of votes, indubitably confirm that Banks was the driving force behind the projected *coup d'état.* A letter to the *Gentleman's Magazine* in 1803 reiterated the same point, referring to the late attempt at revolution which would have made the Society of Antiquaries dependent upon the Royal Society, as Holland was upon France, by filling the chair with a botanist.[102] The letter was anonymous, but it could easily have been penned by Gough, particularly given that the concluding sentence attacked the society for having become too fashionable, too polite and too rich to remember the original design of its institution. The bitter feelings which the quarrel of 1797 had provoked festered and soured relations within the society in the early years of the nineteenth century.

Whether the society at that point was actually too rich was something of a moot point, given that its finances were heavily encumbered by the enormously expensive engravings of Cathedral Antiquities, which Gough himself had been instrumental in promoting. The retail price for these rose from £2 8s for the first volume to six guineas for the fifth, but as most of the copies were distributed free to the members there was little money to be made from their sale. Gough had carped at the costs of engraving the historical prints, but they did not begin to match the £600 charged by Basire for engraving Carter's drawings of Durham.[103] The society was forced to increase revenue by expanding the membership even further, but it was nevertheless left with a loss of over £5000.[104] By 1803 it numbered over 800 members and in 1807 membership stood at 849. Many of these were drawn from London's fashionable elite, headed by the prince of Wales and the dukes of Gloucester and Cumberland, who, it has to be said, were not generally known for their antiquarian proclivities. By this time the Antiquaries had overtaken the Royal Society in terms of membership, if not in wealth. In 1800 the membership of the Royal Society numbered only 531. Its capital, however, stood at a satisfactory £11,000, whereas the Antiquaries were forced to sell some of their own investments to make up the losses sustained on their publications.[105] The value of the books and prints which the fellows had been receiving as members (and which was one of the main reasons for seeking membership – unscrupulous fellows took their copies straight to the book dealers) far exceeded the value of the admission and subscription fees, a situation which was exacerbated by arrears of payment which amounted to over £1300 by 1810.[106] As a consequence of the dire financial situation in which the society found itself, the admission fee in 1804 was raised to eight guineas, with an annual fee of four guineas. Even taking inflation into account, this was substantially more than in the years following incorporation. All of which developments served to heighten the aura of social exclusivity with which the society was associated rather than to enhance its scholarly credentials.

Social exclusivity was also written into the very structure of the society. Even in the early years of the eighteenth century, when the son of a shoemaker such as John Bagford could be elected, the Antiquaries had never admitted quite the diversity of social backgrounds that could be found in the Royal Society. Personal knowledge of potential candidates to the Society of Antiquaries was essential: in 1773 the council ruled that in future no candidates should be nominated unless known personally to the members making or subscribing to the nomination.[107] Family connections often weighed more heavily than mere antiquarian aptitude. Michael Tyson reported to Richard Gough that Sir John Cullum of Hawsted was desirous of being made a member and commented upon his good credentials, placing his family before his antiquarian interests.[108] Members of the aristocracy had always been welcomed as fellows, regardless of their claims to be well versed in antiquities or the likelihood of their being useful members. Membership was automatic upon their making it known that they would welcome admission. Special provision was also made to fast track the sons of peers for membership, bypassing the normal election procedure. Deference became institutionalised in the 1780s when council ruled that all letters to peers should be delivered by the porter, rather than suffering the indignity of being sent through the post. James Douglas's observation that the society had 'become one of our most fashionable weekly rendezvous's' [sic] was more than just another ironic jibe.[109] Charles Clarke of Gravesend sought nomination to the society in 1796 in order to gain access to the society's collections for studying architecture, but, as he explained to Samuel Denne, the fact that he had not attended either university and had no paternal estate to his name had inhibited him from making an earlier application for membership.[110] The anonymous correspondent in the *Gentleman's Magazine* complained that the membership of the society had become nothing more than an 'indiscriminate rabble'; wealth and rank were given preference over any ability to contribute to the study of antiquities.[111]

Recommendations for membership did not record the candidate's occupation, so beyond the obvious categories of the church and the aristocracy a detailed membership profile cannot be established. Crude patterns can, however, be discerned. In 1776 the peerage and the bishops taken together constituted 6.3 per cent of the fellows; ten years later the proportion had risen to 8 per cent and by 1798 to 13.6 per cent, a proportion that continued to rise into the nineteenth century.[112] A comparison with the Royal Society, where peers and bishops together constituted 21 per cent of the membership, suggests the possibility that at least part of the motivation for attracting more members of the aristocracy to the society lay in the constant comparisons which were being made with the fellows of the Royal Society, where men of 'wealth and station' who would 'promote, adorn and patronize science' had always been welcome.[113] The Royal Society clearly had the advantage here. Some individuals professed genuinely to seek admission in order to participate in antiquarian correspondence,[114] but for many others the prime motivation in joining the society was to form social contacts or simply to add to their collection of engravings (which would account for the number of artists and architects who were enrolled but who scarcely ever attended the meetings). The close proximity to the Royal Academy in Somerset House evidently facilitated social interaction between members of the society, and, as with the Royal Society, there was a considerable overlap in membership during these years. The blackballing inflicted upon the architect James Wyatt in protest against his architectural innovations at Durham Cathedral was the more pointed in that membership was being granted to other artists and architects with increasing frequency. In addition to Joseph Farington, from whose diaries we have so much personal and anecdotal detail of the social world in which these people moved, fashionable artists such as Benjamin West and Richard Cosway, or engravers such as Valentine Green and Thomas Byrne were being elected. Joseph Farington and his ilk were part of a lively social and cultural elite who moved easily from the drawing rooms of the nobility and artists' studios to meetings of the Royal Academy or the Society of Antiquaries.

The Antiquaries represented just one other social forum, where connections might be made, introductions effected, news exchanged and commissions sought after. Even at the contested election in 1799, when Farington estimated that 400 of the 800 plus members were within 'penny post' distance of London, only 200 or so members turned up. Membership for many was just an additional status symbol.

'I think this Society is going fast to the D ——', fumed Francis Douce in 1809. The complaint was not a new one. Fellows had been lamenting intermittently that the society was no longer what it was since the 1720s. In almost every decade someone could be found commenting gloomily upon low attendance or the poor quality of papers. Douce, however, has not been alone in arguing that the society had lost its way in the early nineteenth century.[115] The very public wrangling of 1797–99 had left a perception of internecine quarrelling in the public mind. 'The world calls us old women,' complained one antiquary, 'we can quarrel too like them.'[116] Attendance at meetings was by some accounts poor, but since the names of those attending ceased to be recorded in 1770, such complaints are hard to substantiate. The only time at which the meetings were full, according to Douce, was when there was a contested election; otherwise the room was empty, with a dearth of papers. There was some truth in this. Samuel Lysons regaled the assembled company with 'interesting extracts' from his *History of the Berkeley Family*, for want of alternative fare, no less than twenty-two times between 1799 and 1801.[117] Even before the *querelle de Wyatt*, complaints of low attendance and lacklustre papers cropped up during the 1780s and 1790s in the correspondence of antiquaries such as Samuel Denne, who saw themselves as the 'working bees' of the society.[118] The earl of Leicester had never been a dynamic figure as president, and his interest in antiquities was largely limited to heraldry and his own pedigree. Francis Douce accused him of being a 'drunken, whoring' president, under whom the society was a body without a head, a 'corporation with a brainless caput'.[119] After 1801 Leicester's role in the society became increasingly marginal, as his attendance at meetings became more and more infrequent until his death in 1811. Sir Henry Englefield was initially elected as his successor, and did at least have claims to genuine antiquarian scholarship. Englefield's open support for Carter in the 1790s and his own Catholicism, however, had earned him enemies amongst the council and the earl of Aberdeen was elected in his stead. Aberdeen was no more committed an antiquary than Leicester, and even more erratic in attendance. Any assessments of his presidency will always be influenced to some extent by Cruikshank's famous cartoon, *A meeting of the Antiquarian Society* of 1812.

The other officers were hardly more suited to exercise leadership. Lysons was a more than competent antiquary, as his work at Woodchester and the unfinished *Magna Britannia* shows, but he did not use his position as director to further the role played by the society in sponsoring the study of antiquities in any readily discernible way. His energies were directed towards his own publications. He did at least ensure that *Archaeologia* continued to appear on a regular basis; the content changed in tone, however, becoming more miscellaneous, with shorter essays. That is not to say that nothing of value was published: the society did attract papers of antiquarian merit upon subjects such as Gothic architecture or the history of Anglo-Saxon poetry. *Archaeologia* was becoming more widely known at home and abroad, and its transactions more frequently referred to in other literature. In 1808 there was even a proposal from the publishers Baldwin & Co. for issuing an abridgement of *Archaeologia*.[120] The proposal was rejected out of hand, but it indicates that the publishers at least perceived the potential of a wider market for the society's transactions. Thomas Frognall Dibdin penned some caustic comments upon Lysons's record as director, but given that he avowedly saw him as his enemy, his comments should be treated with some scepticism. Lysons was, wrote Dibdin, 'opinionated, dogmatical, and at times, overbearing. There was only *one* dictum to which he, apparently, deferred – and *that* was the opinion of ... Sir Joseph Banks.'[121] The secretary, Nicholas Carlisle, was even less active, treating the position, which came with free accommodation and a comfortable salary of £200 p. a., as little more than a sinecure, never doing more than was absolutely required of him.[122] Criticisms were expressed in the pages of the *Gentleman's Magazine*; the council was charged with having become an unaccountable oligarchy which failed to exercise responsible stewardship over the society's resources.[123] From having been a supplement to the proceedings of the society, the *Gentleman's Magazine* had, since the 1790s, become an arena where antiquaries aired their differences and settled scores.

There was a clear irony here. At a time when antiquarianism was enjoying greater popularity than in previous periods, and when an awareness of the importance of the preservation of buildings and the potential historical value of excavation work was becoming more widely established, the society was not in a position to capitalise upon the situation. Individual members might take an interest in preservation or excavation, but the society as a body did next to nothing. It failed to mobilise the growth in sentiment in favour of preservation or to assert itself in an advisory capacity to the government with respect to, for example, the Record Commission. It had still to be established where the priorities of the society lay. Its failure to take a stand over the election of Wyatt in the case of Durham Cathedral had dented its reputation as a body concerned for the preservation of antiquities. Its expansion in size had enhanced its public profile but diluted its antiquarian credentials. It was known for high quality, expensive engravings – but little else. The influence of Sir Joseph Banks opened up channels of communication to the royal family and secured the advantages of royal patronage for a number of members, but he did not assist the society in achieving the ends for which it had been established. Rather, the strength of his personal influence left it vulnerable to the same factionalism which had bedevilled the Royal Society. The election of the earl of Aberdeen as president in 1812 ensured that the society's social standing was not damaged but held out little chance of strong leadership which would allow the society to assume a more active role. If the achievements of the society in the eighteenth century were questionable, circumscribed or disappointing, how much more so was this the case in the first half of the nineteenth century.[124]

By the 1840s members were in despair; the society appeared to serve no useful function and the meetings were held to be insupportably dull. There was a dearth of papers; the publications were of questionable value; few people attended and the officers treated their posts as sinecures. The best antiquaries of the day no longer published their researches in *Archaeologia* and rarely contributed anything to the meetings. The society had better be dissolved, admitted Joseph Hunter, or root and branch reform be imposed on it.[125] It was not dissolved, and reform, when it happened, was of the incremental rather than the radical variety. Thanks to its charter and its institutional identity it could not simply slide into abeyance or reinvent itself as a subscription library as other more informal gatherings did. Its existence was in a sense artificial during this period. The considerable energy and enthusiasm for investigating the past which was much in evidence during the first half of the nineteenth century was flowing through different channels, which eventually gave rise to the British Archaeological Association, the Camden Society and the local antiquarian and archaeological societies which formed a network of antiquarian activity across Britain from the 1840s onwards.[126] Had the society not been incorporated and thereby possessed of considerable assets, a public identity and a constitution, it is reasonable to suppose that it would have quietly folded.

The experience of the Society of Antiquaries was far from being unique, however, and its failure to give a strong lead in the study of antiquities at this point should not be seen as symptomatic of a malaise in antiquarianism – which as we shall see was, in fact, in a relatively flourishing state. It had always struggled to stake out a clearly defined area of intellectual space, distinct from the Royal Society, which had the advantage of an earlier foundation and greater resources of wealth and patronage. It struggled too to find a balance between fashionable appeal, necessary to secure a place in metropolitan society, and the kind of intellectual endeavour which would allow it to remain true to its founding principles.[127] Societies were essentially cyclical bodies, going through periods of activity and decline on a regular basis. Incorporation meant that a society could persist through a period of inactivity; for societies with a less secure institutional basis, the pattern would be that one society would sink into abeyance and disappear, only to be revived later, or to be replaced by another with similar aims.

The story of the Scottish Society of Antiquaries during this period was hardly more positive. Founded in 1780 and incorporated in 1783 its existence had come about primarily upon the whim of its founder, the earl of Buchan, rather than out of a gathering of like-minded individuals. The manner of its establishment was in itself not without controversy. Buchan was a genuine enthusiast for antiquities and a member of the London society (albeit chronically in arrears with his membership payments). He had identified a need for a forum in which to encourage and develop antiquarianism within Scotland, which he saw as crucial to maintaining a spirit of Scottish patriotism. It was certainly true that there was little organised antiquarian activity in Scotland – the Philosophical Society of Edinburgh did not devote much attention to antiquities, and since the days of Sir Robert Sibbald, antiquarian research had been somewhat overshadowed in the world of the Edinburgh literati by other disciplines.[128] There was definitely a case to be made for establishing a Scottish Society of Antiquaries that could encourage and coordinate antiquarian activity in Scotland. For a number of years Buchan certainly provided the kind of vigorous leadership which his antiquarian brethren missed in the London society, setting before his members a series of ambitious projects which would establish Scotland's history and enhance its reputation – and bring to an end the superiority which English antiquaries had always asserted over Scotland. In brief, it was a plan to equip Scotland with the equivalent to the *opera magna* of English antiquarianism. The parochial survey would surpass *Britannia*; there would be a 'Monasticon Scoticum' to set alongside Dugdale and Tanner and a collection of state papers to match Rymer's *Foedera*; a *catalogue raisonée* of Scottish coinage would be executed and there would be a 'Biographica Scotica', honouring the names of all the Scottish worthies of the past.[129] He met, however, with only very partial success. Enthusiasm for Buchan's projects was limited; his museum never took off; income from members was inadequate; and the house which was purchased for the use of the society proved too expensive to maintain and cheaper accommodation had to be found. Buchan had contributed £500 out of his own pocket, but this was insufficient to cover the costs. In 1784 he upbraided the assembled members for their disappointing contributions at the anniversary dinner; he had not expected that, in a society devoted to a matter of such general concern as the illustration of Scotland, over one hundred gentlemen should have allowed 'the labouring Oar' to remain continually in his own hands.[130] After the first flush of enthusiasm he withdrew from any kind of active participation, disillusioned with what he saw as the selfish, sordid views of his countrymen and their frivolous abdication of serious intellectual inquiry for 'idle shows and sports'.[131] Others were more sceptical of Buchan's own commitment. 'I am doubtfull Ld Buchan's project will not succeed', George Paton confided in Richard Gough, 'His Lordship is happy enough in opening a Scheme but too frequently deserts the prosecution of it before finishing the same'.[132] Between 1802 and 1815 the society was virtually in abeyance and Buchan had withdrawn to his estate at Dryburgh.

The failure of the Scottish society to attract more widespread support can be accounted for in a number of ways.[133] Buchan's personal eccentricity had not a little to do with it. 'On Tuesday last there was a meeting at the earl of Buchan's for the purpose of forming an Antiquarian Society in Scotland', recorded James Boswell. 'I had a card from his Lordship inviting me to it. But as I think him a silly affected being, I did not go.'[134] Buchan's own explanation, which he offered to Richard Gough, was that the nobility were too careless of everything that did not enrich their families and that the middling classes were too poor or engaged in professional activities.[135] Even allowing for Buchan's jaded cynicism, he had a point. He was not alone in suggesting that Edinburgh could only support one learned society, and that to promote another would simply divide the existing learned community which was accustomed to attend the Philosophical Society for discussion of matters of science, antiquities and literature. London, as we have already seen, was exceptional in supporting two distinct learned societies at this time. The recruitment base for a society was certainly much smaller in Edinburgh than in the metropolis; and if the London society was having problems with attendance, it was only to be expected that the same would apply in Edinburgh, where there were equally many other societies and activities with which to compete.[136] The Philosophical Society itself had hardly enjoyed an existence of uninterrupted stability and had almost failed on at least three occasions prior to its dissolution in 1783.

The likelihood of Buchan's society succeeding looks even more improbable when the political context of Edinburgh in the 1780s into which he launched it is taken into account. It was this, rather than any particular problem with apathy for antiquities, which blighted the chances of Buchan's fledgling society. Although there is no doubting the genuine quality of his enthusiasm for antiquarianism, his decision to establish a society for the study of antiquities in Scotland was on one level nothing more than an attempt to strike a blow against the hegemony of the Dundas despotism, which was steadily gathering most of the intellectual institutions of Edinburgh under its sway by the judicious use of patronage. Dundas boasted in 1801 that for the past twenty years every professor in Edinburgh and St Andrews had been appointed either by himself or upon his recommendation.[137] Buchan, by contrast, was on the side of parliamentary reform, had been a supporter of Wyvill and Fox, was a friend of Benjamin Franklin and supported the Americans in the war of independence; in the 1790s he would become a member of the Society of the Friends of the People.[138] He repeatedly protested against the interference of the ministry in Scottish affairs. Buchan's political views were certainly widely known and he made no effort to conceal his ulterior motives in establishing a Society of Antiquaries. Little love was lost between him and the professors of the University of Edinburgh – whom he freely identified with the Tory despotism. Moreover, he accused the university authorities of having failed to discharge their responsibilities, in particular with respect to the natural history museum which had been bequeathed to them by Sir Robert Sibbald, Buchan's model as a patron of antiquities and natural history. Buchan's society has also been interpreted as an affront to the evangelical Presbyterianism which had taken hold in Edinburgh in the aftermath of the Catholic Relief Bill and the Gordon Riots. He had close ties to a number of Scottish Catholic scholars, and a startling number of leading Catholic names appear in the membership lists for the 1780s.[139] All these issues came to a head when Buchan sought incorporation from the king, provoking anxiety on the part of the university and the faculty of advocates that he would succeed in setting up a rival establishment. They made furious, albeit unsuccessful, efforts to block the charter, which resulted in a lively exchange of pamphlets and very public acrimony. Eventually both Buchan's society and the newly established Royal Society of Edinburgh secured incorporation, but the reputation of the Scottish Society of Antiquaries in Edinburgh society was irredeemably tarnished and its prospects severely compromised.

Buchan's experience also highlights again the importance of exercising a discriminatory policy over candidacy for membership; a delicate balancing act between raw numbers, talent and social status had to be performed. He managed initially to sign up a distinguished roster of people for membership, including the third earl of Bute, whom he persuaded to take on the role of president. Few of these, however, attended the meetings, and the political controversy which surrounded Buchan's provocative campaign to acquire incorporation ensured that many of the Edinburgh social and intellectual elite would have nothing to do with the new society. Buchan was therefore dependent upon the support of less socially distinguished personages drawn from the trading and professional classes. George Paton, an excise official and Richard Gough's indispensable informant on matters antiquarian in Scotland, was a member, but seldom attended. William Smellie, who became secretary in 1790, was a noted natural historian who had completed a translation of Buffon, but by trade he was a printer. Only four years earlier Jeremiah Milles, president of the London society, had objected to the proposed candidacy of another well-known printer, John Nichols. However, Nichols was granted honorary membership of the Scottish society, as was the Birmingham historian William Hutton, who was never even proposed for membership of the London society.[140] Of even lower social standing than Smellie was James Cummyngs, who acted as secretary in the earlier years of the society. Critics claimed that Buchan had established a society of 'ragamuffins'. As we have seen, there were weighty reasons of a political nature to account for the more distinguished figures absenting themselves, but the fact that the active membership was not of a socially elevated caste indisputably counted against the society and diminished its standing in the eyes of the Edinburgh elite.

Beyond the metropolitan centres of Edinburgh and London gentlemen across provincial England and Scotland gathered together for the discussion of antiquities in societies of varying degrees of formality. The discussion of antiquities had always been a staple part of the meetings of the provincial learned societies, such as the Gentleman's Society of Spalding and its sister societies in Peterborough, Stamford and other Lincolnshire towns.[141] At the Peterborough Society, which was active between 1730 and 1748, papers on numismatics and antiquities accounted for over a quarter of the contributions, and at Spalding were almost as strongly represented (in both cases papers on antiquities outweighed any other subject category).[142] Antiquities also featured in the transactions of library societies and the later 'lit and phil' societies which sprang up in urban centres across the country towards the end of the century. The Fraternity of the United Friars, established in Norwich in 1785 for philanthropy, learning and good fellowship, espoused a Strawberry Hill 'Gothick' in its choice of name and the Gothic-style chairs upon which its members sat. Its transactions which covered an extremely eclectic range of interests, included contributions on inherently antiquarian topics such as Queen Elizabeth, Henry VII, the formation of the county of Norfolk, the use of parish registers, the history of Suffolk and Norwich castle.[143] The catalogues of library societies show a preponderance of historical and topographical works over other genres, offering a fair indication of the interests which their members wished to pursue in their reading, even if not active antiquaries themselves.[144] Such societies drew on the local urban elite of literate and respectable professions: the clergy, lawyers, schoolmasters, physicians, booksellers and merchants, as well as the resident gentry. Fashion and social status were less significant than in the metropolitan gatherings.[145] The subject of antiquities lent itself readily to local inquiry and presentation; no technical expertise or equipment was required to discourse upon such matters, and as such it featured regularly in these provincial gatherings.

Of all these provincial societies, the Gentleman's Society of Spalding is the only one which can claim a continuity of existence comparable to the London society; most of these eighteenth-century societies depended upon the dynamism of a single individual, or a coterie of like-minded friends, for their existence and as such enjoyed relatively brief periods of flourishing activity, followed by long intervals of dormant inanition. If the lacklustre reputation of the Society of Antiquaries in the early nineteenth century can be largely attributed to the vacuum of leadership at the top, the ability of one individual to shape the interests and fortunes of a society was even more true of these smaller bodies. The Gentlemen's Society of Spalding, established in 1710, flourished under the genial auspices of the Spalding lawyer, Maurice Johnson, who found it 'a true Observation that without a Cheerfull Glass and sober Pipe we Englishmen can't well keep up Conversation'.[146] In recognition of this coffee, tea, chocolate, wine, cider, ale (and a chamberpot), as well as pipes, tobacco and snuff, were regularly supplied at the meetings. Johnson dragooned the local clergy, gentry, schoolmasters and lawyers into attendance, and enrolled his numerous offspring and their spouses as well. The fact that he fathered twenty-six children, of whom sixteen survived to adulthood, should not be underestimated in accounting for the ability of the Spalding Society to flourish when other provincial societies failed. Johnson was well aware of this himself, explaining with disarming frankness to Roger Gale how he depended upon the support of his children and near relations, 'whom I have taken care to train up to a liking of it from their infancy'.[147] Johnson's interests encompassed legal history, numismatics, heraldry and sepulchral monuments, as well as fossils, natural history and gardening. As a member of the London Society of Antiquaries, he was able to persuade over thirty members of that gathering to become corresponding members. Although not all of these fulfilled their obligations, the communications of antiquaries such as George North or Browne Willis contributed to the prominence of antiquarian subjects at the Spalding meetings. Johnson's energy and his unwavering insistence that the members should engage in discussion and correspondence ensured that the society did not, as did many others, degenerate into a convivial drinking society. It met without fail fifty-two weeks a year (the London

Society managed only thirty meetings at its peak) and at each meeting Johnson kept meticulous minutes. They were, he argued, crucial to the society's reputation and an incentive to rise above desultory discussion. A formal record of proceedings was public testimony that the society was answering the ends for which it was established, of intellectual improvement and inquiry.[148] But as Johnson's health declined, so too did the fortunes of his society. He began to complain of the difficulty of maintaining the spirit of inquiry and 'inducing the members to give their own thoughts on any subject'.[149] After his death in 1755 the impetus went out of proceedings. There was no one who would take over his coordinating role, or who shared Johnson's vision of mutual improvement and sociability. By the end of the century the society, whilst still formally in existence, had degenerated into little more than a lending library.[150] The Peterborough Society had already become precisely that, and the others had simply petered out.[151]

Attracting sufficient members and ensuring regular attendance over the long term was clearly a problem. Neither Spalding nor Peterborough could be described as major urban centres – the population of Peterborough in the early eighteenth century stood at around 3000 and Spalding at around 2000, and their success or failure hinged upon the commitment of a few individuals.[152] Nine of the forty-eight regular members at Peterborough and fifteen of the thirty-three members, regular and honorary, at the Stamford Brazenose Society also belonged to the Spalding Society. The Literary and Antiquarian and the Library Societies of Perth similarly shared a considerable number of members, and a common core of a few active individuals.[153] The fortunes of societies in the larger towns such as Newcastle or Edinburgh proved almost as erratic. The first provincial society to be devoted exclusively to the study of antiquities was the Newcastle Society, the forerunner of the Victorian associations such as the Surtees Society, the Chetham Society, and the many historical, archaeological and antiquarian societies which sprang up across mid-Victorian Britain. The Newcastle society was originally founded by a local bookseller, Joseph Bell, in 1813. The north of England, with its rich heritage of Roman antiquities, had obvious attractions for the antiquary and in Newcastle and its environs there would be no shortage of materials to discuss at meetings. The promoters of the scheme initially secured a considerable coup in persuading the duke of Northumberland to act as patron, which instantly rendered the society much more attractive, as it could now be seen to be offering a possibility (however remote) of contact with the duke and his enormous powers of patronage. Hearing of the duke's gracious condescension, David Smith, commissioner of the ducal estates, went back on an earlier refusal to join the society: 'As the Duke I understand has accepted the Presidency of your Society, I feel it a duty to be incorporated in your original foundation ... and beg that you will consider the first of the difficulties I stated are done away.' Despite this incentive to join, the antiquaries found it hard to attract members. They too found themselves competing with a rival gathering: the Newcastle Literary and Philosophical Society had been founded only twenty years earlier in 1793, and although its interests were directed towards scientific rather than antiquarian subjects, the pool of interested individuals upon which it drew proved to be very similar to that of the Society of Antiquaries: 70 per cent of the antiquaries were also members of the literary and philosophical society.[154]

The world in which learned societies operated in the early nineteenth century was very different from that in which they had originated. The highly informal and ad hoc procedure which characterised the early days of the Society of Antiquaries had not adapted well to the changing expectations of what a learned society should achieve or to the more *dirigiste* modes of information gathering which were being introduced by the nineteenth century. Publication was now far more important than the simple exchange of ideas, and failure to publish was correspondingly more of an indictment upon the society's deficiencies. Early meetings had been centred around the discussion of objects of 'curiosity'. Such an approach had lost all intellectual credibility by the early nineteenth century, as both naturalists and antiquaries strove to distance themselves from the eclecticism and undiscriminating methods of the early part of the eighteenth century. As early as 1783 this had been identified as a major weakness of the society. 'It is a melancholy truth', one reviewer observed, 'that all literary Societies are at best but Repertories; bodies without souls, too numerous to concert, too dissonant, or too complaisant to execute one grand design.'[155] The miscellaneous and unsystematic mode of proceeding which had traditionally been taken in the meetings of the society seemed less attractive features in a world where it had to compete against the attractions of more specialist gatherings. Alongside the more systematic methodologies which had been developed in all branches of inquiry, expertise and disciplinary specialisation had become much more pronounced, as evidenced in the establishment of learned societies devoted specifically to the study of mineralogy, geology or chemistry; interests were less general and the area of common ground in which exchange of ideas and mutual improvement could take place was correspondingly diminished. The society's claims to the custodianship of native British history came under increasing pressure from the historical profession, and their own discipline appeared to fragment into sub categories of architectural history, art history, archaeology or palaeography. Even attitudes to sociability, the governing principle of early eighteenth-century societies, had also changed. Whereas Roger Gale had deemed the consumption of a pint of wine or so an important element in the feast of reason and the flow of soul, one hundred years later attitudes had shifted a considerable distance and the Antiquaries attracted satirical derision for their provision of tea and coffee with buttered toast and muffins after their meetings.[156]

In the mid nineteenth century the antiquarian and historical societies of provincial England acquired a cultural force of 'amazing vigour'. The pursuit of antiquities flattered local attachments and fuelled local pride; historical studies provided a link between the glories of the past and the triumphs of the present.[157] Provincial societies were, if anything, more dynamic than those of the metropolis. In Victorian Britain the critical mass of educated men (and women) who had the time, leisure and inclination to study local antiquities and history was significantly higher than in the previous century. The cultural climate too was now more accommodating to the study of domestic antiquities. Victorians, triumphant in their self-appointed role as the agents of Christian imperialism, reacted against what they perceived as the superficial disdain of eighteenth-century classicising taste and its misplaced confidence in a foreign classical ideal. Antiquarianism, however, had by this time taken second place to the increasingly professionalised disciplines of history and archaeology. Nevertheless, the study of the past, whether it was termed archaeology, history or antiquarianism, continued to offer a means of establishing identities and offered a sphere in which sociability could combine with a sense of intellectual endeavour and the attainment of a public good. It was a powerfully attractive formula which arguably proved to be even more successful in the nineteenth than in the eighteenth century.

4

The Ancient Britons

The history of Britain before the arrival of the Romans had always been regarded as the province of the antiquary rather than the historian. History literally began with the Romans. Both the subject matter and the methods of inquiry which antiquaries were necessarily forced to adopt distanced them from the writers of history proper. Antiquaries had little in the way of literary documentation to go upon and therefore resorted to other methodologies, drawing upon cognate disciplines and employing what was often regarded as an unjustifiable degree of speculation and conjecture. The occasionally wild hypotheses of eighteenth-century antiquaries concerning this period probably did more to discredit them with their critics than any other branch of antiquarian study. For modern historians, however, the eighteenth-century approach to the study of British or 'Celtic' past is revealing on a number of counts. The study of pre-Roman antiquities was necessarily interdisciplinary, drawing upon biblical chronology, the techniques of surveying in the course of fieldwork and rudimentary geology in excavations, as well as the traditional humanist skills of textual criticism and philology. The efforts of the eighteenth-century antiquaries highlight the extent to which antiquarianism was part of an intellectual world in which modern disciplines such as geology, archaeology, anthropology and comparative religion were pursued interchangeably, with little sense of disciplinary boundaries. In this respect antiquarianism was as much a part of the Enlightenment project of discovery as was natural history. But at the same time these antiquaries were highly conscious of their dependence upon classical and biblical authorities and their debt to the traditions of antiquarian scholarship which went back over two hundred years.

Antiquaries were also convinced of the importance of their studies to their contemporary world, not least because of the patriotic importance of establishing the earliest history of national origins. For the historian of eighteenth-century Britain these attempts to trace back the lineage of the nation illuminate the process by which national histories and a national identity were constructed and highlight the differences between the self-perceptions of the constituent parts of the kingdom. A sense of British nationhood was forged in the eighteenth century, drawing upon a common

Protestantism, the experience of war, imperial expansion, commercial and manufacturing strength, and the largely peaceful union of England, Scotland and Wales. But Britishness operated at what was often a largely political and rhetorical level; the stronger sense of national identity which historians have identified in the eighteenth century was arguably more evident in the formulation of Scottish, Welsh and English, not to mention Irish, identities during this period.[1] The history of the ancient British inhabitants was probably more sharply contested than any other period of antiquarian research.

For some antiquaries, of course, there was little of interest in the antiquities of pre-Roman Britain. Sir Robert Atkyns explained to the readers of *Ancient and Present State of Glostershire* (1712) that it was not possible to give an account of the kingdom prior to the arrival of the Romans, because the whole country was under the confused power of a 'multitude of barbarous kings' who kept changing the territorial boundaries.[2] National history at this point was primarily conceived as the history of the religious and legal institutions of the state; there was no story to be told of a time before such institutions had taken root.[3] For an antiquary such as Atkyns, for whom the truth of history lay in delineating the descent of property, a period in which the boundaries of ownership had no stability or permanence was not worth inquiring after. Those who emphasised the benefits of Roman rule were reluctant to concern themselves with barbarian inhabitants who could, they argued, be studied with little edification or profit. They represented mankind in its most unpolished form and the uncertainty with which their history was surrounded rendered study of their antiquities futile.

But, commanding though the Roman influence over eighteenth-century antiquarianism was, it could never be forgotten that the Romans were foreign invaders who had conquered the native inhabitants from whom the modern British nation traced its descent. Patriotic sentiment demanded that the earliest inhabitants of the British Isles should not be neglected, and it was the task of the antiquary to establish all that could be known relating to the progenitors of the British race. This ambivalence between admiration for the conquering Romans, and patriotic pride in the barbarian Britons who resisted conquest, created a tension which marked antiquarian literature from William Camden's *Britannia* onwards. Camden, who had embarked upon his project intending to record the antiquities of Roman Britain, found himself devoting progressively more attention to the antiquities of the native Britons, as successive editions of *Britannia* show.[4] Even the most laudatory accounts of the Roman presence in Britain were tempered with acknowledgements of the strength of resistance offered by the native inhabitants. The province of *Britannia* had never comprised the whole of Great Britain and patriotism demanded that the Welsh and Scottish antiquaries should celebrate the failure of the Romans to bring their freedom-loving forebears under the imperial yoke. Similarly, English antiquaries experienced little difficulty in identifying their earliest ancestors as the ancient Britons, whilst simultaneously setting a disdainful distance between themselves and the modern heirs of the original Britons, the Welsh. The true-born Englishman, as Defoe had it, was a mixture of Briton, Roman, Saxon, Dane and Norman, in a mongrel race.[5]

This is a theme which we can trace through the antiquarian literature of the eighteenth century, as the rolling bandwagon of British chauvinism collided with the elegant edifice of classical culture. Upon his election to the Society of Roman Knights, Alexander Gordon, author of *Itinerarium septentrionale*, had taken the name of the hero of Caledonian resistance and architect of the collapse of Agricola's campaign, Galgacus, whose fiery speeches of defiance were recorded by Tacitus. Sir John Clerk, his patron, who had himself taken the name of Agricola in the same society, remarked wryly to Roger Gale on what he saw as Gordon's overly enthusiastic representation of ancient Caledonian valour. But Gordon was deliberately trying to challenge the prevailing assumption that the earliest inhabitants, as described in the standard works of history by Innes, Ussher and Stillingfleet, were little more than, to adopt his own phrase, 'Hottentots': ''Tis worthy of a Curious Man and a Schollar', he wrote to Sir John Clerk, 'to set as much of their History to rights as possible.' Even Clerk, than whom no man could be more admiring of the Romans, expressed himself amazed that his fellow countrymen had not shown more interest in the Roman Wall, which, he told Roger Gale, did their forefathers more honour than any of the other events of Scottish history. The Romans had indeed 'walled' the ancient Caledonians out from civilisation, but did so because of the severity of the threat which they posed to their empire.[6] The less voluble John Horsley, whose documentation of Roman antiquities in Britain was the most authoritative account to be published in the eighteenth century, desisted from pressing admiration for the Roman achievement too far. His respect was tempered by an awareness of the oppression of the native Britons that it must have entailed, and the loss of liberty.[7]

In general, admiration for the Romans was offset by pride in the strength of the resistance put up by the native Britons, whilst the civilising influence of Rome was acknowledged to have been won at the cost of loss of liberty and independence. Native hardiness, courage and virtue were contrasted with the effete corruption of the Roman Empire, particularly in its later stages. Taking their cue from Tacitus, historians and antiquaries lamented the loss of manly virtue and independence which conquest entailed and which left the Britons vulnerable to the marauding, but undeniably virile, Saxon invaders. The Romans, like the Normans (who were also acknowledged to have brought with them the arts of civility) imposed a yoke of servitude. Philip Morant, antiquary and historian of Essex, wrote in stirring terms of Boudicca, the 'brave virago' who when 'provoked by the brutish and unnatural usage of the Romans ... made a vigorous effort to shake off their yoke'. Morant hinted at a slight ambivalence in weighing Roman oppression against the benefits of civilisation: it was 'a *sort* of recompence for the loss of their Liberty (and indeed nothing can be a *sufficient* recompence for it) that the Britons were polished and civilised by their Conquerors'.[8]

This period of ancient British history was, moreover, a deeply problematic area into which to venture given that, bar the comments of foreign (Roman and Greek) observers, and the somewhat remote authority of the Bible, there were no textual sources. From this perspective, the reluctance of eighteenth-century antiquaries to jettison entirely the Brutus legend recorded by Geoffrey of Monmouth in the *Historia regum Britanniae*, according to which Britain had been first settled by refugees from the burning city of Troy, is less surprising, despite the fact that Camden had effectively dismissed its claims as an authentic historical source in *Britannia*.[9] In default of Geoffrey of Monmouth there was but 'a blank table in Chronology' of all that had passed in that 'vast tract of time' before the coming of Caesar. Aaron Thompson's new edition of Geoffrey of Monmouth, published in 1718, argued that 'there was at least some Foundation of Truth discoverable in the ruins of this ancient Story of Brutus and his Successors'. This view was endorsed by a number of other respected antiquaries, including William Borlase, Francis Drake and Philip Morant, not least because the Brutus legend reflected some glory upon the places of which they wrote.[10] The Brutus legend aside, beyond the act of Creation in 4004 BC and the Deluge, which was the prelude to the diaspora peopling the countries of Europe, there were no chronological sign-posts by which to navigate ancient British history. No names of rulers, the conventional method of marking the passage of history, had survived.[11] Without a framework of historical events or personages – 'the exact periods of Life and Action, which are the soul of History, and the Criterion of all Truth' – it was extremely difficult for the antiquary to conceptualise a period about which so little was known.[12] The process by which antiquaries, or those whom we would now consider archaeologists, came to appreciate a period of 'pre-history', and the possibility of recovering the facts of the past through non-textual means, involved a shattering of an intellectual paradigm which had determined the way in which the past had hitherto been conceived. By the end of the eighteenth century that paradigm was showing

A Briton of the Interior, from Samuel Rush Meyrick and Charles Hamilton Smith, *The Costume of the Original Inhabitants of the British Islands from the Earliest Period to the Sixth Century* (London, 1821). (*Society of Antiquaries*)

severe stress fractures, and would soon be irreparably broken. It is important to bear this in mind in order to appreciate the way in which antiquaries approached the history of pre-Roman Britain and the study of what was then understood as the Celtic past.

Camden, whose influence over antiquarianism and history throughout the seventeenth and eighteenth centuries cannot be overestimated, had set the pattern for future antiquaries to follow. In *Britannia* he traced out the distribution of the British tribes; he identified monuments and barrows; and he collated the sources of Roman history which yielded information on the ancient British inhabitants. Rejecting the fleeing Trojans as progenitors of the British people, he argued instead for a settlement from mainland Gaul. The earliest inhabitants were Gomerians or Cimbri, descendants of Noah through his son Japhet, who had spread out over Europe from the East after the Deluge and the fall of the tower of Babel.[13] Due to the unprecedented success of *Britannia*, this view of the early peopling of the British Isles acquired widespread acceptance as the authoritative version. During the seventeenth century that interest in the ancient British inhabitants was rather superseded by the flourishing of Anglo-Saxon studies, particularly given the fact that the discrediting of Geoffrey of Monmouth denuded the historical landscape of any recognisable figures around which a historical debate could be initiated. That is not to say, however, that there was no debate at all. The identity of the first inhabitants continued to arouse discussion. Camden's Gomerian thesis was widely accepted, but was further complicated by an alternative theory which argued that the British were descended from Phoenician settlers who had reached the south-west coast in search of trade; a view which was most famously articulated by Aylett Sammes. Given the almost complete dearth of information about the Phoenicians and their colony at Carthage, so comprehensively destroyed by the Romans, this thesis was hard to prove or disprove (which in itself could present a powerful attraction to the more speculative antiquary).[14]

The monuments of ancient British antiquity had already been identified in the seventeenth century. Under the influence of Scandinavian scholars such as Ole Worm, English antiquaries had begun to show a more critical awareness of stone monuments and earthworks.[15] The Druids, the only constituency of the ancient British population which the classical authorities discussed in any detail, were also subjects of admiration and speculation, featuring in the verse of John Milton and Michael Drayton.[16] The link between stone circles and druidical worship, however, which was the axis around which so much of eighteenth-century writing on Druids and ancient British antiquity revolved, had not yet been made. John Aubrey is now the most famous of those, who in the seventeenth century began to take an interest in the ancient British or druidic monuments, but in his own lifetime his attempt to publish his antiquarian treatise 'Monumenta Britannica', of which the essay, 'Templa Druidum' comprised a sizeable element, failed to attract sufficient subscribers.[17] His influence can be detected, however, in Robert Plot's histories of Oxfordshire and Staffordshire. Plot, a personal friend of Aubrey, included descriptions of stone circles and similar monuments, which were described as British, rather than Roman or Saxon, constructions.[18] Aubrey's simple thesis that such curiosities were to be found in many regions where neither the Romans nor the Saxons had penetrated presented a convincing argument. Aubrey's views were far from finding universal acceptance at this stage. Thomas Tanner, who relied on Aubrey's notes for his revisions of Wiltshire in *Britannia*, simply listed them amongst a number of possible interpretations of Stonehenge.[19] There were still many who believed with Walter Charleton that it was the work of the Danes; or, with Inigo Jones, that the technology and skill which would have been required would have been far beyond such a primitive people, and that it could therefore only be the work of the Romans. Such too was the belief of Jones's Vitruvian heir, the earl of Burlington, who in the eighteenth century was greatly discomfited at William Stukeley's identification of Stonehenge as a British monument.[20]

Just as the revision of Camden's *Britannia* can be seen to have stimulated inquiries into Roman antiquities, the project had a similarly galvanising effect upon the study of ancient British antiquities. Thomas Tanner's contribution ensured that Aubrey's suggestions met a far more extensive readership than a single publication on the subject could have been expected to have done. Aubrey's influence is also discernible upon another of the most important contributors to the 1695 edition, Edward Lhwyd, the Welsh antiquary and naturalist and keeper of the Ashmolean Museum.[21] Lhwyd carried out extensive surveys of megalithic monuments through Wales, Scotland and Ireland, as a result of which he was able to offer conclusive proof for Aubrey's observation that such monuments were to be found in areas which had never known Roman or Danish occupation. His correspondence with Scottish antiquaries, such as James Garden of Aberdeen and Martin Martin in the Orkneys, confirmed him in the belief that according to local lore these stone circles had been places of worship and sacrifice in pagan times. From general tradition, wrote James Garden, these monuments were used in religious ceremonies, and given the fact that the superstition of the time was known to have been that of the Druids, he suggested that it was reasonable to suppose that the circles were Druid temples, although he had found little proof to support this inference.[22] Lhwyd's additions to Wales in *Britannia* included passages of considerable length on Welsh megalithic monuments, transforming what had been an extremely sketchy and ill-informed treatment of Wales. In preparation he had toured Wales for two months, making detailed observations of the antiquities. He was amongst the first to develop a form of classification for the different types of stone monument: the carnedd, cromlech or mein gwyr and the kistvaen.[23] The stones at Kerrig y Druidd he argued add 'not a little to Mr Aubrey's conjecture, that those rude Stones erected, in a circular order, so common in this Island, are also Druid Monuments', but he was far from assuming that all such monuments had an automatic connection with the priestly order, who, as he reminded his readers, were known to worship in open groves.[24] Lhwyd was able to appreciate the technical skill and social organisation which would have been necessary for such monuments to be erected and brought some substantive evidence to bear on the case for pre-Roman British civilisation. He had intended to expand considerably upon the findings outlined in *Britannia* in a publication of his own but, as with so many antiquarian enterprises, Lhwyd's ambitious *Archaeologia britannica* never appeared in its entirety. Only the first volume, the *Glossography*, which dealt with the language of the ancient Britons, was presented to the public.

Lhwyd was one of the first antiquaries to make the case for a sophisticated British civilisation on the basis of artefactual evidence. His defensive stance over the issue of a native British coinage and the primacy of British over Saxon letters raised eyebrows amongst some of his fellow antiquaries, but the insights of his evident etymological skill inspired respect and admiration.[25] Lhwyd's *Archaeologia britannica*, incomplete though it was, was nevertheless of considerable importance in influencing further researches into Celtic antiquity. His achievement was to demonstrate the affinity between the different Celtic tongues and to demonstrate how etymology and comparative philology could be used to elucidate periods of history for which there was no other historical testimony. Lhwyd's work, combined with publications from the Continent such as Paul Pezron's *Antiquities of Nations*, aroused considerable interest in the pre-Roman era within the scholarly community.[26] Whilst archaeologists today might hail Lhwyd's unpublished findings as expressions of precocious insight into archaeological method, it was Lhwyd as an archaeologist of language who exerted most influence.[27] His rigorous approach to philological studies seemed to offer a system of rules and the possibility of certainties to which conjectures surrounding earthworks and monuments could not aspire. Some readers, or so Lhwyd acknowledged in his preface, might consider his researches as time ill spent, but they would, he promised, contribute towards a better understanding of the first inhabitants of the three kingdoms, and the ancient names of persons and places. Lhwyd's apprehensions that his work would be dismissed as mere etymology were unfounded. Although there were always some who carped at what they considered to be entirely speculative and self-referential exercises, the etymological method appeared to most antiquaries to be the most reliable way of investigating the unrecorded past.

In addition to Lhwyd's etymological insights, the early years of the eighteenth century were remarkable for the development of scholarly interest in the Druids. Lhwyd's suggestion that Kerrigg y Druidd was derived from the name of the Druids who used to worship there anticipated much of the future direction of antiquarian studies of the ancient British period. The tradition of a learned druidical culture which was to be so widely discussed amongst eighteenth-century antiquaries was no innovation; it could be traced back well into the sixteenth century and there was a very substantial volume of literature, upon which antiquaries could draw, consisting of both classical authorities and the more recent commentaries of the past two hundred years.[28] Druidical religion and the physical evidence for it, such as stone circles, became a matter of broader interest in the 1720s. In 1723 Lhywd's fellow Welsh antiquary and collaborator, Henry Rowlands, published *Mona antiqua restaurata*. Rowlands, guided by Lhwyd, had undertaken his own observations of the standing stones in his native Anglesey, which was, according to Tacitus, the last stronghold of the Druids.[29] He was also, however, strongly influenced by Aylett Sammes's arguments for the Phoenician origins of the ancient Britons and for the affinity between the Phoenician, Hebrew and Welsh languages. The quality of his fieldwork was superficial in comparison with that of Lhwyd or Stukeley; and his mode of 'enquiry' to modern eyes appears even more dubious, with its reliance upon inference and conjecture. Rowlands concluded that the Druids were descendants of Japhet and that the Welsh language could be traced back to Babel, being closely related to Hebrew, and was thereby able to claim with patriotic pride that 'our nation hath kept its ground, what few or no other Tongues or Nations in the World have done, for about the space of three thousand and five Hundred Years'. The Phoenicians brought with them 'true' religion, being recently descended from Noah, of which the stone altars and cromlechs which he identified on Mona were testimony. The standing stones and pillars were, he decided, evidences of the religious ceremonies and customs described in the Pentateuch and similar to those to be found in Syria and Palestine. As monotheists, the Druids and the ancient Britons were naturally predisposed towards Christianity, which Rowlands argued had originally been brought to Britain during the Roman period by St Paul, thus establishing an origin for the British church which predated the corrupting influence of the sixth-century Augustinian mission from Rome.[30] Rowlands's views were not particularly original, but his publication was a first in terms of presenting a case study drawing upon local topography and antiquities, rather than simply being based upon a discussion of the classical authorities.

Three years later a very different kind of interpretation of the Druids was presented to the public in John Toland's highly polemical *History of the Druids* (1726). Toland, an Anglo-Irish scholar and deist, suspected by some of atheism, never professed himself to be an antiquary. He had not carried out any fieldwork himself and his volume was based entirely upon evidence supplied by others as well as his own reading of the relevant classical authorities.[31] Another antiquary, William Borlase, remarked rather sourly that he doubted whether Toland had ever gone to the trouble of examining or measuring one of the monuments he wrote of, 'and the authorities upon which he asserts many extraordinary particulars have never yet been produced'.[32] Whereas Henry Rowland's Druids had been virtuous, learned and uncorrupted priests, whose monotheism had prepared the way for the rapid reception of Christianity amongst the ancient Britons, in Toland's account the Druids were rendered as the prototype for the priestcraft of the Church of England, which as a deist he railed against. His Druids kept the people in a state of subjugation, maintaining a monopoly over education, and encouraging superstitious and idolatrous practices.[33]

At around the same time that Rowlands and Toland were publishing their interpretations, William Stukeley was refining his views on Stonehenge and Avebury. Stukeley had first visited the monuments in 1719. His interest had been heightened by reading a borrowed copy of Aubrey's manuscript, and was further fuelled by his concern at the destruction which was threatening such monuments from landowners who saw them only as quarries for building materials. When Stukeley began his researches at Avebury a number of the features described by Aubrey had already been lost, and during his lifetime the remaining stones were blown to pieces in order to clear the land for agriculture. In 1719 Stukeley's religious interpretation was barely adumbrated, beyond the fact that he shared the conventional view of his time that the Druids had practised a form of monotheistic faith, which he believed they shared in common with the patriarchs of the Old Testament. Stukeley proceeded to build upon the hints in Aubrey and the material from Scotland, such as Martin Martin's *Western Isles*, with the aim of developing a typology of stone temples which he believed, through comparative analysis, would ultimately explain themselves.[34] He used a theodolite and the latest surveying techniques to draw up an exact geometrical representation of the layout and the orientation of the monuments, calculating the original number of stones and the mathematical relationship of their arrangement, as well as establishing what he believed to be the basic unit of measurement, the Hebrew cubit.[35] Stukeley's painstaking surveying of the sites revealed the sophistication and complexity of the design. He also discovered in them a particular beauty which was something ruder and simpler than that demanded by conventional standards of taste. The stones were carefully proportioned and the harmonies of light and shade nicely calculated, 'Tho' the contrivance that put this massy frame together, must have been exquisite, yet the founders endeavourd to hide it, by the seeming rudeness of the work.'[36]

Over the years, Stukeley's views on the Druids became increasingly complex and elaborate, as he read into the structures of Stonehenge and other stone circles not just evidence of the advanced state of their civilisation, in terms of architectural design, mathematics and the social organisation necessary to erect them, but also statements of their religious belief. 'All my studys in antiquity', affirmed Stukeley to William Borlase, the Cornish antiquary in 1749, 'have ever had a regard to religion. Nor do I think any other studys are worth cultivating, but what have some aspect that way.'[37] The Druids, due to their 'abhorence of writing', he informed Roger Gale, 'have left us little on record of their principle (sic) doctrine of thir (sic) religion, yet they have left us the largest draught of the trinity that ever was [Avebury], where one cannot reasonably doubt of their faith of that divine truth.'[38] His main motive, as he informed Gale in another letter, had been to combat the deists from an 'unexpected quarter'. This threat, it has recently been argued, was not the deism of John Toland, as has often been supposed, but the anti-trinitarianism of William Whiston and other Cambridge Arians, including Sir Isaac Newton. In fact, Stukeley always entertained a favourable opinion of Toland's druidical writings, if not his religious beliefs. According to Stukeley the Druids, who were the heirs of Abraham's religion, had been able to discern a 'perfect notion of the Trinity' through the application of reason, thereby refuting the anti-trinitarian objections that the doctrine was antithetical to reason.[39] The beauty, regularity and complexity which he discerned in these monuments, taken with the evident mechanical and architectural skill which must have been involved in erecting them, strengthened him in his conviction that the Druids had been highly learned and cultivated in the arts.

Historians eager to trace back the origins of modern archaeology have taken a somewhat proleptic view of eighteenth-century antiquarianism.[40] They identify the origins of fieldwork in John Aubrey; it was carried on by Edward Lhywd (but cut short by his death in 1709) and resumed in Stukeley's hands, until he lamentably compromised his work by imposing upon it fantastic theological and metaphysical theories. Rather than regretting

Stukeley's lapse from empirical and accurate field work into wayward speculation, it is important to remember that Stukeley, like Henry Rowlands, was engaging in a debate upon the nature of primitive religious beliefs that was currently engaging the attention of many scholars. The validity of inquiring into the tenets of druidical doctrine was not in itself held up to question. They were both writing in the context of widely held 'euhemerist' views of ancient religion, which had an intellectual lineage going back to Renaissance neo-platonism and interest in the *prisca theologica.* The origins of all religious myths, it was believed, could be traced back to real events and characters in human history. Pagan deities and superstitions were later accretions upon an essentially pure and uncorrupted monotheism. Stukeley's theory that the Druids were the heirs of a learned culture derived from the Egyptians, and that they had practised a monotheistic faith, had long-standing credence, going back to the authority of the classical world. His parallel interest in Egyptian antiquities should similarly be viewed as topical rather than eccentric. He and a number of other antiquaries established a short-lived Egyptian Society in 1741, which discussed the practice of patriarchal religion and the inheritance of the traditions of the Old Testament.[41]

Indeed, the theme of eastern connections in ancient British antiquity was one which ran through the entire eighteenth century and beyond; and, as knowledge of oriental languages and antiquities increased, it gathered new strength rather than being refuted. Enlightenment scepticism tended to reduce all religious beliefs, Christian, classical or oriental, to the status of allegory, reducible to natural, erotic or astronomical meanings. The interest in druidic mythology and the attempt to identify within it and other primitive religions evidence of the patriarchal religion was part of the conservative reaction against a scepticism which appeared to threaten infidelity. This was the concern which lay behind a number of influential publications such as William Cooke's *An Enquiry into the Patriarchal and Druid Religion* (1754) and Jacob Bryant's *A New System or Analysis of Ancient Mythology* (1774), both of which drew on Stukeley's arguments to corroborate their own attempts to find physical evidence of scriptural narratives in the pagan mythologies. There were in every country, wrote Bryant, some shattered remnants of the ancient religion, and he called upon antiquaries in India and China to pay more attention to the antiquities there.[42]

The discovery of affinities between European languages and those of India apparently confirmed earlier suppositions. Charles Vallancey, an eccentric but influential antiquary, was initially convinced that the earliest inhabitants of Ireland had been Spaniards and Carthaginians, who brought with them the learning of ancient Egypt.[43] By the end of the century he was still insistent upon the eastern origins of the ancient Irish, but, inspired by recent publications such as Thomas Maurice's *Indian Antiquities* and Sir William Jones's researches into Sanskrit, he now traced the origins of Irish civilisation and culture further back to India. Irish 'abounded' with 'hindostanee' words, as well as Arabic and Persic, and the deities of the Brahmins were recorded in the Irish manuscripts. The word *Druid*, he argued, derived from the Irish *Draoi*, which in turn was derived from the Persian *Daru* – all of which signified a priest. The round towers of Ireland, which had mystified generations of antiquaries, were temples held to contain sacred fire like those of the 'ancient hindoos'.[44] The pages of *Asiatic Researches* (published from 1799), and in particular the essays of Captain Francis Wilford, offered further confirmation of the connections between the Druids and the Brahmins; the Druids, he argued, were Brahmins beyond a shadow of a doubt.[45] To the eighteenth-century mind, therefore, the notion of investigating ancient British antiquities by studying Egyptian, and latterly oriental antiquities, was an obvious means of progression in a subject where there were few other guides.[46] At the same time the discomfiting realisation that sophisticated civilisations had existed independently of the Graeco-Roman and Judeao-Christian traditions which had shaped the European consciousness could be postponed; the civilisation of India and the East was at least temporarily accommodated within the standard narrative and epistemological framework.

A belief in ancient knowledge also underpinned the masonic movement which was rapidly establishing itself in Britain and across Europe, to which Stukeley and a number of other leading antiquaries of his day belonged.[47] Stukeley appears to have been drawn to freemasonry as a means of discovering more about the mysteries of the ancients, from whom the masonic rituals were supposed to derive. Although he himself did not make an explicit link between Druids and masons, others did, and the two traditions were conflated in another interpretation of Stonehenge published shortly after Stukeley's own account, by the architect and antiquary John Wood.[48] Whilst Wood's interpretation of Stonehenge may now seem little more fanciful than that of Stukeley, the latter, sensing that Wood was encroaching upon his territory, was scathing in his dismissal, taking particular objection to Wood's attempts to interpret the 'rude' dimensions of the megaliths in accordance with proportions derived from the classical orders. Never one to mince his words, Stukeley described Wood's book as 'the fermented dregs and settlement of the dullest, and most inveterate mixture of ignorance, malice and malevolence'.[49] Stukeley need not have worried, because John Wood's theories acquired little recognition and, when noted at all, were secondary to his own. Stukeley's well-established profile as both a scientist and antiquary, and his close connections with many of the leading antiquaries and natural historians of the day, are probably sufficient in themselves to account for the greater fame enjoyed by his own works. Wood, by contrast, was a provincial architect, largely self-taught; he had not been educated at either of the universities or the inns of court, nor was he a member of the Royal Society or the Society of Antiquaries. Without entrée to the same circles as Stukeley, Wood's interpretation was largely unnoticed.

Stukeley's account of Stonehenge was published in 1740 and *Abury: A Temple of the British Druids* made its appearance in 1743. The volumes were not cheap (one guinea each) but, if Stukeley is to be believed, they were soon hard to come by.[50] Stukeley, who styled himself Archdruid and had adopted the name of the Druid Chyndonax as a member of the Society of Roman Knights, acquired the reputation for being the foremost authority on Druids in the country. He even went to court to discuss with the Princess Augusta the subject of patriarchal religion and its parallels with the Church of England.[51] That is not to say, however, that the full range of Stukeley's arguments was accepted without equivocation. Some were convinced and enormously excited by his theories: John Moulding wrote to Charles Lyttelton to thank him for the loan of the recently published *Abury*, 'which has given me the greatest pleasure of any Treatise of this kind, that ever fell into my hands'.[52] Another of Lyttelton's correspondents, John Stephens, was much more sceptical. Whilst acknowledging that Stonehenge, Avebury and Rollright were in all probability Druid temples, he could not accept Stukeley's 'serpentine theory', which was, he said, more suited to a poet than an antiquarian.[53] Stukeley's own personal eccentricities and somewhat cavalier attitude to scholarly conventions did nothing to mitigate the suspicion with which his views were received in some quarters. 'I am sensible', wrote Samuel Pegge, 'the Doctor has his admirers; but I confess I am not one of the number, as not being fond of wildness and enthusiasm upon any subject.'[54] 'Had the author been less infected with Hutchinsonianism', remarked Richard Gough, 'his book would be a useful compendium ... Determined to fathom the utmost depth of druidical science, he almost lost himself in an abyss which nothing but his strong imagination could have carried him through.'[55] By the 1750s Stukeley's views were being received with barely veiled ridicule by his fellow members of the Society of Antiquaries.[56] As we shall see, many took issue with the more extreme elements of his theory, but there were also many who were prepared to take a large part of it on trust and who recognised the inestimable value of the fieldwork which he had carried out.[57] At the very least, it proved impossible in the light of Stukeley's publications for anyone seriously to challenge the theory that Stonehenge, and other stone circles like it, were of Celtic construction.

Even Sir Richard Colt Hoare, that most empirical of antiquaries, used Stukeley's terminology of a 'serpent's head' to describe the arrangement of the stones at Avebury – even if he did not adopt the theological premise behind it – and fully acknowledged the quality of Stukeley's observations and the accuracy of his descriptions.[58]

One of those who admired Stukeley, whilst declining to follow him all the way, was William Borlase, the Cornish antiquary whose *Antiquities Monumental and Historical of the County of Cornwall* represented another important contribution to the systematic recording of megalithic monuments. Borlase was more of a natural historian than an antiquary, and brought to his study of the stone monuments of Cornwall and the isles of Scilly a rigorous and meticulous method of observation and description.[59] He followed the conventional view that the Druids had come originally from the East, identifying them with the Persians, but fell far short of Stukeley's vision of a patriarchal religion that anticipated Christianity.[60] He felt uneasy about the extent to which he had himself been forced to rely on conjecture, although he defended it as a means of illuminating truths which might not otherwise be arrived at; he was no doubt well aware of the criticisms being levelled against Stukeley's thesis.[61] Jeremiah Milles, the dean of Exeter and fellow antiquary, reassured him: 'What you assert is founded on authority, but he makes a system out of his own head, and never cares whether he has any authority to support it.'[62] Borlase's reputation amongst the antiquarian community was always one of greater solidity and reliability than the notorious Stukeley.[63] Other antiquaries felt more comfortable with his theory that the cromlechs were sepulchral monuments, rather than altars, as Stukeley had suggested; an argument which allowed the antiquary to sidestep the uncomfortable question of druidical human sacrifice. Thomas Pennant recommended Borlase as a guide to druidical antiquities and stone circles to his Orkney researcher George Low, on the grounds that Stukeley's *Stonehenge* was too fanciful, whilst Sir Joseph Ayloffe recommended Sheringham, Rowlands and Borlase as essential reading in druidical antiquities, but omitted all mention of Stukeley.[64]

Fanciful or not, it should be recognised that Stukeley's account of Stonehenge, or versions of his original text, became the standard guide for all those visiting the monument and his opinions echo through the comments of those visiting it, shaping their perceptions and influencing their language. Mrs Lybbe Powys visited Stonehenge in 1759 en route from Bath and Bristol, and noted in her journal that her description was 'as I took it down in reading Dr Stukeley's book concerning it'. She had her servants chip fragments of stone from the monuments as souvenirs, noting as she did so that Dr Stukeley had objected to this practice. For her own part, she confessed, she could see little danger in such a custom: the Royal Society itself had done as much in the interests of scientific inquiry.[65] Stonehenge was rapidly becoming one of the most famous monuments on the English landscape, not least because it was sited at a convenient distance between London and Bath, near to Salisbury (where the cathedral was widely regarded as the finest specimen of Gothic architecture in the country) and Wilton House (with the earl of Pembroke's collection of Roman marbles), greatly facilitating its attractiveness as a site of interest to the travelling *beau monde.* 'Salisbury Cathedral and its Neighbour Stonehenge', wrote Samuel Johnson, 'are two eminent models of art and rudeness, and may show the first essay and the last perfection in architecture.'[66] Stukeley's own highly charged account of his reaction to viewing Stonehenge – the sense of awe with which he was filled, and his eloquent praise of its majestic form and symmetry – appealed to the eighteenth-century sense of the sublime and helped to make it accessible to the imagination of a wider public. 'When you enter the building', enthused the author of a guide published in 1776, 'and cast your eyes around upon the yawning ruins, you are struck into an ecstatic reverie, which none can describe, and they only can be sensible that feel it. Other buildings fall by piecemeal, but here a single stone is a ruin.'[67] Stonehenge was presented as a unique monument to the skill and strength of the ancient Britons, and as such a symbol of patriotic pride as well as an object of curiosity. Guides to Salisbury and the surrounding attractions plundered Stukeley, omitting only those passages which were most likely to stretch the credulity or the tolerance of their readers.

The interest which Stonehenge aroused amongst the travelling public, however, had less to do with any widespread credence attached to Stukeley's views than a much broader swelling of interest in the Druids and ancient British or Celtic antiquities, which extended far beyond the circle of antiquaries narrowly defined. The antiquaries' interest in Druids had become caught up in the fashion for primitivism and a rising tide of nationalist sentiment, which was notably manifested in, for example, the cult of the Highlander Ossian and in the Welsh rediscovery of bardic literature and music. This cultural trend has been described as a 'Celtic Revival' and it exercised a powerful influence over both art and literature as well as antiquarianism. The Druid was elevated as a symbol of patriotic valour and, following Jean-Jacques Rousseau, the literary world lauded the 'primitive' qualities of a society uncorrupted by the commerce of a more advanced civilisation. Druid enthusiasts projected back the qualities of simplicity, honour, courage and virtue on to ancient British society and celebrated them in the poetic antiquities of supposedly bardic literature.[68] These literary and artistic effusions are of course antiquarian only in the loosest sense of the word, but poetry and art were not antithetical to antiquarianism. The one informed the other. John Thomas of Beaumaris could use an extract from Mason's poem *Caractacus* in order to illustrate his comments upon the Druid temples in Anglesey.[69] Thomas Gray, whose epic poem *The Bard* (1757) has been identified as the crucial precipitant in bringing about the Celtic Revival, was a man of strong antiquarian leanings himself, and his reading of Camden's *Britannia* can be traced through the details of the poem.[70] William Blake's voracious consumption of antiquarian literature – including Stukeley – and its influence upon his own thought, is similarly well documented.[71] The Druid, thanks to frequent representations in art, literature and even landscape gardening, was becoming a familiar cultural symbol. The very act of giving the admittedly hazy character of a Druid a corporeal form had the effect of endowing it with an imaginative presence and a stronger historical reality.[72]

If one manifestation of the Celtic Revival was a sharply increasing tally of publications on the subject of Druids and bardic literature, this pattern was replicated in the publications of the Society of Antiquaries itself. In most volumes of *Archaeologia* there was at least one paper which dealt with druidical remains in some form or other, but the number of such papers rose steadily during the 1780s, with a peak in 1785 of no fewer than seven, the same year which is supposed to represent the apex of Celtic enthusiasm more broadly defined.[73] Stukeley's *Stonehenge* and *Abury* were not republished, but were becoming 'scarce and dear'.[74] Henry Rowlands's *Mona antiqua* was republished in 1766. Borlase's *Antiquities of Cornwall*, of which a large element concerned the druidical remains, went into a second edition in 1769, and in other local antiquarian and topographical publications the description of druidical antiquities became a standard element. There was a strong sense that there was still much to be recorded: Borlase's efforts in Cornwall alerted antiquaries to the fact that many apparently natural features might in fact be places of former druidic worship. 'The subject', wrote John Watson to Samuel Pegge in 1763, 'wants further illustration' and a plan was proposed for mapping out all such monuments on a nation-wide basis on the model of John Horsley's *Britannia romana*.[75] Watson and Pegge both attempted to fill the lacunae, clutching at straws of evidence as they did so. Watson speculated that the rocks of Stansfield, near his parish of Halifax in the West Riding, were a Druid marriage temple, arriving at this conclusion from the principle that similar formations in Staffordshire and Cornwall were known as the Bride Stones and the Wedding respectively – 'for why should names of this sort be used, except to keep up the remembrance of some antient custom'.[76]

Pegge's contributions took the form of various papers presented to the

Society of Antiquaries during the 1780s on the druidical remains to be found in his home county of Derbyshire. He mixed speculation with a dose of pragmatism, identifying stones as part of a primitive agricultural economy in which they were used for grinding corn, rather than looking for altars upon which the Druids had performed human sacrifices. He also guarded against leaping to conclusions – the large mounds of earth with which Derbyshire was richly endowed could plausibly be heaps of rubbish from the centuries of lead mining rather than burial mounds.[77] Nevertheless, as he pointed out, any remarkable natural feature or monument was likely to have been used as a place of worship and religious rites and would thereby have acquired superstitious significance.[78] When a barrow or tumulus, or any other feature, could not with any confidence be attributed to the Danes, Saxons or Romans, it was easy to conclude that it must, therefore, pertain to the Druids. Without evidence to the contrary, there was enormous potential for constructing elaborate theories on very insubstantial evidence. Whereas the absence of any mention of a settlement or monument in Domesday Book or in the Anglo-Saxon Chronicle might prove a stumbling-block to the antiquary, no such objections could be raised against an era for which no written records survived.[79] Hayman Rooke, another enormously enthusiastic antiquary based in Derbyshire, was particularly adept at identifying druidical remains where none had been located before, and in the absence of contrary indications, such as Roman coins or inscriptions, was willing to identify a site enclosed by a ditch or vallum as a druidical court of justice, whilst a wall of undressed stone nearby was assumed to be the hut of a British chieftain, it being the mode the Britons would 'naturally' have adopted after quitting their caves and subterraneous dwellings.[80]

The flowering of Celticism and druidic antiquities in the later eighteenth century has, above, all, to be seen in the context of the fashion for primitivism and the 'discovery' of Ossian by James Macpherson in 1761. Macpherson presented the poems as authentic survivals from the period of ancient Celtic history, before the arrival of Christianity. The poems told a story of kingship in a primitive society, governed by principles of valour, honour and loyalty. They were the northern world's equivalent to Homer.[81] In *Ossian*, and his subsequent *Introduction to the History of Great Britain*, Macpherson elevated the Celt at the expense of the Gothic tribes, and in particular the Angles and the Saxons, from whom the English were descended.[82] The Celts were ennobled by a religion which anticipated Christianity in its most important tenets; they were philosophers who taught the Greeks and Romans; they were freedom loving, noble and virtuous. Even the Romans were descended from the Celts. The Saxons by contrast were barbaric, violent, unrestrained by any veneer of civilisation and brutally destroyed the peoples whose lands they conquered. The allusion to the recent Hanoverian punishment meted out in Scotland, and the Highlands in particular, was obvious. Nevertheless, such thinly-veiled criticism could not undermine the widespread enthusiasm with which the poetry, and its evocation of ancient primitive simplicity, was received.[83] As well as making the Celtic era fashionable the poems were regarded as a valuable source in themselves upon the manners and customs of the time. William Stukeley (himself a staunch Hanoverian supporter), still elaborating upon his extravagant construction of ancient British society in 1763, welcomed them as further confirmation of his arguments, and ones which brought back memories of his own excavations: 'I was capable of relishing *Fingal*', he boasted, 'more than many readers, and consequently with more plesure.'[84]

The literary furore which arose surrounding the poems' authenticity encouraged English travellers, of whom Samuel Johnson was only one, to travel to Scotland and seek out 'evidence' which would corroborate the testimony of the poems. In the logocentric world of the eighteenth century that meant manuscripts – it was, of course, a largely futile quest in this instance.[85] Others travelled north to experience the sublimity of landscape which the poetry evoked and sought out the remnants of the Highland culture which it celebrated. Interest in the Highland region was further encouraged by its becoming more accessible. In the wake of the 1745 rebellion the region was surveyed by engineers carrying out the military survey of Scotland (1747–55). Geographical knowledge of Scotland increased and went hand in hand with the construction of roads along which armies could move, but which also enabled civilian travellers to take to their chaises, describing the topography and landscape as they passed through.[86] As well as providing a quest for the polite traveller to pursue in Scotland, the Ossianic poems provided a structure around which questions could be framed and evidence ordered, in the same way that the classical sources such as the Antonine Itinerary provided a starting point for the investigation of Romano-British antiquities. The popularity of Ossian rendered the subject of Celtic antiquities in any form more palatable to the reading public, despite the anti-Hanoverian sub-text which Macpherson also employed. This in turn encouraged the publication of poetry and other material and helped revive the study of Celtic languages in Scotland, Ireland and Wales, which had lapsed somewhat since Lhwyd's day. The academic study of Gaelic was given an important stimulus and the first dictionary was drawn up by William Shaw for his *Analysis of the Galic Language* (1778). Up to this point, Scotland had lagged behind England very noticeably in terms of antiquarian publications; a point which English antiquaries such as Richard

Gough were not slow to remark upon.[87] In the last three decades of the eighteenth century, however, there was a rapid upsurge, almost all of which addressed the subject of Ossian and Celtic or Gaelic antiquities.

Given that one of the major stumbling-blocks for the acceptance of the authenticity of Ossian was the absence of a manuscript tradition, barrows, standing stones and other objects of antiquity offered evidence of a more convincing, physical nature for the veracity of the poems than did the elaborate, but ultimately intangible, constructions of the etymologists.[88] Hence James Anderson published papers in *Archaeologia* on ancient monuments in the Scottish Highlands, commenting on the lack of attention which had hitherto been given to antiquities in Scotland.[89] Each nation which had occupied Scotland in its early history, it was argued, would have erected barrows for its warriors, and would have practised their own particular burial practices. It should therefore be possible, with reference to the evidence of Ossian, to establish to whom the barrows belonged by disinterring them. Scotland, it was said, needed a Borlase to describe its monuments.[90] Thus Scottish antiquaries inspired by such notions located the probable birthplace of Fingal or the sites of his battles.[91] Vitrified forts, discovered by engineers involved in surveying the Highlands, were presented to the public as the habitations of Fingal.[92] Druidical remains were quickly identified. Thomas Pennant found them throughout the Highlands and the Hebrides in his tours of 1769 and 1772. By 1773 George Paton was informing Richard Gough that articles upon the Druids were regularly appearing in the weekly magazines in Edinburgh.[93] The poems themselves, however, were not in fact an exercise in druidical hagiography: Macpherson entertained a similar view to that to be found in John Toland's *History of the Druids* and was primarily interested in how their abuse of supposed powers of magic and divination enabled them to exercise control over the populace and to engross the management of civil as well as religious matters.[94] But for John Smith, author of *Galic Antiquities*, druidical remains represented important evidence of culture and civility amongst his Celtic forebears, on a scale to match those found elsewhere in the British Isles. He protested against the negative terms in which the classical authorities had written of the Druids. They wrote only from hearsay and prejudice: a surer guide, and one which reflected much more positively upon the ancient Gaelic culture, was to be found in the customs and idioms of the common people which still held echoes of primitive superstitions. The Highlands, claimed Smith, retained their ancient religion longer than any other part of Great Britain.[95]

There were, of course, always those who refused to accept the authenticity of Macpherson's publications and rejected the entire construction of a Celtic past. Foremost amongst these was John Pinkerton, an immoderate critic of

14. 'A Peep into the Sanctum Sanctorum', from William Stukeley, *Stonehenge: A Temple Restored to the Druids* (1740). (*Special Collections, University of Leicester*)

15. Prospect of Stonehenge from the south west, from William Stukeley, *Stonehenge: A Temple Restored to the Druids* (1740). (*Special Collections, University of Leicester*)

16. Buck Stone, from the *Antiquarian Repertory*, 4 vols (1776–84). (*Society of Antiquaries*)

17. A Maoeata and Caledonian, from Samuel Rush Meyrick and Charles Hamilton Smith, *The Costume of the Original Inhabitants of the British Islands from the Earliest Period to the Sixth Century* (1821). (*Society of Antiquaries*)

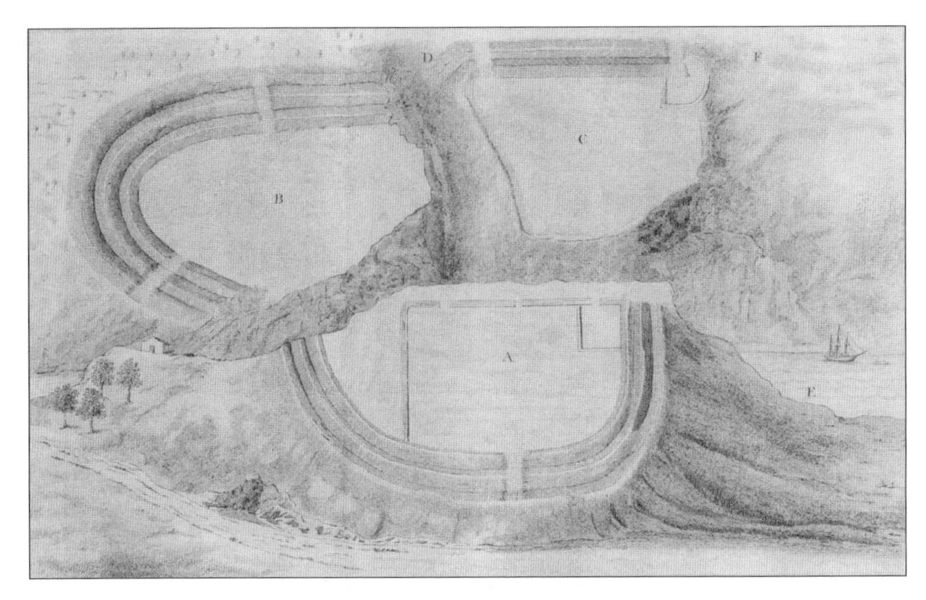

18. Roman camps on the River Avon above the Bristol Hotwells, from William Barrett. *The History and Antiquities of Bristol* (1789).

19. A view of part of the Roman road on Bramham Moor, leading towards Tadcaster, from Francis Drake, *Eboracum: or The History and Antiquities of the City of York, from its Original to the Present Times* (1736). (*Special Collections, University of Leicester*)

20. Danish habits, from Joseph Strutt, *A Complete View of the Dress and Habits of the People of England*, 2 vols (1796). (*Society of Antiquaries*)

21. Anglo-Norman youths, from Joseph Strutt, *A Complete View of the Dress and Habits of the People of England*, 2 vols (1796). (*Society of Antiquaries*)

22. Military costume of the Gothic nations on the western coast of the Baltic, from Samuel Rush Meyrick and Charles Hamilton Smith, *The Costume of the Original Inhabitants of the British Islands from the Earliest Period to the Sixth Century* (1821). (*Society of Antiquaries*)

23. The Eleanor Cross at Waltham (Essex), from William Stukeley, *Itinerarium curiosum* (2nd edn, 1765). (*Special Collections, University of Leicester*)

the enthusiasm for Celtic culture. Pinkerton developed an alternative model of early British history in which successive waves of Gothic invasions brought civilisation to the barbaric Celts. He took violent exception to the attribution of stone monuments to the Druids: 'This century has been overwhelmed with nonsense concerning druidism, and druidic monuments, as being universal amongst the Celts', he complained. They were but 'another idle dream of antiquists'.[96] These so called druidic monuments were actually Gothic courts of justice, similar to those found in Scandinavia, for which he referred to the same Scandinavian authorities who had encouraged Walter Charleton to identify Stonehenge as a Danish monument in the seventeenth century. Pinkerton's vehemence in claiming the so-called druidic monuments for his own 'Gothic' history reflects the extent to which the elevation of Celtic culture and druidical learning had become a crucial element in the rediscovery of a national past for Scottish Highlanders, and by extension the Scottish nation; it also demonstrates the reciprocal importance of establishing the antiquarian credentials of any alternative position.[97] In this sense the Celtic Revival in Scotland was important not just in terms of fabricating a Celtic past which would substantiate the myths of the ancient Scottish constitution or in offering a means of articulating deeply felt resistance to the Hanoverian regime, but also in establishing antiquarianism on a broader base and giving it an institutional presence in the Scottish Society of Antiquaries (founded 1780) and its sister society at Perth (founded 1782) from which more empirical versions of ancient Scottish history might eventually be produced.[98]

It was in Wales, however, that the elevation of the Druid and the study of druidical antiquities assumed its highest importance and enjoyed the closest connections with literary culture and nationalist sentiment. The Welsh, it has been observed, 'began to see that they had a special relationship with him [the Druid] that was different from Druidism in England'.[99] It is not the place here to discuss how the figure of the bard became caught up in the invention of a Welsh national past and character – an area which has been admirably treated by other scholars – save to note how much strength the study of antiquities derived from this incipient national consciousness. The figure of the bard, who was identified as the heir to the druidic traditions, was the symbol chosen by the members of the Honourable Society of Cymmrodorion, whose purpose was the promotion of Welsh culture and history.[100] The bardic tradition was believed to stand in a line of unbroken continuity from the earliest inhabitants until the massacre of the bards by Edward I. It appeared to offer a direct link to the time of the Roman invasions when the influence of the Druids was at its height.[101] The patriotic potential inherent in the study of Welsh antiquities was already apparent in Rowland's *Mona antiqua.* The volumes on Welsh antiquities and language which came forth from the press in response to fashionable demand and nascent Welsh nationalist sentiment were based upon 'discovered' manuscripts of bardic verse, specimens of the bardic oral culture which had been transcribed, accompanied by studies of the Welsh language. These carried on in the tradition of Lhwyd's *Archaeologia britannica.*[102] Lewis Morris, the leading figure of the Welsh network of antiquaries, compiled extensive collections which were published in the nineteenth century under the title *Celtic Remains* as a continuation for *Archaeologia britannica*, but these collections were chiefly concerned with studying the language and analysing the manuscripts that he and his circle had collected.[103] Evan Evans's *Specimens of Antient Welsh Poetry* (1764) claimed its authority from a manuscript which had survived from the period before Edward I's bardic bloodletting, rather than, as in the case of Ossian, being manufactured for contemporary tastes.[104] Evans always insisted that his own collection had been conceived prior to the fame of *Ossian*, but when it came to publication it was almost inevitable that the verses should be presented as the Welsh equivalent, with the ancient bard Taliesin as the counterpart to Homer.[105] In the early nineteenth century the movement for the recovery of Welsh literary antiquities steadily gathered momentum, with publications such as Edward Davies's *Celtic Researches* (1804), the *Myvyrian Archaiology* (1801) and Peter Roberts's *Cambrian Popular Antiquities* (1815).[106] The poems, wrote the editors of the *Myvyrian Archaiology*, were not to be compared with the Ossianic fictions of modern times: 'we pretend to give nothing from oral tradition; we produce many hundreds of manuscripts of undoubted antiquity, marked with all the genuine characteristics of authenticity'.[107] The Welsh antiquaries were almost equally attached to the legends of Geoffrey of Monmouth, despite the fact that he enjoyed little credence in England. However, in Wales antiquaries and historians clung to the myths as part of the same bardic tradition and continued to search for the Welsh original on which they assumed it must have been based.[108] The most creative of the Welsh enthusiasts for druidical antiquities was the radical nationalist and poet, Iolo Morgannwg, who under the influence of laudanum did more to invent the druidical tradition than any one else, including the creation of the Eisteddfod.[109] Thus the Welsh antiquarian tradition of the second half of the eighteenth century was predominantly based upon etymological research, bardic literature and music, rather than fieldwork of the kind that Lhwyd had pioneered. This became a distinguishing feature between the Welsh and English traditions of antiquarianism.

'In observing the manners and customs of this people', noted one tourist in 1770, 'some idea may be formed of their ancestors, the ancient Britons. They have preserved themselves almost intirely distinct from all other nations.'[110] National pride derived from the fact that the Welsh were (in their own eyes at least) the indisputable descendants of the earliest inhabitants. 'Men reckon it always a glorious and an honourable thing to be of the race of the first possessors and maintainers of a country.'[111] Their claims to have the best preserved remains of ancient British antiquity met a challenge in the form of the stone circles of Avebury and Stonehenge, for which there was no equivalent in Wales. Welsh antiquaries, therefore, often revived the argument that Stonehenge was of Saxon rather than ancient British construction.[112] Wales was rich in Roman antiquities in certain areas, such as Monmouthshire and Gwent, but the Welsh prided themselves on having successfully resisted the Roman invaders and on having preserved their traditions distinct from those of other nations.[113] They did not, on the whole, devote much effort towards locating Roman camps or identifying Roman roads. Lewis Morris and his circle showed little interest in tracing the path of the Julia Strata or identifying the remains of Roman stations at Caerleon. Thomas Pennant, better known as a naturalist, although also a man of keen antiquarian interests, was well integrated into London-based literary and intellectual culture, being a leading figure in the Royal and Linnean Societies and intermittently of the Society of Antiquaries.[114] His widely read *Tour in Wales*, published in 1778, celebrated his country of birth 'for the stand it made against the *Romans*'. Agricola, he claimed, did not dare attempt his Caledonian expedition leaving behind him so tremendous an enemy unconquered.[115] South Wales, which bore much more obvious evidence of Roman and Anglo-Norman occupation, never attracted Pennant's topographical attention.

The Roman presence in Wales was pursued instead by English antiquaries. John Strange and John Harris both presented their observations on Roman antiquities around Monmouth and Gwent to the Society of Antiquaries, in papers which were later published in *Archaeologia*.[116] The publication of Richard of Cirencester's spurious itinerary, providing much wanted detail on the course of the Roman roads through Wales, was as welcome to those seeking to elucidate Roman antiquities in Wales as it was to those attempting to trace the course of the campaigns of Agricola or Severus in Scotland. English tourists, led by the popular pioneer of Welsh tourism, Henry Penruddocke Wyndham, searched out the Roman antiquities at Caerleon and followed William Coxe in travelling along the Julia Strata from Bath through Glamorganshire.[117] Richard Fenton, a Welshman by birth, was closer to the antiquarianism of Sir Richard Colt Hoare, to whom he dedicated his history, than his fellow countrymen. His account of Pembrokeshire sought to vindicate the authenticity of Richard of Cirencester (recently challenged by T. D. Whitaker in his history of Whalley) by identifying the remains of the Roman road, which the forgery showed passing through Pembrokeshire.[118]

The attitude of most English antiquaries to the remains of druidic antiquity encountered in Wales tended towards the sceptical. On one level, part of the experience of the Welsh tour was to visit the sublime and awe-inspiring landscapes of Cader Idris and to lose oneself in imaginative reveries provoked by a reading of Gray or Mason. Tourists expected to be struck by the primitive simplicity of rural Wales and to encounter blind Welsh harpists regaling them with ancient bardic verse at the local inns. Cromlechs and carnedds were as much a part of the tour as the castles of Harlech and Caernarvon or the picturesque delights of the Wye Valley. At the same time, however, there was also a tradition of robust scepticism that ridiculed the tendency to convert any large stone into a druidical antiquity. Wyndham had set the tone in 1773, suggesting that many of the piles of rubble, so often identified as carnedds, were actually nothing to do with the Druids. Rather, they were simply the creation of shepherds, who had piled up stones when clearing a field for pasture; a suggestion which was repeated in a number of other tours. Such monuments as there were, in his opinion, were anyway inferior to those of Stonehenge and Avebury.[119] Sir Richard Colt Hoare took a similarly pragmatic view, commenting wryly upon the propensity for tourists and canny locals to attribute any standing stone, set up for cattle to scratch against, as some monument of druidic religion.[120] His own accounts of ancient British barrows excavated in his native Wiltshire did not indulge in speculations upon druidical religious rites.[121] The patronising tone adopted by most English tourists in discussing the supposedly simple and unrefined manners of the Welsh also attributed to Edward I's conquest the same kind of civilising impact that antiquaries and historians associated with the earlier Roman conquest upon their own forebears: 'surely this subjection', wrote Wyndham, 'is esteemed a most happy circumstance, by every reasonable Briton'.[122] If the Welsh stood in a line of unbroken succession from the original ancient Britons and the Druids, the English saw themselves as completing the conquest which had eluded the Romans. It is hardly surprising, therefore, to find the Welsh defending their druidic antiquities and bardic literature and raising the stakes of its importance.[123]

The study of Celtic antiquities in Ireland followed a rather different trajectory from that of England and Wales.[124] The tradition of topographical antiquarianism which dominated the English movement was considerably weaker,[125] but by contrast the extent to which antiquarian research was tied to political debate was much stronger. The gulf which divided rival schools of thought in the later eighteenth century with respect to the supposed Milesian golden age of Irish history was wider than any comparable differences of opinion in England, and was informed by political and sectarian issues. The Milesian model assumed a period of high civilisation spanning both the pre-Christian and early Christian eras, during which Ireland led the rest of Europe in learning and the arts. This culture was only destroyed by the Danish invasions of the ninth and tenth centuries.[126] In its most extreme expression, as for example articulated by the English-born antiquary Major General Charles Vallancey, it was argued that Ireland had originally been peopled by eastern tribes, descendants of the Phoenicians, who had arrived in Ireland via Carthage and Spain. They brought with them language, literacy and other skills, as well as practising a monotheistic brand of religion which anticipated Christianity. The Romans, rather than being the harbingers of civilisation destroyed it. The Carthaginian manuscripts were burnt, and their true history, written by their enemies the Greeks and Romans, was lost.[127] This interpretation of Ireland's past fitted the agenda of both Catholics and patriots, both of whom stressed the negative impact of the subsequent invasions from the east, from the Danes and latterly from the Anglo-Normans (the Normans being simply another branch of the Danes).[128] As in Wales, the publication and success of the Ossian poems provoked a response from Catholic and patriot antiquaries in Ireland. Whereas the Welsh had simply responded in kind, producing a supposedly more 'authentic' Welsh alternative to the Scottish oral tradition, there was considerably more at stake for the Irish antiquaries. In their view Macpherson had appropriated elements of Irish history and antiquities for his own Caledonian history, and in the process had constructed an image of early Irish society which was hardly flattering. At a time when the Catholics were attempting to secure the repeal of the penal laws, the claims of Catholic Irish society to civility, past and present, were of some importance.[129] The necessity of refuting Macpherson's position was a crucial stimulus to the work of Catholic antiquaries such as Charles O'Connor and Sylvester O'Halloran. It also directed attention towards Ireland's own traditions of bardic culture and poetry, which bore fruit in publications by Joseph Cooper Walker and Charlotte Brooke.[130]

The Druids of Irish history were rather hazier figures than those of Ancient Britain and their role in ancient Irish history was correspondingly ambivalent. Stone circles and standing stones were seldom noticed in Irish topographical literature until the early nineteenth century, when an element of convergence between the Irish and mainland traditions becomes apparent.[131] Amongst Irish antiquaries John Toland's image of the Druid held considerable sway, and Druids were somewhat peripheral to broader questions of Milesian culture of which they were simply one element. Although the orientalists amongst the Irish antiquaries shared Stukeley's belief in the eastern origins of druidic and Celtic culture, Stukeley's assertion of the trinitarian nature of druidical religion, for example, was not much regarded, and his approach to fieldwork was less influential in Ireland than in England and Scotland. More frequently cited were the remarks of John Whitaker, who, due to his entry into the Macpherson debate over the origins of Scottish and Irish history, was more easily assimilated into both Irish and Scottish antiquarian traditions.[132] There was an indigenous tradition of Irish antiquarian literature upon the Druids which emphasised the magical element rather than the supposed parallels and continuities with the Old Testament and Christianity. This had been described by Geoffrey Keating, who was a major source for Toland.[133] Irish antiquaries, it has been suggested, were uncomfortable about the implications that a magical religion which practised human sacrifice held for the image of Celtic civility which they were seeking to promote. Hence Charles Vallancey was more interested in exploring the linguistic connections between the eastern civilisations and the Milesian culture of Ireland and elucidating the ancient Brehon laws – although he did suggest that Stonehenge was actually an Irish monument.[134] The most positive evaluation came from the Catholic antiquary Sylvester O'Halloran, whose account was driven by indignation at the way in which the Irish were represented by English and Scottish writers. O'Halloran did not trace the Druids back to Phoenician origins, but argued rather that they originated in Ireland, whence they spread over the rest of Europe. Druidism was a Celtic, not a Greek institution; turning the traditional patterns of migration on their head, he argued that Greece and Egypt were populated from Ireland, rather than vice-versa: the name of the River Nile – the same as that borne by many Irishmen – was an obvious proof.[135]

The alternative interpretation argued that Ireland had been peopled from Britain; it emphasised the Gothic migrations, which brought the elements of civilisation from the mainland, and rejected the theory of an indigenous Celtic culture. The Gothicist theory of migration, therefore, assumed a common origin for all the peoples of Great Britain and Ireland. Given that the Normans who had perpetrated the Anglo-Norman conquest of Ireland were also a Gothic race, this could be represented as simply another wave of the same migratory pattern. The political implications were obvious, and ensured that in Ireland antiquarianism could pretend to none of that impartiality which antiquaries tried to claim for it in England.[136] The leading critic of Vallancey and O'Halloran in this debate was the Anglo-Irish cleric and antiquary Edward Ledwich. Ledwich was a fellow of the Society of Antiquaries of London and incumbent of a living near Salisbury until 1772, when he returned to a parish in Ireland. He had already expressed considerable scepticism concerning Stukeley's theories in a short account of the history and antiquities of Salisbury published anonymously in 1772.[137] His naturally dissentient attitude combined with a staunchly 'Gothicist' approach to Ireland's early history. He became the most eloquent of those who attempted to demonstrate the flaws in Vallancey's argument, as well as vigorously upholding the positive benefits which Ireland had derived from union with Britain. Ledwich contributed papers to *Collectanea de rebus hibernicis*, but, given that Vallancey edited the series, he was restrained from marshalling the full destructive force of his arguments. This he accomplished in *Antiquities of Ireland* (1790).

The opposition between Vallancey's position and that of Ledwich split the antiquarian community in Ireland and certainly contributed to the demise of the Hibernian Society, the predecessor of the Royal Irish Academy.[138] Although the issues were less cogent outside the context of Ireland, the London Society of Antiquaries was certainly aware of the heat with which matters of ancient Irish antiquity were being debated, chiefly through communications from Vallancey himself, Ledwich and Thomas Pownall.[139] English antiquaries were for the most part wary of the eccentricity of Vallancey's arguments and suspicious of their obvious political repercussions. The accepted view in England during the eighteenth century was that antiquarianism, unlike history, should not be made to serve political purposes, and it was this, as much as the lack of evidence with which to substantiate his arguments, that discredited Vallancey in their eyes.[140] Vallancey's influence was more marked in Scotland where his *Irish Grammar* and his observations on the Ogham alphabet were eagerly taken up by Gaelic scholars.[141]

Ledwich's 'Dissertation on the Religion of the Druids', published in the seventh volume of *Archaeologia* in 1785 (the highwater mark of druidical publications), was an unusual piece in that it was directed at antiquaries of both Britain and Ireland. It drew on the same vein of pragmatic scepticism that characterised the comments of Wyndham and Colt Hoare. Although he did not go as far as David Hume or William Robertson in denying the very possibility of monotheism within a primitive society, Ledwich expressed incredulity at the notion that such a barbarous, forest-dwelling people could have anticipated the discoveries of Pythagoras, Archimedes or Newton without the aid of letters or experiments. He insisted that a proper idea of the Druids could only be arrived at by studying what the ancients had written upon the subject, and by acknowledging the agenda and preconceptions of those who had written the accounts upon which such heavy reliance was placed. Julius Caesar's description of the Druids was, he pointed out, tantamount to a description of the Roman priesthood. Caesar was merely projecting on to the Druids exactly those qualities of a priestly order which he expected to find. The Druids, he concluded, possessed no internal or external doctrine; there was no symbolic veil or mystery. They practised only the charlataneries of barbarian priests and gentile superstition.[142] By 1790, when *Antiquities of Ireland* was published, he had divorced himself from all connection with Vallancey and had also imbibed deeply of John Pinkerton's Gothicist theories; he applied them with enthusiasm to the early history of Ireland, taking a pedant's delight in highlighting the confusion between Celts and Goths that reigned in many authorities. The Druids were Celts, he argued, and, as a primitive people with none of the skills of a civilised society, worshipped in groves. The first of the Danish (that is Gothic) invasions took place well before the birth of Christ. By the time that the Romans were making observations on what they took to be Celtic society, the Celts had assimilated much of the incoming Gothic culture and religion, building the carns, carnedds and cromlechs with which Ireland was still littered.

It would be wrong, however, to consider approaches to the pre-Roman history of Britain purely in terms of Druids, bards and Ossian. It was not necessary to subscribe to an implicit belief in the authenticity of Ossian or the trinitarianism of the Druids in order to take an interest in British or 'Celtic' antiquities. Growing national self-confidence, even in the face of loss of the American Colonies, was manifested in a stronger sense of nationhood in history writing, which focused attention ever more strongly upon the antiquities of the original inhabitants. Against those who maintained that the ancient Britons had not even the basis of civility amongst them, there were always some who projected back on to the Britons literacy, social organisation and commercial structures – all characteristics of a society which had progressed beyond a primitive state of barbarism. The need to find supporting evidence encouraged antiquaries to identify signs of urban habitations or an ancient British coinage, which indicated both the skills of minting and participation in a system of commercial exchange.[143] One of the foremost exponents of this view of the ancient Britons was John Whitaker, the historian of Manchester. Whitaker was a polemicist, who liked nothing better than an academic cat fight, and had no qualms about launching *ad hominem* attacks in print. He did not set out to belittle the importance of the period of Roman occupation, but he was determined to salvage the reputation of the ancient Britons: 'The Britons did not live, as Mr Hume describes them, like so many hords (sic) of Tartar or tribes of wild Indians.'[144] Manchester, Whitaker asserted to the disbelief of many of his readers, had been a town even prior to the Roman invasion. Amongst the signs of civilisation that he was sure he could detect amongst the Britons were literacy (reviving a case made at the start of the century by Edward Lhwyd), a feudal system, and the use of manure in agriculture – a skill which, according to Whitaker, the Britons imparted to the Romans. 'It is one principal design of the present work, to strip the Britons of the strange disguises in which she [history] has hitherto drest them up, and exhibit them in their natural and genuine appearance.'[145] Echoes of Whitaker subsequently found their way into many an antiquarian or topographical work. Due to the paucity of literature attempting, as Whitaker did, to shed some light on what might be called the domestic history of Roman and Saxon England, he was a frequently consulted source. Passages reminiscent of Whitaker's enthusiastic endorsement of pre-Roman British society cropped up in a long and heterogeneous list of publications.[146]

William Hutton did not fit the typical antiquarian mould; he was a self-made businessman, a dissenter, who took a provocative delight in flouting the expectations of the educated world. His *History of Birmingham*, however, ranked with Whitaker's *History of Manchester* as one of the most popular and widely read local histories of its day. For all its deliberate subversion of some of the established antiquarian conventions, his ironic stance did not extend to disregarding the importance of establishing the outlines of ancient British society. Hutton was not brought up in the traditions of classical humanist scholarship, nor was he a member of the landed elite; we should not therefore be surprised to find him elevating the achievements of the Britons at the expense of the invading Roman armies. He adopted a cynical view of the reliability of the Roman authorities, so much revered by his classically educated fellow antiquaries. The Romans, he argued, were obliged to make the Britons warlike, or there would have been no merit in conquering them. Similarly they were bound to depict them as ignorant savages, or there would have been no point to their efforts to improve them. If the Britons really had been as wretched as the classical authors had made them out to be, they would certainly not have occupied the Roman armies for over a century before they could be subdued. Like Whitaker, whose history Hutton had clearly read with profit, Hutton argued largely from conjecture, although he occasionally adduced some empirical observations, based upon finds of iron work in the area around Birmingham, for a civilised British society, in which the inhabitants had acquired considerable sophistication in the sciences of iron manufacturing and animal husbandry, as had, of course, Birmingham in his own century.[147]

Given the powerful political resonances which liberty and independence held for eighteenth-century society, the theme of the enslavement of the ancient Britons was always an emotive one. As the campaign against slavery gathered pace in the later eighteenth century, the enslavement of their own forebears by an earlier imperial power aroused increasingly ambivalent sentiments amongst British antiquaries, and nowhere more so than in that perennially fascinating topic of antiquarian study, the Roman road system. Whilst antiquaries were deeply impressed with the feats of engineering which the network of roads represented, they were not unaware of the enforced labour which must have been demanded in their construction. Growing appreciation of the extent of the Roman achievement in Britain, therefore, went along with a sharper realisation of the British labour which must have been extracted under duress. Their own imperial experience was subtly reshaping their view of the past. Whitaker had been an eager spectator of the Roman remains revealed in the course of digging a canal for the duke of Bridgewater; his admiration, was, however, qualified. The roads which they built were, he suggested, often along the course of roads originally laid down by the native Britons. He allowed that they were admirable in their straightness, but pointed out that in a time when the laws of property had been entirely superseded by the rights of conquest, there was nothing extraordinary in the ability to drive a straight line through the countryside. He found fault in their design – they were not well adapted for cart and wagon. Those responsible for the construction –accomplished with considerable skill – were not, of course, Romans, but the native Britons, who had been reduced to the status of slave labour.[148]

The relative civilisation which the Britons had achieved immediately prior to the arrival of the Romans was, by the end of the century, being differentiated with greater confidence from preceding periods. Caesar had commented that the southern coastal areas were inhabited by the Belgic Gauls, in a more advanced stage of civility; the inland regions were inhabited by Celts who were the more barbarous the further they were away from the southern shore. Whilst some argued that the Belgae were Celts, a number of antiquaries adopted a 'Gothicist' model to explain this comparative difference in civilisation: the southern Belgic tribes were assumed to be Gothic tribes (of the same origins as the later Saxon and Danish invaders). The original, more primitive people were Celts. The foundations for nineteenth-century arguments for Teutonic supremacy and Celtic inferiority were gradually being laid, but there was as yet nothing to match the vitriol poured by John Pinkerton upon the Celtic peoples in Scotland south of the border. The simple contrast between the two societies that Caesar had described was still the basic model which antiquaries used, but they were becoming somewhat more sophisticated in relating antiquarian finds to their observations. Discoveries of stone implements, for example, dated back to the sixteenth century or earlier. William Dugdale was one of several seventeenth-century antiquaries who had suggested that they were used by the ancient Britons as weapons. Charles Lyttelton agreed that the stones were most probably weapons, but pointed out the problem of attributing them to the ancient Britons inhabiting the country at the time of the Roman invasions. These were a people, he proposed, with some knowledge of metallurgy:

> How low an idea soever some people may entertain of the Antient Britons, they can hardly be thought so barbarous and ignorant as to have made their battle-axes and spear heads of stone, and this with great labour and difficulty in the execution, when, at the same time, they were mechanics sufficient to make iron scythes, and had such plenty of iron as to arm their chariots of war with this destructive weapon.[149]

The stone axes, he suggested, were 'by far the most antient remains existing' of our ancestors, and probably coeval with the first inhabitants. The distinction between a people accustomed to working metal and those who used only flints was further elaborated by James Douglas in his analysis of barrow excavations, *Nenia Britannica.* He used the differences which he discovered in the burial goods within the barrows as a means to bring greater certainty to the dating of burial sites. Douglas's points were eagerly taken up by other antiquaries such as Hayman Rooke, working in Derbyshire, and John Skinner in Somerset. William Cunnington took a similarly discriminating approach to the excavation of what he identified as early Celtic barrows in Wiltshire, criticising the casual approach of Borlase and Stukeley and their tendency to identify barrows and artefacts uncritically as 'British'. His co-worker in Wiltshire, Thomas Leman, adumbrated three stages of development: in the first period weapons of stone or bone were used; this was followed by the use of brass instruments, and, finally, iron was introduced shortly before the arrival of the Romans.[150] Douglas, Cunnington, Leman and Colt Hoare are the best known of a growing number of antiquaries who were realising the importance of accurate excavation work and the possibilities it held for elucidating pre-Roman history.

Antiquaries were also applying the ethnographic data brought back from voyages of exploration from the South Pacific, popularised in publications such as Hawkesworth's *Voyages* to their own investigation of national origins. Primitivism endowed the noble savage, whether South Sea Islander or North American brave, with admirable qualities which the antiquary was more than willing to identify in the original inhabitants of the British Isles. Current evolutionary theory assumed that all societies progressed through the same stages of civilisation, albeit not synchronically. Accounts of the weapons used by the native inhabitants of North America had encouraged antiquaries of the late seventeenth and early eighteenth century to conjecture that the stone implements that were being uncovered were similarly the weapons of a primitive people.[151] The antiquaries of the later eighteenth century likewise drew heavily upon comparisons with the North Americans and, increasingly, the South Sea Islanders. James Douglas rejected earlier theoretical approaches to the early colonisation of Britain, which argued that similarities in the monuments to be found in Britain, Asia, Palestine, Syria or Egypt inevitably meant that they belonged to the same peoples. Rather, he proposed, these were simply the monuments and artefacts of primitive peoples in any part of the world.[152] It was legitimate to assume, therefore, that customs and manners amongst the primitive inhabitants of the South Pacific would have had their parallels in ancient British society. Stories of Maori cannibalism corroborated the accounts of human sacrifice amongst the Druids which had been inherited from the classical authorities. Images of the tattooed bodies of the Tahitians evoked descriptions of the painted warriors which had struck the invading Romans so forcibly. Thomas Pownall, however, drew upon the reports of tattooing amongst the North American Indians and the South Sea Islanders to reject the traditional etymology of 'Picti' from the Latin 'pictus' or painted. All primitive peoples employed this method of body ornamentation, he argued, and Caesar would have found nothing so unusual about such a practice to merit coining such an epithet.[153] In general, modern ethnography seemed to promise an element of empirical certainty which otherwise eluded the frustrated antiquary. Such thinking was pervasive and exerted a clearly discernible influence over a wide range of antiquarian literature. The most striking use to which it was put, however, and one which probably exerted more influence over the image of the ancient Briton in the public imagination than any other work of antiquarianism, was in Meyrick and Smith's *Costume of the Original Inhabitants of the British Islands* published in 1821. Celtic tribes, they argued, in the progress of migration to the British Isles, had lost the antediluvian art of working metals, like the inhabitants of the South Seas islands. Material drawn from the pages of *Archaeologia* or the *Collectanea de rebus hibernicis* on bronze celts and stone implements was imaginatively combined with descriptions of North American Indians and South Sea Islanders to produce a compelling and vivid realisation of ancient British dress, husbandry and martial arts.[154]

The stadial model of social development allowed antiquaries to conceptualise a framework around which they could relate finds such as stone implements or primitive pottery, but it was a framework with no chronological signposts, and the problem of accommodating it within the time span allowed by biblical authority was never confronted straight on. It was far easier simply to suggest that stone implements predated the era of brass and iron, rather than to try to fit those findings into the timetable of post-diluvian history and the Noachite diaspora. The eighteenth century had no concept of prehistory nor was there any meaningful anticipation of a three age theory. The conceptual barrier to be overcome in arriving at an understanding of differentiated temporality in the pre-historic past was immense. In this context it is important to appreciate that 'archaeology' as it was understood in the eighteenth century was not necessarily based upon excavation or field work. Henry Rowlands described it as the 'Account of the Origin of Nations after the Universal DELUGE'. To recover this past, he relied not so much on the evidence of the physical remains which had first inspired his inquiries, but upon etymological reasoning.[155] When *Mona antiqua* was republished in 1766 the advertisement soliciting subscriptions alluded to the 'general principles of archaeology' which Rowlands had established through his etymological mode of enquiry.[156] Looking further forward, the *Archaeologia cornu britannicae* published in 1790 perpetuated this tradition, emphasising the study of language as the first starting point for all inquiries into the antiquities of a country.[157] For the antiquary, still in thrall to the hegemony of the written text, the study of etymology was the only clue by which they could make their way through the labyrinth of ancient history or 'determine with any degree of probability the early migrations conquests or Colonisations of the first ages of the World'.[158]

For the eighteenth-century antiquary an excavation was of value because it could establish the location of Roman camps, distinguish the different era of burial sites, or provide evidence for commercial links through traded goods. Antiquaries were looking for coins which might date the barrow, or for urns which might suggest whether a pagan or Christian burial had taken place, or for artefacts which would indicate Roman, Saxon, or ancient British provenance. The questions which excavation was expected to answer were limited and before more purposeful excavation could take place a more systematic discussion of what could be derived from such excavations was necessary.

It was the material evidence of geology that eventually did most to unravel the biblical chronology which had provided the framework for the history of the world. Although a few individuals, including the geologist James Hutton, were suggesting that the world was substantially older than the Old Testament indicated, such views were far from being part of general intellectual currency and were represented only in terms of 'conjecture'.[159] John Frere, author of an article upon flints found at Hoxne in Norfolk in 1797, expressed the view that they might have been deposited there at 'a very remote period indeed; even beyond that of the present world'. Frere was unusually observant in his description of the strata which overlaid the site and in which the flints had been found and put forward some interesting attempts to explain the deposition of the flints so far below the surface. His suggestion, however, was hedged about with the word 'conjecture' and, as others have not been slow to point out, was not followed up with any enthusiasm by his fellow antiquaries or geologists. The article is now well known in the context of the history of archaeological studies, as an early attempt to formulate the concept of prehistory; it made less of an impact in his own time.[160] Frere was nudging at a door which was beginning to be pushed open as geological science became more precise.

The development of archaeology as 'excavation' was advancing along with the emergent disciplines of geology and palaeontology.[161] Greater sophistication in stratigraphical analysis went hand in hand with improved excavation techniques in which the exact position of antiquities within the different strata was observed and recorded. Most antiquaries, it should be remembered, were equally interested in geology and collected fossils, but until the critical mass of evidence made the biblical narrative of Genesis untenable there was an enormous ideological impediment to establishing an explicit chronology of antediluvian history and a full articulation of a gradual evolution of society was thwarted. When the Danish antiquary Christian Jurgensen Thomsen proposed a progressive model based on stone to bronze to iron for arranging the museum of antiquities – a suggestion which has generally been accepted as the first elaboration of a three stage system – he was suggesting little that would have been alien to the thought of many of the eighteenth-century antiquaries. The analysis of form and function, and the comparisons with ethnographic data upon which he built were already well established in the British antiquarian tradition. The eighteenth-century antiquaries' contribution to the establishment of archaeology as a positive science should not be underestimated, simply because they stopped short of exploring the full implications of their researches.

The antiquary's sense of Ancient British society at the start of the nineteenth century was, however, in many senses still closer to that of the seventeenth-century antiquaries than that of modern archaeologists. Few had ventured to press the implications of their research to expand the truncated chronology of prehistory; the biblical narrative of the peopling of the antique world, coupled with the evidence of classical literature, still provided the conceptual structure by which they understood the earliest periods of antiquity. The Celtic Revival of the latter part of the century had given the Ancient Briton a literary and artistic persona, but had hardly contributed to a more informed understanding of British society before the arrival of the Romans. Yet the study of antiquities should not be assessed solely on the strength of its contribution to modern archaeological knowledge. The romanticised images of Welsh bards and Ossianic warriors or the tottering edifices of Druidic theology and learning – elaborated by so many antiquaries – may not have greatly enhanced the corpus of knowledge surrounding pre-Roman society, but they do remind us how closely antiquarianism was connected to the broader culture in which it was pursued. The study of ancient British antiquities made a highly significant contribution to the discussion of national origins from which a sense of national identity and national difference could grow. In this context the obscurity of the ancient Britons could be a positive advantage, giving them an endlessly protean quality that allowed antiquaries the possibility of manipulating and reshaping the image of the ancient Briton according to need.

5

The Romans in Britain

The dominant view of ancient Rome in the eighteenth century saw its empire as an agent of civilisation, taming the savage barbarians with the restraint of law, bringing wisdom, discipline and the liberal arts to the 'rude, unpolish'd world', and introducing a code of virtue and manners. In short, under the Roman Empire human potential was fully realised. Unlike other periods of antiquity, whose very barbarism set the civility and politeness of the eighteenth century in sharper relief, the greater part of the fascination in the recovery of Roman antiquities in Britain lay in their association with a civilisation which dominated the eighteenth-century cultural imagination. The study of Roman antiquities was 'not only a study of Curiosity and Instruction' but was 'highly auxiliary to Taste'.[1] Roman antiquities offered a point of connection with the period of history that was held in higher esteem than any other, and traces of Rome were to be found throughout Britain. The observation and recovery of such antiquities was, unsurprisingly, the commonest, and in the eyes of many, the most important element of the antiquarian project. 'Too long', wrote William Stukeley, 'has wretched ignorance and neglect of the valuable pledges of Roman Greatness and Art spread a dark and almost indissoluble Cloud over our Island.'[2]

Antiquarianism was originally born of Renaissance humanism and its revival of classical antiquity.[3] The antiquaries of eighteenth-century Britain had been educated within that tradition and were simply following the example of Italian humanists from Petrarch to Poggio Braccolini, who had annotated their copies of the classics with antiquarian and topographical observations, or had built up collections of Roman coins and inscriptions. The ambitions of British antiquaries, the skills they used and the questions they sought to answer were little different.[4] They regarded their age as particularly enlightened in that scholars recognised the richness of Roman antiquities within their own country, but they were also conscious of belonging to the European community of scholars for whom antiquarianism and humanism had long been complementary studies. The antiquaries of the eighteenth century who recorded the remains of the Roman occupation of Britain were, as they saw it, completing and improving upon the project first outlined by William Camden in 1598 at the instigation of the Dutch humanist and antiquary Ortelius, to 'restore Britain to Antiquity and Antiquity to Britain'.[5]

No antiquary could afford to ignore the legacy of Rome, but the interpretation of that legacy divided those who sought to recover Britain's antiquity. There were those for whom Roman civilisation represented a peak in human achievement to which the modern age could only aspire. As John Spelman had declared, 'in truth that [invasion] of the *Romans* had more of Benefit than of Calamity in it. The *Britons* (we may imagine) were then in the lowest Declension of corrupted Nature, captivate Slaves of all vile Affections, mutually practising and suffering in them'.[6] These were the Ancients in the Battle of the Books, which split the learned world towards the end of the seventeenth century as the discoveries of new science threatened the authority of Antiquity. For those who took up the position of the Ancients, Antiquity could only be emulated; it could not be outdone.[7] By the early eighteenth century the conflict had lost its edge: it took some perversity of spirit not to join the ranks of the Moderns in the fields of science and philosophy. But the unquestioning admiration for the classical achievement in the arts and literature, in comparison with the backwardness of the British both ancient and modern, lived on. The binary opposition of barbaric Britons against the superior civilisation and refinement of the Romans was the fundamental paradigm through which the early history of Britain was understood. The combination of Roman civilisation and the associated first conversion of the island to Christianity ensured that there was no serious challenge to the view of the seismic impact of the Roman invasions for the subsequent development of Britain. This assumption gives a thread of continuity to antiquarian studies throughout our period.

There were others, however, who, whilst appreciating the importance of Rome in the historical development of the civilised world, regarded the conquest of Britain with rather more ambivalence, and even questioned the benefits pertaining to the Roman occupation. The period of Roman colonisation brought into focus the conflict between the cultivation of the arts and civility with the loss of liberty and independence which Tacitus had first outlined.[8] British patriotism sat somewhat uneasily with the elevation of what was essentially a foreign Roman culture and Roman conquest. As pride in British domestic and imperial achievements grew over the course of the century, the inherent tension between celebrating Roman dominion over Britain and establishing a genealogy of British liberty, independence and civilisation deepened. Britain's growing empire, the first to exceed that of Rome in its extent, and its role in bringing civilisation and liberty to the savages and barbarians of the modern world, occasioned frequent comparisons and heightened interest in the remains of the Roman Empire in Britain.

The recovery of the antiquities of native British resistance to Roman power, however, could also become a means of asserting resistance to the expansion of the eighteenth-century British state which identified so obviously with Rome, or of challenging the hegemony of a ruling elite whose own values were closely identified with those of Rome.

At a more pragmatic level, the era of Roman occupation was also the best-documented period of the country's history until the late eleventh century, when monastic chronicles, charters and Domesday Book began to clear some of the obscurity in which the past was shrouded. The conquest of Britain had been documented by the Roman authorities, including Tacitus, Caesar, Diodorus Siculus and Ammianus Marcellinus, and in a language that was understood by any educated person. The Antonine Itinerary, a description of 225 of the major roads of the Empire, listed the place-names and the distances between them of all the major Roman stations; fifteen routes within Britain were described and over a hundred different stations were mentioned. It was first published in 1512. Not long after that the first attempts at identifying the modern location of the ancient Roman roads and cities was begun by an antiquary named Robert Talbot, a friend of Henry VIII's historiographer royal, the antiquary John Leland. Talbot's notes, never published, nevertheless provided the starting point for later antiquaries.[9] The Antonine Itinerary supplied William Camden with a basic framework for *Britannia*, and thereby directly or indirectly influenced the work of any subsequent antiquary working on Romano-British antiquities.[10] Further aids to elucidating the geography of the classical world were to be found in Ptolemy's Geography; the Ravenna Cosmography (a list of place-names compiled in Ravenna in the early eight century) and the *Notitia dignitatum* (an imperial army list from the early fifth century). Camden's mode of proceeding, as he presented it in his preface, was to search out and illustrate those places 'which Caesar, Tacitus, Ptolemy, Antoninus Augustus, Provinciarum Notitia, and other ancient writers have recorded; the names whereof Time has either chang'd lost or corrupted'.[11] Considerable weight was also attached to the histories of Bede and Gildas, for whom the Roman presence was a comparatively recent memory. All of these sources were problematic and the wealth of alternative readings which they allowed ensured constant debate, if not ultimate illumination.[12] This was the methodology, however, which was appropriated by all successive antiquaries in the eighteenth century and overwhelmingly determined the structures through which Roman Britain was conceptualised.

The emphasis on Romano-British antiquities which characterises so much of the antiquarian research of the eighteenth century united antiquaries of Great Britain to their European counterparts, but also set them apart from the antiquaries of Ireland, a country which had never been brought under Roman rule. Whilst there was a considerable amount of common ground between the respective antiquarian communities of the British Isles in other areas, most notably in the study of Celtic antiquities or druidical remains, the fact that the Irish mainland even in Roman times was essentially beyond the pale entailed a fundamental difference in the orientation of antiquarian research. British antiquaries saw the period of Roman occupation as pivotal in the historical development of the country, but it was an experience from which the Irish antiquaries were excluded. The narrative of Irish history and the configuration of Irish antiquarian studies was consequently rather different to the English, Scottish and Welsh models, and knowledge of Irish antiquities in England was correspondingly more muted and even less well informed than interest in the antiquities of Wales or Scotland. Antiquarian itineraries and tours which attempted to retrace the routes of the Roman military ways generated much of the published and unpublished antiquarian research in Great Britain. This kind of topographical literature, however, was simply not in evidence in Ireland. Nor was there a corpus of classical authorities upon which to draw for insights into early Irish history, although by sleight of hand one Irish antiquary managed to commandeer Caesar's account of Druids in Britain for Irish purposes by adjusting the translation to read that Druidism had originated in the British Isles rather than Britain. By contrast, the Celtic and early Christian eras were correspondingly more important. For an English antiquary the exclusion of Ireland from the Roman Empire was yet another indication of the backwardness and underlying barbarism of that country. For the Irish patriots, chafing against Ireland's neo-colonial status, the legends of Milesian civilisation provided Ireland with a history which gave it a higher antiquity than either the Roman Empire or its modern counterpart, Britain.[13]

Although the study of classical literature and history provided the framework of the curriculum at grammar and public schools, if not the universities, and as such was the basis of education for any gentleman, interest in domestic Roman antiquities did not gain much momentum until the late seventeenth century. The outstanding strengths of seventeenth-century antiquarianism lay in legal and ecclesiastical antiquities, and in the Anglo-Saxon scholarship associated with the Oxford antiquaries of the late seventeenth century.[14] Thomas Browne's *Urn Burial* (1686), an account of 'sepulchral remains' excavated in Norfolk, was written as a treatise on Roman burial practices, although it is now clear that the barrows and earthworks described were for the most part Saxon.[15] William Somner's *Treatise on the Roman Forts in Kent*, a pioneering attempt to identify Roman coastal fortifications, was published posthumously in 1693.[16] The Roman Wall was virtually unknown: Sir Roger North described it as a 'heap of old stones' and William Grey's *Chorographia*, a topographical account of Newcastle published in 1649, simply described its course through the town.[17] In its attempt to match the stations of the Antonine Itinerary with modern locations, William Burton's commentary on the Antonine Itinerary published in 1658 stood out in the seventeenth century as a lone enterprise to envision the reality of Rome in Britain.[18]

In the early eighteenth century, however, the genre of antiquarian publications was dominated by some notable contributions to the field of Romano-British antiquities. This shift was not unrelated to the fact that the religious and political debates, which had generated so much of the ground-breaking research in medieval and Anglo-Saxon antiquities in the seventeenth century, began to dissipate in the aftermath of the Revolution settlement. There was a general reaction amongst historians and antiquaries against the highly politicised controversies of the previous era. Antiquarianism began to distance itself from overtly religious or political issues as gentlemen antiquaries sought out a field in which scholarship was not marred by partisan sentiment. Yet it is dangerous to press this argument too far: Roman antiquities could and did provide common ground on which men from very different political and religious persuasions could correspond, but to suggest that the study of antiquities was no longer politically or religiously motivated would be fundamentally to misunderstand the nature of these studies; such motivations would always remain. The antiquaries of the early eighteenth century, however, looked to put the memory of such dissension and instability behind them. The cultivation of Roman antiquities within Britain offered the attractiveness of a pursuit for which all gentlemen were prepared by virtue of their education, whilst at the same time conforming with notions of propriety, patriotism and virtue, with the added benefit that it did not necessitate venturing into areas fraught with political implications. 'I cannot but observe', wrote the Oxford antiquary Francis Wise to the collector Richard Meade, 'that the study of this branch of our antiquities is not only entertaining, but vastly useful and improving; as it insensibly leads us to an acquaintance with the affairs and customs of the greatest conqueror that ever gave laws to mankind.'[19]

Beyond this generalised gentlemanly interest in matters of Roman antiquity, however, it is possible to identify a number of additional factors which, in the first half of the eighteenth century at least, contributed to unprecedented levels of interest in Romano-British antiquities and a number of highly important publications. The publication of a new edition of Camden's *Britannia* under the editorship of the youthful Edmund Gibson in 1695 has, rightly, often been identified as a crucial stimulus in awakening interest in

British antiquities, and not just those of the Roman period.[20] 'The new edition of that immortal work *The Britannia*', noted Francis Wise, 'seems to have inspired our natives with a new desire, of prying more closely into our remotest antiquities.'[21] The process of correcting and updating Camden's original text gave those already interested in antiquarian matters a purpose and a goal towards which to direct their researches and accelerated the process by which networks of correspondence between antiquaries were established, as individuals engaged on a common project exchanged information, advice and materials.[22] It provoked interest and disagreement, which in turn generated more publications. For Roger Gale, who was himself involved in revising the materials for Yorkshire, the success of *Britannia* appears to have encouraged him to publish his father's edition of the Antonine Itinerary in 1709 as well as to compose an essay upon the Roman roads himself.[23] The further revisions for a second edition of *Britannia* in 1722 ensured that a measure of continuity in antiquarian studies was maintained throughout the period. This in turn contributed to the generation of a sense of momentum which bore fruit in a number of other notable publications and the foundation of the Society of Antiquaries, informally in 1707 and formally in 1717.

There was a sense, too, that England had much ground to make up in recording antiquities, having fallen behind her continental counterparts in Italy, France and the Netherlands, where the recovery and recording of Roman antiquities had received greater attention. All the notable works on coins and inscriptions were by continental scholars. Abbé Bernard de Montfaucon's *L'antiquité expliquée et représentée en figures*, a collection of over 30,000 illustrations of anything relating to antiquity from continental sources, for example, had been published in 1719, and was translated into English in 1726. The common European heritage of both classical antiquity and Renaissance humanism meant that in this area, more than any other branch of domestic antiquarian inquiry, British antiquaries were most conscious of the need to match the achievements of their counterparts on mainland Europe. Thus we may detect a note of defensiveness when Alexander Gordon, whose explorations into the Roman antiquities of Scotland were published in 1726, asserted that the wealth of remains which he described 'shews the Value they had for our island', and made the further boast that no nation in Europe had done more to collect and preserve the monuments of antiquity than the English.[24]

Under the Act of Union of 1707, twelve years after the publication of Gibson's *Britannia*, the ancient Roman province of Britannia became a territorial reality once more. It was now possible to imagine eighteenth-century Britain, with its expanding empire, as the heir to imperial Rome.

Romano-British antiquities assumed a new pertinence as a means of highlighting the connection between modern Britain and ancient Rome. 'Old Rome' in time would be rivalled by Britain, promised John Warburton, as he encouraged his countrymen to acquaint themselves with the monuments of ancient Rome in their native country.[25] The level of civilisation which had been achieved under Roman rule became in itself a source of patriotic congratulation and a spur to emulate and outdo the feats of ancient Rome. The profusion of Roman remains, recorded by William Stukeley in the course of his travels, proved Britain, in his opinion, to have been as civilised as any other European country apart from Italy. The British had achieved peacefully what the Romans during an occupation of over four hundred years had failed to achieve by arms: the integration of the whole of Scotland with a greater British state. It is particularly appropriate that one of the most important scholars and patrons of Roman antiquities in Britain, Sir John Clerk of Penicuik, was himself a leading figure in the negotiations leading to the Act of Union on the Scottish side.[26] If the union of Great Britain restored the geopolitical unit, the recovery of antiquities restored the physical presence of the ancient Roman cultural unity and brought an additional stimulus to the study of Roman antiquities in the north of England and the Border regions.

The Roman Wall, the symbol of the limits of Roman imperial power, became a fixed point on the tourist itinerary. John Warburton puffed the publication of his own study of the Roman Wall, *Vallum romanum* (1753) with the declaration that the study of Roman antiquities had lain dormant in Britain until 1716 when 'the publication of my map of Northumberland again revived it'.[27] Warburton, an excise officer turned herald, was not without a sense of his own self-importance and his claims were received with scepticism by his fellow antiquaries, who were not slow to point out his largely unacknowledged borrowings from other authors.[28] Warburton was right in arguing that the Roman Wall had become the subject of much broader interest, but of greater significance than his map was an account written by the antiquary Robert Smith in 1708, published in the 1722 edition of *Britannia*. This represented the first attempt to survey the Wall as a monument in its own right and to describe the individual forts and the mile-castles stationed along its length.[29] The northern regions now began to assume a new cultural importance on account of the richness of the Roman remains to be found there. As travel north of the Border increased after 1745, interest in the Wall grew proportionately.[30] Visitors were amazed to find altars used as watering troughs and monumental inscriptions functioning as door lintels. The very profusion of antiquities was almost overwhelming: 'we were surprised with the august scene of Romano-British antiquities', wrote William Stukeley of his visit to the Wall in 1725, 'in the most neglected condition: a dozen most beautiful and large altars; as many fine *basso relievo*'s, nearly as big as the life, all tumbled in a wet meadow by a wall side, or one on the top of another, to make up the wall of the close'.[31] A network of collectors and antiquaries ranged along the length of the Wall was gradually established, upon whom visitors would call in a kind of antiquarian progress.[32] John Horsley's magnum opus, *Britannia romana* (1732), which dominated Romano-British antiquarian scholarship for the remainder of the eighteenth century and beyond, would have been far less complete, as he acknowledged in his preface, had he not been able to draw upon the expertise of collectors such as Mr Hunter of Durham, Mr Gilpin of Scaleby Castle or Mr Appleby of Cleugh.[33]

England's relationship to Scotland was explicitly compared to that of Rome and the ancient Caledonians. The English would bring civilisation and prosperity, as the Romans had brought the liberal arts and domestic stability to the ancient Britons. In later years the Hanoverian pacification of the Highlands, with its programme of road and fort construction, bore striking parallels to the Roman attempts to secure their own conquests; a similarity which was not lost upon contemporaries. Suggestions were made that monumental pillars 'to distinguish the happy reign to Posterity' should be erected along the new military highway, even as the Romans had done with their roads.[34] In a telling semantic shift the Picts Wall of the seventeenth century became the Roman Wall of the eighteenth-century English antiquaries. The Wall was not just a monument of Roman engineering and military strength unparalleled through the rest of Europe, but, in its modern condition of dilapidation and ruin, it served to highlight the superior achievement of the peaceful political union. Thus James Thomson's celebration of burgeoning empire in *The Seasons* (1728) evoked a scene of military ruins in a peaceful, pastoral landscape, where flocks of sportive lambs frolicked on

> ... the massy round
> That runs around the hill – the rampart once
> Of iron war, in ancient barbarous times,
> when disunited Britain ever bled
> Lost in eternal broil ere yet she grew
> To this deep-laid indissoluble State,
> Where *Wealth* and *Commerce* lift the Golden Head;
> And, o'er our Labours, *Liberty* and *Law*
> Impartial watch, the Wonder of a World![35]

The appeal of Roman antiquities in this first half of the eighteenth century has also to be seen in the context of aristocratic patronage. The founding members of the Society of Antiquaries of London prided themselves that they numbered amongst them the earls of Pembroke, Hertford, Winchelsea and Oxford and Lord Coleraine. 'It is the glory and felicity of the present age, that we have a HERTFORD, a PEMBROKE, an OXFORD, with other illustrious persons of high rank and dignity, who have both apply'd themselves with industry and success to these polite and agreeable studies, and have generously encouraged them in others.'[36] The audiences which Stukeley, Gordon and Horsley were addressing in their lavishly illustrated and expensive volumes comprised the increasing number of British aristocrats and gentlemen who had travelled to Italy on the Grand Tour. There they were confronted with the physical remains of the Roman Empire and found themselves able to trace out the topography of ancient Rome with which they were so familiar from their reading of classical literature. They read the steadily increasing number of topographical and antiquarian publications on Italy, all heavily dominated by accounts of the classical monuments rather than descriptions of contemporary culture.[37] The ambitions, literary traditions and conventions of continental antiquarianism were carried back to England.

Britain could not boast monuments to rival the Colosseum or works of art to rival the statuary with which the earl of Pembroke furnished the galleries of Wilton. Many connoisseurs of classical antiquity professed to scorn what they considered to be the inferior products of provincial Roman culture. Horace Walpole dismissed the Roman remains in Britain on the grounds that they were 'upon a foot with what ideas we should get of Inigo Jones, if somebody was to publish views of huts and houses that our officers run up at Senegal and Goree'.[38] The true antiquary, however, scorned the connoisseur, the man of *virtù*, who sought only perfection in the individual object. The exploration of domestic antiquities, as an illustration to the classical texts in which the landed elite had been educated, was a natural extension of the practice of collecting which was so marked a feature of the *virtuoso*.[39] Roman coins uncovered in the course of agricultural improvement and rebuilding were added to the cabinets of aristocratic collectors. Monumental inscriptions and votive altars ornamented the gardens of a number of seats in the north of England, whilst Humfrey Wanley, librarian to Robert Harley, the earl of Oxford, tried to secure a selection of Roman altars from the collection of the antiquary John Warburton in order to furnish the new library at Wimpole Hall in Cambridgeshire. Negotiations broke down over the price to be paid.[40]

These graduates of the Grand Tour believed the study of ancient Rome and its antiquities to be 'the most proper studie any man should take him to' and sought to encourage 'at home a Taste for those objects which had contributed so much to their entertainment abroad'.[41] Sir John Clerk's memoirs offer a disarmingly frank recognition of his wholehearted admiration for classical and, in particular, Roman civilisation. His imagination had been captured by the 'exploits about which all my time had been hitherto spent in reading the classicks', and his visit to Italy was represented as the ultimate pleasure and satisfaction which he could have achieved. 'The study of Roman antiquities', explained the educationalist Joseph Wilcocks, 'attracts the attention of all. For we all have, from our earliest childhood, been daily hearing or reading something relative to antient Rome.'[42] Clerk's fascination with ancient Rome was in part a romantic identification with an idealised notion of Roman patriotism and civic virtue, but this elevation of Roman culture and values also validated his own social status and offered him a model of taste, learning and political virtue. For Sir John, whose villa at Mavis Bank was a tribute to the Palladian vision of ancient Rome, the recovery of the remnants of Roman imperial grandeur in Britain was a crucial element in establishing a basis for British patriotism. Britain would be shown to be the site of some of Rome's greatest achievements. Sir John's determination to recover the Roman antiquities of his own country originated in the same sentiments which inspired Richard Boyle, earl of Burlington, to lead the way in reviving ancient architecture through the dissemination of Palladian models. Burlington was certainly not uninterested in native Roman antiquities and was an important source of patronage for Francis Drake, the antiquary and historian of York, whose *Eboracum* (1736) might never have been published but for Burlington's intervention.[43] Burlington's interest and patronage no doubt influenced the heavily romanising approach of Drake's history, in which the Roman era was writ large and in which any antiquity, even including the medieval gate of Micklegate Bar with its twelfth-century rounded arch, was confidently attributed to Roman workmanship.[44]

Aristocratic involvement in the Roman antiquities of Britain was briefly given institutional form in 1722 when William Stukeley established the short-lived, but eminently aristocratic, Society of Roman Knights. Its members took the names of distinguished Romans and ancient Britons and were committed 'to adorn the truly noble Monuments of the Romans in Britain and give them Roman eternity'. The roll call of knights, which never amounted to more than forty, included in addition to Sir John Clerk (whose pseudonym was Agricola) the three earls of Pembroke, Winchelsea and Hertford. Stukeley's opening address proclaimed the society's mission to 'to save citys and camps, temples, amphitheatres, walls, monuments, roads, inscriptions, coins, buildings and whatever has a Roman Stamp on them' from the ravages of time and the inroads of Gothic barbarism. This society, like so many others in the eighteenth century, and those established by Stukeley in particular, did not enjoy great longevity.[45] A few of its number – the Gale brothers, Alexander Gordon, William Stukeley, Sir John Clerk – maintained their correspondence on matters Roman, using the classical names each had taken on joining the society.[46] The knights, however, were too widely dispersed for regular meetings and its origin as an informal gathering was never stabilised into more permanent form. Although the various members continued to correspond with each other and, as individuals, to subscribe to works such as Gordon's *Itinerarium septentrionale*, it cannot be said that the society was ever an active force in encouraging the study of Roman antiquities in Britain, to be compared with, for example, the Society of Dilettanti, which famously sponsored the expedition of Richard Chandler, Nicholas Revett and William Pars to Ionia.[47]

The apparent interest of the aristocracy in a number of high-profile antiquarian publications in the 1720s and 1730s gives a slightly distorted sense of the antiquarian movement. Although Sir John Clerk enthusiastically traced the course of the Roman road through his own estate and the earl of Winchelsea joined Stukeley in his fieldwork, the brunt of antiquarian activity in the eighteenth century was not carried out by the members of the aristocracy, or even under their auspices. Even Sir John Clerk was content to make general observations on the Roman Wall, leaving the minute description to Stukeley or to Gordon.[48] Aspiring antiquaries, however, were able skilfully to exploit their aristocratic patrons' self-conscious identification with the Augustan age, and their flattering dedications which eulogised aristocratic taste and classical virtue also made clear the aristocratic responsibility to assist those who sought to recover the physical remnants of this antique past.[49] Undoubtedly the Winchelseas, the Oxfords, the Pembrokes, the Hertfords and the Coleraines were enthusiastic supporters of the search for British Roman antiquities. Dedicatory prefaces and names on a subscription list say more about the ties of patronage, however, than about the levels of interest in antiquities amongst the nation's fashionable elite. Hence, although it has been suggested that the names on Gordon's subscription list represent an index of the interest in Romano-British antiquities amongst the English aristocracy, what it really indicates is that Gordon was using his connections with Sir John Clerk, and connections established through the membership of the Society of Antiquaries, to persuade people to subscribe to his volume.[50] On 4 March 1725, he wrote in triumph to William Stukeley, 'My Lord Pembroke has this morning gott Eleven Bishops to Subscribe to my book the Lord Chief Justice King and the President of the Counsel and the first Baron of the Exchequer. The Duke of Devonshire subscribed yesterday morning and some more lords *so I hope it will prove a profitable work.*'[51] Gordon needed the money: this was no vanity publication, and his patrons saw it as their obligation to secure subscriptions for him. Gordon's contacts certainly did their best on his behalf: it was a glittering subscription list, with no less than forty-nine members of the peerage as well as Pembroke's eleven bishops from a total of 224 subscribers. The earl of Burlington's patronage of Francis Drake's history of York, *Eboracum*, must also account for the similarly impressive social profile of the subscription list. In Drake's case 22 per cent of the subscribers belonged to the peerage, a figure which was far in excess of the proportion shown by other urban histories published at any point in the eighteenth century.[52]

William Stukeley's *Itinerarium curiosum* (1724) was another work which benefited from the publication of *Britannia* and the antiquarian networks it had helped to establish. The title alludes to seventeenth-century publications on the antiquities of Italy such as Montfaucon's *Itinerarium italicum* and was conceived as a patriotic riposte to the fascination of the Grand Tour. Stukeley shifted attention away from the north of England to the midlands and the south and included his own discovery of Roman amphitheatres at Dorchester and Silchester. His own observations on the Roman Wall, however, were not published until 1776 as *Iter boreale* in the second and posthumous edition of the *Itinerarium curiosum*. Stukeley's starting point was to trace the various Roman ways of Britain in a series of peregrinations in which he recorded his observations on the antiquities and monuments encountered along the way. It was essentially the record of Stukeley's ramblings across England in pursuit of antiquities, social contacts and better health. (Stukeley, along with a number of other antiquaries, found the activity involved in antiquarian fieldwork beneficial for his gout.) It was not an exercise in the accurate mapping of Roman civil engineering, although the essential framework was based upon the Antonine Itinerary. Stukeley used it to explore his own imaginative relationship with ancient Rome, and to contrast his idealised vision of Roman virtue and patriotism with the depravity which he feared was encroaching upon modern society. The accuracy of his observations and his ability to interpret the evidence of landscape and ruins brought a vivid clarity to his account of Roman antiquities which was lacking in other publications of that genre. His identification of Roman stations and his interpretation of the classical sources were highly influential throughout the century. Not all antiquaries were convinced, however, by his rendition of the Roman street plans of towns such as Leicester, which at the time were deemed to be somewhat too visionary, whilst Thomas Hearne dismissed with incredulity Stukeley's perceptive identification of an amphitheatre at Silchester.[53]

Alexander Gordon, with whom Stukeley was in close correspondence, was the protégé of Sir John Clerk of Penicuik and under his auspices published *Itinerarium septentrionale* (1726), which endeavoured to establish the route followed by Agricola in his campaigns in North Britain. It included some of the first systematic measurements and observations upon the Roman Wall and Graham's Dike (also known then as the Antonine Wall). By Gordon's own account the volume was well received, and, unusually for a British antiquarian and topographical publication, was soon published in Holland in a Latin edition, demonstrating the extent to which the collection of Roman antiquities was also perceived as part of a broader European humanist project. Gordon's motives in undertaking this project are not entirely transparent: he evidently possessed considerable antiquarian curiosity on his own part, and had spent a number of years in Italy, during which he had become familiar with antiquarian literature and the taste of the aristocracy for such curiosities. He was also a failed opera singer, a would-be artist and surveyor, a part-time customs official and above all, desperate to improve himself. Whilst Gordon's personal interest in Roman antiquities should not be challenged, it is also clear that this was a publication compiled at the behest of Sir John Clerk.

Its influence upon British antiquarianism was somewhat overshadowed by the publication of John Horsley's *Britannia romana* eight years later, covering similar ground, but executed on a broader scale and with greater accuracy and erudition. Horsley, a Presbyterian minister and mathematics teacher, was not primarily an antiquary, and the book was, according to his prefatory disclaimer, originally intended as a work of private amusement. He had been prevailed upon by friends, however, to expand and publish it. Subsequently he was introduced to Sir John Clerk, who allowed him to view his collections and encouraged him in the enterprise, but the two men did not share the same kind of patron-client relationship as that of Clerk and Gordon. No subscription list survives either, if indeed there ever was one: with a *frisson* of distaste Clerk remarked that he believed Horsley to be writing it 'for bread'.[54] Horsley's motivation in undertaking such an intimidating project is less than clear. He presented his work simply as an exercise in the pursuit of truth and beauty, and the intellectual satisfaction to be gained therefrom. It was, he wrote, a 'real pleasure to a well turn'd mind'. Implicit to Horsley's understanding of the value of history was the same priority awarded to classical learning and culture that shaped the outlook of Sir John Clerk or the trio of earls whose beneficent patronage he acknowledged. Gordon was more than a little put out that Horsley was apparently moving in on an area which he thought to have staked out as his own. It was not just his scholarly reputation that Gordon wished to protect, but the access to the patronage that he hoped it would secure, and in which he evidently saw Horsley as a competitor. He moved quickly to claim for himself the credit for having first alerted the public to the antiquities of North Britain. 'It was easy', he caustically remarked in anticipation of Horsley's publication, 'for other People to sail to America after Columbus had found it.'[55]

Of all the publications on Romano-British antiquities in the first half of the eighteenth century, indeed arguably for the entire century, Horsley's was probably the most important in terms of its scope, its innovatory approach and its influence upon subsequent antiquaries. Although his reputation is now diminished, his accuracy and attention to detail continued to set standards that were largely unmatched until well into the nineteenth century. *Britannia romana* was composed of three volumes published as one. It combined a summary of what was known of the Roman occupation of Britain, with a comprehensive listing of all the monumental inscriptions then discovered, drawn and recorded with unprecedented accuracy. The third part was a historical geography of Roman Britain, comprising a review of the extant literature and an attempt to interpret it in the light of current knowledge of Roman antiquities in Britain. The collection of inscriptions in the second volume, which represented the greatest effort and labour on Horsley's part, was regarded at the time as the most important element of his researches, rather than his painstaking measurements and observations of the Roman Wall or his attempts to relate what was known of the physical remains to the various sources discussed in the third volume. The inaccuracies of continental scholars such as Gruter with regard to British monumental inscriptions were demonstrated.[56] Nearly a third of the inscriptions which he illustrated were previously unknown and many more were 'as good as new, tho' extant before, because not published in an intelligible manner'. The attraction of monumental inscriptions lay in the fact that they represented a direct and tangible link with the Roman presence, and, as Horsley pointed out, were to be preferred to numismatic evidence, as they were generally found near to the place in which they were produced, unlike coins, which were easily conveyed away or even counterfeited.[57] The text with which they were inscribed could be studied with the same techniques which had been developed for manuscripts, enabling even a fragment to be dated. To this end Horsley included a plate which illustrated the different types of letter formation to be found in monumental inscriptions and the approximate dates to which they could be assigned. Although, in broad terms, Horsley surveyed the whole of Roman Britain, his own field work took place predominantly in the northern counties, where, as he pointed out, Roman antiquities were found in greater

Britannia Romana, according to the Antonine Itinerary, from John Horsley, *Britannia Romana: or The Roman Antiquities of Britain* (1732). (*Special Collections, University of Leicester*)

abundance than in any other part of Britain, and it is for this work he is chiefly remembered.[58]

Horsley has always excited admiration for the accuracy of his fieldwork and his eye for detail. Yet, for all his precocious skill, it is important to go beyond simply placing Horsley in a neat teleology of the emergence of archaeology. Horsley's purpose as he defined it (and in this he was entirely typical) was to trace out the chronology and geography of ancient monuments in order to confirm and illustrate the literature of ancient history. Antiquities were the adjunct to literature, and his ambition was to illustrate and confirm what had been handed down from the accounts of classical antiquity, rather than to generate new knowledge through excavation or landscape analysis. Although certain of his illustrations, such as the plate of the entrenchments at Dealgin Ross, supposedly where Agricola defeated Galgacus at Mons Graupius, are severely distorted into what a later scholar has termed a 'wholly impossible form', this should not be seen as a reflection on the reliability of Horsley as an antiquary. Rather, it is a reminder that the accurate visual representation of ruins was less important than identifying the location of the names of stations derived from Ptolemy's Geography, the *Notitia imperii* or the Antonine Itinerary.[59]

The subsequent reputation of Gordon and Horsley has obscured those other publications which were more concerned with the antiquities of the southern regions, but had less to offer in terms of new material or scholarship. Nevertheless, these publications add further confirmation of the romanising tendencies in antiquarianism in the 1720s and 1730s. Another aspect of what might be called the '*Britannia* effect' was that publications, which condensed and abridged the original began to make their appearance, contributing to the ever-increasing flow of publications on antiquarian matters. John Pointer's ambitiously titled *Britannia Romana: or Antiquities in Britain* (1724) anticipated Horsley's weightier volume in title, if not in content, which was almost entirely derivative. This in itself suggests that Pointer saw the subject of Romano-British antiquities as a likely bandwagon on which to ride, even if he did not have a great deal to contribute in antiquarian terms. He divided antiquities into the three categories of coins, camps and public roads. The majority of his treatise dealt with the most familiar category of the three, that of coins, for which there was a far more extensive literature and upon which it was far easier to pronounce with a degree of authority. Nathaniel Salmon, author of a history of Hertfordshire and collections for a history of Essex, was also a prolific writer upon Roman antiquities, although his researches drew heavily upon Camden, and lacked the depth of Horsley.[60] Salmon's mainstay, as with Pointer, was coins, camps and roads. The identification of the various itinera he offered is easily faulted now, and his etymologies can be shown to be largely spurious, but what is interesting is that he explicitly identified himself with a new tradition in Romano-British antiquarian scholarship which attached singular importance to observation and field work, of which he regarded Stukeley and Roger Gale as leading exponents: 'There have been of late, great Advances made towards Recovering this sort of Learning', he announced, and 'more is yet to be expected of modern Antiquaries'.[61]

For his part Roger Gale expressed the hope that other gentlemen would endeavour to recover the courses of the Roman roads through their own counties and issued a manifesto for all future students of Roman roads:

> In short, the only means to recover the tract of these *Ways*, besides what we may pick out of our Historians, is diligently to trace what is still left of them where any footsteps or names of them are yet apparent; and where no such are to be found, by observing where they show themselves again after any discontinuance, and filling up the intermediate loss upon the best conjectures we can make either from the Situation of *Roman* stations, or other Antiquities that may offer themselves.[62]

The gradually accumulating body of knowledge had therefore to be accommodated to the roads and stations described in the Antonine Itinerary, corroborated by comments about distances, landscape and other topographical remarks from more literary sources such as Caesar or Tacitus. The discrepancies between the different authorities, the evident inaccuracies of observers such as Ptolemy, who had never even been to Britain, and the numerous errors introduced by generations of careless scribes in the course of transcription all served to heighten the problem of positive identification for any Roman site. The study of Roman antiquities was something akin to a perpetual guessing game in which each antiquary attempted to join the dots of the Antonine Itinerary in such a way as would demonstrate the importance of his own locality within the Roman imperium. It was, as one antiquary noted, 'an endless fund of enquiry, where any one is at liberty to form conjectures'.[63] Camden's ambition had been to search out and identify all the places mentioned in the classical sources; the eighteenth-century antiquaries, in contrast, began to expand their horizons as they realised that there were traces of Roman occupation in areas about which the written sources were silent. William Borlase, the Cornish antiquary, was convinced that he had found evidence which showed that the Romans had penetrated as far as Land's End, in spite of Camden's assertion that there were no Roman remains in Cornwall.[64] The uncertainty surrounding the extent of the Roman advance into Scotland had fired Alexander Gordon's curiosity in *Itinerarium septentrionale*, and the search for Mons Graupius continued to dominate the antiquarian inquiries of Robert Melville, William Roy and the earl of Buchan until the end of the century.

In the many parochial and county histories compiled in the course of the eighteenth century we see the efforts of numbers of antiquaries to fill in their local corner in the map of *Britannia*. The search for Roman origins was one which could be readily taken on by local antiquaries across the country. They were inspired by the proximity which the pursuit of antiquities seemed to bring them to the glory of imperial Rome. Local patriotism, *amor loci natalis*, was demonstrated in the authentication of Roman origins. The study of Roman antiquities could claim the same didactic value as did the study of Roman history and lent some lustre to the intellectual drabness of parochial histories. Both Alexander Gordon and John Horsley drew considerable pride from the richness of Roman remains to be found in their areas; and the northern region acquired a new identity as the heartland of Roman military activity in Britain in contrast to the south, where the Romans became domesticated and lost their military vigour. In an age when the foundation myths of towns which drew on the fables of Geoffrey of Monmouth were rapidly losing credibility, a Roman origin was greatly to be preferred. It established the antiquity upon which towns prided themselves and linked the town to the ideals of Roman citizenship and virtue – a matter of no little importance to the gentlemen of Warwick who objected to Dr Thomas's revised edition of Dugdale's county history because – despite their having encouraged the work all they could – the antiquity of Warwick 'had been brought so low as the Saxon times instead of the Romans'.[65] As the Tory MP Charles Gray, a patron of antiquarian research in his home town of Colchester, wrote to William Stukeley, 'When we see the splendor and number of our cities and towns as they describe them, may it inspire the thinking part of the Brittish people to encourage true religion, morality, liberty, industry and commerce, by which means our cities may become more numerous, and everything desireable for the happiness of mankind may be promoted.'[66] Stukeley, whose critical faculties in this respect were not beyond reproach, commented caustically to Roger Gale, on reading Francis Peck's account of Stamford (a town in which he had a more than passing interest), that 'I have just read over his account of the Roman antiquitys there, which I thought very little satisfactory. He seems desirous of making a vicinall Roman road goe through his town, without the least ground of probability.'[67] Stukeley, on the other hand, had arrived at the even more implausible conclusion that the covered walkways which he saw in Chester, the Rows, were the remains of Roman porticos.[68]

Equally important for the local antiquary was the accessibility of Roman remains. The physical landscape of Britain bore very visible traces, still, of the Roman occupation in the form of Roman roads, camps and brickwork. If not on the same scale as the Wall, coins, masonry, pottery and other artefacts were constantly turned up in the course of daily activities of building or agricultural work. Antiquaries were gradually becoming aware of the extent to which Roman structures had been routinely incorporated into the physical fabric of towns such as Colchester or Leicester. Camden's *Britannia*, despite its bulk and price, offered an immediate starting point for antiquarian researches. It was probably the most widely available of antiquarian works, to be found in gentlemen's libraries, subscription libraries and book clubs. It was probably the most widely available of antiquarian works, to be found in gentlemen's libraries, subscription libraries and book clubs, and it enjoyed a magisterial reputation as the ultimate authority on all matters antiquarian. The fact that Camden was the first point of reference for all antiquarian inquiry encouraged the amateur antiquary to adopt a similar approach and line of reasoning in identifying a former Roman presence in his own locality. Thus Camden's etymological speculations provided the model for others to follow, even where no other evidence existed.

Coins had always been an antiquarian staple, but tracing the roads of the Roman province became an increasingly significant aspect of antiquarian researches. Francis Drake surveyed the Roman roads around York, and claimed the credit for having discovered some that had not previously been identified. Moreover, the confluence of these roads at York gave added weight to his argument for York's unparalleled importance within the Roman polity of Britain.[69] John Hutchins took particular pains to establish the route of the Roman roads through Dorset in his county history, eventually published in 1774.[70] Kennet Gibson, who completed the manuscript of *A Comment upon Part of the Fifth Journey of Antoninus through Britain* in 1769, never lived to see his researches, which definitively established the identity of the Northamptonshire town of Castor with the Roman station Durobrivis, through the press.[71] The interest in Roman antiquities, and roads in particular, noticeably quickened in the 1760s and 1770s. During this period John Watson's *History of Halifax* and John Whitaker's *History of Manchester* both included extensive discussion of the Roman antiquities in their respective areas. There was also a second edition of William Stukeley's *Itinerarium curiosum* issued with the previously unpublished *Iter boreale*, and numerous papers were presented to the Society of Antiquaries and published in *Archaeologia*. Of over 430 papers published in *Archaeologia* between 1770 and 1796 nearly 25 per cent were on the subject of Roman antiquities, and nearly 20 per cent dealt with specifically Romano-British antiquities.[72] There was still much uncertainty, however, even in the late eighteenth century, and the impatience bred from trying to piece together such indistinct fragments in the mosaic of Roman occupation was well articulated by Richard Wilkes, a Staffordshire antiquary. Lovers of antiquity, he noted somewhat grimly, had endeavoured to trace the itinerary through the remaining roads, but without success: their efforts were 'nothing more than endeavours to wash the blackamore white'.[73] George Ashby, labouring in a different part of the country expressed a similar view: ''tis but a barren heath, and one is more likely to discover the faults of others than to make any important discoveries of one's own'.[74] A contemporary satire on the study of antiquities, *Origines Divisianae*, was able to perceive the unforeseen benefits which had arisen from the carelessness of the Roman copying clerks in taking down the distances between the stations in the itineraries – a source of much confusion to subsequent antiquaries: 'Had it not been for this delicious puzzle, many a dull learned man would not have been able to have employed his time, in a tedious peregrination thro' a muzzy life.'[75]

At one level the particular interest in roads was clearly linked to the contemporary expansion of the turnpike road network and the opening up of opportunities for travel. Tracing a Roman road gave a journey purpose and could be easily combined with a constitutionally beneficial summer tour in the manner of Stukeley's *Itinerarium curiosum*. Experience of travel upon modern roads enhanced the respect felt for the achievements of Roman forebears, and, as the turnpike system improved, even allowed the modern tourist to feel that Britain had surpassed its imperial predecessor. The visible progress of improvement – particularly as manifested in travel and communication – 'ought ever to be the prime object of our researches and the object of our leisure hours'.[76] Evidence pertaining to Roman roads was easily integrated into existing bodies of knowledge. Connections could be drawn between stations and camps; military ways could be established and the logistics of the Roman occupation could be unravelled. Contemporary interest in surveying and cartography heightened interest in the maps of Roman Britain and enabled the amateur antiquary to plot with much greater accuracy the remains of Roman occupation. The roads themselves, as antiquaries often lamented, were a source of materials for the construction of the new turnpikes.[77] And here was the irony: the spread of turnpikes offered revealing evidence of Roman roads on an unprecedented scale, but this very programme of road construction was destroying the evidence of the Roman network, as the distinctive ridges and the characteristic strata were levelled out and destroyed. Antiquaries eagerly collated the information, whilst the Roman feats of engineering aroused their admiration and enthusiasm for a culture with which they could find so much to identify. Richard Warner, the historian of Bath, professed himself astonished at their 'stupendous and extensive military ways' built with 'unbaffled perseverance' regardless of terrain in 'undeviating rectilinear lines'.[78]

Another crucial spur to the study of Roman roads in the latter half of the century was the 'discovery' and publication of a supposed medieval manuscript by a monk who became known as Richard of Cirencester. As Andrew Coltée Ducarel remarked to Philip Morant, 'By that Book a great Number of (unknown) Roman Stations are discovered and Antoninus becomes a mere Sketch.'[79] This manuscript, now regarded as an unsophisticated forgery, appeared to offer a more detailed version of the itineraries of Roman Britain, and in particular it provided additional information on the northern regions, which had been left so frustratingly bare in the Antonine Itinerary and other sources. Perpetrated by Charles Bertram (1723–65), an English teacher in the school for naval cadets in Copenhagen, this forgery led many of the antiquaries of the eighteenth century (and much of the nineteenth century) seriously astray; but it also stimulated considerable interest, reviving ambitions of mapping out Roman Britain which had been latterly somewhat flagging.[80] Bertram also published works on English grammar and was a keen antiquary on his own account, with a particular interest in Danish barrows and megaliths. His motives for undertaking the fraud have never been established, but the fact that he chose to concoct a forgery of a Roman itinerary is a good indication of what were regarded as the most pressing issues amongst the antiquaries of the day; there would not have been much point in manufacturing a document on a subject in which there was little interest.[81] In 1747 he began a correspondence with William Stukeley, informing him that he had in his possession an 'old manuscript fragment called Ricardi Monachi Westmonasteriensis' which concerned the ancient geography of Britain and the stations built by the Romans.[82] The forgery was allegedly written by a fourteenth-century monk, Richard of Westminster, who had access to manuscripts describing Roman Britain, which had subsequently been lost, in particular the memoirs of a certain anonymous Roman general. Stukeley was not quite so credulous as has sometimes been made out, and did try to establish the provenance of the manuscript and to persuade Bertram to deposit the original in the British Museum, offering him five guineas for it. Bertram responded with evasion and indicated that the original had been 'pirated … out of a volume of Treatises in a Public Library' by a nobleman who was so embarrassed by this incident from a misspent youth that Bertram could not betray his identity. Stukeley procured a copy of Bertram's manuscript and attempted to authenticate it for himself in England. He presented it to Mr Casley, the keeper of the Cottonian Library, who pronounced the handwriting to be four hundred years old, and to

Francis Widmore, the librarian at Westminster Abbey. Widmore identified a genuine monk of Westminster called Richard, who had come from Cirencester and had written the *Speculum historiale*, and it was upon him that Stukeley pinned the authorship of the manuscript. Despite initial misgivings, Stukeley was soon unreservedly enthusiastic and secured the election of Bertram to both the Society of Antiquaries and the Royal Society in 1756. The manuscript was eventually published in 1757, alongside texts of the British historians Gildas and Nennius (which gave the manuscript some vicarious authenticity) as *Britannicarum gentium historiae antiquae scriptores tres*. An abridged version, which Stukeley had originally read to the Society of Antiquaries the previous year, was published shortly afterwards as, *An Account of Richard of Cirencester, Monk of Westminster, and of his Works: With his Antient Map of Roman Britain; and the Itinerary thereof*.[83]

By 1809, when a new edition with commentary was published by Henry Hatcher, the monk's biography had been considerably fleshed out. Richard of Cirencester had been reinvented in the mould of an eighteenth-century gentleman antiquary, who like William Stukeley or Richard Gough, travelled the country in search of antiquarian information.[84] The fictitious itinerary offered a structure to which antiquaries could fix their hitherto unnoticed localities. The map which accompanied the forgery included over two hundred and fifty place names, of which a hundred were 'wholly new', whilst others were placed in different positions, opening up even more possibilities for the reconfiguration of Roman Britain. It also purported to delineate the geographical distribution of the native British tribes with much greater clarity, giving unprecedented detail on areas such as the north of England and Scotland which the traditional sources had left notoriously hazy – the Scottish antiquary Sir Robert Sibbald had even made the implausible claim that the Silures and Brigantes inhabited Scotland.[85] Given the heightened interest in the native British population in the second part of the century, Richard of Cirencester represented valuable information for the student of ancient British antiquities as well Roman ones.

The archaeologist and biographer of William Stukeley, Stuart Piggott, could hardly contain his frustration at what he saw as a decay in standards of historical scholarship which the success of this forgery appeared to represent. From the heights of palaeographical acumen and medieval textual scholarship which characterised antiquarianism in the early eighteenth century, critical standards and scholarly methods had declined to the point at which the learned community at large was deceived by a palpable fake. 'It is surely inconceivable that such a forgery could have succeeded sixty years earlier', he complained.[86] The eagerness with which the Cirencester deception was received and the rapidity with which it was incorporated into the antiquarian literature should not, however, be seen simply as a regrettable testimony to the gullibility and poor judgement of eighteenth-century antiquaries. A more constructive and illuminating approach would be to consider why antiquaries in the second half of the century were apparently so willing to lay aside their critical faculties. In his disgust at the slovenly scholarship of the later eighteenth century Piggott, and others, have given less weight to the minority who questioned the authenticity of the manuscript. An evaluation of the process by which the forgery escaped detection illuminates the systems of thought behind the production and transmission of antiquarian knowledge as well as throwing the limitations of the epistemological frameworks into sharp relief.

It is important to remember that the forgery appeared at a time when the richness of antiquarian remains being discovered far exceeded the capacity of the traditional explanatory structures, and when antiquarian thought was still only tentatively exploring the possibilities of recovering historical facts from the evidence of material artefacts alone rather than from written texts. The forgery offered a welcome solution to this problem of empirical overload in that it facilitated the incorporation of an abundance of new material and evidence into the old framework, and without the need to challenge or discard traditional notions of the primacy of the written text. It came in a form which was entirely familiar and did not challenge any widely held beliefs on Roman Britain, but simply offered more detail and greater clarification on areas upon which the classical authorities were frustratingly silent. In this respect it differed significantly from the other forgeries of the time: Rowley and Ossian, both of which aroused suspicion because they represented historical evidence of an unfamiliar and unconventional kind in the form of poetry and oral traditions. They also challenged many assumptions about ancient Celtic history or the medieval past – to that extent Bertram's was a clever forgery in that he did not overreach himself. He simply provided the antiquaries with what they wanted to hear, in a format with which they were familiar. The survival of a random manuscript from the wholesale dispersal of the monastic libraries during the Reformation was, moreover, an entirely plausible proposition.

John Whitaker's *History of Manchester*, which became one of the most widely read works on the British and Roman period, owed a particularly heavy debt to the forgery. Somewhat ironically, the preface begins with the exhortation: 'With a judicious Incredulity of Spirit, let us enquire and think for ourselves.' Whitaker confronted head on the challenge of writing about the remote eras of the British past, offering explanations and certainties, promising the reader that he would 'ascertain the doubtful, retrench the false, and clear up the obscure'.[87] His 'certainties' would have been significantly less expansive had not

> in that year [1757] the science of Roman antiquities received an extraordinary illumination, from the discovery of a work which contains a very curious account of Roman Britain, and exhibits to us a new Itinerary for the whole of it. And, what greatly enhances the value to a Roman-British antiquarian, the latter is more antient than that of Antonine, more extensive in its design, and more circumstantial in its execution.

Furthermore, 'This Itinerary has thrown a particular lustre upon the Roman antiquities of Lancashire, and acquainted us with one whole road, a part of another, and two or three stations, that we were ignorant of before.'[88] Thanks to Whitaker's enthusiastic reception, the forgery made its way into many other publications which took Whitaker as their authority; not the least of which was Edward Gibbon's *Decline and Fall.* Although Gibbon referred to the evidence for Richard of Cirencester as feeble, he did not chose to challenge its authority, or the claims which Whitaker made on that basis.[89]

Although the text had been published in its Latin version, *De situ*, by Bertram, it was more widely available in Stukeley's English translation; the Latin version had been published only in Copenhagen. Working with the English translation, the stylistic problems with the Latin and the orthography of the text, which eventually alerted scholars to its inauthenticity, were not immediately obvious. Antiquaries always preached the importance of returning to the original text, but this was a recommendation observed in the breach as much as the observance. When a manuscript was distant or unobtainable, information derived from printed sources had to be taken on trust. This was particularly the case in the later eighteenth century when the upsurge in publishing meant that information was available from a widely heterogeneous range of authorities. With the rise of what were essentially derivative publications, the evidence of Richard of Cirencester achieved a kind of de facto credibility by virtue of its inclusion in histories such as Whitaker's account of Manchester, and the reproduction of the map in popular publications such as the series *The Beauties of England and Wales* in the early nineteenth century.[90] Thomas Pennant, whose topographical works were amongst the most popular of their kind, was another who made frequent reference to the forgery in some of his most successful publications, the tours in Wales and Scotland. There is evidence to suggest, however, that he was not entirely convinced of the authenticity of the document at first. He wrote to George Ashby, regarded by his peers as one of the leading authorities on Roman Britain, that 'I have no thoughts of reprinting the map from R.C. indeed I am a little sceptical about that work.'[91] But whatever disquiets he may have had, Pennant suppressed them for the purposes of publication. The evidence of the text was too valuable a resource to abandon lightly, and if used it did not do in a publication of that kind, aimed at a more general readership, to express misgivings as to authenticity. Thus the forgery acquired additional validity on account of its citation by respected writers and achieved a kind of ubiquity which made its authority even less likely to be contested.

It is undeniable that many leading antiquaries, including Sir Richard Colt Hoare, William Roy and Thomas Leman, were taken in by the forgery and made extensive use of it in their own publications. Leman was widely regarded as the leading authority upon Roman roads in his day and contributed essays on Roman roads to various county histories and regional surveys such as the Lysons's *Magna Britannia.* But it is also true that others expressed misgivings. A short pamphlet by 'Muscipula', entitled *Curious Remarks on the History of Manchester* (1771), published in response to Whitaker's *History of Manchester*, ridiculed a number of the author's pretensions and stylistic idiosyncrasies, and took issue with his scholarly methods and sources, of which the Richard of Cirencester manuscript was one. What were the authorities for it beyond the testimony of some unidentified Roman general? Where had the manuscript been until it was 'discovered' about twenty-four years ago? Muscipula professed to being especially puzzled by the discrepancies between Bertram's edition and that published by Stukeley, particularly as there was no guide as to which was the more authentic. Whitaker's reliance on the questionable authority of Ossian was also queried. The history was built on tottering foundations, said Muscipula, illuminated by the 'glow worm tail' of Richard of Cirencester and Ossian: Charles Bertram, he suggested, was 'the Macpherson of Richard's Itinerary'.[92]

Just as those who were sceptical of Ossian's authenticity demanded to see the original manuscripts upon which the poems were based, those who were unconvinced by Richard of Cirencester wanted to see authentic documentation. It was this, rather than the internal evidence, which ultimately demonstrated its falsity. George Ashby, who like Thomas Pennant had reservations, wrote in 1777 to a contact in Copenhagen, John Lettice, asking him to investigate the whereabouts of the original manuscript, now that Bertram was dead. Lettice, unsurprisingly, was unable to locate the original, but did recover the Bertram–Stukeley correspondence, a copy of which he sent back to Ashby. Ashby's annotations reveal some of the causes of his disquiet: ''Tis very remarkable that B never describes the size etc of his MS nor account for the defects. He should have printed it just the same black letter size and shape as original and then we might have judg'd how many letters were wanting.' He was troubled too by the fact that there was a province named Vespasiana in Scotland – it was not mentioned by any of the other sources. Moreover, the itinera in Cornwall and Scotland (those blank areas which the forgery so conveniently filled in) had no numbers in 'their accidental' – that is there were no distances given between the different camps and stations, a curious inconsistency.[93] For those antiquaries who had no contacts in Copenhagen, however, the fact that the originals were supposedly in a library could allow them to suspend their critical judgement, in that they accepted the desirability of seeing the original, but at the same time could reassure themselves that it was not easily obtainable. Therefore, until evidence appeared to the contrary, they were prepared to give the Richard of Cirencester forgery the benefit of the doubt.

The problems inherent in the forgery continued to vex antiquaries. Richard Gough's review of James Johnstone's *Antiquitates celto normaniae* in the *Gentleman's Magazine* of 1786 referred to the doubts which some critics had entertained and which had yet to be attended to or cleared up.[94] Further reservations were expressed by Thomas Reynolds in *Iter britanniarum* (1799), a new critical edition of the Antonine Itinerary. Reynolds was prepared to consider Richard of Cirencester as a commentator upon the Antonine Itinerary, but refused to accept that the manuscript contained information derived from any other source more ancient than the fourteenth century. He pointed out the essential conformity between the *De situ* and the other traditional resources, and the various solecisms such as the naming of a Scottish province Vespasiana and the anachronistic reference to London as Augusta. It was, he allowed, an 'ingenious fiction ... very admissible in the fourteenth century', but 'it cannot bear the test of historical investigation'.[95] Two years later, T. D. Whitaker expressed even greater reservations in his *History of Whalley* (1801). The authority of the manuscript, he complained, was adopted by the other (John) Whitaker, the historian of Manchester with, 'too little investigation of the evidences on which it rested'. Whitaker's denunciation acquired some notoriety. The Pembrokeshire antiquary Richard Fenton denounced T. D. Whitaker for his temerity in questioning the authenticity of a source 'with more pertinacity than argument'. Not uncoincidentally it also shed considerable lustre and illumination upon the Roman presence in Pembrokeshire, the county of which he was writing the history.[96] Others, such as the Somerset antiquary John Skinner, the Northumberland antiquary John Hodgson and Joseph Hunter, author of a history of Hallamshire, continued to express a sceptical view.[97] In the early nineteenth century John Conybeare, antiquary and professor of Anglo-Saxon at Oxford became convinced it was a forgery because the Latin was not that of the fourteenth or fifteenth century, but of 'preface writers of the eighteenth century'. Although the deception was not conclusively nailed until 1866, when B. B. Woodward published a lengthy article in the *Gentleman's Magazine*, it is evident that there was a long tradition of dissent and suspicion amongst the antiquarian community which dated back to the years soon after its original publication.[98]

Roman roads, which were the object of so much antiquarian inquiry, were built for the transit of armies, and the Roman histories which survived, such as Tacitus's life of Agricola or Caesar's commentaries, were essentially accounts of military campaigns. It is not surprising therefore that for most antiquaries 'Roman antiquities' were synonymous with military antiquities; nor should we wonder that their understanding of the Roman occupation centred upon the movement of troops, the logistics of supplies and the construction of roads, camps and other fortifications. Even in the mid nineteenth century most Roman sites were referred to simply as stations, and no clear distinction was drawn between military and civilian remains.[99] Nathaniel Salmon found it impossible to conceive of a Roman presence in Britain which was not a camp or a garrison.[101] Drake's history of York discussed the city as the military fortification of choice for the emperors Severus, Carausius and Constantine, as the base for the sixth legion, and as a focal point in the Roman road system. The commercial and civic life of the city under Roman rule was scarcely even hinted at, let alone discussed.[101] The Roman Wall, which aroused so much interest amongst antiquaries and visitors to the north of England, assumed new importance because of the military context in which it was viewed after the 1745 rebellion. The construction of the new road after that rebellion, however, placed the fabric in jeopardy, a victim to the depredations of the military engineers. It was this that moved Stukeley to petition the princess of Wales for its better preservation in 1754.[102] Despite Stukeley's heated denunciations of the military, some of the most important antiquarian fieldwork in Scotland was carried out by army surveyors and engineers working in the Highlands. Indeed, the most important work on Romano-British antiquities in the second half of the century was William Roy's *Military Antiquities*, published posthumously under the auspices of the Society of Antiquaries in 1793. Roy, an officer of the British army stationed in Scotland, spent much of the 1750s and early 1760s identifying temporary camps and stations constructed during Agricola's series of campaigns in the Scottish Lowlands, of which no written record survived. Military men, he argued, were far better placed to trace the motions of the Roman army given their familiarity with both the principles of war and the local topography through which the army was moving. Roy also drew on the work of other officers such as Robert Melville, who had discovered a series of Roman camps on a tour into the Strathern region in 1754, where he believed the confrontation between the Romans and Caledonians described in Tacitus's life of Agricola had taken place. Roy's identification of temporary camps demonstrated the existence of a system of 'castramentation' whereby he was able to deduce the route which Agricola's army followed through Scotland.[103]

Other artefacts were interpreted with reference to the presence of camps or a military presence. Monumental inscriptions and coins were easily accommodated in this militarised view of Roman society, particularly given that the majority of surviving inscriptions came from the garrisons stationed in the north of England; hoards of coins, moreover, were easily related to the presence of any army. Antiquaries, however, were slow to conceive of an alternative view of Romano-British society to which evidence with no obvious military connection could be accommodated. There was also a sense that, whilst Britain could boast a richer array of Roman military antiquities than any other country in Europe (where else was there a feat of engineering comparable to the Roman Wall to be found?), the specimens of civilian architecture and art excavated in York or Bath were inferior, provincial constructions which compared very poorly with the architectural glories of Rome. Describing the remains of the temple excavated in Bath in 1790, Sir Henry Englefield was damning with faint praise. The capital was of good form, but nothing different from the usual. The base, however, was 'of so very bad a design, that it was quite disgusting to put in on paper'.[104] Moreover, baths as such did not have the same contemporary appeal as, for example, temples, which provided the model for contemporary architects.[105] There were no discussions of baths in Vitruvius's writings. The qualities of Roman virtue and patriotism may have shaped the code of eighteenth-century gentlemanly behaviour, but the Romans' cult of cleanliness had not won the same widespread admiration. The progressive accumulation of more and more antiquities which were clearly of a non-military origin, however, hastened the process of re-visioning Roman Britain. News of the discoveries being made in Herculaneum and Pompeii also played a part, revealing unprecedented insights into the life-style of civilian Romans, encouraging English antiquaries to identify modest parallels in their own country.[106] Thus antiquaries became increasingly aware that many of the material remains being recovered were actually the remnants of a domesticated Roman society, which was after all established for over four hundred years, and not simply the vestigia of a series of military camps and fortifications. The process by which it became possible to think of a domesticated Roman presence was a slow one, and cannot be divorced from the reorientation of historical writing away from the political and military to the private and domestic. By 1799, when Thomas Reynolds surveyed the various types of antiquities available for the study of Roman Britain, in addition to the traditional trinity of coins, inscriptions and roads, he also listed baths and mosaics.[107]

The most spectacular of the artefacts which prompted this re-evaluation of the Romans in Britain were the tessellated pavements which were uncovered at regular intervals in the wake of farming activities and building projects. These pavements were one of the most impressive testimonies of the extent to which Britons had become civilised under a benign Roman presence – nor did they carry with them the implications of oppression and forced labour with which the road system was associated. They were bright, visually attractive and could be appreciated even without specialist knowledge. A number had been listed in the 1695 edition of *Britannia* and further discoveries were reported in the *Philosophical Transactions.*[108] One of the earliest to receive any kind of notoriety was the Stonesfield pavement in Oxfordshire (depicting Bacchus), which excited an unusual amount of interest amongst the members of the Royal Society and flurries of correspondence between the Oxford and London antiquaries. When he visited the pavement in 1712, Thomas Hearne initially played with the idea that it was the floor of a medieval manor house, representing an image of St Michael fighting a dragon. He eventually convinced himself, on the authority of Robert Plot's *History of Oxfordshire*, that it was a Roman pavement which had been constructed for the temporary residence of a general.[109] The Bacchic figure confused him, however; he was reluctant to associate Roman military virtue and ascetic rigour with a celebration of bacchanalian drinking; the figure of Bacchus, he decided, was Apollo Sagittarius.[110] Confronted with what appeared to be the remains of a Roman villa with pavements at Wellow in Somerset, Samuel Carte could only account for this by suggesting that the military tents of the generals supervising the construction of the nearby Fosse Way were fixed there so long that it was 'jocosely called Villa', to be corrupted later to Wellow by the Saxons.[111] By the 1770s such attitudes had been considerably modified. Thomas Warton, commenting on Hearne's remarks in his *History and Antiquities of Kiddington*, found this conclusion implausible and argued rather that the pavement had been constructed for domestic use; it was the product of the long periods of peace during which the Britons assimilated Roman culture.[112] Discoveries in the second half of the century were regularly reported in the press and attracted the attention of casual visitors as well as antiquaries. Pavements which had been discovered in earlier periods were uncovered once more – excavations were renewed at the behest of the duke of Marlborough, on whose estate the Stonesfield pavement lay, in 1802. By the early nineteenth century pavement excavation was becoming quite a vogue, sought out by curious spectators. The pavement at Woodchester, first mentioned in the 1695 *Britannia*, was excavated by Samuel Lysons in 1794. From Woodchester, he moved on to Frampton in Dorset, and from then to Horkstow in Lincolnshire in 1797, where yet another pavement was awaiting his excavation. A few years later, in 1811, he led another excavation at Bignor in Sussex.[113]

In 1813 a collection of highly detailed, hand-coloured engravings was being advertised by William Fowler in *Reliquiae Britannico Romanae: Containing Figures of Roman Antiquities Discovered in Various Parts of England.* Fowler was a master builder from Lincolnshire, who developed his skills of draughtsmanship in drawing antiquities; his speciality was in depicting mosaic pavements.[114] The volume comprised twenty sets of engravings, most of which were of Roman mosaic pavements; some of these were copies from earlier drawings or engravings (for example, a pavement discovered at Denton in 1727 and drawn by Stukeley), and a new version of the Stonesfield pavement. The scope of Fowler's project illustrates the much more comprehensive knowledge of Roman antiquities which had been acquired since the earlier part of the century, and the extent to which a taste for British Roman antiquities had become fashionable amongst the social elite. It was no longer regarded as a whimsical enthusiasm. Engravings, such as those published by Fowler, were part of the business of the consumption of luxury. At a cost of twelve guineas, and with a print run of only two hundred copies, this was a highly exclusive product – as the names of those who subscribed demonstrates. Lysons's account of Woodchester, printed in folio with hand-coloured engravings, was similarly extravagant: only fifty copies were printed and Lysons was said to have expended over £6000 on the publication.[115] But Fowler and Lysons were simply operating at the upper end of a market which also dealt in publications of a rather lower quality and lesser expense, such as Lysons's own pamphlet written for the visitors who came to view the mosaics at Bignor.[116]

The interest aroused by the finds of Roman antiquities in Bath is instructive in this context. Bath's origin as a Roman city was an obvious asset in enhancing its cachet and attraction to visitors, but comparatively little was known about the Roman origins of the city – unlike York, which as Eboracum and the temporary seat of the second legion had had a much more significant role to play in the Roman occupation. In John Wood's history of Bath, republished in 1765, the Roman period of the city's history was subordinate to his personal obsession with establishing a case for an indigenous British civilisation. This civilisation predated the arrival of the Romans, and was presided over by Druids whose metropolitan seat and university were located at Bath.[117] He recorded the discovery of mosaics, walls and a hypocaust in 1738, but, in keeping with the military paradigm through which the eighteenth century viewed Roman Britain, assumed that it was all part of a praetorium. The finds were actually the remains of a Roman town house. The baths and hypocaust system which were discovered in the process of building the duke of Kingston's baths in 1755 provoked comparatively little attention from the antiquarian world: the Society of Antiquaries received reports from its member on the spot, Mr Mundy, but no publication was forthcoming.[118] 'The baths', reported one visitor, 'cannot be called good specimens of the famous and splendid Roman architecture, but it is so obvious that they were built of bricks, without any great art or science, and probably by the Roman soldiers themselves, and it was not worth our while to go and see them.'[119] The inferior provinciality of Bath could not compete with the riches which were concurrently being uncovered from the ruins of Herculaneum and Pompeii. The substantial finds of 1790, however, including over seventy inscribed stones, the gorgon's head and pieces of the Temple of Minerva, provoked much more interest. Sir Henry Englefield and Thomas Pownall presented their own interpretation of the finds in papers before the Society of Antiquaries.[120] Englefield's paper was also reprinted as an appendix to Richard Warner's *History of Bath* (1801), and in 1813 Samuel Lysons published a meticulous and elaborate reconstruction of the temple in *Reliquiae romanae britannicae.* The museum of Roman antiquities established under the auspices of the corporation also dates from this period – established, if Warner is to be believed, upon his own instigation. In Warner's history of Bath far more attention was given to the Roman history than in Wood's *Description*, even though the taste and workmanship of the recent finds were found wanting. Warner pieced together a plausible account of the process by which Bath became a place of 'bustle and business' with lengthy footnotes on the bathing habits of the Romans.[121]

By the early nineteenth century the amount of detail recovered concerning Roman Britain dwarfed the information which had been available in 1695 for Gibson's first revision of *Britannia.* When Thomas Reynolds compiled his *Iter britanniarum*, in 1799, he calculated that he had included at least one hundred sites where Roman antiquities had been found which had not been mentioned by Richard Gough in his edition of *Britannia*, published only ten years previously.[122] The information was, however, somewhat unstructured. Roger Gale had ruefully commented in 1709 that it was beyond the capacity of any single individual to build up a comprehensive survey, given the degree of local, specialist knowledge which could only be acquired by long residence in an area, and expressed the hope that his example might induce other gentlemen 'as our lovers of our *English Antiquities*' to 'endeavour the Recovery of the Courses these *Ways* formerly took, near their residence'.[123] Gale's appeal for collaboration was echoed in the frequently expressed call to arms for antiquaries to build upon Horsley's achievement. Soon after the publication of *Britannia romana* the need for an expanded edition was making itself felt; in the 1770s Richard Gough was making persistent inquiries as to the whereabouts of the original plates, with the intention of publishing a revised edition which would bring together all the inscriptions subsequently discovered and published in the pages of the *Philosophical Transactions* and the *Gentleman's Magazine*. Gough's efforts to purchase the plates were frustrated, and other projects assumed a more urgent priority. His *Anecdotes of British Topography* (1768), revised in 1780 as *British Topography*, plus his revision of Camden's *Britannia* of 1789, went some way towards summarising the extant literature, but he did nothing towards a synthesis. His ambition was shared by Samuel Pegge, one of the most productive and long-lived of eighteenth-century antiquaries, who was particularly assiduous in charting the Roman remains of Derbyshire.[124] Pegge repeatedly called upon the Society of Antiquaries to organise a nationwide network of antiquaries to map out Roman remains on a systematic basis. Gentlemen in their respective counties, he suggested, should draw up accounts of Roman remains as he had done – this would add up to an excellent *Britannica romana*, 'whereby it would appear that our island was indeed a favourite province of that great people and that they had occupied or visited almost every part of it'.[125] John Whitaker, whose account of the Roman occupation of Britain in his *History of Manchester* was one of the most widely read authorities of the time, was similarly reported to be planning a history of the Roman occupation of Britain, based upon a historical arrangement of inscriptions.[126] The failure of any of these projects to be realised reflects upon the voluntarist manner in which antiquarian activity was undertaken within Britain: it was largely the activity of leisured gentlemen, who were resistant to organised, collaborative research and preferred to undertake it as a private enterprise. The structures necessary for the systematic coordination of antiquarian inquiry were simply not in place.

By the early nineteenth century, the study of Roman antiquities had been consolidated. The admiration for all things Roman, however, no longer commanded the same position of intellectual dominance that had characterised the antiquarian world of the early eighteenth century. Admired though they were as men of taste, it was now recognised that figures such as Sir John Clerk or the earl of Burlington had been prone to let their enthusiasm for things Roman distort their critical faculties. In theory, Clerk had been able to recognise the dangers of ascribing everything to Roman civilisation, arguing that only objects which were inscribed with Latin letters or were found in the neighbourhood of a Roman station should be identified as Roman. In practice, when confronted with the antique artefact, his first instinct was to establish a Roman provenance for it.[127] Similarly, it was Burlington's influence over Francis Drake, or at least Drake's endeavours to satisfy Burlington's vision of reviving the glories of Roman Eboracum, which directed Drake's attempts to ascribe Roman origins for every remnant of antiquity found within the city.[128] As Sir Henry Englefield was to remark on this very issue, Lord Burlington's expertise in Greek and Roman antiquities had 'rather been an hindrance to his forming a proper judgement of the different styles of architecture in the lower ages, than any help to him in that respect'.[129] There had always been a tension between the admiration for the Roman achievement and the reality that the Romans had indisputably slain and conquered the native Britons. Anglo-Roman antiquities, wrote one nineteenth-century antiquary, were the 'vestigia of a hoarde of plunderers' who, after subjugating the country and enslaving its inhabitants, occupied their property for four hundred years.[130] The history of the Romans in Britain became an increasingly contested territory. As antiquarian culture was appropriated by classes beyond the landowning elite and drew ever more on the historical traditions of Scotland, Wales and Ireland, the coherence of the Roman vision of antiquity was fractured and complicated by competing histories of national origins.

6

The Anglo-Saxons

In 1722 Edmund Gibson, bishop of London and one of the leading antiquaries of the early eighteenth century, dedicated the revised edition of his translation of William Camden's *Britannia* to George I in the following manner:

> Not only our Histories, but our Language, our Laws, our Customs, our Names of Persons and names of Places, do all abundantly testify, that the greatest part of your Majesty's Subjects here, are of SAXON Original. And if we enquire from when our Saxon Ancestors came, we shall find, that it was from your Majesty's Dominions in *Germany*.[1]

In terms of content, this edition differed from that of 1695 in the additional coverage given over to Roman antiquities, reflecting the considerable accretion of knowledge which had taken place in the early part of the century. Gibson's decision to attach the science of antiquarianism firmly to the Hanoverian cause, however, was a politically astute one, given that a significant number of the antiquarian circle who had contributed to this and the earlier edition were non-jurors and, in the politically sensitive days of the early Hanoverian regime, suspect.[2] The dedication to George I and the connection made between the common Saxon heritage of the English and the German Hanoverians gave a new poignancy to the Saxon period of history and its historical importance for the development of English culture and the English state. The Hanoverians, Gibson explained, were Saxons; the origin of the word came not from the Sacae of Asia, but the two short swords called sachs carried by the north Germans and to be found to this day upon the arms of Saxony. Samuel Gale, the friend and fellow antiquary of Gibson, had made an equally politic gesture in his *History and Antiquities of the Cathedral Church of Winchester*, in which he had expressed the hope that King George would once again make Winchester the royal residence of the Saxon kings.[3] Gale's brother-in-law, William Stukeley, another firm supporter of the Hanoverian regime, similarly argued that the Hanoverian line was descended from the Saxon line of Hengist.[4] The interest of the antiquaries in the Saxon period, however, was more than simple patriotic posturing. Whilst in the hands of some writers the Saxons, like the ancient

Britons or the Druids, were simply another part of a historical bric-a-brac, without any specific historical provenance, in the view of many antiquaries, the Saxon period demanded greater attention on account of its very obscurity.

Britannia was ostensibly about the whole island of Great Britain but it had always had an Anglocentric conception. Gibson and his fellow antiquaries derived satisfaction from the fact that the Act of Union of 1707 had restored the historic unity of the Roman province, but they simultaneously welcomed George I, monarch of Great Britain, as the modern incarnation of Saxon kingship. Gibson's dedication encapsulates the importance of Saxon antiquities for the construction of a sense of nationhood in eighteenth-century England; it was crucial to all that defined the English nation. The period following the departure of the Romans marked the point at which national differences within Britain become more clearly differentiated in the study of antiquities. 'And here', as Francis Wise observed, 'our history may be said to begin.'[5] Saxon antiquities were never identified as such in Wales or Scotland; they represented a specifically English concern. The Saxons were a Gothic people who with the Jutes and the Angles were the progenitors of the English nation; they brought with them from Germany principles of liberty and justice, which provided the basis of the traditions of English freedom and the common law.[6] They were marked by daring courage, fondness for war, steady perseverance in their old traditions, love of liberty, zeal for the religion of their forefathers, and a contempt for death grounded upon a belief in a 'happy futurity'.[7] The cult of Alfred, the most famous of the Anglo-Saxons kings and often portrayed as the greatest English monarch, embodied the identification of the Anglo-Saxon polity with all that was most prized by Englishmen: the traditions of Parliament, limited monarchy, common law, the jury system, and Christianity in its truest expression – the Church of England. As the author of one popular account of Alfred's reign put it, 'How ought Englishmen to venerate the name of Alfred, the institutor of such noble prerogatives, which raises their nation to an envied pre-eminence above every other, and which, as the great bulwark of their constitution, will ever secure them from the oppression of tyrants.'[8] To study Saxon antiquities, Saxon histories and Saxon literature was therefore not just the preserve of the pedant but also the duty of the patriot.

On this basis, it might seem natural to assume that an interest in Saxon antiquities was widespread amongst eighteenth-century Englishmen. In certain respects, as will be seen, that was certainly true. But the eighteenth century is not normally noted for its contribution to the study of Anglo-Saxon history or culture; and, despite Gibson's fulsome dedication, the prevailing attitude towards the Saxon period was deeply equivocal. Although its significance for England's constitutional, ecclesiastical and legal development was questioned by few, it could not command the widespread interest which surrounded Roman antiquities. Nor did it capture the literary and artistic imagination in the way that Thomas Gray's Bard or Mason's Caractacus had done. The Saxons had betrayed the ancient Britons who had appealed to them for help; they had ravaged the nation and destroyed the tender shoots of imported civilisation. As pagan invaders they had persecuted the fragile early church which had become established during the Roman occupation. The Saxons were barbaric, rude, unedifying. John Spelman's life of Alfred – the basic source for most exercises in Alfredian hagiography in the eighteenth century – was unstinting in his adulation of this greatest of English kings. But the darkness and depravity of the English nation prior to his reign served to highlight Alfred's own achievements with greater clarity. Quoting the chronicler Roger of Hoveden, Spelman concluded that 'in process of time all Virtue became so wholly abolished in them, as no Nation whatsoever might compare with them for Treachery and Villany. So precipitate a Depravation did the Licentiousness of mutual Rapine bring upon them.'[9] Despite the frequency with which Alfred's name was invoked as an exemplar of kingship, this was not in itself sufficient to counteract the general image of rude barbarity with which the 'Dark Ages' were associated. In the opinion of the historian Sir William Temple the rough course of those lawless times and actions was too ignoble a subject for the historian or antiquary to engage with.[10]

Those who studied Saxon antiquities were quick to counter-attack. Such times, wrote William Nicolson in response to Temple, 'were not so *lawless*, nor the Authors so *few* and *mean*, as he imagines'.[11] Eighty years later another Northumberland antiquary, William Hutchinson, was making the same point: 'Authors, in the warmth of accusations, neglect the consideration of the advantages we finally derived form the Saxons; no less than THE MAXIMS OF OUR COMMON LAW, AND THE ORIGINAL PRINCIPLES OF OUR INESTIMABLE CONSTITUTION.'[12] Thomas Pownall, better known as a governor of New England and critic of colonial policy but also, on his return to Britain, a keen antiquary, argued that a close examination of the manner in which the Saxons possessed and governed the counties which they conquered demanded admiration for the state of advancement to which their community had arisen, 'both in civil polity, as well as the art military'. He blamed the 'home bread (sic) ideas' of the 'poor cloistered Monks' who had depicted the era of Saxon and Danish invasions 'as though they were the inroads only of a mere rabble rout of savage pirates'.[13] The taste for 'Travelling and Classick Learning' prejudiced most readers against Saxon antiquities; whereas Roman antiquities were easily identifiable and readily abundant, the Saxons had left few buildings, coins, inscriptions or roads. The Saxon presence in the landscape was elusive and the burden was always on those who sought, in Charles Lyttelton's words, 'to stamp a proper Reputation' upon the Saxon period.[14]

The traditional view of the eighteenth century's contribution to Anglo-Saxon studies has always been that Saxon scholarship flourished in the late seventeenth and early eighteenth centuries, with significant advances being made in the scholarly appreciation of language and literature and the publication of Anglo-Saxon texts. Thereafter little progress was made until the nineteenth century. The scholarship of George Hickes, Humfrey Wanley, Edward Thwaites and the 'Oxford' Saxonists was neglected rather than improved upon; the academic study of Anglo-Saxon virtually disappeared from the curricula of the universities.[15] This analysis carries much truth and there are eminently convincing explanations as to why this lapse in interest should have occurred. It is also true, however, that within the circle of antiquaries a considerable number resisted this trend and continued to endeavour to develop and promote the study of the Anglo-Saxon period. During the same period the dominance of Rome and classical antiquity over the cultural imagination of the eighteenth century became less secure and the identification of the English nation with its specifically Saxon or Teutonic origins became more pronounced.[16] There was a 'recovery' of Saxon literature and architecture, giving rise to a re-evaluation of the Saxon heritage to which antiquaries and the antiquarian movement made an important contribution. The nineteenth-century rediscovery of Anglo-Saxon culture was only made possible through the research and activities of the eighteenth-century antiquaries.

The Saxon period had originally claimed the attention of the antiquary and the historian for two particular reasons. The first, and that which generated the initial scholarly interest in Saxon studies, was the imperative to establish a historical model of the Saxon church which would show it to be the precursor of the newly established Church of England and thereby endow it with historical legitimacy. In the sixteenth century Matthew Parker had sponsored research into Anglo-Saxon literature in order to demonstrate the ancient purity of the English Saxon church before the corrupt pretensions of the papacy had reduced the medieval church to a state of submission to Rome.[17] The necessity of demonstrating the errors of the Roman Catholic Church through historical argument was still a powerful impetus driving the study of Anglo-Saxon language and literature forward in the early eighteenth century. The publication of Saxon homilies, it was hoped, would provide undeniable evidence to posterity 'that the belief of our Papists at this day is a very different thing from that of our Saxon ancestors'.[18] The

The Saxon king in his martial habit, from Joseph Strutt, *A Complete View of the Dress and Habits of the People of England*, 2 vols (1796). (*Society of Antiquaries*)

Convocation Controversy of the early eighteenth century, which arose out of the disputed balance of power between the upper and the lower houses of the deliberative body of the Church of England, brought a new urgency to the study of ecclesiastical antiquities. Arguments based upon historical precedent, drawn from Bede's *Ecclesiastical History* or the records of earlier synods, dominated the debate.[19]

The second reason, and one which had more lasting influence in the eighteenth century, was political: the Saxon period was the era during which the system of common law and the principles of the constitution were believed to have been established. According to the Whig interpretation of history, the Saxons brought with them from Germany the principles of freedom and representation that Tacitus had described in the *Germania*, from which the Anglo-Saxon constitution had evolved. The Saxons 'used their Victory fairly, planted, built, manured and inhabited, established Laws of Equity and Peace'.[20] The precise contours of this constitution, indeed its very existence, was politically contentious in the seventeenth century. Political and legal antiquarianism provided much of the ammunition in the constitutional struggles being waged between the theorists of Stuart absolutism, the defenders of the common law tradition, and the proponents of the most radical interpretation of the Norman Yoke.[21] Historical precedent, in both the seventeenth and eighteenth centuries, was one of the most important legitimating strategies of political rhetoric; the significance of the Saxon constitution and political antiquarianism in wider debates should not therefore be underestimated.

The extreme urgency of the issues surrounding the political and religious debates of the seventeenth century, however, was somewhat diminished in the eighteenth century. Antiquarian research was not necessarily harnessed to ideological motives, and determined efforts were made by some to break the close relationship between politics and antiquarianism. Antiquaries such as White Kennett and Edmund Gibson positively welcomed the possibility of dissociating antiquities from the politics in which it had been embroiled in the previous century. The dominant genre of antiquarian literature in this period, that of topographical and local antiquities, was certainly more easily pursued independent of such ideological imperatives. Later in the century the rise of 'sceptical Whiggery' amongst the Scottish social theorists, and most influentially in David Hume's *History of England*, undermined the credibility of an ancient constitution and Anglo-Saxon liberties. But belief in Saxon liberties died hard and could be repackaged as part of an 'evolutionary Whiggism' which accommodated the historical reality of constitutional change, which was itself demonstrated through the researches of antiquaries such as Henry Spelman and Thomas Madox.[22] In the political realm, however, antiquarian arguments continued to play a crucial role in debate. Whether one subscribed to notions of Saxon immemorialism or not, it was impossible to ignore the prevalence of Anglo-Saxon constititutionalism. 'Other parts therefore of our antiquities may be either known or passed by as matters of curiosity and entertainment rather than of public benefit,' argued the antiquary Samuel Squire, 'but the history of the civil constitution cannot be too carefully studied, or too minutely enquired into'; particularly, he noted, in a country where all sides appealed to the ancient constitution for the truth of its opinions.[23] The publications of the period offer numerous instances of the manipulation of historical evidence for political argument rather than for their insights into the Anglo-Saxon past. The classic statement of the thesis of Anglo-Saxon liberties, Nathaniel Bacon's *An Historicall Discourse of the Uniformity of the Government of England*, was originally published in 1647 but had gone through six editions by 1760. His arguments resurfaced in *An Historical Essay on the English Constitution* (1771) and continued to feature in radical literature through the period of reform. The association between the Saxon period and the legal, political and ecclesiastical constitution of the eighteenth-century state was crucial to legitimate academic interest in the period, particularly given the prejudices against the period on the grounds of taste. Further to this, however, the strength of legal and political antiquarianism also demonstrates the pervasiveness of antiquarian models of thought and must alert us to the cogency which arguments for the contemporary relevance of antiquarian pursuits were able to command.[24]

The question whether the Anglo-Saxon polity was feudal in nature was probably the most consistently debated aspect of Anglo-Saxon history. It engaged the attention of numerous antiquaries, who studied the terms of charters and other legal documents in the hope of establishing the complex system of landholding with greater certainty.[25] But it was also of weighty importance to those who sought to understand the processes by which Britain had arrived at the unique balance of its eighteenth-century constitution. A system of feudal tenure was necessarily based upon a system of land held in reward for services rendered in return for privileges, including political representation. Feudalism could therefore be constructed as the historical ancestor of the eighteenth-century system of parliamentary representation which awarded the franchise to the propertied elite. It also represented a crucial evolutionary stage between a primitive state of nature and the security of private property enjoyed in the eighteenth century and upon which liberty, prosperity and civilisation were assumed to depend. The assumption that feudalism had existed across Europe during the medieval period corroborated the universalist view of mankind's development which prevailed for much of the eighteenth century, lending itself to the comparative, conjectural approach which was characteristic of much antiquarian and historical writing. The rise and fall of feudalism offered the explanatory structure for the emergence of modern commercial society and the establishment of political liberty and private property. As such it was the preoccupation of not only antiquaries but also the leading thinkers of the Scottish Enlightenment.[26] Thus antiquarian research had a particularly pertinent application for philosophers, political economists and social theorists. The evidence of antiquity, from laws, charters, or etymological speculation, provided the basic raw materials of social theorists from Lord Kames to John Millar.

In the late seventeenth century Robert Brady had taken up Henry Spelman's contention that the Normans had imposed feudalism upon a free people to argue for the monarch's absolute power by right of conquest. To counter these royalist arguments the Whigs were under pressure to develop a theory of feudalism under the Saxons; they had to be able to demonstrate some continuity through the period of the Norman invasion in order to refute the case for absolute discontinuity and disruption. Although there were significant variations upon this basic premise, a belief in Saxon feudalism commanded a majority (although not total) consensus during the eighteenth century. John Whitaker's *History of Manchester* considered not just the feudal polity of the Saxons, but its presumed earlier genesis under the Britons. In so doing he aimed some blows at David Hume's dismissive summary of the Saxon heptarchy, whose account was 'strange and wild in itself', although Whitaker's reasoning was hardly based upon more secure foundations.[27] *An Essay on the English Constitution* (1771) reinvented the Saxons as a democratic, largely urban society, in which the franchise was enjoyed by all those who paid their taxes and elections were held on an annual basis. This radical Saxonism persisted alongside the arguments of the natural rights theorists into the nineteenth century, featuring in the arguments of James Burgh's *Political Disquisitions*, the London Corresponding Society, and in the claims of radicals who turned to urban charters in order to collect the proofs which would lend their arguments the authoritative stamp of evidence from antiquity.[28] Thus Thomas Oldfield turned to the evidence of antiquity in penning his polemical *History of the Boroughs* (1792). This was a far cry from Brady's drier, more technical scholarship, which had been written for a minority of the political elite. But the appeal to antiquity as the basis for further argument was the same. The Tory Samuel Henshall responded with a counterblast of antiquities. His *Specimens and Parts* (1798) was, he said, written specifically to silence the Towers and Oldfields who were yelping after the imagined liberties of the Saxon constitution. His object was to demonstrate continuity before and after the Norman Conquest. There was no usurpation of ancient liberties, he argued: Saxon England had been fully feudalised prior to the Norman Conquest, and it was only the gripes of disgruntled monkish chroniclers that painted William in such a negative light.[29]

Oldfield was no antiquary; he was a political hack. But there were others who were carrying out rather more careful research into the documents of borough history as a means of pressing their case for political reform.[30] Charter scholarship enjoyed a resurgence in the years leading up to the reforms of 1832 and 1835 as local antiquaries across the country resorted to the charters and related documents of borough history to press the case for reform. This was not the charter scholarship of a Brady or a Madox, but the parameters of political debate had changed from those of over a century earlier and demanded a different kind of research. What was at issue now was not so much the relationship between the king and parliament, or the rights of the House of Commons, as the distribution of the franchise within the borough. This was a new form of polemical, legal antiquarianism aimed at the expanded community of the political nation of the early nineteenth century rather than the tiny political elite of late Stuart England. The original borough charters in which the franchise had been granted in the act of incorporation provided the evidence with which reformers sought to overturn oligarchy, or occasionally by which oligarchy defended its own comfortable position. Reformers of an antiquarian turn of mind studied the charters of their respective towns for evidence of an Anglo-Saxon householder franchise in a movement which culminated in Merewether and Stephen's classic statement arguing the case for municipal reform, *The History of the Boroughs and Municipal Corporations* (1835).[31]

Eighteenth-century interest in Anglo-Saxon antiquities was undoubtedly also a beneficiary of the heightened sense of collective consciousness or national identity which steadily intensified over the course of the eighteenth century. It was in this context that increasing currency was given to the importance of antiquities to patriotism and to national honour. This patriotic turn likewise helps to explain the popular currency of Anglo-Saxon constitutionalism in the rhetoric of political debate. Saxonists had always emphasised the patriotic dimension to their researches, but such arguments acquired greater plausibility as Englishmen became more conscious of their Saxon descent and were correspondingly willing to project back upon the Saxons the qualities upon which they prided themselves.[32] Rather than pursuing antiquities in foreign lands, as did the Grand Tourists, the domestic antiquary could contribute far more to his nation's honour and reputation by recovering those remnants of the past which remained and which might, if judiciously collected, further elucidate the obscurities of that dark period of English history. Richard Gough, provoked to irritation by the aristocracy's continued fascination with the Mediterranean and the Near East, issued a manifesto for antiquarian studies in the preface to *Anecdotes of British Topography*: 'Among other desiderata in our antiquities must be reckoned a connected history of the Saxons, both in and out of England. If the traces of this people, before they quitted the Continent, are dark and confused, we have good materials for their history after this island submitted to them.' John Whitaker, not normally one to give unconditional agreement to anything that Gough wrote, echoed these sentiments: the period of Saxon history was 'The great seed plot of our national history, as it gives us the origin and institution of all our government, all our civility and all our religion.' This represented a deliberate attempt to secure some of the didactic high ground for the study of Saxon history and antiquities, which was at best conventionally allowed to the reign of Alfred the Great alone. Sharon Turner's history, the first volume of which was published in 1799, consolidated this shift. Whilst identifying the Anglo-Saxon period as crucial to the formation of the English nation, he used his knowledge of Anglo-Saxon sources to challenge the hackneyed generalisations which featured in histories with a weaker basis in antiquarian research, including the tendency to attribute every noteworthy achievement of the Anglo-Saxons to Alfred's reign.

Given these pressing considerations in favour of the study of Anglo-Saxon history and its antiquities, it remains to be considered why it is that the eighteenth century does not boast a better reputation in the wider history of Anglo-Saxon studies. In the opinion of both contemporaries and subsequent observers, the progress made in the study of Saxon history and antiquities was limited. In 1693 Edmund Gibson wrote to his fellow antiquary, Thomas Tanner, on the frustrations of studying the period: 'We forsooth, are to thrash among the Saxons and Danes, where the materials for a History are soe narrow and have in them soe little of connexion, that after a man had done all he could, it should look more like dry Annals than a just History.'[33] One hundred years later, the situation was apparently not much different: 'The great want of materials for furnishing a complete history of the Anglo-Saxons', wrote Joseph Strutt in 1796, 'and the confusion of circumstances ... has deterred many of our best writers from making deep researches into the abstracted remains of antiquity, concerning them.'[34] There is an evident discrepancy between the obvious significance of Saxon antiquities to English culture and the apparent disregard for that period of history. Many accounts have been premised upon a teleological framework of the emergence of Old English scholarship and a canon of scholarly editions of Anglo-Saxon texts, and have consequently found the eighteenth century wanting. Others have taken at face value the disparaging comments on the subject which punctuate the literature. The apparent failure of antiquarian nerve in following up the achievements of earlier periods of scholarship needs to be reconsidered.

Gibson's comment quoted above is telling: the Saxons had no Tacitus or Livy to record their history for posterity. The primary sources available to the aspiring historian were few: Bede's history, Nennius, Gildas, the Anglo-Saxon Chronicle, Asser's life of Alfred and later compilations of Saxon laws and charters. After the catastrophic fire at the Cottonian Library in 1731 they were fewer still. The lack of familiarity with Old English, or Saxon as it was then known, presented a serious impediment to further study. William Nicolson questioned Edward Thwaites' decision to publish the Heptateuch in Saxon only: 'I wish you had given us the Vulgar Latin with it ... the world is not yet so well stocked with men skilled in our Saxon language and antiquities as we may hope to see it.'[35] Even those texts which had been written in Latin, or had been translated into Latin, could not be accepted, however, on the same terms as the corpus of the Roman historians. Not only was the Latin 'barbarous', showing none of the elegance of the Roman authors, the 'models of chaste diction, elocution, and sound sense',[36] but these were monkish chroniclers who had been confined to the monasteries, at the mercy of hearsay, blinded by superstition and religious prejudice. In the indolence of the 'age of monkery' the chroniclers took all things upon trust: 'they are, indeed, to be consulted', wrote Nathaniel Salmon, 'but with Grains of Allowance. Some History we are altogether obliged to them for, finding no Footsteps of it in Foreigners.'[37] These were histories which contravened all the criteria by which the man of letters judged a historical work. Even Francis Wise, one of those who struggled to keep alive the traditions of Anglo-Saxon scholarship in Oxford in the eighteenth century, judged the Anglo-Saxon historians by a Roman yardstick. The Saxons' bias to superstition, he wrote, rendered them less useful than the Roman historians; even Bede was defective in this respect.[38]

Nor were the stories of constant warfare, feuds and plunder such as to excite admiration. The barbarism and violence with which it was inevitably associated repelled those eighteenth-century Englishmen who prided themselves on their progress towards greater civility and refinement. Whereas the polite gentleman could take pleasure in constructing himself in what he believed to be the image of a Roman patrician, the Anglo-Saxon invader inspired no comparable associations. Even the illustrations to the masque *Alfred* showed the eponymous hero lying on a bank in a distinctly neo-classical pose, remodelled as a Roman.[39] The tradition that the Saxons had destroyed every element of civilisation they encountered was long established. All the civilised qualities of the Roman Empire, which inspired the English antiquary to further research, were obliterated by the marauding Saxon. Whilst the Whig consensus accepted that the Saxons represented liberty and freedom, it disdained the finer detail of Saxon history, with all its petty feuds and bloody violence, comparable only, it was said, to the hissing of cats. The classical humanist conception of history, which saw it as providing a model for political action, could find little to admire in the period following the departure of the Romans. With an almost tangible shudder of distaste, Richard Warner described the Anglo-Saxon period as 'gloomy and disgusting', a time when 'every vestige of refinement disappeared ... commerce and husbandry [were] neglected for war and hunting, clouds of ferocity, ignorance and superstition'.[40]

Despite the academic interest in matters Anglo-Saxon in both universities – Cambridge in the sixteenth and Oxford in the later seventeenth century – in neither university had it become securely established; its strength was always in the enthusiasms of a number of like-minded scholars and patrons, and as such extremely unstable. In Cambridge Sir John Spelman had endowed a lectureship for the study of 'domestique Antiquities touching our Church and reviving the Saxon tongue' shortly before the outbreak of the Civil War, but it 'failed by the confusion of the times'. The deaths of both Henry and John Spelman by 1643 deprived the movement of leadership.[41] A number of notable contributions to Anglo-Saxon studies were produced in the second part of the century by Cambridge scholars such as Thomas Gale, Robert Sheringham and John Smith. The impetus for the study of Saxon antiquities appears to have been lost by the end of the seventeenth century, however, overshadowed by the intellectual might of Newtonian natural philosophy and mathematics.[42] The dynamic centre for Anglo-Saxon studies had, by this time, shifted to Oxford, where plans were made to establish a regular lectureship in Saxon studies, a post which was held 1679–82 by William Nicolson, who had been sent to Leipzig for a year in order to study German and Scandinavian languages.[43] Rivalry with Cambridge had not a little to do with the enthusiasm with which Nicolson was encouraged by his superiors to work upon an edition of the Anglo-Saxon Chronicle, a grammar and a dictionary, which taken together would not only match but surpass those projected by Cambridge.[44]

Political events conspired against the consolidation of this community of Saxon scholars. Given their respect for tradition and continuity, it was no coincidence that many antiquaries were high churchmen; in the years following the Glorious Revolution a high proportion of these became non-jurors. Their Saxon studies became a means of resisting the Whigs (who similarly drew on historical precedent to justify the Revolution).[45] George Hickes, the leading Saxonist at Oxford, was forced into hiding, and the prospects of less highly placed scholars such as Thomas Hearne or Humfrey Wanley were heavily compromised. Others were elevated by the new regime and eventually left Oxford and active antiquarian research behind them. The study of Anglo-Saxon at Oxford did not go into immediate eclipse, however, and under the sympathetic guidance of Arthur Charlett the university press continued to publish Saxon texts, whilst Edward Thwaites presided over a steady stream of neophyte Saxonists, and, in collaboration with other scholars from Queen's, continued work on various projects related to the publication of Saxon history and literature.[46] During the 1690s, and even into the first years of the eighteenth century, there was a sense of gathering strength: William Nicolson, whose robust defence of Anglo-Saxon studies has already been noted, wrote to his fellow antiquary Ralph Thoresby in consistently upbeat terms as to the extent of interest in antiquarianism which he detected amongst the public. Hickes's grammar, he claimed, met with far more encouragement than he could have hoped for; Rawlinson's edition of Boethius in Saxon had been published, with a print run of two hundred and fifty copies – all of which had been subscribed for. Furthermore, he had subscribed for twelve copies of the Saxon Pentateuch with the intention of dispersing it amongst all 'lovers of antiquity' in order to promote the study of the Saxon tongue.[47]

The grammar by Hickes to which Nicolson referred was the *Linguarum vett. septentrionalium thesaurus grammatico-criticus et archaeologicus* (Oxford, 1703–5) in which the Oxford Saxonist laid bare his unrivalled understanding of the Saxon (and other 'Gothic') languages. It provided the learned world with irrefutable evidence that Anglo-Saxon, like Latin and Greek, had an orderly grammatical structure, as opposed to being a rude and barbarous language with no order or system to it. The momentum in publishing Anglo-Saxon antiquities did not stop with Hickes: Thwaites condensed some of Hickes's findings in *Grammatica Anglo-Saxonica* (1711), whilst in 1715 Elizabeth Elstob's *Rudiments of Grammar for the English-Saxon Tongue* revealed the logical structure and beauty of the Saxon language in a more widely accessible format. She and her brother William Elstob, himself a former pupil of Hickes, had in preparation other items including an edition of Saxon homilies. These she particularly valued as demonstrating the purity of doctrine in Anglo-Saxon times.[48] William Wotton produced an abridgement of Hickes's *Thesaurus* in 1708 which was intended to broaden access to that work, and was itself translated into English by Maurice Shelton in 1735 in a further bid to broaden its accessibility.[49] David Wilkins produced an edition of the *Leges Anglo Saxonicae* in 1716. Seven years later, in 1722, John and George Smith's critical edition of Bede's *Ecclesiastical History* was published, which has been described as a crowning achievement of the seventeenth-century Saxonists.[50] Even then the seventeenth-century momentum had not petered out. The transactions of the church synods between the fifth and the seventeenth centuries, on which Sir Henry Spelman, Archbishop Wake and Thomas Tanner had all laboured, were finally published in 1737 under the editorship of David Wilkins.[51]

Thwaites died in 1715, however, as did William Elstob, and Hickes had died in 1711. Nicolson, Gibson and Thomas Tanner had all been deflected into ecclesiastical careers and were climbing the ranks of the episcopacy. Nicolson never gave up his enthusiasm for Anglo-Saxon studies and did his best to establish a permanent lectureship in Anglo-Saxon at both universities; his efforts bore fruit in the appointment of David Wilkins in 1716, but his lectureship was not permanently endowed and there was no one to succeed him. Nearly forty years later Anglo-Saxon scholarship looked set to acquire a permanent presence in 1754 when Richard Rawlinson bequeathed money to Oxford to establish a chair in Anglo-Saxon studies, but the terms of Rawlinson's will made it virtually impossible to appoint anyone who was eligible on the grounds of scholarship, and it was further tainted by Rawlinson's own Jacobite associations. Following a violent dispute with the Society of Antiquaries, Rawlinson had decreed that no one from that society, or the Royal Society, was to fill it; nor could anyone of Scottish descent, nor anyone who was involved in the colonies or the stock market. He also stipulated that the first holder should be a St John's man. This narrowed the field somewhat. 'His intention', as Richard Gough later remarked, 'defeats itself.' The chair was not actually filled until 1795.[52]

By the 1720s and 1730s the remaining Saxonists in Oxford were uttering constant laments at the neglect of Saxon studies; the excited enthusiasm with which William Nicolson had corresponded with Ralph Thoresby on the Saxon history of the Northumbrian kingdom had dissipated into nervous defensiveness and uncertainty. The small circle of remaining scholars engaged in rounds of mutual condolence, lamenting the contraction in their numbers and bemoaning the failure of public spirit amongst their fellow scholars, who neglected to encourage the study of this most important period of English history. Francis Wise put his finger on the problem in a letter dated 10 September 1754 to Edward Lye, following the departure of his fellow Saxonist George Ballard; there was a good disposition in some of the young people, he said, towards the northern languages, but they had made little progress. This could be remedied 'if they had but the countenance of two or three leaders here, to keep them from being laughed out of the study'.[53] Lye, to whom Francis Wise made these rather pointed comments, was a shy scholar who preferred the retirement of his Northamptonshire parish to Oxford life. He was, however, the most competent Saxonist of his day, whose contributions to the study of Saxon were of long-term significance, and not just in terms of the eighteenth-century's rather weak traditions.[54] Wise's lament also smacks of an older man looking back upon his youth, and endowing it with the more attractive hues of nostalgia. Ultimately the eclipse of Anglo-Saxon studies at Oxford was a reflection of the lack of leadership and encouragement at the higher levels of the university and demonstrated the importance of maintaining a critical mass of like-minded individuals who could sustain the momentum.

Yet it would be wrong to consider the study of Anglo-Saxon antiquities purely in terms of the academic interest it attracted (or failed to attract) at the universities of Oxford and Cambridge. As the Society of Antiquaries became established as a focal point for those interested in antiquities after its formal establishment in 1717, the role played by the universities, whilst still important, became less central to the antiquarian enterprise. The earliest minutes of the society stated that its business should be limited to the subject of antiquities, and 'more particularly, to such things as may Illustrate and Relate to the History of Great Britain'. Humfrey Wanley, one of the founder members, subsequently elaborated upon this basic founding principle in a memorandum of the society's objective which he drew up for Edward Harley, later second earl of Oxford (who he evidently intended should provide the patronage for the fledgling society). Many were conceived in very general terms and implicitly included Saxon history within them. Under the heading of 'Good Books Wanted', Wanley specifically cited a number of the favourite projects of the Oxford Saxonists, but clearly did not regard these as projects to be undertaken only under the auspices of the university. He wished to see an enlarged edition of the Saxon laws, the homilies and the Anglo-Saxon Bible as well as a *Britannia saxonica* which would provide an inventory of all the Saxon antiquities to be found within the kingdom.[55] From its inception the study of Saxon antiquities was one of the society's foremost concerns. The frontispiece for the minute book of the Society of Antiquaries designed by William Stukeley shows three warriors, clad in Roman-style garb, united over a Roman altar, but the romanisation of the British past is not complete: one of the warriors holds a series of medallions displaying a pair of clasped hands, a portrait of Charles I and also one of Alfred the Great. Interest in Anglo-Saxon matters continued, albeit with a diminished profile, even through the period from the 1740s when the academic study of what would now be termed Old English was entering into decline.

Edward Rowe Mores provides another example of continuity between the earlier periods of Saxon scholarship and the late eighteenth century, when the academic study of Anglo-Saxon began to revive once more. He acquired his interest in Saxon antiquities at Oxford under the influence of scholars such as Francis Wise and George Ballard. In the 1750s he was involved in proposals for the publication of the Junius Caedmon manuscript held in the Bodleian Library.[56] Initially the Society of Antiquaries expressed interest in the scheme, it falling very evidently within their founding principles. However, although the society contributed towards the costs of engraving the illustrations – which were published as *Figurae quaedam antiquae ex Caedmonis monachi paraphraseos in Genesin* (1754) – further financial commitment was not forthcoming. The society's reluctance to invest in such a project is partially explicable by the fact that its finances at this point were still recovering from the considerable costs of obtaining a charter. Any such publication was almost bound to involve substantial losses; this at least was the interpretation put upon the proceedings by Richard Rawlinson. 'Caedmon was talked of but our Expence not approved of, so that the dean's interest must work it up. Those of my Friends of the Society, who think at all about expences and our revenue know that large works will not do.' Rawlinson's account of the meeting makes it clear that there was a division of opinion, with some members supporting the proposals for publication, whilst others demurred on account of the cost and the limited market to which it would appeal.[57] What Rawlinson did not remark upon was that his known Jacobitism would not have helped his cause amongst a council dominated by ministerial Whigs.

Had Rowe Mores remained on the council of the Society of Antiquaries it is possible that he would have been able to influence the society into taking assuming a more active role in publishing Saxon materials. In 1754 there were rumours that he had access to manuscripts not even known to Hearne, leading to hopes of a resurgence of Saxon and medieval publications emanating from the Oxford collections. 'The progress he has made in our English Antiquities is amazing', enthused Andrew Coltée Ducarel to William Cole, 'and his Discoveries of Antiquities now extant in Oxford, unknown to Tom Hearne, and even to the present Antiquaries there, tho' very obvious when he shew'd 'em to them, make me believe that he will make a very great figure hereafter.'[58] It is, however, a largely hypothetical issue, because in 1754 he was voted off the council.[59] Although he never abandoned his interest in Saxon literature entirely, his interests took an increasingly topographical and typographical turn, provoking the ire of Richard Gough who rounded on him sharply, complaining of his sloth and luxury. His failure to produce any further works of antiquarian scholarship ranked as a betrayal of the antiquarian cause. The fact that Rowe Mores failed to fulfil his early promise was doubly unfortunate given that Edward Lye also preferred his Northamptonshire rectory to Oxford, where his presence might have given much needed direction to Anglo-Saxon studies.[60]

In the second half of the century the study of Anglo-Saxon was largely a lost cause in Oxford, but at the Society of Antiquaries it continued to be a subject of discussion for fruitful discussion. Saxon coins were regularly presented for inspection and Samuel Pegge was developing his arguments concerning the existence of a gold Saxon coinage.[61] George Vertue and Charles Lyttelton, who sponsored the engraving of the images from the Caedmon manuscript, also promoted the publication of engravings of what were taken to be Saxon buildings.[62] Rawlinson regularly produced Saxon charters, particularly illuminated ones, for the society's edification. There was a genuine zeal to proselytise on behalf of Saxon studies, as Daines Barrington enthused to his fellow member Samuel Pegge: 'I must own I cannot but think that every Saxon treatise be it of what kind it may should be published as the language can only be thoroughly understood from several such publications'.[63] Neither of these two had claims to any real competence in Anglo-Saxon, but between them they achieved the long-awaited publication of an edition of Alfred's Saxon translation of *Orosius* in 1773.[64]

Moreover, those who took up the study of Anglo-Saxon antiquities did not necessarily have the classical training of Oxford or Cambridge fellows, and in common with other branches of antiquarianism, it acquired a rather broader social basis and readership. One of the results of this shift in the centre of gravity was that there was mounting pressure for Saxon texts to be translated into English. It was increasingly a matter for regret, for example, that there were no Saxon-English dictionaries. The eventual publication of Edward Lye's dictionary, completed by Owen Manning, in 1772 was welcomed, but not without reservations.[65] Lye had insisted upon working in Latin, not least because he wished his work to be accessible to scholars in Scandinavia who were similarly working upon Gothic antiquities. Yet, however much in tune Lye may have been with the ethos of a cosmopolitan community of learning, his fellow antiquaries saw the need to secure Saxon studies upon a firmer footing in the English language as a more urgent priority. Foote Gower complained to Richard Gough: 'Old English Words themselves, or a literal English Translation of the Saxon Word tho' it was a bald One, wou'd have show'd us the real Meaning of this Saxon Word at the first light.'[66]

Not only was the custom of translation into Latin an obstacle to the growing numbers with an interest in antiquities but without facility in classical languages, it was also increasingly regarded as a distortion of the

Saxon language, whose idiom and peculiar beauty were lost when forced into the latinate mould, whilst the connections with the modern English tongue were obscured. The insistence upon translating into Latin had played into the hands of those, like Horace Walpole, who contemptuously dismissed the Anglo-Saxon language as unworthy of study: 'there never did exist a more barbarous Jargon than the Dialect, still venerated by Antiquaries and called Saxon'.[67] Walpole's sneering provoked some disquiet amongst other antiquaries: Richard Gough complained to Foote Gower that 'Mr Walpole has abused the Saxon language so grosly in his last publication'. He was even moved to give expression to his indignation in verse:

> Bid us recall the *Saxon* tongue, whose boast
> Is comprehensive phrase, which we have lost,
> Nor pithy sense it wants, nor nervous force,
> Tho' *Walpole* deem it dissonant and coarse.[68]

Gough aired these sentiments rather more publicly, if less poetically, in the preface of *Anecdotes of British Topography* (1768). 'A Saxon dictionary', he wrote, 'with a literal English version would contribute more than any thing to bring us acquainted with that language, which, however we have suffered it to be corrupted by the heterogeneous mixture of Latinisms, Gallicisms, and Scotticisms, is our mother tongue.'[69]

By 1797 such was the reaction against the earlier practice of Latin translations that Samuel Henshall, a clergyman and self-proclaimed expert in Saxon literature, was arguing that earlier antiquaries had been severely in error, due to their having pursued their study of Anglo-Saxon learning through the medium of Latin.[70] Building on the linguistic similarity between Saxon and the modern tongue, Henshall tried to persuade his readers that the Saxon language was far easier than the enormous and forbidding erudition of Hickes and Lye would suggest; the aspiring student, he suggested, should first become thoroughly acquainted with the characters and then begin with the Saxon Gospel of St John without any translation and pronounce the consonants of any word which was not understood distinctly. The English meaning of the word would thereby suggest itself. The fallibility of Henshall's approach was shown up in the highly critical review in the *Gentleman's Magazine* 1798, written by Gough with assistance from Charles Mayo, the first Rawlinson Professor of Anglo-Saxon. 'Mr H.', thundered Gough, 'has undertaken a task for which he is totally unqualified.' Such utterances provoked in turn a bitter response from Henshall. Yet, wrongheaded though Henshall may have been, his project is representative of a late eighteenth-century attitude which emphasised the relevance of the study of Anglo-Saxon to contemporary culture and for a non-specialist audience.[71]

Henshall's suggestions for the private study of Anglo-Saxon highlight another important aspect of Saxon antiquarian scholarship. Although in the heyday of Anglo-Saxon studies Edward Thwaites had prided himself on his clutch of students studying the language with him, it was essentially a subject which was acquired through private study.[72] Given that it effectively had no institutional presence, the numbers of those who acquired any proficiency in the Saxon language during the second half of the eighteenth century is extremely difficult to assess. The papers and correspondence of antiquaries, however, suggest that a reading knowledge, at least, was not such an uncommon acquisition. The grammars of Hickes and Elizabeth Elstob enabled those with sufficient interest to navigate their way through Saxon texts. Hickes's grammar was essentially a reading course for the autodidact, taking him (or her) through the grammar, then the Anglo-Saxon Gospels and then successively more complex texts. Shelton's English translation of Wotton's *Short View* was undertaken with the determination to encourage those who might be put off by the 'old dry stuff' of Saxon characters to apply themselves to the study of the Saxon language and its antiquities.[73] The anticipation with which Lye's dictionary was awaited shows that there was an interested constituency, albeit not very numerous.[74] Most of the century's noted Saxonists, including Edward Lye, were essentially autodidacts. Ralph Thoresby's contributions to *Britannia* mainly concerned Roman antiquities in the area, but the contact which it brought him with other Saxonists evidently inspired him to pursue these studies, the fruits of which were made evident in the much more detailed treatment he gave to Saxon material in *Ducatus Leodiensis.* His diary records the hours he spent in studying Saxon, under the tutelage of Hickes's grammar.[75] Whilst still apprenticed to a staymaker, George Ballard taught himself and his sister Elizabeth the Saxon language. Later in life he acted as mentor to his friend William Saunders, a physician, whose imagination had been captured by reading Saxon history and who longed to study it in the original.[76] Richard Gough had appealed to his close friend Foote Gower for guidance on the best Anglo-Saxon grammar to use (Gower's advice was the more user-friendly Elstob rather than Hickes). Although Gough always deprecated his own abilities, he was sufficiently competent to undertake a translation of the original version of the Anglo-Saxon Chronicle. His bequest of books to the Bodleian Library included nearly one thousand volumes on Saxon literature, which show clear evidence of his comparative method, being interleaved with his Latin translations.[77] Other antiquaries acquired their knowledge on an ad hoc basis. John Whitaker, the historian of Manchester, found his researches led him to the Anglo-Saxon charters and he taught himself Saxon in order to read the originals.[78] Samuel Baldock, who was making collections for the history of

Devon, undertook to learn it in order better to be able to judge the veracity of Gibson's translation of the Anglo-Saxon Chronicle.[79] The importance of the autodidactic tradition is demonstrated in the number of notable female Saxonists, from Elizabeth Elstob to Mrs Anne Schimmelpennick, whose progress in Saxon studies can be traced through her borrowings from Lichfield Cathedral Library, and Miss Ann Gurney, who completed a translation of the Anglo-Saxon Chronicle, which was printed, albeit not published, in 1819.[80]

Some of the weightiest achievements of antiquarian scholarship during this period were in the field of topographical and antiquarian literature and interest in Saxon antiquities is often evident in these publications, even if the period was not rich in the publication of Anglo-Saxon texts. The pursuit of local antiquities frequently confronted the local antiquary with the need for a working knowledge of Old English, whether as a means to elucidate the etymology of local placenames, or in order to decipher ancient charters which would clarify the changes in tenurial possession or the pattern of administrative boundaries. The basic text for all antiquarian topographers, *Britannia*, set a model in this respect: Camden had routinely given the Saxon for any placename and in many cases the Saxon etymology was often the only clue from which the aspiring antiquary could work in tracing out the history and antiquities of that period. The late seventeenth-century flowering of Anglo-Saxon scholarship was well represented in Gibson's 1695 edition of *Britannia*, both in terms of much more sophisticated etymological derivations and a fleshing out of the narrative of Saxon history which greater familiarity with the chronicles made possible. The 1722 edition went further and provided a list of common Saxon placenames and their meanings to help the amateur in the etymologies of his own locality.

William Nicolson, archdeacon and later bishop of Carlisle, who was one of the leading Saxonists, had undertaken the revisions for Northumberland. Today he is remembered for his *English Historical Library*, an early and very successful, historiographical and bibliographical guide for aspiring students of history and antiquities, but this was secondary to his role as mentor to northern antiquaries.[81] He assumed this role not simply as a means of exercising patronage, but because his abiding interest was in the history of the ancient kingdom of Northumbria. He had acquired the manuscripts of the seventeenth-century Cumbrian antiquary Thomas Machell, and had also made substantial collections himself, although he was never able to bring this cherished project to completion.[82] Northumbria was a creation of the Saxon period, one of the kingdoms of the Saxon heptarchy, and, although Nicolson planned to include British, Roman and Danish antiquities within his survey, it was in the Saxon period that the kingdom acquired its identity and its importance. Bede's *Ecclesiastical History*, one of the most important sources for the period, was first and foremost an ecclesiastical history of the Northumbrian kingdom. Ecclesiastical and political obligations of his own, however, checked the appearance of such a work. The recipient of many of Nicolson's letters, Ralph Thoresby, shared a similar regard for the Saxon period of history, as well as a high regard for the Venerable Bede and the piety of his Saxon forebears. In *Ducatus Leodiensis* this was given expression as a celebration of the victory of Christianity over the pagans in the north of England during the Saxon era. The Saxon presence in Yorkshire was believed to have left tangible remains, such as barrows, camps, coins and other artefacts, which fell within the antiquary's scope. In the absence of an Antonine Itinerary or more detailed information on the history of the Saxon polity, however, it was extremely difficult to fit these stray monuments of antiquities to any kind of chronological framework. This was where Thoresby was fortunate, in that Bede's history referred to specific locations, which Thoresby persuaded himself he had identified within the vicinity of Leeds.[83]

The conceptual and methodological framework which was adopted in most county histories, however, did not lend itself easily to the integration of such miscellaneous antiquities and curiosities with any kind of historical narrative. As a result, the narrative coverage of the Saxon period was often very brief, based entirely on secondary sources, or passed over in almost complete silence. Once Rapin's *History of England* was available in an English translation by 1731, this, along with one of the various editions of Asser's life of Alfred, provided a basic narrative outline for many topographical writers. The nature of the market for which the antiquaries were writing was equally important in determining the format and content of such volumes. The subscribers to county histories were the gentry whose education naturally equipped them to recognise and appreciate the remnants of Roman history in the vicinity. Their main interest, however, was generally in the account of the manors and estates; they looked to the county history to provide a delineation of the descent of property, accompanied by appropriate pedigrees and monumental epitaphs. For such readers, the key event in English history was the compilation of Domesday Book, which first gave evidence for the possession of property. The radical discontinuity which the Norman appropriation of the landed estates of the Saxon lords was believed to represent rendered the period prior to the Norman invasion of comparatively little interest to the property-holding elite.

For the county historian the most important aspect of the Saxon period was that this was the point at which the territorial divisions of the counties and the subdivisions within them were laid down. These were the administrative units which defined the sphere of gentry activity and provided the parameters through which they conceptualised their own place in the wider English state. It is very noticeable that although the historic continuity of the county and the administrative units of hundreds and tithings were important themes in antiquarian topographical literature, the Saxon kingdoms were seldom alluded to specifically. Their historical identity was very weak. William Nicolson and Ralph Thoresby were distinctly unusual in their explicit interest in the Northumbrian kingdom. By contrast, such was Francis Drake's disaffection from the Saxon period that he even ventured to dispute the orthodoxy that Alfred had established shires and counties in the country at large. These administrative divisions were, he argued, effected much later in the north of England. 'I shall not', he promised, 'trouble the reader with the lives of the *Northumbrian* Kings in the *Heptarchy*, any more than suits my purpose.'[84] The exception to this pattern was a city such as Winchester, whose identity was closely bound up with its status as the first capital of the united kingdom under Egbert, and with its association with Alfred, under whom the city 'daily advanced in greatness and popularity' and in whose time 'Winchester may be said to have arisen at the summit of her glory'.[85] Alfred's power base, the kingdom of Wessex, however, was barely mentioned. For the most part, such references as were made to the Anglo-Saxon kingdoms (beyond the recital of the internecine conflicts of the heptarchy) smack of literary affectation. Richard Gough informed William Cole that he was his only correspondent in the kingdom of the East Angles and referred to Thomas Pennant's journey from Chester to London as an excursion through the kingdom of Mercia.[86] William Stukeley, too, had a particular interest in the kingdom of Mercia; he liked to argue that his native town of Stamford was the ancient seat of Hengist and Horsa, who had laid the foundations of the 'potent Mercian kingdom'.[87] Northumbria and Mercia, rather than East Anglia or Wessex, appear to have enjoyed the strongest imaginative presence. It was only with the publication of Sharon Turner's *History of the Anglo-Saxons* (1799–1806), that local antiquaries and historians began to display a greater interest in the period of the Saxon heptarchy and were able to harness local patriotism to it. Under King Offa, wrote the Lincolnshire antiquary Adam Stark, Mercia reached the acme of its glory, and the capital of that kingdom was Lincoln,[88] whilst Alexander Hay, author of the *History of Chichester*, claimed that Chichester had been the metropolis of the South Saxons; that Caedmon had been a South Saxon poet and that the kingdom of the South Saxons, though the least and weakest in the heptarchy, was the most civilised and the most enlightened.[89]

Some antiquarian topographers were ambitious to consolidate and extend their knowledge of the Saxon presence in England and realised the importance of fieldwork in so doing. It was accepted that Saxons frequently adopted Roman camps and settlements for their own use, and modified them. The old rules that square camps were Roman and Saxon camps were round had been refined; not least because antiquaries had realised that the Saxons often reused what had been Roman sites. It was also accepted that, prior to their conversion to Christianity, the Saxons had engaged in pagan rites of burial, such as burning bodies. John Watson, another fellow of the Society of Antiquaries, similarly held that it was time to devote more systematic attention to the mapping out of Saxon as opposed to Roman remains. 'It is something remarkable', he remarked, 'that the general plan of the Roman military stations in this island is better known than those of the Saxons and Danes.'[90] He called for better searches to be made and the findings to be made public; but here again the would-be Saxonist encountered obstacles. Even distinguishing Saxon burial urns from Roman was problematic, due to a predisposition amongst antiquaries to attribute antiquities indiscriminately to the Roman period.[91] Antiquaries professed themselves uncertain as to what they should be looking for. George North, a numismatist, longed for a publication that would illustrate specimens of Saxon monuments, camps and buildings which could be use for reference, for 'I own I do not yet, with all my enquiries, for a certainty, know how to distinguish a Saxon camp.'[92] North's diffidence stemmed at least in part from his innate suspicion of the Saxons, who had destroyed so much of the noble magnificence of Roman civilisation, but it is also symptomatic of the nervousness which antiquaries felt when approaching the Saxon era, for which they had so little textual material to guide them.

A notable milestone in identifying Saxon remains was reached by James Douglas, a military chaplain, natural historian and antiquary, whose interest in barrows had first been excited by the excavations of the military engineers behind Chatham Lines. Douglas's insistence upon first-hand observation and systematic excavation, and his comparison of different types of tumulus, enabled him to draw up a more sophisticated typology of tumuli than any previously produced. According to this typology, he was able to claim with some confidence that the small conical barrows to be found in parts of Kent, the southern counties and other parts of England were Saxon.[93] William Cunnington, who excavated barrows around Wiltshire under the patronage of Sir Richard Colt Hoare, also developed considerable expertise in Saxon barrows, distinguishing between the camps of the 'barbarous' Saxons of the fifth century and those of the civilised (and Christian) Saxons of the ninth and tenth centuries.[94] The increasing sophistication of archaeological fieldwork provided important confirmation and illustration for a more sympathetic treatment of the Saxon era, which laid greater emphasis upon the gradual evolution of a more civilised culture rather than seeing it purely in terms of undifferentiated cruelty and barbarism.

There were no Saxon roads or Saxon camps to match those of Roman Britain, but the position was rather better with respect to coins, that other staple of eighteenth-century antiquaries. This was an area where contemporaries were confident that considerable progress had been made. There were always some who found it hard to credit that the arrangement of Saxon coins in the manner of tables of classical coinage was a worthwhile exercise, assuming that a coherent system of coinage was beyond the barbarous state of civilisation to which the Saxons belonged. Ralph Thoresby's son, responding to Samuel Pegge's inquiries about the weight of the Saxon coins in his father's collection, expressed himself somewhat surprised, given that 'I apprehend our Antiquaries thought those Antient Minters too inaccurate to build any hypothesis upon their Authority'.[95] But the publication of tables of coinage was an essential step towards gathering further knowledge, as the engravings facilitated comparison between scattered collections and thereby consolidated whatever information was available. Gibson's edition of *Britannia* in 1695 had included a new section on the Saxon coinage drawn up by Obadiah Walker, matching that which Camden had originally compiled to illustrate the Roman coinage. It was the first study of its kind to be published, yet the deficiencies were soon recognised and Sir Andrew Fountaine composed a much more comprehensive and satisfactory account, 'Numismata Anglo-Saxonica et Anglo Danica breviter illustrata' for Hickes's *Thesaurus.* Building on these achievements, one of the earliest projects initiated by the Society of Antiquaries was to plan a table of the English coinage through all its different ages. This grandiose scheme was never brought to completion. Other efforts, however, were made to provide a comprehensive account of the Saxon coinage. The latter part of the period saw publications by William Clarke, Thomas Snelling and Rogers Ruding to this end. The efforts of Walker and Fountaine had laid out a framework from which to proceed in the *Thesaurus*, but, as William Clarke pointed out, it would be absurd to think that the coinage remained unchanged during such a long period. In his *Connexion of the Roman, Saxon and English Coins* (1767), Clarke endeavoured to chart some of the changes which had taken place, and, in consequence, his account of the coinage amounted to considerably more than a simple listing, offering extended comments upon the Saxon polity and society. His argument was open to criticism: 'he had built a system and was too considerable a man to submitt it to criticism', but he and others ensured that the history of Saxon coinage remained an area of debate and active research.[96] Samuel Pegge's essays on Saxon coinage had also given rise to a lively correspondence on the subject of Saxon coins and the interest generated had apparently caused a dramatic inflation in the availability and price of such coins.[97] Gough's annotated copy of his 1789 edition of *Britannia* bears testimony to the confidence which antiquaries felt in their own progress in the science of Saxon numismatics: 'As this branch of our numismatic science has been more fully understood since Mr Walker, Mr Thoresby, or Dr Wotton commented on those tables ... it has been thought not amiss to annex a series of such Saxon coins whose genuineness may be depended upon.'[98]

Given the costs of engraving plates and the somewhat specialised market for such publications, only a fraction of the researches and collections of the eighteenth-century numismatists was ever published, and these men collectively embodied far more knowledge concerning Anglo-Saxon England than their publications would suggest. Richard Southgate, who owned one of the most significant private collections of Saxon and Danish coins, had planned a history of that period based upon their coinage, but died before he could complete the project, as did Charles Combe, who had planned a similar work.[99] Rogers Ruding, a clergyman from Surrey, was more fortunate in this respect and managed to bring his history, *Annals of the Coinage of Britain*, to completion. Ruding's work marks a significant departure from previous numismatic histories in its methodological approach and reflects the transformation in historical sympathy towards the Saxons which had taken place over the previous century. He used numismatic evidence to argue that the Saxons were more advanced than commonly given credit for, rejecting the theory that they had only acquired their knowledge of minting and coinage from contact with the Romans. A knowledge of Saxon coins not only assisted in establishing the identity and chronology of the Saxon kings, it contributed to the knowledge of dress, buildings and the 'manners and customs' of the times. Other sources, such as the illustrations from illuminated manuscripts, could be used in a similar way. It was for this reason that Charles Lyttelton was keen to sponsor engravings of the illustrations from the Junius Caedmon manuscript: regardless of the value of the text itself such illustrations would 'point out the mode of Building, Habits, etc of that age'.[100] It remains the case, however, that without the collections of Combe, Southgate and others, fully acknowledged in the preface, Ruding's synthesis would not have been possible.[101] The study of coins was always redolent of the antiquary's study and did not lend itself to more general consumption, but material of this kind could relieve the dryness with which Saxon studies were often associated, and the visual legibility of coins could break down the barriers to understanding of the Saxon period engendered by unfamiliarity with the Saxon scripts.

The full potential of this approach was realised by the engraver turned antiquary, Joseph Strutt, whose work acquired a far larger circulation than the specialist publications produced by the Society of Antiquaries or its fellows. In the course of his career Strutt set out to illustrate the antiquities of English history largely through engravings of images taken from manuscripts in the British Museum. Although Strutt's volumes were not confined to the Anglo-Saxon era, he became particularly renowned for his illustrations of this period, not least because there was so little material published upon the subject against which his publications could be compared. Strutt recognised that the problematic lack of materials and the consequent narrative uncertainty had largely contributed to the scholarly neglect of the Anglo-Saxon period. As an artist and engraver, rather than a professed scholar, he was representative of the trend towards antiquarian works which appealed to a broader readership, and he was determined to make an apparently unappealing subject accessible to the generality of readers. The letterpress was entirely reliant upon secondary literature, but the illustrations, which lay at the heart of his publications, were drawn from his own researches amongst the manuscripts in the Harleian and Cottonian collections. Strutt brought before a wider public the richness of the art and culture of the Saxons and demonstrated how such visual sources could be exploited for histories of the 'manners and customs'. He covered not just victories and defeats of warfare, but also the weapons used by Saxons and their design. Architecture was an important theme, but, as well as the conventional surveys of public buildings of churches and castles, he also described the domestic housing of ordinary Saxons. Costume and dress were discussed at some length – this being a topic which particularly lent itself to study through illustrated manuscripts, and from the analysis of dress Strutt ventured further to discuss the domestic employment of Saxon women. From scrutinising the depiction of feasts and banquets in the illuminated manuscripts, he was able to sketch the outlines of Saxon dietary and culinary practice. Even the coiffure and the bathing habits of the Saxons fell within his purview. Understated and diffident though his scholarship was, Strutt's freedom from the preconceptions of classical scholarship enabled him to follow a much more wide-ranging approach, in which he combined close observation of the manuscripts with remarkably perceptive insights into their interpretation. His recurrent theme, through all his publications, was the need for a greater recognition of the Saxon cultural and social achievement, which was the basis of the English nation. Even a partial examination of their drawings, he argued, would demonstrate evidence of 'natural genius under some degree of cultivation, and convince us that more than the mere dawn of civilisation had taken place among them'.[102] Publications such as

James Macpherson's heated denunciation of Saxon barbarity in the *Introduction to the History of Great Britain and Ireland* (1771), which was making its impact just when Strutt embarked upon his project, can only have fuelled his endeavours to cast the Saxon period in a more favourable light.

Strutt was not alone in defending the claims of the Saxons to a more advanced state of civilisation. He was a product of, and contributed to, a gradual shift in sentiment towards the Anglo-Saxons which was characteristic of the later eighteenth and early nineteenth centuries. It would have been impossible to challenge the assumption that Saxon society was in some measure rude and backward. The Saxons were unquestionably rooted at a primitive stage in mankind's progression from barbarism to civilisation. There was scope for modification, however, and with the rise of primitivism a new value could be placed on simplicity and a lack of refinement. The dominance which Roman remains were able to exercise over antiquarian imaginations, although strong, was becoming less invincible.[103] Britain's own imperial status, dwarfing that of Rome, combined with a stronger sense of national confidence and identity, served to temper the earlier Augustan admiration of Rome.[104] The inherent tension between admiration for the Romans as the bringers of civilisation and the knowledge that they had enslaved and weakened the indigenous British population had never been resolved, and it was awarded greater prominence as historians and antiquaries became more confident in asserting the claims of native traditions. The interest in Saxon history and antiquities undoubtedly drew strength from the same vogue for primitivism and search for national origins which nurtured interest in ancient British and Celtic antiquities. Whilst the reputation of Anglo-Saxons could never match that of the Romans in the cultivated arts, the balance began to shift in their favour, as admiration for the moral virtues of liberty, valour and simplicity grew in reaction to the formal classicism of Roman civility. By the end of the century the Saxons were being awarded greater credit for having purged the nation of the corruption and decadence of the late Roman presence in Britain. They were rehabilitated as the shadowy precursors to the freeborn Englishman of the eighteenth century, with a balanced constitution to match that of the king in parliament. Bede's reputation underwent a similar transformation, from being regarded as a credulous monkish chronicler to a historian employing high standards of scholarship, and a more reliable source than the Roman historians.[105] John Spelman's life of Alfred remained one of the standard works on Saxon history, but challengers appeared, written in a rather easier style for the eighteenth-century readership and reflecting the increasingly positive and more fully informed evaluation of Saxon history. Interest in Alfred was no longer simply a question of Alfredian hagiography, but was broadening out into a much more inclusive interpretation of Saxon society. John Spelman had suggested that the only positive aspect of the Saxon heptarchy was that that they 'did not more wast and consume, every one the Potency of his Neighbour, than corrupt and ruin the Manners of their own People'.[106] Alexander Bicknell, however, the author of an enormously popular *Life of Alfred*, acknowledged that the polity and civilisation of the Romans had been lost, but put much greater emphasis on the fact that the Saxons had brought with them a considerable store of military knowledge from their native country. Since Germany, where they originated, was never totally conquered by the Romans, their courage and skill in war must have been formidable.[107]

If the cultural climate of the late 1770s was becoming more sympathetic to Anglo-Saxon antiquities, by the 1790s the tenor of contemporary comment had discernibly changed and become more positive. As Richard Gough set about the revisions of *British Topography* for a third edition in the final years of the century, at the passage where he had originally lamented the failure of Rawlinson's efforts to encourage the study of Saxon antiquities at Oxford, he glossed it with the comment that it was 'now just beginning to operate again'.[108] Gough looked back on the recent works which had helped to stimulate an interest in the Saxon period. Publications on architecture had heightened awareness of the Saxon achievement, and moreover had highlighted the extent to which the Saxon era encompassed significant and identifiable changes in the society and polity of England; it was far from being a period of unremitting bloodshed as was often imagined. A more tangible indication of this quickening of interest was that the Rawlinson chair in Anglo-Saxon was actually filled for the first time, by Charles Mayo in 1795. Mayo does not occupy a position of importance today in the pantheon of Old English scholars, but he clearly had some claims to the position – beyond the fact that he met the directive of Rawlinson's will that the first occupant should be a St John's man. Mayo corresponded with Gough on matters of Anglo-Saxon literature and influenced a promising young scholar at St John's, Henry Ellis, to pursue Saxon studies. Ellis spent much of his time in the manuscript collections at Bodley, where Rawlinson's collections were still uncatalogued, following up inquiries from Richard Gough. 'Saxon is in a progressive State', he informed Gough in 1797, 'Professor Mayo and myself are now transcribing one of Ballard's Bodleian Manuscripts entitled "*Flores soliloquorum divi Augustini &c*" translated by King Alfred.'[109] He also embarked upon the collation of three versions of the Anglo-Saxon Chronicle which he had identified in the Bodleian, in preparation for a new edition which would provide an English translation, but left to take up a more remunerative post at the British Museum before it was completed. Ellis carried his interest in Saxon antiquities with him, however, and in 1802 was writing to Gough of his plans for 'Anecdotes of Saxon literature', drawing on the papers and collections of 'Hickes, Thwaites, Nicholson, Wanley, Gibson, Junius, Smith, the Elstobs, and twenty others'.[110]

By now the process of reshaping the Saxons as the Teutonic forebears of the English nation was well under way and the standing of Saxon history and antiquities was in the ascendant, as evidenced by the success of Sharon Turner's two-volume *History of the Anglo-Saxons* (1799–1806), which quickly became the standard history for that period.[111] Turner filled the gap identified by Gough in 1768 for a connected history of the Saxon period, drawing heavily on charters, Saxon poetry and other manuscript sources in the British Museum, as well as the material published in the earlier part of the century, to give depth and breadth to the traditionally cursory accounts of the Anglo-Saxon polity. The *History of the Anglo-Saxons*, like Edward Gibbon's *Decline and Fall*, whose stately epiphrases Turner attempted without any great degree of success to emulate, was conceived upon a broad and comprehensive framework, offering a judicious account of the Saxons which broke with the stereotypical image of the period as one of warfare and barbarism. A strong theme of steady progress towards civilisation, in response to the influence of Rome and Christianity, provided the framework. The individual Saxon kingdoms and their rulers began to assume characters, rather than simply being names in a litany of warring factions. Alfred was still the embodiment of wise kingship, but favours amongst the Saxon monarchs were spread rather more widely, so that other rulers were allowed to exhibit some of the famed qualities of the Saxons that had traditionally been projected exclusively onto Alfred. The Saxons were shown to be imbued with the spirit of freedom and justice, and to have evolved a form of representative government and constitutional monarchy. In the second volume, which dealt with the 'manners and customs', Turner showed considerable ingenuity in exploiting sources such as wills and charters, as well as the illuminated illustrations to manuscripts, to garner details on the lives, clothing, and even cultural practices of the Saxons, gradually reinforcing the argument for a steady progress through the Saxon era towards civility, refinement and politeness, which set them apart from other Gothic nations.

Turner was the first antiquary to explore fully the manuscript sources available in the British Museum; he also drew heavily on the work of Joseph Strutt, particularly in the second volume, and was clearly following the latter's example in using manuscript illustrations as source material. He turned to the surviving examples of Saxon poetry and was the first English antiquary to study the *Beowulf* poems in any detail, arguing that the poems contained much information on battles, campaigns, warriors and kings which was otherwise lost to memory.[112] Moreover, unlike the poems of Ossian or Chatteron's Rowley forgery, these were authentic survivals rather than dubious 'discoveries'. Turner's appraisal of the potential inherent in Saxon poetry as a historical source showed the influence of the Welsh bardic scholars such as David Williams, whose publications he also cited, blending two antiquarian traditions which had threatened to diverge. The Welsh Triads, he argued, provided a glimpse into the first era of the Saxon invasions when the nation was still peopled by Britons. Turner's emphasis on the value of poetry as a means of studying the past was nothing new, but his widely accessible *History of the Anglo-Saxons* gave additional currency amongst a general readership to the arguments for the relative civilisation and culture of that society.[113]

Turner's emphasis on primary sources was scholarly, and gave him impeccable antiquarian credentials, but obscured the extent to which some of the issues he aired had engaged the minds of antiquaries during the intervening period, whilst setting off his own achievements all the more clearly. His footnotes were replete with references to manuscripts in the Cottonian Library and to Wilkins's collection of Anglo-Saxon laws, but there were scarcely any references to the publications that had struggled to deal with matters of Saxon history in the period between Smith's edition of Bede and Joseph Strutt's publications. The issues he raised, such as Saxon literacy, the nature of the coinage or the composition of the Witangemot, had engaged the attention of antiquaries during the eighteenth century. It might be objected that the exchange between Pegge and Barrington in *Archaeologia* on the subject of Anglo-Saxon viticulture, for example, was hardly representative of the highest standards of antiquarian scholarship, but such publications were representative of the gradual shift towards a more positive evaluation of Saxon society, upon which Turner was able to build.[114] He was not the first by any means to make the case for a more sympathetic and nuanced account of the Saxon period; an argument which had already been expressed with particular force in the field of architectural antiquities.[115]

A substantial element of Turner's second volume was devoted to a discussion of Saxon poetry and literature, which he analysed not just as a historical source, but as a form of literature in its own right. John Conybeare, who occupied the Rawlinson chair of Anglo-Saxon from 1808 to 1812, made an important contribution to establishing the study of Saxon literature as a discipline. After nearly a century during which Saxonists had inhabited the shadow cast by Hickes and Wanley, he set out to distance himself from those scholars by demonstrating some of the former's shortcomings. Hickes, he claimed, had been guilty of judging Saxon poetry by the conventions of classical literature, and had thereby failed to grasp the internal patterns of rhyme and alliteration which gave it its structure and its beauty. Meanwhile, Wanley's treatment of the Exeter Manuscript was, he argued, scanty and inaccurate; he pressed the case for further study of the existing manuscripts.[116] Conybeare's essays embody a sea change in the attitudes of antiquaries. Rather than seeing himself as embattled and struggling to maintain a tradition inherited from Hickes and Wanley, Conybeare had the confidence to distance himself from their achievement and to point out the deficiencies in their scholarship. Nor were his the first essays to be published in *Archaeologia* on the subject. In the same volume Robert Willan had written on the poetic culture of the Saxons, directly challenging those who mistakenly supposed that 'the conquering Saxons attended only to the din of arms and operations of war'. Rather, he claimed, even as early as the seventh century, the poets were highly valued and had 'obtained great celebrity'.[117] Meanwhile, Conybeare's predecessor in the chair of Anglo-Saxon, James Ingram (1803–8), was to publish the first revised edition of the Anglo-Saxon Chronicle with an English translation in 1823. It is at this point that the narrative of Old English scholarship is commonly allowed to recommence. Turner, Conybeare and Ingram were riding on the gathering swell of a wave which was to crest later in the Victorian period in the articulation of theories of Teutonic racial superiority. To leap from the world of Thwaites, Hickes and Wanley to that of Turner, Ingram and Conybeare, however, leaves much unexplained and unexplored.

The Saxons, however, were not the only Gothic race. They were one of a number of tribes who had, it was believed, emanated originally from Scythia, and inhabited northern Europe and Scandinavia.[118] To speak of Saxon antiquities and scholarship without reference to the broader scope of Gothic antiquities, as we have done so far, is something of a distortion, but reflects the Anglo-centric agenda of the English antiquaries. The Gothic nations comprehended the Germanic races (Saxons, Angles, Jutes, Friesians) and also those of Scandinavia, notably the Danes, who caused such disturbance to the Saxon kingdoms in the ninth and tenth centuries. The Celts, as we have seen, were an imprecise entity whose origins were hidden in obscurity. Similarly the term 'Goth' had been applied without distinction in the early modern period to describe any non-Roman nation. Considerable confusion reigned amongst authorities such as Philip Cluever, Johann Keysler, Simon Pelloutier and Paul Pezron as to the difference between Celts and Goths; the terms were used with little discrimination.[119] The contrast between Celts and Goths, however, was forcibly drawn for a non-specialist readership by Thomas Percy, who himself was alerted to this misapprehension by the Welsh antiquary Evan Evans.

In the preface to his translation of Paul-Henri Mallet's *Northern Antiquities* (1770), Percy was at pains to correct Mallet, who had indiscriminately referred to all European peoples as Goths.[120] The initial grounds for distinction were based upon the difference in language, but were also elaborated to include literature and culture – which was of particular importance in the context of antiquarian research. The Goths, claimed Percy, were a literate people, who were 'addicted' to writing and were free from the superstition and mystery of the Druids, who had dominated Celtic culture. English, he added, was very like German, the modern descendant of the Gothic people, and most unlike Welsh – the language of the surviving Celts.[121]

The Goths comprised both Saxons and Danes, which in turn subsumed Norwegian and Swedish peoples, and could be taken to cover Icelandic antiquities as well. The term Viking was not one which eighteenth-century antiquaries would have recognised, although *vikingr* was beginning to acquire common currency by the turn of the century.[122] The traditional image of the Viking with horned helmet and long boat, sailing forth to pillage, plunder and rape, was a nineteenth-century invention. English antiquaries were the heirs of the Saxon chroniclers, who, from Bede onwards, saw the Danes as 'the other', the *pagani* who destroyed Lindisfarne, who brought terror and destruction, imposing barbaric practices which further delayed the glimmerings of civilisation which Alfred had begun to nurture. 'The Danes perpetrated such a scene of villainy', wrote Francis Wise, 'as is scarce to be parallel'd in the stories of the most savage nations.'[123] They were a rude and illiterate people who corrupted the Anglo-Saxon language.[124] The raids recorded in Bede or the Anglo-Saxon Chronicle were an essential ingredient in the narrative of British and Irish history, but beyond that the Danes themselves attracted even less attention than the Saxons. The record of the Danish presence in England survived in far fewer manuscripts or inscriptions, and antiquaries had little confidence in distinguishing Danish from Saxon camps and burials. They had, as Francis Wise dryly noted, left a large field for the antiquary to expatiate on.[125] Ralph Thoresby's museum, which comprised one of the largest private coin collections in the country, numbered only one coin with a 'true' runic inscription, and this, claimed Thoresby, was unique in Europe.[126] As interest in the Anglo-Saxon period increased amongst English antiquaries and historians in the latter part of the century and bolder claims were made for Saxon civility and culture, the Danes were cast in a correspondingly more negative role, absorbing all the objectionable traits which formerly had been associated with Saxons, Angles, Goths, Vandals, Danes and Norwegians alike. The Danish invasions, claimed Samuel Squire in his analysis of the Anglo-Saxon constitution, had overturned the regular and beautiful order of government.[127] The atrocities they committed in Northumberland, wrote William Hutchinson, were too painful to describe. Nor did he allow them any part in the heritage of the Northumbrian people, tracing the descent of the present inhabitants only from the Saxon heroes who had resisted the Danish onslaught.[128] Sharon Turner hardly refined this view, commenting that 'the ferocity and useless cruelty of this race of beings almost transcend belief'. In a telling passage on the Anglo-Saxon kingdom of Northumbria, he began to adopt the term 'English' as soon as he started to recount the horrors of the Danish invasions. The English were forged from the Anglo-Saxons as soon as an external threat – 'the other' – in the form of the Danes appeared.[129] The fact that they were assumed to be amongst the last nations of Europe to adopt Christianity seemed further proof of their depravity. The one Dane who came off with any credit was Canute the Great, a man with deeply barbarian elements to his character, but who at least showed some personal improvement during his own life, committing his worst excesses early in his career; the implication being that such improvement was due only to contact with his more civilised Saxon neighbours.[130] The Danes became the scapegoats who were made to assume the worst sins of earlier ages. In the climate of evangelical and moral reform in the late eighteenth century this kind of language became more marked, with a particular emphasis on their excessive drinking.[131]

The standard narratives of English history did not allow the Danes a formative role in any of the key areas of historical interest: they did not bring with them Christianity, the arts, a liberal constitution or even the English language. The Danes were so deeply loathed by the English, it was said, that their settlement made little lasting impact. Their presence was only acknowledged in the commemoration of their departure in the hoketyde festivities which still survived in attenuated form in some of the midlands towns.[132] The problem of language was of equal significance. If Saxon was hard to master for scholars trained in the traditions of classical humanism, the Norse or runic tongues were even further beyond the reach of most antiquaries, and presented a commensurately greater obstacle to the study of Danish antiquities. George Hickes had insisted that the antiquary should not stop at Anglo-Saxon but should go on, and study the other northern languages, but few antiquaries lived up to this recommendation. There were exceptions: according to his sister Elizabeth's testimony, William Elstob had mastered some of the Gothic tongues. Edward Lye prepared an edition of the Gothic Gospels and collated runic poetry with the Latin translations for Thomas Percy. His proposals for the Saxon dictionary promised subscribers an account of Saxon surnames and rules for distinguishing them from those of Danish and Norman extraction.[133]

Other Saxonists, however, openly admitted their limitations and confessed the runic inscriptions which were occasionally found on crosses and other monuments beyond them. When the Danish antiquary and state archivist Grimr Thorkelin came to Britain in 1786, he was greeted warmly by the antiquarian community, given membership of both the English and the Scottish Societies of Antiquaries and allowed free access to the British Museum, where he angled unsuccessfully for the appointment to the vacant keepership. Hopes that he would unlock the mysteries of the runic inscriptions on monuments such as the Ruthwell cross, however, were disappointed. 'He seems to think no Runic monument out of his country of any consequence', complained Gough to George Paton.[134]

Even less was known, therefore, about the Danes than about the Saxons and the framework around which Danish antiquities could be arranged was extremely sketchy. Progress in studying Danish antiquities amounted largely to a narrowing down of what could actually be identified as such. Popular tradition, upon which antiquaries relied for much of their evidence, was replete with stories of the atrocities committed by the marauding Danes, which in turn served to explain a place-name, the appearance of a barrow or the presence of a castle.[135] The influence of Danish antiquaries such as Ole Worm and Thomas Bartholine upon English antiquaries in the seventeenth century served only to confirm this tendency to attribute monuments and objects which otherwise defied identification as 'Danish'. Worm's *Danicorum monumentorum libri sex* (1643) had become established as part of the antiquarian canon by the end of the seventeenth century, and enjoyed a ubiquitous presence in the footnotes of antiquarian publications throughout the eighteenth century.[136] Thus Walter Charleton had argued that the victorious Danes erected Stonehenge for the inauguration of their supreme commander as king of England,[137] but eighteenth-century antiquaries, notably William Stukeley, made the British construction of this and other similar monuments such as the Rollright Stones an orthodoxy. James Douglas, one of the leading excavators of barrows in the later eighteenth century, was able to demonstrate the fallacy by which many other monuments, barrows, obelisks had been attributed to the Danes.[138] It was one thing, however, to establish what were not Danish antiquities: positive identification proved a rather more problematic objective, and often mistaken. Papers presented to the Society of Antiquaries rarely addressed the subject of Danish (as opposed to Saxon) antiquities, and when they did so, it was generally to admit the almost total absence of knowledge. A horn, a camp, a barrow or a series of coins were assigned to the Danish era on purely textual evidence rather than from any confidence in identifying the attributes of a Danish burial or features of Danish antiquities.[139] Samuel Gale's paper on the ancient Danish horn at York was written from the perspective of a virtuoso: the carved ivory horn was of interest because of its aesthetic, surface qualities. The paper soon veered off onto a tangent discussing the practice of investiture and donation (to which it was assumed the horn referred) rather than the horn itself.[140] Arguments were even constructed to explain the absence of the kind of antiquities with which antiquaries were used to work, such as funerary monuments. Daily life was too uncertain, explained Smart Lethieullier to Charles Lyttelton, for thoughts of perpetuating a person's memory after death to evolve. Indeed, it was only in the area of numismatics that antiquaries could venture an opinion with any degree of confidence. Gustavus Brander, whose Swedish origins ensured a personal interest in Danish antiquities, presented a paper to the society discussing the commercial links between the Saxons and the Danes and Swedes, based upon the evidence of Saxon coins in Sweden. But such insights could not be integrated into a history of Britain in which the Danes were hostile invaders, and the implications of the paper remained unexplored.[141]

By the end of the eighteenth century there was considerably more interest in the Nordic ancestors of the English, even if knowledge and understanding of Danish antiquities or familiarity with the Norse language had barely progressed amongst most antiquaries. All these elements were the beneficiaries of the general revival of interest in septentrional society that was a marked feature of northern European culture in the latter part of the century. Nordic poems were admired for their primitivism, the nobility of emotions and their sublime grandeur and simplicity, in the same way that the Ossianic literature was lauded. Indeed the timing of the publication of Thomas Gray's *Norse Odes* (written in 1761 but not published until 1768) and Thomas Percy's *Five Runic Pieces* (1763) can only be understood in terms of a Gothic response to the Celtic *Fragments of Antient Poetry*. Gray and Percy together inspired a considerable sub-genre which took themes from Norse history or mythology as its subject.[142] Horace Walpole professed himself to be 'a perfect hermit … and buried in Runic poetry and Danish Wars' and Richard Gough described the avidity with which all northern literature was being received in England to George Paton in Edinburgh.[143] It took considerably longer for Saxon poetry to be appreciated, due not least to the opinion expressed by Thomas Warton in his highly influential *History of English Poetry* that it was constituted of nothing but religious rhapsodies, and therefore did not merit consideration.[144]

The visit of the Danish King Christian VII in 1768 was an additional factor in giving all things Nordic, including literature, a temporary fashionable cachet, and occasioned closer links between the two countries, diplomatically and culturally. Gray's *Norse Odes* were published in that same year. The heroism of the ancient Scandinavians was celebrated in the *London Magazine* of 1770, whilst Percy's translation of Mallet's *Northern Antiquities* provided readers with an interpretation of Gothic history which claimed superior antiquity for Gothic culture and learning, and located the origins of chivalry in a Gothic past. The Danes were depicted as courageous and possessing a stoicism in the face of death which seemed to match that of classical antiquity, whilst their belief in an afterlife in Valhalla could be seen as anticipating the Christian doctrine of life after death. Poets such as Anna Seward increasingly turned to Nordic themes for inspiration as material from the sagas were made available in English by the Icelandic scholar Grimr Thorkelin and the Scottish scholar James Johnstone in publications such as *Anecdotes of Olave the Black* (1780), *Haco's Expedition* (1782) *Antiquitates celto-scandicae* (1786).[145] In the heroic myths of the Saxons and the Danes, wrote Thomas Burgess, later to be bishop of St Davids, 'we find the fierce spirit of the northern genius combined and tempered with the most enthusiastic zeal of gallantry and courtesy'.[146] Northern literature offered a roundabout means by which English antiquaries could establish an oral tradition to match those of Wales, Scotland and Ireland: the Danish scalds, it was argued, were the ancestors of the minstrels of the medieval period, from whom in turn the literary tradition of Chaucer and English vernacular poetry derived.[147] Important though this literary interest was in breaking down the perception of the Danes (and the Saxons) as rude and barbarous, it ultimately represented only a superficial acquaintance with the period, conditioned by the demands of the reading public for sublimity and romance in poetry. Thorkelin's plans to publish in English a series of works on Icelandic laws, poetry and sagas with a dictionary and a grammar came to nothing. No publisher was willing to take it on.[148]

English antiquaries were aware of the close connection between the Scandinavian, German and English languages, but were almost entirely reliant upon Latin and English translations of Icelandic verse.[149] Although English antiquaries regularly made references to the work of Scandinavian scholars who had published extracts in translation from Norse poems and sagas, such as Ole Worm's *Runer* (1636) or Thomas Bartholine's *Antiquitates danicae* (1689), there was little first-hand familiarity with their works and no attempt to edit or translate them from the Icelandic for an English market until William Herbert's *Select Icelandic Poetry*, published in 1804.[150] Sharon Turner devoted more attention to the history of the Danes and the *vikingr* or sea pirates who had ravaged the Saxon polity, using the Icelandic material in translation, but there is no evidence that he could read any of the so-called Gothic tongues. The use to which he put these sources was largely limited to elaborating upon the depravity of the Danes and their comparative lack of civility and politeness in comparison with the Christian Saxons. Only one antiquary, William Drake, pursued the evident linguistic proximity between the English and the Scandinavian languages with any rigour. He identified a close relationship between English, specifically the Yorkshire dialect, and Icelandic. Refining upon the thesis put forward by Mallet in *Northern Antiquities* for the essentially Gothic origins of English, Drake argued that the British or Celtic language bore little relation to modern English, save the predictable borrowings resulting from long years of proximity. The origins of English were to be found in Gothic (meaning Icelandic and Scandinavian) rather than the Saxon tongues.[151]

Northern antiquities were of rather more direct bearing in Scotland, where a quickening of interest in northern, and particularly Norwegian and Icelandic, is more readily identifiable. Even before the issue of Celtic or Gothic origins became so sharply contested, Scottish antiquaries in the late seventeenth and early eighteenth centuries had been aware of the close connections between the antiquities of Scandinavia and their own country, particularly in the remoter areas of the north and the Orkneys and Shetlands, where the language was audibly related to that of Iceland and Norway.[152] The islands had fallen under Norwegian rule between the tenth and eleventh centuries, and these northern regions bore the evidence of the feuding and conflicts which had marked the gradual withdrawal of Norwegian influence from the area.[153] The histories of the kingdom of Norway, compiled by the Icelandic antiquary Torfaeus for the Danish king Frederick III in the seventeenth century, covered the period during which Scotland was part of a Scandinavian kingdom and offered, as one antiquary put, it 'probably the best, and only authentic record, of transactions in the north that is now to be found'.[154]

Initially much of the interest in northern antiquities in Scotland was stimulated by the inquiries of English antiquaries. Thomas Pennant, whose published tours in Scotland did more to awaken English antiquaries to the existence of Scottish antiquities than any other publication, was particularly interested in the Scandinavian and Icelandic connections with Scotland. He made a particular point of asking his correspondents to address the issue of Norwegian antiquities in the inquiries he circulated amongst them preparatory to his Scottish tours. George Low, his contact in the Orkneys, was provided with translations of Torfaeus and other texts in order to assist him in compiling an account of the antiquities.[155] Pennant's interest was informed less by his view of Celtic or Gothic Scotland – he did not, in fact, show much sensitivity to the difference between Celts and Goths in his writings – than by his own interest in Iceland, and Icelandic connections with Britain. His protégé Joseph Banks, with fellow naturalist Daniel Solander, had recently visited Orkney on returning from their voyage to Iceland, just before Pennant embarked upon his own Scottish tours. It seems probable that Banks was responsible for putting Pennant in touch with Low and alerting Pennant to the antiquarian and natural historical riches to be found in the Orkneys.[156] The success of Pennant's tours ensured that Orkneyan antiquities were brought before a wide reading public, and helped to nurture the growing interest in the Nordic antiquities of North Britain.

The Ossian phenomenon not only provoked interest in the Celtic antiquities of the Highlands, and the manners and customs of the ancient Gaels, but also sparked off a reaction from Lowlanders. Whilst aged Highlanders were pursued by hopeful literary antiquaries in the anticipation of securing some remnant of ancient Celtic poetry, the elderly inhabitants of Orkney were also being pressed to record their traditional verse for antiquarian collectors.[157] The most vocal of those who fought against the Celtic appropriation of Scotland's ancient past was John Pinkerton, who emphasised instead the Gothic heritage in the form of ancient Pictish invasions from Scandinavia.[158] The Picts were identified as the first invaders of Scotland during a Gothic diaspora, of which the Saxons and the Danes represented two different branches, and of which the final wave came about with the Norwegian forays of the ninth to eleventh centuries. There was an obvious political agenda here. In asserting the fundamental similarity of Lowland Scotland with England, Pinkerton gave a historical basis to an Anglo-British identity and demonstrated the superiority of the Lowlands over the Highlands.[159] Macpherson's Celtic civilisation was rebranded as Gothic; Rome itself, still the touchstone of antique achievements, was attributed Gothic rather than Celtic origins. The ancient monuments which, in the first waves of Ossian-inspired Celtic enthusiasm, had been designated the work of the Druids, were controversially reclaimed as monuments of the ancient Norse peoples, and their gods. The supposedly druidic stone circles which had been identified in Scotland were not, according to Pinkerton, the creation of Celts, but were Gothic courts of justice, and similar ones were to be found in Scandinavia and Iceland, where they had been used for that purpose in more recent times.[160] Unlike Sharon Turner, who shared many elements of this more positive assessment of Gothic history, Pinkerton refused to make unfavourable comparisons between the Romans and the Saxons: instead of denigrating a people who brought down the Roman Empire, he argued, they should rather be admired for their success in so doing and for their military skill and organisation. The negative perception of the

Goths handed down through history was the result of viewing their incursions solely from the perspective of histories written by those who belonged to the Roman imperium under attack: 'We look at the Goths thro a most false and imperfect medium, that of the Roman writers of a barbarous age.'[161]

In so far as the Saxons were a Gothic race, John Pinkerton also encouraged the study of their history. In a series of letters written to the *Gentleman's Magazine* upon the study of national history, he poured coruscating scorn on Hume and Bolingbroke, who could only see the utility of studying the recent past. 'One might as well think of building a house by beginning at the garretts', he sniffed. Of the seven topics he identified as being particularly in need of attention, three related to the Saxon period. Given the paucity of *written* sources, the significance of antiquarian studies was therefore all the greater.[162] Yet the Scottish antiquaries had no particular ties to the Saxons who were so crucial to the construction of the English national myth; whilst they had clearly settled in parts of Lowland Scotland, they could not embody the nation as they did in England. The Saxon period in Scottish history carried with it none of the political, legal and cultural implications for Scottish past and the Scottish sense of nationhood which it had in England.[163] As a consequence Scottish antiquaries tended to write in more general terms of 'northern' or 'Gothic' antiquities and were somewhat ahead of their English counterparts in exploring the potential of the northern literature of sagas and myths as a source for the history and antiquities of the early medieval period, which offered a much richer account of the history, customs and manners of Scotland and other northern nations than was to be gained from 'monkish chroniclers', who compiled their narratives from hearsay cloistered away in their cells.[164]

The closer connections with Scandinavia could also become another means of claiming a separate identity from England and for countering the implications of Romano-British antiquarianism, which tended to emphasise the historic unity of England and Scotland. Thorkelin had encouraged Robert Jamieson to develop his argument that Scottish was an older language than English, and that the Scots tongue was derived from Scandinavia rather than being introduced to Scotland from the south; a view which Jamieson presented in his etymological dictionary, published in 1808.[165] Scotland had no Anglo-Saxon constitution to rival that of England, but George Barry, who wrote a history of the Orkney Islands in 1805, argued that the inhabitants were descended from Icelanders, who displayed a wisdom which 'among a barbarous people, has seldom been equalled, and never surpassed, in forming themselves into a regular republic'. There is a danger in reading too much into Barry's celebration of Scotland's Icelandic connections: the location of a golden age of greater political freedom at some point in the past was a standard part of political discourse. It should also be recognised, however, that the more positive conceptualisation of the Vikings, which took place in the nineteenth century within the English antiquarian and literary tradition, was anticipated in Barry's comments.

The debate between Celtic and Gothic antiquities was equally divisive amongst Irish antiquaries, and, given the fraught history of Anglo-Irish and Protestant-Catholic relationships, carried even clearer political implications.[166] For Catholic antiquaries, who clung to the tradition of an island of 'saints and scholars', and a flowering of scholarship and civilisation which far outshone that to be found in any other part of post-Roman Europe, the impact of the Danish invasions in the ninth centuries could be seen only in the most destructive terms. These invasions were just the forerunner to the later incursions of the Anglo-Normans, themselves of Danish descent. Although Charles Vallancey, the leading figure amongst Irish antiquaries, was not himself a Catholic, he was regarded by the Protestant establishment as being too close to the Catholic cause. The thesis of Asiatic or Phoenician origins for Irish culture, which he did so much to promote, was explicitly connected with the Catholic camp. The Gothicists amongst the Irish antiquaries were led by Edward Ledwich, who combined a sceptical approach to conjectural antiquarianism with a mischievous delight in provoking those who carried the case for ancient Hibernian Celtic civilisation to extremes. Ledwich, therefore, combined his scorn for the dubious etymological reasoning employed by Vallancey in presenting the Celtic case with his own inclination to assert Gothic origins for the early history of Ireland. He, and other Protestant antiquaries, argued that the history of Danish (or Gothic) invasions went back much earlier than the ninth century, predating even the birth of Christ. This allowed Ledwich to co-opt the flourishing culture of the early Christian period within his Danish model.[167] The arrival of the Danes in the ninth century, representing one of the earliest fixed points in Irish history, could be presented in a far more positive light as one in a series of invasions from the East, which brought civilisation to the rude and barbaric native inhabitants of Ireland. The Anglo-Norman colonisation of the twelfth century was simply a part of a continuum of migrations from Britain to Ireland.[168] The Danes were a 'mercantile people' who brought commerce to the Irish shores, introduced a system of coinage and founded many of the Irish towns which would later flourish under the Protestant ascendancy.[169] The function of the famous round towers of Ireland was likewise contested between those who wished to locate them in the Milesian golden age and those who insisted that they were the construction of Danes or Ostmen.[170] In terms of studying Irish-Danish antiquities, the Irish contribution was, however, negligible and largely reliant on English and Scottish antiquarian sources.[171]

Whatever else, these debates were symptomatic of the closer interest being taken in the early medieval period, and its necessary significance for the formulation of notions of nationhood and identity. Narrow and pedantic though the concerns of the antiquary might be perceived to be in searching for evidence of coinage amongst the Britons, literacy amongst the Goths or minstrelsy amongst the Saxons, these were not just minor lines of inquiry but contributed to much broader debates concerning the origins of nations, their social organisation, their military capacity and their relative progress in the arts of civilisation. The shift in emphasis is made admirably clear in James Ingram's edition of the Anglo-Saxon Chronicle (1823), which responded to the plea issued by Gough back in 1768 for a vernacular as opposed to a Latin translation. Ingram introduced the Chronicle, along with Domesday Book, as one of the two 'substantial monuments' of England's early history. Every reader would find many interesting facts relative to the nation's architecture, coinage, commerce, naval and military glory, laws, liberty and religion. Without the Anglo-Saxon Chronicle, no person, however learned, could claim to be acquainted with the elements of English history and the British constitution. He compared the Chronicle, as a record of the history of a single people written in the vernacular, to the history of the Jews to be found in the Old Testament. Far from being a race of barbarian plunderers, unacquainted with the arts and sciences, the Saxons were, by implication, a chosen race, with rich traditions in architectural, commercial and political history. Saxon history and Saxon antiquities were no longer simply a context in which the political and religious debates of the time were contested. They had become the basis from which to construct a national identity as 'the faithful depository of our national idiom'.[172]

7

The Middle Ages

Eighteenth-century attitudes to the middle ages were complex, shifting and ambivalent, but the most straightforward reaction was one of distaste. The assumed barbarity of the middle ages acted as a foil to the polite and commercial society of eighteenth-century Britain. It was a period of Catholic superstition, feudal oppression and commercial backwardness, during which learning and the arts were stunted and disregarded. In the opinion of David Hume the period was one of curiosity, not utility. Like the Saxon period, however, the middle ages could never be completely ignored because of its importance as the formative era of the English constitution and for the development of the system of common law. The same impetus to retrieve and record the national past that stimulated enthusiasm for the Saxon and ancient British past in the later eighteenth century exerted its influence over the study of medieval England.

The antiquaries of the eighteenth century were very conscious of the legacy of the seventeenth-century scholars who had made such signal contributions to the study of the origins of parliament and common law. If their own achievements did not match that of their predecessors at every instance, the scholarship of the previous century was not forgotten and continued to exercise a powerful influence in both political culture and historical thought. Eighteenth-century attempts to elucidate the transition from a feudal to a commercial society opened up new lines of inquiry and gave a fresh significance to the middle ages in the narrative of progress towards modern civility. Charters and similar documents acquired a new value in the light of this approach, as they provided not only evidence of the rights and privileges which underpinned the fabric of society, but also material illustrative of the changing manners and customs of the past. It was no longer enough simply to compare past and present constitutions; the thrust of inquiry was shifted to the comparison of past and present society and culture. The eighteenth-century antiquaries were the heirs of the seventeenth century too in the study of medieval ecclesiastical antiquities and for many scholars medieval antiquities were essentially ecclesiastical antiquities. Interest in churches, abbeys and cathedrals considerably outweighed the attention given to the secular remains of the medieval past, be they city walls or baronial castles. Protestant antipathy towards Catholicism notwithstanding, a residual sympathy for the more positive aspects of the pre-Reformation church, its piety, learning and philanthropy, had always existed, surfacing in Laudianism and again in the high churchmanship of the later seventeenth century.[1] Such traditions were kept alive, largely by the non-juring, Tory antiquaries of the early eighteenth century. In the later eighteenth century these traditions blended with the revival of a more benign view of the middle ages as an era of greater social stability, charity and relative simplicity as contemporaries responded with increasing concern to the rapid social and political changes taking place around them. The distaste which the medieval period aroused could never be absolute, and became considerably less so as the very qualities which distinguished the middle ages so markedly from the liberty, prosperity and politeness of eighteenth-century England began to acquire a new value as the sources of sublime horror or picturesque delight. There was much in the eighteenth-century relationship with the 'Gothick', medieval past that was superficial, based upon romanticised notions of chivalry and monkish superstition, or exaggerated views of feudal tyranny and lawlessness. It had only the loosest of associations with the historical past. But the vogue for things 'Gothick' patently rendered the middle ages more attractive as a period of antiquarian or historical inquiry and contributed to a broader interest in more scholarly approaches to the medieval past upon which the historians of the nineteenth century could build.

Despite the pan-European approach to the study of feudalism taken by the historians of the Scottish Enlightenment, such as William Robertson or Lord Kames, the trend towards English insularity noted in the study of Saxon antiquities became even more pronounced in the study of medieval antiquities. English antiquaries writing upon ancient Britons, Druids, the Romans, and to a certain extent the Saxon and Danish periods, were in frequent communication with antiquaries within the other parts of the British Isles. Ethnicities were fluid, territorial boundaries obscure and documentary evidence imprecise. Antiquaries could not afford to be too rigid in their definition of what constituted the national past. In the eighth, ninth and tenth centuries the various Gothic tribes of Europe – the Saxons, Angles, Jutes and Danes – were gradually consolidated into an entity which could be called English, and the approach of the English antiquaries developed simultaneously a stronger Anglocentric focus. The antiquities of the medieval period were entwined ever more closely with the narratives of the English kingdom, rather than simply the recovery of past ages for which, it was believed, no history could be written. Domesday Book marked a kind of caesura from the previous period of obscurity. The historical focus shifted from the northern regions, with the Roman Wall, the military stations and the evidence of Bede's *Ecclesiastical History*, to the south, the centre of royal power and government. From the reign of William the Conqueror the antiquary and historian could tread on more certain ground, with evidence that was increasingly familiar and accessible. The cathedrals, monasteries and castles which punctuated the landscape told an English history of religious reformation and political upheaval from which the alliance of church and state of the eighteenth century had emerged. The charters, chronicles and parliamentary rolls, which mapped out the contours of the terrain in which the antiquary worked, were the testimony of a common English past structured around legal, religious and political institutions, and above all the English monarchy.

The study of medieval texts and documents enjoyed comparable fortunes to the study of Anglo-Saxon antiquities, with a peak of activity in the late seventeenth and early eighteenth centuries, followed by a gradual falling off in publications. There were certainly some important milestones in medieval antiquarian scholarship in the first three decades of the century. Thomas Madox's *Formulare anglicanum* (1702), *The History and Antiquities of the Exchequer* (1711), and *Firma burgi* (1726) were outstanding works of charter scholarship and historical interpretation which were not matched for the remainder of the eighteenth century. Thomas Rymer's *Foedera* (1704–13), which brought together all the diplomatic correspondence between England and other states, was widely recognised as a major contribution to the nation's history and an achievement which set Britain apart from other European nations. Through Rapin's condensed version, *Acta regia*, it penetrated the nation's historical consciousness far more extensively than had been possible for the original publication.[2] *Acta regia* subsequently became a staple work of antiquarian and historical reference. Thomas Hearne's many and accurate editions of medieval texts and monastic historians made important sources for the study of English history much more widely available.[3] Following Hearne, it is argued, few significant editions were published, bar a handful of exceptions such as James Nasmith's edition of the fifteenth-century itinerary of William of Worcester, the earliest indigenous topographical account of England.[4] The optimism expressed by William Nicolson in the *English Historical Library* for the development of medieval historical studies and the further consolidation of the sources available to the antiquary and historian appeared to have been misplaced. The gradual lowering of the temperature of religious and political debate in the eighteenth century has been linked to a loss of ideological potency in antiquarian studies: the sense of urgency which had driven antiquaries in earlier periods was dissipated. Instead, antiquaries were caught up in the fashionable enthusiasm for chivalry and romance, were duped by poetry of dubious authenticity, or engaged in theoretical speculation on the origins of feudalism.[5]

The somewhat cavalier dismissal of later eighteenth-century scholarship put forward by D. C. Douglas in *English Scholars* is not now sustainable. Recent scholarship has been much more sympathetic to the variation and breadth of historical studies of the later eighteenth century. Few would presume to summarise later eighteenth-century attitudes to history and antiquities purely with reference to Walpole, Bolingbroke, Chesterfield and Gibbon – the last's interest in medieval history being portrayed as a personal eccentricity. The simple opposition between polite taste and Gothic barbarity to which Douglas imputes the dissolution of medieval studies is easily shown to be overly simplistic and reductionist. Furthermore, it would be wrong to assume that, simply because the study of medieval texts and charters was no longer the most active area of antiquarian and historical research, antiquaries ceased to be interested in such matters, or that they failed to appreciate the importance of the research which these works represented.[6] Great value was attached to the scholarship inherited from the earlier period, and English antiquaries were conscious that it set them apart from the sister kingdoms. In Scotland, where there had not been a comparable flowering of medieval antiquarian scholarship in the seventeenth century, the desiderata of publications drawn up by the Scottish antiquaries was effectively a list that would match the English corpus work for work. Thomas Madox's scholarship and perspicuity may have been unmatched, but it was not unappreciated. The achievements of the seventeenth and early eighteenth centuries were not forgotten; they were constantly cited and held up as a model of proceeding. The publications of Madox and the other great medievalists were cited by antiquaries throughout the eighteenth century, alongside such other staples of antiquarian inquiry as Camden's *Britannia* and Dugdale's *Monasticon anglicanum*. Thomas Hearne may have become a byword in pedantry and eccentricity, but his editions were far from being ignored; their importance was recognised in the publication of new editions of *Collectanea* and the *Liber niger scaccarii* in 1771. His very industry, like that of Wanley and Hickes in the sphere of Saxon studies, may, too, have contributed to the apparent lack of interest in such texts in the later period. Such was his achievement that the need to carry on this programme of editing and publishing medieval texts was much less apparent. Other aspects of the medieval past – notably the physical legacy – took priority.

Valuable contributions were made to medieval studies, moreover. William Blackstone's edition of Magna Carta in 1759, for example, was a major

24. The door of Barfreston Church in Kent, from the *Antiquarian Repertory*, 4 vols (1776–84). (*Society of Antiquaries*)

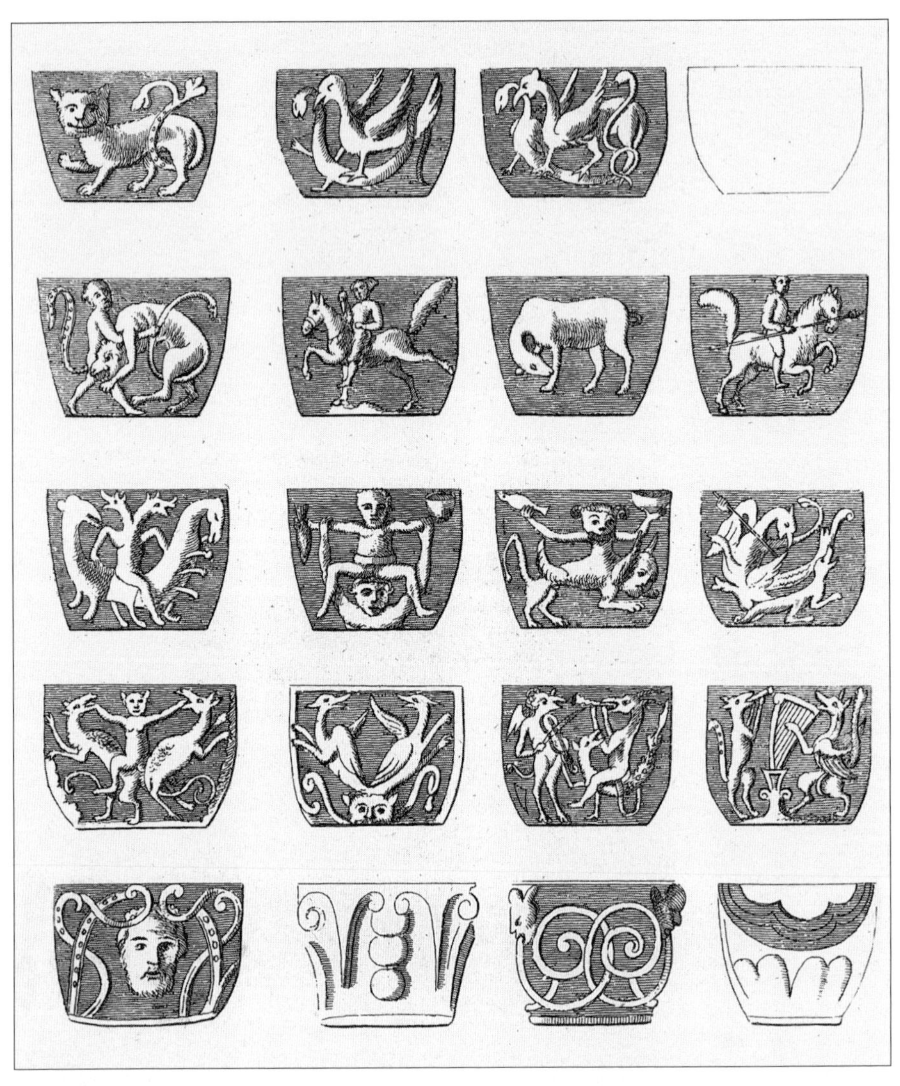

25. Saxon capitals, from the *Antiquarian Repertory*, 4 vols (1776–84). (*Society of Antiquaries*)

26. Tomb of Edward III in Westminster Abbey, engraved by James Basire, from Richard Gough, *Sepulchral Monuments in Great Britain*, 2 vols (1786–96). (*Special Collections, University of Leicester*)

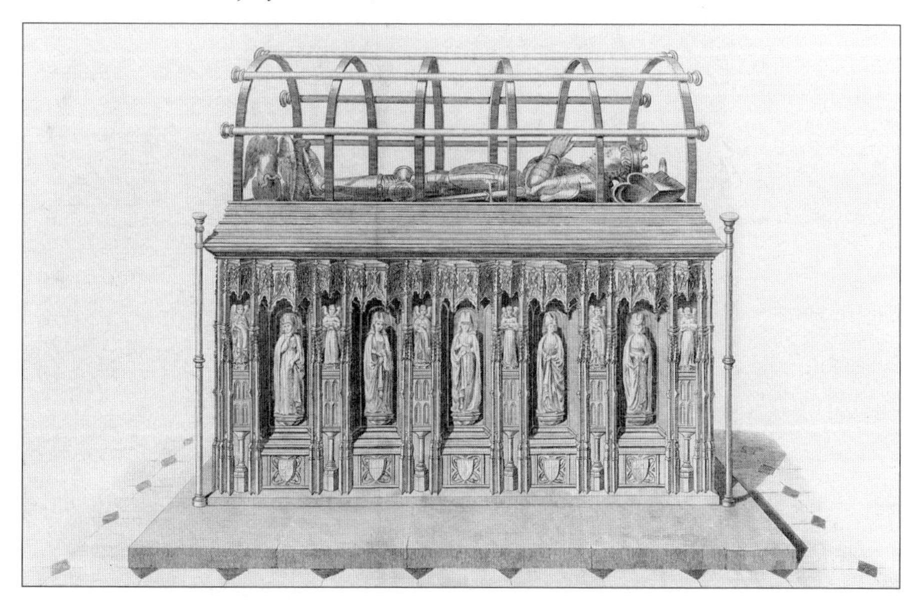

27. Monument of Richard Beauchamp, Earl of Warwick, engraved by James Basire, from Richard Gough, *Sepulchral Monuments in Great Britain*, 2 vols (1786–96). (*Special Collections, University of Leicester*)

28. William Stukeley, 'Sir Mitchil Bruce, Stonekiller', from the *Antiquarian Repertory*, 4 vols (2nd edn, 1809). (*Society of Antiquaries*)

29. Newstead Abbey in Nottinghamshire, from H. Boswell, *Historical Description of New and Elegant Picturesque Views of the Antiquities of England and Wales* (1785). (*Society of Antiquaries*)

30. Cockermouth Castle, Cumberland, from Francis Grose, *The Antiquities of England and Wales*, 4 vols (1772–76). (*Special Collections, University of Leicester*)

31. Raby Castle, Durham, from Francis Grose, *The Antiquities of England and Wales*, 4 vols (1772–76). (*Special Collections, University of Leicester*)

32. Tintern Abbey, Monmouthshire, from the *Antiquarian Repertory*, 4 vols (1776–84). (*Special Collections, University of Leicester*)

33. Netley Abbey, from the *Antiquarian Repertory*, 4 vols (1776–84). (*Special Collections, University of Leicester*)

34. Cross-section of Ely Cathedral, from James Bentham, *The History and Antiquities of the Conventual Church of Ely* (2nd edn, 1812). (*Special Collections, University of Leicester*)

35. Elevation of the west front of the Cathedral Church at Durham by John Carter, from *Some Account of the Cathedral Church at Durham* (1801). *(Society of Antiquaries)*

36. Croyland Bridge, Lincolnshire, from William Stukeley, *Itinerarium curiosum* (2nd edn, 1765). (*Special Collections, University of Leicester*)

37. The Ouse Bridge at York, from Francis Drake, *Eboracum: or The History and Antiquities of the City of York, from its Original to the Present Times* (1736). (*Special Collections, University of Leicester*)

stimulus to polemical interest in the Great Charter – but it was also of a piece with the antiquarian traditions of seventeenth-century scholarship, drawing heavily on the researches of Henry Spelman.[7] It was essentially a continuation of the traditions of legal antiquarianism, with an additional polish of enlightenment phraseology. So too was the publication of a facsimile of Domesday Book in 1783, which represented a major step forward for the study of Anglo-Norman history and antiquities.[8] The desirability of publishing a complete edition had been recognised at an early date, and was one item of many on Humfrey Wanley's highly ambitious agenda drawn up for the Society of Antiquaries in 1707.[9] Its importance for the understanding of constitutional history and the development of feudalism was self-evident and its publication was welcomed by those who saw the opportunity of bringing a foundation of empirical evidence to arguments of specious antiquarian content which were bandied about in the 'cabinet, in parliament and the courts of justice'.[10] The practical advantages of a published version were manifold, it being 'universally esteemed the foundation of English property, the origin from whence Antiquaries have commenced their enquiries, and beyond which it is almost useless for them to search'.[11] As such it provided the earliest certain evidence of legal tenure, and was the starting point from which to trace the myriad pathways through which property had descended. It had become the ultimate evidential proof in all disputed cases; in the words of Sir Robert Atkyns, 'whomever this Book did record to be lawful Owner of any Land, he was deemed to be so in all Courts'.[12] If the researches of the seventeenth-century antiquaries were driven by the ideological imperatives of religious and political conflict, eighteenth-century antiquarianism was equally responsive to the dominant ideology of the sanctity of private property.

The first attempt to collate the different versions was not made until 1755, however, when Philip Carteret Webb set about preparing proposals for the publication of a facsimile copy. Webb spurred his fellow members of the newly incorporated society into pooling their collective knowledge in an undertaking of major national importance.[13] Webb, who as Treasury solicitor was to lead the ministry's proceedings against John Wilkes, was well aware of the importance of antiquarian evidence in the arena of political and constitutional debate; his involvement in the efforts to get Domesday published should not, therefore, be seen simply as an antiquarian aside to his legal career, but as a practical move to ensure the preservation of the constitution and the understanding of political liberties, which he would later defend against Wilkes. In 1768 the House of Commons decided to proceed with the publication of a facsimile of Domesday Book and called upon the Society of Antiquaries to take responsibility for overseeing the publication. The antiquaries were in favour of engraving the entire manuscript, as only by this means could the idiosyncrasies of the handwriting, the scores of abbreviations employed and the physical appearance of the page be reproduced. Engraving was prohibitively expensive, however, and eventually the decision was taken to manufacture a special typeface – in itself hardly an economy measure.[14] The tortuous proceedings were eventually brought to fruition in 1783. The resulting volume was 'monumental, accurate and complete'.[15] The complete text was not made available to the general public; its distribution was confined to official bodies. But the fact that it had been published now rendered reproduction of its various parts much easier. No county history could now afford to be published without a transcription of Domesday Book, and a series of county studies made a quick appearance after 1783.[16] John Nichols even contemplated publishing a reproduction in serial form in the pages of the *Gentleman's Magazine*.[17] By the end of the eighteenth century the corpus of knowledge surrounding Domesday Book, and the recognition of its potential as a historical source were considerably enhanced.[18] Not only had the most important text for English medieval history been made more widely available but the preparations for publication had precipitated a considerable amount of research into the process by which Domesday Book had been compiled and the textual relationship between the various copies to each other.[19]

The latter part of the century may not stand out for pioneering palaeographical studies, but the lessons which had been learnt were not forgotten, and were more widely applied. The earlier generation of antiquaries had done valuable work in the editing and publishing of historical manuscripts. Antiquaries of the later eighteenth century freely acknowledged the significance of what had been achieved, but saw their task as building upon that achievement. The correspondence and publications of eighteenth-century antiquaries shows that their appreciation of the importance of medieval antiquities was undiminished, and in their individual spheres they endeavoured to preserve manuscripts and other documentary records. They realised that any manuscript was of potential historical value, and was worthy of preservation. An interest in palaeography and the publication of medieval texts was particularly marked amongst those antiquaries who were employed in the national record repositories, such as Sir Joseph Ayloffe (editor of *Calendar of Ancient Charters* and a revised edition of some of Thomas Hearne's works) or Thomas Astle, who amassed one of the most significant collections of medieval documents in private hands.[20] Astle's *The Origin and Progress of Writing* (1784) was professedly published to illustrate the 'diplomatic science', to enable readers to form a proper judgement of the age and authenticity of manuscripts, charters and other records. With very audible echoes of Thomas Madox's preface to *Formulare anglicanum*, Astle claimed that diplomatic was the surest guide to all other forms of inquiry, underpinning the study of politics, literature, canon and civil law and even divinity. His contributions to *Archaeologia* similarly distinguished between forged and genuine charters and called antiquaries and historians to account for their anachronism and inaccuracy in establishing the dates of historical transactions.[21] It was essential to demonstrate the bases upon which the rules of antiquarian criticism were constructed. If these rules were shown to be falsely derived or arbitrary, the entire authority of all ancient literature would be destroyed at a stroke. It was the science of antiquities which meant that history represented truth, rather than fiction.[22]

Charters granted from the age of the Saxon kings onwards were the very building blocks of history. They enshrined rights and privileges which were the basis of society – from Magna Carta to the manorial grant of a village's right to hold a market. 'History', in all its generalising scope, was the national story, but the fate of the inhabitants of a region or a town was told through the particularities of its antiquities: the charters which recorded privileges or endowments; the charitable benefactions which had sustained the poor, and the buildings which had been erected out of communal piety or private munificence. Yet, for all the acknowledged importance of charters and other documents, the legacy of the medieval period was most powerfully expressed in the physical presence of cathedrals and monasteries, castles and city walls. If standards of textual criticism failed to live up to the example set by the 'English Scholars', a much stronger case may be made for the increasingly critical and perceptive analysis of the architecture, sculpture and arts of the medieval period. Although the deeply seated prejudices in favour of classical values and culture proved in most cases at bottom ineradicable, it was possible even within that classical mindset to express a more historicist and sympathetic view of this period, and, in the gathering swell of a critique of Roman imperialism, even to assert the superiority of the Gothic over the classical. In the eighteenth century antiquaries began to learn to 'read' these buildings just as in previous generations they had learned to use the skills of diplomatic and palaeography to extract the secrets of ancient manuscripts. Antiquaries applied the same principles of comparison and attention to the fine detail by which the palaeographers dated their manuscripts, to arrive at a far more sophisticated knowledge of medieval architecture, which allowed them to date a building or a tomb on a purely stylistic basis. Although eighteenth-century fieldwork, in the sense of excavation and surveying, may not have fulfilled the early promise of Aubrey, Lhwyd and Stukeley, architectural fieldwork made rapid progress.

The origins of the Gothic Revival and the rise of architectural history in the eighteenth century are now a relatively well-charted area, in which Horace Walpole's contribution has attracted particular attention. Kenneth Clark's famous account of the *Gothic Revival*, coupled with more recent work by other scholars, provides a comprehensive survey of the most significant literature and the key figures involved.[23] The importance of Horace Walpole in encouraging an aesthetic appreciation of the Gothic and in patronising those who could share his interests should not be underestimated and it is certainly a major theme in much of the literature. He was one, and not the first, however, of a circle of antiquaries, who not only attempted to preserve and record the beauties of medieval architecture but sought to establish the underlying principles of Gothic architecture in order to develop a chronological analysis of style. The remainder of this chapter will consider how it was that antiquarian interest began to focus more sharply on medieval buildings and to explore the broader diffusion of this interest during the long eighteenth century. If it is impossible to extrapolate the impetus for Anglo-Saxon and medieval studies at the start of this period from the ideological upheavals precipitated by the Reformation and the Civil War, it is equally futile to divorce the study of medieval antiquities from broader cultural developments, which placed a new aesthetic value upon the sublime and the picturesque, the fascination with all things 'Gothic' and the reinvigoration of chivalry as a romantic cult of honour and martial virtue. More importantly, it was through these essentially more popular media that what contemporaries referred to as architectonical antiquarianism could reach out to a broader audience. Once the focus is drawn away from Walpole's circle of connoisseurs the quickening interest of the early nineteenth century may be rooted more securely in its eighteenth-century precedents.

Appreciation of medieval buildings was not high amongst educated circles at the start of the period. It is a simple matter to find dismissive comments, even revulsion, directed at the nation's medieval fabric, the most ubiquitous and conspicuous part of which was ecclesiastical. For seventeenth-century Protestants monasteries and abbeys, and even churches and cathedrals, represented the idolatry and superstition of Catholicism. Monastic ruins were a salutary reminder of the corruption and greed of the Catholic church, serving only to represent the triumph of reformed religion. 'Cathedrals', John Evelyn had written, were 'Congestions of Heavy, Dark, Melancholy and Monkish Piles without any just Proportion, Use or Beauty, compar'd with the truly Ancient.'[24] Those who admired such buildings or expressed regret at their passing were liable to be suspected of crypto-Catholicism, or 'too superstitious Affection for these Buildings'.[25] Protestant sensibilities alone are not sufficient to account for the degree of distaste expressed by

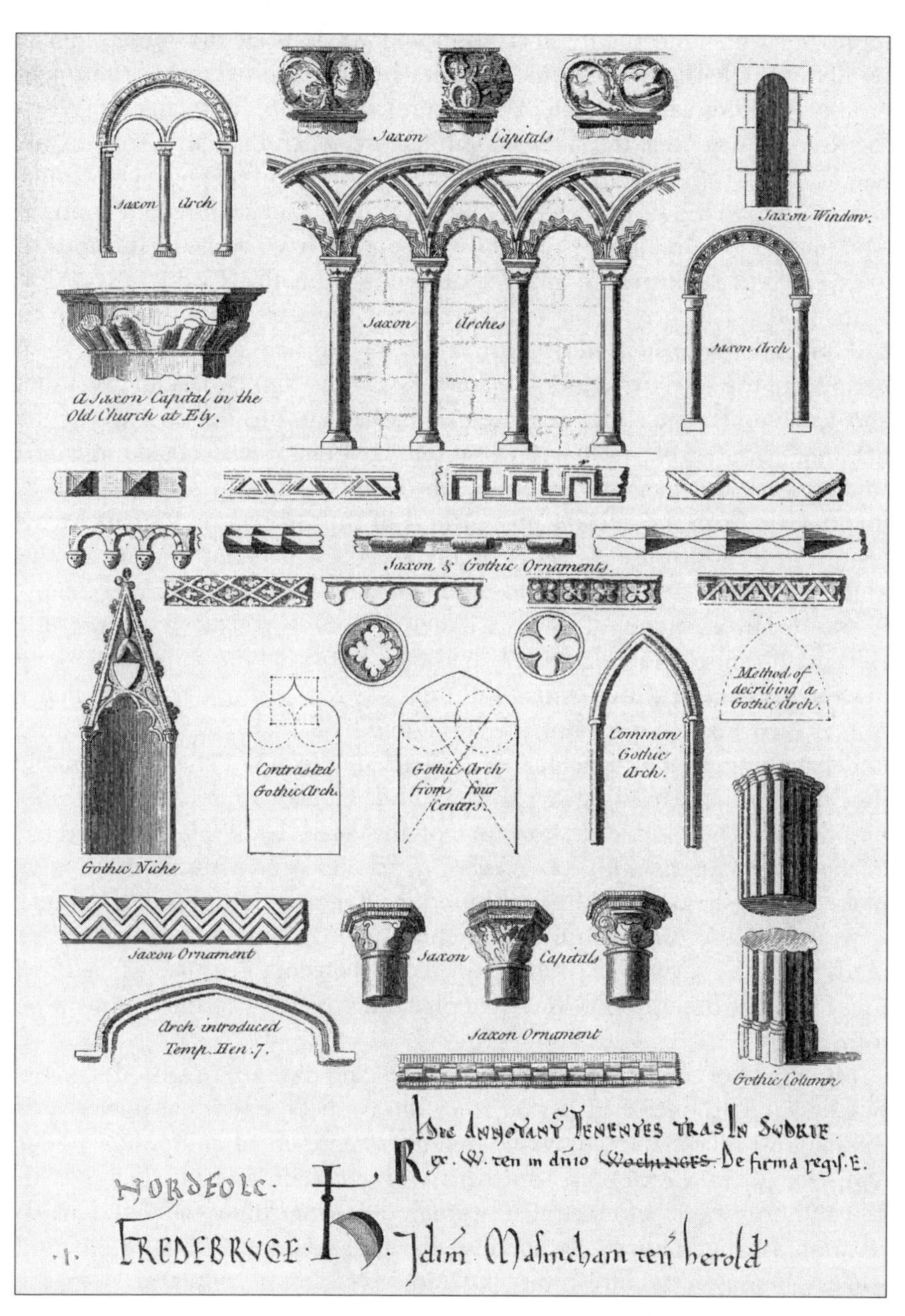

Saxon and Gothic architecture, from the *Antiquarian Repertory*, 4 vols (1776–84). (*Society of Antiquaries*)

Evelyn. For those schooled in classicism the Gothic style of architecture represented an unfortunate aberration and was one of the most tangible results of the barbarian, 'Gothic' invasions which had overcome the might of imperial Rome, bringing the Roman presence in Britain to an end. When the Romans departed, the skills in architecture which the native inhabitants had acquired were rapidly lost under the barbarian onslaughts. The Goths, wrote Sir John Clerk of Penicuik, 'introduced a bad manner not only in Architectory but in all other arts & sciences. We have been for upwards of 200 years endeavouring to recover ourselves from this Gothicism.'[26] The term 'Goths' had been used indiscriminately to describe the peoples who had inhabited north-western Europe in the Roman and early medieval period and the adjective 'Gothic' was applied with a similar lack of precision, and to a similar end, that is to signify barbarism and the absence of the defining features of Roman civilisation.[27] 'Modern writers', complained Charles Lyttelton in 1758, 'have used the term Gothick to signify all kinds that deviate from the ancient proportions of the Grecian or Roman Architecture.'[28] The Saxons, it was generally accepted, had not known how to build in stone – yet another indication of their barbarism. Consequently, it was believed, none of their wooden edifices had survived into the eighteenth century. Only gradually had they recovered the skills of working in stone, as contact with mainland Europe was renewed under the influence of Christian missionaries. But the stone buildings then erected showed no understanding of the principles of Roman architecture. They were purely functional; squat, massy, heavy and dark. They had no grace, elegance or proportion. The Gothic architecture of the later medieval period veered to the other extreme with its excess of detail and ornamentation; the grotesque carvings and the whimsical humour offended the eighteenth-century sense of architectural propriety. Architecture continued in this deviant mode until the revival of antiquity in the seventeenth century, when Inigo Jones brought back proportion, harmony and symmetry to the architectural form.

Yet, however much gentlemen of taste and fashion might decry the buildings of the medieval period, they always held a residual power over the nation's imagination. Physical buildings represented continuity, power and strength in a society in which life was uncertain and in which wealth and authority were demonstrated through the ownership of land and architectural display. Medieval castles and city walls were reminders of a period when defensive structures were all too necessary in times of domestic disorder. The church or the cathedral was a sacred building, an offering *ad maiorem gloriam dei*, but was also an embodiment of the collective memory of society; it was the greatest of all monuments to ancestors and to the spirit of piety, charity and patriotism which held together the community at both the local and national level. As such the buildings demanded respect, irrespective of any perceived architectural shortcomings.

There was, therefore, always a limit to the dominance of classicism and there were always those who were receptive to the beauty of a Gothic building in both its physical and symbolic senses. Buildings such as York Minster transcended conventional expectations and could inspire admiration at any point, regardless of whether they conformed to notions of architectural propriety and taste. 'For a Noble and Lofty Fabrick, lightsomnesse, due proportion and exquisite Architecture', wrote Christopher Hildyard, a seventeenth-century lawyer, '[York Minster], will scarce yield to any Church in Europe.' The external part of the Minster was, according to the York historian Thomas Gent writing in 1730, 'exquisite in all its parts'.[29]

The destruction consequent upon the Dissolution of the Monasteries created a radical discontinuity, a fault line in the passage of history. The monastic ruin and the Gothic architecture in which it was built therefore became emblematic of that past age. The ruins were a reminder of the disjuncture of the past and the present. Even in 1598, when the nation's monasteries were but recently ruined, and when to express sympathy with the Catholic faith which they represented was politically dangerous, William Camden was moved by their physical presence and the destruction of hundreds of years of piety and learning which they symbolised. Buildings were valued for their size and grandeur and for their evocative power. By the seventeenth century it is possible to identify a critique of Tudor avarice and barbarism in bringing about such sacrilege and a total annihilation of so many 'inestimable pieces of antiquity'. William Laud was no antiquary, but in his campaign to recover the beauty of holiness he showed how an attitude more sympathetic to the ideals of monastic piety could be fostered and some of the decay which had afflicted churches and chapels could be repaired. It was in this more benign atmosphere of churchmanship that works which would inspire later antiquaries in the eighteenth century, such as John Weever's *Funeral Monuments* (1633), were prepared. The further iconoclasm and destruction of the Civil War prompted another generation of antiquaries to record the ecclesiastical fabric before it was destroyed and lost for ever. Thus gentlemen such as Sir William Dugdale, John Aubrey and William Backhouse travelled the country in search of ecclesiastical antiquities, identifying the ruins of former monastic foundations whilst they could still be traced.[30] But nevertheless, of all the seventeenth-century antiquaries only William Somner attempted to make anything more than a superficial assessment of the physical structure of buildings. In his account of Canterbury Cathedral he was able to confirm the period at which various parts were built by comparing their architecture against those parts for which he could be sure of a date from documentary sources.[31]

Yet, the importance of recording these foundations was, by the end of the seventeenth century, universally accepted as a desideratum by antiquaries. The emphasis, however, was upon honouring the memory and piety of those who had endowed and inhabited the monasteries, the traditions of learning and the uninterrupted years of religious observance which they represented. The physical ruins aroused admiration, emotion and a powerful sense of the mutability of human fortune, and a warning against the rapine of greedy monarchs, but as objects of interest in terms of their physical appearance they were of secondary importance. The language available to describe them was correspondingly limited. The preservation of the ruin was simply a means of ensuring that the intangible memory of those whose lives and devotion it commemorated were saved from oblivion. The study of ecclesiastical antiquities – from which the study of architectural antiquities would emerge in the eighteenth century – was primarily concerned with recording the names of the founders, the endowments, the officeholders. 'I have shewed their Foundations, endowments, and continuance', wrote Dugdale of the religious houses, hospitals and chantries in Warwickshire, 'with their dissolutions and ruine, which gave the greatest blow to Antiquities that ever England had.'[32] Indefatigable as he was in visiting the churches to which he referred, he was primarily a student of the written word. His account of St Paul's was essentially a catalogue of epitaphs and a summary of its endowments and incumbents. He never described the physical appearance of the buildings he recorded, for all that he employed the leading topographical draughtsman of the time, Wenceslaus Hollar, to make the drawings for the copperplates illustrating the volume.[33] The approach of Dugdale and his contemporaries was also driven by highly practical considerations. Churches and monasteries were important sources of information for those tracing the descent of property and genealogies. The monumental epitaphs and the heraldic glass inside a church could provide valuable genealogical information, which could even be produced in courts of law. Monastic records of estates, which had now largely passed into lay hands, were generally far better kept than those of secular landowners and provided valuable detail on the descent of property and issues such as legal immunities, which could be of considerable import for contemporary proprietors. The materials with which ecclesiastical antiquaries worked were therefore primarily textual ones: the charters granted to monasteries, the endowment of churches, the epitaphs and inscriptions to be found within. The physical structure of the church itself was very much a secondary consideration.

By the end of the seventeenth century ecclesiastical edifices no longer stood in danger from the kind of iconoclastic destruction which had impressed Sir William Dugdale with the need for their preservation. Nor was their wreckage so recent and raw as the scenes of monastic ruin which William Camden had faced when compiling material for *Britannia* at the end of the sixteenth century.[34] From the perspective of the high churchman, however, the church was still in danger: theologically from the low church latitudinarians and physically in terms of the neglect and decay into which its buildings had been allowed to fall during the decades of Puritan neglect. Encroachments had been made upon its properties and rights, made possible by emasculated ecclesiastical authority. It should come as no surprise that many – but by no means all – of the antiquaries who were most concerned with ecclesiastical antiquities in this period were high churchmen and non-jurors. Jacobites and Tories were predisposed towards an antiquarian cast of mind. Their religious sympathies were closer to the Catholic traditions embodied in the monasteries and cathedrals than the non-conformity and deism which they identified in the Hanoverian Church of England. The Tories' nostalgia for a bygone age, their belief in hereditary succession and antipathy to a new dynasty, a new political order and new money, combined with their political exclusion after 1714, sent them to scour the past in search of legitimation for their resistance, for reassurance and for confirmation of their own beliefs.[35]

In the early eighteenth century Browne Willis (1682–1760) stands out amongst the antiquaries for the breadth of his coverage and for the industry with which he pursued the study of 'ecclesiastical antiquities', the institutions and buildings of the Established Church.[36] Willis was a country gentleman from Whaddon Hall, Buckinghamshire; initially a non-juror, he later reneged and took the oaths – much to Thomas Hearne's disgust. He was said to have acquired his love of antiquities as a boy sent to school at Westminster, where he used to walk and contemplate 'the solemnity of the Building, the antique Appearance, the Monuments'. Whether or not Westminster Abbey really did exercise such a formative influence upon the young Willis cannot be established, but his subsequent behaviour was certainly in keeping with such early sentiments. Apart from a brief spell as MP for Buckingham in 1705, Willis devoted his life and his considerable estate to the study of antiquities and the interests of the church. He gave generously on many occasions to funds for repairing, restoring or simply improving churches within the county. He spent much of his life travelling the country to visit churches and cathedrals, always attempting to arrive on the day of their patronal festival, manifesting again his sympathies with the traditions of Roman Catholic piety. His interest took a more practical turn as well. He raised a subscription for building a chapel at St Martin's, Fenny Stratford; he subscribed generously to the cost of restoring the church of St Mary Magdalen in Stoney Stratford following a fire; he gave £200 for the repair of Buckingham church tower and paid for the restoration of Bow Brickhill church which had been disused for over 150 years.[37] Willis, however, was working in the tradition of a Laudian restoration of the beauty of holiness, rather than as a prototype for the Historic Churches Fund. In giving financial assistance in this way he was attempting to restore the place of the church as the focal point of the Christian community and to recover the elements of true religion: charity, piety and devotion, which the physical fabric of the church, with its monuments to ancestral piety and devotion, represented. The medieval church buildings embodied the continuity of the Church of England with the earlier traditions of Catholicism. Willis was angrily dismissive of those who still saw the medieval legacy of religious structures as a threat, to be levelled to the ground, 'as if the superstitious Rites of the former Age had, like the Leprosy of the ancient Jews, penetrated the very Walls'.[38] The Reformation, as he pointed out, was securely accomplished. Further action was not necessary, and these buildings were a vital symbol of the endurance and essential immutability of true religion. Willis, however, was also captivated by the beauty and vulnerability of these buildings. Arguments against the impiety of allowing buildings constructed for the glorification of God to fall into ruin easily transmuted into an argument for the better preservation of a building as a structure of beauty and historical curiosity. 'To this day', he warned, 'many of our Cathedral Churches have lain in such Obscurity, as to have had no particular Notice taken of them.' Posterity would deplore the current negligence and want of esteem for such antiquities.

Willis attempted to take that action and to inspire fellow antiquaries to do likewise. He embarked on two major publications, *A Survey of the Cathedrals* and a *History of the Mitred Abbies.* Making use of a questionnaire he sent out to local inhabitants, he compiled essential information on each cathedral or abbey, much of which was concerned with issues of property or ecclesiastical dignitaries. More importantly in this context, however, there was also a physical description, giving the dimensions, the layout and the condition in which each building was maintained. At Peterborough he found that the cathedral was in a sorry state of dilapidation:

> I cannot but say that it is ill kept in Repair, and lies very slovenly in the inside, and several windows are stopped up with Bricks, and the glazing in others sadly broken; and the Boards of the Roof of the middle Isle or nave which with the Cross-Isle is not archt with stone (but wainscotted with painted boards, as at

> *St Albans*) are several of them damaged and Broken, as is also the Pavement, insomuch that scarce any Cathedral in *England* is more neglected. However, as at the present, the Dean and Chapter have already set apart £700 and design to appropriate more on the Expiration of some Leases.[39]

Browne Willis had none of the vocabulary of architectural description; nor did he have the amateur architect's interest in construction, but he was able to appreciate the beauties of the churches he described, even if he could not articulate in descriptive detail what it was that he so admired. Descriptions such as this actually represented a comparatively small proportion of his total work, but he kept up a relentless attack against the shameful neglect and decay through all his writings on ecclesiastical antiquities.[40] Like Thomas Hearne, Browne Willis was a prolific writer of letters, collecting and coordinating information and research from antiquaries across the country. His letters to the Tory bookseller Thomas Gent of York, with his advice on how to take church notes, are a case in point. 'Pray describe the fabric of York churches', wrote Browne Willis to Gent, 'as, for instance, "All Saints Church has a body and two side aisles, leaded and embattled with a tiled chancel; at the west end is a tower with an octagon dome on which hang three bells"'.[41] Willis's dependence upon this network of correspondents for information about places he had never visited was highlighted by his critics, but they could not deny that his researches consolidated large amounts of materials from other collections, provided a framework for future research and alerted the antiquarian world to the sheer extent of the architectural and historical riches which the cathedrals and abbeys embodied.

Richard Rawlinson, another non-juror and Jacobite, similarly fired with indignation at the neglect and disrepair into which the nation's churches had been allowed to fall, compiled histories of four cathedrals, which complemented those of Willis. His was a very different approach, however, being entirely reliant on the traditional format of inscriptions and incumbents.[42] Rawlinson set out to redress the destruction and profanity of the Protestant reformers and to restore the memory of 'heroick minds' and pious ancestors, and identified himself very deliberately with the tradition established by Sir William Dugdale in the previous century. Willis's interest in the buildings themselves appeared to puzzle him: Mr Willis, he remarked, had written rather 'the Geometrical and Architectonical History of that Church [St David's cathedral]'. Rawlinson's backhanded compliment acknowledged that Willis had helped to set in train a new approach to ecclesiastical antiquities, which later antiquaries acknowledged more openly.[43] 'Our religious foundations are obliged to Mr Willis notwithstanding the many inaccuracies of dates and epitaphs', wrote Richard Gough in 1780.[44] Whatever the shortcomings of these volumes in terms of information and accuracy (and they were, as Gough pointed out, deeply flawed), they were to remain unsurpassed as a basic source of information until the nineteenth century. The survey of cathedral architecture which the Society of Antiquaries sponsored in the 1790s was never completed, and was moreover published at a price which made it all but unaffordable for the majority of readers. When James Storer, a specialist antiquarian engraver, published his series *Cathedral Antiquities* (1814), nearly one hundred years later, Browne Willis's observations were still worth referring to and comprised the major source of information for the Welsh cathedrals, which had attracted far less scholarly attention than their English counterparts.[45]

Thomas Staveley's *History of the Churches in England* was published posthumously in 1712, nearly thirty years after his death in 1683. With this single publication to his name Staveley was rather overshadowed by the prolific Willis, but his history stands out as almost the only publication in the first half of the century to draw attention to what he termed 'church furniture' and the 'materials, workmanship, and fashion' of churches. Staveley's avowed intent, similar to that of Browne Willis, was to honour the genius and devotion of those who had built the churches which adorned the face of the nation. There was, however, a subsidiary aim, which he presented by highlighting the enormous contrast in appearance between the descriptions of the first church at Glastonbury and the magnificence of the cathedrals of the high middle ages. He threw down the gauntlet for antiquaries to establish the differences between Saxon and Norman architecture and the changes which had taken place in the progressive development of architecture: a challenge to which most antiquaries writing on the subject later in the century referred.[46] To this end he made some rudimentary distinctions: Saxons had built low, mean buildings, whereas those of the Normans were more 'stately, lightsome and pleasant'. Given these differences, he suggested, in the absence of any other *textual* evidence for the date at which a church was built, those who 'critically addict' themselves to observation and comparison may well be able to arrive at a reasonable conjecture as to the time of building.[47] It is likely that it was upon a reading of Staveley that Browne Willis called for a more systematic study of architectural form, suggesting that a classification of church buildings on the basis of their structure should be undertaken.[48] His suggestions certainly did not go unheard and were reiterated, for example, in 1727 by Francis Peck, a Lincolnshire antiquary and author of a history of Stamford, who suggested that 'by a nice examination of the different modes in the fabric of parish churches, the different ages when they were in use may be pretty nearly ascertained'. Books of antiquities, he suggested, should contain plates of these structures rather than gentlemen's seats in order to facilitate the comparison.[49] Peck thus outlined a mode of preceding and an agenda for future antiquaries.

Meanwhile, Willis was not alone in his concern at the steady decay and destruction being visited upon church architecture. There was a sympathetic and widespread constituency for his views. Sir Robert Atkyns, for example, another non-juror, a lawyer and MP for Gloucestershire, devoted a considerable proportion of his *History of Glostershire* (sic) to ecclesiastical antiquities. He explained that he had given the dimensions of all the churches in order that it 'may conduce towards the preserving them in Reparation and may prevent the pulling down one part to uphold the rest, and may suggest the Building of more Churches where it is requisite'.[50] We should not, however, be too emphatic in drawing a connection between high church tendencies and a respect for the traditions of worship and spirituality embodied in the nation's ecclesiastical edifices. Such feelings of religious and ancestral piety could operate equally powerfully upon those whose fortunes were more closely identified with the Hanoverian regime. When Thomas Tanner was chancellor of the diocese of Norwich he wrote to the Norfolk antiquary and clergyman Francis Blomefield of his concern that the 'fine Church' at Cromer was being allowed to fall into decay and the ruin of the 'most noble Chancel' was being lost; he offered a plate of the ruin for Blomefield's projected history of Norfolk to preserve its memory.[51] It was not necessary to be a non-juror to acknowledge the losses consequent upon the Dissolution of the Monasteries or to find much to admire in the former monastic institutions and their traditions of piety and learning. William Stukeley, a friend of Browne Willis and fellow member of the Antiquarian, Spalding and Royal societies was a Newtonian, a freemason and a physician who avoided attending church whilst in London during the 1720s in order not to invite ridicule amongst his peers. Yet once he was back in rural Stamford, the sight of ruined monasteries or churches suffered to fall into decay and wilfully denuded of their medieval ornamentation aroused him to similar expressions of regret and indignation. At Crowland (Croyland), he complained, every house was become religious, constructed with materials looted from the ruins of the monumental abbey church, the 'holy shipwreck'.[52]

Interest in monastic ruins and historic churches was not solely triggered by dismay at the state of decay into which they had fallen. Some of the earliest attempts to identify architectural style and to establish a sense of its chronological development came from the circle of antiquaries who were most actively engaged in challenging the dismissive treatment generally given to the Saxon period as one of unrelieved barbarism. In discussing the relative civility of any society in the eighteenth century, various criteria were used: the levels of literacy (hence the debate as to whether the Druids had actually embodied a literate culture); the treatment of women; and the standards of beauty and skill attained in architecture. For those who identified the formative period of what they understood to be the English state as the Saxon period, it was of no little importance to establish larger claims for their Saxon forebears, rather than simply a certain manly vigour and facility with the battle-axe. Just as Elizabeth Elstob had sought to demonstrate the merits of Old English on its own terms, and by demonstrating Saxon literacy had necessarily modified the views of unrelieved barbarism, the next generation of antiquaries reacted against the prevailing view of the 'ignorance of the Saxon Times' and the authority of all those antiquaries who believed that the Saxons knew 'little or nothing of Architecture'.[53] 'New lights upon that subject (Saxon architecture) flow in upon me pretty fast,' wrote one antiquary in 1749, '& I hope God give me life to Digest such Materials as will prove our Saxon Ancestors to have been men of more knowledge in many Arts & Sciences than they have hitherto been esteem'd.'[54]

There were also powerful political reasons behind this desire to elevate the reputation of the nation's Saxon forefathers. The patriot opposition within the Whig party to Robert Walpole's Robinocracy shared common ground with the Tories in looking back to the Saxon constitution as a symbol of the constitutional balance that Walpole's oligarchy had upset.[55] Architectural style could become a potent and expressive statement of political allegiance and ideology. The Tory peer Lord Bathurst of Bathurst Park near Cirencester built a fake 'Gothic' ruin, Alfred's Hall, within his grounds in 1723, alluding to an era of political liberty which the Whig political regime, from which he was excluded, had destroyed. The hall was designed in wood with reference to what was then believed to be the Saxon mode of building – the assumption that the Saxon's had lost the art of building in stone had yet to be decisively challenged.[56] The classic exemplar of garden architecture exploited to articulate an ideological statement was at Stowe, where the opposition Whig, Sir Richard Temple, later Viscount Cobham, constructed a series of buildings which bore witness to his own political stance and presented a critique of the Walpolian regime. The Temple of Ancient Virtue, which included a bust of King Alfred, champion of Anglo-Saxon liberties, contrasted with the ruins of the Temple of Modern Virtue, with a matching decapitated bust of Walpole, whilst the Temple of Liberty was built in Gothic form, recalling to mind the liberties of the ancient Gothic constitution. Gothic architecture symbolised the baronial opposition to the monarchy of the thirteenth century and evoked the triumph of liberty enshrined in Magna Carta.[57] Sir Richard's grandson,

Charles Lyttelton, who was one of the first to attempt a more systematic study of Saxon and Gothic architecture, therefore came from a background in which there was a firm acceptance of the historical and constitutional importance of the medieval period, and in particular the Saxon era, and also a tradition of expressing political ideology through architecture. This, it may be inferred, was an important factor in stimulating his own interest in the antiquities of that period.

Lyttelton later claimed that he had first been inspired to follow this line of inquiry 'from a loose sheet of Mr Aubrey's MSS in the Ashmole Museum; wherein he gives a rude drawing'.[58] This manuscript, now known as 'Chronologica Architectonica', contains Aubrey's sketches of different forms of window, tracing their chronological development from the rounded to the simple pointed arch, to the increasingly ornamented and elongated arches of the later Gothic period, to the flattened appearance of the sixteenth century.[59] It is also apparent that Lyttelton's thinking was influenced by his familiarity with Saxon manuscripts. He had matriculated at University College, Oxford in 1732, where he would have come into contact with the remaining 'Oxford Saxonists' and the traditions of Anglo-Saxon scholarship. He certainly maintained a correspondence with Wise, Mores and Ballard in later years.[60] Hickes, Wanley and Thwaites had not themselves displayed any evident interest in the architectural, as opposed to the literary, achievements of the Saxons. The attention they directed towards Saxon manuscripts and the palaeographical techniques they employed, however, were themselves a stimulus to the study of the architecture. Lyttelton argued that there would be a common style to the ornamentation of both manuscripts and buildings which would offer conclusive proof, where textual evidence was lacking, of a building's antiquity: 'from Books we may find Hints which may lead to this Enquiry, but 'tis the Remains that must speak for themselves'.[61] Smart Lethieullier, with whom he exchanged ideas, went to Oxford specifically to study the Saxon manuscripts there. With Francis Wise he examined St Peters in the East, St Giles, St Mary's Iffley, and Christ Church Cathedral in an attempt to identify the elements of what he supposed to be Saxon construction.[62] The Saxons, it was decided, had adopted the use of stone and rounded arches at the time of their conversion to Christianity: the rounded arch thus acquired a dual valency as a symbol of Saxon civility in the emulation of Roman forms, and as the physical embodiment of the Christian church.[63]

Lyttelton was convinced that he had introduced a wholly new branch of antiquarian inquiry.[64] He and Lethieullier attempted to introduce a more systematic mode in their own observations: 'I am sure 'tis by the Consideration of a Great Number & watching when the Styles are Blended that we shall at last be able to Establish any tolerable Rule to Judge by.'[65] In another letter Lethieuller adumbrated a tentative scheme: 'Allow Tutbury to the Age of the Conqueror, – A Part of Waltham Abby to Edwd the Confessors, & a Part of Christ Church to Ethelred's, & we shall arrive at a sort of series, which by the Rules of Comparison, may lead to Decypher Others, but these I only offer to you as Occasional hints, wch wou'd require much supporting before positive Conclusions could be drawn from them.'[66] Lyttelton encouraged those with whom he corresponded to make similar observations and gave guidance as to what features to look out for. The material and the architectural style of a building, he pointed out, could confirm or even disprove the authenticity of other evidence pertaining to its date. Comparison of buildings – for example the statues on the gatepost of Worcester Cathedral with those at Wells and Exeter, for which dates were already known, could also lead to confirmation.[67] Like Francis Peck, Lyttelton apprehended the possibilities for studying architecture through accurate drawings in order to facilitate comparison. Friends were commissioned to take sketches of any interesting monument or building which they visited. They were referred to the plates in Francis Drake's *Eboracum* and were asked to compare them with sketches from Iffley, St Peters in the East or the church at Tutbury. William Borlase, more used to dealing with fossils and druidical remains, was keen to demonstrate his newly acquired enthusiasm for Lyttelton's interests: 'I must own I could not before I saw them distinguish the Saxon from the common run of the Gothick', he admitted, but having read Lyttelton's observations he felt confident in identifying a Saxon building, and promised to send him a drawing of the first specimen he should come across.[68]

The basic distinctions which Lyttelton and his correspondents were attempting to establish seem obvious from a modern perspective, accustomed as we are to view a building such as a cathedral as an aggregate of different architectural styles. At this point in the eighteenth century, however, it was a commonplace to observe of a cathedral that despite the (documented) fact that it had been built over a great many years, it nevertheless had the appearance of unity, as if built all in one burst of activity. Thus Francis Drake observed of York Minster that such care had been taken in joining and uniting the different elements of the building process that 'it seems to be one entire edifice at this day; though composed of five several tastes of Gothick architecture'.[69] Few would have viewed a building with the expectation of being able to detect a variety of different styles which could be linked to equivalent stages in the building process. Despite the hints that had been put out by Somner and Staveley, for the first half of the century at least, it was still generally accepted that without textual confirmation the date of a building could not be established, and even amongst antiquaries this attitude was well entrenched. George North, better known as a numismatist, was also fascinated by the developments of architectural style, but assumed that this was something which could be established purely with reference to textual sources. Place him in London, he wrote, with libraries and record repositories at his disposal, and he was confident that he would be able to establish the origins of the various styles.[70] The efforts to date buildings simply by comparative analysis, therefore, represented a significant shift of attitude by which buildings were approached as historical evidence.

Lyttelton and Lethieullier were particularly interested in identifying whether there was any significant difference between the Saxon and the Norman periods, and in tracing the gradual evolution of the rounded to the pointed arch in the post-conquest era. This differentiation was in itself a step towards refining the crude notions of unrelieved barbarism which dismissed all architecture deviating from the classical norm as 'Gothic' and unworthy of notice. They did not, however, come to any satisfactory conclusion. Lyttelton believed the Norman style to be plainer, grander, more massive and monumental. The Saxons built on a lesser scale, with a much richer form of ornamentation. Any building which appeared to show greater elegance or sophistication was dated to the earlier Saxon period, rather than allowing for an evolution of style in the eleventh and twelfth centuries. Lyttelton delighted in the luxuriancy of what he took to be the Saxon imagination, which ran riot in the ornamentation of arches and capitals – the artistic manifestation of Saxon liberties. This preference was unusual amongst antiquaries, most of whom thought the early Saxon style inferior to the greater simplicity associated with the post-conquest era and tended to express revulsion at the lack of discipline and the vulgarity of such carvings. It was more usual to regard the Saxon style as 'heavy', 'massy' and 'gloomy'. The transepts at Winchester Cathedral were described by one antiquarian visitor as 'vile and beyond expression clumsy'.[71]

Both Saxon and Norman buildings, however, were identified as being built in the 'Saxon' style in distinction to the Gothic or 'pointed' style. Lethieullier expressed his doubts on the use of the term Saxon and the apparent wilful perversity in describing a building known to be built by William II or Henry I as Saxon. The Saxons, he remarked, had no more title to that name than the Danes, Normans or Lombards, but 'I am affraid the Names Saxon and Gothick are so fix'd it would be difficult to introduce others'.[72] The alternative term 'debased Roman' did not catch on and the confusion persisted up to the end of the century and beyond. The term 'debased Roman' is indicative of the extent to which perceptions were still governed by a classical model. Lyttelton and his circle may have been pressing for a re-evaluation of Saxon architectural achievements, but this did not amount to full-blown historicism. Their attitude was always based upon the assumption that the norms of classical architecture were truest to nature and therefore, when correctly observed, represented the truest beauty. The criteria by which they judged Saxon or Gothic architecture were those laid down by generations of writers schooled in classical architecture: symmetry, proportion and order. Rather than discovering a Saxon architectural idiom or celebrating an indigenous strain of Saxon creativity, antiquaries like Lyttelton and Lethieullier were effectively giving the Saxons, whom they honoured as the ancestors of the English state, a veneer of Roman refinement, in keeping with the sense of their own class of being the eighteenth-century inheritors of the Roman Empire. The superiority of Roman civilisation was not challenged; it was merely deftly reintegrated as part of the Saxon tradition. This was not an anticipation of nineteenth-century Saxonism, but a covert exercise in classicising the Saxon.[73]

Another member of Lyttleton's circle, Andrew Coltée Ducarel, travelled to Normandy with the specific intention of discovering the difference between Saxon and Norman architecture: a goal which he claimed to his friends to have gone some way to achieving. His conclusions were actually very little different from those already put forward by Lyttelton.[74] Given the limited corpus of knowledge with which antiquaries were working, this conclusion is hardly surprising, but the ambiguity should also be seen in the light of the political affiliations of those involved, and those of Lyttelton in particular. With respect to the impact of the Norman Conquest, there was, as we have already seen, a consensus amongst eighteenth-century Whigs that feudalism, and therefore the basis for a representative system of government, had existed in Saxon society prior to the Norman invasion. According to the theoretical accounts emanating from Scotland, feudalism had been developed first in mainland Europe. If cultural exchange in architectural forms throughout the Saxon and Norman periods could be demonstrated it added substance to the argument for constitutional continuity and gradual evolution.[75] To be able to demonstrate that the Saxons had built with stone and had imported masons from the Continent, and that the Norman invasion had not radically altered architectural practice or style, would add further grist to this mill. Lyttelton's own chronology suggested that the Saxon form prevailed until the reign of Henry II. Thereafter it was intermixed with some Gothic, until the reign of King John, from which point he dated the unchallenged rise of the Gothic style of architecture.[76] 'I no more believe there was a round Column with a Circular Arch built in the Reign of King John than I do that there was a true

Corinthian Portico built then.'[77] It was in the reign of John that, according to contemporary Whig thought, property had been rendered secure under the provisions of Magna Carta. The emergence of the distinctive new style was thus linked to the consolidation of private property at a key stage in the historical evolution of commercial society from feudalism, so beloved of eighteenth-century historians. Lyttelton's terms of architectural description did not match the historical periods from which they took their names, but his identification of the chronology of architectural style dovetailed neatly with the chronology of his own understanding of constitutional development.

Neither Lethieullier nor Lyttelton published on the subject on which they corresponded at such length and upon which they both made substantial collections.[78] Despite constant urging from his friends to publish his observations on architecture, Lyttelton's only contributions to reach the public domain were a paper on the origins of building in brick, which he read to the Society of Antiquaries in 1765 and which appeared in the first volume of *Archaeologia* (1770), and the survey of Exeter Cathedral which accompanied the engravings published by the society in 1797.[79] His correspondence, however, reveals that he was using his considerable influence and patronage to activate inquiries in this direction amongst antiquaries and friends through Oxford and through the Society of Antiquaries to which he had been elected in 1746. He put pressure upon the society to publish plates of what he took to be Saxon buildings, such as St Augustine's at Canterbury, and supported the move to commission engravings of the illustrations to the Caedmon manuscript, chiefly because they served to illustrate various Saxon architectural features.[80] He also did his best to encourage his friend Sanderson Miller to draw up a history of architectural antiquities. Miller, a Warwickshire landowner and amateur architect, was responsible for a number of Gothic-inspired buildings erected by his circle of friends, chiefly amongst the midlands gentry. Most of these were country Whigs or Tory in politics and the choice of the Gothic style would have had important political resonances for them.[81] Miller's enthusiasm never took the desired literary turn, largely because of the time and expense that such a project would involve. More fruitfully Lyttelton's influence can be seen in the advice and information he provided for other antiquaries who did venture into print. His observations on churches were the basis for the architectural descriptions in Treadway Nash's *History of Worcestershire* and in William Borlase's *History and Antiquities of Cornwall*, and his notes on Staffordshire (where the family seat of Hagley was located) were used by Stebbing Shaw in the 1798 history of Staffordshire. Most notably, his comments were taken up and pursued at greater length by his correspondent James Bentham, a canon of Ely cathedral, and eventually published in *History and Antiquities of Ely Cathedral* (1771).

By mid century it was becoming more common to distinguish the Saxon or debased Roman style from the 'Gothic' style which had replaced it from, it was believed, the late twelfth century. In its elegance and lightness the Gothic style reached a perfection of beauty in cathedrals such as York or Salisbury. The pointed Gothic arch was identified as the key feature distinguishing that style from the preceding Saxon era. Its implementation enabled the medieval architects to achieve the characteristic qualities of light, height and space, as opposed to the rounded Norman arches, which put a limit on the size of arches and vaults and produced the massy heaviness which so many found distasteful. If a date could be identified when the pointed arch was introduced, it would offer a yardstick by which to date all other buildings in the absence of documentary evidence. This, therefore, provided the basic framework around which antiquaries conducted their inquiries into Gothic architecture.

Various theories surrounding the origin of the Gothic arch circulated during the eighteenth century. Some argued that the inspiration came from observing the intersection of branches of trees, and that the Gothic peoples, who had originally worshipped in woody glades, had sought to recreate the effect of the sylvan setting in more durable materials. William Stukeley, developing his theme of continuity in patriarchal religion, argued that the Druids had worshiped their Supreme Being in just such glades, and that the pointed arch used in church architecture was therefore the physical expression of the spiritual continuity. 'The present Westminster Abby, and generally our cathedrals, the Temple church, and the like, present us with a true notion of those verdant cathedrals of antiquity; and which our Druids brought from the east into our own island, and practised before the Romans came hither.'[82] An influential essay by William Warburton, a longstanding friend of Stukeley's, had similarly suggested that the Goths had been inspired by the arcades formed by arboreal intersection.[83] This approach to identifying the origins of Gothic architecture was not universally discredited, even by the end of the century. In 1797 Sir James Hall suggested a novel refinement on the theme, arguing not only that the pointed arch was modelled upon the branches of trees, but that the whole system of ornamentation could be shown to be derived from an imitation of wickerwork. Despite the detailed illustrations with which he supported his thesis, it was not well received.[84]

The theory of intersecting branches had a certain instinctive appeal, which was particularly appropriate to eighteenth-century constructions of primitive society, but it could never be established with any degree of certainty. More problematically, the thesis did not shed any illumination upon the historical conjuncture at which the arch was first deployed. In 1750 Sir Christopher Wren's writings on architecture were published posthumously in the collection of writings edited by his son, *Parentalia*. This volume included his unfinished 'Tracts on Architecture', and also his reports on Old St Paul's, Salisbury Cathedral and Westminster Abbey. These reports included extensive architectural analysis of the buildings as well as Wren's theory of the origins of the Gothic arch in English buildings.[85] Taken together, the tracts were effectively the first publication to treat a cathedral as an architectural structure, rather than primarily as a site of worship and religious veneration – a distinction of some significance in the development of 'architectonical antiquities' or architectural history, as it would now be called. Such was the respect in which Wren was held that the interpretation he offered rapidly gained a large following. Wren identified a similarity between the pointed Gothic arch and those of Islamic architecture, and suggested that the arch was brought to England by returning crusaders. It was thus dubbed the saracenic arch. This theory, tying the arrival of the new style of architecture to participation in the Crusades, had an obvious attraction in that it offered the possibility of assigning a fixed date to the introduction of the Gothic style. Given both Sir Christopher's reputation, which ensured a broader readership for *Parentalia* than many antiquarian publications could be expected to attract, and the epistemological preference for explaining political, social and cultural change in terms of successive invasions, it was easily assimilated into many architectural studies. A variant of this theme also gave the pointed arch an eastern origin, but the channel by which it was introduced was via the Moorish influence in the Iberian peninsula. It was with the intention of establishing the genesis of the Gothic arch in Spain that Charles Lyttelton's nephew, Thomas Pitt, travelled to Spain in 1760.[86] His account circulated in manuscript amongst the antiquaries, although it never found its way into print, and the Iberian connection was largely unexplored until revived again in James Murphy's analysis of the Gothic architecture of the church at Batalha in Portugal.[87]

Others argued that the pointed arch was developed from observing the patterns created by intersecting rounded arches. This was a view much favoured, lending itself readily to the personal experience of antiquaries who could easily hunt out local examples of intersecting rounded arches from which they could construct their own architectural chronology. It could also be represented as an indigenous innovation – a factor which was to become of increasing significance in the latter part of the century as the Gothic style became more closely tied to the construction of an English national identity. The arcade of intersecting arches on the wall of the hospital of St Cross, Winchester, was a favourite example offered by antiquaries to account for the origins of pointed arches, and St Cross acquired a kind of classic status on the antiquarian itinerary on this account. Another theory, developed notably by the architect James Essex, was that the pointed arch was a structural response to the problems of spanning a wide space with a single arch.[88] John Whitaker, in a typically eccentric fashion, rejected all other theories for the origin of the Gothic arch, and insisted upon its origins in Roman Britain. The cathedral church of St Neots, he argued, had been first established by the romanised Britons who had been converted to Christianity. They had used the pointed arch, whose construction they had learnt from the Romans; the pointed arches survived as evidence both of the sophistication of the Britons' building technique and the continuity of Christianity in Cornwall. As with any object of antiquarian inquiry, the origins of the pointed arch could always be made to serve an ulterior argument.[89]

Despite the frequent objections levelled against Gothic architecture there was a growing realisation that it should be judged on its own terms, rather than as a corruption of the classical norm. Sir William Chambers famously observed that, 'One cannot refrain from wishing that the Gothic Structures were more considered, better understood, and in higher estimation than they hitherto seem to have been' in his *Treatise on Civil Architecture* (1759), although his own designs and publications did little to alter this perception.[90] This new sensitivity was given expression in particularly influential form in Richard Hurd's *Letters on Chivalry and Romance* (1762).

> When an architect examines a Gothic structure by Grecian rules, he finds nothing but deformity. But the Gothic architecture has it's (sic) own rules, by which when it comes to be examined, it is seen to have it's (sic) merit, as well as the Grecian. The question is not, which of the two is conducted in the simplest or truest taste: but, whether there be not sense and design in both, when scrutinized by the laws of which each is projected.[91]

Whereas Saxon architecture was regarded as Roman architecture degenerated, the Gothic style appeared to flout every classical convention. Once this difference had been embraced, it could then be admired for its asymmetry, the extreme slenderness of the pillars and the delicate tracery of the ornamentation, which could inspire a sense of reverence and awe of which no classical building was capable. The fame of Hurd's essay has ensured him a place in the pantheon of early Gothicists, and the literary trend which revived the poetry of more primitive ages was sympathetically receptive to a reinterpretration of Gothic architecture. Richard Hurd was no architectural antiquary, but others within his circle were, such as Thomas Warton and the poet Thomas Gray, both of whom made significant collections of material relating to Gothic antiquities in the 1750s and 1760s.[92] Warton amassed a considerable amount of material towards a history of Gothic architecture – which he never wrote, but fragments of which were published in notes to the second edition of *Observations on Spenser's Fairy Queen* and in a brief history of Winchester.[93] Gray's observations on Gothic architecture and its ornament were the most accurate and perceptive of any produced until the end of the century, but they remained in manuscript form, and were seen only by a small group of friends.[94]

Despite an evident broadening of interest in Gothic architecture, a regular history was not forthcoming. Proposals for a new history of Gothic architecture had been published in 1760 by the architectural draughtsman Thomas Muntz, but nothing came of them.[95] Warton's observations were published in 1750 and 1762 and John Aubrey's 'Chronologica Architectonica' was circulating amongst antiquaries in manuscript through the 1750s and 1760s, arousing considerable interest. A part of it was published in 1766 with engravings by Francis Perry, but had very limited circulation.[96] Horace Walpole's *Anecdotes of Painting* (1762) included brief comments establishing the aesthetic appreciation of the Gothic style, without giving any clear indication of its development or analysis. Such an approach was never his priority anyway. This was a deficiency to which Richard Gough, who established so much of the antiquarian agenda of the later eighteenth century, drew particular attention. He was emphatic in pressing the urgency of the need for a history of Gothic architecture which would not just establish a chronology, but would also elucidate its systems and rules. 'One cannot enough regret', wrote Gough in 1768 as he looked back upon the abortive projects of the past decade, 'the little regard hitherto paid to Gothic architecture ... Had the remains of antient buildings been more attended to, we should have seen a system of Gothic architecture in all its aeras: we should have had all its parts reduced to rules: their variations and their dates fixed together.' Despite the richness of variety of Gothic buildings, antiquaries had not even assigned names by which to distinguish the tracery of windows, the mouldings of arches, or the foliage of capitals.[97] This was not merely a matter of aesthetic appreciation. Along with the lack of any considered history of the Anglo-Saxon period, the absence of a sympathetic but critical analysis of Gothic architecture represented a void in the nation's history. The history of Gothic architecture was now being presented as an essential element in the wider narrative of national history and the Gothic style would soon be hailed as the definitively English form of architecture.

Gough did not relinquish hopes of seeing a regular history, however, because the Cambridge architect James Essex was also said to be planning an architectural history which would trace out the chronological development of the Gothic style. Essex, who had worked on King's College Chapel, and Ely and Lincoln cathedrals, had been identified by William Cole as a 'Gothicist' in the 1740s, and as early as 1756 the architect was planning an architectural history of King's College Chapel.[98] Despite a modest background as the son of a tradesman and a builder-cum-architect, he was taken up by antiquaries such as James Bentham (to whose *History of Ely* he made an important contribution), William Cole, Horace Walpole, Michael Tyson and James Nasmith, as well as Gough himself. In 1772, unusually for a man in his position, his friends secured his election to the Society of Antiquaries, and during the 1770s he accompanied Tyson and Gough on a number of antiquarian tours examining buildings of Gothic interest. Gough was driven to distraction by Essex's reluctance to risk the expense of venturing into print and by his technical prolixity.[99] 'I join my tears with yours', wrote Gough to Tyson, 'when I think of *Gothick Architecture*.'[100] It may be doubted whether one need share the despair of Gough and Tyson over Essex's failure to produce. The surviving manuscript, which would have provided the basis for the history, indicates that Essex had little to contribute in terms of originality of thought or insights into the principles of Gothic architecture.[101] What Gough and Tyson valued, however, was the technical knowledge of building construction which Essex could bring to the subject, which was beyond them, whatever their capacities for aesthetic appreciation and historical contextualisation. For medievalists such as Gough a history of Gothic architecture was an essential step in establishing the academic credibility of their enthusiasm. However much he, or any of his circle, sought to assert the importance of Anglo-Saxon or Gothic antiquities, their approach was indelibly coloured by their own classical training, and their expectations were invariably shaped by their knowledge of classical antiquities. A history of the kind proposed by Essex would elevate a study of Gothic architecture from the realms of taste, such as that outlined in Walpole's *Anecdotes*, and raise the level of discussion from the imprecise and ill-founded generalities which they identified in contemporary publications. It would give the claims being made for medieval proficiency in the arts of building an unarguable basis in a language that could match the architectural treatises of Vitruvius or Alberti.

Essex failed to produce and Gough did not have the architectural expertise to undertake such a project himself, however much he asserted its desirability. But Essex's specialist knowledge was not entirely squandered. In addition to the paper he had contributed to *Archaeologia* he had also advised James Bentham, prebendary and canon of Ely Cathedral, in the historical account that Bentham had drawn up of the cathedral and provided the drawings for the plates with which the volume was illustrated. William Cole, whose touchy pride was slighted because Bentham had curtailed the account of the bishops he had sent him from his own collections, was typically dismissive of Bentham's efforts. His history, he told Walpole, was crawling along, but he laboured under 'dullness and slowness of apprehension' and 'natural poverty of genius'.[102] Bentham's background, he went on by way of explanation, was in trade; moreover his brother was an alderman of Cambridge. Bentham's account of Ely may have been twenty years in gestation, but it exercised considerably more influence over the antiquarian appreciation of Gothic architecture than did anything which either Cole or Walpole produced – despite his unfortunate family background. For many years it stood out as the most detailed and perceptive analysis of a medieval building published in the English language and was the starting point for almost every discussion of the origins of the pointed arch – whether or not the author agreed with the thesis of intersecting arches. Bentham corresponded at considerable length with Charles Lyttelton, and shared his fascination with the relationship between the Saxon and Norman styles, together with Lyttelton's preference for what they considered to be the Saxon mode of building. Saxon churches were 'elegant fabricks' and well constructed, of moderate size; whereas Norman churches were large, sumptuous and magnificent, and of much greater proportions.[103] There followed a detailed analysis of the varieties of ornamentation to be found in Saxon and Norman designs: capitals were plain or decorated with foliage and animals; pillars might be decorated with spiral grooves, or a network of lozenges; arches were plain, but the principal ones were decorated with chevron work or zig-zag moulding, or would be ornamented by embattled frett, triangular frett, nail head moulding, or billeted moulding. These descriptions drew not just on Ely, but also observations on the cathedrals at Lincoln, Durham, Peterborough, Hereford and Old St Paul's (using the evidence of Hollar's engravings for Dugdale's history). With the analysis of Saxon architecture completed, he moved on to discuss the Gothic. At this point Sir Christopher Wren was courteously put right: the 'eminent Architect's memory' must have failed him – for otherwise he could not have confused the buildings constructed before and after the Conquest. Bentham then proceeded to elaborate upon the thesis of intersecting arches, as evidenced by the example of St Cross.[104]

The evolution of the pointed arch, from the simple lancet window and slender pillar of Henry III's reign, exemplified in the architecture of Salisbury Cathedral, to the ornate tracery, multiple pillars and profusion of ornament of the later Plantaganet era, reached the height of perfection in King's

College Chapel – itself a reflection of Essex's contribution to Bentham's analysis:

> The decorations, harmony and proportions of the several parts of this magnificent Fabrick, it's (sic) fine painted Windows, and richly ornamented spreading Roof, it's (sic) gloom, and perspective all concur in affecting the imagination with pleasure and delight, at the same time that they inspire awe and devotions. It is undoubtedly one of the most complete, elegant, and magnificent Structures in the Kingdom.[105]

It must be acknowledged, however, that the most detailed and perceptive element of the history, which analysed the structure and ornament of the cathedral, was heavily dependent upon the unpublished notes of Thomas Gray, the poet and antiquary, who had been compiling observations upon the stylistic development of medieval architecture as early as 1753 in summer tours made around the country. Gray's friend William Mason asserted that Gray had been able 'to pronounce at first sight, on the precise time, when any particular part of any of our cathedrals was erected'.[106] A comparison with Gray's commonplace books reveals just how deeply Bentham was indebted to him, for both terminology and examples.

Despite the considerable milestone which Bentham's history represented, it had not gone far enough, and Richard Gough continued to look for a regular history of Gothic architecture. In the 1780s he pinned his hopes on another protégé, the draughtsman John Carter, who had been 'discovered' by Michael Lort around 1780 as being particularly skilled in drawing Gothic antiquities. Carter had already contributed a number of plates with accompanying commentary for the *Builder's Magazine*, praising Gothic architecture at the expense of classical architecture, which he dismissed as a foreign import.[107] Like Walpole he extolled the mystery and sublimity of Gothic buildings, their capacity to inspire a sense of awe and reverence, but Carter took this admiration to a new plane and exalted it over and above the classical style.

Carter was an extremely competent architectural draughtsman, and was employed by Richard Gough on the drawings for his *History of Croyland Abbey* and *Sepulchral Monuments* (1786). He was also engaged as draughtsman to the Society of Antiquaries and executed commissions for a number of other members of the Society. In 1790 he was directed to take drawings of the medieval palace of Westminster and from 1792 he embarked upon the drawings for the society's *Cathedral Antiquities*, an outstanding series of highly detailed engravings which presented the façades, cross-sections and details of the internal and external ornament of the cathedral. The volumes were printed at great expense on high-quality atlas paper. In the meantime he also undertook his own publishing ventures, *Specimens of Ancient Sculpture and Painting*, 2 vols (1780–86, 1787–94), *Views of Ancient Buildings in England*, 6 vols (1786–93) and *The Ancient Architecture of England*, 2 vols (1795–1814). Through these volumes, and through a journalistic campaign conducted in the pages of the *Gentleman's Magazine*, he developed a passionate defence of Gothic architecture. He was the most vocal and dogmatic exponent of the view that the Gothic style was indigenous to England and owed nothing to foreign influence. Its origins were not saracenic as suggested by Wren, whose derogatory comments upon the Gothic style in *Parentalia* made him fume with indignation, but lay, as Warton had suggested, in the intersection of arches. The term 'Gothic' he disliked, for its pejorative overtones of philistinism and vandalism, and its imputation of foreign origins.[108] Essex had appreciated the architectural logic behind Gothic architecture, but had nevertheless judged it according to the classical principles in which he had been trained. Carter went further and articulated an admiration for the Gothic which saw it not from the perspective of degeneration from a classical ideal, but as a superior, purer and native style.[109] There was no positive system to Gothic architecture, he wrote. It had evolved in a pragmatic, ad hoc way in response to specific structural problems, by 'all commanding-chance, the caprice of architects, or that compelling power necessity, to work within the space or dimensions given.'[110] Gothic architecture, like the Gothic constitution, was distinctively English and had reached its perfection in England; such specimens of Gothic architecture as there were in France (which he had never visited) had been built by Englishmen. Carter was not the originator of this suggestion. William Gilpin, purveyor of the picturesque, for example, had similarly argued that the Gothic style was found nowhere but in England, with the exception of such parts of France as had been in the possession of the English.[111] Carter's soaring flights of eloquence on the sublimity and the exquisite beauty of the pointed style left the plodding comments of other antiquaries far behind. His theories were developed during the 1770s and 1780s and dovetailed neatly with the crescendo of nationalist sentiment. During the 1790s the rhetoric became increasingly strident, even xenophobic. The French Wars not only stimulated enthusiasm for English medieval architecture, but also made the Gothic baronial style of architecture increasingly fashionable and encouraged the taste for medieval romances, ballads and chronicles. 'I know of no way that can so well aid the general cause', wrote Carter, 'as to stimulate my countrymen to think well of their own national memorials, the works of art of ancient times, and not to hold up any foreign works as superior to our own.'[112]

Innovation was identified as the great enemy. Innovation and a desire for novelty had facilitated the introduction of the heathenish classical forms of architecture, and had led to the neglect of these most valuable monuments of antiquity or had permitted their perversion for other uses. Carter's imagination was captured by the fantasy of a chivalric medieval world which drew upon the fashionable taste for medieval romance in literature. He built up an idealised view of a medieval society which reached its apogee under Edward III, the model of the martial king, who humbled the French and his wife, Queen Philippa, the model of womanhood. Wykeham, Edward's bishop of Winchester, was an exemplar of churchmanship and was responsible for the building of some of the finest specimens of Gothic architecture at Winchester. In Edward III's reign 'the English nation ... arrived at its meridian of glory. Laws, arms and arts shone in all their splendor.'[113] The value set upon the medieval era in his interpretation of history no longer depended simply on its importance as the period in which the glories of the English constitution were established. The old antipathies to the middle ages as a period of feudal subjugation or Catholic superstition were steadily eroded. Instead it was celebrated as a golden age of chivalric culture; a period of military valour and virtue, in which the arts flourished and society prospered.[114] In developing this idealised vision, Carter was articulating a deeply conservative reaction to the rapid changes which were becoming increasingly apparent through British economy and society. The elevation of Gothic antiquities went hand in hand with Edmund Burke's *Reflections on the Revolution in France*, and Carter's Gothic style had evolved as organically as Burke's English constitution.

Carter's views were controversial on several counts; he was at this stage still in a small minority in his advocacy of Gothic architecture in preference to the classical system. Further to that his views on preservation and his criticisms of the fashionable architect James Wyatt ensured that he acquired considerable personal notoriety.[115] A third point on which he was often challenged was the thesis of the English origins of the Gothic arch. During the period of the French revolutionary and Napoleonic Wars this interpretation had held an obvious popular appeal. The effective prohibition on foreign travel imposed by war made it problematic to gather continental evidence to the contrary. Carter's argument was echoed by a number of other antiquaries, the most influential of whom was John Milner, whose own essay on the origins of the pointed arch was published in the 1800 collection, *Essays on Gothic Architecture.* Milner, like Carter, espoused the view that the pointed arch had arisen fortuitously from the intersection of rounded arches.

The advocates of foreign origins for the Gothic arch could not be completely silenced, however, and in the early nineteenth century the evidence for earlier continental specimens of Gothic architecture weighed ever more heavily against the chauvinist thesis of Carter or Milner. G. D. Whittington's *Survey of the Ecclesiastical Antiquities of France*, published posthumously in 1809, was much more decisive in locating the European origins of Gothic architecture in France: his explicit intent was to refute the hypothesis that the Gothic style had originated in England, to which Carter had given high profile credence through the Society of Antiquaries' *Cathedral Antiquities.*[116] Names were not mentioned, but it was received as a direct attack on Carter. Whittington was another of those who thought that the style was of eastern origin, imported by twelfth-century crusaders and developed to a peak of ornamentation by the freemasons. It bore no relationship to the Anglo-Norman debasement of Roman form. The claims that England had been first to develop the Gothic style were shown to be unfounded; Suger's work at St-Denis could be demonstrated to predate all the English pretenders to primacy. Even in point of view of excellence of execution, the French cathedrals were found to be superior. Rheims, he argued, excelled anything in England because of the lightness of execution and the intricacy of the pyramidal and spiral form. In a comparison between the cathedral at Amiens, and that icon of English Gothic architecture, Salisbury, the former came off better, reaching a higher state of perfection than any building in England.[117] Carter riposted in typically bullish style in the *Gentleman's Magazine*, condemning Whittington's 'downright apostacy', but the evidence began to mount up against him and his followers.[118]

Other antiquaries continued to chip away at Carter's doggedly insistent assertion about the Englishness of Gothic architecture. Papers published in *Archaeologia* carried on this theme, taking issue with the insularity of Carter's arguments and redirecting attention towards the European contexts in which Gothic architecture had emerged. Taking a wider European perspective allowed Thomas Kerrich to tackle the problem from a different direction. He attempted to move the discussion forward from the narrow obsession with the 'pointed arch' by which it had been dominated throughout the eighteenth century. The question, he argued, was not who had invented the arch first, or where it originated, but why the style, of which it was just one element, appeared across Europe apparently almost simultaneously. He dismissed traditional explanations, which had posited that it had been introduced 'ripe and adult and in its full vigour' from some other country and that western Europe had implicitly adopted it without making any alterations. Reviving James Essex's argument (whose papers he had acquired) that the Gothic arch was conceived in response to the structural challenge posed by vaulting a ceiling, Kerrich proffered a much more sophisticated and evolutionary explanation of the emergence of the new style of architecture, concentrating on the structural elements, rather then relying on a modification of the invasion thesis to account for stylistic change. Kerrich's interpretation thereby lifted the analysis of Gothic architecture above issues of national partisanship. The function of the building, Kerrich suggested, the materials available and the sheer ignorance of classical building technique – combined with the undeniable creative fancy of the artificers – were sufficient to account for the emergence of a new and unheard of style of building.[119] Carter's response to these papers was so intemperate that the council of the Society of Antiquaries ordered that it should not be read 'as savouring of controversy', but even though Kerrich denied the primacy of English Gothic architecture, he and Carter were united in arguing that the Gothic was no aberration of a classical model but was an entirely different and distinct form.[120] Saracenic origins and intersecting arches began now to give place to increasingly intricate and sophisticated analyses of the Gothic arch and to a rapidly escalating lexicon of technical terminology.[121]

Yet the Englishness of Gothic architecture was too attractive a thesis to give up in its entirety, and was therefore modified. In 1810 the fraternal antiquarian partnership behind *Magna Britannia*, Samuel and Daniel Lysons, suggested that there were specimens of Gothic architecture from the twelfth century in Europe which were coeval or might even predate those of England, and some which were certainly superior. As Carter's sworn enemy at the Society of Antiquaries, Samuel Lysons could hardly have been expected to endorse Carter's position, but in the early nineteenth century the importance of asserting English superiority over France was unavoidable. Judicious even-handedness was called for, and so the superiority of the continental cathedrals was acknowledged in a footnote, whilst the main text argued that nowhere was it more generally used and with a greater variety of elegant ornament than in England.[122] Thomas Rickman's *Attempt to Discriminate the Styles of English Architecture* acknowledged the existence of European versions of the Gothic, but he judiciously declined to comment upon the respective precedence of the English and continental traditions. The English style, he suggested, deserved to be treated individually, on the grounds of its very different character of pure simplicity – the Englishness of plain speaking, plain food, sincerity and frankness was translated into the architectural idiom as well.[123] Rickman therefore coined the terms Norman, early English, decorated English and perpendicular English, the terms which continue to serve architectural historians today.[124] John Brewer, writing in the concluding volume of the *Beauties of England and Wales* (1818), was similarly cautious. Whilst sidestepping the controversial issue of English versus continental origins, he pandered to patriotic sentiment in declaring that the 'fairest and most stupendous' specimens were to be found within the British Isles.[125] A. C. Pugin's *Specimens of Gothic Architecture* published three years later offered a much more emphatic dismissal of the English thesis: the attempts to designate the style to England, he observed, was made without due regard to the monuments remaining in France, Flanders and Germany. The fact that Pugin was himself French by birth may not have been immaterial here.[126]

Meanwhile, the number of publications which purported to explain the different terms of Gothic architecture or to chart its historical development steadily grew. James Bentham's *History and Antiquities of Ely* (1771) was itself republished in 1812 with additional notes and some of the correspondence between Bentham and Lyttelton. Francis Grose offered a brief outline in the introduction to his serial publication, *The Antiquities of England and Wales*, accompanied by a plate illustrating different varieties of Saxon and Gothic ornaments. Extracts from Bentham and Browne Willis's *Cathedral Antiquities* and *Mitred Parliamentary Abbies* were published together in 1798 and two years later, a compilation *Essays on Gothic Architecture* (1800) brought together some of the specialist literature of the last forty years into a more accessible format.[127] It included the essays by Bentham from his *History of Ely*, Grose's preface to the *Antiquities of England*, Warton's notes on the *Faery Queen* and culminated with John Milner's essay on the rise of the pointed arch, extracted from his recently published history of Winchester. This was no publication by subscription, but a commercial venture, and one which was sufficiently successful to merit a third edition by 1808: the *Quarterly Review* described it in 1809 as a work in 'everyone's hands'.[128] The editors hoped that by rendering these essays on the ancient architecture of England easily accessible and at a low cost many readers would be 'led to a higher relish' to that branch of antiquarian study.[129] The fact that such a publication was a successful venture is a fair indication that the appreciation and knowledge of Gothic antiquities was no longer the preserve of a small circle of antiquaries. William Rastall Dickinson's *History of Southwell* (1787) and *History of Newark* (1806) performed a similar function, summarising the extant literature on Gothic architecture, and sought to establish for the reader some kind of framework for distinguishing the characteristics of Roman, Saxon, Danish, Norman and Gothic architecture. His intention was to form a 'sort of architectural index, or nomenclature of columns, arches, and ornaments, by means of which the origin of every ancient building might, almost on a first view be dated'.[130] The brothers Lysons accomplished a similar design in *Magna Britannia;* their method was to work through the centuries from the Saxon period onwards, discussing the churches, or elements of churches, which fell into the particular chronological range they were discussing. Within two years of the publication of Rickman's *Attempt to Discriminate the Styles of English Architecture* in 1817, such was the progress that had been made in the refinement of a language of architectural description that one antiquary made it a positive selling-point of his history of Gloucester that in his description of the cathedral he had avoided all technical terms.[131] Architectural antiquities were finally detached from the stultifying complexities of pedigrees and genealogies, and the interminable lists of charitable benefactions. Churches were described *en masse*, as they illustrated particular architectural features, rather than individually as the repository of the memorials of previous generations.

These attempts to educate the amateur and the antiquary in discriminating between the different styles were developed into a commercial publishing venture by John Britton, in a series of publications of which the most important were *Beauties of England and Wales, Architectural Antiquities* and *Cathedral Antiquities.* Britton had started out as a hack writer of letterpress for periodicals. He built up his antiquarian expertise in the course of a career in publishing, in which he constantly asserted that his aims were to bring about a wider appreciation and understanding of the nation's architectural riches amongst the reading public. It cannot be said, however, that he brought any new insights to the subject; he was a synthesiser and an editor, summarising the work of others and packaging it in an attractive format for publication. The value of his publications now may be seen to lie in the quality of the engravings, which were the first to be published at an affordable price whilst doing justice to the architecture, rather than depicting generalised picturesque Gothic. John Carter had provided elevations, sections and attention to fine detail, but had not done so in a format available for widespread consumption. The *Cathedral Antiquities* published by the Society of Antiquaries was prohibitively expensive, with even the cheapest of the series costing five guineas. The expense was such that the project was abandoned with only six cathedrals surveyed.[132] Samuel and Daniel Lysons had followed Carter in using a combination of plans, sections, details of ornament and full elevations in the illustrations to *Magna Britannia*, but their project was abandoned after the publication of Devonshire with the death of Samuel Lysons in 1819. Again, it was priced for the wealthier collector, rather than the general public. Britton's volumes were hardly in the category of cheap prints, but were of a price which did not automatically restrict them to the gentleman connoisseur, and were published with correspondingly larger print runs of a thousand or more. Each number of the *Cathedral Antiquities* for example, which included six prints (four architectural and two sculptural) was to cost 12 shillings, or £1 for imperial paper.[133]

Britton took stock of the enormous growth which had taken place in the discussion of architectural antiquities in England in 1825 in the concluding volume to the series *The Architectural Antiquities of Great Britain*. There was a rapidly expanding genre of specialist literature, much of which was now written by architects rather than amateurs. Prior to 1770 publications on architectural antiquities were few and far between, and many of those Britton mentioned dealt with the subject only tangentially. After that date the rate of publication rose rapidly and he cited fifty different items which had appeared in just over fifty years between 1770 and 1822.[134] Three years earlier Britton had collaborated with A. C. Pugin in a similar retrospective view in *Specimens of Gothic Architecture*: the efforts of the eighteenth-century antiquaries such as Browne Willis were marred by 'gross blunders'. Sir Christopher Wren was daringly dismissed for his 'wild theories'. The inappropriateness of the term 'Gothic' was acknowledged; but, noted Pugin, it was never now used in a contemptuous sense. Pugin was writing in a purely architectural context, but these comments are a fair indication of the cultural shift which had taken place over the course of a century in attitudes to medieval history and culture. The *Specimens* were also manifestly produced with the architect in mind; Pugin, Britton and their collaborator Edward Willson were all members of the Architects and Antiquaries Club, established in 1819 with Britton as treasurer and honorary secretary and boasting nineteen regular and fourteen honorary members. Its immediate aim was to promote scholarly communication on ancient architecture and its relationship with literature and the fine arts. More broadly it set itself the mission of improving the practice of architecture and refining the public taste – to be achieved primarily through the dissemination of high quality engravings of specimens of ancient architecture. To Britton's dismay, the chief absorption of the society revealed itself as conviviality, and, quite predictably, it was felt that it was poaching on the territory of the chartered architectural and antiquarian bodies. By the end of 1822 it had effectively ceased to exist. Despite the brevity of its existence, however, the very fact that Britton was able to coral a corpus of like-minded individuals to join the club indicates that by 1820 architectural history had gone some way towards establishing itself as a discipline distinct from the more general inquiries of antiquarianism.[135]

The preference for the term 'English' to refer to Gothic architecture is not only significant as another manifestation of embattled nationalism. Implicit in the usage of the term was a series of assumptions about English superiority and dominance within the British Isles. Whether or not Carter's thesis of the Englishness of Gothic architecture was accepted, the Anglocentricity by which the style and its origins were discussed in all of the literature was well-nigh absolute. Whilst Thomas Rickman anticipated a time at which it would be possible to distinguish Spanish, Italian or French variants of the Gothic style, his use of the term 'English' subsumed Scottish, Welsh and even Irish variants. It is noticeable that very few of the studies of Gothic architecture or architectural antiquities which were published in this period were written by native Scots, Welsh or Irish antiquaries. The exception was Sir James Hall's *Essay on the Origins and Principles of Gothic Architecture.* Hall was a Scot, and his idiosyncratic wickerwork theory never acquired much of a following amongst English antiquaries.[136] The Gothic style of architecture was an English creation and it was primarily English antiquaries who hunted out specimens through Scotland, Wales and Ireland. 'The ecclesiastical architecture of Wales', commented one writer, 'so closely assimilates, in progressive character and improvement, with that of England, that it scarcely requires separate notice in an endeavour to investigate the rise and history of the different styles of building observable in this island.'[137] The study of architectural antiquities was another means of cultural imperialism within the British Isles, by which the antiquities of Scotland, Wales, and to a lesser extent Ireland, could be appropriated to England.

Gothic architecture in Wales represented English mastery over the Welsh in the castles built by Edward I and in the cathedrals and monasteries that symbolised the displacement of the native Welsh church by that of Roman Catholicism. Daines Barrington, who of all the Fellows of the Society of Antiquaries had some of the strongest ties with Wales and Welsh antiquaries, was one of the first to draw attention to the scale and historical importance of the Welsh castles, which he depicted as unequivocally English. Despite Barrington's evident sympathy for Wales, he believed the country to have been sunk in barbarism until conquest by the English under Edward I introduced some elements of civilisation. The Welsh, he argued, had neither the resources nor the skill to construct such edifices. Even now he doubted whether the most expert of Welsh artisans had the proficiency in masonry to lay such a regular course of stones as was to be found in the Welsh castles.[138] For their part, Welsh antiquaries displayed comparatively little interest in their cathedral antiquities or the monastic ruins. Thomas Pennant, whose *Tour in Wales* was one of the most widely consulted works on Welsh topography and antiquities, did not make this one of his priorities. His draughtsman, Moses Griffiths, provided competent drawings, but Pennant's descriptions showed barely any appreciation of the buildings and ruins depicted. A crude distinction between Gothic and rounded arches was the best that he could muster. The castles, those other monuments of medieval grandeur, were the occasion for recounting the English subjugation of the Welsh, rather than evoking picturesque scenes or making architectural disquisitions. The exception was the description of Conway, a castle of 'matchless magnificence'.[139] It was left to the Welsh tourists, such as Sir Richard Colt Hoare or William Coxe, to draw attention to the ruins at Llanthony or Margam Abbey.[140] The architectural antiquities of St David's were illustrated by an Englishman, Charles Norris, who fully espoused not only Carter's assertion of the superiority of Gothic architecture over the modern Grecian style, but the attribution of the pointed arch to the English.[141]

For the Irish, Gothic architecture was even more sharply evocative of foreign conquest by the English and represented only a minor strand in the agenda of the Irish antiquaries. The subject was barely even mentioned in the course of the six volumes of *Collectanea de rebus hibernicis* (1781–1804) edited by Charles Vallancey. Mervyn Archdall's *Monasticon hibernicum*, a history of the monastic foundations and their estates modelled on Sir William Dugdale's *Monasticon anglicanum*, conveyed almost no information on the physical appearance of the monastic foundations he described, despite the fact that it was written in 1786 when there was already considerable interest in the subject in England. The contiguity of Catholicism in Ireland left no scope for the Protestant antiquaries such as Archdall to indulge in the kind of nostalgic recollection of monastic piety or philanthropy which filled the reveries of English antiquaries. The ruins of the monasteries evoked a threat which was far from dormant, reminding him of the 'fatal delusions', 'religious zeal' and 'mortified ascetics' of the pre-Reformation era.[142] Descriptions of buildings in urban and county histories were brief and perfunctory, consisting of little more than references to 'ancient Gothic piles' and were comparatively reticent as to the picturesque attractions of such ruins.[143] This too is significant: because Ireland never assumed the same place in the English tourist itinerary as Scotland or Wales, there was less interest on the part of English readers – the most important market for a description of the picturesque architectural antiquities of Ireland.[144] The fact that Ireland had never been conquered by the Romans meant that it was impossible to trace out the standard narrative of architectural excellence introduced by the Romans, followed by decline and a descent into barbarism and ignorance, followed by a gradual recovery of taste and elegance. Ireland's ancient and medieval history set it apart from the rest of the British Isles, and such attempts as there were to survey the early history of architectural antiquities by native scholars adopted a very different explanatory framework from that of their English peers – one which was much more open to European influences. The Irish acquired their knowledge of architecture not from the Romans, it was said, but from Spain.[145]

Wales and Scotland, Sir Richard Colt Hoare informed his readers, had attracted the notice and admiration of men of taste for many years. The press teemed with their publications, and there was little remaining to be said upon the subject of military, monastic or natural beauties. But Ireland was unvisited and unknown – 'And why? Because from want of books, and living information, we have been led to suppose its country rude, its inhabitants savage, its paths dangerous.'[146] Ireland, it was agreed, suffered 'unparalleled neglect' from topographers and remained nearly untouched and little regarded by Englishmen of taste.[147] Thus it was that Francis Grose left describing the antiquities of Ireland till the end of his career and died before the volume was completed. The project was taken over by the Anglo-Irish antiquary Edward Ledwich, scourge of the patriot and Catholic antiquaries. Only the year before Grose's arrival in Ireland, he had published the *Antiquities of Ireland* (1790), which had gone some way towards describing some of the architectural antiquities.[148] Grose's *Antiquities of Ireland*, he wrote later, would have united Ireland in the closest association with Great Britain.[149] Ledwich was fully complicit in this project of antiquarian colonialism, and the celebration of Irish medieval or 'Gothic' antiquities was entirely consonant with his own perspective on Irish history and its antiquities. As a Gothicist, second only to John Pinkerton in his assertion of the superiority of the Goth over the Celt, Ledwich saw the English conquest of Ireland as one in a series of 'Gothic' invasions, and as a pivotal step in bringing the Irish towards a state of civilisation. The castles, monasteries and cathedrals which they built, therefore, were the most striking monument to English superiority and the progress of Anglo-Irish civilisation. Ledwich was not one of those picturesque antiquaries who loved to dwell upon the crumbling masonry and delicate tracery of a Gothic building, but was sufficiently well read in the relevant literature to offer some pertinent observations on the subject.[150] His descriptions were concise; he preferred to refer the reader to the English authorities upon the subject – Bentham, Ducarel and Warton – rather than to go into minute descriptive detail himself. The inescapable conclusion was that these antiquities were English in all but location, offering further proof of Irish subordination and inferiority to England.[151] It is hardly surprising that neither the Catholic nor the patriot antiquaries showed much interest in this line of inquiry and sought to recover the history of Ireland's middle ages through the 'authentic' Irish antiquities of ballads and poetry.[152]

Scotland, it was held, could not boast many specimens of Gothic architecture which could even begin to rival those of England. Its history of religious conflict had been even more divisive than in England, and the destructive iconoclasm of the Reformation even more comprehensive. Such monuments as had survived into the eighteenth century had been indiscriminately ravaged by the destructive fury of Protestant zealots during the Reformation era. The low survival rate of ecclesiastical antiquities within Scotland offered yet more proof to the English of Scotland's poor record in allowing religious enthusiasm to gain the upper hand. Significantly, those Gothic antiquities for which the Scots could claim fame, such as Melrose or Jedburgh, were located in the Borders, the area of Scotland closest to English influence. By a cunning sleight of hand the English antiquary William Hutchinson had virtually annexed Melrose, which was believed to be the finest specimen of Gothic architecture in Scotland, to England's architectural heritage, by including an 'excursion to Mailross [Melrose] Abbey' in his *View of Northumberland* (1776).[153] Linlithgow was allowed by a later antiquary to be an elegant edifice – but was claimed for the English, it being built, it was said, by either Edward I or Aylmer de Valence. In general, Scottish specimens of medieval architecture were inferior, clumsy and in poor taste.[154]

English antiquaries held their Scottish brethren to task for a culpable neglect of their architectural antiquities. 'Prudes in divinity, metaphysicians in philosophy, novices in philology, they aspire above the ruse of antiquarian science. By principle averse to religious magnificence, the splendor of the earlier church moulders away unnoticed.'[155] Whilst Catholic and Episcopalian antiquaries with Jacobite leanings, such as Robert Keith, Richard Hay or Thomas Innes, had built up substantial manuscript collections on ecclesiastical antiquities, the Presbyterian majority were not disposed to show a benignly indulgent attitude towards the ruins of the Catholic, Gothic past.[156] Scottish neglect presented further proof of the superiority of English antiquarianism over that of its sister nation. The Scots could write history, but they failed to take the necessary measures to record and observe the monuments upon which history was based. Following his visit to Scotland in 1771, Richard Gough reported in despair to Michael Tyson upon the condition in which the ruins were maintained: 'Except one or two well preserved Abbies there is very little in the Gothic way. One is really shockt to see the inside of a kirk: everything about it debas'd and perverted: not a single antient monument left: nor a modern one worth looking at.'[157] He moderated the trenchant criticisms he had made in 1768 in the 1780 edition, *British Topography*, but still drew attention to the paucity of views and engravings of Scottish buildings.[158]

The following decade saw some small improvement in the description of Scottish antiquities, but these publications were chiefly undertaken by Englishmen, or at the instigation of English antiquaries for an English market. The English antiquaries, therefore, assumed to themselves the credit for having alerted the Scottish to the importance of preserving such remains of antiquity, pointing to publications such as Thomas Pennant's tours or Francis Grose's *Antiquities of Scotland* (1789–91) – a miscellany of Scottish views, largely monastic foundations and castles. A number of these also appeared in the selection which was offered in Thomas Hearne's *Antiquities of Great Britain* (1784 and 1806). Additional views appeared in volumes by Charles Cordiner and Adam Cardonnel.[159] Both these volumes were published in London rather than Edinburgh, prompting George Paton to report to Gough that Cordiner's work was unknown in Edinburgh.[160] Even after the foundation of the Scottish Society of Antiquaries, interest in architectural antiquities – as opposed to the location of Mons Graupius or the habitations of Ossian – was muted. The earl of Buchan, the society's founder, protested vigorously against English appropriation of Scottish archives, manuscripts and monuments, but the recording of architectural antiquities was still something which was largely left to the English and attracted little of his patronage.[161] Scotland's medieval antiquities eventually acquired their own champion in Sir Walter Scott. Scott's romantic world of chivalry, medieval minstrelsy and feudal manners and customs was, as he readily admitted, a blend of fiction, conjecture and antiquarian fact, but his antiquarian instincts were never far away, and amongst his numerous publications must be numbered *Border Antiquities*, which provided a series of engravings with letterpress of all the notable antiquities in the Border region.[162] The English antiquaries continued to level the charges of neglect and destruction of antiquities against the Scots, however, as long as the influence of Calvinism prevailed. 'What misery is it to make a church-tour in Scotland!' wrote J. M. Neale of the Camden Society, 'I think nothing can surpass the desecration there.'[163]

It should not be thought that antiquaries were interested only in the exterior appearance of churches, or that the insights derived from a critical and comparative approach were confined to the exterior form. Their interest in ornament and stylistic evolution extended to the interior, to fonts, painted glass and monumental brasses. This was the church 'furniture' to which Thomas Staveley had drawn attention, and it was upon reading Stavely that Andrew Coltée Ducarel wrote in a burst of enthusiasm to Smart Lethieullier about investigating the variety of different forms in which fonts were carved in antiquity.[164] Fonts could be subjected to the same kind of visual analysis of style as the architecture and ornamentation of the church structure, and dated accordingly. Fonts were, however, something of a minority concern, and their illustration was confined to beautifully executed plates in *Vetusta monumenta* or *Archaeologia*.[165] Painted (that is stained) glass and ornamental brasses had likewise assumed the status of a niche interest amongst antiquaries by the end of the century. Painted glass had always been valued by antiquaries for the genealogical information it conveyed. William Stukeley's anger at the dismantling of the painted glass from the windows of the Stamford churches in the 1720s was only partly a lament for the loss of specimens of exquisite workmanship and beauty; primarily it was a response to the destruction of the historic record of benefactions and piety which the glass recorded.[166] By the end of the century, however, a taste for painted glass for its aesthetic qualities – the air of gloom and mystery with which it endowed a church interior – as well as the craftsmanship involved in its decoration, ensured that it was becoming much more highly prized amongst antiquaries, and along with brasses, epitaphs and monuments represented another item to be checked off in the antiquary's church notes.[167]

Of much wider appeal were sepulchral monuments. Whereas the 'church notes' of many antiquaries did not include any mention of pointed arches or the foliage of capitals, they would always record the tombs and effigies, the monumental inscriptions and the heraldic testimony of escutcheons and painted glass. If arches and capitals were of doubtful date, tombs and monuments offered much more certain hope of identification. The interest of the landed proprietor in the tombs of his ancestors and the genealogists' search for heraldic information evolved into a movement to study monuments in their own right. The cult of the tomb was well developed within eighteenth-century society, irrespective of antiquarian considerations: Addison's meditative reflections upon the tombs in Westminster Abbey must have been one of the most frequently cited of all the essays in the *Spectator*.[168] The move towards examining tombs and monuments critically, rather than simply as a means of inspiring melancholy thought and ancestral piety, was one of the important conceptual advances which antiquaries made in the course of the eighteenth century.

Maurice Johnson, the linchpin of the Spalding Gentleman's Society, had once drawn up an essay on the importance of studying tomb architecture. It circulated in manuscript form but, as with most of Johnson's writings, never met with publication. Smart Lethieullier, himself an honorary member of the Spalding Society, was similarly interested and made the first significant collections of material upon the subject. English antiquaries were always quick to claim their superiority over other countries in many aspects of the antiquarian science, but in the study of monumental sculpture they had to acknowledge their debt to Montfaucon, author of *L'antiquité expliquée et répresentée en figures*, 5 vols (1719) which was translated into English in 1727, and *Monumens de la monarchie françoise*, 5 vols (1729–33). Lethieullier had spent two years in France, where he had been the student of Montfaucon. The Benedictine's influence was deeply felt and, on his return to England,

Lethieullier devoted considerable effort in compiling extensive collections relating to sepulchral monuments and the changing customs of commemorating the dead. Like many antiquaries of his social status, he never published his collections, being deterred by the cost and unwilling to solicit subscriptions. His collections were purchased instead by Horace Walpole in 1761, who briefly contemplated such a history himself. Lethieullier's paper on monuments in Gloucestershire churches, in which he argued for the importance of establishing a chronology of tombs and demonstrated their importance in illustrating the manners and customs of the period in which they were erected, was published posthumously in *Archaeologia*.[169] The one antiquary who did proceed to publication was Richard Gough, who drew on many of these earlier collections and brought them together in the massive, albeit flawed, *Sepulchral Monuments.*

Sepulchral Monuments was welcomed by Gough's fellow antiquaries with great enthusiasm. With *British Topography* and the 1789 edition of *Britannia* it stands as one of his major achievements. Gough had rehearsed the theme of illustrating national monuments in a manner to match Montfaucon in *British Topography*. National pride dictated that England could not be seen to be backward with regard to anything which cast honour upon its history or could add to its reputation abroad. The interest which *Sepulchral Monuments* aroused is partly explained by the strength of familial feeling which was vested in such monuments. Gough himself was sympathetic to this conservative strain of thought, which deplored the loss of family monuments and the evidences of descents, benefactions and property. But Gough's own vision for the project, and the warmth of its public reception, was deeply influenced by the interest in the architecture and ornament of the medieval period which we have already observed. If architecture could be understood to reflect social and political changes, this was even more the case with monumental sculpture, with its shifts in iconography mirroring social, religious and sartorial developments.[170] Gough went to great lengths in procuring the illustrations for the volume, begging them from friends, exploiting the resources of the Society of Antiquaries and commissioning draughtsmen such John Carter and Jacob Schnebbelie to make drawings for him. All this was done at his personal cost, and the copper plates for volume two alone were said to have cost him over 2000 guineas.[171] Gough believed that such an enormous financial investment in building up this visual taxonomy was worthwhile because he saw that this was an area where it was possible to move beyond the standards set by continental scholars. Montfaucon, he explained, had assigned the dates of monuments, but he had not exploited them for illustrations of national manners or modes, or attempted to compare one monument with another, nor yet to establish rules by which they might be judged. It was only from such sources, and *not* from texts, that huge areas of the nation's past, upon which the written sources were silent, could be opened up to investigation.

It would be misleading to stress too far the innovation in Gough's approach. Joseph Strutt had pre-empted Gough to some extent in his own publications drawing upon the visual imagery of tombs and monuments, as well as illuminated manuscripts and other sources. Strutt's intellectual proximity to Gough no doubt accounts in part for the barbed and condescending tenor of the latter's comments on Strutt's efforts, who, he said, did not sufficiently discriminate the subjects of different periods and was too limited in his reading.[172] Strutt had none of the advantages of Gough's education, his contacts or his very considerable wealth, which enabled him to travel widely and commission drawings. It was easy to find fault with Strutt, but arguably his lack of familiarity with the traditions of antiquarian scholarship enabled him to adopt a much fresher, original approach. Fundamentally, however, they shared the same objective, to demonstrate how visual materials deserved closer analysis and were proper objects of antiquarian analysis, yielding historical information rather than simply serving as illustrations to a text.

The success of Gough's achievement is perhaps best seen in the rapidity with which it appeared to be outdated. Despite the enormous financial investment in the illustrations, the drawings in *Sepulchral Monuments* can be faulted; indeed they soon were. 'Whatever information we may receive from his writings', wrote Charles Stothard, 'the delineating part is so extremely incorrect, and full or errors, that at a future period, when the originals no longer exist, it will be impossible to form any correct idea of what they really were.'[173] Stothard was being more than a little disingenuous, however; his comments do, after all, come from his own volume upon the same subject published in 1817. The quality of Gough's engravings was considerably better than he implied, particularly when the long gestation of the book is taken into account, during which buildings and monuments were being depicted with ever increasing accuracy by draughtsmen and engravers.[174] In a sense, by the time that Stothard was writing, the battle had already been won in that the importance of accurate engravings was widely accepted. Stothard was capitalising on forty or fifty years of scholarship in which the publication of antiquarian prints had become steadily more popular and in which sensitivity to non-classical design and ornamentation had become much more pronounced.

By the early nineteenth century it is clear that the attempts of Lyttelton and those with whom he corresponded to build up a chronological 'system' of Saxon and Gothic architecture had been largely fulfilled, and that the hegemony of classicism against which they had railed had been comprehensively challenged. Lyttelton and other antiquaries, such as Strutt and Gough, had effectively shown how the systematic comparison of visual media could elicit historical information and in so doing had made a significant contribution to the evolution of a more sophisticated antiquarian methodology, albeit one which would be subsequently appropriated by other disciplines. The emphasis upon establishing a chronological progression of style played an important role in moving the study of antiquities decisively away from the miscellaneous collection of the virtuoso's cabinet to the ordered arrangement exemplified in the architectural histories of the early nineteenth century. In the process, new sub-genres of scholarly inquiry had been opened up and the historical evaluation of England's medieval past reshaped. Contemporaries were not slow to pick up on the irony that the Goths, who had been attributed with bringing down the greatness of the Roman Empire, had also given their name to a style of architecture which showed breathtaking skill in execution and design. Whitby Abbey, remarked Sir William Burrell, was a terrible proof of the 'Gothick disposition' of its former owner, who had gutted the entire (Gothic) building and allowed it to fall into ruin, a habitation for rabbits.[175] Modern Goths could not appreciate their Gothic heritage. Attitudes to antiquities in the early nineteenth century had clearly undergone a remarkable change within half a century or so. In the second part of the eighteenth century a much more explicit articulation of the need to preserve historic or 'antique' buildings, and other antiquities was being expressed, and not simply by lone individuals who belonged to the Society of Antiquaries. Formerly ancient buildings had excited admiration because of their representational value; the spires and steeples were 'like so many fair Emblems of those gradual Ascents, where we hope to aim'.[176] Fortifications and city walls conjured up memories of social and political instability, whilst the ruins of castles were a testimony to the vanity and futility of man's endeavours. An obsessive and pedantic interest was still considered a social solecism, but an appreciation of the Gothic, informed by antiquarianism, was in itself becoming an important element in the repertoire of the polite gentleman (or woman). The place of antiquities in the constant battles over defining taste had therefore been redefined, and the issue of preservation was moving towards a position which made it the concern of not just those of an antiquarian disposition but also one of public interest.

8

Preservation

Antiquaries had a vested interest in the cause of preservation. Their *raison d'être* was based upon the principle of preserving the memory of the past and ensuring its perpetuation for future generations. The antiquities they studied were the objects which had survived the ravages and vicissitudes of history. They relished the puzzle of piecing together the fragments of the past; they delighted in the patina of age and decay which obscured an image or obliterated a date. The obvious marks of antiquity signified the temporal breach between their own time and that past era which only they, with their accumulated expertise, could recover. The recognition of the past as qualitatively different from the present is obviously fundamental to being able to conceive of the desirability of actively preserving a building or an object simply on account of its age. That awareness, however, of both the transience of the physical fabric and the value of maintaining or even restoring it, which is inherent to our modern understanding of preservation, was barely conceptualised in the early eighteenth century. The evolution towards an antiquarian sensibility which placed a priority upon preservation and conservation can be discerned through the activities and writings of the eighteenth century antiquaries. It is ineluctably tied up with the emergence of a discourse of national antiquities and a concept of national history or heritage, both of which went hand in hand with the expression of national identity. By the end of the century the framework for a discussion of the merits of preservation, the principles upon which it should be enacted, and the bodies with whom responsibility for the nation's antiquities should lie was beginning to be sketched out. The foundations for the construction of the idea of a national heritage – manifested in the history, landscape and buildings of the country – had been laid. Increasing recourse was made to the argument that such monuments were a part of the nation's history and were therefore the property of the nation at large. Their value transcended that of private interest; their importance was such that the state, in its legislative embodiment as parliament, could be called upon to take action for their preservation.

Antiquarianism was presented to society in the language of patriotism and public spirit. Collaboration was essential, but the idea of antiquaries acting together as a lobby or a pressure group did not follow naturally upon the exchange of information between equals which characterised the Republic of Letters. This, quite apart from the conceptual barriers which had to be surmounted, presented a further obstacle to the formation of a concerted movement for the preservation of historic monuments. Antiquaries were primarily collectors – in itself a highly individualistic activity – and sought above all to enrich their private collections by ransacking the past, often at the expense of the integrity or even survival of a larger monument. Manuscripts and books, frequently purloined from libraries, archives and other collections, found their way into the personal collections of many antiquaries. Sir Robert Cotton had removed many of the Roman inscriptions from Housesteads to his own private collection at Connington in Huntingdonshire. Antiquaries regularly took away the tesserae from mosaic pavements and plundered the barrows which they excavated for their own collections. The behaviour of a character such as John Warburton, who happily carved up altar pieces and monumental inscriptions in order to add to his own collection, was regarded by other antiquaries as regrettable, even reprehensible. But the scales were already weighted against him on account of a number of other failings, which did not dispose his fellow antiquaries to extend much generosity towards him in this business.[1] His actions were in principle no different from those of most other eighteenth-century antiquaries. Even Richard Gough was not above taking his own memento from the tomb of Edward I when it was exhumed in Westminster Abbey in 1771. The incident was recorded with macabre relish by William Cole, who had it from Michael Tyson: 'Mr G was observed to put his Hand into the Coffin and immediately to apply it to his Pocket: but not so dexterously but that the Dean of Westminster saw it: he remonstrated against the Propriety of it, and Mr G. denying the Fact, the Dean insisted on the Pocket being searched: when they found that he had taken a Finger; which was replaced.' Cole professed that he could not tell whether to believe it.[2]

The antiquary's personal collecting instinct could therefore be at odds with the public responsibility for preservation. This tension illustrates in microcosm the wider problem raised by the question of preservation in the eighteenth century and one which persists, of course, to the present day. All antiquities, every monument of the past, represented somebody's property. The survival of family papers and manuscripts, private libraries and collections depended upon the whim of the owner. Even the documents of the state were caught up in a web of vested interests; the keepers of the various record repositories had the right to levy fees on all those who wished to use them – their custody was a form of property. Any monument, whether church, stone circle or Roman pavement, lay on a piece of ground that, except in a few very cases, was the property of some private or incorporated body, who retained the right to do as they wished with any antiquities which lay on their land. Hoards of coins could be melted down for bullion, standing stones could be burnt for lime, ruined abbeys and castles could be dismantled for building materials. Any notion of 'preservation' for a wider public good – what might today be called the 'national heritage' – would necessarily invoke the intervention of a higher authority, and had therefore to contend with the deeply entrenched attitudes surrounding the sanctity of private property. Changing attitudes to governance, which justified state intervention in other areas of private property, clearly had some part to play in the shift towards a language of national antiquities and a national heritage by which private property rights could be curtailed in the interests of the wider nation; but there were also other cultural changes at work which arose from the agenda of the antiquaries rather than the political economists.

The desirability of preserving an artefact for future generations on account of its inherent historical interest or cultural value is as relevant to documents as to the grandiose edifices of the medieval church; indeed, the urgency of preserving a document was much more immediately apparent. The truths of history, legal precedents and political rights were all settled by recourse to written documents. The frenzy of editing which took place in the late seventeenth and early eighteenth century arose out of a realisation of the fragility and vulnerability of the past, which the discords of the past two centuries had demonstrated, and an awareness of the political and social value of preserving these records. For the non-jurors in particular, who were the most prominent in this move for publication, not the least of the disasters consequent upon Henry VIII's avaricious assault upon the monasteries was the dispersal and destruction of the libraries and the centuries of learning which they represented. The Reformation was represented as the destruction of a literary heritage long before the architectural losses were appreciated. Manuscripts, the antiquaries discovered, were burnt for kindling, used to wrap food or wipe boots, destroyed by rats and damaged by damp. Fires, such as that at the Cottonian Library in 1731, brought home how vulnerable manuscripts were, even when carefully preserved in a collector's library. The issue of preserving a manuscript, however, posed fewer problems than maintaining buildings, which might serve no apparent practical purpose, were costly to maintain, and could be more profitably deployed as building materials, or the land they occupied put to better use. 'While written documents are preserved with the utmost care', complained one correspondent to the *Gentleman's Magazine*, 'ancient edifices are suffered to moulder into dust.'[3] Documents were relatively cheaper and easier to store and, leaving aside the obvious dangers of being used for lighting fires, wrapping pies or being reused as scrap paper, their preservation did not represent the freezing of a significant amount of capital. Questions of ownership and rights of property rarely conflicted with the ethos of preservation, and the essential utility of documents was easy to argue. The importance of documentary proof in a legal context was incontestable and preserving the written records of state was consonant with the traditional primacy awarded to the written word in the writing of history.

The early eighteenth century represented a high point in the publication of important texts for medieval history. Thomas Hearne's single-handed efforts made available some of the most important sources for medieval history in his editions of the various monastic chronicles and Leland's *Itinerary*. At the same time work had begun on the mammoth task of compilation and publication which would eventually become known as Rymer's *Foedera*.[4] Thomas Madox's scholarship was driven by a similar desire to preserve the original charters he had discovered in the Court of Augmentations.[5] The achievement of the later eighteenth-century antiquaries in the realm of publication of texts has not traditionally enjoyed favourable comparison with either the era preceding or succeeding it. The barren landscape depicted by some scholars is, however, misleading. William Blackstone's edition of *Magna Carta* (1759), for example, was manifestly an important piece of antiquarian scholarship and stirred up considerable political and constitutional debate at the time.[6] Minor texts and documents were published in the pages of *Archaeologia* and antiquarian publications of a local scope. All this was small fry, however, in comparison with two major projects, both of which absorbed the energies of a team of antiquaries and involved the Society of Antiquaries in an advisory capacity.

In 1767 the project to publish the parliamentary rolls was commenced. Like Rymer's *Foedera*, this was a project which was intended for official reference rather than rendering the rolls accessible to the wider public, although this subsidiary aim was inevitably facilitated by the scheme. Whilst rendering ease of access was one issue, another factor which persuaded parliament to go ahead with the costs of this project – and also of publishing Domesday Book – was an appreciation of the vulnerability of the originals. Publication secured the contents for the future and was an insurance against the ever-present risk of fire. The scheme was promoted by Philip Carteret Webb, MP for Haslemere, solicitor to the Treasury and a leading figure in the Society of Antiquaries. The editorial work involved some of the leading antiquaries of both the earlier and the latter part of the century, drawing in scholars such as Philip Morant, who had corresponded with Edmund

St Botoloph's Priory, Colchester, Essex, from Francis Grose, *The Antiquities of England and Wales*, 4 vols (1772–76). (*Special Collections, University of Leicester*)

Gibson and Thomas Hearne, and younger figures such as Thomas Astle and John Topham, both of whom were leading figures on the council of the Society of Antiquaries. As an antiquarian exercise the editorial policy can be faulted, but standards did not show an appreciable decline from the earlier part of the century, and are allowed to have been rigorous and consistent.[7] By 1777 the printing of *Rotuli parliamentorum* was complete. Distribution of the printed volumes was tightly restricted, but, crucially, copies were made available to the State Paper Office and the Tower Record Office, where they could, in theory, be searched by members of the public. The publication of an index and glossary ensured that not just the physical documents but also the contents were made accessible to those who wished to search them.[8]

The second project, that of publishing a facsimile edition of Domesday Book, was likewise instigated by the Society of Antiquaries upon the initiative of Philip Carteret Webb and drew upon the expertise of the society as a body. The prolonged debates over whether to proceed by engraving a facsimile copper plate or whether to cut a specially created typeface hinged upon how best to reproduce Domesday Book in all its idiosyncrasies; the variety of hands, the range of contractions, abbreviations and interlineations, the very appearance of the page were all recognised to be integral to the value of Domesday Book as a monument over and above the more obvious significance of its factual content.[9] Although initially copies of the facsimile, which was eventually published in 1783, were distributed only amongst members of the Houses of Parliament, thereafter a facsimile, accompanied by a translation, was a prerequisite for any county history, and a sub genre of studies relating to Domesday Book soon emerged.[10] The status of Domesday Book as a national monument was confirmed: no other European country had an equivalent survey which approached it in antiquity. The ancient Roman itineraries were trifles in comparison.[11] In Domesday Book, as with the Roman Wall, Stonehenge and Magna Carta, England and the English stood alone.[12]

The printing of the parliamentary rolls and Domesday Book was matched by efforts to publish, or at least bring into greater order, other types of record at a national and a local level, both in order to ensure their better preservation and as a means of making documents more readily available to those who had an interest in them. A succession of antiquaries occupying positions of responsibility in the various state record offices went some way towards overhauling the archives over which they had responsibility. Sir Joseph Ayloffe, with Andrew Coltée Ducarel and Thomas Astle, was appointed one of the three keepers when the State Paper Office was established in 1763 in order to put the national archives upon a better footing. In this capacity he was one of the chief instigators for the transcription and printing of the parliamentary rolls.[13] Ayloffe was acutely conscious of the historical importance of the documents with which he worked. In his *Calendar of the Ancient Charters* (1774) he referred back to the report of the Commons Inquiry made in 1732, following the disastrous fire at the Cottonian Library in 1731, which had recommended that the legislature should take action to make the content of the national records and muniments more generally known and to facilitate public access. He deliberately emphasised the desirability of making the searches 'certain, easy and expeditious', giving notice of where records were stored and drawing up calendars and indices, which he offered as one step towards greater public availability.

Working with Ayloffe in the State Paper Office was Thomas Astle, an ambitious attorney turned archivist from Staffordshire, who was equally energetic both in bringing some order to the chaotic manner in which the various archives were run and in making the records easier for the public to use. Astle fought a long drawn out campaign against damp and anarchic methods of storage. Although it was far from being won by the time of his death in 1803, he left the records in a considerably more healthy state than that in which he had found them.[14] He and his clerk Robert Lemon laboured upon a programme of compiling indices and guides to the various collections which would not only ensure their preservation but would also make them easier to use for those carrying out research. Lemon was kept busy compiling an alphabetical *index locorum* to the charter books of liberties. It would, he hoped, be 'an exceeding good and useful Work'. Researchers, he noted pragmatically, generally knew the place of their inquiry, even if they knew nothing else.[15] Astle's correspondence with Lemon is revealing: in it we find a mission to make the records easier to use for the public and, above all, to improve and rationalise the manner in which they were stored. In a report to a select committee of the House of Commons in 1799, Astle announced that, since his appointment to the position of chief clerk in 1775, he had compiled forty-one volumes of repertories to the records in the Tower, for its use and for the benefit of the public.

Significant inroads were made upon the attitude that records were effectively private property, in that custodianship rested in the officeholder who charged for their use. Some opposition to the printing of the parliamentary rolls had been raised by archivists such as Henry Rooke, deputy keeper of the records in the Tower and a fellow of the Society of Antiquaries. He stood to lose a significant income from fees paid to inspect the documents in his care which would no longer be payable once the rolls were printed. Rooke's protest over his loss of fees signalled a sea change in the culture of record keeping. The archivists responsible for Domesday Book, by contrast, were commended for their willingness in surrendering a valuable perquisite when the volume was published.[16] The sense that these were documents that belonged to the public at large and to which the public should have access had become firmly established. Antiquaries had a crucial role to play in the adoption of a more systematic and conservation-oriented practice of record keeping that took place over the course of the eighteenth century. In so doing, antiquaries such as Thomas Astle and Sir Joseph Ayloffe contributed to the formulation of an argument for the preservation of antiquities, framed in terms of public utility, which stressed the importance of such documents for the national interest.[17] The ethos of officially sponsored preservation went hand in hand with the assumption that these were documents which should be made more widely available; their historical importance for the history of the nation rendered their preservation a matter of public concern. They were a communal property and a part of the national heritage. A clearer articulation of the importance of preserving documentation, therefore, was closely linked to changes in the political culture of the time, which placed an ever stronger emphasis upon the accountability of bodies in authority at both a local and a national level. The ongoing discussion of the need for public access to record repositories, as well as publication projects such as the Domesday Book or the *Rotuli parliamentorum*, gave historical depth to the expansion of the political sphere and the demands for public accountability which were largely the achievement of the newspaper press.

The preservation of other antiquities – whether tessellated pavements, stone circles or ruined abbeys – posed much more problematic issues concerning private property rights and the extent to which these could be curtailed by a broader concept of public ownership, which was in turn based upon the national historical importance of the antiquity in question. From the earliest days of antiquarianism, antiquaries had found themselves at odds with their more present-minded contemporaries, who disregarded the historic associations of buildings and landscape and set their sights on more immediate gains. The very concept of preservation demanded that at least two important premises be accepted. The first was the assumption that it was worthwhile to preserve a building, monument or artefact, or indeed document, purely because it was old. The building or artefact had to be seen as a historical record rather than simply an emblem of antiquity. The antiquaries had here to counter the traditional prejudice that they were 'plodding drudges' whose myopic vision could not penetrate beyond a patina of rust to assess an object's value on aesthetic or historical grounds.[18] Whilst Horace Walpole might protest against the interest of the fellows of the Society of Antiquaries in Romano-British antiquities on the grounds of taste, it was becoming more credible to argue the case for preserving all objects of antiquity on the basis that they could be made to yield up information which contributed to an increasingly wide range of historical inquiries. The rise of primitivism, and the emergence of a historicist approach influencing the study of non-classical antiquities, created a climate of opinion which placed a higher value on these products of a different age, simply because they were so far removed from modern cultural norms. Further to this, however, there also had to be some agreement upon the need actively to preserve monuments of antiquity, rather than simply allowing them to moulder with the passage of time back into the dust whence they originated. Antiquities were memorials which obviated the threat of oblivion; but the mnemonic function of the antiquity was not dependent upon preserving its physical form. A written record of the tomb or the monument would do equally well, as generations of antiquaries testified.

The necessity of physically preserving artefacts, monuments, buildings or landscapes was not at first explicitly formulated; indeed many antiquaries showed a somewhat ambivalent attitude towards the decay and destruction of buildings and antiquities. It was one thing to decry the desecration and damage of the Civil War iconoclasts; another to try to check the insidious and inevitable disintegration brought about by the passage of time, or to oppose the progress of agricultural improvement in the interests of preserving antiquities. Decay was, after all, a natural process and an inherent feature of the fallen world; part of the value in studying antiquities was to be reminded of the fallibility and transitory nature of human creative endeavour. An active commitment to the preservation, let alone restoration, of monuments of antiquities was by no means axiomatic to the profession of antiquarianism. By the end of our period, however, there was a vigorous debate about the importance of preservation, and the principles along which this should be enacted. Crucial to the arguments of those making the case for preservation was the idea that such antiquities in a virtual sense belonged to the nation at large as the physical embodiment of the nation's history.

The origins of an aesthetic which argued for the preservation of historical monuments because of their antiquity and their historical associations has its origins in the Renaissance rediscovery of classical antiquity. Monuments in Rome were esteemed for their literary associations and their power to evoke the classical civilisation that had been lost in the descent into barbarism during the dark ages. Successive popes passed edicts for the preservation of classical ruins in order that future generations might find the buildings, which were the city's greatest charm, intact. Generations of humanists described the ruins in loving detail and protested against their desecration, as the monuments described by Vitruvius were stripped of their porphyry and marble and then rendered into lime.[19] These monuments were illustrations to history; they were proof of its authority, and they were models for artistic and architectural emulation. Tourists such as Sir John Clerk of Penicuik brought back some of these assumptions to Britain. Without the buildings of antiquity there was no means by which architecture could progress; if all ancient monuments were destroyed, there was an end to architecture. Britain had few such monuments, and hence Clerk's fury at the barbarous destruction of the Roman temple in the Borders known as Arthur's O'on. For Sir John this specimen of Roman architecture was significant, not so much because of its import for national history but because it was a symbol of the Roman civilisation to which he aspired.[20] Sir John did not extend his arguments to monuments of Gothic architecture, for which he had much less sympathy and little admiration. The medieval past was in some senses too recent; the ascent from barbarism to civility too freshly made, to engender the sense of historical distance which drove antiquaries to recover, restore and preserve the antiquities of ancient Rome.

The lineage of arguments for preservation can, however, also be traced back along another, neighbouring path. Given the veneration in which churches and their monuments were almost universally held, some of the earliest and sharpest expressions of a sensibility which argued the need to preserve such buildings are to be found directed against those responsible for the neglect or abuse of ecclesiastical foundations. We see this most clearly amongst the high churchmen of the eighteenth century who first drew attention to the study of the architectural form of religious buildings.[21] Browne Willis had no sympathy with the destructive fury of the sixteenth-century reformers, 'the pulling down and desecrating of which was the chief Blemish of the Reformation, and what our Nation stands greatly censured for'.[22] His self-confessed 'affection' for the buildings of the medieval Catholic past arose from his appreciation of what they stood for in terms of faith, piety and man's creative potential, and also a sense that they stood as an ornament and honour to the nation, celebrating as they did the most estimable achievements of Englishmen of past ages. Willis's sentiments were to figure time and again throughout the century, and few if any antiquaries, regardless of their churchmanship, could find it in themselves to condone the blindly indiscriminate destruction of the Puritan iconoclasts. These were actions which insulted not just their religious sensibilities, but offended against the memory of pious benefactors, whose desecrated images had never encouraged idolatry.

Eighteenth-century piety, it has been observed, often found its expression less in building new churches than in the restoration and improvement of the existing fabric.[23] Repair of church buildings undoubtedly contributed to a more informed appreciation of Gothic architecture. Sir Christopher Wren's surveys of Salisbury and Westminster provided some of the first analyses of Gothic architecture to be written in English;[24] James Essex's insights were developed in the context of his restoration work at Ely, Lincoln and King's College Chapel; Francis Price's description of Salisbury Cathedral, which was the outcome of the restoration work undertaken between 1734–53, has been credited as the first publication to discuss a cathedral or church as an architectural structure and can be seen to have stimulated further inquiry along these lines. Similarly Charles Lyttelton's account of Exeter Cathedral (published posthumously to accompany Carter's engravings published by the Society of Antiquaries in 1797) was written as an element in the programme of restoration and improvement he initiated during the 1760s.[25] The works of restoration and repair carried out upon the cathedrals and churches were instrumental in deepening antiquaries' understanding of Gothic architecture. This had the effect, however, of heightening consciousness of the peculiar beauty and value of that architecture, which in turn rendered the eighteenth-century interventions more suspect. Improvement is seldom an absolute good. There were always some who resisted the changes implemented in the cause of beautifying medieval churches. The removal of the painted glass from Stamford's churches, for example, was ostensibly carried out in order to increase the light and counteract the gloominess of the interior. In the opinion of William Stukeley, however, it was simply a ploy on the part of the vicar to lighten the interior and avoid having to purchase spectacles for reading.[26] Richard Gough drew attention to the damage which was being imposed upon the medieval fabric of churches in *Anecdotes of British Topography* as early as 1768, but, unlike his strictures on futile etymologies and verbose disquisitions, his diatribe against the church wardens who plastered over monuments and allowed the Gothic beauty of their churches to be impaired did not capture the imagination of his readers.[27]

Objections to the changes being wrought were muted, diffuse and disparate until the end of the century, when a series of high-profile programmes of cathedral restoration provoked a heated and widely publicised response from members of the antiquarian community. Through these debates we see that the traditional concerns for the church as a commemorative site and a monument to piety retained a latent presence in antiquarian thought, but was increasingly combined with newer arguments which focused upon the integrity of the medieval structure, its value as a historical document and a savage critique of the classicising tendencies of eighteenth-century improvement. To substantiate these criticisms we see also increasing recourse being made to the language of 'national antiquities' and public interest to counter the assumed right of a bishop and chapter to alter buildings of 'national' importance.

During the last three decades of the eighteenth century many of the nation's English cathedrals underwent a programme of restoration and renovation; in some cases extensive structural alterations were deemed necessary. At Hereford, where the west end had collapsed in 1786, they were absolutely essential. Changes were also afoot in other cathedrals under the auspices of James Wyatt, who was making a name for himself as the Gothic specialist of his day. Wyatt was the mastermind behind the alterations at Lichfield, which included the controversial opening up of the choir by removing the altar screen and the monuments to create a larger and more open space.[28] The rebuilding of the west end of Hereford Cathedral according to his designs, it was said, was carried out in a style out of keeping with the Saxon (sic) structure of the original edifice in a pastiche which betrayed an ignorance of the relationship of the different Gothic forms and involved the unnecessary destruction and alteration of much of what remained.[29] Again, at Salisbury, he was employed to stabilise the structure and to 'improve' the interior appearance of the cathedral.

Concern about the proposed changes at Salisbury was first raised through the pages of the *Gentleman's Magazine* in 1785: 'what is doing to this fabric, and what has been done away from it, shall live as long as printing or engraving can contribute to its immortality'.[30] Jacob Schnebbelie, draughtsman to the Society of Antiquaries, was employed to take drawings at Salisbury during the summer of 1789. He wrote to Richard Gough, informing him of the structural and decorative work being carried out under James Wyatt's direction. Gough responded in the *Monthly Review*, the *General Evening Post* and the *Gentleman's Magazine* with a barrage of complaints against the proposed alterations. The outcry was in part a protest against the destruction of the Gothic integrity of the building in conformity with false, modern ideas of beauty and elegance and the threatened loss of the medieval painted ceiling in the Hungerford Chapel. But Gough's ire was also roused by what he perceived to be Wyatt's cavalier handling of the tombs in the Hungerford Chapel; some were now rendered invisible behind wainscoting, those in the Lady Chapel had been summarily moved to the nave, and the bodies disinterred – whether they would be replaced in the right tomb, was he suggested, a matter of doubt.[31] Gough's indignation mounted as he pressed his case: with the monuments of the great bishops and benefactors of the past gone, there was nothing to remind society of the debt owed to the nation's forefathers. If such disrespect was to be paid to history, what surety was there that current or future generations would show any more gratitude?[32] The alterations at Lichfield provoked similar concerns; the elongation of the choir, achieved by taking down and removing the altar screen, wrote Gough, was not only a violation of the 'judicious proportions' of the original Gothic design, but also had the effect of making the preacher impossible to hear. The architect had sacrificed the historic integrity and the essential spiritual function of the building to his own ideas of elegance. 'We shall by and by be told that every variation occasioned by the different repairs or rebuildings must now be reduced to the uniformity of the best age', concluded Gough.[33]

Gough's disgust over Wyatt's alterations at Salisbury, Hereford and Lichfield was merely a prelude to the much more bitter controversy which was to arise over Wyatt's work at Durham. John Carter, at that time draughtsman to the Society of Antiquaries, was sent to Durham to execute the drawings for the society's series of cathedral engravings. He arrived as Wyatt was embarking upon another ambitious programme of restoration and 'improvement'. That was not how Carter saw it. He was horrified by what had been done in refacing and 'repairing' the façade of the east end, but a far worse threat was posed by the plans which had yet to be implemented. The old chapterhouse was to be destroyed and replaced with a modern 'elegant' building; the Galilee Chapel at the west end, the altar, the bishop's throne and the Neville Screen had all been identified to undergo a similar fate.[34] Carter reported back to the Society of Antiquaries in a series of outraged communications, decrying every aspect of Wyatt's so-called restoration. The king, patron of the Society of Antiquaries, should, he suggested, be approached to prevent 'interested persons' from further effacement of the 'remaining unaltered Traits of our Ancient Magnificence' which were 'but faintly to be imitated and perhaps never to be equalled'. In his concluding address, Carter threw down the gauntlet. In conformity with his character as 'an Antiquary, a Lover of my Country and an Artist', he declared, he felt bound to use his best endeavours to preserve 'these national memorials', the cathedral churches, against the destructive 'iron hand' of innovation. Carter's fulminations were received with little sympathy, coinciding as they did with Wyatt's candidacy for membership of the society. The Gothicists, Carter and Gough, were joined in their protests against the depredations at Durham by John Milner and Sir Henry Englefield, both of whom were Catholics – with the inevitable consequence that they became known, inaccurately, as the Catholic party.[35]

When the *Account of Durham* was published, Carter's strictures upon the damage which had been inflicted were toned down, and no overt criticism was allowed to enter the letterpress. The critique was still there, however, a subversive undercurrent, rippling through the apparently polite and anodyne tone of the observations upon the plates.[36] Pointed references were made to the 'intended' plans, not yet begun: 'it is earnestly to be hoped', the commentary smoothly proceeded, 'that these most elegant parts of the edifice may long remain unmoved and uninjured.' In depicting the façade, the reader was told, details were substituted from the authority of views engraved *before* the recent alterations, which had been undertaken in a style 'quite foreign' to that of the original buildings, had been completed.[37] Wyatt disputed Carter's allegations, but whatever his original plans may have been, Carter's view prevailed and no more significant alterations were carried out upon the cathedral.

For all the factional politics which threatened to overshadow the antiquarian considerations at stake, the debate provoked by Wyatt's interventions at Durham, Hereford, Lichfield and Salisbury drew attention to the questions concerning the manner in which buildings of historic interest should be treated. The heightened awareness of the distinctive qualities of different periods of Gothic architecture that was now generally diffused amongst antiquaries, if not society at large, meant that it was no longer possible simply to add, modify or remove in accordance with contemporary taste, as had previously been the practice. Antiquarian sensibilities had evolved, even over a period of only thirty years. In 1758 the architectural antiquary James Essex was the mastermind behind the alterations to Ely Cathedral, for which James Bentham, author of one of the most influential texts on architectural antiquities to be published in the eighteenth century, happily helped to drum up subscriptions and effectively acted as clerk of works. Bentham wrote to Charles Lyttelton informing him of the plans to move the choir to the east end and open up the area underneath the octagon, utterly unconscious that this might damage the historical integrity of the building in which he took such a keen antiquarian interest.[38] Gough and Carter represented a different generation of antiquaries with a strongly historicist outlook, who saw the building as a monument to be preserved rather than adapted to contemporary tastes. Buildings were reflections of the manners and customs of the societies in which they were created; to meddle with them therefore risked jeopardising their value as antiquarian or historical material, as well as demonstrating a lack of taste in failing to appreciate the coherence and integrity of the historical building. It proved impossible to turn back the wheel to a point where this historicist view point had not yet been arrived at. A further question therefore arose: should a building be restored to a particular point in time – if so, at which point in its history? – or should it be preserved with all its historical accretions intact?[39] Such considerations acquired steadily increasing prominence in the early nineteenth century as the foundations for the debates over restoration which would so inflame opinion within the Camden Society were laid.

Gough registered his protest in resigning from the Society of Antiquaries in 1797 when Wyatt was elected to membership; he had by this time become thoroughly disillusioned and largely withdrew from the arena. Carter, however, being a younger man, was full of fight. He carried on his campaign through the pages of the *Gentleman's Magazine* in the series of essays, 'The Pursuit of Architectural Innovation' which ran for nearly twenty years from 1798 to 1817 and numbered 212 contributions in all.[40] This was the war correspondent's report from the front of architectural damage and destruction. He reported on the 'improvements' being carried out, the buildings being pulled down, and the decay which was allowed to persist unchecked in historical buildings across the country. He endlessly recapitulated his themes of the iniquity of innovation, the Englishness of Gothic, and the importance of preserving national antiquities. Carter's antiquarian pen ranged widely across the country, but he constantly returned back to Westminster where he identified a particularly dangerous threat to the architectural heritage. At the Palace of Westminster, where St Stephen's Chapel with its newly uncovered painted chamber had been earmarked for alterations at the hands of Wyatt, he had executed the drawings for the society's publication in 1795.[41] Following the discovery of the paintings he was furious to find his access barred by order of the Surveyor of Works – James Wyatt. At Westminster Abbey, where the glories of the architecture appeared particularly vulnerable to both the hand of time and the hand of Wyatt, he worked himself into a similar state of outraged indignation.

Of the two, the changes being wrought at Westminster Abbey assumed the higher profile. This was partly because of the highly contentious nature of the (anonymous) and vitriolic exchanges between Carter and the Dean of Westminster, William Vincent, which entertained the readers of the *Gentleman's Magazine* for over a decade. Vincent, whilst not unsympathetic to the importance of preserving the medieval fabric of the abbey, took offence at Carter's arrogance and propensity to overstatement. For Carter, those who were not with him in his anti-Wyatt crusade were against him, and he responded accordingly.[42] The fact that in 1803 the entire destruction of Henry VII's chapel by fire was only narrowly averted heightened the image of fragility and vulnerability which Carter built up around the chapel in his campaign against Wyatt. Overriding these considerations, however, was the fact that Westminster Abbey, with its tombs of monarchs and national heroes, appeared to embody the nation's history in a way which Salisbury or Durham, for all their architectural beauty, could not do.

Westminster Abbey was unique in the range of its symbolic meanings; it was the 'mausoleum of kings', the site of coronations where all the ritual of monarchy was enacted before the public. It housed the monuments to the greatest figures of national history.[43] The tombs erected in the abbey occupied a special place in the reading public's imagination, immortalised as they were in Joseph Addison's famous essay in the *Spectator*.[44] When visitors, such as the Frenchman François La Rochefoucauld, visited it, it was the magnificence of the tombs of kings and illustrious personages by which they were most impressed.[45] The abbey had another unique claim to the public's interest, in that the repairs were paid for not solely from the revenues of the dean and chapter or from private subscription, as was the case at other cathedrals, but from funds granted by parliament. The abbey had been in receipt of regular parliamentary grants throughout the first half of the eighteenth century to finance a major programme of restoration. Between 1697 and 1745 over £100,000 was spent on repairing and finishing it.[46] The process of decay had been only temporarily halted however, and by the end of the century the need for further restorative action had become pressing. In a series of articles published in the *Gentleman's Magazine*, John Carter poured scathing criticism upon Dean Vincent and his failure to fulfil his obligations to preserve the historic features of the abbey and accused the chapter of a gross error of misjudgement in appointing James Wyatt, 'the Destroyer', as surveyor of the board of works at Westminster. Carter's journalism had its effect. Earlier accounts of Westminster Abbey had emphasised the significance of the building as the site of royal ritual and display and as the burial place of the monarchy, but this had not been elaborated into a celebration of the abbey as the embodiment of national history and national glory.[47] Carter's relentless campaign, in which he styled himself the 'literary guardian of national antiquities', succeeded in establishing this connection firmly in the public consciousness. Westminster Abbey, 'the sublime repository of departed greatness', was the 'Christian birthright of every Englishman'.[48] The year after these articles appeared, the artist and antiquary J. P. Malcolm (similarly a frequent contributor to the *Gentleman's Magazine*) highlighted the damage and decay which had been allowed to proceed unchecked upon the fabric and windows of Westminster Abbey, describing it as a reproach to the nation and demanding restorative action.[49]

The fate of the chapel of Henry VII featured prominently in Carter's litany of complaints against the irresponsible actions of the dean and chapter and their employee Wyatt. The softness of the stone from which the chapel had been constructed had left it susceptible to erosion and damage; the carvings were becoming shapeless, even obliterated. Writing of the proposed alterations in 1803, Carter had declared that the public were 'highly interested' in the fate of Henry's chapel; it was a 'national glory'.[50] When the dean and chapter petitioned parliament for a grant to underwrite the cost of the repair work, they willingly adopted the same rhetoric as Carter, even if they were less ready to adhere to his admonitions for its restoration.[51] For such requests to succeed they had to be framed in terms of the national interest, which it was parliament's role to uphold. The costs of restoration work therefore drove the abbey dignitaries to emphasise the national significance of the building in order to continue to claim public money for its upkeep. Just over one hundred years previously the dean and chapter had sought money from parliament, arguing their case on the grounds that the repairs were to be undertaken for 'The honour of God, the spiritual welfare of Her Majesty's subjects, the interest of the established Church and the glory of Her Majesty's reign'.[52] By 1807 the centrality of the abbey to the nation was no longer a spiritual matter; rather it was its architectural significance that was emphasised. It was, argued the petition, 'the most beautiful specimen of Gothic Architecture now remaining in this Kingdom, and perhaps in Europe'.[53] Wyatt's 'improving' instincts were kept firmly in check. Most of the repair and restoration was actually overseen by the master mason, Thomas Gayfere, whose work was remarkable for its attempt to emulate the medieval original rather than to make it comply with modern notions of propriety. Significantly, the overall direction of the restoration work rested not with the dean and chapter, but with a Committee for the Inspection of National Monuments (also known as the Committee of Taste), which included amongst its number several individuals sympathetic to the ideals of preservation enunciated by Carter. This arrangement not only recognised the fact that the abbey was accountable to parliament for the expenditure of the moneys granted, it also enshrined the principle that the proper restoration of the chapel was a matter of national interest.[54] Once that principle was acknowledged with such clarity, it was impossible to resist the further assumption that the building was a form of public property. Ackermann's *History of the Abbey Church of St Peter's Westminster*, published at a time when public adulation of national heroes was at a wartime peak, represented an even fuller elaboration of Westminster Abbey as the sublimation of all that was noblest and best in British history. On viewing the abbey, he wrote, 'Who does not feel his best sensibilities awakened, his piety animated, his thoughts dignified, his sense of public duty enlarged, and his moral tendencies, strengthened?'[55]

Carter could be said to have generated almost single-handed the concept of national heritage, to have made the connection between buildings and history as a form of public property and to have pioneered the belief in the Gothic as a distinctively English architectural idiom. More plausibly, he could also be said to be the first consistent campaigner in the cause of preservation, and to have made some of the earliest demands for intervention to protect buildings against the wishes of those who were ostensibly the property owners. Carter was not on his own, however, despite the fact that he tended to present himself as a lone prophet of doom, a voice crying in the wilderness, to whom no one was prepared to listen. There was a growing constituency of antiquaries who similarly saw the need for some higher authority able to intervene in the interests of preserving antiquities. Nor was he entirely disinterested. In all his fulminations, there was an element of professional pique and jealousy at Wyatt's success, and the fact that he held a position as surveyor of the board of works, which Carter considered should rightfully have been his. Yet, in claiming for himself the role of guardian of national antiquities and speaking the language of public good, national honour and patriotism, he transformed a personal vendetta and private obsession into a mission of national importance. But his views, could not have gained the currency they did had he not been able to tap into a swelling tide of nationalist sentiment which was founded on a belief in the exceptionalism of English history. The elision between monarchy and nation that took place in his descriptions of Westminster Abbey was one which was manifest on a much broader cultural front. Under the rule of George III, 'God Save the King' had become the national anthem and the monarchy itself a focus for patriotic celebration.[56]

It was not, of course, only religious edifices which were threatened by improvement and innovation; nor should it be assumed that Carter confined himself to campaigning on their behalf, however much his obsession with Wyatt the Destroyer might leave that impression. A series of articles by Carter in the *Gentleman's Magazine* between 1807 and 1809, for example, took up the cause of the city walls at York, which the corporation had it within their sights to destroy, such was the drain upon their finances of maintaining them in good repair.[57] 'Shocking reflection!' he exclaimed, that superannuated surveyors, purblind carpenters and doting masons should hold the destiny of England's antiquities in their hands. Old walls, replete with historic lore, held fewer charms to them than a new bridewell or a gaol.[58] As urban improvement gathered pace through provincial England in the second half of the century, the medieval townscape gradually disappeared. Demographic growth and economic expansion rendered the narrow streets and gateways of the medieval and early modern town impractical. A town's economy depended on trade; it required broader streets, spacious market houses and imposing exchanges. As corporation restrictions quietly receded into abeyance, the need to regulate the flow of visitors in and out of the town diminished; city walls and gateways were no longer an economic or defensive necessity and were costly to maintain. Market crosses were removed as trade shifted from the open street into purpose-built shambles;

improvement commissioners executed orders of compulsory purchase on old timber-frame housing to be replaced by the crisp, geometrical symmetry of neoclassical terraces and squares. Contemporary medical thought condemned the dark and narrow streets, with their lack of paving, overhanging frontages and primitive drainage. Classically informed notions of taste could see beauty only in uniform frontages, straight streets and dramatic vistas. The disappearance of the medieval urban environment was the most striking evidence of the new, vibrant prosperity of the eighteenth-century town.

The antiquary's outrage joined forces with the less academic concerns of local inhabitants who saw the destruction of these ancient buildings as a loss to the community. Buildings embodied the collective memory and the communal identity of the town or city. In 1732 one anonymous annalist in Bristol recorded with sorrow that in this year the 'finest and neatest cross in the three Kingdoms' had been taken down.[59] William Cowper of Chester wrote to Charles Lyttelton, whom he addressed as 'tutamen antiquitatis' in 1767, informing him of the decision taken by Chester corporation to take down the east gate, 'the principal Ornament of Chester' on the grounds that it had become ruinous, despite his protestations to the contrary.[60] By the 1790s the outbursts were occurring with increasing frequency. John Throsby vilified the 'contracted minds' responsible for the despicable and wanton destruction of the antiquities of his native town of Leicester in the name of improvement: gates, walls and crosses were pulled down and sold for a pittance.[61] James Wallace, the author of a history of Liverpool published in 1795, was sharply critical of the corporation's decision to take down various historic monuments without even securing drawings of them, only to replace them with neoclassical buildings constructed in poor taste, and unsuited to the environment in which they were placed. This abnegation of their responsibility for the conveyance of the town's antiquities to posterity was, he suggested, another instance of their cultural poverty.[62] Every vestige of antiquity around the old harbour at Hartlepool, wrote Sir Cuthbert Sharp, that could be converted to profit was seized 'with merciless and unrelenting grip'.[63] John Milner, who had joined Carter in his crusade against Wyatt, set himself up against the civic leaders of Winchester in a similar cause.[64] His *Civil and Ecclesiastical History of Winchester* voiced an extended lament for the destruction and ruin of the city's medieval fabric, a victim to modern improvement and false notions of taste. Each building was linked to the history's past. It was not just its age, or the beauty of its construction, but its historical associations which gave the city its identity. Only the ordinary inhabitants, uncorrupted by the barbarism and avarice of those of a higher class, resisted the attempts to remove the high cross – 'a valuable ornament to Winchester and a public trophy of its Christianity'

– and drove away the workmen and preserved 'this curious remnant of ancient art and piety'.[65]

John Carter's relentless tirades against the forces of innovation, novelty and philistinism did not identify urban society as the culprit in so many words, but his critique, and that of others like him, was in effect an attack against the growth of modern, commercial and *urban* society. Crude profit was often identified as the motive in bringing about the destruction of a building or a ruin, and profit was associated above all with the commercial ethos of the city. The walls of York were crumbling into obsolescence, not through the passage of time, but through the wanton despoliation of the citizens, who sought actively to undermine them, so that they might be declared beyond repair and rendered a quarry of masonry for building the charmless structures of modern urban life.[66] No less vigorous in his denunciations was John Byng, Viscount Torrington. Byng's tours through England, undertaken in the 1780s and 1790s, bear eloquent and dyspeptic witness to his sense of anxiety and apprehension in the face of the rapid economic, social and political change that he saw in the towns and cities through which he passed. By contrast, the medieval buildings represented stability, continuity and the values of social deference and hierarchy to which he, as a landed gentleman, subscribed. In rural society the landowner's dominance continued unchallenged; in the towns the old social order had gone for ever. 'For antiquity look not into great town churches,' he expostulated, 'for aldermen are ashamed of seeing painted windows, and old tombs.'[67] Neath Abbey epitomised the conflict which modern commercial progress posed for the nation's Gothic fabric and the spiritual values of society: within its ruins he found the copper smelting furnaces of Sir Herbert Mackworth, polluting the once hallowed buildings with sacrilegious industry. 'How Horrid, how infernal, was all before me! Deep in the very centre of its sacred walls were set the furnaces wherein the poisonous ore becomes a prey to fusion.'[68] When the past was held to be of such valuable didactic import, wilfully to destroy its record threatened the order of society. Francis Grose regretted the widespread loss of buildings, pulled down for building materials: 'such buildings,' he wrote, 'had tended to inspire the beholder with a love for the now happy establishment; by leading him to compare the present, with those times when such buildings were erected'.[69] Given that so much of the destruction of the medieval fabric of England took place within an urban environment, it is not surprising that failure to appreciate the past and insensitivity to the value of its monuments was incorporated into the barrage of criticism fired against the growth of urban society by those of a more conservative disposition. A powerful element of antiquarian thought was the search for continuity and durability through time; urban society, with its rapid growth and constant innovations appeared to represent the very antithesis of those values.

The association between antiquity and social stability and continuity was expressed with particular urgency in the 1790s. It is often said that this was the point when domestic tourism began; when Englishmen deprived of the possibility of touring on the European mainland were forced to discover their own country. It is crudely reductionist to explain the rise of domestic tourism simply in terms of events on the Continent, although it is clear that a number of aristocratic tourists and artists, such as Sir Richard Colt Hoare, Sir George Beaumont or even John Byng, certainly turned their attention to their native country as a result of the favoured European destinations being barred to them through war.[70] What is less equivocal is that the scenes of destruction in France, of which the émigrés brought back such horrifying reports, stimulated a sense of urgency for the preservation of domestic antiquities, lest any similar ravages should take place in Britain. Events across the Channel heightened awareness of the symbolic importance of such buildings as the incarnation of the traditions and history that formed the fabric of the constitution upon which the liberties of the freeborn Englishman rested. The twin pillars of the constitution, church and state, were defended in principle by Edmund Burke. Their physical embodiment lay in the ecclesiastical structures and the ruined castles of England, and it was the antiquaries who were in the vanguard for their defence. It is no coincidence that this was the decade in which John Carter commenced his apologia for Gothicism as the national style of architecture in the *Gentleman's Magazine*. The architectural innovation that he lambasted with such vigour consisted of 'innovating and levelling' – terms which could have been equally deployed by the critics of the French Revolution against the politics of Painite radicalism.[71] A significant feature of the conservative reaction to the Revolution in France was, therefore, the greater importance subsequently attached to domestic history and antiquities and the urgent need to ensure their preservation.

Events in France were a proximate cause for an increasingly positive evaluation of Gothic (or, as Carter would have it, English) architecture and its preservation. A more sympathetic approach to Gothic antiquities was also the hallmark of the picturesque movement that dominated the culture of the latter part of the eighteenth century. With its penchant for ruined castles and abbeys, the picturesque aesthetic held somewhat contrary implications for antiquities. On the one hand, the heightened value placed upon ruins of any sort for their sentimental associations and their pictorial qualities endowed them with greater cultural value and therefore ultimately promoted their preservation rather than their demolition. Ruins acquired an economic value as a means of attracting tourists and the custom of well-heeled visitors; their worth was no longer reduced to the value of the building materials they could provide. 'It is a matter of some astonishment', remarked one tourist at Glastonbury, 'that the inhabitants should be so blind to their own interest as to pull down for their own private use what would have made some recompense for the loss of those former revenues spent among them, by bringing to the town a great concourse of people to admire its mouldering fabric.'[72] The discovery of landscape, and the exploration of the nation which topographical literature represented, fostered the sense that the picturesque scenery and antiquities described in such publications were the property of the entire nation. The illustration of monuments of antiquity allowed the public to possess these antiquities, albeit vicariously. It was but a small imaginative leap to regard the buildings themselves as a communal, national heritage. Thus landowners who, like the Duke of Beaufort, had taken pains to maintain a ruin such as Tintern Abbey in good condition, were praised by the editors of the *Antiquarian Repertory* for the pains they took to preserve this and other monuments 'which may be considered as national ornaments'.[73]

From the picturesque perspective, however, the greater the state of decay into which a building had fallen, the better. The history of the ruin was less important than its gradual disintegration back into the soil from which it had originally been erected; such ruins embodied an organic unity between nature and culture. 'A ruin is a sacred thing,' wrote William Gilpin, 'rooted for ages in the soil; assimilated to it; and become, as it were, a part of it; we consider it as a work of nature, rather than of art.'[74] Sprouting saplings, festoons of foliage, and crumbling crenellations were regarded as positive additions. James Moore regretted that so few Gothic buildings in Scotland were adorned with the requisite growth of ivy, which would soften the edges and endow them with the appropriate air of romantic gloom.[75] The grove of trees growing within the body of the church at Netley Abbey 'husbands out the beauties of the scene, and, in appearance trebles its real magnitude'. The ruined Gothic arches echoed the intersecting arches of the trees which had supposedly provided the inspiration for their shape, demonstrating that conformity with nature so important to the observers of the picturesque. William Gilpin's recommendations for knocking off a few additional corbels at Tintern to improve the effect have become something of a picturesque cliché,[76] but there were plenty of other antiquaries who did not demur from his recommendations. Francis Grose, whose *Antiquities of England and Wales* became a standard work of reference for picturesque tourists, was pleased to note that three sides of the tower at Kirkstall Abbey near Leeds had recently fallen down: 'a circumstance which, far from impairing the beauty of the ruin, has rendered it rather more picturesque than before'.[77]

Such picturesque profusion, however, led to a far more comprehensive state of disintegration, as a number of antiquaries recognised. This in turn sharpened their sense of the desirability of intervention to impede the gradual disappearance of such ruins from the landscape. William Bray, the historian of Surrey, was more alert to the long-term dangers of neglect at Kirkstall than was Francis Grose: 'One cannot but regret', he wrote, 'that they (the ruins) should want the little care which would preserve them very long from farther destruction.'[78] For him the cattle housed within the abbey symbolised the wilful neglect of the ruins and were a sacrilege upon the memory of its original use. Yet for the picturesque artist the cattle provided a 'natural' contrast to the man-made ruins in which they grazed.[79] Moreover, ivy obscured the form and proportions of the original building, which was the antiquary's principal interest, and wrought untold damage to the masonry. 'I value my ivy more than this my antient building,' one proprietor informed John Carter, 'and had rather behold this luxuriant state of Nature's beauteous foliage, than all those architectural features which you seem to hold as possessing the greater claim.'[80] Many parts of Llanthony Abbey, observed Sir Richard Colt Hoare in 1798, were threatened with dissolution by the trees and other plants growing out of the fissures. When he revisited the abbey five years later he found Llanthony even further decayed: 'It is a melancholy sight to the traveller who frequently revisits the same ground and object of antiquity to witness the progressive ruin of these fine specimens of ancient architecture ... Llanthony will soon no longer excite nor deserve the attention of the traveller.'[81] Nevertheless, antiquarianism benefited from the sentimental appreciation of ruins which the cult of the picturesque established, even if the kind of publications which promoted such images were superficial and desultory in content. A wider awareness of architectural antiquities was created and a series of buildings had been inscribed upon the collective consciousness of the reading public as monuments to antiquity, whose preservation should be ensured.

There was, however, little that could be done beyond murmurs of disapprobation. If a proprietor wished to plough up a field in which stood a stone circle, and blow up those stones for lime, or to construct a wall on newly enclosed land, he was simply asserting the right of the landowner to exploit the resources of his own property. A ruined abbey was of little practical use to an improving landlord, who saw it as a source of masonry rather than a monument of antiquity. It was one thing to appeal to public spirit, patriotism or matters of taste in pressing a case for the preservation of a building, but for effective action to be taken the authority of some higher body needed to be invoked which could override the sanctity of private property; in eighteenth- or nineteenth-century terms, that meant parliamentary statute. In some European countries, such as Sweden, royal proclamations had been accepted by the provincial assemblies as early as the seventeenth century prohibiting the destruction of historic monuments.[82] The British parliament, however, composed in large measure by members of the propertied elite, was always slow to take the initiative in any sphere that involved interfering in rights which, according to popular understandings of constitutional history, it had been created to protect. It would be wrong, therefore, to make too much of the pamphlet presented to the Society of Antiquaries in 1776 as an early call for a preservation society. Claiming to speak for the ruined abbeys of North Britain, the pamphlet decried the decay and neglect into which the nation's ruins had been allowed to fall and demanded that the Society of Antiquaries should take measures to bring a bill before parliament. Quite what kind of legislative action was anticipated, however, was not elucidated.

The
GROANS
Of the Abbays, Cathedrals, Palaces and other ancient buildings of North Britain.
Illustrious Society, Can you tamely look on, and suffer out bodies
To be basely torn, barbarously mangled, and layed [sic] in ruins by a selfish race of unfeeling Goths:
Can you tamely look on, we say, and not punish these rude offenders?
Many of us are entirely leveled! [sic]
Some of us falling down with Gothic irons!
Some of us tumbling down with old age!
Pity our forlorn situation, and procure us necessary aid, by an Act of Parliament:
Or Soon! Too soon alas! None of us will be left to Groan.[83]

The specific reference to the plight of these buildings in North Britain offers yet another instance of the widespread assumption that the Scottish were particularly remiss in neglecting their Gothic antiquities,[84] but the 'Groans of the Abbays' is chiefly interesting as being possibly the first attempt to secure parliamentary action for the preservation of ancient buildings. As incorporated public bodies, the Society of Antiquaries and its sister institutions in Scotland and in Ireland were the natural vehicles for raising concerns about the threatened loss of antiquities of national importance. They were, however, incapable of taking a proactive stance for the preservation of antiquities and demurred from even assuming this kind of lobbying role. The reaction of the society to Carter's castigation of Wyatt is telling; his 'restoration' work at Durham, it was argued, should be immaterial to his candidacy for membership. The society, argued Thomas

Astle, was not a court of inquest: 'it has nothing to do with Deans and Chapters, or their alterations of buildings – neither is it to attend to the conduct of Architects'.[85] Legislation, as the history of preservation tells us, was a long time in coming.[86] The only recourse in a voluntarist age was to exploit the landed elite's ethos of stewardship and responsibility upon which their hegemony was based.

The other alternative was to take notes and drawings of all and any antiquities before they were lost to posterity for ever. Since the Renaissance this was essentially what had been meant by 'preservation' – the preservation of the memory of the building, its appearance, and the names of those whose epitaphs were inscribed upon the tombs. The impulse to secure drawings and engravings was widespread, and was greatly facilitated by the refinement of the art of engraving within Britain that took place during the eighteenth century.[87] Engravings of antiquities offered yet another opportunity for the collector and the gentleman to exercise his taste and judgement, as evidenced by the craze for grangerisation.[88] The practical purpose of recording and preserving monuments of antiquities therefore neatly dovetailed with a growing market of potential collectors of prints. A tradition of antiquarian engraving was already developing in the seventeenth century, best represented in Britain by the illustrations of Wenceslaus Hollar for Sir William Dugdale's history of St Paul's, but also made familiar to English collectors through his engravings of antiquities in Rome.[89] This tradition was perpetuated in the early eighteenth century in the success of series such as Samuel and Nathaniel Buck's, *Perspective Views of the Ruins of the Most Noted Abbies and Castles of England.* The proposals issued to promote the subscription explained the rationale behind the project:

> The Antiquity of such *Edifices*, together with the pious Intention of the *Founders*, having made the Memory of them justly venerable; and as most of those valuable *Structures* are now mould'ring in *Ruins*, they being already no more than the defac'd *Remains* of what they originally were: The best *Perspective Views* they are at this Day capable of, we find by Experience do not fail of being acceptable to this curious Age: as they greatly contribute to illustrate the History of the former State of this *Island*, and to transmit those things to Posterity, which must otherwise be irretrievably lost: the *Undertakers* have for these Reasons made it their principal Business, at no small Expence, to visit them, and take *Perspective Views* of whatever remains remarkable.[90]

At a time when the lexicon of architectural description for all such buildings as did not fall within the parameters of classical terminology was extremely limited, the engraving substituted eloquently for written description. Words could not express the beauty and elegance of the architecture of York Minster, wrote Browne Willis only an illustration would suffice.[91]

The illustrations, naïve and inaccurate as they may seem today, were an important element of his *Mitred Abbies* and *Cathedrals* series, and distinguished his volumes from Richard Rawlinson's cathedral histories. Willis railed against the limitations of the draughtsmen and engravers with whom he worked and the scope allowed him for illustrating his books, seeing the delineation of the physical fabric of a building as one of the most important means of preserving its memory.

The illustration of antiquities was one area in which the Society of Antiquaries was able to make a significant contribution. Humfrey Wanley's foundation articles for the English Society of Antiquaries had begun with the statement that it would 'bring to light and preserve all old monumental Inscriptions etc, Architecture, Sculpture, Painting ...'[92] It was to this end that fellows of the Society of Antiquaries were given advice on a number of occasions as to the type of antiquity to observe and the form of notes to be taken. The sponsorship of illustrations of antiquity was fully compatible with the ethos of a gentlemanly society, and it was in this area that eighteenth-century antiquaries notably distinguished themselves from their forebears. For all their scholarly acumen, the 'English Scholars' of the early eighteenth century had been textual scholars rather than students of the visual record.

William Stukeley, a keen amateur draughtsman himself, was foremost amongst those who sought to ensure that the society lived up to these principles, encouraging it to commission engravings of ancient monuments.[93] It was Stukeley's own drawing of Waltham Cross, damaged and threatened with destruction, which George Vertue engraved for one of the earliest plates to be published by the Society of Antiquaries in the series *Vetusta monumenta*.[94] Medieval antiquities – castles, palaces, churches and crosses – predominated, even over the Roman antiquities favoured by the gentlemen of taste, such as Sir John Clerk, who could not stomach the society's fascination with Gothicism. Yet amongst those interested in architectural antiquities, as opposed to, for example, numismatics, there was a feeling that there was scope for greater activity in this area. Particularly after the society was incorporated in 1751, it was argued that as a public body the society had a leadership role to play in encouraging its members to take a more active part in recording national antiquities. James Bentham suggested to Charles Lyttelton, by then president of the Society of Antiquaries, that it should do more to collect information about Gothic architecture, instructing its members on how best to make observations and securing drawings, but no action was taken in this direction.[95] The suggestion was revived in the 1790s as part of the same spirit of Gothic enthusiasm which drove forward the project for engraving the entire series of English cathedrals. Sir Henry Englefield and Joseph Windham (who comprised the society's 'committee for publishing the Church Antiquities of England') drew up directions for the use of members on surveying, measuring and describing buildings of Gothic architecture.[96]

The engraving of antiquities was something of a crusade for Gough in his capacity as director of the Society of Antiquaries, and one in which he achieved rather more success than he was to do in his opposition to Wyatt. Only one year after his election to the society in 1768 he commented rather caustically on its failure to produce more of such 'presents' (that is engravings of antiquities) for the public.[97] The pressing need for better engravings was highlighted in both editions of *British Topography*. His own *Sepulchral Monuments* was itself born of his conviction of the value of visual imagery in conveying historical truths, as well as the importance of preserving the memory of such monumental antiquities for future generations. Engravings of buildings or sepulchral monuments were not to be regarded as mere ornament or light relief for the eye from the tedium of the printed page. He was a zealot for the cause of accurate engravings in which perspective and proportion were properly observed; such images would illuminate the study of the manners and customs of the time in which they were constructed and would also facilitate comparison and preserve such details for posterity. It was a reproach to the English as a nation, argued Gough, that so little effort had been made to record antiquities, or to procure proper drawings illustrative of the history and antiquities of the country. He uttered dire warnings to the readers of *Sepulchral Monuments*, that soon the foundations for such a work would no longer be in existence. Statues were crumbling away, paintings were being whitewashed over and other antiquities were being allowed to fall into neglect and dissolution.[98]

The minutes of the Society of Antiquaries, the plates of *Vetusta monumenta* and the pages of the *Gentlemen's Magazine*, for which he acted as editor of reviews from 1786, show the importance of Gough's influence in directing the attention of antiquaries towards engravings of antiquities. It is very noticeable that in the 1780s and 1790s when the society resumed publication of *Vetusta monumenta* the content was heavily medieval. In volume three, for example, a single plate illustrating a Roman tessellated pavement interrupted a sequence of medieval antiquities. (This did not win approval from the more classically minded members such as Sir George Yonge, who fulminated against the society's preoccupation with Gothic antiquities in its publications.)[99] Gough was rigorous and demanding in his standards of draughtsmanship and ensured that the quality of the drawings and the engravings was high. He directed Grimm, Jacob Schnebbelie and John Carter, the society's leading draughtsmen, as to what they should draw and encouraged them to develop an expertise in the depiction of Gothic antiquities.[100] He also introduced much more extensive commentary, in English rather than Latin as had been the case in volume one, to accompany the engravings, discussing both the objects or buildings represented, as well as giving the historical context.

Carter's drawings and engravings were a meticulous record of the ornament and appearance of the cathedrals. They represented a significant point of departure in the depiction of Gothic architecture. Earlier prints, such as those engraved by George Vertue and published under the auspices of the society, had presented an idealised version of the Gothic in which decay and damage was repaired; clean lines and sharp outlines gave a misleading homogeneity to the appearance; the texture of the stonework was smoothed over, and the finer details of disintegration and decay were seldom observed. Accurate, unadorned by any extraneous detail and presented in identical format, they were the visual equivalent to the precise mode of factual representation and empirical observation demanded of antiquarian writing.[101] Vertue's exactitude was valued by antiquaries but diminished his reputation as an artist. James Basire, who followed him as engraver to the Society of Antiquaries and engraved many of Carter's drawings, was similarly despised for his old-fashioned reluctance to soften the lineal sharpness of his style with fashionable mezzotints or stipple work. It was this sharpness, allowing for minute detail, which so endeared him to the antiquaries.[102] Other draughtsmen and engravers, with less understanding or appreciation of the Gothic, simply distorted it according to their expectations of classical architecture, resulting in the curious interpretations of the Gothic which were closer to the designs in Battey Langley's pattern books than the originals upon which they were based.

The picturesque style went to the other extreme: 'Topographical draughtsmen', remarked J. T. Smith, 'introduce more than they see, in order to make their productions picturesque.'[103] Picturesque artists emphasised the contrast of light and shade, revelled in the crumbling masonry, and embedded the building deep into the middle ground of a suitably arranged landscape. The niceties of ornamentation or architectural structure, which were so often shrouded by ivy and other vegetation, were generally lost.[104] Accuracy was sacrificed to pictorial effect. Carter, as one might expect, was especially eloquent on this subject, particularly when it was a question of defending the costly format adopted in the *Cathedral Antiquities*. Most prints were too small; they were contrived simply for picturesque effect and to show off the skills of the delineator rather than the ancient architect. His drawings, however, endeavoured to render the architectural features conspicuous and intelligible, so that they would not only delight the eye, but provide exemplars for the professional imitators of 'our national architecture'.[105]

It was one thing to publish prints of antique monuments or buildings in order to preserve their memory; it was another to call for their actual preservation. In the midst of this proliferation of antiquarian prints and engravings, there was a danger that the fashion for Gothic antiquities could engender a dangerous complacency that would ultimately be counter-productive. Prints and engravings could certainly educate society to be more discerning and sensitive to the buildings in its midst, but they could also foster the attitude that once an antiquity had been drawn its physical preservation was thereafter of less importance; its destruction could be contemplated with equanimity. In an essay on the use of inscriptions and medals, Scipione Maffei had drawn attention to the paradox that antiquities were engraved and kept in fine bindings and gilded presses, whilst the originals were left exposed to weather and unwitting destruction, or were pillaged by foreigners. His comments, translated into English and published as an appendix to Richard Rawlinson's translation of du Fresnoy's *A New Method of Studying History* in 1728, may well have influenced the author of an article which appeared in the *Gentleman's Magazine* in 1788.[106]

> The art of engraving, which helps to make ancient buildings known, and preserves their form to a certain degree, contributes, I fear, to their demolition. 'Is such a thing engraved?' – 'O, yes' – 'Then it is preserved to posterity' ... 'The Corporation intend to blow up the castle; but it is engraved! ... No matter if the engraving be inaccurate – or exhibiting only a *partial* view – ... when the engraving is made, farewell to the thing engraved! ... While written documents are preserved with the utmost care, ancient edifices are suffered to moulder into dust; we are contented to read a description of them, and we are not solicitous to rescue them from dilapidation and decay.[107]

Charles Norris expressed similar reservations in 1811 in a work devoted to describing the neglected ecclesiastical antiquities of Wales. Where the security of the building in question was under no threat, Norris was wholly in favour of its delineation, but he too feared that the ready availability of such engravings dulled the public's awareness of the rapid loss of buildings; even as he wrote, 'admirable specimens of ancient taste and magnificence' were being irretrievably destroyed.[108]

The preservation of antiquities as engravings was made out to be a matter of public interest, just as the physical conservation was, and it was similarly dependent upon the whim, munificence or public spirit of the individual (or a collective of individuals in the case of the Society of Antiquaries). Indeed, the responsibility for preserving the antiquities of the past was to lie with private individuals for some considerable time yet. In this, the

British experience contrasted with that of France. Here the destruction consequent upon the Revolution, which caused so much consternation amongst English antiquaries, provoked even stronger outrage amongst the French antiquarian community. In an attempt to check the wholesale desecration which was taking place, the antiquary Aubin Louis Millin presented the Constituent Assembly with the first volume of his *Antiquités nationales ou recueil de monuments* in 1790. The sale of ecclesiastical properties, he argued, had undoubtedly endowed the nation with invaluable resources, but the nationalisation of the church had also brought fatal consequences for the arts and sciences, by allowing for the devastation of so many historic monuments that served to illustrate the greatest episodes in the nation's history. The revolutionary government was hardly in a position to outlaw further damage to former ecclesiastical properties at a time when it was itself in dire need of exploiting these resources for the prosecution of war, but in the *Suite d'instructions* issued in 1791, the Legislative Assembly stipulated a list of exceptions from those items which it otherwise demanded should be requisitioned for the state; these included all such assets as were of interest on account of the beauty of their workmanship, or their historic or didactic value. In the early nineteenth century successive French governments asserted responsibility for improving the nation's taste and for safeguarding the nation's history; the preservation of the nation's antiquities was demonstrably essential to both these aims. By 1830 the preservation and conservation of the nation's historic buildings had become the responsibility of a civil servant, the Inspector of Historic Monuments.[109] The contrast with the laissez-faire attitude prevailing at home was not lost upon British observers, not the least of whom was John Britton, whose admiration for John Carter was manifested in a determination to perpetuate Carter's crusade for the better preservation of medieval architecture. The following year he made the first of his attempts to persuade parliament to establish a historical commission for arts and monuments and for protecting national antiquities; but in this, as in so many other of his enterprises, he was frustrated.[110]

It is premature to speak of a 'preservation movement' in early nineteenth-century Britain, and we should be wary of attributing to eighteenth-century antiquaries the concerns and preoccupations of the modern conservators of the nation's antiquarian heritage. Yet some of the framework on which modern attitudes to the preservation of the physical remains of the past, however ill-defined, would be built up, had been laid. No longer could 'preservation' be synonymous with simply taking a drawing. Nor could 'restoration' any longer be taken to comprehend within its meaning the alternative sense of 'improvement'. The principles of fidelity to the medieval original which drove the Gothic revival and the hostility to whitewash and false accretions, which roused the members of the Camden Society, were all anticipated by antiquaries of the eighteenth century. The antiquaries developed the critical vocabulary with which to describe these monuments and identified their historical importance, rescuing them from the generalised and dehistoricised embrace of the picturesque. The contribution of antiquarian literature was to define in the public mind the assumption that historic buildings, whether monastic ruins, city walls or Roman fortifications, had a national importance and were a vital element of the nation's distinctive heritage and identity. It was the antiquarian attachment to cathedrals which ensured their place as definitive symbols of the national heritage, just as it was also the antiquaries' perennial fascination with stone circles such as Stonehenge which placed these monuments to the forefront of any tourist itinerary. The arguments the antiquaries pressed in order to persuade their readers of the value and importance of their inquiries necessarily invoked the language of the nation and the public good. Buildings such as Westminster Abbey, supported by parliamentary grants, or cathedrals restored by the generosity of public subscription, were readily described as public buildings and part of the national heritage, but so too were privately owned monuments, such as Tintern Abbey. A convenient linguistic sleight of hand allowed collections of antiquities, monuments and buildings held as private property to be described as part of the national heritage, belonging in some nebulous, transcendent sense to the nation; in turn this allowed the proprietors – generally members of the ruling elite – to present themselves, somewhat opportunistically, as the disinterested custodians of the nation's past.[111] The antiquarian publication that placed castle, abbey and cathedral in close succession in the same volume, contributed to the assumption that these were a communal property and equally a part of the national heritage.

9

Popularisation

Antiquities and history belonged to the public at large. The word 'heritage', with all its modern connotations, was not used in the eighteenth century, but there was an assumption that, like the liberties of the freeborn Englishman that were every man's birthright, antiquities were in some sense a communal possession. As national identity waxed stronger over the course of the century, the adumbration of a common ancestral past through the description of the nation's history and antiquities assumed a weightier significance. The patriotic imperative to render antiquarian works more widely available and in a format to suit every pocket became increasingly pronounced and signalled an appreciation that antiquities, like the political franchise, should not remain the perquisite of a social elite, but should be freely available to all. Patriotism alone, however, does not account for the increasing popularity of antiquarianism. The re-evaluation of domestic antiquities was considerably indebted to the aesthetic preference for the picturesque and the sublime which dominated the second half of the century. This placed a different kind of value upon ancient monuments, particularly Gothic ruins, castles and medieval churches, and created a demand for a new type of publication which illustrated scenes of picturesque antiquities. The rise of domestic travel, which helped to fuel picturesque tourism, encouraged the publication of books that provided information upon antiquities in an accessible, less unwieldy format and at a more affordable price. Engravings assumed an increasingly important place; indeed, they were often the *raison d'être* of such publications. The nation's historical past, in the form of picturesque scenes of antiquities, was undergoing a process of reinterpretation for popular consumption. Alongside agricultural surveys such as Sir Arthur Young's *Tours* or Sir John Sinclair's *Statistical Account of Scotland*, the nation was coming to know itself through topographical literature, and to define itself through the monuments and antiquities as well as the agriculture and manufactures.

This chapter will examine the process by which antiquarianism became more widely accessible to a broader readership, how it was marketed and how it was received. It cannot be said that antiquarianism was truly popularised or consumed by a mass readership. The technology of eighteenth-century printing did not permit the kind of print runs which allow one to talk of mass consumption and popularisation in meaningful terms.[1] It is, however, possible to argue that antiquarianism lent itself to an increasingly commercialised format. Its practitioners had to respond to the interests of the book-buying public in an age in which the pressures of the market place exerted ever weightier influence. The subject of antiquities gradually came to be seen as one with potential commercial opportunities, and entrepreneurs began to exploit the historical and picturesque appeal which antiquities held. The consumption of antiquities was thereby extended beyond the professional and propertied classes to a readership based more solidly upon the middling sort. The purist's delight in antiquarian minutiae would always be a minority interest, but a generalised – at times superficial – acquaintance with the nation's antiquities was being subsumed into a historical package for the wider reading public; a process of commodifying the past that would become typical of the 'heritage industry'.

Even at the start of the eighteenth century there had been those who attempted to realise the commercial potential in antiquities. Not all books on antiquarian subjects were so highly priced as to be inaccessible to those of more modest means. The cachet of 'antiquities' commanded an element of prestige which could be exploited to lend an air of learning and authority to something rather more lightweight – a fact which publishers traded on, although they would not be numbered amongst the antiquarian fraternity themselves. Thomas Gent, for example, published historical and antiquarian accounts of three urban centres, York, Hull and Ripon, as well as a volume on the history and antiquities of York Minster. His books were aimed explicitly at the visitor market and were modestly sized and priced. In York he stole a march on Francis Drake, bringing out his own history six years before the latter's ponderous labours had been completed. He exploited his connections in the bookselling world to obtain antiquarian material and collections which gave greater gravitas to his own reflections and facetious asides.[2] His book, he wrote, was 'intended not so much to adorn a Library, as to be Pocket Companion in City or Country, the parlour, the Garden or the Field'.[3] Francis Howgrave of Stamford, another publisher, performed a similarly pre-emptive trick to Gent, in bringing out a brief account of the history and antiquities of Stamford in advance of Francis Peck's erudite and weighty *Academica tertia anglicana* (1727), which according to Michael Tyson was essentially comprised of collections made by his grandfather.[4]

Camden's *Britannia* was unaffordable for those of modest means, but cheaper serialised versions and abridgements of more expensive works, such as Cox's *Magna Britannia* (essentially an abridgement of Camden), were available for purchase by numbers through the local newspapers. *Britannia* itself was serialised in 1733 as a supplement to the *British Observator*.[5] The connection between local topographical and antiquarian publications and newspapers was a close one, and a number of urban histories, derivative of more expensive and erudite volumes, were published by newspaper proprietors in serialised form. Andrew Hooke of Bristol offered subscribers to his newspaper, the *Oracle*, the opportunity of purchasing his account of the history and antiquities of Bristol, *Bristollia* for six pence per quarterly pamphlet, as opposed to two shillings per issue to non-subscribers. In 1780 Thomas Brice, the proprietor of the *Exeter Chronicle*, offered readers a heavily abridged version of Samuel Izacke's *Remarkable Antiquities of the City of Exeter* for a halfpenny per issue, with a copy of the newspaper thrown in gratis – this was, in fact, a ploy to circumvent the stamp tax.[6] Serial publication made available works of antiquarianism, history and geography to a class of readers who would not otherwise have encountered them. John Cannon, an excise collector, was an autodidact who developed a passion for 'searching after antiquity', which he sustained by subscribing to *Magna Britannia* through the local newspaper. His memoirs record his reading in Speed, Dugdale, Camden, Rapin, William of Malmesbury and Geoffrey of Monmouth, and end with him in debt (due to antiquarian purchases), attempting to get hold of a copy of Browne Willis's *Notitia parliamenta*.[7] Cannon's case reminds us that even expensive antiquarian volumes were not invariably confined to a readership of the social elite.

Local historians and topographical writers alike were responding to commercial demand. They exploited the curiosity of the growing numbers of domestic travellers, providing information about antiquities, alongside a wide range of other types of information. Despite the fact that improvements in transport had reduced the duration of journeys so dramatically in the eighteenth century, travel was still a time-consuming and potentially dreary business, often necessitating long stops in provincial towns whilst horses were changed. In purely practical terms, the observation of antiquities offered a diversion to the tedium of travel and made it less irksome. Travellers liked to go to read sepulchral inscriptions in nearby churches at 'leg-stretching turns at change-horse places in the country'.[8] The observation of monuments of antiquity, suggested William Borlase, would set aside the thoughts of fatigue: barrows, stone circles, Roman camps and medieval ruins offered welcome diversions.[9]

In response to this need, a significant proportion of urban histories were written to inform the visitor rather than simply out of a sense of civic patriotism. The content varied from the solidly antiquarian material of

Francis Drake's *Eboracum* (1736) or John Brand's *History of Newcastle* (1789) to the limited recital of a few unspecified objects of antiquarian curiosity, unearthed during road building. Others, like Gent and Howgrave mentioned above, took advantage of the willingness of antiquaries to provide them with information which could be interpolated into an otherwise largely ahistorical work. Thomas Fisher, an enterprising bookseller in Rochester, notably achieved some success in persuading the Kent antiquaries Samuel Denne and John Thorpe to assist him in *The History and Antiquities of Rochester and its Environs* (1772).[10] The guide to Knaresborough – an up and coming watering place situated near monastic ruins – which was produced by the local publisher, Ely Hargrove, went through five editions between 1769 and 1798, each one displaying a greater depth of antiquarian detail.[11]

Another option was to take an antiquarian work and abridge it for easier consumption. This was patently the case in York in the second half of the century, where Drake's massive volume was long since out of print. The account of the minster was extracted for a publication in 1758, and in 1785 the first of several abridged histories made its appearance. The content was entirely derivative, the only new material being a section bringing the history up to date to cover the eighteenth century (a period which Drake, largely for political reasons, had not ventured upon). The history was issued in a much more manageable octavo format, with fewer and smaller illustrations, and with much of the potentially intimidating antiquarian apparatus removed. Long and discursive footnotes no longer crowded the bottom of the page, and the transcribed charters, the perusal of which delighted the antiquary but not the tourist, ceded place to accounts of assemblies, race meetings and the progress of polite sociability.[12] Conversely there were antiquaries who realised the potential profit of a smaller publication aimed at a more numerous market of urban purchasers and published the history and antiquities of the town separately from a county history. Thus Samuel Rudder published accounts of Gloucester and Cirencester in octavo volumes priced at six shillings, in addition to *A New History of Gloucestershire* (1778), a folio volume, for which subscribers had had to pay two and a half guineas.[13] Richard Gough, who had undertaken responsibility for publishing the *History of Dorset* for John Hutchins, planned to publish the section dealing with Corfe Castle separately, hoping thereby to earn some additional revenue for Hutchins' widow and daughter.[14]

Given the very mixed readership for which they were writing, local historians attempted to distance themselves from the dry pedantry with which antiquarianism was so often associated. They explored the possibilities of making antiquities more attractive: thus they eschewed lengthy footnotes and appendices, provided translations of Latin charters and offered rather more zest in the narrative than a more serious-minded antiquary would normally have allowed himself. Despite the denunciations of Gough, the practice of rendering passages of Latin text into English, or simply summarising the contents of a document, became increasingly common. Lionel Charlton, a surveyor and schoolmaster from Whitby, explained his decision to translate the numerous charters upon which his *History of Whitby* was based into English, and his avoidance of lengthy footnotes, on the grounds that few of his readers (the 'vulgar' as he referred to them) would have been interested in seeing the original texts. Inclusion of such material, he said, would have swollen the volume too far, making it unaffordable for precisely those purchasers for whom it should have held most interest.[15] The issues of proof and the need to secure the rhetorical high ground of truth, which had so preoccupied the antiquaries engaged in the ideological and political debates of an earlier generation, took second place to the necessity of making the subject palatable and accessible. The success of publications such as these indicates how a taste for antiquities had been disseminated beyond a narrow and socially exclusive community of scholars and gentlemen to reach an increasingly varied readership amongst the middling sorts.

William Hutton, the Birmingham business man and author of a number of local historical and topographical works, took delight in flouting all the conventions of antiquarian scholarship. His volumes dealt with much material that was inherently antiquarian, not least the Roman Wall. He styled himself as an 'antiquary' and proudly displayed the initials FSAS (fellow of the Society of Antiquaries of Scotland) after his name in publications, but what he wrote was effectively an anti-type of antiquarianism. He did not deny the interest or the importance of the Roman Wall, but in his eyes the interminable array of inscriptions which dominated the descriptions to be found in accounts from Camden's *Britannia* to John Warburton's *Vallum romanum* were nothing more than 'dry husks'. Antiquities needed spirited language to dress them up: 'meer dull description, like a burnt cinder, is dead matter'. The traditional emphasis of the antiquary upon detailed and minute observation was summarily dismissed: it was the 'dullest of all descriptions' and rendered more dull by the use of abstruse terms and as much Latin as the page could hold. As a bookseller himself, Hutton was well aware of the desirability of a cheap, compact volume: 'if I load it with parings, like putting garlic into his [the bookseller's] repast it will swell the book, the price, and the disgust'.[16] The popularity and success of Hutton's account lay in his ability to present the antiquarian object of the Wall in terms of his personal experience and to convey it as something living rather than dead. He described the remains of the fortifications directly as he saw them – there was no discussion of coins and inscriptions, no attempt to dazzle the reader with a show of erudition by citing classical authorities.[17] The Wall and the ditches were anthropomorphised as the general (Agricola) and the emperor (Hadrian or Severus) respectively. At Port Gate he found the united works of Agricola and Hadrian intact: 'I surveyed them with surprize; with delight, was fascinated, and unable to proceed; forgot I was upon a wild common, a stranger, and the evening approaching. I had the grandest works under my eye, of the greatest men of the age in which they lived, and of the most eminent nation then living.' But at Axeldonum, 'I was taken into a garden where a stone with a Roman inscription was shewn me; but none of us could read it.'[18] The Latin inscription, which for John Horsley had been the point of departure for all his inquiries concerning the Roman Wall, was in practical terms illegible to Hutton and as such redundant. It could not offer that point of personal communion with the past, which for Hutton – who had little interest in pinning down the precise location of the different stations of the Wall – was the essence of all antiquarian experience. His argument was simple: the vast store of learning, upon which antiquaries such as Gough prided themselves, was not necessary for an appreciation of the country's antiquities and the historical legacy of the past. Hutton was the antithesis of all those qualities which are often associated with antiquarianism: social status, landed property, Anglicanism and Tory politics. He was a dissenting bookseller who had worked himself up from a position of poverty to amass considerable wealth – facts which he made no attempt to disguise.[19] He was, however, positive as to the didactic value of history and antiquities and the inherent pleasure to be derived from them. His mission was to prove that the nation's history belonged to everyone and anyone, not just those who chose to lock it up in impenetrable prose and Latin quotations.

Alongside local history flourished the topographical tour. As many contemporaries observed, there was a very rage for travel writing in the eighteenth century. Daniel Defoe had notably declared in the first edition of his *Tour through the Whole Island of Great Britain* that he would take no notice of antiquities, being more interested in the modern state of the nation. Of Ely, he wrote, there was nothing remarkable, save the minster, and there was nothing remarkable about the minster, save that it was so ancient that it tottered and threatened to collapse in every gust of wind. Nor was it of any moment whether Julius Caesar landed first at Deal or Ramsgate, and the question would never by proved either way. This did not, however, prevent him from plagiarising the text of *Britannia* when it suited him, and despite himself, he found it impossible to ignore the presence

William Hutton. (*Julian Pooley*)

of a monument such as Stonehenge, or the antique remains which littered the city of Lincoln.[20] Successive editions of Defoe's *Tour* incorporated a steadily increasing element of antiquarian information, as the sources from which such material could be lifted became more readily available to the editorial assistants in Samuel Richardson's printing house. Readers were referred to other publications for fuller accounts of, for example, the antiquities of Richborough, upon which earlier editions had cast such scorn.[21]

Not all travel writers followed this trend: there were always some who made a very virtue of the fact that they included no dry antiquarian material, but most paid at least lip-service to describing the antiquities passed along the way – not least because so many, like Defoe, were dependent upon Camden's *Britannia* as a basic starting point for information. Others writers, like John Collinson, the author of a history of Somerset, compiled a handy octavo volume for travellers, composed of extracts from authors on 'the more remarkable antiquities', entitled *The Beauties of British Antiquity.* Another county historian, Stebbing Shaw, who published *A Tour in the West of England* (1789) was unapologetic about his decision to include a considerable amount of antiquarian material, but promised to accommodate 'those readers, whose taste cannot relish the unadorned narration of history'. This populist aim was to be achieved by 'digressions of the fancy and descriptions of the muse'.[22] George Lipscombe specifically targeted his *Journey into South Wales* at 'men of business and persons of very moderate incomes' – not the landed elite who purchased the county histories. He wrote for the tourist who did not have the leisure or inclination to wade through the various county histories; those who felt no extraordinary emotion at 'the sight of a rusty shield or a corroded statue' but could rejoice in the triumph of civilisation over barbarity. Lipscombe set himself up in opposition to the tedium of antiquaries, who clogged their text with notes, offering instead the 'pleasant and flowery paths' of miscellaneous history. But even his breezy generalisations betrayed a fundamental familiarity with the topics of antiquarian discourse which he passed on to his readers.[23]

Antiquities could not provide much relief from tedium, however, if the traveller did not already have a prior flickering of curiosity. Here we must acknowledge the fashionable influence of the picturesque movement and incipient romanticism in arousing the interest of even the most casual visitors in ruins of any description. Castles and abbeys had always had some claim to interest because they symbolised key elements of national history in the passage of feudalism and the triumph of reformed religion over Catholicism. Similarly, the value of ruins as *memento mori*, reminders of the fragility of human endeavour, was well established: castles erected by once mighty families were now laid low, as were the family fortunes. Further to this, the theorisation of the picturesque that was developed by Edmund Burke in the *Philosophical Essay on the Sublime and the Beautiful*, in the oeuvre of William Gilpin, or more latterly in the writings of Uvedale Price, Humphry Repton or Richard Payne Knight, established aesthetic criteria upon which the ruin could be appreciated and according to which it was made the object of fashionable taste. William Gilpin, the medium through which many readers gained their appreciation of the picturesque, informed his readers that 'among all the objects of art, the picturesque eye is perhaps most inquisitive after the elegant relics of ancient architecture; the ruined tower, the Gothic arch, the remains of castles, and abbeys'.[24] Crumbling masonry, ivy-clad walls and fallen arches were prized as a pleasing contrast to the regularity of classicism, as an exercise in the contrasts of light and shade, and for the imaginative associations which they provoked. Alternatively the ruin could be viewed as the object of sublime awe, horror or melancholy in a deeply personal and emotionally charged relationship with the beholder.[25] One must have taste to be sensible of the beauties of Grecian architecture, wrote Walpole; one only wants passion to feel Gothic.[26] Gothic buildings inspired wonder and reverence; their gloom and obscurity heightened the sense of mystery; they were eminently more suited for the worship of a deity than the symmetrical uniformity of classical temples. For the traveller in search of heightened emotional impact, the sight of a ruined abbey such as Tintern was enough to send him or her into ecstasies of appreciation. Whereas once the man of taste had spurned the Gothic, by the later eighteenth century no sentimental traveller could afford not to be moved by the sight of physical decay and over-abundant vegetation: 'Heavens what a noble pile of Gothic Architecture is Tintern Abbey. I was in extase and speechless.'[27]

One cannot, however, make hard and fast distinctions between the antiquaries and those whose appreciation of the Gothic was conceived solely in terms of the picturesque. The relationship was generally complementary, as was that which developed between the champions of bardic literature and antiquarianism narrowly defined. Although an antiquary such as Richard Gough was prone to deride those like Gilpin, whom he considered to be mere landscape artists, there was a common language and set of assumptions to which most antiquaries also laid claim. Whilst William Gilpin could expound on the distinctions between Roman, Saxon and Gothic architecture in his picturesque tours, Edward King, one-time president of the Society of Antiquaries, could introduce his history of castles, *Munimenta antiqua*, with a meditation on the 'rude sublimity of thought and design manifested in their Architecture'.[28]

It was the taste for the picturesque, rather than historical curiosity, or a fascination with the evolution of the pointed arch, which accounted for the rapid growth in volumes devoted to delineating Gothic antiquities. This was a genre which demanded illustration. The picturesque was a visual phenomenon: it was the appearance of the building or the ruin which mattered, not its date of foundation or the granting of a charter. Engravings, as was well established, considerably enhanced the appeal of a volume. Compilers of topographical collections, noted one reviewer, generally attempted to compensate for the tedium of the contents by the splendour of the engravings.[29] The accompanying letterpress commonly took second place, and was derivative if not derisory in its content. For all that, the growing number of volumes illustrating picturesque antiquities made a significant contribution to broadening the market for works devoted to the illustration of architectural antiquities. This visual emphasis dovetailed neatly with the concomitant shift in emphasis in antiquarian studies towards the artefact and the building, rather than the written record.

As early as 1726 Nathaniel and Samuel Buck had commenced publication of *Views of the Ruins of Castles and Abbeys in England and Wales*, a work which anticipated many of the later picturesque publications, and indeed very often proved to be the source of unacknowledged borrowings. It was not, however, published at a price which would appeal to any but the social elite; appearing in seventeen annual sets costing two guineas each, the complete series would have cost the prospective purchaser the substantial sum of thirty-four guineas. The list of subscribers was correspondingly dominated by names drawn from the nobility, gentry and professional classes.[30] In 1774, however, the series was reissued by Edward Sayer, as *Buck's Antiquities*, in response, as seems likely, to the success which another publication on a similar subject was enjoying – Francis Grose's *Antiquities of England and Wales* (1772–76). Grose, former Richmond Herald, militia captain and a fellow of the Society of Antiquaries, undertook the project in order to rescue his precarious fortunes, rather than as an exercise in antiquarian self-indulgence. Published in parts the volumes were relatively affordable, costing one shilling and six pence for twenty-four pages plus three plates (he later charged two shillings for four plates). This worked out as six pence a plate: half the price, or less, of any of the comparable publications available at the time (although few purchasers, it must be allowed, would have bought only a single plate).[31] The volumes could be found in many provincial subscription libraries as well as in private collections, alongside other standard works of reference such as *Britannia* and *British Topography*. Although Grose presented the *Antiquities* to a non-specialist market, it was still one in which familiarity with Latin and French was assumed, and the four volumes in quarto format were evidently aimed at the upper end of the 'popular' market.

Grose's intentions were stated in the preface: he did not pretend to inform the 'Veteran Antiquary', but had drawn up the accounts for the use of those who wished to acquire a general rather than a specialist knowledge of the subjects discussed in his publication. He promised to point out the principal characteristics of Gothic and Saxon architecture and to explain all the terms and allusions. Recommendations for further reading in Wren, Warton and Bentham were made to assist those who sought further illumination.[32] Despite his own background as a fellow of the Society of Antiquaries, amongst whom he numbered several close friends, Grose was clearly writing for a readership whose imagination had been captured by tales of knightly chivalry and for whom the Gothic was primarily a source of sublime *frissons* and picturesque delight. The frontispiece of a ruined abbey and the tomb of a knight, followed by another composite scene of a knight in armour below a castle, riding towards a monk outside a chapel, offered a visual summary of the popular appeal of Gothic antiquities. It was a *mélange* of medieval antiquities in which temporal precision and factual accuracy were sacrificed for a pleasing pictorial effect. As promised, Grose did offer a summary of the characteristics of Saxon and Gothic architecture, together with a history of castles, abbeys and other monastic foundations. But the introduction aside, the letterpress was brief and superficial, consisting of little more than a summary of the owners of the property and, in the case of ecclesiastical foundations, wealth at the time of the Dissolution of the Monasteries – not even the picturesque could usurp the eternal antiquarian preoccupation with property and its value.

Additional comments appealed to the developing picturesque aesthetic within polite culture. Tintern Abbey had been so opened up by the duke of Beaufort that it had become too light – it had lost that sought after air of mystery and horror. The more decayed a building, the better: the ash trees which had taken root amongst the ruins of Lannercost Priory and 'flourished amongst the disjointed stones' afforded a very picturesque appearance. The church of St Mary Magdalen at Colchester, meanwhile, earned its inclusion on the basis of its very picturesque appearance, rather than its perceived historical importance. It should be acknowledged, however, that Grose's decision to highlight the church's picturesque appeal says as much about the sources available to him as the actual appearance of the buildings in Colchester. He was always working under considerable pressure to produce the letterpress in time for each issue, and the inadequacy of some of the accounts reflects the commercial exigencies of the situation rather than a reluctance to deliver information of antiquarian value. Whereas his account of Ely, for which he relied upon Bentham, was detailed and informative, in Colchester his source was Philip Morant's *History of Colchester* (1748). Morant was no architectonical antiquary; he was of the earlier school of antiquarianism which described a church in terms of dimensions and benefactions. There was little in Morant which Grose could seize upon to enliven his prose. Thus the quality of the descriptions of Colchester's antiquities deteriorated to the level of hackneyed picturesque banalities. The impatient voice of the printer's compositor is almost audible in the background. *The Antiquities of England and Wales* swiftly established itself as a standard work of reference for the polite traveller, and such was its success (and also such were the financial difficulties in which Grose found himself) that the series was followed up by *Antiquities of Scotland* and *Antiquities of Ireland*, although Grose died before the latter was completed. Furthermore, a second and cheaper edition was called for, appearing in eight volumes in 1783. Ultimately the enterprise earned Grose £800, saving both himself and his publisher from bankruptcy.[33]

Grose's *Antiquities of England and Wales* was soon joined by a range of other publications illustrating buildings and sites of historical interest, accompanied by descriptive letterpress of varying degrees of antiquarian content. In addition to *Buck's Antiquities* already noted, William Stukeley's *Itinerarium curiosum*, which boasted many illustrations as well as antiquarian observations, was reissued two years later in 1776 with the previously unpublished *Iter boreale*. Paul Sandby offered the *Virtuosi's Museum* (1778–81) and Thomas Hearne and William Byrne responded with *The Antiquities of Great Britain* (1778–86, 1806). Hearne and Byrne's series, like that of Francis Grose, was dominated by picturesque views of monasteries and castles; indeed there was a significant overlap in subject matter. With their irregular outlines and overgrown interiors, ruined monasteries and castles were closer to the picturesque ideal than were the churches and cathedrals which had not been allowed to fall into a similar state of decay. Accordingly they tended to dominate in such publications. In most images the historical and social contexts of the ruin would be ignored in the creation of a generalised landscape; what was important was the impact upon the sensibilities of the viewer rather than the documentary record of the past.[34] Hearne's engravings were not simply exercises in picturesque composition, however, but showed meticulous attention to architectural detail and a high level of accuracy. This unusual feature won the approval of Richard Gough, who told his friend Michael Tyson that Hearne was 'wonderfully happy in hitting off Gothic architecture, which he much attends to'.[35] The letterpress, also provided by Hearne, was not without merit either. He was largely reliant upon secondary authorities and the goodwill of antiquaries such as Richard

Gough and Thomas Percy. The level of information fluctuated accordingly, but he cut and pasted from his sources effectively, alerting the reader to the variations in ornamentation which indicated the period of construction, or singling out Gothic structures of particular beauty. He clearly had an instinctive sympathy for medieval architecture which was reflected in both his draughtsmanship and the tenor of his comments. The emphasis was if anything upon the antiquarian, rather than the picturesque importance of the antiquities engraved. Hearne's engravings were published at three shillings each, whilst Sandby's were a shilling a piece. Neither of these, therefore, could be said to have been readily affordable to any but the interested collector, but the views, and indeed the letterpress, were reworked and reproduced in numerous other histories and collections of views, and thereby reached a much broader market.

They featured, for example, in magazines and periodicals such as the *Universal, European, London* and *Ladies Magazines.* The *Copper Plate Magazine*, which commenced publication in 1778, offered its readers a variety of views of landscapes, gentlemen's seats and scenes of picturesque antiquity. The *Gentleman's Magazine* had always provided a forum in which information and news on antiquities could be exchanged and discussed. Under the editorship of John Nichols the antiquarian element was substantially increased, and it regularly carried illustrations of objects and buildings of antiquarian interest. One correspondent referred to it as 'a kind of Supplement' to *Archaeologia.*[36] In 1782–83 a debate was conducted as to when the Gothic style had been introduced, and how the term should be used, a belated response to Bentham's *History of Ely* (1771).[37] Between 1798 and 1817 its pages were taken up with numerous articles on the subject of Gothic architecture and its preservation from the pen of John Carter.[38] The vigour, not to say vitriol, with which Carter conducted his campaign against the philistines who showed no appreciation of the superior qualities of the Gothic style, and who connived in the destruction of medieval buildings, must have attracted many readers who would otherwise have passed over the more measured and restrained architectural descriptions normally produced by antiquaries – controversy and debate, particularly if *ad hominem* remarks are involved, will always succeed in garnering interest.

In 1775 the first periodical devoted specifically to the subject of antiquities, the *Antiquarian Repertory*, was published by the engraver Richard Godfrey. Francis Grose has often been wrongly identified as its editor, but although he promoted its publication and contributed a number of views and short pieces, he was not actively involved in its production.[39] Four volumes had been issued by 1786, whereupon it ceased publication. This may be taken as indicative of a lack of interest – although it should also be remembered how many other periodical ventures failed in this period. The first number in 1775 offered a stirring manifesto for the study of antiquities which confronted head-on the popular prejudices against antiquarianism. 'It has long been the fashion to laugh at the study of Antiquities, and to consider it the idle amusement of a few humdrum, plodding fellows ...' Antiquaries, it was said, lacked the genius for nobler pursuits and instead busied themselves with a futile quest for illegible manuscripts and obliterated coins. This perversion and abuse of scholarship was unjust, declared the editorial, and it proceeded to explain precisely how the study of antiquities was the *sine qua non* for any gentleman or liberal profession. The contents of the *Antiquarian Repertory* were widely varied and miscellaneous, largely comprising 'fugitive pieces' which could not find a place of publication elsewhere: they ranged from short pieces on Westminster Abbey or the Queen's Cross at Northampton, to extracts from Hollinshed or John Taylor, the Water Poet. A number of respected antiquarian names such as Sir John Cullum, Hayman Rooke, Thomas Astle, Thomas Pownall and William Hutchinson were listed amongst its correspondents. Richard Gough, however, was conspicuously absent.[40]

The first edition was well received in some quarters. William Cuming, Gough's co-editor in the business of Hutchins's *History and Antiquities of Dorset*, was enthusiastic, but Gough, predictably, held it in small esteem and encouraged it only in the hope that it would eventually improve in quality.[41] Michael Tyson was contemptuous of its superficiality and outraged by the editor's failure to live up to his promise only to publish views which had never been issued before. 'I would set fire to my study rather than give them a line', he concluded.[42] The subject matter of the articles published is revealing of both the intended readership and also the obvious difficulties the editors were encountering in the latter numbers in securing sufficient copy. Views of picturesque rather than strictly antiquarian interest, such as the Waterfall at Lodore on Keswick Lake, were frequently included as space fillers, whilst a letter about inscriptions from modern tombstones was found a place on the grounds that the 'variety' would make up for the undeniable want of antiquity. Over the course of a couple of years the reliance upon extracts from easily plundered sources such as John Taylor or Hollinshed became much more evident. Although the *Antiquarian Repertory* struggled and was forced to cease publication at the end of 1786, it did find its way into a number of libraries. Arguably, it suffered from being slightly ahead of its time in offering a dedicated, accessible and affordable medium for antiquarian matters. In 1807 it was reissued in response, it was claimed, to popular demand, as well as the availability of additional material with which to enrich and enhance a new edition.[43]

There was also an increasing number of publications that were wholly derivative of more expensive volumes, amongst which those put forth by Alexander Hogg are particularly notable. His *England Displayed* (1769) listed antiquities to be seen in each county, but had no illustrations. This was followed by similar publications, *The Complete English Traveller* (1771) and *The Modern Universal British Traveller* (1779). G. A. Walpoole's *New British Traveller* (1784) was ornamented with plates of execrable quality, including a number of views of antiquarian interest, combined with gentlemen's seats and urban prospects. The *Historical Description of New and Elegant Picturesque Views of the Antiquities of England and Wales* (1785), published under the name of Henry Boswell, was Hogg's first real attempt to exploit the commercial potential of antiquities, and the considerable quantity of published material which was by this point available for him to plagiarise.[44] For these volumes Hogg drew on the *Antiquarian Repertory*, the *Antiquities of England and Wales* and also Hearne and Byrne's, *Antiquities of Great Britain.* Hogg was said to have employed a servant by the week to 'cut up books' for the printer and to read the proofs. Despite the blatant plagiarism of his own publications, evident in both engravings and letterpress, Francis Grose was listed as a subscriber. According to John Britton, however, Grose successfully sued Hogg for damages.[45] Hogg's preface, in which he outlined to the reader the importance of antiquities, struck a note which was less elitist than those prefatory statements which graced volumes with sounder antiquarian credentials. Mankind in general, it was said, has a propensity to admire everything relating to antiquities or ruins; even a clown – however rude his manners – has an inclination to become acquainted with the history of any building of antiquity in his neighbourhood. All ranks of people sought views of antiquities, but hitherto only the affluent had been able to afford the extravagant prices. This publication therefore was 'cheap and elegant' and designed to accommodate all possible readers. The price was calculated for 'Public Advantage', not private emolument, and would fit all pockets and dispositions. Rich, poor and middle class alike could 'improve their Minds, please their Taste, ornament their Libraries, decorate their Apartments, and in various Ways afford Sentiments of Pleasure and Delight to all around them'. For those who were uncertain of what they might expect to gain from purchasing such a volume, the didactic value was spelled out. The changes undergone by the memorials of 'grandeur and dominion' would offer a striking lesson in the mutability of human greatness. Readers were promised that their minds would be improved and their eyes delighted.

This promise of self-improvement and edification, combined with a repeated emphasis upon the cheapness of the volume and the deliberately inclusive tone of the preface, betokens an important shift towards the democratisation of antiquities and the history which they represented. It places it within that booming genre of 'self-help' literature for the middling sort with aspirations to gentility. This was yet another way to acquire those trappings of politeness so necessary on the way to becoming 'rich and respectable'.[46] Although the *Antiquarian Repertory* had declared that 'every man is naturally an Antiquarian', the self-evident assumption was that the readers would be gentlemen or at least pretenders to genteel status. Hogg, however, whilst reproducing almost word for word much of the preface to the *Antiquarian Repertory*, down to the statement that 'without a competent fund of Antiquarian Learning, no one will ever make a respectable figure, either as a Divine, a Lawyer, Statesman, Soldier, or even private Gentleman', added to this list the categories of 'Tradesman or Mechanic'. In this version of antiquarianism for all, nobody – whatever their sphere of life – could be properly qualified without it.[47]

In the early nineteenth century the trend for antiquarian material in an accessible format and at an affordable price continued, and Hearne, Grose and Sandby continued to be regularly plagiarised in lesser publications. The works that stand out in this period followed the same format, of offering a fairly random series of views of monuments and objects, presented simply as engravings attractive in themselves, rather than serving to illustrate a broader thesis or thematic treatment of an antiquarian subject. There was not as yet any system of chronological or even geographical organisation to these volumes. James Storer, an engraver, was behind the publication of a number of antiquarian volumes, all of which were published serially over a number of years, including the *Antiquarian and Topographical Cabinet* (1807), *The Antiquarian Itinerary* (1815) and the *History and Antiquities of the Cathedral Churches of Great Britain* (1814). Storer and his co-editor Brierely were responsible for the engravings. The letterpress was compiled by their compositor, a Mr Brown, from a variety of secondary sources such as Camden, Gough, Grose and Hearne or contributions sent in by correspondents.[48] Given that the latter two in particular were themselves generally extrapolating from the observation of others, a considerable superstructure of accumulated borrowings was being built up. The first two series were published in matching format, octavo, with small engravings, accompanied by a short passage of letterpress, generally two pages long. The very broad margins to the printed page and the quality of the engraving, which whilst being very small was finely detailed and accurate, pronounced that these were primarily visual rather than informative volumes. The 'proprietors' expressed the hope that the volumes would not only be an agreeable pocket companion to the 'Antiquarian Traveller' but would also provide a more complete repertory of antiquarian illustrations than any offered hitherto to the public.

The type of antiquities that they chose to illustrate was still heavily dominated by the aesthetic of the ruin. Artefacts were rarely engraved – occasionally a Roman inscription would be reproduced – and secular buildings, particularly in an urban context, were comparatively infrequent subjects. At Beaconsfield, near Canewdon church (the subject of one of the plates), for example, it was simply noted that a 'great variety' of urns had been uncovered there at different times during the previous century, without any further elaboration of the finds or their significance. The dominant theme of the volumes, therefore, was upon illustrating the continuity of both the church and the landed elite who commanded the castles and the great houses: a continuity which was the more important at a time when both church and nobility had been recently overthrown in France.[49] The brevity of the text and the absence of footnotes made few demands upon the reader; the information offered was of a general kind and tended towards the historical, as in the case of castles, for which the letterpress was chiefly concerned with the histories of the families with which they were associated. Architectural descriptions were largely unsophisticated. Whilst the text showed a nicer appreciation than Paul Sandby, for example, had displayed, the simple dichotomy between Saxon and pointed styles was hardly at the cutting edge of antiquarian expertise.[50] In some cases the descriptions were of laconic brevity: the ruins at Kirkham Priory were described simply as 'respectable'.[51] The quality of the engravings might have met with Richard Gough's grudging approval, despite the cramped format adopted. It is unlikely, however, that he would have been impressed by the display of antiquarian learning in the text.

At roughly the same time that Storer's publications were making their appearance, another, and considerably more ambitious project, was also getting under way, that is the series *Beauties of England and Wales* under the joint editorship of John Britton and Edward Brayley. Britton, the son of a shopkeeper from Kingston, began his career apprenticed to a wine merchant before becoming an actor. He was initiated into topography and antiquarianism when he began writing the letterpress for the *Copper Plate Magazine* published by Samuel Ireland.[52] In his autobiography he described how as a young man he had struggled with the conventional antiquarian fare such as Camden's *Britannia*, Gough's *British Topography* or King's *Munimenta antiqua*. It was only on reading Richard Warner's *Walk through Wales*, which itself owed a heavy debt to Gilpin, that Britton discovered his own delight in antiquities. Here he found information about history and antiquities blended with reflections and anecdotes, all written in a polished and conversational style. He realised that antiquities did not have to be presented in a distasteful or obscurantist manner; the subject could be compelling, pleasurable and democratic in its appeal to all types of readers. Britton's virtual walk through Wales was his road to Damascus.

> I read it with avidity, was pleased with it, and found that such writing did not require much recondite learning, and need not be encumbered and confused by technical terms, or dull details of genealogy, manorial and parochial history, and useless lists of rectors and vicars, with long inscriptions on tombs, in Latin, Greek and bad English.[53]

Such was his enthusiasm that he immediately embarked upon his own extended picturesque pedestrian tour through the midlands, the Wye Valley and north Wales. In later life Britton would move away from the blandly picturesque approach towards a more specialist antiquarian stance, but his approach to antiquarian literature was always based upon the assumption that it should be made palatable for a non-specialist readership.

In 1798 Britton embarked upon a project to compile a topographical work entitled the *Beauties of Wiltshire.* This eventually led to his much more ambitious scheme, *The Beauties of England and Wales*, for which Britton had been approached by the publishers Vernor and Hood, who wanted to cash in on the growing topographical market. He undertook the project in collaboration with another writer-cum-antiquary, Edward Brayley. Published in numbers at a cost of two shillings and six pence each, the series was aimed at the general market. The sales reflected this. Whereas most antiquarian publications had print runs of anything between 200 and 1000 copies, the *Beauties of England and Wales* sold in the thousands.[54] It was still, however, a readership dominated by the gentry and the more prosperous middling sort; evidence that even a series such as this made its way into the hands of a truly popular readership is hard to come by.

Britton, whose antiquarian interests were now well established, however, was emphatic that the series should be based upon original sources and illustrated by accurate engravings of antiquities, as opposed to the crowd-pleasing combination of country seats and picturesque woodland scenes which Vernor and Hood had envisaged. The volumes became progressively more detailed as the two editors broadened their reading and built up their expertise. They insisted on carrying out their own research and conducted lengthy field trips to collect the information, claiming to have consulted between twenty and thirty books per county.[55] Relations with Vernor and Hood were permanently strained, however, as neither Britton nor Brayley ever felt that they received their due in remuneration for the venture, for which they were paid by the sheet, rather than being allowed a share as proprietors. The partnership between the two editors was hardly harmonious either – not that Britton gave any hint of this in his own self-aggrandising memoirs. Brayley complained that he was left to do all the work of writing the letterpress, whilst Britton just executed directions. 'I find I am only considered as Mr Britton's assistant when by *right* I am as fully intitled to be regarded as a Principal as he is.'[56] Both individuals withdrew from the project before it was completed, although Britton was persuaded to come back to finish the volume on Wiltshire in 1810.

The focus was upon the architecture, rather than the effects of ivy and crumbling masonry, and this tradition was carried on in the subsequent volumes, even after Britton and Brayley had withdrawn from the enterprise. An impressive team of artists and engravers was enrolled to produce the illustrations, which were, in the opinion of Britton at least, superior to any that had gone before. John Varley, Thomas Hearne, J. M. W. Turner and even Benjamin West, better known for his history paintings, all contributed drawings. It was soon apparent that the series would far exceed the original six volumes which had been projected; in fact it ran to twenty-seven volumes published over the course of twenty years. It included more than 700 illustrations, and was reputed to have cost over £50,000 to produce (the total price for an entire set was £30 2.6d.).[57] Britton, never one to underestimate his own importance, claimed in his autobiography that the series had 'greatly assisted in rendering *local history* an object of fashionable study' and had effected a memorable improvement in the quality of the engravings of antiquities offered to the public. He was, moreover, sufficiently encouraged by the success of the *Beauties of England and Wales* to embark upon another project which enabled him to pursue more closely what was rapidly becoming his dominant interest, architectural antiquities.[58]

The *Beauties of England and Wales* was also accompanied by the *British Atlas*, comprising a series of maps of all the counties of England and Wales, showing, amongst other items of interest, the course of the Roman roads and the location of the principal Roman camps and stations in any county. What was being offered was a systematic and comprehensive coverage of the whole of England and Wales, which encouraged the reader to compare and contrast antiquities across the country, rather than the jumbled and unsystematic collections that characterised the earlier topographical collections. In the final volume published in 1818, readers were offered a retrospective introduction to the history and antiquities of England which provided the chronological framework for the preceding volumes. Information was presented in a rationalised form – as in, for example, the tables of Celtic and British tribes with their geographical location. This drive to systematise knowledge was particularly in evidence in the section devoted to architectural history where, for each 'period' of architecture identified, tables were compiled, listing churches and monastic ruins which displayed specimens of the particular style in question. The search for order, which antiquaries were imposing upon the study of architectural antiquities, was gradually permeating the presentation of antiquities for popular consumption as well.[59] Prior to the *Beauties of England and Wales* few of the volumes purporting to illustrate picturesque antiquities had shown anything more than the barest semblance of thematic, geographical or temporal organisation. Plates were published apparently at random: Ripon Minster might be followed by Roslin Castle, after which there was a sudden leap south to the abbey gate at Bury St Edmunds.[60] Indeed, the assumption was that collectors should be left to bind the plates at their discretion. Jacob Schnebbelie, draughtsman to the Society of Antiquaries, issued proposals for publishing the *Antiquaries Museum* in 1790. Each number, he promised, would be complete in itself so that gentlemen could arrange them as they wished.[61] This was the visual equivalent to arranging one's own cabinet of curiosities – and the content was almost equally miscellaneous.

Publications such as Grose's *Antiquities of England and Wales* or the *Beauties of England and Wales*, along with the articles in the *Gentleman's Magazine* or the *Antiquarian Repertory* became an important mean of filtering information, initially confined to a small antiquarian coterie, through to a much wider readership. This was particularly evident in descriptions of medieval architecture for which the levels of analysis and vocabulary of description became considerably more sophisticated. The process, however, was certainly not instantaneous. Even the apprehension of the difference between Saxon and Gothic, which had first been crudely drawn by Sir Christopher Wren, was far from universal. For a long time rounded arches were variously debased Roman, Saxon, Norman, or in some cases Danish. The church at Nantwich, the reader was informed, was likely to have been built by Canute, given that its octangular tower, low doors and lofty windows were very clearly of Danish construction.[62] John Watson, who was noted for his contributions to the study of Roman antiquities, druidical and Saxon remains in Yorkshire, betrayed very little sign of sharing the interests of Richard Gough and other members of the Society of Antiquaries in his history of Halifax published in 1775. The fabric of the parish church was identified laconically as 'Gothic'; it had a 'good appearance', and touched with local patriotism, Watson claimed that it excelled in several respects most parochial churches of its kind. The age of the building, he explained, could not be determined, but he suggested that it had been re-edified at different periods, since parts of the north side looked older than the rest, and were 'worse built'.[63]

At the same time other writers saw the potential for fleshing out their guides and histories and assimilated the new materials with alacrity. A history of Winchester, published anonymously in 1773, lifted long passages verbatim from Thomas Warton's account of the cathedral and the hospital of St Cross, and also cited the authority of James Bentham, whose volume on Ely Cathedral had been published only two years earlier. The visitor was informed that the pillars of the chapel at St Cross were Saxon, but neater than those which were commonly so called, and that they also had more ornamentation on the capitals than was usually the case. It was therefore presumed that the chapel had been erected at the point when the 'plain Saxon' was changing and partly succeeded by the 'Saracen style', which used the pointed arch and slender column. Thus the chapel was likely to have been founded after the reign of Henry I.[64] The surgeon turned antiquary William Barrett, describing the cathedral at Bristol, remarked that the gate house was in the 'stile of what Sir Christopher Wren calls the Saxon architecture, before the Gothic or rather the Saracenic with pointed arches was introduced in this island after the crusades'. But thereafter he floundered, completely lacking the words or the concepts with which to describe the ornamentation or the design. It was, he wrote, impossible to give any idea of the decorations. 'The scrolls, twists, and other ornaments are so interwoven and intricate, that the eye is puzzled in surveying them, and is at loss where to fix and trace them out'. He later interpolated a description of the cathedral written by Charles Lyttelton, which had been traced for Barrett amongst the records of the Society of Antiquaries and which displayed all Lyttelton's preoccupation with detecting the evolution from 'Saxon' to 'Gothic'.[65] Barrett's account of St Mary Redcliff, the most outstanding specimen of perpendicular architecture in Bristol, was by contrast singularly uninformative, and he returned to his own style of bald description. Despite Barrett's incorporation of Lyttelton's observations, he was clearly unable to engage with what Lyttelton was trying to achieve and failed to see the difference of approach that it marked. Rather, his own comments betray some of the prejudices of conventional eighteenth-century notions of taste against the Gothic style and illustrate the limits of an antiquarian Gothic sensibility.

William Reader, a newspaper proprietor, who published a history of Coventry in 1810, candidly admitted that his account of the 'venerable pile' of St Mary's Hall had been drawn entirely from 'letters inserted at different periods in the *Gentleman's Magazine* by the late Mr Gough and Mr Carter'.[66] John Britton similarly confessed in his autobiography that much of his knowledge in the early stages of his career derived from reading Carter's articles.[67] John Blackner, another newspaper proprietor, who developed an interest in antiquities and wrote a history of Nottingham, was able to dismiss an earlier identification of St Mary's Nottingham as Saxon by another local antiquary, Charles Deering, on the authority of John Carter's articles in the *Gentleman's Magazine*, John Moffat's *History of Malmesbury* and the *British Encyclopedia*. Deering, he said, had made a 'gross error' which had not the smallest trace of architectural evidence to support it. Rather than studying the architecture of the building itself for a clue to its age, he explained, Deering had been led astray by workmen who had reported finding a date on a beam.[68] Moffat's history of Malmesbury, referred to by Blackner, had been published in 1805 and was itself indebted to the accounts published by Carter, as well as the discussion of Gothic and Saxon in Bentham's account of Ely Cathedral. The expansion of antiquarian and topographical publishing thus created and sustained a new constituency of readers with an interest in history and antiquities, which existed independently of either the universities or the learned societies, and which was open to anyone who could gain access to periodicals or afford a few shillings for these cheaper publications.

Guides, histories and topographical tours all contributed to the gradual dissemination of this more easily digestible antiquarianism. The dedicated and wealthy travellers made extracts from weighty volumes and took with them plates of the views which they expected to see; and in their journals, which they wrote up subsequently, they compared their own experience with the descriptions of Grose or Gilpin, or whoever had been their *vade-mecum*. For those who took their antiquarian tourism less seriously there were many cheaper guides and abridgements. The literary hacks, who compiled the topographical tours, histories and guides, were reliant on the publications of antiquaries and therefore reflected the current preoccupations of the antiquarian world in their own less specialist literature. Even the casual traveller who purchased one of these volumes would be seeing the places through which they passed in antiquarian terms. By the early nineteenth century the traveller was being offered compact guides which purported to highlight all that was most worthy of notice – whether in antiquities, botany, mineralogy or scenery.[69] Antiquities, plants and landscapes were reduced to a list of items to be ticked off, with the implied assurance that doing so would render one a truly polite and scientific tourist. Some published tours had even introduced a system of asterisks to denote the relative interest of different sites.[70] Antiquities had become part of a common cultural experience for the aspirational member of the middling sort, as well as the gentleman of leisure. Camden's *Britannia* had restored antiquity to Britain and Britain to antiquity, but publications such as these not only restored antiquities, in the sense of preserving their memory, but ensured that their physical appearance became an integral part of the cultural identity of early nineteenth-century Britain.

Topographical literature, however, was far from being the only medium through which antiquities could be presented to a wider readership. If, as has been argued, the aloof dignity of the didactic imperative in history was being challenged by the mission to entertain, the same was equally true of antiquarian literature.[71] By the late eighteenth century the prefatory advertisements of authors were more and more likely to express the hope that not only would their work instruct but also amuse the leisure hours. The admission of entertainment as legitimate grounds for publication in turn rendered it more acceptable to produce studies of what would formerly have been deemed trivial subjects, beneath the dignity of history and hardly worthy of scholarly inquiry. Histories of subjects as diverse as armour, dress, playing cards or cookery could provide 'entertainment' and could also be presented as illustrative of the customs and manners of the time. Some of these treatises were to be found in the pages of *Archaeologia* but they also increasingly featured in publications that aimed at a less specialist market.

The study of antiquities, wrote Joseph Strutt, was both 'amusing and useful'. Strutt's humble origins ensured that he suffered the condescension of other antiquaries, such as Richard Gough, who derided his lack of formal antiquarian learning, but his series of illustrated antiquarian works, starting with *Regal and Ecclesiastical Antiquities* (1773), *Manners and Customs* (1775–76), *Complete View of the Dress and Habits of the People of England* (1795–96) and *Sports and Pastimes of the English People* (1801) were successful and influential publications within Britain and further afield – the *Manners and Customs* was translated into French in 1789, which was more than could be said for any of Gough's publications. In *Manners and Customs*, the most widely read of his works in his own time, the material was organised so that not only did armies and military affairs precede royal processions and coronations, but historical dress, banquets, music, sport and the theatre all took priority over the more morally edifying subject of burials and religion. Although hardly within the category of cheap literature, it was certainly aimed at a less specialist readership, and became one of the most widely read antiquarian sources of the time. The appeal of Strutt's volume lay in the originality of the subject matter and in the accompanying plates which illustrated historical subjects that had never been given visual realisation before. They conveyed a picture of ancient times in which 'we seem to behold their very thoughts unveiled'. It was, he assured his readers, 'the first attempt of this sort ever made in this kingdom'. Strutt's antiquarianism, like that of John Carter, was structured around a strongly articulated sense of English, Protestant national identity. National pride inspired him to provide England with volumes to match both Bernard de Montfaucon's *L'antiquité expliquée et représentée en figures* and his *Les monumens de la monarchie françoise.* Strutt's view of history was an unequivocally triumphalist one, a Whiggish narrative of progressive improvement and civilisation, in which the present age was greatly superior to all those which had gone before. In his emphasis upon the distinctiveness of the English religious and constitutional experience, going against the grain of the universalising histories of the Scottish Enlightenment, he anticipated the popular histories of the nineteenth century.[72] His confidence in the pre-eminence of the English nation provided comfortable certainties at a time when the British Empire was beleaguered by a war against the American colonies and a hostile Europe. Such was the success enjoyed by *Manners and Customs* that Strutt embarked upon a third volume in 1776, in addition to the two which subscribers had originally been promised. Although Strutt's fame now rests chiefly on his *Sports and Pastimes*, during his own life time *Manners and Customs* was more frequently referred to than any other of his works.[73]

Strutt's volumes were also puffed in terms of their value in illustrating the poetry of former times, made increasingly popular by collections such as Percy's *Reliques* and Chatterton's Rowley forgeries. In a sense Strutt was reinventing the traditional argument of the numismatist, who pleaded for the value of coins and medals for the illustration of classical poetry, but his arguments contributed to the notion that a measure of historical background was necessary for the appreciation of such poems. The provision of such information came not from the historian but from the antiquary, who could provide the reader with the details concerning the manners and customs of the period with which the poetry dealt. Furthermore, it was the antiquary, and Strutt in particular, who provided the artistic world with the visual resources for their historical reconstructions, with results that have been described as 'revolutionary'.[74] The latter part of the eighteenth century was a formative period in the establishment of a tradition of British history painting in which increasing emphasis was placed upon the historical verisimilitude of the scenes portrayed. The accuracy with which dress in historical scenes (and also theatrical costume) was depicted has been directly attributed to the publication of antiquarian prints. *Manners and Customs* and particularly the *Complete View* became an essential source book for all artists and illustrators – as indeed Strutt had hoped that they would.[75] One might postulate that the incessant changes in fashion, which were so important a barometer of social standing in eighteenth-century society, also made consumers more sensitive to changes in dress and the evolution of style and therefore receptive to a book describing its historical development. Strutt certainly made very pointed comparisons between the changes of costume which he depicted in his engravings and the fluctuations of fashion in his own time. The indecencies and absurdities against which moralists inveighed were not, as he showed, confined to the eighteenth century. Strutt himself was particularly disgusted by the 'abominable and beastly' sixteenth-century custom of wearing cod-pieces of ostentatious proportions.[76]

Francis Grose, whose success with the *Antiquities of England and Wales* has already been noted, was quick to exploit this more commercial approach to antiquarianism, which presented antiquities as auxiliary to other fashionable diversions and pursuits. In addition to the *Antiquities of England and Wales*, he also published a volume on military antiquities – in effect a history of the army – and a separate study of the historical development of armour.[77] Like Strutt, he explained that he intended these volumes not just for the antiquary but also for sculptors, painters and designers, and anyone else involved in the depiction of historical dress, and hoped that it would enable them to avoid anachronistic violations of costume. Grose's choice of subject matter was indubitably influenced by the contemporary fascination with medieval chivalry, the tournament and medieval romance. As early as 1707 the Society of Antiquaries had identified chivalry, along with heraldry, as an area in need of antiquarian inquiry, but by the later eighteenth century the emphasis was less on antiquarian erudition than the evocation of a bygone period in which knights inhabiting Gothic castles led lives governed by a strict code of honour, attending tournaments, performing acts of gallantry and being entertained by troubadours. Richard Hurd's *Moral and Political Dialogues* (1759–65), followed by *Letters on Chivalry and Romance* (1762), had encouraged readers to look beyond the apparent barbarism of the middle ages and to consider the latent causes which had given rise to Gothic chivalry. Thomas Percy continued along this train of thought, developing the romantic theme of the medieval troubadour in the *Reliques of English Poetry* (1765). The French scholar Jean-Baptiste de la Curne de Sainte-Palaye covered the subject in even more detail in *Mémoires de l'ancienne chivalerie* and *Histoire des troubadours*, which were translated for an English readership in 1779 and 1784 respectively.[78] The *Antiquarian Repertory* was prompt to respond to fashionable enthusiasms: the first item which it published was the transcription of a manuscript of ordinances used at tournaments. Brasses in churches, it was suggested, were illustrative of the manners and customs of former times, in particular the high honour paid to the fair sex in the days of chivalry. Part of the attraction of castles came to reside not in their historical importance, or even their picturesque qualities, but in their capacity to conjure up images of gallant actions and chivalry – associations which antiquaries were quick to exploit, to give their own effusions a patina of chivalric appeal. Thus Stebbing Shaw described the antiquarian delight of revivifying the features of the mouldering figures of the bold knights of chivalry. Castles, wrote Thomas Burgess in *An Essay on the Study of Antiquities*, reflected the very genius of chivalry: 'Amid such a scene the manly exercises of knighthood recur (sic) to the imagination in their full pomp and solemnity; while every patriot feeling beats at the remembrance of the generous virtues which were nursed in those schools of fortitude, honour, courtesy and wit, the mansions of our ancient nobility.'[79] It is not surprising then to find that antiquaries such as Grose sought to exploit the fashionable interest in chivalry by turning their own researches towards its illustration.

Joseph Strutt's final antiquarian venture represents what may perhaps be seen as the logical conclusion of the popularisation of antiquarianism through the illustration of manners and customs: the historical novel. He did not, of course, ever refer to it as such; rather it was a 'History of the Times Past: or, A View of the Domestic Manners and Amusements of the Fifteenth Century; exemplified under the form of a Legendary Romance'. The (unpublished) preface explained that the author's purpose was to use the form of a romance as a means of 'conveying much useful instruction, imperceptibly, to the minds of such readers as are disgusted at the dryness usually concomitant with the labours of the antiquary'. He died in 1807 with the novel, *Queenho Hall*, uncompleted, and it was passed by the publisher John Murray to a Scottish writer and antiquary, Walter Scott, to edit and complete.[80] It was this experience, it has been argued, that first alerted Scott to the potential of the historical novel as a literary form. Scott considered that Strutt had displayed his antiquarian knowledge too liberally; for a historical novel to succeed it needed to be 'more light and obvious to the general comprehension'.[81] Scott evidently learnt his lesson well. For Richard Gough, protesting against the absence of scholarly references and seriousness of purpose in the books which he reviewed, the worst indictment that he had been able to formulate was that the work in question bore more resemblance to a novel or a romance than a work of antiquarianism.[82] Scott turned this into a positive virtue. *Ivanhoe*, as he explained in the dedicatory epistle, was a historical pastiche; the emphasis was on atmosphere rather than accuracy, plausibility rather than authenticity, narrative rather than detail.[83]

If antiquarianism was becoming more popular, the popular was itself becoming the subject of antiquarian inquiry. Local customs and beliefs had formed a standard part of the antiquarian questionnaire since Robert Plot's queries were circulated in the 1670s, and comprised a common appendix or addenda to many antiquarian publications. John Aubrey had been intrigued by the local customs and superstitions that persisted in his native Wiltshire, and the recording of these beliefs constituted a major element of his collections. The work which is generally credited as being the starting point for subsequent studies of popular customs, however, was Henry Bourne's *Antiquitates vulgares* (1725). Bourne was a clergyman from Newcastle whose own origins were humble enough; he had been apprenticed to a glazier, and it was only due to the generosity of friends that he was sent to Oxford and entered into holy orders. He embarked upon his survey of popular customs and beliefs in order to establish such practices as were beneficial and such as were dangerous and which ought properly to be suppressed. In this sense his work, despite the title, was not antiquarian, in that it was only incidentally a project for the recovery or preservation of the past. *Antiquitates vulgares* was an exercise in reportage, a survey of religious belief amongst the common people. This was no nostalgic illustration of bygone manners and customs. 'I would not be thought a Reviver of Old Rites and Ceremonies to the Burdening of the People,' he avowed, 'nor an Abolisher of innocent customs, which are their Pleasures and Recreations.' Rather he sought to regulate those which were benign and to abolish those which were 'sinful and wicked'.[84]

The publication of John Brand's *Observations on Popular Antiquities* (1777) may be seen as a significant landmark in the evolution of popular customs as a distinct area of inquiry.[85] Brand had been approached by the Newcastle publisher, Thomas Saint, to update and extend Bourne's original volume. The project was from the outset a commercial, rather than purely antiquarian, undertaking. Brand's method was simply to add additional comments and observations to the end of each of Bourne's chapters, with further chapters on practices and beliefs of which Bourne had failed to take notice. Brand viewed these 'antiquities' as objects of curiosity whose origins were a matter of intellectual interest, rather than of pressing moral and religious concern. He was explicit in his denunciation of papistry (Bourne, who had high church leanings, had been more tolerant where he had deemed a practice harmless), and followed the convention of identifying any practice which seemed redolent of superstition to the rituals of the Catholic pre-Reformation era, which could in turn be traced back to some pagan, superstitious rite. Bourne's agenda of reformation and regulation was entirely lost: 'I know not how the present Generation will relish his Reflections', observed Brand, 'serious Animadversions of this Sort seem by no Means pleasing to the *refined* Taste of our Age'.[86]

The popular custom had completed its metamorphosis into the object of curiosity and entertainment; like the oral traditions of the Scottish Highlands which supposedly went back to the time of Ossian, these 'fancies of the multitude', it was held, had survived substantially unchanged from the earliest periods of history, through religious and political upheaval. The games held around the obelisks at Boroughbridge (believed to be a druidical monument) at the time of the fair were identified by eighteenth-century antiquaries as the attenuated rituals of druidic rites of celebration.[87] Antiquaries had been accustomed to think in terms of a common law passed down through the generations, essentially unchanged from its inception amongst their Saxon forebears since the seventeenth century. It required no great intellectual leap to apply the same reasoning to the supposed survival of manners and customs of an earlier age. Popular antiquities therefore illuminated some of those periods of history otherwise lost in gloom, and, like the common law, were a defining element of English society. 'Our enlightened age', wrote Richard Gough, 'laughs at the rudeness of our ancestors, and overlooks that rank of men whose simplicity is the best guardian of antiquity.' Local customs and usages could guide the antiquary back to the truth, the ancient facts upon which they were founded: 'Aids to tradition, they are its most faithful interpreters!'[88] Popular antiquities could also be constructed as contributing to that ever topical subject, the study of society. 'The Antiquities of the Common People', explained John Brand, 'cannot be studied without acquiring some useful Knowledge of Mankind. The People, of whom Society is chiefly composed ... is a respectable Subject to every one who is the friend of Man.' The study of primitive customs surviving within the British Isles thus complemented the ethnographic literature describing the manners and customs of the primitive peoples of the South Seas. Of all branches of antiquarianism, 'popular antiquities' – the study of the manners and customs of the past – had the most general and widespread appeal.

Francis Grose's *Provincial Glossary with a Collection of Local Proverbs and Popular Superstitions* (1787) owed a heavy debt to Brand's publication, containing a significant amount of very similar material relating to popular customs and sayings. As with his publications on armour and the army, he was also tapping into the fascination with chivalric romance and 'ancient poetry'. Like Joseph Strutt, he argued that antiquities – in this case those of regional dialects and popular customs – could be an aid to understanding and appreciating the poetry of the past ages. As the title suggests, the *Provincial Glossary* was a compilation of words and phrases of local dialect, organised on a regional rather than county by county basis. He drew on his own experience of travelling around England in the course of militia duties, but, as the preface acknowledged, Grose was hardly the first in the field here. He pointed to John Ray's *Proverbs*, Tim Bobbin's *Lancashire Dialect* (no date), John Lewis's *History and Antiquities Ecclesiastical and Civil of the Isle of Thanet* (1723), Sir John Cullum's *History and Antiquities of Hawsted in the County of Suffolk* (1784) and numerous county histories and communications in the *Gentleman's Magazine.* Local dialects could provide evidence of Danish or Saxon settlement, but beyond that Grose's linguistic and philological analysis was weak. His strength never lay in pushing back the frontiers of historical inquiry, but in presenting the miscellaneous inquiries and researches of others as an attractive commodity for a non-specialist readership.

Brand carried on collecting materials for a revised edition of *Popular Antiquities* for the remainder until his death in 1806, and had planned to bring out the second edition in 1795. He was apparently overwhelmed by the task of arranging systematically so much material, however, and did not live to complete the project. Instead, the collections were purchased for £600 after his death by a bookseller, incorporated into a new edition by Sir Henry Ellis and published in 1813.[89] Despite the success of *Popular Antiquities*, it was not without its critics; Brand's arrangement (mirrored in his management of the Society of Antiquaries' affairs) was confused, not to say chaotic, and he was overly reliant on second-hand authorities, the accuracy of which were open to question. Brand's eclectic approach and apparently random organisation were faults which came to be seen as increasingly culpable as antiquaries and their readers moved further away from the collecting habits of the previous generations of antiquaries. Nevertheless, the volume gathered together vast quantities of miscellaneous material, providing a starting point for other more rigorous inquiries, from which the discipline of folklore studies would emerge.[90]

When Henry Bourne had compiled his materials, most of the customs which he described were not in any apparent danger of disappearing, and where they were he exhibited no regret at their passage. Grose, Brand, Strutt and others, by contrast, looked upon the disappearance of such popular customs as a loss: they were sliding into oblivion with the spread of modern manners in the same way that the physical fabric of medieval buildings was vanishing in the wake of urban 'improvement'. Danish and Saxon words had fallen into general disuse, explained Francis Grose, and they survived only in areas at a great distance from the capital, where modern refinements had not found their way.[91] The disappearance of popular customs could be seen as smoothing off the rust of barbarism from the fabric of society, but such practices had seemed also to represent values of social harmony and stability which modern improvements placed under threat. Traditional expressions of nostalgia for a lost golden age, which appeared in eighteenth-century guise in poems such as Goldsmith's *Deserted Village*, acquired a sharper edge as the pace of social and economic change accelerated. Fear of innovation fostered a benign view of the days gone by, which existed in tension with the characteristically enlightenment perception of the past as a period of backward barbarism and religious oppression.[92] Thus John Brand also identified a political utility to the study of *Popular Antiquities*, expressing the hope that the revival of the innocent sports and pastimes in question would counteract the general spread of luxury and dissipation which imperilled the manliness and virtue of the national character.[93] Rising poor rates made commentators particularly sentimental for the days of monastic philanthropy and the benevolent paternalism of feudal landlords before such impositions had ever been dreamed of.[94] Monasteries were seldom identified as the haunts of greedy abbots and loose-living monks in this latter period. The earlier Protestant emphasis upon their corruption and parasitism was muted. Rather, monastic institutions were lauded as the providers of charity and care for the elderly and infirm.[95] Castles were not the symbols of an oppressive feudal overlord, but the sites of baronial hospitality. From the 1770s a language of benevolent paternalism, simple piety and dutiful charity suffused the accounts of both monastic and feudal foundation in many antiquarian publications. The artist Thomas Hearne could accompany his engravings of medieval hospitals, such as St Cross at Winchester or St Thomas at York, with a tribute to the practice of medieval charity and communal responsibility.[96] Lionel Charlton was particularly struck by how monastic traditions of hospitality had enabled even the poorest travellers to embark upon journeys across the country without fear of cost.[97]

Francis Grose conjured up images of a similarly nostalgic hue as he described the disappearing relics of a passing era in the *Provincial Glossary*. These were stories collected from the mouths of village historians, narrated by a village elder to a close circle of attentive hearers, gathered around a fire in an old hall or manor house on a winter evening. It was a picture of the 'good old days', where the only entertainment to be had in remote places was to be found in tales of ghosts and fairies, before newspapers and stage coaches had opened up intercourse with the metropolis, importing scepticism and making every ploughman a politician.[98] Brand's revisions for *Observations on Popular Antiquities* made during the 1780s and '90s expressed appreciation of the political value of popular customs as a means of keeping the labouring sort contented and uncorrupted, in a state of innocence immune from the insidious spread of metropolitan luxury and insubordination.[99] In the *Antiquities of England and Wales* Grose's readers were informed that the enormous chimney in the kitchen at Cockermouth

Castle conveyed an idea of the scale of ancient hospitality; and, with a sense of *déjà vu*, the persistent reader learnt that the oven at Raby Castle was of dimensions suitable to the hospitality of those feudal times.[100] Such images of baronial largesse and feudal philanthropy confirmed a hierarchical, paternalist and essentially aristocratic view of society. Meanwhile, the vulgar superstitions and credulity which marked the popular customs and beliefs confirmed the superiority of the elite and their claims to exercise authority on behalf of those below them. This conservative ideology of antiquarianism, apparent in a range of publications from popular customs to Gothic antiquities, could be hitched on to current anxieties aroused by the growth of the metropolis and the apparent breakdown of the traditional structures of society in a manner that certainly heightened its appeal amongst certain constituencies. Nostalgic antiquarianism became part of the conservative arsenal to be launched against the innovations of the modern era and the threats of popular radicalism and revolution emanating from France.

There is some obvious continuity between the Victorian celebration of 'Merry England' and the romanticised notion of medieval society that is to be found in so much of eighteenth-century literature. The antiquarian oeuvre written by and for the social elite of the nineteenth century continued to display many of the preoccupations and prejudices of the previous century: the fascination with popular customs and the evocation of a simpler, primitive society in the eighteenth century was one of perennial service to the interests of the ruling classes. But there was nothing in the eighteenth century to match the mass appeal of the 'olden times' and 'Merry England' manufactured in the popular histories and illustrated periodicals of the Victorian era. The latter publications portrayed an era of social harmony, egalitarianism, hospitality, philanthropy and domesticity, that flourished under the Tudors and Stuarts rather than looking back to the middle ages.[101] The Victorians placed a markedly democratic emphasis upon popular antiquities as a common heritage, as the expression of true Englishness and embodying the most praiseworthy attributes of ancestral England. The customs and pastimes of Merry England were generated by the common people, not the elite. Hence, it is argued, there was a Victorian preference for Tudor and Stuart settings, which evoked the time when the middling sort first assumed a role upon the historical stage, rather than the aristocratic, chivalric world of medieval England favoured in the previous century. The emphasis in Victorian literature was upon the dimensions of the baronial hall at Penshurst, where all joined together in commensality, rather than the size of the ovens producing the food, which could, after all, be partaken of in a socially segregated setting. The popular market which consumed this kind of literature was presented with a view of sixteenth-century England that was fundamentally at odds with the elitist perspective upon popular culture characteristic of the eighteenth century.

It is possible, however, to see antecedents to this more democratic view, which triumphed in the Victorian era, amongst the antiquaries of the eighteenth century. The conservative perspective on the past was dominant, but not absolute. Take, for example, Joseph Riston, the north country lawyer, antiquary and radical man of letters. Ritson was another antiquary, who, like William Hutton, was denied membership of the Society of Antiquaries.[102] Whilst Ritson's profession as a lawyer did not count against him, his direct challenge to Thomas Warton's *History of English Poetry*, and the aspersions which he cast upon Thomas Percy's scholarship, amounted to a breach of the gentlemanly behaviour expected of an antiquary and undoubtedly influenced those who blackballed his candidature. Ritson had taken particular objection to Percy's representation of medieval minstrelsy in *Reliques of Ancient Poetry*. Percy's minstrels inhabited court circles; the ballads which they performed and which had survived for inclusion in the *Reliques* were therefore essentially remnants of an aristocratic taste. As such Percy had 'improved' the diction and the form, smoothing off some of the barbarisms of popular usage, to make them more acceptable to the ears of his polite audience. Ritson, however, denied that the medieval minstrels had been figures at court; the court at that time was, he pointed out, French speaking – the ballads, by contrast, were all handed down in English. Rather than being valued entertainers the 'minstrels' would have been regarded as rogues and vagabonds (as indeed they were under Tudor legislation). The literary titivation Percy had performed upon the ballads themselves provoked his greatest wrath. This to Ritson represented systematic deceit and the theft of an oral tradition which belonged to the people. Percy had distorted the genuine character of the ballads and had uprooted them from their popular context; he had appropriated them for an elitist view of culture and its history which prioritised the classical over the vernacular.[103] In similar vein Ritson protested against the attempt to cast Shakespeare in a classical model rather than recognising his roots in native English traditions. Ritson's own contributions to the genre of balladry and medieval poems were scholarly, based on a close study of the original manuscripts, and supported by introductory and prefatory material which demonstrated his familiarity with the antiquarian context; the poems were presented in a rude and unadorned state, preserving all their metrical and linguistic aberrations. These collections of ancient English poetry told a history of the vulgar people, the illiterate masses whose culture was suppressed, but not destroyed, by monastic writers and Norman francophone rulers, only to triumph and blossom forth in the sixteenth century in the verse of Edmund Spenser and William Shakespeare.

Ritson's efforts to restore ballads and other popular antiquities to the people with whom they originated went hand in hand with his heated attack on Warton for dismissing the relevance of Saxon verse for a history of English poetry.[104] Saxon, as Ritson argued, was the language from which modern English evolved and it lived on in the vocabulary of the vernacular. Ritson was also at odds with that other enthusiast for popular verse, Walter Scott, whose own view of the plebeian origins of the Border ballads which he collected was decidedly ambivalent.[105] Ritson's democratising views on antiquities were shaped by and were subordinate to his political views, which became increasingly radical, to the extent that he was espousing full-blown republicanism in the notes and prefaces to his publications in the 1790s. Beyond the literary sphere Ritson used his knowledge of legal antiquities to defend the autonomy of the duchy of Savoy and the rights and liberties of its inhabitants.[106] The study of popular antiquities (including ballads, vernacular dialect, manners and customs) could lend themselves either to a conservative interpretation of the past or, as in the hands of Ritson and other antiquaries with similar political sympathies, a radicalised antiquarian perspective with deeply subversive implications. The elevation of manners and customs to the realm of academic inquiry meant that even the credulous superstitions of the vulgar and the most commonplace objects of quotidian existence acquired a historical significance, disrupting the hierarchies of value which had reproduced the social order in the collections of the aristocratic collectors of *virtù*.

John Blackner, the newspaper proprietor and radical from Nottingham, published his history of the town in 1815. Much of it represented a far cry from the normal antiquarian fare, being primarily suited to the interests of the commercial and manufacturing classes in Nottingham, whose prosperity it celebrated. There was, however, a substantial element of antiquarian subject matter being made available in a format to suit those who were not interested in the rarefied cogitations of the antiquarian circle – his use of the proliferating genre of architectural antiquities has already been commented upon. In this context it should also be noted how Blackner appropriated the antiquities themselves to the people at large, whose cause he promoted elsewhere in his advocacy of political reform. The emphasis on the Gothic as a national, *English* style of architecture, as advocated by John Carter, lent itself to a democratising view of architectural antiquities which placed them back in the communities in which they were created, rather than in an abstract lineage of deviation from and return to a classical norm. Not only did Blackner denominate the Gothic '*our* pointed style', he specifically honoured it as a monument to the labour of the people.[107] In a similar manner William Hutton subverted the emphasis upon the landed elite which dominated so much antiquarian topographical literature. The pretentious pedigrees, lovingly traced back to Domesday Book, which provided the framework for many county and parochial histories, were summarily dismissed. The descendants of the conquering heroes of the Saxons and Normans were either extinct or reduced to poverty as he provocatively concluded 'for antiquity, alliance, and blood, the advantage is evidently in favour of the lowest class'.[108]

Martin Dunsford, wool merchant, west country radical and historian of Tiverton, was also willing to use antiquarian materials where it suited him: Whitaker's *History of Manchester* provided information on the prices of provisions; John Brand's *Popular Antiquities* illustrated the rhymes used by the common people in the medieval period; Joseph Strutt was his source for the manners and customs of the Saxons and Danes. His history, however, omitted any discussion of Tiverton Castle (despite its obvious interest as an architectural antiquity) or the Redvers family, whose influence as landowners was of considerable significance for Tiverton's historical development. Nor did the heraldry of funeral escutcheons or the armorial bearings emblazoned in the windows find any place in the description of the church. Dunsford's dedication eschewed the customary paeans of praise to an aristocratic patron; instead the book was inscribed to the 'virtuous and industrious poor of Tiverton', whose rights to the misappropriated charitable benefactions of the parish he hoped his researches would restore. Dunsford challenged the principles which underpinned the political dominance of the landed elite explicitly in political terms and implicitly by undermining the accepted orthodoxies of antiquarian and topographical literature, whilst using the genre and its materials to disseminate his political message, which asserted the rights of the common people.[109] The legal antiquarianism of political reformers, who searched out borough charters and demanded a restoration of the original forms of municipal government, represented the same appropriation of antiquarianism by those who opposed the status quo and demanded a restoration of an assumed status quo ante.[110]

By the end of the eighteenth century antiquarianism had broadened both its scope and its appeal; there was, therefore, more substance than is often allowed to its advocates' claims for its universal interest and relevance. In achieving this transformation, antiquarianism had shifted away from earlier preoccupations with property, genealogy, ecclesiastical antiquities and philology. These were still important elements of the antiquary's expertise, but they no longer defined the subject as such. Architecture, art, manners and customs and private as well as public life, had all inspired the antiquarian imagination, and it was these elements which appealed successfully to a wider reading public. A basic knowledge of antiquities and history had become essential elements of the foundation upon which perceptions of national identity and difference could be constructed. The proliferation of illustrated topographical antiquarian literature had begun to map out a landscape of historic Britain which shaped views of both the contemporary landscape and that in which the national past was located. The subject matter comprehended by the term 'antiquities' had become more varied and eclectic, and information derived from antiquarian sources was now available in a wide range of literature. It was no longer confined to the academic volumes of scholarly erudition – and, as such, the subject of antiquities found its way to a much more diverse and inclusive readership. Few of those who styled themselves 'antiquaries' made the necessary concessions to the demands of a more popular readership. It was the publishers and printers who spotted the potential in works of an antiquarian nature and were behind many of the more populist presentations of antiquarian material. Thus the authorship, as well as the readership, of such publications can correspondingly be seen to have broadened out in social terms. It was this development that created the constituency to which appeals to a sense of national heritage could be made.

10

Achievement

The process of popularisation and commercialisation of the antiquarian genre, surveyed in the previous chapter, can hardly be attributed to the antiquaries themselves. For all their emphasis upon the importance of antiquities to the national interest and their zeal in defending the antiquary's place in society, they did not, as a rule, embrace the possibilities of long print runs with popular appeal. The proliferation of printed media in the later eighteenth century highlighted the tension which had always been inherent in the study of antiquities. A subject which defined itself by its empiricism and its attention to detail was never going to lend itself to facile generalisations or breezy narratives. In the earlier part of the century the problem facing antiquaries who ventured into print was that of how to reconcile the erudition – or, as many saw it, pedantry – of antiquarianism with the of demands 'polite literature'. By the turn of the nineteenth century the issue was not so much one of satisfying gentlemanly taste, but of rendering the subject palatable to a broader readership which did not share the gentleman scholar's depth of learning and expertise. The antiquaries' arguments for the importance of their subject were validated in the evident popularity of works with an antiquarian element, but many felt that they could not exploit this favourable development and still maintain their scholarly standards.

The history of antiquarianism has generally been treated as the rise of archaeology in the eighteenth century; a narrative written around the work of a handful of field archaeologists, starting with John Aubrey and Edward Lhwyd in the late seventeenth century, peaking with William Stukeley's fieldwork at Stonehenge and Avebury. Thereafter there was a decline in standards of accuracy and observation until James Douglas, William Cunnington and Sir Richard Colt Hoare joined forces at the end of the century and stressed the importance of speaking from 'facts not theory'. Systematic and accurate investigation, conclusions based upon observation and comparison, together with a strictly empirical approach, took precedence over tradition or etymological derivations, whilst abstruse debates over the Celtic or Belgic origins of the original inhabitants were put to one side.[1] This tells us who the key figures were in the emergence of modern archaeology, but offers little insight as to what the antiquaries hoped to discover or how their excavations related to their other branches of inquiry.[2]

It also diminishes and disregards the activities of those apart from Stukeley who were engaged upon the excavation of the past. There was plenty of detailed fieldwork and observation going on, but it has tended to be overlooked – cast into a shadow by the towering size of Stukeley's reputation. Antiquaries did set higher standards of accuracy in recording their finds (inadequate though they may now seem to modern archaeologists) and were no longer satisfied with the records their forebears had made. In the 1730s John Horsley had uttered severe strictures upon the standards of accuracy with which monumental inscriptions had been copied by his predecessors. Subsequent antiquaries sought to match or improve upon his standards.[3] A greater precision can be identified, whether in recording inscriptions, describing excavations or drawing the physical remains. The contrast between Samuel Lysons's account of his excavations at Woodchester and Samuel Carte's perfunctory account of recent Roman finds in Leicester gives a powerful illustration of the methodological and conceptual distance that had been travelled. Lysons set out his methodology, detailed the precise order in which the site was dug, itemised every artefact uncovered and drew up meticulous plans of the layout of the site, whilst Carte simply noted that 'There are many other remains of the Romans which it would be tedious to mention particularly such as the walls & foundations of Houses &c under ground, but here follows an account of two or three.'[4] What Lysons achieved in his account of Woodchester was essentially a reconstruction of the layout of the Roman villa; he was making an imaginative leap from the evidence of excavation to recreating the probable appearance of the original building.

As has been emphasised throughout, antiquarianism should never be equated with fieldwork and the development of archaeology. Fieldwork was just one facet of the antiquary's activity, and in order to understand the approaches which the antiquaries employed we need to look not only at the development of geological science but also to other areas of antiquarian practice. The gradual appreciation of the value of oral history and verse as vehicles for the transmission of historical knowledge about undocumented periods of the past helped to break down some of the dependence upon written authorities. Yet the demands faced by James Macpherson, the author of the Ossian forgery, to produce the original manuscripts from which he had worked, and the importance of the manuscript tradition for the students of Welsh and Nordic bardic culture, show up the limitations of this conceptual shift. Similarly, as we saw in the context of medieval antiquities, antiquaries were rapidly establishing their independence from documents and dealing increasingly with the artefact, or in this case, the building alone. Just as the precise observation of strata and the position of objects within them could provide a clue to the antiquity of a burial, observation of variations in the style of buildings could establish their antiquity. The techniques of collecting data, making comparisons, drawing inferences and testing a hypothesis against the evidence which Douglas outlined in *Nenia Britannica* did not represent a sudden breakthrough in archaeological method. Lyttelton and his followers had been applying precisely the same principles for some time in their study of ecclesiastical architecture. Douglas's recommendations represented a distillation of good practice – a practice which had been being consolidated over the century in a range of antiquarian endeavours. It was one to which most of Douglas's fellow antiquaries would have subscribed and which they attempted to follow, to a greater or lesser extent, in their own observations.

The academic success of the antiquarian project is clearly evinced in the progress which was made towards combining the fruits of antiquarian researches with a historical narrative. Here the antiquary and historian of Anglo-Saxon England Sharon Turner provides an illuminating example. Turner cannot be said to rank with Edward Gibbon in terms of erudition or urbanity. The *History of the Anglo-Saxons* falls far short of encompassing a comparable scale of time and place to *The Decline and Fall of the Roman Empire*, but Turner was following in the same tradition – and evidently wished to have cast himself in the same mould. He wrote a history, but his methods and his sources were antiquarian, implementing precisely the kind of methodology that we have seen advocated by antiquaries such as Richard Gough. The reputation and authority of Turner's history rested upon solid empirical foundations. He brought far more detail to the period than had any previous historian, not through supposition and conjecture, but through a careful reading and analysis of charters, wills, chronicles and poetry. Turner collated and compared. He rejected the authority of the medieval Icelandic historian Snorro on the grounds that the chronology was unfounded. He searched out the different variants of the Anglo-Saxon Chronicle. He exploited Thomas Astle's collection of charters and the largely unexplored territory of the Cottonian and Harleian collections in the British Museum. Moving away from the hackneyed images of Saxon history, which had done service for most historians and many antiquaries up to that point, he attempted to build up his history from first principles in precisely the antiquarian manner advocated by Thomas Madox. He made a point of emphasising his reliance on primary evidence, and his avoidance of conjecture, promising to leave the reader to draw his own conclusions, rather than imposing a system upon him.[5]

Turner presented himself as a historian, but both the period which he covered and his reliance upon manuscript sources were typically the preserve of the antiquary. His insistence upon citation and upon comparing and assessing the reliability of his sources, and his rejection of 'fallacious' theories, drew on what were essentially antiquarian traditions. There had never been an insuperable barrier between the study of history and antiquities; there had always been a process of frequent borrowings and mutual influence. *The History of the Anglo-Saxons* is a testimony to the extent to which the gap between history and antiquarianism had closed over the eighteenth century. As historians began to place more emphasis upon the value of research in the nineteenth century they quietly appropriated much of the traditional territory of the antiquary. Antiquarianism was still a catch-all term, but was becoming increasingly denuded of its content as history, and other specialisms – geology, philology architectural history and particularly archaeology – established themselves, taking with them much of the traditional material of the antiquary. What has been left is the husk of pedantry, tedious minutiae and a futile accumulation of the detritus of the past. This partially accounts for the less than sympathetic treatment that antiquarianism has often received in historical studies.

If the present age, wrote Francis Wise to Richard Meade, notwithstanding all its boasted light and knowledge 'should run into a contempt of Antiquity [it] would want one of the most infallible characteristicks of learning, and true politeness'.[6] Wise's defence of the study of antiquities seems particularly pertinent at a time when the Secretary of State for Education has openly opined that the idea of learning for its own sake is 'a bit dodgy' and is reputed to have dismissed the study of medieval history as simply 'ornamental'.[7] Without wanting to draw too many false parallels, there is a certain continuity from the eighteenth century to the present in the criticisms to which those who profess to study the more remote periods of the past are vulnerable. Similarly, the disdain evinced by an antiquary such as Richard Gough for the attempts to render the subject of antiquarianism more acceptable to a popular readership resurface in the tension between academic historians and those who attempt to present the subject through more user-friendly media.[8] In many senses the world of the eighteenth-century antiquary – the methodologies, the subject matter and the debates in which they were involved – is one which is entirely familiar to that of the modern academic historian. But simply looking to the past to find a reflection of the present is not very illuminating. The 'discovery of the past' upon which eighteenth-century antiquaries embarked is much more important for what it tells us about the culture of eighteenth-century Britain than for the reassuring confirmation it offers that our current preoccupations are nothing new. The eighteenth-century culture of 'improvement' and 'progress', of enlightened rationality and commercialised leisure, in which the modern world, to paraphrase one historian, was created, was also one in which tradition held powerful sway, where high regard was paid to antiquity, in which the study of history was a public good and the most important basis for patriotism. Studies of the church and religion, political debate, literature, art, landscape gardening and topographical literature have all individually drawn attention to the presence of arguments based upon history, historical motifs and antiquarian materials. Taken together these constitute an undeniable argument for the significance of the antiquarian cast of mind – a significance which this study has attempted to elucidate and illustrate.

Antiquarian research was deeply embedded within eighteenth-century culture and society. It helped to shape, and was in turn shaped by, religious debate and political conflict; it was invoked by the ruling elite to legitimate their position but was also appropriated by those who looked to the past to undermine the very foundations of that rule. The antiquities of Britain provided the basis for the construction of a national past and it was the growth of interest in national history that was the crucial factor in bringing antiquarianism out of the gentleman's study and before the broader public at large. But most of those who corresponded in the pages of the *Gentleman's Magazine* or who collected the epitaphs in their local church or sought out the contours of ancient camps and barrows in the landscape through which they passed, were moved in the first instance by a delight in the past which they did not even presume to interrogate. 'An insatiable Desire of knowing what is past, as well as what is to come', remarked one antiquary, is 'so fix'd in Humane Nature, as never to be eradicated.'[9] The timeless impulse to discover one's origins had never been stronger.

Given the evident importance of antiquarian scholarship and the widespread interest it generated, it is curious that the subject should have attracted so little academic interest. Even now it is remarkably underconceptualised. The antiquaries' subsequent reputation – like that of so many other aspects of the eighteenth century – suffered first at the hands of the Victorians, who belittled their scholarship and exaggerated their faults, taking offence against the perceived superficiality and classicising tendencies of so much eighteenth-century culture. For too long the perception of antiquarianism of the eighteenth century has oscillated between the dilettante persona of Horace Walpole, who prized elegance over erudition, and Scott's chaotic creation of Jonathan Oldbuck. The Lunar Society, with a limited membership and elusive identity, has often been taken as more emblematic of the eighteenth century, with its polymathic approach to science, literature, business and politics.[10] The Society of Antiquaries, however, with far more members and a far stronger institutional presence, has never exercised quite the same charisma, but the antiquarianism which it and its members represented was of great significance in shaping British culture and identities. It is time for a re-evaluation. Antiquarianism should become, like politeness, improvement, progress or reason, a key word for understanding the eighteenth century.

Notes

Note to Preface

1. William Stukeley, *The Medallic History of Marcus Aurelius Valerius Carausius Emperor in Britain* (London, 1757).

Notes to Introduction

1. John Earle, *Micro-Cosmographie: or A Peece of the World Discovered* (7th edn, London, 1660), pp. 33–34.
2. A useful overview of some of the literary representations of antiquaries during this period can be found in Iain Gordon Brown, *The Hobby-Horsical Antiquary* (Edinburgh, 1980), pp. 1–18, and J. M. Levine, *Dr Woodward's Shield: History, Science and Satire in Augustan England* (Ithaca and London, reprinted 1991), pp. 114–29.
3. Stuart Piggott, *Ruins in a Landscape: Essays in Antiquarianism* (Edinburgh, 1976), pp. 50–51.
4. Roy Porter, *Enlightenment: Britain and the Creation of the Modern World* (London, 2000). Porter implies, pp. 230–31, that after some notable scholarly achievements in the seventeenth century, antiquarianism was sidelined by the rise of an erudite breed of philosophic historians in the eighteenth century.
5. Richard Gough, *Anecdotes of British Topography* (London, 1768), p. iii.
6. William Borlase, *Antiquities Historical and Monumental of the County of Cornwall* (2nd edn, London, 1769), p. v.
7. See, for example, Glyn Daniel, *The Idea of Prehistory* (London, 1962); Piggott, *Ruins in a Landscape*; idem, *William Stukeley: An Eighteenth-Century Antiquary* (2nd edn, London, 1985); idem, *Ancient Britons and the Antiquarian Imagination: Ideas from the Renaissance to the Regency* (London, 1989); Barry M. Marsden, *Pioneers of Prehistory: Leaders and Landmarks in English Archaeology, 1500–1900* (Ormskirk, 1984); idem, *The Early Barrow Diggers* (Stroud, 1999).
8. Bodleian Library, MS Gough Gen. Top. 44, fol. 55v, Michael Tyson to Richard Gough, 30 January 1772.
9. Graham Parry, *The Trophies of Time: English Antiquarians of the Seventeenth Century* (Oxford, 1996); Daniel Woolf, *Reading History in Early Modern England* (Cambridge, 2000); idem, *The Social Circulation of the Past: Historical Culture in Early Modern England, 1500–1730* (Oxford, 2003).
10. Levi Fox, *English Historical Scholarship in the Sixteenth and Seventeenth Centuries* (London, 1956); Daniel Woolf, *The Idea of History in Tudor and Stuart*

England (Toronto, 1990); Kevin Sharpe, *Sir Robert Cotton, 1586–1631* (Oxford, 1979); J. G. A. Pocock, *The Ancient Constitution and the Feudal Law: English Historical Thought in the Seventeenth Century* (Cambridge, 1987).

11. D. C. Douglas, *English Scholars, 1660–1730* (London, 1939).
12. Richard Cust, 'Catholicism, Antiquarianism and Gentry Honour: The Writings of Sir Thomas Shirley', *Midland History*, 23 (1998), pp. 40–63.

Notes to Chapter 1: The Rise of Antiquary

1. Daniel Woolf, 'A Feminine Past? Gender, Genre, and Historical Knowledge in England, 1500–1800', *American Historical Review*, 102 (1997), pp. 645–79.
2. The classic exposition of this relationship is Arnaldo Momigliano, 'Ancient History and the Antiquarian', in *Studies in Historiography* (London, 1966), pp. 1–39.
3. Daniel Woolf, *The Idea of History in Early Stuart England* (Toronto, 1990).
4. White Kennett contributed to the revisions to *Britannia* in 1695, was the author of *Parochial Antiquities Attempted in the History of Ambrosden, Burcester and Other Adjacent Parts in the Counties of Oxford and Bucks* (Oxford, 1695), and was employed by a group of London booksellers in 1706 to compose a history of the seventeenth century for a compilation entitled *A Complete History of England*. Gibson's antiquarian fame rests upon his editorship of the revised editions of William Camden's *Britannia* in 1695 and 1722 and an edition of the Anglo-Saxon Chronicle published in 1693.
5. Momigliano, 'Ancient History and the Antiquarian', pp. 10–14; Justin Champion, *The Pillars of Priestcraft Shaken: The Church of England and its Enemies, 1660–1730* (Cambridge, 1992), pp. 25–52; J. G. A. Pocock, *Barbarism and Religion: The Enlightenments of Edward Gibbon, 1737–1764* (Cambridge, 1999), pp. 152–68.
6. Arnaldo Momigliano, 'Gibbon's Contribution to Historical Method', in *Studies in Historiography* (London, 1966), pp. 40–55. See also J. M. Levine, 'Edward Gibbon and the Quarrel between the Ancients and Moderns', in *Humanism and History: Origins of Modern English Historiography* (Ithaca and London, 1987), pp. 178–90; Mark Salber Phillips, 'Reconsiderations on History and Antiquarianism: Arnaldo Momigliano and the Historiography of Eighteenth-Century Britain', *Journal of the History of Ideas*, 57 (1996), pp. 297–316.
7. On history writing in this period see Thomas Preston Peardon, *The Transition in English Historical Writing, 1760–1830* (New York, 1933); Laird Okie, *Augustan Historical Writing: Histories of England in the English Enlightenment* (Lanham, Maryland, 1991); J. M. Levine, *The Battle of the Books: History and Literature in the Augustan Age* (Ithaca and London, 1991); Philip Hicks, *Neoclassical History and English Culture from Clarendon to Hume* (Basingstoke, 1996); Karen O'Brien, *Narratives of Enlightenment: Cosmopolitan History from Voltaire to Gibbon* (Cambridge, 1997); Mark Salber Phillips, *Society and Sentiment: Genres of Historical Writing in Britain, 1740–1820* (Princeton, 2000); Daniel Woolf,

Reading History in Early Modern England (Cambridge, 2001); idem, *The Social Circulation of the Past in Early Modern England: English Historical Culture, 1500–1730* (Oxford, 2003).

8. On the influence of classical history upon eighteenth-century historians see Levine, *Humanism and History*, pp. 155–90, and *The Battle of the Books*, pp. 267–90.
9. Isaac Kramnick (ed.), *Lord Bolingbroke: Historical Writings* (Chicago and London, 1972), p. 8.
10. O'Brien, *Narratives of Enlightenment*; Pocock, *Barbarism and Religion*, p. 129.
11. Notable examples of eighteenth-century satire include Anon., *Origines Divisianae: or The Antiquities of the Devizes* (London, 1754); John Clubbe, *The History and Antiquities of the Ancient Villa of Wheatfield* (London, 1758); Muscipula, *Curious Remarks on the History of Manchester* (London, 1771); Francis Grose, *The Grumbler* (London, 1791); idem, *The Olio* (London, 1792); Sir Walter Scott, *The Antiquary* (Edinburgh, 1815). See also J. M. Levine, *Dr Woodward's Shield: History, Science and Satire in Augustan England* (Ithaca and London, reprinted 1991), pp. 114–29.
12. M. Langlet du Fresnoy, *A New Method of Studying History*, trans. Richard Rawlinson (London, 1728), p. 237.
13. Joseph Addison, *The Spectator*, ed. Donald Bond, 5 vols (Oxford, 1965), i, pp. 437–38.
14. Joseph Addison, *Dialogues upon the Usefulness of Ancient Medals: Especially in Relation to the Latin and Greek Poets* (London, 1726), p. 11. Addison's arguments upon the utility of medals and the dangers of pedantry were still being rehearsed, with little variation in discussions of numismatics much later in the century. See for example, John Pinkerton, *An Essay on Medals* (London, 1784).
15. John Nichols (ed.), *Reliquiae Galeanae: or Miscellaneous Pieces by the Late Learned Brothers Roger and Samuel Gale* (London, 1784), p. 74, Sir John Clerk to Maurice Johnson, no date. On Clerk see I. G. Brown, 'Sir John Clerk of Penicuik (1676–1755): Aspects of a Virtuoso Life', unpublished Ph.D. thesis, University of Cambridge (1980).
16. West Suffolk Record Office, E2/22/2 unfoliated collection, William Stevenson to George Ashby, no date.
17. Thomas Warton, *The History and Antiquities of Kiddington: First Published as a Specimen of a History of Oxfordshire* (3rd edn, London, 1812), p. 1.
18. Francis Drake, *Eboracum: or The History and Antiquities of the City of York, from its Original to the Present Times* (London, 1736), preface.
19. John Whitaker, *The History of Manchester in Four Books*, 2 vols (2nd edn, London, 1773), i, p. v.
20. William Stukeley, *Abury, a Temple of the British Druids, with Some Others Described: Wherein is a More Particular Account of the First and Patriarchal Religion* (London, 1743), p. 1.
21. William Holman to Humfrey Wanley, 10 August 1723, quoted in C. F. D. Sperling, 'William Holman', *Essex Review*, 3 (1894), p. 263.

22. British Library, Add. MS 29944, fol. 324, Richard Gough to Foote Gower, 26 February 1772; Foote Gower, 'Address to the Public Relative to the Proposed History of Cheshire' (Chelmsford, 1772), p. vii.
23. Quoted in Mark Salber Phillips, 'Adam Smith and the History of Private Life: Social and Sentimental Narratives in Eighteenth-Century Historiography', in Donald R. Kelley and David Harris Sacks (ed.), *The Historical Imagination in Early Modern Britain: History, Rhetoric and Fiction, 1500–1800* (Cambridge, 1997), p. 326. Anthony Grafton, *The Footnote: A Curious History* (London, 1997), charts the evolution of the footnote through Western traditions of literature and scholarship.
24. National Library of Scotland, Adv. MS 29.5.7 (II), fol. 48, Richard Gough to George Paton, 8 April 1787. John Callander of Craigforth was similarly irritated: 'Whitaker is not the single instance of writers putting their Readers to great trouble in this way, and Doctor Robertson has oft put me out of Temper in his History of Charles the Fifth by a similar error', National Library of Scotland, Adv. MS 29.3.8, fol. 40, Callander to George Paton, 23 March 1784.
25. Steven Shapin, '"A Scholar and a Gentleman": The Problematic Identity of the Scientific Practitioner in Early Modern England', *History of Science*, 29 (1991), pp. 279–327.
26. Barbara Shapiro *Probability and Certainty in Seventeenth-Century England* (Princeton, 1983), pp. 119–52, explores the methodological and intellectual relationship between science, antiquities and history in the seventeenth century. 'Contemporaries', she writes, 'saw nothing incompatible about pursuing historical and scientific topics simultaneously, as intimately related parts of a larger intellectual endeavour' (p. 120). On the virtuoso figure in the eighteenth century see John Gascoigne, *Joseph Banks and the English Enlightenment: Useful Knowledge and Polite Culture* (Cambridge, 1994), especially pp. 119–84; Harold Carter, *Sir Joseph Banks* (London, 1988). David Haycock's recent biography of William Stukeley elucidates the close relationship between Stukeley's scientific inquiries and his antiquarianism: David Boyd Haycock, *William Stukeley: Science, Religion and Archaeology in Eighteenth-Century England* (Woodbridge, 2002).
27. Usually around 30 per cent of members of the Antiquarian Society also belonged to the Royal Society; see chapter 3.
28. See pp. 114–17.
29. Francis Bacon, *De Augmentia Scientiae*, II c. 6, quoted in Nicolson, *English Historical Library*, p. i.
30. *A Speech Delivered by Edward King, Esq. President of the Society of Antiquaries of London* (London, 1784), p. 5.
31. John Pinkerton, *An Essay on Medals* (London, 1784), p. 257, 'And tho' your starched and bigotted medallist may sneer, because such a sequence would controvert his formal and narrow way of thinking, common sense will authorise us to laugh at the pedant in our turn, and to pronounce such a series more various, rich, and interesting, than if the collector had only arranged one metal, and rejected a curious article because he did not collect gold or

silver.' For the traditional mode of arranging medals, attacked by Pinkerton, see, for example, Louis Jobert, *The Knowledge of Medals: or Instructions for Those who Apply Themselves to the Study of Medals, both Ancient and Modern*, trans. Roger Gale (London, 1697).

32. Robert Plot, *The Natural History of Staffordshire* (London, 1686), p. 392.
33. Quoted in Gascoigne, *Joseph Banks and the English Enlightenment*, p. 120; M. D. Eddy, 'Geology, Mineralogy and Time in John Walker's University of Edinburgh Natural History Lectures', *History of Science*, 39 (2001), pp. 95–119.
34. J. Webster, 'The Construction of the Old Wall at Verolam: The Roman Bricks Compared with the Modern, &c', *Archaeologia*, 2 (1773), pp. 184–87.
35. Richard Sorrenson, 'Towards a History of the Royal Society in the Eighteenth Century', *Notes and Records of the Royal Society of London*, 50 (1996), p. 37.
36. G. S. Rousseau and David Haycock, 'Voices Calling for Reform: The Royal Society in the Mid-Eighteenth Century – Martin Folkes, John Hill and William Stukelely', *History of Science*, 37 (1999), pp. 377–406. See also chapter 3 below.
37. Richard Gough, *The History of Carausius: or An Examination of What has Been Advanced on that Subject by Genebrier and Stukeley* (London, 1762), preface.
38. Society of Antiquaries, MS 447/3, fol. 154, Samuel Pegge to Jeremiah Milles, 6 April 1778: 'We have already Accounts of three or four of the like blocks [lead pigs], in the *Philosophical Transactions*, and in the *Gentleman's Magazine*, but the *Archaeologia* has not yet afforded any, so that I hope Gentlemen will think proper to approve & Print this Paper of mine.'
39. Bodleian Library, MS Gough Gen. Top. 44, fol. 65, Richard Gough to Michael Tyson, 24 February 1772; or Nichols (ed.), *Literary Anecdotes*, viii, p. 582.
40. Joan Evans, *History of the Society of Antiquaries* (Oxford, 1956), p. 152.
41. For various reasons Buchan met with considerable opposition to his plans for a separate antiquarian society, of which one of the arguments was that Edinburgh was not sufficiently large to support two such learned societies devoted to different ends. See pp.
42. Richard Gough, *British Topography*, 2 vols (London, 1780), ii, p. 436.
43. On the alterations at Salisbury Cathedral and the wider controversy which this aroused see pp. 288–89. John Milner, *A Dissertation on the Modern Style of Altering Ancient Cathedrals, as Exemplified in the Cathedral of Salisbury* (London, 1798), pp. 20–21.
44. Sir Henry Lyons, *The Royal Society, 1660–1940: A History of its Administration and its Charters* (Cambridge, 1944), pp. 216–17.
45. Roger L. Emerson, 'The Scottish Enlightenment and the End of the Philosophical Society of Edinburgh', *British Journal for the History of Science*, 21 (1988), pp. 33–66; Roy Porter, *The Making of Geology: Earth Science in Britain, 1660–1815* (Cambridge, 1977).
46. See pp. 90–91.
47. The development of topography and natural history in the seventeenth century has been reviewed by Mendyk in *Speculum Britanniae*.

48. Stuart Piggott, *William Stukeley: An Eighteenth-Century Antiquary* (2nd edn, London, 1985), pp. 21–22, lists the earliest surviving questionnaires, all of which included questions on both natural and antiquarian curiosities. John Nichols surveyed the history of such inquiries in *Bibliotheca topographica britannica*, 1 (1780), pp. i–iv.
49. C. J. Withers, 'How Scotland Came to Know Itself: Geography, National Identity and the Making of a Nation, 1680–1790', *Journal of Historical Geography*, 21 (1995), pp. 371–97, especially pp. 374–75. Richard Gough's *Anecdotes of British Topography* (London, 1768) was primarily concerned with antiquities, but he encompassed publications upon natural history within his purview, regarding them as complementary to his main interest.
50. David P. Miller, 'Into the Valley of Darkness: Reflections on the Royal Society in the Eighteenth Century', *History of Science*, 27 (1989), p. 157.
51. Gough, *Anecdotes of British Topography*, p. xviii.
52. William Clarke, *The Connexion of the Roman, Saxon, and English Coins, Deduced from Observations on the Saxon Weights and Money* (London, 1767), p. xii.
53. Lambeth Palace Library, Topographical Collections, MS 2214, fol. 107, Richard Gough to Samuel Rudder, no date, *c.* 1768. Gough was here echoing the opinion of Richard Rawlinson in *The English Topographer* (London, 1720), p. 54: 'It were to be wish'd that the Author, or Editor had for many Things given us his Authorities, and not expected an implicit Faith without them, as well as given us his Charters and Grants in the Language he found them, as translations in Books of this Nature seem a Reflection on the Understanding of his Readers.'
54. Krystztof Pomian, *Collectors and Curiosities in Paris and Venice, 1500–1800* (Cambridge, 1987); Patricia Kell, 'British Collecting, 1656–1800: Scientific Inquiry and Social Practice', unpublished D.Phil. thesis, University of Oxford (1996); Katherine Edgar, 'Edward Daniel Clarke (1769–1822) and the Collecting of Classical Antiquities', unpublished Ph.D. thesis, University of Cambridge (2001).
55. Ezekiel Spanheim, *Dissertatio de praestantia et usu numismatum antiquorum* (Rome, 1664); Charles Patin, *De numismate antiquo Augusti et Platonis* (Basle, 1675); *Imperatorum romanorum numismata ex aere, mediae et minimae formae* (Paris, 1697) and *Histoire des médailles* (Paris, 1697); Jobert, *History of Medals*; Obadiah Walker, *The Greek and Roman History Illustrated by Coins and Medals* (London, 1692). See also Alain Schnapp, *The Discovery of the Past: The Origins of Archaeology* (London, 1996), pp. 182–85; Woolf, *Social Circulation of the Past*, pp. 231–38.
56. Addison, *Dialogue upon the Usefulness of Ancient Medals*, pp. 18–23.
57. John Pointer, *Britannia Romana: or Antiquities in Britain, viz, Coins, Camps, and Public Roads* (Oxford, 1724).
58. John Strange, 'A Further Account of Some Remains of Roman and Antiquities in or near the County of Brecknock in South Wales', *Archaeologia*, 4 (1777), p. 26.

59. Pinkerton, *An Essay on Medals*, p. 12.
60. Thomas Astle, *The Origin and Progress of Writing* (London, 1784), p. iii.
61. On Thomas Rymer see Douglas, *English Scholars*, pp. 285–301, and M. M. Condon and Elizabeth M. Hallam, 'Government Printing of the Public Records in the Eighteenth Century', *Journal of the Society of Archivists*, 7 (1984), pp. 348–59.
62. Hickes, *Neoclassical History and English Culture*, pp. 146–48.
63. See for example Thomas Madox's preface addressed to Lord Somers in *Formulare Anglicanum: or A Collection of Ancient Charters and Instruments of Divers Kinds, Taken from the Originals* (London, 1702). On Madox as an antiquary and historian see Douglas, *English Scholars*, pp. 301–15; Levine, *Battle of the Books*, pp. 368–73.
64. Thomas Madox, *The History and Antiquities of the Exchequer* (London, 1711), pp. iv–v; idem, *Firma Burgi: or An Historical Essay Concerning the Cities, Towns and Boroughs of England* (London, 1726), p. ix.
65. Nicolson's role in the study of Anglo-Saxon antiquities will be discussed in chapter 6.
66. William Nicolson, *The English Historical Library in Three Parts* (2nd edn, London, 1714), pp. 209, 240. The first edition was published between 1695 and 1699. Public demand and the rapidly apparent need for new additions necessitated this second edition in 1714.
67. Levine, *The Battle of the Books*, p. 340.
68. Madox, *Firma Burgi*, p. ix (my italics).
69. Richard Gough, 'Introduction', *Archaeologia*, 1 (1770), p. ii.
70. Thomas Pownall, *A Treatise on the Study of Antiquities as the Commentary to Historical Learning* (London, 1782), p. 54.
71. *Antiquarian Repertory*, 1 (1775), p. vii.
72. Pinkerton, *An Essay on Medals*, p. xxiv: 'They who make a pursuit of it ought to reflect that, tho it is a most innocent pursuit, and such as never engaged the attention of a bad man, it is yet a far more laudable amusement. They ought, in consequence, not to make of it an article of faith, but to treat all the parts of it with coolness and candour, as matters of the merest indifference, and certainly of no necessity or importance. Instead of this, the conversation of some medallists is commonly vehement about trifles, and condemnatory of every opinion, of either living or dead authors, which accords not with their own. Like other pedants they are fierce and stern: for there are many analogies between men and other animals, and other animals, and none stronger than this, that they get fierce from being kept in the dark.'
73. Society of Antiquaries, MS 477/1, fol. 110, Jeremiah Milles to Richard Gough, 14 November 1774. Thomas Chapple had been making collections for a history of Devonshire which were eventually published as *A Review of Part of Risdon's Survey of Devon* (Exeter, 1785).
74. British Library, Stowe MS 5841, fol. 25, Sir Peter Thompson to Browne Willis, 30 August 1749.

75. White Kennett, *A Treatise on the Roman Ports and Forts in Kent by William Somner: To Which is Prefixt the Life of Mr Somner* (Oxford, 1693), p. 39.
76. Bodleian Library, MS Eng. Lett. c. 364, fol. 230, Sambrooke Russell to John Nichols, 19 February 1791.
77. *Analytical Review*, 5 (1789), p. 169, reviewing John Brand, *The History and Antiquities of the Town and County of the Town of Newcastle upon Tyne*, 2 vols (London, 1789).
78. Extract taken from *Monthly Review*, October 1766, p. 311, in Richard Gough's copy of Charles Carracioli, *The Antiquities of Arundel* (London, 1766), Bodleian Library, Gough Sussex 8.
79. Henry Rowlands, *Mona Antiqua Restaurata: An Archaeological Discourse on the Antiquities Natural and Historical of the Isle of Angelsey, the Antient Seat of the British Druids* (Dublin, 1723).
80. William Hutton, *History of the Roman Wall* (London, 1802), p. v; John Whitaker, *The History of Manchester in Four Books*, 2 vols (2nd edn, London, 1773), i, p. xi.
81. W. S. Lewis (ed.), *The Yale Edition of Horace Walpole's Correspondence* (Oxford, 1937–83), i, p. 369, Cole to Walpole, 29 April 1775.
82. According to Whitaker, Gibbon had 'solicited' his acquaintance following the publication of the *History of Manchester* in 1771 and they corresponded on literary and historical matters for four or five years. Whitaker cannily exploited the connection thus forged to call upon him, in his capacity as MP for Liskeard, to introduce additional clauses modifying an improvement Bill for Manchester; see British Library, Add. MS 34886. Whitaker was initially full of enthusiasm for Gibbon's history; he later claimed that Gibbon had sent him a bowdlerised version of the work, omitting the final two chapters. His enthusiasm declined as he appreciated the full force of Gibbon's critique of the church and when a mutual friend made him aware of Gibbon's opinion of his *Mary Queen of Scots*. By 1788 Whitaker was penning vigorous denunciations of Gibbon's apostasy in the *English Review* (collected as *Gibbon's History of the Decline and Fall of the Roman Empire … Reviewed* (London, 1791), and prided himself on having 'laid bare his historical defects'. Chetham Library, Manchester, MS A 6 93, fol. 74, and Whitaker, *The Ancient Cathedral Church of Cornwall Historically Surveyed*, 2 vols (London, 1804), ii, pp. 315–16. See also *Notes and Queries*, 5th series, 7 (1877), pp. 444–45, 489–90. Whitaker's response to Gibbon is explored by David Womersley, *Gibbon and the 'Watchmen of the Holy City': The Historian and his Reputation, 1776–1815* (Oxford, 2002), pp. 335–40.
83. Whitaker, *History of Manchester*, i, p. 165; Percival's essay on Roman roads in Lancashire was published as 'Part of a Letter from Mr Thomas Percival', *Archaeologia*, 1 (1770), pp. 62–64.
84. Muscipula, *Curious Remarks on the History of Manchester* (London, 1771), pp. v, 7, 10; see also the annotations to Francis Douce's copy of *The History of Manchester … Containing the Saxon Period* (London, 1775), in the British Library, C 28 16 and 17.

85. Bodleian Library, Gough Gen. Top. 364, p. 496, annotated copy of Gough, *British Topography.*
86. See chapter 4, pp. 128–29.
87. Whitaker, *History of Manchester*, ii, pp. 17–18.
88. West Suffolk Record Office, E2/22/2, unfoliated collection, Thomas Pennant to George Ashby, 9 February 1776.
89. Bodleian Library, MS Gen. Top. 47, fol. 137, Robert Masters to Richard Gough, 28 January 1769.
90. See in particular Piggott, *William Stukeley.*
91. Haycock, *William Stukeley*, pp. 136–88.
92. William Stukeley, *The Medallic History of Marcus Aurelius Valerius Carausius, Emperor in Britain* (London, 1757), p. xxi. Contrast Stukeley's approach with the careful warning given by Joseph Strutt: 'where my authority is in any point doubtful, or deficient, I have acquainted the Reader how far he has to depend upon conjectural evidence, which from necessity occurs in several instances', *A Complete View of the Dress and Habits of the People of England*, 2 vols (London, 1794–96), i, 'Address to the Reader', p. iv.
93. Gough, *History of Carausius*, advertisement. The suspicion of system was equally widespread amongst natural historians (accounting for the initial scepticism with which the Linnaean method of classification was received in Britain). Emmanuel da Costa's remarks to the Cambridge botanist Thomas Martyn could equally have been made between two antiquaries: 'Systems & Systemmakers I most generally abhor. Facts I prize as you do but they must be truly & authentically respected ... They are often perverted to prove what can never be deduced from them. Science is now in a bad company wit pedantry & imagination & forsaking her former friends & associates Reason Judgement and Truth.' Quoted in Gascoigne, *Joseph Banks and the English Enlightenment*, pp. 114–15.
94. British Library, Add. MS 22936, fol. 80v, Foote Gower to Richard Gough, 9 June 1767.
95. Edward Ledwich, 'A Dissertation on the Religion of the Druids: Addressed to Governor Pownall', *Archaeologia*, 7 (1785), p. 303.
96. James Douglas, 'On the Urbs Rutupiae of Ptolemy and the Linden-Pic of the Saxons', *Bibliotheca topographica britannica*, 1 (1780), pp. 474–75; William Somner, *A Treatise on the Roman Forts and Ports in Kent*, ed. White Kennett (Oxford, 1693); John Battely, *Antiquitates Rutupinae*, ed. T. Terry (Oxford, 1711).
97. James Douglas, *Nenia Britannica: or A Sepulchral History of Great Britain* (London, 1793), p. v.
98. Bryony Orme, 'Governor Pownall', *Antiquity*, 48 (1974), pp. 117–24, and Caroline Robbins, 'An Active and Intelligent Antiquary: Governor Thomas Pownall', in Barbara Taft (ed.), *Absolute Liberty: A Selection from the Articles and Papers of Caroline Robbins* (Hamden, Connecticut, 1982), pp. 247–63.
99. R. Meek, *Social Science and the Ignoble Savage* (Cambridge, 1976).

100. Gascoigne, *Joseph Banks and the English Enlightenment*, pp. 125–83; Kathleen Wilson, *The Island Race: Englishness, Empire and Gender in the Eighteenth Century* (London, 2003), pp. 54–91.
101. See for example, the critique offered by John Pinkerton, *An Enquiry into the History of Scotland Preceding the Reign of King Malcolm III, Including the Authentic History of that Period*, 2 vols (London, 1789), i, p. 401. Nigel Leask, 'Mythology', in Iain McCalman (ed.), *An Oxford Companion to the Romantic Age: British Culture, 1776–1832* (Oxford, 1999), pp. 338–45.
102. Thomas Pownall, 'A Description of the Sepulchral Monument at New Grange, Near Drogheda, in the County of Meath, in Ireland', *Archaeologia*, 2 (1773), pp. 236–75.
103. See also chapter 4, pp. 148–53.
104. Thomas Pownall, 'Observations Arising from an Enquiry into the Nature of the Vases Found on the Mosquito Shore in South America', *Archaeologia*, 5 (1779), pp. 318–22.
105. Thomas Pownall, *A Treatise on the Study of Antiquities as the Commentary to Historical Learning* (London, 1782); idem, *An Antiquarian Romance: Endeavouring to Mark a Line by Which the Most Ancient People, and the Processions of the Earliest Inhabitancy of Europe, May be Investigated* (London, 1795).
106. Pownall, *Treatise on the Study of Antiquities*, p. 10.
107. E. H. Harvey Wood, 'Letters to an Antiquary: The Literary Correspondence of G. J. Thorkelin (1752–1829)', unpublished Ph.D. thesis, University of Edinburgh (1972), p. 310. On Monboddo see also Porter, *Enlightenment*, p. 237.
108. Pownall, *Antiquarian Romance*, p. xiii. His theories were not always happily conceived: his suggestion that the pieces of earthenware frequently washed up upon the shore of Kent indicated that at the time of the Romans there had been an earthenware manufactory, which had since been submerged by the encroaching seas, was quickly and effectively demolished by his fellow antiquaries. Thomas Pownall, 'Memoir on the Roman Earthen Ware Fished up Within the Mouth of the River Thames', *Archaeologia*, 5 (1779), pp. 282–90; Edward Jacob, 'Observations on the Roman Earthen Ware Taken from the Pan-Pudding Rock', *Archaeologia*, 6 (1782), pp. 121–24; George Keate, 'Observations on the Roman Earthen Ware Found in the Sea on the Kentish Coast, between Whitstable and Reculver on the Borders of the Isle of Thanet', *Archaeologia*, 6 (1782), pp. 125–29.
109. Pownall did not specifically refer to particular writers who may have influenced him upon these points, but his thinking would appear to have been informed by, for example, Dugald Stewart's *Dissertation on the Origin of Language* (1761), in which Stewart adumbrated a theory of conjectural history, arguing that speculative accounts had real value in showing how change may have come about through natural causes. The logical conclusion of Pownall's 'antiquarian Romance' might seem to be the historical novel, and there are certainly echoes of Pownall's arguments in Sir Walter Scott's dedicatory epistle to Dr Dryasdust in *Ivanhoe*. Scott freely admitted that he had been eclectic in his historical

borrowings, but argued that minute historical accuracy was less important than giving a plausible account of the manners and customs of the time unmarred by obvious anachronisms.

110. *Gentleman's Magazine*, 53 (1783), p. 241–42, review of Pownall, *A Treatise on the Study of Antiquities.* The secretary of the Society of Antiquaries, William Norris, confessed to Samuel Pegge that 'his Matter and Manner are so very abstruse & metaphysical, that I can't pretend to give you an Idea of it'. Undated letter bound with Richard Gough's annotated copy of *Archaeologia*, 7 (1785), Bodleian Library.
111. See chapter 4, pp. 130–31, 143–46.
112. Edward Ledwich 'A Dissertation on the Religion of the Druids: Addressed to Governor Pownall', *Archaeologia*, 7 (1785), p. 303.
113. Letters dated 17 April 1782 from Governor Pownall to the Society of Antiquaries and 6 May 1782 from J. C. Brooke in Gough's copy of vol. 5 of *Archaeologia*, Bodleian Library. See also the review of vol. 6 in *Gentleman's Magazine*, 53 (1783), pp. 148–49.
114. Pownall, *Treatise on the Study of Antiquities*, p. 2, and idem, 'A Letter from Governor Pownall to the Rev. Michael Lort, D.D.V.P.A.S. Inclosing Mr Ledwich's Letter on the Ship Temples in Ireland', *Archaeologia*, 7 (1785), p. 272. Pownall did not actually carry out his threat; papers by him continued to appear in vols 8, 9 and 10 of *Archaeologia.*
115. Paul-Henri Mallet, *Northern Antiquities: or A Description of the Manners, Customs, Religion and Laws of the Ancient Danes, and Other Northern Nations*, trans. Thomas Percy, 2 vols (London, 1770), i, p. 55.
116. William Robertson, *The History of the Reign of the Emperor Charles V* (London, 1769).
117. Stephen Howard, 'Biography and the Cult of Personality in Eighteenth-Century Britain', unpublished D.Phil. thesis, University of Oxford (1998).
118. Phillips, 'Adam Smith and the History of Private Life'. On sentiment and sensibility see Janet Todd, *Sensibility: An Introduction* (London, 1986).
119. George Hadley, *A New and Complete History of the Town and County of the Town of Kingston upon Hull* (Hull, 1788), preface. These issues are discussed at greater length in Rosemary Sweet, *The Writing of Urban Histories in Eighteenth-Century England* (Oxford, 1997), pp. 223–29, 248–49.
120. T. D. Whitaker, *An History of the Original Parish of Whalley, and Honor of Clithero in the Counties of Lancaster and York* (London, 1801), p. iv.
121. National Library of Scotland, Adv. MS 29.3.14, fol. 78, earl of Buchan's anniversary discourse to the Scottish Society of Antiquaries, 15 November 1784.
122. Thomas Burgess, *An Essay on the Study of Antiquities, to Which are Added Some Cursory Remarks on the Origin of Language in General, and of the Greek Language in Particular* (Oxford, 1781), p. 19.
123. Richard Gough, *Sepulchral Monuments in Great Britain*, 2 vols (London, 1786–96), i, p. 4. Gough had in mind the practice of many historians, including David Hume, of relegating such matters to the end of the chapter under the

heading 'miscellaneous transactions of this reign'. The reconfiguration of the historical genres which Gough's comments reflect is discussed in detail by Phillips, *Society and Sentiment.*

124. On Montfaucon and his influence on eighteenth-century antiquarianism and art history see Francis Haskell, *History and its Images* (New Haven and London, 1993), pp. 131–44, and Françoise Choay, *The Invention of the Historic Monument*, trans. Lauren M. O'Connell (Cambridge, 2001), pp. 41–48.
125. Gough, *Sepulchral Monuments*, i, p. 7. See also William Clarke's criticisms of Montfaucon's approach to the study of numismatics in *The Connexion of the Roman, Saxon, and English Coins, Deduced from Observations on the Saxon Weights and Money* (London, 1767), p. 199. Montfaucon was a scholar 'whose views were only to produce specimens of the antiquities, he was explaining' rather than seeking to understand how the system of coinage worked.
126. Pownall, *A Treatise on the Study of Antiquities*, pp. 76, 101.
127. Addison, *Dialogues upon the Usefulness of Ancient Medals*, p. 26.
128. J. M. Levine, 'Eighteenth-Century Historicism and the First Gothic Revival', in *Humanism and History*, pp. 190–213.
129. Edward King, 'Observations on Antient Castles', *Archaeologia*, 4 (1777), p. 365.
130. It is possible here to detect the influence of continental scholars, in particular the Comte de Caylus, who emphasised that a study of the art and antiquities of the ancients could lead to a better understanding of their institutions, beliefs and histories. Pomian, *Collectors and Curiosities*, pp. 130–34, 173–83; Haskell, *History and its Images*, pp. 180–86; Schnapp, *The Discovery of the Past*, pp. 240–41.
131. Edward King, *Munimenta Antiqua: or Observations on Antient Castles*, 4 vols (London, 1799–1804), i, pp. vii–viii.
132. See chapter 3 below, pp. 100, 102.
133. *A Speech Delivered by Edward King*, pp. 9–11.
134. Bodleian Library, MS Don. d. 90, fol. 247 et seq., '*Prospectus* for a General History of the County of York' (1816).
135. T. D. Fosbroke, *Abstracts of Records and Manuscripts Respecting the County of Gloucester* (Gloucester, 1807), preface.

Notes to Chapter 2: People

1. James Boswell, *The Life of Johnson*, 2 vols (London, 1949), ii, p. 200. Johnson was speaking of Thomas Percy and comparing him with the Scottish antiquary and historian Lord Hailes. Percy, he suggested, outdid Hailes both in minuteness of research and elegance of composition. Percy won his approval for the grace and splendour which he brought to what seemed to Johnson an essentially unattractive pursuit.
2. *The Antiquarian Repertory*, 1 (1775), p. ii.
3. On classical collections see Philip Ayres, *Classical Culture and the Idea of Rome in Eighteenth-Century England* (Cambridge, 1997); Ian Jenkins and Kim Sloan,

Vases and Volcanoes: Sir William Hamilton and his Collections (London, 1996); Jeremy Black, *The Grand Tour in the Eighteenth Century* (London, 1999); Timothy Mowl, *William Beckford* (London, 1998); David Constantine, *Fields of Fire: A Life of Sir William Hamilton* (London, 2001); Bernard D. Frischer and I. G. Brown, *Allan Ramsay and the Search for Horace's Villa* (Aldershot, 2001).

4. The importance of antiquarianism and natural history as demarcators of social status has recently been discussed by H. R. French, '"Ingenious & Learned Gentlemen": Social Perceptions and Self-Fashioning among Parish Elites in Essex, 1680–1740', *Social History*, 25 (2000), pp. 44–66.
5. Bodleian Library, MS Eng. Misc. e. 121, fos 9, 16; Nichols (ed.), *Literary Anecdotes*, v, p. 107; Theodor Harmsen, *Antiquarianism in the Augustan Age: Thomas Hearne, 1678–1735* (Bern, 2000), p. 33.
6. Norfolk and Norwich Record Office, MS Bradfer Lawrence II a/1, fol. 2, Sir John Fenn, 'Memoirs of Thomas Martin'.
7. Richard Warner, *Literary Recollections*, 2 vols (London, 1830), i, pp. 84–85.
8. Stebbing Shaw, *The History and Antiquities of Stafforshire*, 2 vols (London, 1798–1801), i, p. v.
9. John Hodgson, 'On the Study of Antiquities: Read before the Society [of Antiquaries of Newcastle] at its Second Monthly Meeting' (Newcastle, 1813), p. xv.
10. Antiquarianism can clearly be included as one of the 'historical genres' which are the focus of Mark Salber Phillips's study, *Society and Sentiment: Genres of Historical Writing in Britain, 1740–1820* (Princeton, 2000). Phillips argues that 'eighteenth-century sentimentalism played an enormously important role in encouraging the idea that we go to history in order to experience a sense of the evocative presence of other places and other times', p. 28. The boundaries between antiquarianism and history here are clearly fluid.
11. John Callander, proposals for *Bibliotheca septentrionalis* (Edinburgh, 1778), p. iii.
12. Bodleian Library, MS Gough Gen. Top. 39, fol. 180, Samuel Denne to Richard Gough, 7 August 1797, quoting Joseph Addison, *Spectator*, no. 447.
13. Joseph Addison, *The Spectator*, ed. David Bond, 5 vols (Oxford, 1965), iii, pp. 527–31.
14. British Library, Add. MS 37220, fol. 46v, Lord Dacre to Philip Morant, 26 December 1762.
15. Bryan Faussett, *Inventorium sepulchrale*, ed. Charles Roach Smith (London, 1856), p. 36.
16. British Library, Add. MS 33638, fol. 134v, John Skinner, 'Observations on the Roman Wall'. The domestic antiquaries were, of course, echoing the sentiments of the tourist and the antiquary in Rome, for whom the site of the imperial ruins was assumed to bring the past back to life in the imagination and illustrate the literature upon which they had been educated. Many of the guides to Rome were deliberately composed to lead the tourist through the sites as they illustrated the passages of Roman history and literature with which he was familiar. See also Francis Haskell and Nicholas Penny, *Taste*

and the Antique: The Lure of Classical Sculpture, 1500–1900 (New Haven and London, 1991), pp. 44–48.

17. Mrs Charles Stothard, *Memoirs, Including the Original Journals, Letters, Papers and Antiquarian Tracts of the Late Charles Alfred Stothard, FSA, Author of The Monumental Effigies of Great Britain* (London, 1823), p. 146.
18. Thomas Madox, *Formulare Anglicanum* (London, 1702), preface, sig. b.
19. British Library, Harleian MS 7055, quoted in Joan Evans, *History of the Society of Antiquaries* (Oxford, 1956), p. 44.
20. Harmsen, *Antiquarianism in the Augustan Age.* For a broader discussion of the significance of conservative religious and political ideologies in eighteenth-century society, see J. C. D. Clark, *English Society, 1660–1832* (revised edn, Cambridge, 2000).
21. John Collinson, *The History and Antiquities of the County of Somerset*, 3 vols (London, 1790), i, p. viii.
22. See for example, John Warburton, *Vallum Romanum: or The History and Antiquities of the Roman Wall, Commonly Called the Picts Wall* (London, 1753), pp. vii–viii.
23. William Borlase, *Antiquities Historical and Monumental of the County of Cornwall* (2nd edn, London, 1769), p. v. See also William Stukeley, *Itinerarium curiosum* (London, 1724), p. 3; Richard Gough, *British Topography*, 2 vols (London, 1780), i, pp. xiii–xiv; and Thomas Madox, *The History and Antiquities of the Exchequer* (London, 1711), p. vii: 'they [gentlemen] have travelled into Foreign Countries, where politeness is planted, to observe and learn their Laws, customs, and manners. But do the Political Constitution, Laws, and Manners of Ancient *Greece* or *Rome* bear a nearer affinity or resemblance to Those of *Britain* at this day, than the Ancient Constitution, Laws, and Manners of *Britain* do to Those of *Britain* in the modern or present times? Are we concerned to know the manners and customs which were in use amongst the *Grecians* and *Romans* many ages ago: and not concerned to know the customs and manners of our Own ancestours,[sic] at a far less distance of time? Do we think it beneficial to be versed in the history, both ancient and modern, of Foreign nations: and are we at the same time content to despise or neglect the ancient history of our Own?'
24. William Nicolson, *The English Historical Library in Three Parts* (2nd edn, London, 1714), p. 5.
25. White Kennett, *Parochial Antiquities Attempted in the History of Ambrosden, Burcester and Other Adjacent Parts in the Counties of Oxford and Bucks* (Oxford, 1695), preface.
26. Studies which focus on the county as a unit of political and administrative activity in the eighteenth century include David Eastwood, *Governing Rural England: Tradition and Transformation in Local Government, 1780–1840* (Oxford,1994); idem, *Government and Community in the English Provinces* (Basingstoke, 1997); Paul Langford, *Public Life and the Propertied Englishman* (Oxford, 1990).

27. The county club as a distinct variant on eighteenth-century habits of sociability is discussed by Peter Clark, *British Clubs and Societies, 1580–1800: The Origins of an Associational World* (Oxford, 2000), pp. 290–93.
28. W. C. Lukis (ed.), 'Family Memoirs of William Stukeley, vol. ii', *Surtees Society*, 73 (1883), p. 73, Rev. Mr Patten to Roger Gale, 30 January 1730/1.
29. *The Topographer, Containing a Variety of Original Articles, Illustrative of the Local History and Antiquities of this Kingdom*, 1 (1789), p. iv.
30. With reference to an earlier period Philip Styles has argued that antiquarian knowledge was a means to making feudal tenure profitable: 'This combination of family pride and business acumen made antiquaries out of many country squires in Stuart England'. See Philip Styles, 'Sir Simon Archer, 1581–1662', *Dugdale Society Occasional Papers* (1946), pp. 1–51 (quotation from pp. 23–24).
31. John Hutchins, *History and Antiquities of Dorset*, 2 vols (London, 1773), i, p. v.
32. John Watson, *The History and Antiquities of the Parish of Halifax in Yorkshire* (London, 1775), dedication.
33. Prospectus (1791) for William Hutchinson's *The History of the County of Cumberland and Some Places Adjacent*, 2 vols (Carlisle, 1794).
34. Bodleian Library, MS Top. Gen. c. 8, fos 247–49, Nathaniel Templeman to Richard Gough, 25 January 1774.
35. James Raine, *A Memoir of the Revd John Hodgson*, 2 vols (London, 1857), i, pp. 269, 272.
36. Hutchins, *History of Dorset*, i, p. vi. Some of his fellow antiquaries, however, did consider that he had gone too far towards satisfying the vanity of his gentry subscribers. George North to Andrew Coltée Ducarel, 29 May 1750, bound in Richard Gough's copy of *Archaeologia*, 1 (1770), Bodleian Library.
37. Robert Atkyns, *The Antient History of Glostershire* (London, 1712), preface, 'This has its peculiar Use; it stimulates and excites the Brave, to imitate the generous Actions of their Ancestors; and it shames the Debauch'd and Reprobate, both in the Eyes of others and in their own Breasts, when they consider how they have degenerated.'
38. For the importance of ancestry to constructions of nobility and familial honour, and its place in antiquarian scholarship in an earlier period, see Richard Cust, 'Catholicism, Antiquarianism and Gentry Honour: The Writings of Sir Thomas Shirley', *Midland History*, 23 (1998), pp. 40–63.
39. West Suffolk Record Office, E2/22/2, unfoliated collection, Samuel Pegge to George Ashby, 20 January 1773.
40. Edward Hasted, *The History and Topographical Survey of the County of Kent*, 12 vols (2nd edn, Canterbury, 1797–1801), i, p. x. Hasted's sentiments expressed here were almost identical to those articulated by Robert Atkyns almost one hundred years earlier.
41. A Mr Coosens of Margate claimed in 1822 to have identified over 2000 errors in Hasted's *History of Kent*. George M. Arnold, *Robert Pocock: the Gravesend Historian, Naturalist, and Printer* (London, 1883), p. 117.

42. Ralph Bigland, *Observations on Marriages, Baptisms, and Burials, as Preserved in Parochial Registers* (London, 1764), p. 95. Bigland was actually quoting from William Maitland's description of the College of Arms in *The History of London from its Foundation by the Romans to the Present Time* (London, 1739).
43. British Library, Add. MS 37221, fol. 93, Charles Gray to Philip Morant, 21 January 1767.
44. Gough was put out that Morant had not made better use of the collections which had already been made by William Holman and Nathaniel Salmon. British Library, Egerton MS 2382, fos 179–200. See also W. Raymond Powell, 'Antiquaries in Conflict: Philip Morant versus Richard Gough', *Essex Archaeology and History*, 20 (1989), pp. 143–47. Morant's response to Gough, in a review of Gough's *Anecdotes of British Topography* was published in *Monthly Review*, 40 (1769), p. 455; a draft survives at Essex Record Office, D/DCm Z19, fos 291–93.
45. British Library, Add. MS 37220, fos 32v, 26v, 34, 36v, 42. Nathaniel Salmon, *The History and Antiquities of Essex* (London, 1740). Salmon died in 1742 with 154 parishes still to cover. Edward A. Fitch, 'Nathaniel Salmon', *Essex Review*, 2 (1893), pp. 238–45.
46. Richard Gough, *Anecdotes of British Topography* (London, 1768), p. xviii.
47. *Gentleman's Magazine*, 72, pt 2 (1812), p. 104.
48. *Gentleman's Magazine*, 62 (1802), pt 2, pp. 702–3, proposals for a history of Yorkshire by Robert Townson.
49. See p. 9.
50. Norfolk and Norwich Record Office, Rye MS, fol. 43, Thomas Tanner to Francis Blomefield, 31 October 1735.
51. British Library, Add. MS 37220, fol. 55, Lord Dacre to Philip Morant, no date, 1764.
52. 'Collections towards the History and Antiquities of Bedfordshire, Containing the Parishes of Puddington, Luton and Dunstaple', in John Nichols (ed.), *Bibliotheca topographica britannica*, 4 (1783), p. iii.
53. Bodleian Library, MS Eng. Lett. d. 44, fol. 367, John Hawkesworth to Samuel Pegge, 28 April 1758.
54. Bodleian Library, MS Eng. Lett. c. 357, fol. 13, William Hamper to John Nichols, 21 May 1810. Hamper, a successful businessman turned magistrate and landed gentleman, had hoped to employ John Britton on this project, but was thwarted by the publisher who had another (cheaper) candidate in view. Britton *Autobiography*, i, p. 156. Henry Penruddocke Wyndham produced a plan for a committee of gentlemen to subscribe between £1500 and £2000 towards employing 'the most able Historians, Antiquarians, Draughtsmen, Heralds, Botanists, Engravers &c &c' in writing the history and antiquities of Wiltshire. Wyndham, *Wiltshire Extracted from Domesday Book*, p. xxii.
55. British Library, Add. MS 22936, fol. 62 Richard Gough to Foote Gower, 2 March 1767.

56. Tony Brown and Glen Foard, *The Making of a County History: John Bridge's Northamptonshire* (Leicester, 1994), pp. 154–56; Leicestershire, Leicester and Rutland Record Office, 23 D 57 (papers of Sir Thomas Cave). See also A. H. Smith, 'John Nichols and Hutchins' *History and Antiquities of Dorset*', *The Library*, 5th series, 15 (1960), pp. 81–95, and introduction to the facsimile edition of the third edition by Robert Douche (Wakefield, 1973). See also correspondence in Bodleian Library, MSS Top. gen. d. 2; Top. gen. c. 7; Top. gen. c. 8 and Gough Gen. Top. 42.
57. The fire destroyed 'the whole of six portions' of the history of Leicestershire, as well as much of Nichols's other stock. See the report in *Gentleman's Magazine*, 68 (1808), pp. 99–100. Bodleian Library, MS Eng. Lett. b. 19, fol. 78, W. Ruding writing to John Nichols, 17 September 1808, informed him that the gentlemen of Leicestershire had agreed to advance the cost of the final volume to 5 guineas to make up for the losses consequent upon the fire.
58. Philippa Levine, *The Amateur and the Professional: Antiquarians, Historians and Archaeologists in Victorian England, 1838–1886* (Cambridge, 1986), pp. 59–61, 69.
59. Benedict Anderson, *Imagined Communities: Reflections on the Origin and Spread of Nationalism* (revised edn, London, 1991).
60. National Library of Scotland, Adv. MS 29.5.7, fol. 51, George Paton to Richard Gough, 25 June 1787. See also fol. 36.
61. Sir Robert Sibbald, *The History, Ancient and Modern, of the Sheriffdoms of Fife and Kinross, and of the Firths of Forth and Tay* (Edinburgh, 1710); Sir Robert Sibbald, *The History, Ancient and Modern, of the Sheriffdoms of Linlithgow and Stirling* (Edinburgh, 1710); Lachlan Shaw, *The History of the Province of Moray* (Edinburgh 1775); George Crawfurd, *A History of the Shire of Renfrew, Containing a Genealogical History of the Royal House of Stuart* (Edinburgh, 1782); William Nimmo, *A General History of Stirlingshire* (Edinburgh, 1777); William Hamilton, 'Descriptions of the Sheriffdoms of Lanark and Renfrew', compiled *c.* 1710, was published in 1831.
62. Harmsen, *Antiquarianism in the Augustan Age*, pp. 273–77, discusses the Jacobite networks amongst the Scottish antiquaries.
63. Gough, *British Topography*, ii, p. 479.
64. Quentin Deakin, 'The Early County Histories of Wales and Western England, *c.* 1570–1656', unpublished Ph.D. thesis, University of Wales (1982).
65. Theophilus Jones, *A History of the County of Brecknock*, 2 vols (Brecknock, 1805); Samuel Rush Meyrick, *The History and Antiquities of Cardiganshire* (London, 1808); Richard Fenton, *A Historical Tour through Pembrokeshire* (London, 1810).
66. Philip Jenkins, 'The Creation of an 'Ancient Gentry': Glamorgan, 1760–1840', *Welsh Historical Review*, 12 (1984), pp. 25–49; see also his *The Making of a Ruling Class: The Glamorgan Gentry, 1640–1790* (Cambridge, 1983), pp. 235–39.
67. Jenkins, *The Making of a Ruling Class*, p. 272.
68. Gough's chief correspondents for the revisions of *Britannia* were Thomas

Campbell, Joseph Cooper Walker and Samuel Ledwich. His correspondence with Campbell and Ledwich is reprinted in Nichols (ed.), *Illustrations of Literature*, vii, pp. 799–855, and see also the Gough manuscripts at Enfield Local History, Library, D 1624.

69. *A Topographical and Chorographical Survey of the County of Down* (Dublin, 1740); Charles Smith, *The Ancient and Present State of the County and City of Waterford* (Dublin, 1746); idem, *The Ancient and Present State of the County and City of Cork*, 2 vols (Dublin, 1750); idem, *The Ancient and Present State of the County of Kerry* (Dublin, 1756). On Charles Smith see William Fraher, 'Charles Smith, 1715–62: Pioneer of Irish Topography', *Decies: Journal of the Waterford Archaeological and Historical Society*, 53 (1997), pp. 33–44.
70. The predominance of members of the Inns of Court was also a function of the metropolitan bias of the membership.
71. The travel journals upon which Bray drew for the *Sketch of a Tour* are at Surrey History Centre, MS 85/2/5. William Mavor, author of bowdlerised topography and didactic literature, commented of Bray that as 'A professed antiquary, he seems to have been more solicitous to display his skill in tracing the history of former times, than to delineate the existing state of the country through which he past.' *The British Tourist, or Traveller's Pocket Companion, through England, Wales, Scotland and Ireland*, 6 vols (London, 1798), ii, p. 303.
72. Owen Manning, *The History and Antiquities of the County of Surrey ... Continued to the Present Time by William Bray*, 3 vols (London, 1804–14), ii, p. v.
73. Surrey History Centre, MS 85/1/46, diary entry for 22 August 1803.
74. Wyndham, *Wiltshire Extracted from Domesday Book*, p. xxii.
75. David Stoker, 'The Compilation and Production of a Classic County History', unpublished M.Phil. thesis, University of Reading (1982), p. 69.
76. Manning and Bray, *History and Antiquities of Surrey*, ii, p. iii; Surrey History Centre, MS 85/1/50, diary entry for 6 October 1808.
77. On Richard Wilkes and his Staffordshire Collections see M. W. Greenslade, 'The Staffordshire Historians', in *Collections for a History of Staffordshire*, Staffordshire History Society Publications, 4th series, 11 (1982).
78. Nichols (ed.), *Illustrations of Literature*, iv, p. 581, William Barrett to Andrew Coltée Ducarel, 20 July 1772.
79. Le Neve resigned as president in 1724. His antiquarian collections towards a history of Norfolk were inherited by Thomas Martin (who married his widow) and formed the basis for much of Blomefield's history. Stoker, 'Compilation and Production of a Classic County History'.
80. Anthony Wagner, *Heralds of England: A History of the Office and College of Arms* (London, 1967), pp. 329–42.
81. Bodleian Library, MS Gough Gen. Top. 45.
82. Francis Grose is remembered chiefly for *Antiquities of England and Wales*, 4 vols (London, 1773–87) and his work on dialect and armour; John Warburton, *Vallum Romanum: or The History and Antiquities of the Roman Wall* (London, 1753); John Ives published Henry Swinden's *The History and Antiquities*

of the Ancient Burgh of Great Yarmouth (Norwich, 1772), for which he wrote an introduction. He also issued proposals for a history of Lothingland in Suffolk, which was never printed (British Library, Add. MS 19098). A selection of shorter papers was printed under the title *Select Papers Chiefly Relating to English Antiquities* (London, 1773–5); Ralph Bigland made extensive collections for a history of Gloucestershire, see Bodleian Library, MSS Top. Glos. e. 10–12.

83. Calculated from membership lists of the Society of Antiquaries, bound with Richard Gough's annotated copies of *Archaeologia* in the Bodleian Library.
84. Rosemary Sweet, *The Writing of Urban Histories in Eighteenth-Century England* (Oxford, 1997), appendix B, pp. 288–92.
85. I am very grateful to Michael Honeybone for sharing his research on the Spalding and Peterborough societies with me.
86. David McKitterick, *Cambridge University Library: A History. The Eighteenth and Nineteenth Centuries* (Cambridge, 1986); J. G. Milne, 'The Oxford Coin Collections of the Seventeenth and Eighteenth Centuries', *Oxoniensia*, 14 (1969), pp. 53–62.
87. McKitterick, *Cambridge University Library*, p. 250.
88. David McKitterick, 'From Camden to Cambridge: Sir Robert Cotton's Roman Inscriptions, and their Subsequent Treatment', in C. J. Wright (ed.), *Sir Robert Cotton as Collector: Essays on an Early Stuart Courtier and his Legacy* (1997), pp. 105–28; Katharine Edgar, 'Edward Daniel Clarke (1769–1822) and the Collecting of Classical Antiquities', unpublished Ph.D. thesis, University of Cambridge (2001), pp. 22–25.
89. British Library, Add. MS 5886, William Cole, 'A Short Account of Such Antiquaries as Received their Education in Corpus Christi College Cambridge'; Bodleian Library, MS Gough Gen. Top. 44, fol. 302, Michael Tyson to Richard Gough, 4 May 1778. See also Nichols (ed.), *Literary Anecdotes*, viii, p. 631.
90. Michael Lort told Richard Gough that proposals for James Nasmith's *Itinerary of William of Worcester* had been placed in all the common rooms of Oxford. Society of Antiquaries, MS 447/2, fol. 98v, 24 May 1777.
91. Patricia Bell (ed.), *Episcopal Visitations in Bedfordshire, 1706–1720*, Bedfordshire Historical Record Society, 81 (2002), p. xv.
92. British Library, Add. MS 33665, fol. 41v, James Douglas to John Skinner, 9 December 1817.
93. Peter Muilman writing in the *Morning Post*, 7 November 1769.
94. Quoted in Douglas, *English Scholars*, p. 20.
95. John Whitaker, *The Origin of Arianism Disclosed* (London, 1791); idem, *The Real Origin of Government* (London, 1795); idem, *The Ancient Cathedral of Cornwall Historically Surveyed*, 2 vols (London, 1804); James Storer, *History and Antiquities of the Cathedral Churches of Great Britain*, 4 vols (London, 1814).
96. James Bentham, *History and Antiquities of the Conventual Church of Ely* (Cambridge, 1771); John Milner, *A Dissertation on the Modern Style of Altering Antient Cathedrals* (London, 1798); idem, *The History Civil and Ecclesiastical*

and Survey of the Antiquities of Winchester, 2 vols (Winchester, 1799–1801); John Haggitt, *Two Letters to a Fellow of the Society of Antiquaries on the Subject of Gothic Architecture: Containing a Refutation of Dr Milner's Objections to Mr Whittington's Historical Survey of the Ecclesiastical Edifices of France* (Cambridge, 1813); William Gunn, *An Inquiry into the Origin and Influence of Gothic Architecture* (London, 1819); Robert Darley Waddilove, 'An Historical and Descriptive Account of Ripon Minster', *Archaeologia*, 17 (1814), pp. 128–37; Thomas Kerrich, 'Observations on the Gothic Buildings Abroad', *Archaeologia*, 16 (1812), pp. 292–325; Richard Yates, *An Illustration of the Monastic History and Antiquities of the Town and Abbey of St. Edmund's Bury* (London, 1805).

97. Simon Bradley, The Gothic Revival and the Church of England, 1790–1840', unpublished Ph.D. thesis, University of London (1996), p. 121; Arthur Burns, *The Diocesan Revival in the Church of England* (Oxford, 1999), pp. 82–83.
98. Thomas Rickman, *An Attempt to Discriminate the Styles of English Architecture, from the Conquest to the Reformation* (London, 1817), p. iii.
99. Bradley, 'Gothic Revival', p. 122.
100. William Borlase to William Stukeley, 10 November 1749, quoted in William Borlase, *Antiquities Historical and Monumental of the County of Cornwall*, ed. P. A. S. Poole and Charles Thomas (Wakefield, 1973), p. vii.
101. British Library, Stowe MS 752, fol. 130, William Borlase to Charles Lyttelton, 13 March 1750.
102. Howard and Peter Coombs (ed.), *Journal of a Somerset Rector, 1803–4* (Oxford, 1984), p. 115.
103. Bodleian Library, MS Eng. Lett. d. 46, fos 171–465 correspondence on antiquarian and related topics between Ray and Pegge. Ray would receive copies of papers read at the Society of Antiquaries of London, which he would then pass on to Pegge. Ray was also an active member of the Gentlemen's Society of Spalding.
104. Bodleian Library, MS Eng. Lett. d. 45, fol. 505, William Norris to Samuel Pegge, no date, 'I am at a loss at what Period to commence my Detail of the Proceedings of the A.S. not being able to recollect precisely the time of your being last in Town, & taking a Survey of what had been done in the Course of this or the preceding Year ...' There follows seven sides of abstracts of papers read and business conducted at the meetings in a closely written hand. Society of Antiquaries, MS 447/3, fol. 167, 29 January 1779, Pegge (who by this date had moved to Derbyshire) thanks Richard Gough for his letters as he has so few correspondents and in this remote place there is little chance of discussing literary matters. Bryan Faussett complained to Ducarel that all his acquaintances in Kent could talk about was horses, dogs, hunting and shooting, 'but I must bear with it or live alone'. British Library, Add. MS 23900, fol. 88, 13 September 1766.
105. Philip Falle, *An Account of the Isle of Jersey* (London, 1694); the second edition was published in 1734.

106. C. F. D. Sperling, 'Philip Morant', *Essex Review*, 3 (1894), pp. 27–41.
107. Morant's extracts from Rapin in British Library, Stowe MSS 79 and 1053. Edward A. Fitch, 'Nicholas Tindal', *Essex Review*, 2 (1893), pp. 168–79; Morant's correspondence with Tindal is at British Library, Add. MS 37222, fos 1, 9, 22, 23, 87.
108. Christine E. Cobbold, 'The Writing of Essex County History, *c.* 1600–1768', *Essex Journal*, 8 (1973), pp. 2–10. British Library, Add. MS 37216, fol. 115v, Philip Morant to Philip Falle, 16 September 1735. Of Morant, Tindal, Salmon, Holman, Holbrook, Ouseley and Booth, Booth was the only layman.
109. By April 1733 Morant had been nominated to the chaplaincy of the English Episcopal Church at Amsterdam and had been offered the rectory of Shellow Bowells in Essex.
110. British Library, Add. MS 37221, fol. 29v, Morant to Gibson, 24 April 1738.
111. British Library, Add. MS 37221, fol. 55, Gibson to Morant, 7 August 1739; fol. 59, Morant to Gibson 22 December 1739. See also ibid., fos 130, 131, 161, 251, 258, and British Library, Add. MS 37216, fol. 133v.
112. Thomas Dudley Fosbroke, vicar of a parish in Gloucestershire and author a history of Gloucester and of the monastic orders, complained in the preface to *Encyclopaedia of Antiquities and Elements of Archaeology, Classic and Medieval*, 2 vols (London, 1825), that his antiquarian publications had failed to secure for him the preferment which he had anticipated: 'I had hopes, that my literary efforts would have obtained me some moderate preferment, tending to render my feelings easy with regard to my declining years.'
113. Stebbing Shaw, *The History and Antiquities of Staffordshire*, 2 vols (London, 1798–1801), i, pp. x–xi.
114. The tensions surrounding clerical attempts to maximise the income from their property are discussed in Eric Evans, 'Some Reasons for the Growth of English Rural Anticlericalism, *c.* 1750–1830', *Past and Present*, 66 (1975), pp. 84–109. 'The church', he writes, 'was determined to assert its ancient rights in conditions which were now becoming advantageous to the landed interest.'
115. Atkyns, *Ancient and Present State of Glostershire*, preface.
116. Corpus Christi College Cambridge, Parker Library, Stukeley MS 610, fol. 3. Cf. White Kennet, *Parochial Antiquities*, sig. b. 2: 'Thus tithes have been appropriated to the uses of the church within this realm for a term of more than one thousand years, a term in which the whole property of the kingdom has passed through several hands, and been held by different titles and claims; which they would do well to consider who cannot without envy and malignity look on the ordinary revenues of the church, as if they were deprived of their just dues by those payments, which their estates were liable to at their first acquisition.'
117. Jeremy Gregory, *Restoration, Reformation and Reform, 1660–1828: Archbishops of Canterbury and their Diocese* (Oxford, 2000), pp. 157–58.
118. Shirley Burgoyne Black, *A Scholar and a Gentleman: Edward Hasted, the Historian of Kent* (Otford, 2001), pp. 276–78.

119. Henry Home, Lord Kames, *Historical Law Tracts* (3rd edn, London, 1776), p. 88.
120. Nicolson, *English Historical Library*, p. 13.
121. J. Hunter (ed.), *The Life of Thomas Gent* (London, 1832), p. 179.
122. Nichols, *Illustrations of Literature*, iv, p. 855–7, John Whitaker to Andrew Coltée Ducarel, 13 June 1772.
123. Daines Barrington, 'Observations on the Practice of Archery in England', *Archaeologia*, 7 (1785), p. 68.
124. Bodleian Library, MS Top. Gen. 44, fol. 190, Tyson to Gough, no date, 1774. See also Nichols (ed.), *Literary Anecdotes*, viii, p. 610.
125. In addition to Hearne and Bagford the group included Richard Graves, George Ballard (the son of a staymaker), Thomas Granger and John Murray. Harmsen, *Antiquarianism in the Augustan Age*, pp. 118–19; on Bagford see M. M. Gatch, 'John Bagford, Bookseller and Antiquary', *British Library Journal*, 12 (1986), pp. 150–71.
126. On Vertue see Martin Myrone, 'Graphic Antiquarianism in Eighteenth-Century Britain: The Career and Reputation of George Vertue (1684–1756)', in Martin Myrone and Lucy Peltz (ed.), *Producing the Past: Aspects of Antiquarian Culture and Practice, 1700–1850* (Aldershot, 1999), pp. 35–54.
127. Valentine Green, *The Survey of the City of Worcester* (Worcester, 1764); idem, *The History and Antiquities of the City and Suburbs of Worcester*, 2 vols (Worcester, 1796); idem, *An Account of the Discovery of the Body of King John in the Cathedral Church of Worcester* (Worcester, 1797).
128. Brenda Lilian Hough, 'A Consideration of the Antiquarian and Literary Works of Joseph Strutt, with a Transcript of a Hitherto Inedited Manuscript Novel', unpublished Ph.D. thesis, University of London (1984).
129. Nichols (ed.), *Literary Anecdotes*, v, p. 670, Joseph Strutt to his future wife, Anne Blower, 27 June 1771.
130. National Library of Scotland, Adv. MS 29.5.6, fol. 167, Richard Gough to George Paton, 4 March 1778.
131. Gough, *British Topography*, i, p. xli.
132. Thomas Hearne and Edward Byrne, *Antiquities of Great Britain*, 2 vols (London, 1786–1804); Jacob Schnebbelie, *The Antiquary's Museum* (London, 1791); J. P. Malcolm, *Londinium Redivium: or An Antient History and Modern Description of London. Compiled from Parochial Records, Archives of Various Foundations, the Harleian MSS and other Authentic Sources*, 2 vols (London, 1802); J. T. Smith, *Antiquities of Westminster* (London, 1807).
133. C. A. Stothard, *The Monumental Effigies of Great Britain* (London, 1817).
134. On Carter see J. Mordaunt Cook, *John Carter and the Mind of the Gothic Revival* (London, 1995).
135. Kenneth Garlick and Angus Macintyre (ed.), *Diary of Joseph Farington*, 12 vols (New Haven and London, 1978–84), iii, p. 919, 9 November 1797.
136. *Gentleman's Magazine*, 79 (1809), pt 1, pp. 523–24, pt 2, 1097–98. See also *Gentleman's Magazine*, 71 (1801), pt 1, pp. 309–10. Carter's dispute with Whittington is discussed in chapter 7, pp. 263–64.

137. See also the careers of William Hutton, Joseph Ritson, John Britton and John Blackner.
138. I. G. Brown, 'Sir John Clerk of Penicuik (1676–1755): Aspects of a Virtuoso Life', unpublished Ph.D. thesis, University of Cambridge (1980), pp. 174–217; National Archives of Scotland, GD 18/5023 and 18/5029. Gordon's flattery of Sir John runs through *Itinerarium septentrionale.*
139. Bodleian Library, MS Ballard 42, fol. 173, Charles Lyttelton to George Ballard, 2 January 1752.
140. On the concept of the Republic of Letters see Anne Goldgar, *Impolite Learning: Conduct and Community in the Republic of Letters, 1680–1750* (London, 1995), although her thesis that the Republic was essentially redundant by the mid eighteenth century is difficult to sustain in the context of this study. Correspondence networks in the Royal Society are discussed by Andrea Rusnock, 'Correspondence Networks and the Royal Society, 1700–1750', *British Journal for the History of Science*, 32 (1999), pp. 155–69 and amongst provincial scientists by Vladimir Jankovic, 'The Place of Nature and the Nature of Place: The Chorographic Challenge to the History of British Provincial Science', *History of Science*, 38 (2000), pp. 79–113. For a comparative view of correspondence networks amongst French antiquaries see Laurence Brockliss, *Calvet's Web: Enlightenment and the Republic of Letters in Eighteenth-Century France* (Oxford, 2002).
141. Bodleian Library, MS Gough Gen. Top. 43, fol. 263, Thomas Pennant to Richard Gough, 2 June 1775.
142. Nichols (ed.), *Illustrations of Literature*, iv, p. 587, 'I have not the pleasure of being personally known to you, but the interest I take in every thing that tends to illustrate our National Antiquities will, I trust, be my apology for the liberty I take to inquire after your "History of the Counties of Cumberland and Westmoreland"', Richard Gough to Richard Burns, 28 June 1775.
143. British Library, Stowe MS 752, fos 27, 35v, Smart Lethieullier to Charles Lyttleton.
144. National Library of Scotland, Adv. MS 27.5.7 (1), fol. 1, William Cuming to Mr Balfour, 31 July 1771.
145. National Library of Scotland, Adv. MS 29.5.6 (1), fol. 234, Richard Gough to George Paton, 30 March 1780, fos 67–68; Gough to Paton, 25 February 1775.
146. National Library of Scotland, Adv. MS 29.5.7, fol. 208, Richard Gough to George Paton, 24 March 1800.
147. For an analysis of a similar network of patronage and correspondence see Geoffrey Cantor, 'The Rise and Fall of Emmanuel Mendes da Costa', *English Historical Review*, 116 (2001), pp. 584–603.
148. Bodleian Library, MS Eng. Lett. c. 358, fos 162–213; Leicestershire, Leicester and Rutland Record Office, DE 5463/11. See also Rosemary Sweet, 'John Nichols and his Circle', *Transactions of the Leicestershire Archaeological and Historical Society*, 74 (2000), pp. 1–20.
149. National Library of Scotland, Adv. MS 29.5.6 (2), fol. 93, Richard Gough to George Paton, 18 December 1787.

150. Nichols (ed.), *Literary Anecdotes*, viii, p. 739, Thomas Pennant to George Allan, 17 February 1778; Lewis (ed.), *Correspondence of Horace Walpole*, i, p. 327, William Cole to Horace Walpole, 19 May 1774.
151. National Library of Scotland, Adv. MS 29.5.7, fol. 136, George Paton to Richard Gough, 23 June 1789.
152. National Library of Scotland, Adv. MS 29.5.5 (2), fol. 112, Richard Gough to George Paton, 15 August 1784.
153. National Library of Scotland, Adv. MS 29.5.5 (2), fol. 175, Thomas Pennant to George Paton, 10 December 1791.
154. George Low *A Tour through the Islands of Orkney and Schetland: Containing Hints Relative to their Ancient, Modern and Natural History Collected in 1774* (Kirkwall, 1879), p. xlix. Pennant gave a rather different account of their dealings in his preening memoirs published as *The Literary Life of the Late Thomas Pennant* (London, 1793), pp. 37–38. 'Certain reasons', he said, 'discouraged him' from publishing Low's voyages as he had Cordiner's. Gough used information supplied by Low in *Sepulchral Monuments* and the revisions to *Britannia.*
155. Harold Carter similarly finds evidence of Pennant's unprincipled methods of obtaining information in his relationship with Joseph Banks, who was initially his protégé. He draws particular attention to Pennant's use of Banks's materials from his voyage to Iceland in *Arctic Zoology*, 2 vols (London, 1784–87), and the account of Staffa and Fingal's Cave in Pennant's, *Tour in Scotland and Voyage to the Hebrides 1772*, 2 vols (Chester, 1774–76). See Harold B. Carter, *Sir Joseph Banks* (London, 1988), pp. 42–48, 104–19.
156. Bodleian Library, MS Eng. Lett. d. 45, fol. 281v, James Philipps to Samuel Pegge, 26 July 1760. Alexander Gordon similarly fell foul of Sir John Clerk for publishing letters written by him to Roger Gale without permission in the appendix to *Itinerarium septentrionale* (London, 1727), pp. 169–87.
157. M. Summerlad, 'The Historical and Antiquarian Interest of Thomas Tanner', unpublished D.Phil. thesis, University of Oxford (1962), p. 139; British Library, Add. MS 5834, fol. 108v, William Cole to Richard Gough, 20 August 1781, 'I am going to do what I never yet did to any one, except to Mr Walpole; entrust you with one of my volumes.'
158. Norfolk and Norwich Record Office, MS Rye 32, fol. 58, Beaupré Bell to Francis Blomefield, 10 December 1735.
159. Quoted in D. C. Coxe, *'This Foolish Business': Dr Nash and the Worcestershire Collections*, Worcestershire Historical Collections, 7 (1993), p. 21.
160. The phrase comes from Mark Noble, *A History of the College of Arms* (London, 1805), p. 433, quoted in Wagner, *Heralds of England*, p. 415. Brooke, who had started life as the son of a doctor apprenticed to an apothecary, died aged forty-five in 1794, killed in a stampede at the Haymarket Theatre with fellow herald Benjamin Pingo. He was said to have been worth at least £14,000 – evidently most of his clients were more profitable than Nash.
161. Bodleian Library, MS Eng. Lett. b. 13, fol. 32, Treadway Nash to Richard Gough, 6 August 1779; ibid., fol. 33v, Gough to Nash, 7 August 1779; see also

Bodleian Library MS Eng. Lett. e. 98, fos 53v, 78; see also Nichols (ed.), *Literary Illustrations*, vi, p. 351, Nash to Gough, 6 August, 1778 and Coxe, *'This Foolish Business'*.

162. Raine, *Memoir of the Revd John Hodgson*, i, p. 167, John Hodgson to Nicholas Carlisle, March 1815.
163. Bodleian Library, MS Eng. Lett. c. 364, fos 83–193
164. Bodleian Library, MS Eng. Lett. c. 360, fos 128–60. William Bray, the Surrey antiquary, was also lending Ruding money. Surrey History Centre, MS 85/1/46, diary entry for 14 November 1803.
165. Nichols (ed.), *Illustrations of Literature*, v, p. 354, Peck to Blomefield, 27 June 1734. Blomefield was the author of *An Essay Towards a Topographical History of the County of Norfolk*, 5 vols (Fersfield, 1739–75).
166. British Library, Stowe MS 752, fol. 136.
167. Alan Everitt, introduction to Edward Hasted, *The History and Topographical Survey of the County of Kent*, 12 vols (Wakefield, 1972), i, p. xvi.
168. Lewis (ed.), *Correspondence of Horace Walpole*, ii, pp. 164–65, Walpole to William Cole, 2 June 1779.
169. National Library of Scotland, Adv. MS 29.3.8, fol. 125, George Chalmers to George Paton, December 1775.
170. Raine, *Memoir of the Rev John Hodgson*, i, p. 169, Rogers Ruding to John Hodgson, 8 May 1815.
171. Francis Drake, *Eboracum: or The History and Antiquities of the City of York from its Original to the Present Time* (London, 1736), preface. See also the earl of Pembroke's efforts on behalf of Alexander Gordon's *Itinerarium septentrionale* described in chapter 5 above.
172. On the place of women in the Republic of Letters, albeit in a French context, see Dena Goodman's interpretation, *The Republic of Letters: A Cultural History of the French Enlightenment* (London, 1994).
173. On Sarah Banks see John Gascoigne, *Joseph Banks and the English Enlightenment: Useful Knowledge and Polite Culture* (Cambridge, 1994), p. 67. Her collections were bequeathed to the British Museum.
174. Bodleian Library, MS Eng. Lett. b. 2, fol. 50. Mrs Bertram was so moved by the reading that she had to get up and wipe the image of the 'dear Dr's face' that was hanging on the wall.
175. Susanna Watts, *A Walk Through Leicester* (Leicester, 1804). Watts was an evangelical campaigner on abolition and political reform and a correspondent of John Nichols (Bodleian Library MS Eng. Lett. c. 368 et seq). Her *Walk through Leicester* was essentially an antiquarian tour, based upon the learning of 'Mr Nichols, Mr Camden, Mr Peck and Mr Throsby'. Watt also prepared a translation of Tasso which was advertised in the *Gentleman's Magazine* in 1797 and attracted a number of aristocratic women subscribers; it was, however, never published. On Watts and her political activities, see Kenneth Corfield, 'Elizabeth Heyrick: Radical Quaker', in Gail Malmgreen (ed.), *Religion in the Lives of English Women, 1760–1930* (Bloomington and Indianapolis, 1986), pp. 41–67.

176. Samuel Pegge, 'An Historical Account of that Venerable Monument of Antiquity the Textus Roffensis; including Memoirs of the Learned Saxonists Mr William Elstob and his Sister', *Bibliotheca topographica britannica*, 1 (1784), p. 26.
177. Bodleian Library, MS Eng. Lett. c. 355, fol. 16, Anna Clarke to John Nichols, 10 June 1819.
178. George Ballard, *Memoirs of Several Ladies of Great Britain who have been Celebrated for their Writings or Skill in the Learned Languages, Arts and Sciences* (Oxford, 1752).
179. Bodleian Library, MS Ballard 42, fol. 30v, George Ballard to Charles Lyttleton, no date.
180. Bodleian Library, MS Ballard 43, fol. 29, Elizabeth Elstob to George Ballard, 4 December 1736. On Elstob see Sarah Huff Collins, 'The Elstobs and the End of the Saxon Revival', in Carl T. Berkhout and Milton McC. Gatch (ed.), *Anglo-Saxon Scholarship: The First Three Centuries* (Boston Massachusetts, 1982), pp. 107–18, and ibid., Shaun F. D. Hughes, 'The Anglo-Saxon Grammars of George Hickes and Elizabeth Elstob', pp. 119–47; Richard Morton, 'Elizabeth Elstob's *Rudiments of Grammar* (1715): Germanic Philology for Women', *Studies in Eighteenth-Century Culture*, 20 (1990), pp. 267–87; M. J. Murphy, 'The Elstobs, Scholars of Old English and Anglican Apologists', *Durham University Journal*, 58 (1966), pp. 131–38; Kathryn Sutherland, 'Editing for a New Century: Elizabeth Elstob's Anglo-Saxon Manifesto and Aelfric's St Gregory Homily', in D. G. Scragg and Paul E. Szarmach (ed.), *The Editing of Old English: Papers from the 1990 Manchester Conference* (Cambridge, 1994), pp. 213–37.
181. British Library, Add. MS 4312, fol. 314, Charles Lyttelton to Thomas Birch, 9 April 1753.
182. This issue is discussed at some length by Daniel Woolf, 'A Feminine Past? Gender, Genre, and Historical Knowledge in England, 1500–1800', *American Historical Review*, 102 (1997), pp. 645–79.
183. Mark Salber Philips, '"If Mrs Mure be not Sorry for Poor King Charles": History, the Novel, and the Sentimental Reader', *History Workshop Journal*, 43 (1997), pp. 111–31.
184. J. Hunter (ed.), *The Diary of Ralph Thoresby, 1677–1724*, 2 vols (London, 1830), ii, p. 302, 19 October 1720.
185. There were exceptions: the surveyor and antiquary Thomas Wright was employed by a number of aristocratic families to teach the ladies mathematics, geometry, the use of globes and surveying. The duchess of Kent managed to produce a plan of the gardens at Wrest Park as a result. Edward Hughes, 'The Early Journals of Thomas Wright of Durham', *Annals of Science*, 28 (1951), p. 14. My thanks to Paul Elliott for providing information on this and other points.
186. John Rylands Library, MS 1124, fol. 200.
187. R. P. Harris, *A History of the Library of the British Museum* (London, 1998). In the 1820s John Hodgson was assisted by Emma Trevelyan, niece of Sir Walter Cavlerley Trevelyan, who was a frequent copyist in the British Museum

on his account during family trips to London. Raine, *Memoir of the Revd John Hodgson*, i, pp. 302–3.

188. Francis Griffin Stokes (ed.), *The Blecheley Diary of the Rev. William Cole, 1765–67* (London, 1931), p. 263.
189. These findings are largely consonant with those of Woolf in *Reading History*, pp. 309–11, where he analyses the subscription lists to twenty-seven historical works, many of which were antiquarian. The Boyle women were also amongst the twenty-seven women (17 per cent of the total list) subscribing to Aaron Thompson's edition of Geoffrey of Monmouth's *British History*.
190. Gordon, *Itinerarium septentrionale*; Woolf, 'A Feminine Past?', notes that there were no female subscribers to Francis Wise's edition of Asser, *Annales rerum gestarum Alfredi magni* (Oxford, 1722) or Edward Lhwyd's *Archaeologica britannica* (Oxford, 1707). See also Woolf, *Reading History*, pp. 302–10.
191. Woolf, 'A Feminine Past?', p. 647.
192. Woolf cites the example of the Essex antiquary, William Holman, who was referred by local gentry and fellow antiquaries to wives, mothers and sisters as sources of genealogical information.
193. Lewis (ed.), *Correspondence of Horace Walpole*, i, p. 218, Walpole to Cole, 11 June 1771; ibid., x, p. 148, Walpole to George Montague, 18 February 1765; ibid., ii, p. 250, Walpole to Cole, 20 November 1780.
194. Lewis (ed.), *Correspondence of Horace Walpole*, ii, p. 182, Cole to Walpole, 30 December 1779.
195. Archdall was the author of *Monasticon Hibernicum: or A History of the Abbeys, Priories, and Other Religious Houses in Ireland* (London, 1786), and a revised edition of John Lodge, *The Peerage of Ireland: or A Genealogical History of the Present Nobility of that Kingdom* (London, 1789). Information on Mrs Archdall from *Dictionary of National Biography*.
196. British Library, Add MS 37219, fol. 137, Philip Morant to Andrew Coltée Ducarel, 7 October 1758; Add MS 37218, fol. 57, Morant to Ducarel, 28 December 1762; Add MS 37219, fol. 123, Ducarel to Morant, 30 September 1758.
197. British Library, Add MS 37219, fol. 12, Ducarel to Morant, 15 September 1753.
198. Thomas Cocke, *The Ingenious Mr Essex, Architect* (Cambridge, 1984), p. 3.
199. Edward King, *Munimenta Antiqua: or Observations on Ancient Castles*, 4 vols (London, 1799), i, p. xii.
200. Ronald Jessup, *Man of Many Talents: An Informal Biography of James Douglas, 1753–1819* (Buckingham, 1975), p. 137.
201. Robert H. Cunnington, ed. James Dyer, *From Antiquary to Archaeologist. A Biography of William Cunnington, 1754–1810* (Buckingham, 1975), p. 46.
202. Stuart Piggott, *William Stukeley: An Eighteenth-Century Antiquary* (2nd edn, London, 1985), pp. 53–56. Piggott describes Mrs Stukeley as 'a woman of some intellectual attainments' who had been a pupil of Mattaire, the classical scholar (p. 76). On the Society of Roman Knights see Bodleian Library, MS Eng. Misc. c. 401.
203. National Archives of Scotland, GD 18 5023/1, William Stukeley to Alexander Gordon, 25 September 1723.

204. Nichols (ed.), *Illustrations of Literature*, ii, p. 16, William Warburton to William Stukeley, 9 May 1732. Warburton had no high opinion of Peck, commenting that, like the woodcock, his guts were better than his brains, ibid., p. 38.
205. Quoted in Piggott, *William Stukeley*, p. 142. At the time that Anna Fairchild (as she then was) was writing the White Horse was commonly believed to have been the work of the Saxons. Piggott points out that it was not attributed to the ancient Britons (i.e. Iron Age) again until the end of the nineteenth century.
206. Marcia Pointon, 'Abundant Leisure and Extensive Knowledge: Dorothy Richardson Delineates', in *Strategies for Showing: Women, Possession and Representation in English Visual Culture, 1665–1800* (Oxford, 1997), pp. 89–130.
207. John Rylands Library, MS 1122, fos 178–89; MS 1125, fol. 84
208. John Rylands Library, MS 1155, fos 154–55.
209. Nichols (ed.), *Illustrations of Literature*, i, p. 245; Joseph Thomas Fowler (ed.), *The Correspondence of William Fowler of Winterton in the County of Lincoln* (privately printed, 1907), p. 46.
210. Nichols (ed.), *Illustrations of Literature*, i, pp. 225–52.
211. *Vetusta monumenta*, iii, plate 43.
212. Mark Girouard, *The Return of Camelot: Chivalry and the English Gentleman* (New Haven and London, 1981), p. 22; J. B. de la Curne de Sainte Palaye *Mémoires de l'ancienne chevalerie*, 2 vols (Paris, 1759), third volume (Paris, 1781), and idem, *Histoire littéraire des troubadours* (Paris, 1774). Both works were translated into English by Susan Dobson (d. 1795) and published as *Literary History of the Troubadors* (London, 1779; 2nd edn, 1807); *Memoirs of Ancient Chivalry* (London, 1784).
213. See for example, John Rylands Library, MS 1123, fol. 40 (describing West Wycombe).
214. John Rylands Library, MS 1122, fol. 108.
215. John Rylands Library, MS 1122, fol. 182; William Gilpin, *Observations on the Mountains and Lakes of Cumberland and Westmoreland*, 2 vols (London, 1786), ii, p. 188. Gilpin was less specific in his objections than Richardson, referring to a 'ridiculous figure' raised upon the 'fragments of the old pavement'.
216. See chapter 9.
217. Clark, *British Clubs and Societies*, pp. 111, 444–45; on local societies see chapter 3.

Notes to Chapter 3: Antiquarian Societies

1. Joseph Hunter (ed.), *Letters of Eminent Men, Addressed to Ralph Thoresby, FRS, Now First Published from the Originals*, 2 vols (London, 1832), i, p. 138, William Nicolson to Ralph Thoresby, 23 June 1693.
2. Ibid., p. 162, Nicolson to Thoresby, 7 May 1764.
3. Larry Stewart, *The Rise of Public Science: Rhetoric, Technology, and Natural Philosophy in Newtonian Britain, 1660–1750* (Cambridge, 1992), and idem, 'Other Centres of Calculation: or Where the Royal Society Didn't Count.

Commerce, Coffee-houses and Natural Philosophy in Early Modern London', *British Journal for the History of Science*, 32 (1999), pp. 133–53.

4. Nichols (ed.), *Illustrations of Literature*, iii, p. 413, Thomas Tanner to Peter Le Neve, 18 March 1701/2.
5. Peter Clark, *British Clubs and Societies, 1580–1800: The Origins of an Associational World* (Oxford, 2000). See also R. Allen, *The Clubs of Augustan England* (Cambridge, Massachusetts, 1933).
6. Richard Gough, 'Introduction', *Archaeologia*, 1 (1770), pp. iii–xxiv; Linda van Norden, 'Peiresc and the English Scholars', *Huntington Library Quarterly*, 12 (1949), pp. 369–90, and eadem, 'Sir Henry Spelman and the Chronology of the Elizabethan College of Antiquaries', *Huntington Library Quarterly*, 13 (1950), pp. 131–60. See also F. S. Fussner, *The Historical Revolution: English Historical Writing and Thought, 1580–1640* (London, 1962), chapter 4; C. E. Wright, 'The Elizabethan Society of Antiquaries and the Formation of the Cotton Library', in F. Wormald and C. E. Wright (ed.), *The English Library before 1700* (London, 1958).
7. Nichols (ed.), *Literary Anecdotes*, v, p. 466.
8. Thomas Clerk, *A List of the Royal Society of London* (London, 1718), reprinted in Charles Weld, *A History of the Royal Society*, 2 vols (London, 1848; reprinted 1975), i, p. 427.
9. Wanley's draft for a constitution referred to an Antiquity Society set up in Germany by the last emperor, a college at Uppsala and a meeting in Edinburgh, as well as the Académie des Belles Lettres in France. Joan Evans, *A History of the Society of Antiquaries* (Oxford, 1956), p. 41.
10. Society of Antiquaries, MS 265, fol. 73 v, articles of foundation.
11. National Archives of Scotland, GD 18/5030/3; Gough, 'Introduction', p. xxxviii, attributing the decline in attendance to the death of Winchelsea, the departure of Stukeley and the failure of members such as Roger Gale and Peter Le Neve to attend.
12. Richard Rawlinson was particularly pressing that the society should secure a charter. The quarrel he had with the society, which caused him to bequeath his collections to the Bodleian Library instead, took place after incorporation.
13. 'At the Antiquarian Society they debated the affair of Lord Colrain's donation to them of all his books of prints and antiquitys, but by the advice of the learned in the law, they cannot receive that donation, their society being nominal only. Dr Rawlinson spoke that it was high time to think of obtaining a charter, and of removing from a tavern to a place where they could be secure of what they already had.' W. C. Lukis (ed.), 'Family Memoirs of William Stukeley, vol. ii', *Surtees Society*, 73 (1883), p. 366, diary entry, 9 November 1749.
14. John Evans, *History of the Society of Antiquaries* (Oxford, 1956), pp. 44, 100–12.
15. Folkes was elected to the presidency of the Royal Society in 1745 and to the Society of Antiquaries in 1750, following the death of the duke of Richmond.

On Folkes's role in proceedings see David Boyd Haycock, '"The Cabal of a Few Designing Members": The Presidency of Martin Folkes, PRS, and the Society's First Charter', *Antiquaries Journal*, 80 (2000), pp. 273–84.

16. George Vertue, who was one of those who opposed incorporation, claimed that several attempts had already been made to unite the Antiquaries with the Royal Society. Gough, 'Introduction', p. xxxviii.
17. Lukis (ed.), 'Family Memoirs of William Stukeley, vol. ii', *Surtees Society*, 73 (1883), p. 373, diary entry, 27 February 1752.
18. Nichols (ed.) *Literary Anecdotes*, v, p. 441, George North to Andrew Coltée Ducarel, 21 March, 1750/1.
19. Society of Antiquaries, Minute Books vii, fol. 5, 19 December 1751.
20. British Library, Add. MS 23900, fol. 28, Robert Lumley Kingston to Andrew Coltée Ducarel, no date.
21. Clark, *British Clubs and Societies*, pp. 97–98.
22. Society of Antiquaries, Minute Books, vii, fol. 60v, 26 April 1753.
23. Of the sixty-three individuals named in Sir Hans Sloane's will as trustees of the British Museum half were members of the Society of Antiquaries and forty were fellows of the Royal Society. Arthur MacGregor (ed.), *Sir Hans Sloane: Collector, Scientist, Antiquary, Founding Father of the British Museum* (London, 1994), p. 48.
24. Evans, *Society of Antiquaries*, p. 104.
25. Society of Antiquaries, Minute Books, vii (typescript), p. 240, 2 May 1754: motion that the society should apply for copies of the plan followed by the Académie des Belles Lettres et Inscriptions.
26. Evans identifies Theobald as one of those trying to impose reforms upon the society in the 1730s.
27. During the following year he received only one other parochial account from Hopton Norfolk. In 1756 an account of Elton in Huntingdonshire was sent in, followed by accounts from Monmouthshire in 1758 and Sherborne in 1759. See Sociaty of Antiquaries, MS 115. The questionnaire reappeared in various guises throughout the century, however, not least in that drawn up by Peter Muilman, which eventually provided the grounds for his expulsion from the society (see below), and in another abortive proposal to coordinate a series of county surveys of antiquities from the members in 1771. See Society of Antiquaries, Council Minute Book, i, 3 March 1771.
28. Society of Antiquaries, Minute Books, vii (typescript), p. 478, 11 November 1756.
29. Theobald provided accounts of the water gate at the end of Buckingham Street in York Buildings, which was soon to be dismantled; of the fate of the collection of Arundel marbles (he was able to report that one of the columns was currently in use as a roller for his bowling green at White Waltham); and of the rise and progress of the Society for the Encouragement of Arts and Manufactures, of which both he and Baker were founder members. Society of Antiquaries, Minute Books, viii (typescript), p. 66, 5 May 1757; p. 219, 11

May 1758; p. 228 1 June 1758. See also David G. C. Allan and J. H. Appleby, 'James Theobald's "Missing" MS History of the Society of Arts and his "Chronological Register of the Present Age"', *Antiquaries Journal*, 76 (1996), pp. 201–14. Other antiquaries who also belonged to the Society of Arts included Thomas Brand, Gustavus Brander, Sir Henry Cheere, Thomas Hollis, the earl of Macclesfield, James Stuart, Charles Morton and Philip Carteret Webb.

30. J. B. Harley, 'The Society of Arts and the Surveys of English Counties, 1759–1809', *Journal of the Society of Arts*, 112 (1963–4), pp. 43–46, 119–24, 269–75, 538–43. Competition with France was a driving force behind this project also: there was a strong sense that Britain lagged behind France, where Louis XV had commissioned a map of the whole country upon a trigonometrical framework.
31. Nichols (ed.), *Illustrations of Literature*, vi, p. 502, earl of Buchan to John Nichols, 8 June 1783. Two parochial accounts were published in the *Transactions* of the Scottish Society of Antiquaries (1792), and were described by George Paton as being executed upon a more extensive plan than those of the *Statistical Account*. National Library of Scotland, Adv. MS 29.5.7 (4), fol. 179, 4 July 1792.
32. Rosalind Mitchison, *Agricultural Sir John: The Life of Sir John Sinclair of Ulbster, 1754–1835* (London, 1962), pp. 120–36.
33. Sir Henry Lyons, *The Royal Society, 1660–1940* (Cambridge, 1944), p. 163.
34. The only member who specifically responded to this was, predictably, James Theobald, who reported in the following December that he had collected addenda to Lewis's history of Thanet which he proposed to insert in the society's copy of the book. Minute Books, vii (typescript), p. 466, 24 June 1756; p. 489, 9 December 1756.
35. Society of Antiquaries, Minute Books, vii (typescript), p. 385, 20 November 1755; Minute Books, viii (typescript), p. 224, 25 May 1758.
36. Society of Antiquaries, Minute Books, vii (typescript), p. 438, 1 April 1756; viii (typescript), pp. 41–42, 24 March 1757; p. 110, 8 December 1757. See also Henry Ellis's interleaved copy of Philip Carteret Webb, *A Short Account of Some Particulars Concerning Domesday Book* (London, 1756) which includes much of the correspondence generated from this project and the negotiations which took place over publication, British Library, Add. MS 38541.
37. Bodleian Library, MS Top. London c. 2, fos 187–88.
38. Martin Folkes, *A Table of English Gold Coins from the 18th Year of King Edward III when Gold was first Coined in England* (London, 1736); idem, *A Table of English Silver Coins from the Norman Conquest to the Present Time* (1745); idem, *Tables of English Silver and Gold Coins, First Published by Martin Folkes Esq, 1736–45, and Now Reprinted* (London, 1763).
39. Bodleian Library, MS Top. London c. 2, fol. 192.
40. Society of Antiquaries, Minute Books, vii (typescript), p. 156, 28 June 1753; p. 207, 24 Jan 1754.
41. Evans, *History of the Society of Antiquaries*, p. 139.
42. William Blackstone observed that 'it were much to be wished that all

gentlemen, who are possessed of similar curiosities [a copy of the Great Charter], would follow so laudable an example, by placing them in some public repositary. The collecting and hoarding of antiquities, which, when confined to private amusement and self-satisfaction only, are too justly the object of ridicule, would then be of singular advantage to the public. However, we may congratulate the present age on the prospect there is of seeing the paths to these hidden treasures made sufficiently easy and commodious, not only by the immense fund of antient learning which the wisdom of the legislature has amassed together and deposited in the British Museum; but also by a plan which has long employed the attention of the noble and honourable trustees of the Radcliffe library in Oxford, for transferring to that august edifice, all the MSS which are at present the property of the university, and the appropriating it for the future to the reception of MSS only.' William Blackstone, *The Great Charter and the Charter of the Forest, with other Authentic Instruments: To Which is Prefixed an Introductory Discourse, Containing the History of the Charters* (Oxford, 1759), p. xxxv.

43. Lionel Cust, *History of the Society of Dilettanti*, ed. Sidney Colvin (London, 1898). Although none of the founder members belonged to the Society of Antiquaries, in the course of time several antiquaries would hold dual membership with the Dilettanti, such as Sir Joseph Banks and James 'Athenian' Stuart, joint author with Nicholas Revett of *Antiquities of Athens* (London, 1762).

44. A scheme for establishing an Academy of Arts was mooted in 1748/9 but foundered on resistance on the part of the artists concerned (members of the St Martins Academy) to the Dilettanti's attempts to assert overriding control over the proposed academy. In 1774 it was decided to devote the interest on £4000 at 3 per cent annuities to sending two young artists abroad to study in Greece or Italy for a period of three years. Cust and Colvin, *History of the Society of Dilettanti*, pp. 52–57. See also John Brewer, *The Pleasures of the Imagination: English Culture in the Eighteenth Century* (London, 1997), pp. 257–61.

45. By 1760 444 fellows had been elected to the society; excluding the honorary fellows, this left 419 members, of whom only forty-seven, or just over 10 per cent, are known to have travelled to Italy. John Ingamells, *A Dictionary of British and Irish Travellers in Italy, 1701–1800* (New Haven and London, 1998). Seven of these travellers were, or would become members of the Society of Dilettanti, for which, according to Horace Walpole, the nominal qualification was to have travelled to Italy, the real one, to have been drunk. W. S. Lewis (ed.), *The Yale Edition of Horace Walpole's Correspondence* (Oxford, 1937–83), xviii, p. 211, Walpole to Horace Mann, 14 April 1743.

46. Brinsley Ford, 'James Byres: Principal Antiquarian for the English Visitors to Rome', *Apollo*, 99 (1974), pp. 446–61, and 'Thomas Jenkins: Banker, Dealer and Unofficial English Agent', ibid., pp. 416–25.

47. Society of Antiquaries, MS 264, fos 44–45, 'Extract of Two Letters from Signor Camillo Paderni at Rome to Mr Allan Ramsay, Painter in Covent Garden,

Concerning Some Ancient Statues, Pictures and other Curiosity's Found in a Subterranean Town, Lately Discovered near Naples, Translated from the Italian by Mr Ramsay and Sent by him to Mr Ward', dated 20 November 1739 and 20 February 1740; *Memoirs Concerning Herculaneum, the Subterranean City* (London, 1750); Monsignor Bellicard, *Observations upon the Antiquities of the Town of Herculaneum, Discovered at the Foot of Mount Vesuvius: With some Reflections on the Painting and Sculpture of the Ancients and a Short Description of the Antiquities in the Neighbourhood of Naples* (London, 1753); Thomas Martyn and John Lettice, *The Antiquities of Herculaneum: Translated from the Italian* (London, 1757).

48. Don Francesco Valetta, a member of the 'Academy for explaining the antiquities of Herculaneum instituted by the King of Naples', was elected in 1756; his election was followed a few months later by that of Signor Camillo Paderni, keeper of the museum at Herculaneum.
49. Gough's influence is discussed in greater detail in Rosemary Sweet, 'Antiquaries and Antiquities in Eighteenth-Century England', *Eighteenth-Century Studies*, 34 (2001), pp. 181–206.
50. British Library, Add. MS 29944, fol. 134v, Richard Gough to Foote Gower, 18 February 1768.
51. Average attendance in 1752 was twenty, in 1762 it was fifteen. This does not include attendance at the meeting on 23 April when numbers were always much higher on the occasion of the elections and the anniversary dinner.
52. In 1773 bound copies of the second volume of *Archaeologia* were presented to the Society of Mannheim, the Society of St Petersburg and the University of Göttingen. In 1777 volumes were exchanged with the Imperial College and Royal Academy of Sciences and Belles Lettres of Brussels and the Society of Antiquaries at Hesse Cassell (Society of Antiquaries, Council Minute Book, ii, 1 December 1777 and 3 February 1778).
53. John Whitaker, *The History of Manchester in Four Volumes*, 2 vols (2nd edn, London, 1773), i, p. 136.
54. John Watson, *The History and Antiquities of the Parish of Halifax* (London, 1775), p. v.
55. Society of Antiquaries, MS 447/1, fol. 82, Jeremiah Milles to Richard Gough, 17 May 1774, fol. 88, Gough to Milles, 18 May 1774, fol. 99 v, Gough to Milles, 30 Sept 1774, fol. 101, Milles to Gough, 8 Oct 1774, fol. 111, Milles to Gough, 27 November 1774. The paper which so offended Percy was Samuel Pegge's, 'Observations on Dr Percy's Account of Minstrels among the Saxons', *Archaeologia*, 2 (1773), pp. 100–6.
56. Bodleian Library, MS Gough Gen. Top. 44, fol. 458, Richard Gough to Michael Tyson, 20 March 1780. Nichols (ed.), *Literary Anecdotes*, viii, p. 664. Edward Hasted made similarly scathing comments to Andrew Coltée Ducarel: 'Our Transactions of the Antiquarian Society have done us so little credit, that we are rather out of humour with the compilers of it.' Nichols (ed.), *Literary Illustrations*, iv, p. 648, 18 February 1771.

57. British Library, Add. MS 5834, fol. 105, Richard Gough to William Cole, 22 January 1781.
58. See for example, Gough's letter to Michael Lort, Society of Antiquaries, MS 447/2, fos 124–26, 29 Januray 1778.
59. West Suffolk Record Office E2/22/2, unfoliated collection, Michael Lort to George Ashby, 6 March 1781.
60. Society of Antiquaries, MS 447/2, fol. 88, Richard Gough to Michael Lort, 11 December 1776. The papers in question were Daines Barrington, 'Observations on Patriarchal Customs and Manners', *Archaeologia*, 5 (1779), pp. 119–36, and Samuel Pegge, 'Examination of the Mistaken Opinion that Ireland and Thanet Were Void of Serpents', *Archaeologia*, 5 (1779), pp. 160–65.
61. Society of Antiquaries, Council Minute Book, ii, 21 June 1775.
62. Society of Antiquaries, MS 447/2, fol. 134, Michael Lort to Richard Gough, 26 January 1778.
63. Society of Antiquaries, Council Minute Book, ii, 8 July 1778.
64. Ibid., ii, 23 November 1779.
65. It was so large that it could not be accommodated within a wagon and had to be transported from Kent to London by hoy instead.
66. Roy Strong, *And When Did You Last See your Father? The Victorian Painter and British History* (London, 1978), pp. 13–29; Peter Cannon Brookes (ed.), *The Painted Word: British History Painting, 1750–1830* (Woodbridge, 1991).
67. 'From the judicious Investigation of ancient Science, and Art, a more general and useful Field of Knowledge is opened to the modern Artist. The most valuable Hints for the Direction of his Studies are to be collected from the Works of Antiquaries; and the Repositories of Arts have been enriched with a Variety of necessary Information from the same Source.' Society of Antiquaries, Minute Books, xvii, p. 220, 11 January 1781.
68. Society of Antiquaries, Minute Books, xvi, p. 223, 25 February 1779. Michael Lort had written to Lord Hardwick the previous year, telling him how a 'good puffing' description of the print had been drawn up at the last council meeting: 'we had almost thought of sending Hawkers down to the respective encampments to circulate that & Sir Joseph's [Ayloffe] historical description, but this the Baronet thought would be degrading his & our own dignities', British Library, Add. MS 35614, fol. 277, Michael Lort to Lord Hardwick, 9 July 1778.
69. Society of Antiquaries, MS 447/2, fol. 59, Michael Lort to Richard Gough, 11 May 1775.
70. West Suffolk Record Office, E2/22/1 unfoliated collection, Richard Gough to George Ashby, 14 February 1776. See also Gough's letter to Samuel Pegge, Society of Antiquaries, MS 447/3, fol. 91, 8 May 1775. The outcome of the ballot to go ahead with the Cowdray print was won by a narrow majority of 8:6. Society of Antiquaries, Council Minute Book, ii, 21 June 1775.
71. West Suffolk Record Office, E2/22/1, unfoliated collection Richard Gough to George Ashby; Gough, *British Topography*, i, p. xli.
72. Society of Antiquaries, MS 447/1, fol. 215, Richard Gough to Jeremiah Milles,

undated letter, *c.* 1780. The text of the letter is reproduced in Evans, *History of the Society of Antiquaries*, p. 180.

73. As Alexander Chalmers put it in his biographical memoir: 'His talents, his rank in society, and his years, gave him claims to respect, which were, what he thought them, undeniable; and even where he shewed any symptoms of resentment, they were never beyond the limits which his superior character and long services amply justified.' Bodleian Library, MS Top. Gen. c. 7, p. 14.
74. Society of Antiquaries, Council Minute Book, ii, 17 January 1776; 6 February 1776; 9 March 1776. See also the account by Evans in *History of the Society of Antiquaries*, pp. 170–77, although she confuses Lord North with his brother.
75. Society of Antiquaries, MS 447/1, fol. 157, Jeremiah Milles to Richard Gough, 12 February 1776. It was decided to have moreen curtains (a stout woollen or wool and cloth fabric) in the meeting room and to order twelve chairs with horsehair seats for the library at a cost of twenty shillings each, and a couple of brass chandeliers. The mace had to be regilded, the president's chair 'beautified' and the timepiece and the ballot box were both deemed to be unsuitable to the dignity of the society. One of the largest items of expenditure was a marble bust of their royal patron, costing 100 guineas.
76. West Suffolk Record Office, E/2/22/1, unfoliated collection, Michael Lort to George Ashby, 3 March 1781.
77. *A Speech Delivered by Edward King, Esq., President of the Society of Antiquaries of London* (London, 1784), p. 4.
78. See for example, Thomas Shadwell's play *The Virtuoso*. W. E. Houghton, 'The English Virtuoso in the Seventeenth Century', *Journal of the History of Ideas*, 3 (1942), pp. 51–73, 190–219. As John Gascoigne points out in *Joseph Banks and the English Enlightenment: Useful Knowledge and Polite Culture* (Cambridge, 1994), p. 61, Houghton's argument that the figure of the virtuoso disappeared as a cultural type in the early eighteenth century is untenable in view of the life and interests of individuals who combined natural history, antiquities and travel such as Sir Joseph Banks, or, on a lesser scale, many of the individuals discussed in this volume. See also chapter 1.
79. W. S. Lewis (ed.), *Correspondence of Horace Walpole*, i, p. 265, Walpole to Cole, 7 July 1772, and p. 270, Walpole to Cole, 28 July 1772.
80. Francis Grose, *The Grumbler: Being a Collection of Sixteen Essays* (London, 1791) and *The Olio: Being a Collection of Essays, Dialogues, Letters, Biographical Sketches, Anecdotes, Pieces of Poetry, Parodies, Bon Mots, Epigrams, Epitaphs &c., Chiefly Original* (London, 1792).
81. *A Speech Delivered by Edward King*, pp. 5, 11.
82. John Pinkerton 'Letters to the People of Great Britain on their Cultivation of their National History', *Gentleman's Magazine*, 58 (1788), pt 2, p. 1150.
83. Pinkerton, 'Letters to the People of Great Britain on the Cultivation of their National History', pp. 1149–51.
84. Three years earlier Michael Lort had rejected the notion of premiums of this kind, on the grounds that 'the determination of which is often unpleasant

and invidious'. Nichols (ed.), *Illustrations of Literature*, vii, p. 469, Michael Lort to Thomas Percy, 24 June 1785.

85. The Hibernian Society of Antiquaries (1780–83) was founded by William Burton Conyngham, Mervyn Archdall, Charles Vallancey, Edward Ledwich, Charles O'Connor and William Beauford. Matters went 'very well' at first, but the strain upon Ledwich of moderating his comments on Vallancey's wilder speculations proved too much. 'By the lively jocular way in which he wrote, [Ledwich] offended Colonel Valancey [sic], who expatriated him from his Collectanea, and from a Society which immediately ceased.' *Gentleman's Magazine*, 66 (1796), p. 528. Following the failure of the Hibernian Society, the Royal Irish Academy, established in 1788, comprehended antiquities within its inquiries. On the latter society see T. O'Raifeartaigh (ed.), *The Royal Irish Academy* (Dublin, 1985).
86. Nichols (ed.), *Illustrations of Literature*, vii, p. 469, Michael Lort to Thomas Percy, 24 June 1785.
87. John Nichols (ed.), *Bibliotheca topographica britannica*, 1 (1780), pp. i–iii, drew particular attention to this failure of the society to produce anything of note.
88. Society of Antiquaries, MS 891/1, unfoliated collection, Hayman Rooke to Samuel Pegge, 18 May 1785.
89. Harold B. Carter, *Sir Joseph Banks* (1988), p. 32. Two of the sponsors were the same in each case: Charles Lyttelton and Charles Morton. Gascoigne, *Joseph Banks and the English Enlightenment*, p. 123.
90. His correspondence with Gough on Lincolnshire history and antiquities is printed in Nichols (ed.), *Illustrations of Literature*, iv, pp. 694–99. See also Gascoigne, *Joseph Banks*, pp. 124–26.
91. Lyons, *The Royal Society*, pp. 212–14; P. H. Maty, *An Authentic Narrative of the Dissensions and Debates in the Royal Society* (London, 1784); Andrew Kippis, *Observations on the Late Contests in the Royal Society* (London, 1784).
92. Gascoigne, *Joseph Banks and the English Enlightenment*, p. 121.
93. Lindsay Fleming, *Memoir and Select Letters of Samuel Lysons VPRS and VPSA, 1763–1819* (Oxford, no date), pp. 17, 21–22. On 2 January 1794 he wrote to Banks reporting on progress made to date: 'As you have been so good as to furnish me with the means of carrying on a winter Campaign, I think I ought to give you some account of my proceedings.'
94. See chapter8, pp. 288–95.
95. Society of Antiquaries, MS 891/1, unfoliated collection, Samuel Pegge junior to Hayman Rooke, 13 March 1798.
96. J. Mordaunt Crook, 'The Surveyorship of James Wyatt', in Howard Colvin (ed.), *A History of the King's Works*, 6 vols (London, 1973), vi, pp. 49–76.
97. Society of Antiquaries, Minute Books, xxiv, pp. 225, 335–37, 345–47, 360–66, 368. See also Kenneth Garlick and Angus Macintyre (ed.), *The Diary of Joseph Farington*, 12 vols (New Haven and London, 1978–84), iv, pp. 1227, 1235.
98. Evans, *History of the Society of Antiquaries*, p. 212. A committee was deputed to report on the state of affairs vis à vis Carter's cathedral engravings in 1799.

Carter had completed Exeter, Bath and Durham (yet to be engraved) and had work in hand for Gloucester and Wells, for which he had not been paid.

99. Details of the negotiations preceding the election were recorded by Joseph Farington; see Garlick and Macintyre (ed.), *Diary of Joseph Farington*, iv, pp. 1161, 1163, 1168, 1169, 1173, 1174, 1176, 1182, 1185, 1187, 1188, 1191, 1192, 1193, 1204, 1208–10.
100. 'There were more violent contests in the Society of Antiquaries on St George's day. A Set of Gentlemen, who wish to remove the President and all the Officers, set up a new Candidate (Lord Lewisham) for the Chair, with an Intent to discard the Secretaries, and every other Officer in the present Establishment who did not accord with their Wishes.' Society of Antiquaries, MS 891/1, unfoliated collection, Samuel Pegge junior to Hayman Rooke, 8 May 1799.
101. Nichols (ed.), *Illustrations of Literature*, vi, pp. 776–77, Samuel Denne to Richard Gough, 13 May 1799: 'I was much obliged to you for your favour received by the post on Sunday; and join heartily with you in the congratulation on the victory obtained over Magog Banks.'
102. *Gentleman's Magazine*, 73 (1803), p. 316.
103. Society of Antiquaries, Council Minute Book, iii, 30 May 1799.
104. Society of Antiquaries, Council Minute Book, iv, pp. 166–67, 25 May 1810, statement of accounts; Evans, *History of the Society of Antiquaries*, p. 214.
105. Richard Sorrenson, 'Towards a History of the Royal Society in the Eighteenth Century', *Notes and Records of the Royal Society of London*, 50 (1996), p. 30.
106. *Gentleman's Magazine*, 72 (1802), pt 2, p. 1181; Society of Antiquaries, Council Minute Book, iv, p. 128, 8 February 1810.
107. Evans, *History of the Society of Antiquaries*, p. 148.
108. Bodleian Library, MS Gough Gen. Top. 44, fol. 112, Michael Tyson to Richard Gough, 9 September 1772. See also Nichols (ed.), *Literary Anecdotes*, viii, p. 595.
109. James Douglas to Bryan Faussett, 4 February 1785, quoted in Ronald Jessup, *Man of Many Talents: An Informal Biography of James Douglas, 1753–1819* (London, 1975), p. 28.
110. Nichols (ed.), *Illustrations of Literature*, vi, p. 662, Clarke to Denne, 13 February 1796. Clarke's fears proved unfounded and he was elected that same year.
111. *Gentleman's Magazine*, 73 (1803), pt 1, p. 125.
112. Figures calculated from membership lists bound with Richard Gough's annotated copies of *Archaeologia* in the Bodleian Library.
113. Membership is analysed by Sorrenson, 'Towards a History of the Royal Society', pp. 36–37. See also Lyons, *The Royal Society*, p. 211.
114. Robert Lumley Kingston assured Andrew Coltée Ducarel that he wished more than anything to become a member of the society, because by correspondence with other members he could improve himself in that branch of knowledge in which he was most interested. British Library, Add. MS 23900, fol. 24, Kingston to Ducarel, 6 April 1752.
115. Evans, *History of the Society of Antiquaries*, pp. 225–51; Levine, *The Amateur*

and the Professional: Antiquarians, Historians and Archaeologists in Victorian England (Cambridge, 1986), pp. 49–51; Linda Ebbatson, 'Conditions of the Emergence and Existence of Archaeology in the Nineteenth Century: The Royal Archaeological Institute, 1843–1914', unpublished Ph.D. thesis, University of Durham (1999), p. 110.

116. Corpus Christi College Cambridge, Parker Library, Kerrich MS 601, fol. 123v, Edward Balme to Thomas Kerrich, 21 November 1803.
117. Evans, *History of the Society of Antiquaries*, p. 213, on the basis of the index, suggests that it was only fifteen times.
118. Bodleian Library, MS Top. Gen. 39, fol. 24, Richard Gough to Samuel Denne, 9 August 1792.
119. Corpus Christi College, Cambridge, Parker Library, Kerrich MS 606, fol. 68, Francis Douce to Thomas Kerrich, 17 April 1809.
120. Society of Antiquaries, MS 782/5, unfoliated collection, Nicholas Carlisle to Samuel Lysons, 17 November 1808.
121. T. F. Dibdin, *Reminiscences of a Literary Life*, ii, p. 751, quoted in Evans, *History of the Society of Antiquaries*, p. 222.
122. Evans, *History of Society of Antiquaries*, p. 224.
123. *Gentleman's Magazine*, 72 (1802), pp. 1181–83; ibid, 73 (1803), pp. 123–25.
124. The account offered by Evans in the *History of the Society of Antiquaries*, pp. 225–51, is particularly damning, laying the blame squarely on the inefficacy of the officers who should have been responsible for a more effective use of the society's considerable resources and who should have offered a firmer leadership.
125. The development of antiquarian studies more generally in the nineteenth century is surveyed by Levine, *The Amateur and the Professional.*
126. Stuart Piggott, 'The Origins of the English County Archaeological Societies', in idem, *Ruins in a Landscape. Essays in Antiquarianism* (Edinburgh, 1976), pp. 171–95; Levine, *The Amateur and the Professional*, pp. 31–69; F. J. Levy, 'The Origins of the Camden Society', *Victorian Studies*, 7 (1964), pp. 295–305.
127. The same tension is implicit in Lyons's *The Royal Society*, although he attributes the decline in the Royal Society's reputation to a culpable lack of effective leadership, rather than an inherently problematic balancing act.
128. Roger Emmerson, 'Sir Robert Sibbald, Kt, the Royal Society of Scotland and the Origins of the Scottish Enlightenment', *Annals of Science*, 45 (1988), pp. 41–72. Sibbald was at the centre of a circle of 'virtuosi' in Edinburgh and evidently established some kind of informal gathering of antiquaries; it did not survive beyond Sibbald's death in 1711. Steven Shapin, 'Property, Patronage, and the Politics of Science: the Founding of the Royal Society of Edinburgh', *British Journal for the History of Science* (1974), pp. 1–41, finds little evidence of antiquarianism in the Philosophical Society, a view which has been challenged by I. G. Brown, 'Sir John Clerk of Penicuik (1676–1755): Aspects of a Virtuoso Life', unpublished Ph.D. thesis, University of Cambridge (1980), pp. 209–17.

129. Nichols (ed.). *Illustrations of Literature*, vi, pp. 502–11.
130. National Library of Scotland, Adv. MS 29.3.14, fol. 80. In 1794 and 1795 only one paper was given in each year. Shapin, 'Property, Patronage and the Politics of Science'.
131. Nichols (ed.), *Illustrations of Literature*, vi, p. 515, earl of Buchan to Richard Gough, 9 March 1787.
132. National Library of Scotland, Adv. MS 29.5.7 (4), fol. 187, Paton to Gough, 10 May 1793.
133. The following paragraphs are heavily indebted to Ronald G. Cant, 'David Steuart Erskine, 11th Earl of Buchan: Founder of the Society of Antiquaries of Scotland', in A. S. Bell (ed.), *The Scottish Antiquarian Tradition: Essays to Mark the Bicentenary of the Society of Antiquaries of Scotland and its Museum, 1780–1980* (Edinburgh, 1981), pp. 1–30.
134. Hugh M. Milne (ed.), *Boswell's Edinburgh Journals, 1767–1786* (Edinburgh, 2001), p. 416.
135. Nichols (ed.), *Illustrations of Literature*, vi, p. 514, earl of Buchan to Richard Gough, 10 January 1786.
136. R. Houston, *Social Change in the Age of Enlightenment: Edinburgh, 1660–1760* (Oxford, 1994); D. McElroy, 'The Literary Clubs and Societies of Eighteenth-Century Scotland', unpublished Ph.D. thesis, University of Edinburgh (1952); Emmerson, 'Sir Robert Sibbald', p. 59, highlights the problem of a small recruitment base throughout the eighteenth century.
137. Ian D. L. Clark, 'From Protest to Reaction: The Moderate Regime in the Church of Scotland', in N. T. Phillipson and Rosalind Mitchison (ed.), *Scotland in the Age of Improvement* (Edinburgh, 1970), p. 203.
138. Cant, 'David Steuart Erskine, 11th Earl of Buchan', pp. 1–30; Shapin, 'Property, Patronage and the Politics of Science, pp. 1–41 and Emmerson, 'The Scottish Enlightenment and the End of the Philosophical Society of Edinburgh', pp. 33–66.
139. Mark Goldie, 'The Scottish Catholic Enlightenment', *Journal of British Studies*, 30 (1991), pp. 20–62.
140. Society of Antiquaries, MS 447/1, fol. 189, Jeremiah Milles to Richard Gough (no date, *c.* 1778).
141. Societies are recorded to have met at Doncaster, Boston, Wisbeach and Lincoln, although no records of their transactions survive. 'An Account of the Gentlemen's Society at Spalding', in John Nichols (ed.), *Bibliotheca topographica britannica*, 3 (1784), p. ii. See also Nichols (ed.), *Literary Anecdotes*, vi, 1–68.
142. Antiquities represented roughly 27 per cent of papers read at Peterborough and 20 per cent of those read at Spalding. Michael Honeybone, 'The Ideology of Provincial Learned Societies, 1700–1750', unpublished paper presented to the early modern seminar, University of Leicester, October 2002. I am most grateful to Dr Honeybone for permission to cite this and other information. Meetings of William Stukeley's short-lived Brazenose Society at Stamford were

almost entirely taken up with papers on antiquities and astronomy. Bodleian Library, MS Eng. Misc. e 122. The period during which Stukeley took notes was 1736–37. The author of 'An Account of the Gentlemen's Society at Spalding', p. ii, referred to the foundation of a society at Stamford in 1721, which Stukeley revived – records of this earlier society have not survived. Stukeley's own memoirs refer to a botanical society at Boston, a monthly book club at Stamford, the Brazenose Society, and gatherings at Grantham, Market Overton, West Deeping and Greetham Bodleian Library, MS Eng. Misc. e. 260, fos 88–89.

143. Norfolk and Norwich Record Office, MS COL/9/ 193/1–7, M. Knights, 'History of the Fraternity of the United Friars'. The catalogue of its library (MS COL/19/8) includes a substantial number of antiquarian works. Its founding members included bankers, merchants, artists, architects, newspaper proprietors, civic officers and surveyors. Its last recorded meeting was in 1828.
144. David Allan, 'Provincial Readers and Book Culture in the Scottish Enlightenment: The Perth Library, 1784 – *c.* 1800', *The Library*, 3 (2002), pp. 367–89. The Perth library had an 'obsessive' interest in history, which accounted for 86 per cent of its initial purchases, of which a majority were concerned with regional history and antiquarianism; see also idem, 'The Scottish Enlightenment and the Readers of Late Georgian Lancaster: "Light in the North"', *Northern History*, 36 (2000), pp. 278–79; Paul Kaufmann has observed that for the period 1764–1800, Dugdale's *Antiquities of Warwickshire* was the ninth most frequently borrowed volume from Lichfield Cathedral Library; Montfaucon's *L'antiquité expliquée*, Dugdale's *Monasticon* and Browne Willis's *Cathedral Antiquities* were also particularly popular works. Paul Kaufman, 'Readers and their Reading in Eighteenth-Century Lichfield', *Library*, 5th series, 28 (1973), pp. 108–15. See Allan, 'Perth Library', pp. 382–83, for further evidence of a preference for history and antiquities in other English provincial libraries.
145. Clark, *British Clubs and Societies*, pp. 111, 444–45, stresses the social heterogeneity of most literary associations and their role in bringing together old and new elite groups.
146. Bodleian Library, MS Eng. Misc. c. 113, fol. 325v, Maurice Johnson to William Stukeley, 8 January 1732.
147. 'An Account of the Gentlemen's Society at Spalding', p. vi.
148. Gentlemen's Society of Spalding, Minute Books, iv, 21 February 1744.
149. 'An Account of the Gentlemen's Society at Spalding', p. xvii.
150. On the Spalding Society see also William Moore, *The Gentleman's Society of Spalding: Its Origin and Progress* (Pickering, 1851); Marten Perry, 'Spalding Gentlemen's Society', *Memorials of Old Lincolnshire* (Spalding, no date); G. W. Bailey, 'Spalding Gentlemen's Society' (reprinted from *Lincolnshire Magazine*, no date); Dorothy M. Owen (ed.), *The Minutes Books of the Spalding Gentlemen's Society, 1713–55*, Lincoln Record Society, 73 (1981); Michael Honeybone, 'The Spalding Gentlemen's Society: The Communication of Science in the East Midlands of England, 1710–1760', unpublished Ph.D. thesis, Open

University (2001). The society reconstituted itself as the Gentlemen's Society in Spalding and Subscription Library in 1814.

151. On the Peterborough Society see C. Dack, 'The Peterborough Gentleman's Society', *Journal of the British Archaeological Society*, 5 (1899), pp. 141–60. It metamorphosed into the Peterborough Book Club in 1810.
152. Owen, *Spalding Society*, p. vii, states that there were at least 500 families in Spalding in the early eighteenth century.
153. Allan, 'Perth Library', p. 371. Clark, *British Clubs and Societies*, p. 443 comments more generally on the relatively limited achievements, instability and financial problems of learned societies in this period.
154. George Jobey, 'The Society of Antiquaries of Newcastle upon Tyne', *Archaeologia Aeliana*, 5th series, 17 (1990), pp. 197–216 (quotation at p. 197); D. Orange, 'Rational Dissent and Provincial Science: William Turner and the Newcastle Literary and Philosophical Society', in *Metropolis and Province: Science in the Provinces, 1780–1850*, ed. I. Inkster and A. Morrell (London, 1983), pp. 205–30.
155. *Gentleman's Magazine*, 53 (1783), p. 241.
156. National Archives of Scotland, GD 18/5030/3, Roger Gale to Sir John Clerk, 26 April 1726; Evans, *History of the Society of Antiquaries*, p. 240, quoting Nicholas Harris Nicholas in the *Westminster Review*, October 1829.
157. Levine, *The Amateur and the Professional*, p. 61; Piggott, 'The Origins of the English County Archaeological Societies'.

Notes to Chapter 4: The Ancient Britons

1. There are numerous studies on the formation of national identities during this period including Gerald Newman, *The Rise of English Nationalism: A Cultural History, 1740–1830* (London, 1987); Linda Colley, *Britons: The Forging of a Nation, 1707–1832* (New Haven and London, 1992); Colin Kidd, *British Identities Before Nationalism: Ethnicity and Nationhood in the Atlantic Worlds, 1600–1800* (Cambridge, 1999); Murray G. H. Pittock, *Celtic Identities and the British Image* (Manchester, 1999).
2. Sir Robert Atkyns, *Ancient and Present State of Glostershire* (London, 1712), p. 35.
3. On the problems inherent in the concept of 'national history' prior to the post French revolutionary period see J. C. D. Clark, *The Language of Liberty, 1660–1832: Political Discourse and Social Dynamics in the Anglo-American World* (Cambridge, 1994).
4. Graham Parry, *The Trophies of Time: English Antiquarians in the Seventeenth Century* (Oxford, 1995), pp. 1–21; William Rockett, 'The Structural Plan of Camden's *Britannia*', *Sixteenth-Century Journal*, 26 (1995), pp. 829–41.
5. Daniel Defoe, *The True Born Englishman* (London, 1720).
6. Scottish Record Office, GD 18 5023/3/57, Alexander Gordon to Sir John Clerk, June 1732; GD 18/5031/14, Sir John Clerk to Roger Gale, 19 August 1739.
7. John Horsley, *Britannia Romana: or the Roman Antiquities of Britain in Three*

Parts (London, 1732), p. 355: 'although it may afford an agreeable pleasure to an inquisitive mind to view those marks and traces of slavery and subjection to a foreign power; yet it is certainly a more substantial happiness to feel ourselves a free people, and to find our country in most parts a pleasant garden, instead of a series of *Roman* garrisons'.

8. Philip Morant, *The History and Antiquities of the most Ancient Town and Borough of Colchester in the County of Essex* (London, 1748), p. 15.
9. Camden, *Britannia*, ed. Gibson (1695), cols iv–xii. On the comparative popularity of Geoffrey of Monmouth as a historical work see Daniel Woolf, *Reading History in Early Modern England* (Cambridge, 2000), pp. 302–3, 309, 313.
10. Aaron Thompson, *The British History, Translated from the Latin of Jeffrey of Monmouth, with a Large Preface Concerning the Authority of the History* (London, 1718), p. vii–xi; Francis Drake, *Eboracum: or The History and Antiquities of the City of York from its Original to the Present Time* (London, 1736), p. 2, wrote that 'The verity of *Geofry's* history has been excellently well vindicated by Mr *Aaron Thompson*, in the preface to an *English* edition of that author, *London* printed 1718.' See also Morant, *History and Antiquities of Colchester*, p. 17; William Borlase, *Antiquities Historical and Monumental of the County of Cornwall* (2nd edn, London, 1769), p. 26. See also T. Kendrick, *British Antiquity* (London, 1950), pp. 99–102.
11. For this reason attempts to recover the earliest history of mankind often merged into religious antiquities and chronology and biblical exegesis. See, for example, David Boyd Haycock, *William Stukeley: Science, Religion and Archaeology in Eighteenth-Century England* (Woodbridge, 2002).
12. White Kennett, *Parochial Antiquities Attempted in the History of Ambrosden, Burcester and other Adjacent Parts in the Counties of Oxfordshire and Buckinghamshire* (Oxford, 1695), preface.
13. The highly speculative accounts of the Noachite diaspora and their relationship to the earliest inhabitants of Britain and Europe are elucidated by Kidd, *British Identities Before Nationalism*, pp. 9–72.
14. Aylett Sammes, *Britannia antiqua illustrata* (London, 1676). Sammes had not been the first to propound this view: it had already been outlined by John Twyne (1501–81) *De rebus albionicis* (London, 1590), and by Samuel Bochart, *Geographia sacra* (London, 1646). See also Parry, *Trophies of Time*, pp. 308–30. There was always a large constituency which remained unconvinced by Sammes's arguments. William Nicolson commented wryly that Sammes 'if left to himself, could as easily have brought the *Britains* from *New Spain*, and the *Saxons* from *Madagascar*', William Nicolson, *The English Historical Library in Three Parts* (2nd edn, London, 1714), p. 38.
15. Ethel Seaton, *Literary Relations of England and Scandinavia in the Seventeenth Century* (Oxford, 1935), pp. 157–251; Klindt Jensen, *A History of Scandinavian Archaeology* (London, 1975), pp. 18–24
16. John Curran, 'The History Never Written: Bards, Druids, and the Problem of Antiquarianism in "Poly Olbion"', *Renaissance Quarterly*, 51:2 (1998), pp. 298–526.

17. John Aubrey, *Monumenta Britannica: or a Miscellany of British Antiquities*, ed. John Fowles, 2 vols (Sherborne, 1980), i, pp. 14–228.
18. Michael Hunter, *John Aubrey and the World of Learning* (London, 1975), pp. 205–6; Robert Plot, *The Natural History of Staffordshire* (Oxford, 1686), p. 398; idem, *The Natural History of Oxfordshire* (2nd edn, Oxford, 1705), pp. 351–52.
19. Camden, *Britannia*, ed. Gibson (1695), pp. 108–11.
20. Scottish Record Office, GD 18 5023/3/12, William Stukeley to Alexander Gordon, 24 October 1724; Walter Charleton, *Chorea Gigantum: or The Most Famous Antiquity of Great Britain, Vulgarly Called Stone-Heng, Standing on Salisbury Plain, Restored to the Danes* (London, 1663); Inigo Jones, *The Most Notable Antiquity of Great Britain, Vulgarly Called Stone-Heng on Salisbury Plain, Restored*, ed. John Webb (London, 1655); Thomas Twining, *Avebury in Wiltshire: The Remains of a Roman Work* (London, 1723), made the case for the Roman construction of Avebury.
21. On Aubrey's relationship to Tanner and Lhwyd and their contributions to *Britannia* see Hunter, *John Aubrey and the Realm of Learning*, pp. 85–6, 205–6.
22. James Garden, 'A Copy of the Letter from the Reverend Dr James Garden, Professor of Theology in the King's College at Aberdeen, to John Aubrey Esq on the Circular Monuments in Scotland', *Archaeologia*, 1 (1770), pp. 336–42. Martin Martin, *A Description of the Western Islands of Scotland c. 1695 and a Late Voyage to St Kilda*, ed. C. J. Withers (repr. Edinburgh, 1999), pp. 17–18, 217. Martin's *Description* was first published in 1703.
23. Camden, *Britannia*, ed. Gibson (1695), cols 588, 618, 636–38, 681–84.
24. Ibid., col. 683.
25. J. Hunter (ed.), *Letters of Eminent Men Addressed to Ralph Thoresby FRS, Now First Published from the Original*, 2 vols (London, 1832), i, pp. 269, 271, 413; Bodleian Library, MS Eng. Lett. d. 44, fol. 97, Charles Lyttelton to Samuel Pegge, 5 March 1767.
26. Paul Pezron, *The Antiquities of Nations: More Particularly of the Celtae or Gauls, Taken to be Originally the Same People as our Ancient Britains* (1703, trans. D. Jones, London, 1706); Prys Morgan, 'The Abbé Pezron and the Celts', *Transactions of the Honourable Society of Cymmrodorion* (1965), pp. 286–95; Kidd, *British Identities before Nationalism*, pp. 66–67, 97.
27. On Lhwyd as an archaeologist see Glyn Daniel, 'Edward Lhuyd: Antiquary and Archaeologist', *Welsh History Review*, 3 (1966), pp. 345–59; Frank Emery, 'Edward Lhwyd and the 1695 *Britannia*', *Antiquity*, 32 (1958), pp. 179–82; Michael Hunter 'The Royal Society and the Origins of British Archaeology', *Antiquity*, 45 (1971) pp. 119–20; David McGuinness, 'Edward Lhuyd's Contribution to the Study of Irish Megalithic Tombs', *Journal of the Royal Society of Antiquaries of Ireland*, 126 (1996), pp. 62–85.
28. A. L. Owen, *The Famous Druids: A Survey of Three Centuries of English Literature on the Druids* (Oxford, 1962); Stuart Piggott, *The Druids* (London, 1974); Haycock, *William Stukeley*, pp. 160–67; Parry, *The Trophies of Time.*

29. Their correspondence is published at end of the second edition of *Mona Antiqua* (London, 1766). See also J. Gareth Thomas, 'Henry Rowlands: The Welsh Stukeley', *Transactions of the Anglesey Antiquarian Society* (1958), pp. 33–45.
30. Rowlands, *Mona antiqua*, pp. 51, 140–51.
31. Owen, *Famous Druids*, pp. 113–17. Toland drew on the evidence supplied by John Aubrey, Martin Martin, James Garden, Edward Lhwyd and the Irish antiquary George Keating.
32. Borlase, *Antiquities of Cornwall*, p. vi.
33. Justin Champion, 'John Toland, the Druids, and the Politics of Celtic Scholarship', *Irish Historical Studies*, 32 (2001), pp. 337–41; Owen, *Famous Druids*.
34. Bodleian Library, MS Eng. Misc. c. 323, 'Templa Celtica'.
35. Peter J. Ucko, Michael Hunter, Alan J. Clark, Andrew David (eds), *Avebury Reconsidered from the 1660s to the 1990s* (London, 1991), p. 67. Stukeley termed the unit the 'Hebrew cubit' because he believed that the stone temples shared the same basic proportions as the temple of Solomon of the Old Testament.
36. William Stukeley, *Stonehenge. A Temple Restored to the Druids* (London, 1740), p. 5.
37. W. C. Lukis (ed.), 'Family Memoirs of William Stukeley, vol. ii', *Surtees Society*, 76 (1883), p. 55, 17 October 1749.
38. Bodleian Library, MS Eng. Misc. c. 323, fol. 140
39. Lukis (ed.), 'Family Memoirs of William Stukeley, vol. i', *Surtees Society*, 73 (1880), p. 228, letter believed to date from 1729 and to have been intended for Roger Gale. These views were more fully elaborated in the conclusion to *Abury. A Temple of the British Druids* (London, 1743), pp. 89–90. Haycock, *William Stukeley*, pp. 189–216, modifies the standard accounts best represented by Stuart Piggott's biography, *William Stukeley: An Eighteenth-Century Antiquary* (2nd edn, London, 1985).
40. Stuart Piggott's extremely valuable work does not do full justice to the intellectual context in which Stukeley formulated his theories, or address the agenda which Stukeley had as an antiquary, rather than a proto-archaeologist.
41. Bodleian Library, MS Eng. Misc. e. 124, fos 85, 90. Another member was Alexander Gordon, who had been interested in Egyptian antiquities since the 1730s when he was employed by William Lethieullier to draw the Egyptian antiquities he had collected. Gordon then proceeded to record those in the collections of Sir Hans Sloane and Richard Meade and was planning a volume which would illustrate all those antiquities held in Britain entitled 'An Essay towards Illustrating the History, Chronology and Mythology of the Ancient Egyptians'. This survives as British Library, Add. MS 8834; Gordon's comments upon his Egyptian interests are at National Archives of Scotland, GD 18 5023/3/60, 62, 63, 68, 71. Sir John Clerk, his patron, was not impressed; he wrote to Roger Gale on 23 September 1734: 'But as to Mr Gordon's Egyptian Antiquities I wish you cou'd dissuade him from proceeding further. Their Learning at best as well as the Worship of their Gods was rediculous mean & contemptible. Men who cou'd design so ill the Works of Nature that were

constantly in their Eyes were not fit for enquireing into her more Mysterious operations. I have always observed that learning went hand in hand with sculpture & declined as it did.' Scottish Record Office, GD 18/5031/5. Other members of the Egyptian Society included Frederick Ludvig Norden and Richard Pococke, whose comments drawing attention to the similarities between Irish monuments and those in Egypt were to exercise a powerful influence over a later generation of Irish and British antiquaries; see, for example, *Pococke's Tour in Ireland in 1752*, ed. George T. Stokes (Dublin, 1891), p. 65. On Egyptian antiquarianism see also F. L. Norden, *Drawings of some Ruins and Colossal Statues at Thebes in Egypt* (London, 1741); R. Pococke, *A Description of the East and Some Other Countries* (London, 1743). See also M. Craske, 'Entombed Like and Egyptian: An Eighteenth-Century Surgeon's Extravagant Mausoleum to Preserve his Mortal Remains', *Church Monuments*, 5 (2000), pp. 71–88.

42. Jacob Bryant, *A New System: or An Analysis of Ancient Mythology* (London, 1774), p. xiii. Nigel Leask, 'Mythology', in Iain McCalman (ed.), *An Oxford Companion to the Romantic Age: British Culture, 1776–1832* (Oxford, 1999), pp. 338–45, and Haycock, *William Stukeley*, pp. 240–48.
43. Vallancey also frequently referred to these first settlers as Phoenicians. Charles Vallancey (ed.), *Collectanea de rebus hibernicis*, 6 vols (2nd edn, Dublin, 1786–1804), ii, preface.
44. Charles Vallancey, 'Proem', in *Collectanea de rebus hibernicis*, vi, pp. xv–xxiii. Vallancey's essays on the ancient history of Ireland, the Ogham alphabet and the round towers of Ireland in this volume were all essentially elaborations on this theme, as were the majority of the essays which he contributed to the other five volumes. Thomas Maurice used comparative religion and astronomical arguments to substantiate his claims for an affinity between the Brahmins of India and the Druids and claimed to have identified elements of patriarchal religion within the 'Hindoo' superstition. See Thomas Maurice, *Indian Antiquities*, 7 vols (London, 1792–1800), particularly volume six containing the essay, 'Dissertation on the Indian Origin of the Druids: And the Striking Affinity which the Religious Rites and Ceremonies Anciently Practised in the Brittish Islands, Bore to those of the Brahmins', and his *Sanscreet Fragments: or Interesting Extracts from the Sacred Books of the Brahmins, on Subjects Important to the British Isles* (London, 1797).
45. Quoted in Nigel Leask, 'Francis Wilford and the Colonial Construction of Hindu Geography 1799–1822' in Amanda Gilroy (ed.), *Romantic Geographies: Discourses of Travel, 1775–1844* (Manchester, 2000), p. 204.
46. See for example Richard Gough's compilation of variously authored essays, *A Comparative View of the Antient Monuments of India, Particularly Those in the Island of Salset near Bombay* (London, 1785); Maurice, *Indian Antiquities*. See also Owen, *Famous Druids*, pp. 96–97, 188 and Haycock, *William Stukeley*, pp. 241–45. The earl of Buchan in an address to the Scottish Society of Antiquaries in 1787 expressed a wish to compare 'the authentic description ... of

the religious ceremonies and customs of the ancient Highlanders ... with those described by the Asiatic Society of antiquaries'. O'Halloran, 'Golden Ages and Barbarous Nations', p. 112.

47. On the rise of freemasonry in eighteenth-century Britain see David Stevenson *The Origins of Freemasonry: Scotland's Century, 1590–1710* (Cambridge, 1988). Stukeley became a freemason in 1721 and established a lodge at Grantham later, after he left London: Haycock, *William Stukeley*, pp. 174–80. Other masonic antiquaries included the duke of Montague, earl of Coleraine, Martin Folkes, Maurice Johnson, Francis Drake and William Hutchinson. See also Evans, *History of the Society of Antiquaries*, pp. 54–55, 186. Drake delivered a speech on the history of the craft to the York Grand Lodge in 1727, printed in York by Thomas Gent and in several collections of masonic essays, for example, B. Cole (ed.), *The Antient Constitutions of Free and Accepted Masons* (London, 1731).
48. John Wood, *Choir Gaure, Vulgarly called Stonehenge, on Salisbury Plain, Described, Restored, and Explained* (Oxford, 1747); Wood elaborated upon some of these themes in his *Description of Bath* (London, 1742–43) and in the second edition published in 1765; see also T. Mowl and B. Earnshaw, *John Wood: Architect of Obsession* (London, 1988); William Hutchinson, *The Spirit of Masonry in Moral and Elucidatory Lectures* (2nd edn, Carlisle, 1795), p. 48; see also his *History and Antiquities of the County Palatine of Durham*, 2 vols (Newcastle, 1785), i, pp. ii–iii. The freemasonic element amongst the subscription to Gordon's *Itinerarium septentrionale* is analysed in G. C. Shadwell, '"Itinerarium septentrionale" 1726', *Ars Quatuor Coronatorum*, 60 (1950), pp. 91–98.
49. Lukis (ed.), 'Family Memoirs of William Stukeley, vol. iii', *Surtees Society*, 80 (1885), p. 275, diary entry, 3 August 1763.
50. The delay between composition and publication hinged on pecuniary problems. It was only in 1740 after marrying Elizabeth, the sister of Roger and Samuel Gale, who brought with her a dowry of £10,000, that Stukeley was in a position to finance the publication of the two volumes.
51. Lukis (ed.), 'Family Memoirs of William Stukeley, vol. iii', p. 211, 5 October 1754.
52. British Library, Stowe MS 753, fol. 41, John Moulding to Charles Lyttelton, 25 March 1744.
53. British Library, Stowe MS 754, fol. 73, John Stephens to Charles Lyttelton, 22 October 1760. Stukeley's serpentine theory, outlined in Abury proceeded upon the principle that the temple had been constructed as a 'hieroglyph' of the snake and circle, being the ancient symbol for the deity. For a detailed discussion of Stukeley's thinking on this point see Haycock, *William Stukeley*, pp. 208–9.
54. Samuel Pegge, *An Essay on the Coins of Cunobelin* (London, 1766), quoted by John Whitaker, *The History of Manchester in Four Books*, 2 vols (London, 1773), ii, p. 17, n. 52.
55. Richard Gough, *British Topography*, 2 vols (London, 1780), ii, p. 373–74. John Hutchinson, author of *Moses's Principia* (London, 1724) was little noticed in

his own time, but received more attention in the second half of the century when, according to Horace Walpole, he was more influential than Methodism in Oxford. Arguments for and against his views appeared for over fifty years in the *Gentleman's Magazine.* Hutchinson set out to counter the perceived atheism of Newtonianism: he argued that the Hebrew text of Genesis was the source for all understanding of the natural and spiritual universe and that the Old Testament was full of evidence for the primeval origins of revealed Christianity, and the doctrine of the Trinity in particular. Albert Kuhn, 'Glory or Gravity: Hutchinson *vs* Newton', *Journal of the History of Ideas*, 22 (1961), pp. 303–22.

56. Charles Goodwyn informed John Hutchins that Stukeley 'sometimes tires the patience of the Antiquarian Society with a dissertation, which never fails of exciting laughter'. Goodwyn to John Hutchins, 23 December 1763, Bodleian Library, MS Top. Gen. d. 2 fol. 108. The various papers which Stukeley presented to the Society of Antiquaries during the late 1750s and 1760s were recorded by the secretary with thinly veiled scepticism. Society of Antiquaries, Minute Books, viii (typescript), pp. 35–37, 47–48, 54–59, 69–71, 320–23, 397–401, 760.
57. See, for example, the geologist and antiquary Charles Mason's use of Stukeley in his travel journals. Cambridge University Library, Add. MS 7762.
58. M. W. Thompson, *The Journeys of Sir Richard Colt Hoare through Wales and England, 1793–1810* (London, 1983), p. 102. See also Haycock, *William Stukeley*, pp. 249–50.
59. Borlase, *Antiquities of Cornwall*; idem, *Observations on the Ancient and Present State of the Islands of Scilly, and their Importance to the Trade of Great Britain: In a Letter to the Reverend Charles Lyttelton* (Oxford, 1756).
60. British Library, Stowe MS 752, fos 126, 134.
61. Borlase, *Antiquities of Cornwall*, p. ix.
62. Jeremiah Milles to William Borlase, 25 April 1754, quoted in William Borlase, *Antiquities Historical and Monumental of the County of Cornwall*, ed. P. A. S. Poole and Charles Thomas (Wakefield, 1973), p. xi.
63. John Watson, *The History and Antiquities of the Parish of Halifax in Yorkshire* (London, 1775), p. 29, referred to Stukeley as being a better authority upon the Druids than any other person.
64. National Library of Scotland, Adv. MS 29.5.5, fol. 76, Thomas Pennant to George Low, 23 January 1774; Nichols (ed.), *Literary Anecdotes*, viii, pp. 486–87.
65. E. J. Climenson (ed.), *Passages from the Diaries of Mrs Lybbe Powys, 1756–1805* (London, 1899), pp. 51–52.
66. R. W. Chapman (ed.), *The Letters of Samuel Johnson* (Oxford, 1952), iii, p. 86, Johnson to Mrs Thrale, 9 October 1783.
67. Anon., *A Description of Stonehenge, Abiry, etc in Wiltshire, with an Account of the Learning and Discipline of the Druids, to which is Added an Account of Antiquities on Salisbury Plain* (London, 1776), p. 7.
68. Edward Snyder, *The Celtic Revival in English Literature* (Cambridge, 1923); see

also Owen, *Famous Druids* and Pittock, *Celtic Identities and the British Image*, pp. 35–40.

69. John Thomas, *History of the Island of Anglesey, from its First Invasion by the Romans, until Finally Acceded to the Crown of England … Serving as a Supplement to Rowland's Mona Antiqua Restaurata* (London, 1775), pp. 11–14.
70. Snyder, *Celtic Revival*, pp. 34–37.
71. Jon Mee, *Dangerous Enthusiasm: William Blake and the Culture of Radicalism in the 1790s* (Oxford, 1992), pp. 75–109; Peter Ackroyd, *Blake* (London, 1996), pp. 43–51; Owen, *Famous Druids*, pp. 224–36.
72. Sam Smiles, *The Image of Antiquity: Ancient Britain and the Romantic Imagination* (New Haven and London, 1994); David Boyd Haycock, '"A Small Journey into the Country": William Stukeley and the Polite Landscapes of Stonehenge and Avebury', in Lucy Peltz and Martin Myrone (ed.), *Producing the Past: Aspects of Antiquarian Culture and Practice, 1700–1850* (Aldershot, 1999), pp. 67–82.
73. Snyder, *Celtic Revival*, p. 162.
74. National Library of Scotland, Adv. MS 29.5.6, fol. 18, Richard Gough to George Paton, 11 September 1772. The topographer and antiquary John Britton acquired many of Stukeley's papers and had a plan for republishing them in the early nineteenth century, but never implemented it.
75. Bodleian Library, MS Eng. Lett. 45, fol. 531, John Watson to Samuel Pegge, 13 December 1763; Society of Antiquaries, MS 443/3, fol. 143, Michael Lort to Richard Gough, 27 September 1778.
76. John Watson, *The History and Antiquities of the Parish of Halifax in Yorkshire* (London, 1775), p. 24.
77. Samuel Pegge, 'Illustration of Some Druidical Remains in the Peak of Derbyshire' and 'A Disquisition on the Lows or Barrows in the Peak of Derbyshire, Particularly that Capital British Monument Called Arbelows', *Archaeologia*, 7 (1785), pp. 19–24, 131–48; Hayman Rooke, 'A Further Account of Some Druidical Remains in Derbyshire', ibid., pp. 175–8; Samuel Pegge, 'Observations by the Rev. Mr Pegge on the Stanton Moor Urns and Druidical Temple', *Archaeologia*, 8 (1787), pp. 58–62; Hayman Rooke, 'Observations on the Brimham Rocks in Yorkshire', *Archaeologia*, 8 (1787), pp, 209–27; Samuel Pegge, 'Discoveries in Opening a Tumulus in Derbyshire', *Archaeologia*, 9 (1789), pp. 189–92.
78. Thomas Pownall, 'Account of a Singular Stone among the Rocks at West Hoadley, Sussex', *Archaeologia*, 6 (1782), pp. 56–57.
79. See for example Samuel Pegge, 'A Disquisition on the Lows or Barrows in the Peak of Derbyshire, Particularly that Capital British Monument called Arbelows', *Archaeologia*, 7 (1785), pp. 131–148.
80. Hayman Rooke, 'Antiquities in Cumberland and Westmoreland', *Archaeologia*, 10 (1792), pp. 110–11. The druidical circle which he identified in his paper on the Brimham rocks, see note 77 above is actually a natural formation of gritstone.

81. Clare O'Halloran, 'Irish Re-Creations of the Gaelic Past: The Challenge of Macpherson's Ossian', *Past and Present*, 124 (1989), pp. 69–95.
82. James Macpherson, *An Introduction to the History of Great Britain and Ireland* (3rd edn, London, 1773).
83. The political implications to Macpherson's position are particularly emphasised in Howard Weinbrot, *Britannia's Issue: The Rise of British Literature from Dryden to Ossian* (Cambridge, 1993), pp. 516–24.
84. William Stukeley, *A Letter from Dr Stukeley to Mr Macpherson on his Publication of Fingal and Temora* (London, 1763), p. 7.
85. The critical reception of and response to Ossian is discussed by Fiona Stafford, *The Sublime Savage: A Study of James Macpherson and the Poems of Ossian* (Edinburgh, 1988).
86. C. J. Withers, 'How Scotland Came to Know Itself: Geography, National Identity and the Making of a Nation, 1680–1790', *Journal of Historical Geography*, 21 (1995), p. 378.
87. Richard Gough, *Anecdotes of British Topography* (London, 1768), pp. 617–68: 'Attentive to humanize themselves and mankind we see the Scots, a nation of philosophers, without an antiquary to lay open to us their original state.' By the time that Gough published the second edition, *British Topography*, 2 vols (London, 1780), ii, pp. 553–54, he was already in a position to comment upon the increase in interest in antiquarianism which was evident in Scotland at this date. Scottish antiquarian literature was reviewed, ibid., pp. 553–78.
88. The importance of manuscripts in the authentication of origins is discussed in Ian Haywood, *The Making of History* (London, 1986), pp. 21–69.
89. James Anderson, 'An Account of Antient Monuments and Fortifications in the Highlands of Scotland', *Archaeologia*, 5 (1779), pp. 241–66, and idem, 'A Further Description of Antient Fortifications in the North of Scotland', *Archaeologia*, 6 (1782), pp. 87–99.
90. Robert Riddell, 'Observations on Vitrified Fortification in Galloway', *Archaeologia*, 10 (1792), p. 147.
91. William Nimmo, *A General History of Stirlingshire: Containing an Account of the Ancient Monuments and Most Important and Curious Transactions of that Shire, from the Roman Invasion of Scotland to the Present Times, with the Natural History of the Shire* (Edinburgh, 1777), pp. 39, 67; John Callander, proposals for *Bibliotheca septentrionalis* (Edinburgh, 1778); M. D. Eddy, 'Geology, Mineralogy and Time in John Walker's University of Edinburgh Natural History Lectures (1779–1903)', *History of Science*, 39 (2001), pp. 95–119; John Smith, *Galic Antiquities: Consisting of a History of the Druids, Particularly those of Caledonia; a Dissertation on the Authenticity of the Poems of Ossian* (Edinburgh, 1780), pp. 16–18, 90–124
92. John Williams, *An Account of Some Remarkable Ancient Ruins, Lately Discovered in the Highlands, and Northern Parts of Scotland in a Series of Letters to G.C.M. Esq* (Edinburgh, 1777), p. 19.
93. Thomas Pennant, *A Tour in Scotland, 1769* (Chester, 1771); idem, *A Tour in*

Scotland and Voyage to the Hebrides, 1772, 2 vols (Chester, 1774–76); National Library of Scotland, Adv. MS 29.5.7, fol. 90, George Paton to Richard Gough, 26 February 1773.

94. Stafford, *The Sublime Savage*, p. 157.
95. Smith, *Galic Antiquities*, p. 3. See also Owen, *Famous Druids*, pp. 155–62.
96. John Pinkerton, *A Dissertation on the Origin and Progress of the Scythians or Goths: Being an Introduction to the Ancient and Modern History of Europe* (London, 1787), and *An Enquiry into the History of Scotland Preceding the Reign of Malcolm III Including the Authentic History of that Period*, 2 vols (London, 1789), i, pp. 17–18. Pinkerton's views are discussed in Colin Kidd, 'Teutonist Ethnology and Scottish Nationalist Inhibition, 1780–1880', *Scottish History Review*, 74 (1995), pp. 45–68.
97. The debate between the Gothic and the Celtic interpretation of Scotland's ancient history was satirised in Sir Walter Scott's novel, *The Antiquary* (Edinburgh, 1816).
98. The identification and recording of druidical monuments from the time of Ossian was identified by the earl of Buchan as one of the most urgent tasks of the Scottish society in the address which he gave at the founding of the society. See William Smellie, *An Account of the Institution and Progress of the Society of the Antiquaries of Scotland* (Edinburgh, 1782), p. 5. On the changing constructions of Scotland's ancient history during the eighteenth century see Colin Kidd, *Subverting Scotland's Past: Scottish Whig Historians and the Creation of an Anglo-British Identity, c. 1680–1830* (Cambridge, 1993).
99. Prys Morgan, 'From a Death to a View: The Hunt for the Welsh Past in the Romantic Period', in Eric Hobsbawm and Terence Ranger (ed.), *The Invention of Tradition* (Cambridge, reprinted 1997), p. 63.
100. Prys Morgan, *The Eighteenth-Century Renaissance* (Llandybie, 1981), pp. 70–161. See also Geraint H. Jenkins, *The Foundations of Modern Wales* (Oxford, 1987), pp. 386–426.
101. Bards were believed to have been an order of Druids who had the power of prophecy; after the extirpation of the Druid religion, the vatic function was continued in the tradition of the bard, who acted as adviser to princes, prophet and bearer of the oral traditions of poetry and history.
102. Thomas Richards, *Antiquae linguae britannicae thesaurus* (Bristol, 1753); John Walters, *A Dissertation on the Welsh Language* (London, 1770); Rowland Jones, *Origin of Language and Nations* (London, 1764); William Owen (Pughe), *Myvyrian Archaiology of Wales* (London, 1801–7).
103. Lewis Morris, *Celtic Remains*, Cambrian Archaeological Association (1878).
104. There were also attempts to assert a comparable Irish bardic tradition, see Joseph Cooper Walker, *Historical Memoirs of the Irish Bards* (London, 1786). Walker's identification of seminaries for Irish bards was found to be less than convincing by some of his English reviewers. His career is reviewed by Monica Nevin, 'Joseph Cooper Walker, 1761–1810', *Journal of the Royal Society of Antiquaries of Ireland*, 126 (1996), pp. 152–66.

105. Evans protested (vainly) in the preface that he was not trying to compete with Ossian, nor had the success of Ossian prompted him to undertake the project. *Some Specimens of the Poetry of the Antient Welsh Bards* (London, 1764), pp. ii–iii
106. The bardic literature exercised a profound influence on Sharon Turner – see chapter 6 below. It was also an importance source for Samuel Rush Meyrick, *The History and Antiquities of Cardigan* (London, 1808).
107. *Myvyrian Archaiology of Wales*, i, p. xvi.
108. Morgan, 'From a Death to a View', p. 46, and, *The Eighteenth-Century Renaissance.* See also Evan Evans's defence of Geoffrey of Monmouth to Thomas Percy in Aneirin Lewis (ed.), *The Correspondence of Thomas Percy and Evan Evans* (Baton Rouge, Louisiana, 1957), p. 9 and in the letters of Lewis Morris to the English antiquary Samuel Pegge printed in *The Cambrian Register* (London, 1796), pp. 347–72.
109. Morgan, 'The Hunt for the Welsh Past', pp. 62–66.
110. Joseph Cradock, *Letters from Snowdon Descriptive of a Tour through the Northern Counties of Wales* (London, 1770), p. 62.
111. Morris, *Celtic Remains*, p. vii.
112. The Wiltshire antiquary William Cunnington opined that 'this monument of the Britons is more ancient than our Welch antiquarians are willing to allow is very clear in my opinion ... I think it impossible that the Romans, Saxons, or Danes can have any claim either to Abury or Stonehenge'. Robert Cunnington, ed. James Dyer, *From Antiquary to Archaeologist: A Biography of William Cunnington* (Buckingham, 1975), p. 110 See also Meyrick, *History and Antiquities of Cardigan*, p. xcv.
113. Horsley, *Britannia Romana*, pp. 320–22 (one of the briefest sections on inscriptions in different regions of Britain), 465–66 (on Roman roads in Wales); William Harris, 'Observations on the Julia Strata and on the Roman Stations, Forts, and Camps, in the Counties of Monmouth, Caermarthen, and Glamorgan', *Archaeologia*, 2 (1773), pp. 1–24; John Strange, 'A Further Account of Some Remains of Roman and Other Antiquities in or near the County of Brecknock in South Wales', *Archaeologia*, 4 (1777), pp. 1–26; idem, 'An Account of some Remains of Roman and Other Antiquities in Monmouthshire', *Archaeologia*, 5 (1779), pp. 33–80; idem, 'Remarks on the Reverend Mr William Harris's Observations on the Roman Antiquities in Monmouthshire and the Neighbouring Counties of Wales', *Archaeologia*, 6 (1782), pp. 6–38.
114. On Pennant see R. Paul Evans, 'Thomas Pennant (1726–1798): "The Father of Cambrian Tourists"', *Welsh History Review*, 13 (1987), pp. 395–417, and 'The Life and Works of Thomas Pennant, 1726–1798', unpublished Ph.D. thesis, University of Wales (1993); Donald Moore, 'Thomas Pennant's Vision of the Landscape', *Archaeologia Cambrensis*, 146 (2000 for 1997), pp. 138–77; Colin Matheson, 'Thomas Pennant and the Morris Brothers', *Annals of Science*, 10 (1954), pp. 258–71.
115. Thomas Pennant, *A Tour in Wales in 1773* (London, 1778), p. 1.

116. See note 113 above.
117. Henry Penruddocke Wyndham, *A Gentleman's Tour through Monmouthshire and Wales, in the Months of June and July 1774* (London, 1775); William Coxe, *An Historical Tour in Monmouthshire: Illustrated with Views by Sir Richard Colt Hoare* (London, 1801), pp. 1–26. Coxe substantially modified the overly enthusiastic attributions of Harris, who had attributed any antiquity which he encountered to the Romans
118. Richard Fenton, *An Historical Tour through Pembrokeshire* (London, 1810), pp. 41–48.
119. Wyndham, *Gentleman's Tour*, pp. 142–43; see also W. Bingley, *A Tour round North Wales Performed during the Summer of 1789*, 2 vols (London, 1800), i, p. 431; John Evans, *A Tour through Part of North Wales in the Year 1798* (London, 1800), p. 134.
120. Thompson, *Journeys of Sir Richard Colt Hoare*, p. 43.
121. Sir Richard Colt Hoare, *The Ancient History of South Wiltshire* (London, 1812); idem, *The Ancient History of North Wiltshire* (London, 1819).
122. Wyndham, *Gentleman's Tour*, p. 47.
123. Theophilus Jones, *A History of the County of Brecknock*, 2 vols (Brecknock, 1805), i, pp. 199–279.
124. The authoritative account of Irish antiquarianism in the eighteenth century is O'Halloran, 'Golden Ages and Barbarous Nations'. On Druids see especially pp. 255–69.
125. Rosemary Sweet, 'Provincial Culture and Urban Histories in England Ireland during the Long Eighteenth Century', in P. Borsay and L. Proudfoot (ed.), *Provincial Towns in Early Modern England and Ireland: Change, Convergence and Divergence*, Proceedings of the British Academy, 108 (Oxford, 2002), pp. 223–40.
126. Clare O'Halloran, '"The Island of Saints and Scholars": Views of the Early Church and Sectarian Politics in Late Eighteenth-Century Ireland', *Eighteenth-Century Ireland*, 5 (1990), pp. 7–20.
127. Charles Vallancey, *An Essay on the Antiquity of the Irish Language, Being a Collation of the Irish with the Punic Language* (Dublin, 1772), p. 3.
128. The connection between the patriot movement and antiquarian interest in the Carthaginian connection has been explored by Norman Vance, 'Celts, Carthaginians and Constitutions: Anglo-Irish Literary Relations, 1780–1820', *Irish Historical Studies*, 22 (1981), pp. 216–238; Joep Leerssen, 'On the Edges of Europe: Ireland in Search of Oriental Roots, 1650–1850', *Comparative Criticism*, 8 (1986), pp. 91–112; see also O'Halloran, 'Golden Ages and Barbarous Nations'.
129. This issue is fully explored in Clare O'Halloran, 'Irish Re-Creations of the Gaelic Past: The Challenge of Macpherson's Ossian', *Past and Present*, 124 (1989), pp. 69–95, and Colin Kidd, 'Gaelic Antiquity and National Identity in Enlightenment Ireland and Scotland', *English Historical Review* (1994), pp. 1197–1214; Charles O'Connor, *Dissertations on the History of Ireland* (2nd edn, Dublin, 1766); Sylvester O'Halloran, *An Introduction to the Study of the History*

and Antiquities of Ireland in which the Assertions of Mr Hume and Other Writers are Occasionally Considered (London, 1772).

130. J. C. Walker, *Historical Memoirs of the Irish Bards* (London, 1786), and Charlotte Brooke, *Reliques of Irish Poetry* (Dublin, 1789).
131. There is a reference to stone circles in *The History of the Town of Belfast* (Belfast 1823), pp. 263–64. Thomas Wright's slim volume *Louthiana: or An Introduction to the Antiquities of Ireland* (London, 1748) included a brief section on driudical remains, showing the influence of Rowlands and Stukeley. Wright, a surveyor, was originally from Durham. Irish Druids, he argued, differed from their British counterparts, in having the use of letters and in having established universities (iii, p. 6).
132. John Whitaker, *The Genuine History of the Britons Asserted against Mr Macpherson* (2nd edn, London, 1773). There were also many references to Ossian in his *History of Manchester.*
133. Geoffrey Keating, *The General History of Ireland*, trans. Dermod O'Connor (Dublin, 1723).
134. Vallancey, *Collectanea de rebus hibernicis*, vi, p. xxvii.
135. O'Halloran, *An Introduction to the Study of the Antiquities of Ireland* (London, 1772).
136. See Vance, 'Celts, Carthaginians and Constitutions', pp. 222–28.
137. [Edward Ledwich], *Antiquitates Sarisburienses* (Salisbury, 1771), p. 15, 'I must observe in general, that we have no instance existing of any place built in the regular manner he supposes Old Sarum to have been, the number of towers and the disposition of the streets never had a being out of Stukeley's brain, any more than the wonderful order of Stonehenge.'
138. Ledwich described the break up in a letter to Richard Gough, 18 September 1787, Nichols (ed.), *Illustrations of Literature*, vii, pp. 849–51. See also pp. 386 n. 85.
139. Vallancey had presented the London society with a copy of his *Irish Grammar* in 1773 and communicated a paper in 1773 in response to Pownall's essay (Bodleian Library, MS Top London c. 2, fol. 93v). He was elected to the society in 1784 and his essay on the Ogham alphabet was published in *Archaeologia*, 7 (1785), pp. 276–85. A further paper on inscriptions found in North America appeared in *Archaeologia*, 8 (1787), pp. 302–6. His name was dropped from the members list in 1794 for being over three years in arrears (Society of Antiquaries, Council Minute Books, xv, 5 April 1794). Pownall struck out his own idiosyncratic path which combined Gothicism with Vallancey's theories upon fire worship amongst the ancient Irish.
140. See for example Michael Lort's comment to Thomas Percy that 'To what do Vallancey's researches tend, but to prove she [Ireland] is the elder sister?' Nichols (ed.), *Illustrations of Literature*, vii, p. 465, 19 August 1784. Some, however, for example J. Graves, *The History and Antiquities of Cleveland in the County of York* (London, 1808), pp. 3–4, adopted Vallancey's views.
141. National Library of Scotland, Adv. MS 29.3.14, fol. 78, where the earl of Buchan in his anniversary discourse of 1784 referred to Vallancey as an authority on

the Gaelic language. John Callander of Craigforth was delighted to hear that Vallancey had been made a member of the Scottish Society of Antiquaries (National Library of Scotland, Adv. MS 28.3.8, fol. 51, John Callander to George Paton, 29 May 1781).

142. Edward Ledwich, 'A Dissertation on the Religion of the Druids: Addressed to Governor Pownall' *Archaeologia*, 7 (1785), pp. 303–23. Ledwich's criticisms were as much about antiquarian methodology as about the contested ethnic origins of Ireland or the nature of Celtic civilisation.

143. See for example, Daines Barrington, 'An Account of Certain Remarkable Pits or Caverns in the Earth, in the County of Berks', *Archaeologia*, 7 (1785), pp. 236–43 and Hayman Rooke, 'Description of Certain Pits in Derbyshire', *Archaeologia*, 10 (1792) pp. 114–17. Both antiquaries argued that the 'pits' under discussion were actually houses and indicative of the presence of an ancient British city. 'The regular manner in which these pits are placed', argued Rooke, 'forming a kind of street, obviates a supposition that they were hiding places of people pursued by a victorious army.'

144. Whitaker, *History of Manchester*, ii, p. 318.

145. Ibid., i, p. 16.

146. See, for example, Coxe, *Historical Tour in Monmouthshire*, p. 5, 'Mr Whitaker has plainly proved, in opposition to the assertions of Gildas, which are adopted by Hume and others, that the Britons did not act with pusillanimity, but defended themselves with great vigour and industry.'

147. William Hutton, *History of Birmingham* (2nd edn, Birmingham, 1783), pp. 16–18.

148. Whitaker, *History of Manchester*, i, pp. 45–52, 71, 105–8, 124–25, 309–10, 336–38.

149. Charles Lyttelton, 'Observations on Stone Hatchets', *Archaeologia*, 2 (1773), pp. 122–23. The paper was delivered on 5 December 1765.

150. William Cunnington, 'Account of Tumuli Opened in Wiltshire in Letters to Aylmer Bourke Lambert Esq FRS FSA', *Archaeologia*, 15 (1806), pp. 122–28, 338–45. Cunnington, a tradesman from Devizes, worked closely with Sir Richard Colt Hoare on the *Ancient History of Wiltshire* and was the leading excavator of the early nineteenth century. Cunnington, ed. Dyer, *From Antiquary to Archaeologist*; Kenneth Woodbridge, *Landscape and Antiquity* (London, 1971); Thomas Leman to William Cunnington (no date), quoted in J. Simmons and D. D. A. Simpson, 'Introduction', in *The Ancient History of Wiltshire* (Wakefield, 1975), p. 15.

151. Matthew R. Goodrum, 'The Meaning of Ceraunia: Archaeology, Natural History and the Interpretation of Prehistoric Stone Artefacts in the Eighteenth Century', *British Journal for the History of Science*, 35 (2002), pp. 255–69.

152. James Douglas, *Nenia Britannica: or A Sepulchral History of Great Britain* (London, 1793), pp. 154, 184; see also Thomas Pownall, 'A Description of the Sepulchral Monument at New Grange near Drogheda', *Archaeologia*, 2 (1773), pp. 236–75, where he argued that certain types of artefact belonged to people of any race or country at specific stages in the progress of civilisation.

153. Thomas Pownall, *An Antiquarian Romance* (London, 1795), p. 70.

154. Samuel Rush Meyrick and Charles Hamilton Smith, *The Costume of the Original Inhabitants of the British Islands from the Earliest Period to the Sixth Century* (London, 1821).
155. Rowlands, *Mona Antiqua*, preface.
156. *Proposals for Printing by Subscription, Mona Antiqua Restaurata: An Archaeological Discourse on the Antiquities Natural and Historical of the Isle of Angelesy, the Antient Seat of the British Druids* (London, 1764).
157. William Pryce, *Archaeologia cornu britannica* (London, 1790). This was based upon the text of Thomas Tonkin's study of the Cornish language, compiled in the first half of the eighteenth century.
158. National Library of Scotland, Adv. MS 29.3.14, fol. 78, earl of Buchan's anniversary discourse to the Scottish Society of Antiquaries, 15 November 1784.
159. James Hutton, *Theory of the Earth* (London, 1799).
160. John Frere, 'An Account of Flint Weapons Discovered at Hoxne in Suffolk', *Archaeologia*, 13 (1800), pp. 204–5; Glyn Daniel, *The Idea of Prehistory* (London, 1972), pp. 23–41; James Parkinson, *Organic Remains of a Former World* (London, 1804), especially pp. 6–12, was similarly replete with vague references to former worlds and antediluvian remains, but was very unforthcoming as to their age, relative or absolute. See Porter, *The Making of Geology*, p. 168.
161. Porter, *The Making of Geology*; M. S. J. Rudwick, *The Great Devonian Controversy: The Shaping of Scientific Knowledge among Gentlemanly Specialists* (Chicago, 1985); Alain Schnapp, *The Discovery of the Past: The Origins of Archaeology* (London, 1996), pp. 275–316, examines the problem from a European perspective.

Notes to Chapter 5: The Romans in Britain

1. T. D. Fosbroke, *Encyclopaedia of Antiquities and Elements of Archaeology, Classic and Medieval*, 2 vols (London, 1825), i, p. iv.
2. Bodleian Library, MS Eng. Misc. c. 401, fol. 6.
3. On Renaissance antiquarianism on the Continent see Peter Burke, *The Renaissance Sense of the Past* (London, 1969); Anthony Grafton, *Joseph Scaliger* (Oxford, 1983), and idem, *Defenders of the Text* (Cambridge, Massachusetts, 1991); Peter Millar, *Peiresc's Europe: Learning and Virtue in the Seventeenth Century* (New Haven and London, 2000); Arnaldo Momigliano, *Studies in Historiography* (London, 1966); Roberto Weiss, *The Renaissance Discovery of Classical Antiquity* (Oxford, 1969).
4. J. M. Levine, 'The Antiquarian Enterprise', in *Humanism and History: Origins of Modern English Historiography* (Ithaca and London, 1987), p. 75.
5. Edmund Gibson, *William Camden's Britannia, Newly Translated into English: with Large Additions and Improvements* (London, 1695), 'Mr Camden's preface'.
6. Thomas Hearne, *The Life of King Aelfred the Great by Sir John Spelman Kt from the Original Manuscripts in the Bodleian Library; with Considerable Additions, and Several Historical Remarks* (Oxford, 1709), pp. 3–4.

7. J. M. Levine, *The Battle of the Books: History and Literature in the Augustan Age* (Ithaca and London, 1991).
8. Alexander Gordon, *Itinerarium Septentrionale: or, a Journey thro' most of the Counties of Scotland and those in the North of England* (London, 1726), p. 32, 'Iam vero principum filios liberalibus artibus erudire, et ingenia Britannorum studiis Gallorum anteferre, ut qui modo linguam Romanam abnuebant, eloquentiam concupiscerent. Inde etiam habitus nostri honor et frequens Toga. Paulatimque discessum ad delinimenta vitiorum etc.', was translated by Gordon thus: 'so that gradually they slipt into the Blandishments of Vice and Effeminacy, building sumptuous Galleries, Bagnios and making delicate entertainments; which Things passed among the Ignorant of them, for *Politeness*, but at the Bottom were nothing but Baits of *Slavery*.'
9. For a contemporary summary of the various attempts to establish the 'Roman Geography' see Richard Gough in *British Topography*, 2 vols (London, 1780), i, pp. xiv–xv.
10. William Rockett, 'The Structural Plan of Camden's *Britannia*', *Sixteenth-Century Journal*, 26 (1995), pp. 829–41.
11. Camden, *Britannia*, ed. Gibson (1695), preface.
12. For an overview of these sources see Barri Jones and David Mattingley, *An Atlas of Roman Britain* (2nd edn, Oxford, 1998), pp. 16–42.
13. On Irish antiquarianism see Clare O'Halloran, 'Golden Ages and Barbarous Nations: Antiquarian Debate on the Celtic Past in Ireland and Scotland in the Eighteenth Century', unpublished Ph.D. thesis, University of Cambridge (1991); Sylvester O'Halloran, *Introduction to the Study of the History and Antiquities of Ireland* (London, 1772), p. 268.
14. D. C. Douglas, *English Scholars, 1660–1730* (London, 1939); Levi Fox (ed.), *English Historical Scholarship in the Sixteenth and Seventeenth Centuries* (London, 1962); T. Kendrick, *British Antiquity* (London, 1950); Graham Parry, *The Trophies of Time: English Antiquarians of the Seventeenth Century* (Oxford, 1995); Levine, *The Battle of the Books*, pp. 327–73.
15. Parry, *Trophies of Time*, pp. 250–256.
16. William Somner, *A Treatise on the Roman Ports and Forts in Kent*, ed. White Kennett (Oxford, 1693). Daniel Woolf, *The Social Circulation of the Past: Historical Culture in Early Modern England, 1500–1730* (Oxford, 2003) charts early interest in Roman antiquities, pp. 229–33, 238–26.
17. Roger North quoted in Eric Birley, *Research on Hadrian's Wall* (Kendal, 1961), p. 9; W. Grey, *Chorographia: or A Survey of Newcastle upon Tyne* (Newcastle, 1649), p. 37.
18. Parry, *Trophies of Time*, p. 261.
19. Francis Wise, *A Letter to Dr Mead Concerning Some Antiquities in Berkshire* (Oxford, 1753), p. 9.
20. G. Walters and Frank Emery, 'Edward Lhwyd, Edmund Gibson and the Printing of Camden's *Britannia*', *Library*, 5th series, 32 (1977), pp. 109–37.
21. Wise, *Letter to Dr Mead*, p. 5.

22. The correspondence generated by the process of revision is evident in a number of collections. Gibson's letters and materials are in the Bodleian Library; see also Joseph Hunter (ed.), *Letters of Eminent Men, Addressed to Ralph Thoresby, FRS, Now First Published from the Originals*, 2 vols (London, 1832).
23. Roger Gale (ed.), *Antonini iter Britanniarum commentariis illustratum Thomae Gale* (London, 1709); see also Roger Gale 'An Essay towards the Recovery of the Courses of the Four Great Roman Ways', in Thomas Hearne (ed.), *The Itinerary of John Leland the Antiquary*, 9 vols (Oxford, 1711), vi, pp. 93–122.
24. Gordon, *Itinerarium septentrionale*, unpaginated preface.
25. Warburton, *Vallum romanum*, p. vii.
26. I. G. Brown, 'Sir John Clerk of Penicuik (1676–1755): Aspects of a Virtuoso Life', unpublished Ph.D. thesis, University of Cambridge (1980), pp. 116–18. Clerk's own account of the proceedings are to be found in John M. Gray (ed.), *Memoirs of the Life of Sir John Clerk of Penicuik*, Scottish History Society, 13 (1982).
27. John Warburton, *Vallum Romanum: or The History and Antiquities of the Roman Wall, Commonly Called the Picts Wall* (London, 1753), p. vi. Warburton claimed that he had caused the map which he published in 1715 to be surveyed himself; it was, in fact copied by one executed for the Board of Ordnance. Sir George Macdonald, 'John Horsley, Scholar and Gentleman', *Archaeologia Aeliana*, 3rd series, 10 (1933), p. 53.
28. Macdonald 'John Horsley', p. 51, estimates that six out of 159 pages of text can be attributed to Warburton; the remainder being plagiarised from Horsley.
29. Camden, *Britannia*, ed., Gibson, 2 vols (1722), ii, pp. 1051–60. On Robert Smith see R. C. Bosanquet, 'Robert Smith and the "Observations upon the Picts Wall", 1708–9', *Transactions of the Cumberland and Westmoreland Antiquarian Society*, 55 (1956), pp. 154–71; Smith differed from later writers such as Gordon or Horsley in that he did not make any use of the *Notitia* or other contemporary Roman sources in order to interpret the remains, but relied instead upon the description to be found in Bede. His kinsmen John and George Smith were preparing a new edition of Bede's history (see chapter 6 below).
30. The publication of John Warburton's *Vallum romanum* was a direct reflection of the upsurge in interest which was generated in the Roman Wall. He presented it to the public as a cheaper and portable alternative to the heavy folio volumes of Camden, Gordon or Horsley.
31. William Stukeley, 'Iter boreale', published with *Itinerarium curiosum* (2nd edn, London, 1776), p. 61.
32. See, for example, the journey made by Sir John Clerk of Penicuik in 1724 during which he called upon antiquaries in Newcastle and Durham as well as landed gentlemen such as Mr Shaftoe of Benwell. Eric Birley (ed.), 'Sir John Clerk's Visit to the North of England in 1724', *Transactions of the Durham and Northumberland Archaeological and Architectural Society*, 11 (1962), pp. 221–46.
33. Birley, *Research on Hadrian's Wall*, pp. 1–60.

34. *Gentleman's Magazine*, 1 (1731), pp. 487–88, quoted in I. G. Brown, 'Sir John Clerk of Penicuik', p. 137.
35. James Thomson, 'Spring', from *The Seasons*, ed. James Sambrook (Oxford, 1981), p. 42.
36. John Horsley, *Britannia Romana: or The Roman Antiquities of Britain* (London, 1732), p. iv.
37. Edward Chaney, 'The Grand Tour and the Evolution of the Travel Book', in A. Wilton and I. Bignamini (ed.), *Grand Tour: The Lure of Italy in the Eighteenth Century* (London, 1996), pp. 95–96.
38. Lewis (ed.), *Correspondence of Horace Walpole*, ii, pp. 116–17, Horace Walpole to William Cole, 1 September 1778.
39. On collecting practices in the eighteenth century see Francis Haskell and Nicholas Penny, *Taste and the Antique: The Lure of Classical Sculpture, 1500–1900* (New Haven and London, 1991) and Francis Haskell, *History and its Images: Art and the Interpretation of the Past* (New Haven and London, 1993), pp. 13–130; Krzysztof Pomian, *Collectors and Curiosities in Paris and Venice, 1500–1800* (Cambridge, 1987); Patricia Kell, 'British Collecting, 1656–1800: Scientific and Social Practice', unpublished D.Phil. thesis, University of Oxford (1996); Arthur Macgregor (ed.), *Sir Hans Sloane: Collector, Scientist, Antiquary. Founding Father of the British Museum* (London, 1994); Ian Jenkins and Kim Sloan, *Vases and Volcanoes: Sir William Hamilton and his Collections* (London, 1996). For a comparative French perspective see Laurence Brockliss, *Calvet's Web: Enlightenment and the Republic of Letters in Eighteenth-Century France* (Oxford, 2002), pp. 193–280.
40. Horsley, *Britannia Romana*, p. 182; William Hutchinson, *A View of Northumberland with an Excursion to the Abbey of Mailross in Scotland*, 2 vols (Newcastle, 1776–78), i, p. 60, quoting a letter from Warburton to Gale, 21 November 1717. The largest single collection of British Roman antiquities was that amassed by Sir Robert Cotton in the early seventeenth century at his seat at Connington, although, by the time that Horsley viewed it, the antiquities had suffered considerable weathering and defacement. The fifteen remaining marbles were later presented to Trinity College, Cambridge, in 1759 by Sir Robert's heirs. Gough, *British Topography*, i, p. xv.
41. This was the ethos of the Society of Dilettanti founded in 1732; Lionel Cust, *History of the Society of Dilettanti*, ed. Sidney Colvin (London, 1898) p. 4. On some of the wider influences of neoclassicism see James William Johnson, *The Formation of English Neo-Classical Thought* (Princeton, 1967), especially pp. 62–68, 90–105; Philip Ayres, *Classical Culture and the Idea of Rome in the Eighteenth Century* (Cambridge, 1997), and J. M. Levine, 'Why Neoclassicism? Politics and Culture in Eighteenth-Century England', *British Journal for Eighteenth-Century Studies*, 25 (2002), pp. 75–93.
42. Joseph Wilcocks, *Roman Conversations*, 2 vols (London, 1792), i, p. v.
43. Drake had been persuaded by the MP Sir Harry Slingsby to put his name to a bond for £600. Sir Harry repudiated the debt, and as an MP escaped

imprisonment; Drake, however, was arrested and imprisoned in the Fleet in early 1736. Burlington intervened, telling Sir Harry that 'he would use all his interest to prevent his being rechosen for Knaresborough unless he paid the debt and made a compensation to Mr Drake', Nichols (ed.), *Illustrations of Literature*, v, p. 298.

44. Rosemary Sweet, 'History and Identity in Eighteenth-Century York', in Jane Rendall and Mark Hallett (ed.), *Eighteenth-Century York: Culture, Space and Society* (York, 2003).
45. See note 3, pp. 144–17.
46. Bodleian Library, MS Gough Gen. Top. 15 comprises a collection of plans of Roman sites dedicated to individual knights and their seats. See Iain G. Brown, 'Chyndonax to Galgacus: New Letters of William Stukeley to Alexander Gordon', *Antiquaries Journal*, 67 (1987), p. 125, n. 43.
47. Cust and Colvin, *History of the Society of Dilettanti*, pp. 82–106; R. Chandler, N. Revett and W. Pars, *Ionian Antiquities* (London, 1769). This is contrary to the interpretation put forward by Ayres in *Classical Culture and the Idea of Rome*, in which he awards the Society of Roman Knights considerable agency in stimulating the study of Roman antiquities. On Stukeley's role in the society see the biographies by Piggott and Haycock.
48. Brown, 'Sir John Clerk of Penicuik', p. 119.
49. See for example the dedication to the earl of Winchelsea for 'Iter Romanum V' in Stukeley's *Itinerarium curiosum* (London, 1724), p. 72: 'the delight you take in rescuing the monuments of our ancestors, your indefatigable zeal in collecting them, your exquisite knowledge in the Greek, Roman and British antiquities, and especially your great love for those of your own country, which you continually commit to writing, in your private commentaries, add a reputation to these studies, and make the Muses hope for a sunshine, when men of your Lordship's noble birth entertain them with that familiarity and condescension which was one great glory of the Augustan age'.
50. Ayres, *Classical Culture and the Idea of Rome*, p. 101.
51. National Archives of Scotland, GD 18/3/8, Alexander Gordon to William Stukeley, 4 March 1725 (my italics).
52. Sweet, 'History and Identity in Eighteenth-Century York'.
53. Haycock, *William Stukeley*, p. 222; Theodor Harmsen, *Antiquarianism in the Augustan Age: Thomas Hearne, 1678–1735* (Bern, 2000), p. 183, 'Dr Stukely was much talk'd of by us before Mr Burton came in, particularly his new Book of an hundred Cuts, wch some very deservedly call Dr Stukely's hundred Fancies, wch I have not yet seen, but 'tis universally condemn'd as strange, weak ridiculous Stuff, even worse, as it were, than Poynter of Merton's Things. He indulges his Fancy to that degree, as to endeavour to impose any Thing upon the World for Antiquity, whereas at the same time his Draughts do not agree to the Originals'; William Bray, *Sketch of a Tour into Derbyshire, Yorkshire, Including Part of Buckingham, Warwick, Leicester, Nottingham, Northampton, Bedford and Hertfordshire* (2nd edn, London, 1780), pp. 77–78.

54. National Archives of Scotland, GD 18/5033, Sir John Clerk in a letter of introduction for Horsley addressed to Mr Crawfurd, professor of church history at the university of Edinburgh, 6 January 1729.
55. National Archives of Scotland, GD 18 5023/3/41, Gordon to Stukeley, 7 September 1728.
56. Janus Gruter, *Inscriptiones antiquae totius orbis romani* (Amsterdam, 1707).
57. Horsley, *Britannia romana*, p. 178; Horsley's views expressed here suggest that he had recently read Scipione Maffei's essay on the use and inscription of medals published in Richard Rawlinson's translation of M. Langlet du Fresnoy, *A New Method of Studying History* (London, 1728).
58. Horsley did make special journeys to Bath and to Caerleon (Monmouthshire) in order to view the antiquities there. He was at pains to vary the route which he took each time he travelled to London in order to maximise the number of different Roman stations through which he passed.
59. Horsley, *Britannia romana*, p. 44. The criticism is made in Sir George Macdonald, 'John Horsley, Scholar and Gentleman', *Archaeologia Aeliana*, 3rd series, 10 (1933), p. 21. On Horsley's achievement, see also J. M. Levine, *The Battle of the Books: History and Literature in the Augustan Age* (Ithaca and London, 1991), pp. 387–402.
60. Nathaniel Salmon, *The History of Hertfordshire; Describing the County, and its Antient Monuments, Particularly the Roman* (London, 1728); Edward A. Fitch, 'Nathaniel Salmon', *Essex Review*, 2 (1893), pp. 238–45; S. Doree, 'Nathaniel Salmon: Hertfordshire's Neglected Historian', in D. Jones Baker (ed.), *Hertfordshire in History* (London, 1991), pp. 206–16.
61. Nathaniel Salmon, *Roman Stations in Britain* (London 1726), p. ii; idem, *A New Survey of England: Wherein the Defects of Camden are Supplied* (London, 1731).
62. Gale, 'Essay Towards the Recovery of the Courses of the Four Great Roman Ways', p. 97.
63. Wise, *Letter to Dr Mead*, p. 8.
64. British Library, Stowe MS 752, fol. 112, William Borlase to Charles Lyttelton, 21 August 1749. See also Borlase's paper published in *Philosophical Transactions* (1751); even now the extent of Roman occupation in Cornwall remains unclear.
65. Quoted in H. M. Jenkins, 'Dr Thomas's Edition of Sir William Dugdale's Antiquities of Warwickshire', *Dugdale Society Occasional Papers*, 3 (1931), p. 15. See also Rosemary Sweet, *The Writing of Urban Histories in Eighteenth Century England* (Oxford, 1997), p. 154.
66. W. C. Lukis (ed.), 'Family Memoirs of William Stukeley, vol. i', *Surtees Society*, 73 (1880), p. 397, Charles Grey to William Stukeley, 28 April 1749.
67. Lukis (ed.), 'Family Memoirs of William Stukeley, vol. ii', *Surtees Society*, 76 (1883), p. 260, William Stukeley to Roger Gale, 31 January 1727/8; Francis Peck, *Academica Tertia Anglicana: or The Antiquarian Annals of Stamford in Lincolnshire* (London, 1727). Stukeley compiled his own manuscript history of Stamford, Corpus Christi College, Cambridge, Parker Library, Stukeley MSS 618–19. 'Stanfordia Illustrata or an Account of the Antiquities of Stanford

[sic], in the way of Dialogue, between Panagaeus and Palaephatus 1736'. Stukeley had attempted to secure Peck's appointment to the wardenship of Brown's Hospital in Stamford, and Peck was a fellow member of an informal society meeting on a monthly basis, which Stukeley had established, first at Grantham and then Market Deeping. Bodleian Library, MS Eng. Misc. e. 260, fol. 88v; Eng. Misc. c. 121, fol. 34. See also Lukis (ed.), 'Family Memoirs of William Stukeley, vol. i', *Surtees Society*, 73 (1880), p. 123.

68. Stukeley, *Itinerarium curiosum*, pt 2, p. 59.
69. Drake, *Eboracum*, p. 18.
70. John Hutchins, *The History and Antiquities of the County of Dorset*, 2 vols (London, 1774), i, pp. xii–xx. William Coxe, however, complained to John Nichols that his account was full of mistakes which had been left uncorrected even in the second edition. Bodleian Library, MS Eng. Lett. c. 355, fol. 123v.
71. Gibson died in 1772; the manuscript was acquired by John Nichols in 1795 and was published in 1800.
72. Calculation based upon the essays published in *Archaeologia*, 1–12 (1770–1796).
73. Stebbing Shaw, *The History and Antiquities of Staffordshire*, 2 vols (1798–1801), i, p. 22.
74. West Suffolk Record Office, E2/22/1, unfoliated collection, George Ashby to Thomas Granger, no date.
75. Anon., *Origines Divisianae: or The Antiquities of the Devizes in Some Familiar Letters to a Friend, Wrote in the Years 1750 and 1751* (London, 1754), pp. 62–63.
76. Stebbing Shaw, *A Tour in the West of England* (London, 1789), p. 433; on turnpikes see E. Pawson, *Transport and Economy: The Turnpike Roads in Eighteenth-Century Britain* (London, 1977).
77. Corpus Christi College, Cambridge, Parker Library, Stukeley MS 618, fos 21–23.
78. Richard Warner, *The History of Bath* (London, 1801), p. 25.
79. British Library, Add. MS 37219, fol. 53v, Andrew Coltée Ducarel to Philip Morant, 4 October 1755.
80. The deception is discussed in Stuart Piggott's biography of Stukeley: *William Stukeley: An Eighteenth-Centry Antiquary* (2nd edn, London, 1985), pp. 129–38. Stukeley's own version of the discovery was delivered in a paper to the Society of Antiquaries in 1756, 'An Account of Richard of Cirencester, Monk of Westminster, and of his Works, with his Ancient Map of Roman Britain and the Itinerary thereof', and published with the second edition of *Itinerarium curiosum*, pt 2, pp. 109–68.
81. Possible motivations for Bertram's forgery are discussed by Stephen Bann, 'The Truth in Mapping', in *The Inventions of History* (Manchester, 1990). Bann interprets the forgery as an attempt to 'recover Britain symbolically' after the estrangement caused by his father's improvidence which forced the family to go abroad: 'Bertram's engraving of the map seems almost the condensation of his desire to take possession of what he had lost.' (p. 206). The most obvious explanation is that Bertram hoped to be able to advance his career by securing credit with Stukeley and the antiquarian community in England. He informed

Stukeley that election to the Royal and Antiquarian Societies would assist in winning him promotion.

82. Bodleian Library, MS Eng. Lett. b. 2, fos 7–8.
83. Piggott, *William Stukeley*, pp. 126–38.
84. Henry Hatcher (ed.), *The Description of Britain, Translated from Richard of Cirencester* (London, 1809), pp. xix–xxi.
85. Gordon, *Itinerarium septentrionale*, p. 43; the Silures are generally accepted to have inhabited Glamorgan and Gwent and the Brigantes were spread over areas of Yorkshire, Northumberland, Cumbria and Lancashire.
86. Piggott, *William Stukeley*, p. 138.
87. John Whitaker, *The History of Manchester in Four Books*, 2 vols (2nd edn, London, 1773), i, pp. v, vii.
88. Whitaker, *History of Manchester*, i, p. 83, 89.
89. *Gentleman's Magazine*, 57 (1787), p. 566.
90. See for example, J. Hodgson and F. C. Laird, *The Beauties of England and Wales*, 18 vols (London, 1813), xii, pt 1.
91. West Suffolk Record Office, E/2/22/2, unfoliated collection, Thomas Pennant to George Ashby, 14 November 1773.
92. Muscipula, *Curious Remarks on the History of Manchester* (London, 1771), pp. vii, 10. According to Michael Tyson 'Muscipula' was John Collier, also known as Tim Bobbin, whose other works included *A View of the Lancashire Dialect* (London, 1770). Bodleian Library, MS Gough Gen. Top. 44, fol. 43, Tyson to Gough, 30 November, 1771. See also Nichols (ed.), *Literary Anecdotes*, vii, p. 573.
93. West Suffolk Record Office E2/22/2 unfoliated collection John Lettice to George Ashby, 25 December 1777.
94. *Gentleman's Magazine*, 56 (1786), p. 1061. The reviewer was principally concerned that Johnstone (like Stukeley and Bertram) had not fulfilled this 'first duty to the public' in that he had not satisfied them as to the authenticity of the materials; he had not stated the number of the manuscript taken from the British Museum collection or demonstrated how it differed from that used by Camden.
95. Thomas Reynolds, *Iter Britanniarum: or That Part of the Itinerary which Relates to Britain, with a New Comment* (Cambridge, 1799), pp. ii, xiv, 119–36.
96. Richard Fenton, *A Historical Tour through Pembrokeshire* (London, 1810), p. 41.
97. Donald Haigh, 'Antiquities, Artifice and Error: The Ramification of Richard of Cirencester in the Township of Barkisland, Parish of Halifax', *Transactions of the Halifax Antiquarian Society*, new series, 7 (1999), pp. 13–37; for Skinner's doubts see British Library, Add. MS 28795, fos 132–50.
98. Nichols (ed.), *Illustrations of Literature*, vi, pp. 439–40. Sir Richard Colt Hoare, whilst defending the testimony of Richard of Cirencester himself, commented upon the fashion 'even amongst distinguished authors' to accuse him of 'incorrectness'. See his *Ancient History of North Wiltshire*, 2 vols (London, 1821), ii, pt 2, p. 29. B. B. Woodward, 'A Literary Forgery: Richard of Cirencester's

Tractate on Britain', *Gentleman's Magazine*, new series, 1 (1866), pp. 310–18, 617–24; 2 (1866), pp. 458–66. See also J. E. B. Mayor, *Ricardi de Cirencestria speculum historiale de gestis regum angliae*, Rolls Society, pt 2 (1869) who identifies the 'credulous' and the sceptics amongst the published antiquarian and topographical works of the period.

99. Linda Ebbatson, 'Conditions of the Emergence and Existence of Archaeology in the Nineteenth Century: The Royal Archaeological Institute, 1843–1914', unpublished Ph.D. thesis, University of Durham (1999), p. 143.
100. Salmon, *New Survey of England*, p. 30.
101. Drake, *Eboracum*, pp. 8–66.
102. Lukis (ed.), 'Family Memoirs of William Stukeley, vol. iii', *Surtees Society*, 80 (1885), p. 140. Owen Salusbury Brereton, who made a tour of Scotland in 1768, informed the Society of Antiquaries that 'so much of the Stone has been borrowed of late years to build with; and so many Parts of it serve as the Foundation for the grand military Road cross the island, lately made, that the Remains of this once noble Work, at present, are but small'. Society of Antiquaries, Minute Books, xi (typescript), p. 62, 16 February 1769.
103. Robert Melville, *A Critical Inquiry into the Constitution of the Roman Legion* (Edinburgh, 1773); William Roy, *The Military Antiquities of the Romans in North Britain, and Particularly their Ancient System of Castramentation, Illustrated from Vestiges of the Camps of Agricola Existing There* (London, 1793), pp. i–ix.
104. Sir Henry Englefield, 'Account of Antiquities Discovered at Bath 1790', *Archaeologia*, 10 (1792), p. 331.
105. William Stukeley drew attention to this anomaly in a paper on the structure and use of Roman baths in England presented to the Society of Antiquaries, 28 May 1761. Tellingly it was not one of those selected later for publication. Society of Antiquaries, Minute Books, viii (typescript), pp. 677–78.
106. Ibid., xvii, p. 164, 16 November 1780, Daines Barrington described antiquities lately found near Cirencester and Stunsfield [Stonesfield], in Oxfordshire. The (mosaic) pavement, he wrote 'is not great, yet it equals that of several Rooms at Herculaneum'.
107. Reynolds, *Iter britanniarum*, pp. 56–57.
108. William Stukeley listed twenty which had been found between 1667 and 1739, Society of Antiquaries, MS 264, fol. 39.
109. Thomas Hearne, 'A Discourse Concerning the Stunsfield Tessellated Pavement', in *The Itinerary of John Leland the Antiquary*, 9 vols (Oxford, 1712), viii, pp. vii–xxxv; J. M. Levine, 'The Stonesfield Pavement: Archaeology in Augustan England', in *Humanism and History*, pp. 107–22.
110. Hearne, 'Stunsfield Tessellated Pavement', pp. xv–xvi; Harmsen, *Antiquarianism in the Augustan Age*, p. 176.
111. Samuel Carte, 'An Account of Roman Pavements; particularly of those discovered at Wellow in Somersetshire, 1737', Society of Antiquaries, MS 264, fol. 103. Carte was aware of the logistical problems of carting around large

quantities of stone tesserae in the military baggage train, but ingeniously suggested that this was the reason for generals such as Caesar using elephants in military campaigns (fol. 102).

112. Thomas Warton, *History and Antiquities of Kiddington* (3rd edn, London, 1815), p. 67.
113. Samuel Lysons, *An Account of the Roman Antiquities Discovered at Woodchester* (London, 1797); idem, *An Account of the Remains of a Roman Villa Discovered at Bignor in the County of Sussex in the Year 1811, and the Four Following Years* (London 1820); Lindsay Fleming (ed.), *Memoir and Select Letters of Samuel Lysons VPRS and VPSA, 1763–1819* (Oxford, no date), pp. 21–23, 25–26.
114. His success was due not least, to the patronage of Sir Joseph Banks, his Lincolnshire compatriot. Joseph Thomas Fowler (ed.), *The Correspondence of William Fowler* (privately printed, 1907), pp. 51, 228.
115. Malcolm Todd, 'From Romanticism to Archaeology: Richard Colt Hoare, Samuel Lysons and Antiquity', in Mark Brayshaw (ed.), *Topographical Writers in South-West England* (Exeter, 1996), p. 94.
116. Lysons, *Account of the Remains of a Roman Villa Discovered.*
117. John Wood, *A Description of Bath* (Bath, 1765), p. 170. The context in which Wood developed his views on early British society is discussed more fully in the following chapter.
118. Society of Antiquaries, Minute Book, vii (typescript), p. 370, 19 June 1755.
119. Friedrich Kielmansegge, *Diary of Journey to England in the Years 1761–1762* (London, 1902), pp. 127–28, quoted in Trevor Fawcett, *Voices of Eighteenth-Century Bath* (Bath, 1995), p. 115.
120. Sir Henry Englefield, 'Account of Antiquities Discovered at Bath 1790', *Archaeologia*, 10 (1792), pp. 325–33; Thomas Pownall, *Descriptions and Explanations of Some Remains of Roman Antiquities Dug up in the City of Bath in the Year MDCCXC* (Bath, 1796).
121. Richard Warner, *The History of Bath* (London, 1801); see also Barry Cunliffe, *Roman Bath Discovered* (London, 1971), pp. 17–18, 224 and Peter Borsay, *The Image of Georgian Bath* (Oxford, 2000), pp. 55–57.
122. Reynolds, *Iter britanniarum*, p. xii.
123. Gale, 'An Essay Towards the Recovery of the Courses of the Four Great Roman Ways', pp. 121–22.
124. Samuel Pegge, *The Roman Roads, Ikenild Street and Bath Way through the Country of the Coritani or County of Derby* (London, 1769); eight papers specifically on Roman roads in Britain were published in *Archaeologia* between 1770 and 1796.
125. Society of Antiquaries, MS 477/3, fol. 261, Samuel Pegge to Richard Gough, 2 August 1788; he expressed similar views in 'Derbeiescira romana', *Archaeologia*, 10 (1792), pp. 35–36.
126. West Suffolk Record Office E2/22/1, unfoliated letter, Richard Gough to George Ashby, no date.
127. Iain G. Brown, 'Critick in Antiquity; Sir John Clerk of Penicuik', *Antiquity*,

51 (1977), p. 207; see also Roger Gale's letter to Sir John, National Archives of Scotland, GD 18/2, 24 March 1725/6, in which Gale agreed with him on the danger of ascribing all brass weapons to the Romans.

128. Drake, *Eboracum*, especially pp. 26–37.

129. Sir Henry Englefield, 'Observations on the Antient Buildings at York', *Archaeologia*, 6 (1782), p. 106. Englefield was referring in particular to Drake's identification of Mickelgate Bar as belonging to the Roman period on the basis of its being constructed with a rounded arch. As Englefield pointed out, Saxon and Norman buildings were also raised on segments of arches and built of grit; moreover, the Bar was itself well above ground level still, in contrast to all other known remnants of the Roman city.

130. John Britton, *The Autobiography of John Britton*, 2 vols (London, 1850), i, p. 241.

Notes to Chapter 6: The Anglo-Saxons

1. William Camden, *Britannia: or A Chorographical Description of Great Britain and Ireland*, 2 vols (London, 1722), ed. Edmund Gibson, i, dedication.
2. Robert Mayhew, 'Edmund Gibson's Editions of *Britannia*: Dynastic Chorography and the Particularist Politics of Precedent', *Historical Research*, 73 (2000), pp. 239–61.
3. Samuel Gale, *The History and Antiquities of the Cathedral Church of Winchester* (London, 1715), p. 7.
4. Corpus Christi College, Cambridge, Parker Library, Stukeley MS 19, 'Stanfordia Illustrata, or an Account of the Antiquities of Stanford [sic], in the Way of Dialogue between Panageus and Palaephatus 1736', fol. 34.
5. Francis Wise, *A Letter to Dr Mead Concerning some Antiquities in Berkshire* (Oxford, 1753), p. 10.
6. Thor J. Beck, *Northern Antiquities in French Learning and Literature*, 2 vols (New York, 1934), i, pp. 1–65; Samuel Kliger, *The Goths in England: A Study in Seventeenth and Eighteenth-Century Thought* (Cambridge, Massachusetts, 1952); Hugh A. MacDougall, *Racial Myth in English History: Trojans, Teutons and Anglo-Saxons* (London, 1982), pp. 1–86; J. W. Burrow, *A Liberal Descent: Victorian Historians and the English Past* (Cambridge, 1981), pp. 109–25.
7. Samuel Squire, *An Enquiry into the Foundation of the English Constitution: or Historical Essay upon the Anglo-Saxon Government both in Germany and England* (London, 1745), p. 9.
8. A. Bicknell, *The Life of Alfred the Great, King of the Anglo-Saxons* (London, 1777), p. 196.
9. Thomas Hearne, *The Life of King Aelfred the Great by Sir John Spelman Kt from the Original Manuscripts in the Bodleian Library; with Considerable Additions, and Several Historical Remarks* (Oxford, 1709), p. 8.
10. William Nicolson, *The English Historical Library in Three Parts* (2nd edn, London 1714), p. 41.

11. Nicolson, *English Historical Library*, p. 41
12. William Hutchinson, *A View of Northumberland with an Excursion to the Abbey of Mailross in Scotland*, 2 vols (Newcastle, 1776–78), i, pp. vi–vii. All that the English had inherited from their British ancestors was ferocity, instability and ingratitude. Hutchinson did not go so far as the Gothicist John Pinkerton in identifying these qualities exclusively with the Celts.
13. Thomas Pownall, 'A Description of the Sepulchral Monument at New Grange, near Drogheda, in the County of Meath, in Ireland', *Archaeologia*, 2 (1773), p. 294.
14. Bodleian Library, MS Ballard 42, fol. 76, Charles Lyttelton to George Ballard, 20 January 1748/9.
15. David Fairer, 'Anglo-Saxon Studies', in *The Eighteenth Century*, L. G. Mitchell and L. S. Sutherland (ed.), *The History of the University of Oxford*, ed. T. H. Aston, 8 vols (Oxford, 1986), v, pp. 807–28.
16. Colin Kidd, *British Identities before Nationalism: Ethnicity and Nationhood in the Atlantic World, 1600–1800* (Cambridge, 1999); Reginald Horsman, 'Origins of Racial Anglo-Saxonism in Great Britain before 1850', *Journal of the History of Ideas*, 37 (1976), pp. 387–410; MacDougal, *Racial Myth in English History*.
17. Angelika Lutz, 'The Study of the Anglo-Saxon Chronicle in the Seventeenth Century and the Establishment of Old English Studies in the Universities', in Timothy Graham (ed.), *The Recovery of Old English: Anglo-Saxon Studies in the Sixteenth and Seventeenth Centuries* (Kalamazoo, 2000), pp. 1–82.
18. Nichols, *Literary Anecdotes*, iv, p. 143, Edmund Gibson to Thwaites, 20 May 1697. George Hickes, *Several Letters which Passed between Dr George Hickes and a Popish Priest* (1705), p. 70, argued that the purity of Saxon worship gave no popish titles to the Virgin Mary and no adoration of saints' images or the real presence. Fairer 'Anglo-Saxon Studies', p. 808; see also, M. J. Murphy, 'The Elstobs, Scholars of Old England and Anglican Apologists', *Durham University Journal*, 58 (1966), pp. 131–38.
19. D. C. Douglas, *English Scholars, 1660–1730* (London, 1939), pp. 249–84; Mayhew, 'Edmund Gibson's Editions of *Britannia*', pp. 251–54.
20. Hearne (ed.), *Life of Aelfred* p. 9.
21. Richard T. Vann, 'The Free Anglo-Saxons: A Historical Myth', *Journal of the History of Ideas*, 19 (1958), pp. 259–72; Glen Burgess, *The Politics of the Ancient Constitution: An Introduction to English Political Thought, 1603–1642* (Pennsylvania, 1993), pp. 1–78; Christopher Hill, 'The Norman Yoke', in idem, *Puritanism and Revolution* (London, 1958), pp. 50–122.
22. R. J. Smith, *The Gothic Bequest: Medieval Institutions in British Thought, 1688–1863* (Cambridge, 1987), pp. 113–26, on Edmund Burke. Smith's study surveys the continuing resonance of the myth throughout this period.
23. Squire, *Enquiry into the Foundation of the English Constitution*, p. 3. On the relationship between Squire's antiquarian scholarship and his politics see Reed Browning, *Political and Constitutional Ideas of the Court Whigs* (Baton Rouge, Louisiana, 1982), pp. 117–44; Christine Gerrard, *The Patriot*

Opposition to Walpole: Politics, Poetry and National Myth, 1725–42 (Oxford, 1994), pp. 101–41.

24. The classic study being J. G. A. Pocock, *The Ancient Constitution and the Feudal Law* (Cambridge, 1987); see also Smith, *Gothic Bequest.*
25. Robert Brady, *An Historical Treatise of Cities and Burghs, or Boroughs* (London, 1690); Thomas Madox, *Firma Burgi* (London, 1727); Squire, *Enquiry into the Foundation of the English Constitution*; James Ibbetson, *A Dissertation on the Folclande and Boclande of the Saxons* (London, 1777); idem, *A Dissertation on the National Assemblies under the Saxon and Norman Governments* (London, 1781); Francis Maseres, 'A View of the Ancient Constitution of the English Parliament', *Archaeologia*, 2 (1773), pp. 301–41; Charles Mellish, 'Observations on Mr Maseres' View of the Ancient Constitution of the English Parliament', *Archaeologia*, 2 (1773), pp. 341–53.
26. Smith, *Gothic Bequest*, pp. 71–84; David Allan, *Virtue, Learning and the Scottish Enlightenment* (Edinburgh, 1993), pp. 168–69; Kidd, *British Identities before Nationalism*, pp. 279–86.
27. John Whitaker, *The History of Manchester ... Containing the Saxon Period*, 2 vols (London, 1775), ii, p. 139.
28. John Cartwright, *Take Your Choice!* (London, 1776); Granville Sharp, *An Account of the Constitutional English Policy of Congregational Courts, and More Particularly of the Great Annual Court of the People Called the View of the Frankpledge* (London, 1786); James Burgh, *Political Disquisitions*, 3 vols (London, 1774–75). On radical patriotism see Linda Colley, 'Radical Patriotism in Eighteenth-Century England', in Raphael Samuel (ed.), *Patriotism: the Making and Unmaking of British National Identity*, 3 vols (London, 1989), i, pp. 169–87.
29. Samuel Henshall, *Specimens and Parts: Containing a History of the County of Kent, and a Dissertation on the Laws from the Reign of Edward the Confessor to Edward I* (London, 1798), pp. 7, 12, 16.
30. Rosemary Sweet, *The English Town: Government, Society and Culture, 1680–1840* (Harlow, 1999), pp. 141–62, and 'Freemen and Independence in English Borough Politics, c. 1780–1820', *Past and Present*, 161 (1998), pp. 84–115.
31. Edward Griffith, *A Collection of Ancient Records, Relating to the Borough of Huntingdon* (London, 1827); Joseph Parkes, *The Governing Charter of the Borough of Warwick* (London, 1827); Benjamin Strutt, *The Constitution of the Burgh of Colchester* (Colchester, 1822); H. Merewether and A. J. Stephens, *The History of the Boroughs and Municipal Corporations of the United Kingdom, from the Earliest to the Present Time: With an Examination of Records, Charters and Other Documents Illustrative of their Constitution and Powers*, 3 vols (London, 1835); Smith, *Gothic Bequest*, pp. 101–2; Asa Briggs, *Saxons, Normans and Victorians* (Historical Association, 1966), pp. 6–8.
32. G. Newman, *The Rise of English Nationalism: A Cultural History, 1740–1830* (London, 1987), pp. 116–18, 184–85, 189; Colley, 'Radical Patriotism'; Kathleen Wilson, *The Island Race: Englishness, Empire and Gender in the Eighteenth Century* (London, 2003), pp. 84–89.

33. Bodleian Library, Tanner MS 25, fol. 251, Edmund Gibson to Thomas Tanner, 21 October 1694.
34. Joseph Strutt, *A Complete View of the Dress and Habits of the People of England, from the Establishment of the Saxons in Britain to the Present Time, Illustrated by Engravings Taken from the Most Authentic Remains of Antiquity*, 2 vols (London, 1796), i, p. 14.
35. Nichols, *Literary Anecdotes*, iv, p. 145, William Nicolson to Edward Thwaites, no date.
36. British Library, Add. MS 33665, fol. 35v, John Skinner to his daughter Laura Skinner, 6 September 1817.
37. Nathaniel Salmon, *A New Survey of England* (London, 1731), p. 32.
38. Wise, *A Letter to Dr Mead*, p. 10.
39. Michael Burden, *Garrick, Arne and the Masque of Alfred: A Case Study in National, Theatrical and Musical Politics* (Lampeter, 1994), p. 45.
40. Thornhaugh Gurdon, *Essay on the Antiquity of Norwich Castel* (sic) (Norwich, 1728), p. 14; Richard Warner, *History of the Isle of Wight* (London, 1795), p. 23.
41. Richard Gough, *Anecdotes of British Topography* (London, 1768), p. xvii.
42. John Gascoigne, *Cambridge in the Age of Enlightenment: Science, Religion and Politics from the Restoration to the French Revolution* (Cambridge, 1989).
43. Lutz, 'Study of the Anglo-Saxon Chronicle', pp. 52–53; Fairer, 'Anglo-Saxon Studies'.
44. Francis Godwin James, *North Country Bishop: A Biography of William Nicolson* (London, 1956), pp. 9–14.
45. The connections between George Hickes's religious and political stance and his antiquarian studies are examined in greater detail by Richard L. Harris, 'George Hickes, White Kennett and the Inception of the *Thesaurus Linguarum Septentrionalium*', *Bodleian Library Record*, 10 (1983), pp. 169–86.
46. E. N. Adams, *Old English Scholarship in England from 1566–1800* (New Haven, 1917; reprinted, 1970); C. T. Berkhout and M. McC. Gatch (ed.), *Anglo-Saxon Scholarship: The First Three Centuries* (Boston, Massachusetts, 1982).
47. J. Hunter (ed.), *Letters of Eminent Men, Addressed to Ralph Thoresby, FRS: Now First Published from the Originals*, 2 vols (London, 1832), i, pp. 221, 316, 318. William Nicolson to Ralph Thoresby, 17 March, 7 May, 22 October 1698.
48. Hunter (ed.), *Letters of Eminent Men*, ii, p. 198, Elizabeth Elstob to Ralph Thoresby, 10 October 1709.
49. Maurice Shelton, *Wootton's Short View of George Hicke's Grammatico-Critical and Archaeological Treasure of the Northern Languages* (London, 1735).
50. This edition of the *Ecclesiastical History* comprised the Latin original, King Alfred's Saxon version, the prose and metrical *Lives of St Cuthbert*, the *Lives of the Abbots of Wearmouth and Jarrow*, the treatises *On the Holy Places*, the *Life of St Felix* and a *Martyrology* and Mabillon's *Life of Bede* as well as a series of appendices. See Douglas, *English Scholars*, pp. 73–6; Terence Towers, 'Smith and Son, Editors of Bede', in Gerald Bonner (ed.), *Famulus Christi: Essays in Commemoration of the Thirteenth Centenary of the Birth of the*

Venerable Bede (London, 1976), pp. 357–65. This enormous piece of scholarship was published by subscription at 30 s. small paper and 50 s. large paper

51. Douglas, *English Scholars*, pp. 273–84; F. M. Powicke, 'Sir Henry Spelman and the Concilia', *Proceedings of the British Academy*, 16 (1930), pp. 345–82; E. F. Jacob, 'Wilkins' Concilia and the Fifteenth Century', *Transactions of the Royal Historical Society*, 4th series, 15 (1932), pp. 91–131.
52. Georgian R. Tashjian, David R. Tashjian, Brian J. Enright, *Richard Rawlinson: A Tercentenary Memorial* (Kalamazoo, 1990); Gough, *British Topography*, i, p. xxxviii.
53. British Library, Add. MS 32325, fol. 117, Francis Wise to Edward Lye, 10 September 1754.
54. Margaret Clunies Ross, 'Re-evaluating the Work of Edward Lye, an Eighteenth-Century Septentrional Scholar', in *Studies in Medievalism*, 9 (1997), pp. 66–79. As well as the dictionary, Lye published an edition of Francis Junius's *Etymologicum Anglicanum* in 1745 and an edition of the Gothic Gospels in 1750. Nineteenth-century scholars were particularly critical of Lye's scholarship: see *Gentleman's Magazine*, new series, 1 (1832), p. 392, 'for if ever book was calculated to do harm, to retard the progress of a study, to perplex and fill with trouble the mind of a learner, Lye's Dictionary is assuredly that Book'.
55. Joan Evans, *A History of the Society of Antiquaries* (Oxford, 1956), pp. 40–44.
56. Nichols (ed.), *Literary Anecdotes*, v, pp. 403–4, Edward Rowe Mores to Andrew Coltée Ducarel, 13 January 1753.
57. Bodleian Library, MS Ballard 2; quoted in Edward Rowe Mores, *A Dissertation upon English Typographical Founders and Founderies (1778) with a Catalogue and Specimen of the Typefoundry of John James (1782)*, ed. Harry Carter and Christopher Ricks, Oxford Bibliographical Society (1961), p. xxiii.
58. Carter and Ricks (ed.), *Dissertation upon Typographical Founders*, p. xxix; British Library, Add. MS 6401, fol. 10, Andrew Coltée Ducarel to William Cole, 17 October 1751.
59. Mores's position on the council had been largely due to the influence of Richard Rawlinson. Following Rawlinson's breach with the society over his Jacobite politics (for which see Tashjian, Tashjian and Enright, *Richard Rawlinson*, pp. 63–64), Mores lost his place on the council.
60. National Library of Scotland, Adv. MS 29.5.6, fol. 211, Richard Gough to George Paton, 30 July 1779.
61. Samuel Pegge, *A Series of Dissertations on some Elegant and very Valuable Anglo-Saxon Remains* (London, 1750); H. E. Manville, 'Square Pegges and Round Robins: Some Mid Eighteenth-Century Numismatic Disputes', *British Numismatic Journal*, 60 (1990), pp. 109–12.
62. See for example plates 7 (Greensted church) and 15 and 16 (the cathedral church at Canterbury, parts of which were believed to be Saxon) in the second volume of *Vetusta monumenta*.
63. Bodleian Library, MS Eng. Lett. d. 43, fol. 321, Daines Barrington to Samuel Pegge, 15 June 1771.

64. Daines Barrington, *King Alfred's Orosius: The Anglo-Saxon Version, from the Historian Orosius. By Aelfred the Great. Together with an English Translation from the Anglo-Saxon* (London, 1773). The manuscript upon which this edition and translation was based was originally the work of William Elstob. It had been purchased by Joseph Ames, and then acquired by Samuel Pegge. Pegge did not have the means to publish it and entrusted it to Daines Barrington. His own interest in Anglo-Saxon literature and its study was evidently aroused by possession of the manuscript and led him to complete a history of the Elstobs and their contribution to Saxon scholarship which was published as 'An Historical Account of that Venerable Monument of Antiquity the Textus Roffensis', in J. Nichols (ed.), *Bibliotheca topographica britannica*, 1 (1784).
65. Lye was working on the dictionary from the 1750s and left it uncompleted at his death in 1767. It was finished by Owen Manning, better known now as the historian of Surrey.
66. British Library, Add. MS 22936, fol. 85, Foote Gower to Richard Gough, 5 July 1767. Lye's proposals are to be found at British Library, Add. MS 32325.
67. Quoted in Samuel Henshall, *The Saxon and English Languages Reciprocally Illustrative of Each Other* (London, 1797), p. 41.
68. Nichols (ed.), *Literary Anecdotes*, vi, p. 335.
69. Gough, *Anecdotes of British Topography*, p. xvii.
70. Henshall, *Saxon and English*, p. 29. The author of his obituary in *Gentleman's Magazine*, 77 (1807), p. 1176, commented with some irony that Henshall 'had persuaded himself that he was the best Saxon scholar in the kingdom'.
71. *Gentleman's Magazine*, 68 (1798), pp. 861–65; Bodleian Library, MS Eng. Lett. c. 359, fol. 77.
72. Fairer 'Anglo-Saxon Studies'; M. Murphy, 'Edward Thwaites: Pioneer Teacher of Old English', *Durham University Journal*, 73 (1981), pp. 153–59; Nichols (ed.), *Literary Anecdotes*, iv, pp. 141–49.
73. Shelton, *Wootton's Short View*, dedication.
74. British Library, Add. MS 32325, fol. 245, lists subscriptions for the dictionary which had been received by John Price of Oxford by the time of his death.
75. J. Hunter (ed.), *The Diary of Ralph Thoresby, 1677–1724*, 2 vols (London, 1830), i, pp. 258, 303.
76. Bodleian Library, MS Ballard 37, fos 180–87.
77. Gough's translation of the chronicle, for example, survives interleaved in a copy of Gibson's edition as Bodleian Library, MS Gough Saxon Lit 93. James Ingram acknowledged his debt to Gough in *The Saxon Chronicle, with an English Translation and Notes, Critical and Explanatory* (London, 1823), pp. xvi–xvii.
78. Chetham Library Manchester, MS A 6 93, fol. 142, John Whitaker to George Chalmers, 9 April 1809.
79. Richard Polwhele, *Reminiscences in Prose and Verse*, 3 vols (London, 1836), i, p. 63, Samuel Baldock to George Yonge, 15 February 1787.
80. T. A. Birrell, 'The Society of Antiquaries and the Taste for Old English 1705–1840',

Neophilogus, 50 (1966), pp. 109–10; Ingram, *The Saxon Chronicle*, p. xvii. On Elizabeth Elstob's Anglo-Saxon scholarship and a 'matrilineal conception of history', see Kathryn Sutherland, 'Editing for a New Century: Elizabeth Elstob's Anglo-Saxon Manifesto and Aelfric's St Gregory Homily', in D. G. Scragg and Paul E. Szarmach (ed.), *The Editing of Old English: Papers from the 1990 Manchester Conference* (Cambridge, 1994), pp. 213–37.

81. First published in three parts in between 1696 and 1699; and then reprinted, 'in response to earnest demand' in 1714, p. v.
82. J. Nichols (ed.), *Letters on Various Subjects, Literary, Political and Ecclesiastical, to and from William Nicolson DD, Successively Bishop of Carlisle and Derry; and Archbishop of Cashell*, 2 vols (London, 1809), i, p. 24; Hunter (ed.), *Letters of Eminent Men*, pp. 116, 126, 220, 349; James, *North Country Bishop*, pp. 65–89. On Thomas Machell see Eric Birley, 'Thomas Machell, the Antiquary', *Transactions of the Cumberland and Westmoreland Archaeological and Antiquarian Society*, new series, 33 (1956), pp. 132–53, and J. M. Ewbank, 'Antiquary on Horseback', *Cumberland and Westmoreland Archaeological and Antiquarian Society*, extra series, 19 (1963).
83. Ralph Thoresby, *Ducatus Leodiensis: or The Topography of the Ancient and Populous Town and Parish of Leedes and Parts Adjacent in the West Riding of the County of York* (London, 1715), pp. v, 112, 143.
84. Francis Drake, *Eboracum: or The History and Antiquities of the City of York from its Original to the Present Time* (London, 1736), pp. 68, 85.
85. Anon, *The History and Antiquities of Winchester*, 2 vols (Winchester, 1773), ii, p. 40.
86. British Library, Add. MS 5834, fol. 105, Richard Gough to William Cole, 20 December 1780: 'I have no Correspondent in the Kingdom of the East Angles, that can give me literary Intelligence but yourself.' National Library of Scotland, Adv. MS 29.5.6 (i), fol. 272, Richard Gough to George Paton, 12 June 1781.
87. Society of Antiquaries, Minute Books, viii (typescript), p. 303, 9 February 1759.
88. Adam Stark, *History of Lincoln* (Lincoln, 1810), p. 33.
89. Alexander Hay, *History of Chichester* (Chichester, 1804), pp. 110, 138–39.
90. John Watson, 'An Account of Some Hitherto Undescribed Remains of Antiquity', *Archaeologia*, 5 (1779), p. 87.
91. The Kent antiquary Bryan Fausset, for example, invariably described objects as belonging to 'Britons Romanised or Romans Britonised'. Charles Roach Smith, *Inventorium Sepulchrale: An Account of Some Antiquities Dug up at Gilton, Kingston, Sibertswold, Barfriston, Beakesbourne, Chartham, and Crundale, in the County of Kent from AD 1757 to AD 1773. By the Revd Bryan Faussett* (London, 1856), pp. 36, 102.
92. Nichols (ed.), *Literary Anecdotes*, iv, p. 439, George North to A. C. Ducarel, 11 October 1750.
93. James Douglas, *Nenia Britannica: or A Sepulchral History of Great Britain* (London, 1793).
94. William Cunnington to Thomas Leman, 1809, quoted in K. Woodbridge,

Landscape and Antiquity (London, 1971), p. 279. On Cunnington see Robert H. Cunnington, ed. James Dyer, *From Antiquary to Archaeologist. A Biography of William Cunnington, 1754–1810* (Buckingham, 1975).

95. Bodleian Library, MS Eng. Lett. d. 43, fol. 217, Ralph Thoresby junior to Samuel Pegge, 2 November 1741.
96. Bodleian Library, MS Eng. Lett. d. 44, fol. 461, Jeremiah Milles to Samuel Pegge, 6 March 1772.
97. Bodleian Library, MS Eng. Lett. d. 43, fol. 187, George Vertue to Samuel Pegge, 27 June 1754.
98. Camden, *Britannia*, ed. Gough (1789) annotated copy, Bodleian Library, Gough Gen. Top. 140, fol. 169.
99. J. S. Martin, 'Some Remarks on Eighteenth-Century Numismatic Manuscripts and Numismatists', in R. H. M. Dolley (ed.), *Anglo-Saxon Coins: Essays Presented to F. M. Stenton* (London, 1960), p. 234.
100. Bodleian Library, MS Ballard 42, fol. 176 v, Charles Lyttelton to George Ballard, 6 February 1752.
101. Rogers Ruding, *Annals of the Coinage of Britain and its Dependencies* (London, 1818). See also his correspondence with Nichols in Bodleian Library, MS Eng. Lett. c. 364.
102. Joseph Strutt, *Horda Angel Cynnan: A Compleat View of the Manners, Customs, Arms, Habits, etc of the Inhabitants of England from the Arrival of the Saxons to the Present Time; with a Short Account of the Britons during the Government of the Romans*, 3 vols (London, 1775–76); idem, *A Complete View of the Dress and Habits of the People of England, from the Establishment of the Saxons in Britain to the Present Time, Illustrated by Engravings Taken from the Most Authentic Remains of Antiquity*, 2 vols (London, 1796), i, p. 14. On Strutt and his career see Brenda Lilian Hough, 'A Consideration of the Antiquarian and Literary Works of Joseph Strutt, with a Transcript of a Hitherto Inedited Manuscript Novel', unpublished Ph.D. thesis, University of London (1984).
103. One important manifestation of this cultural shift, the challenge to neoclassical architectural norms from the Gothic revival, will be considered in the following chapter.
104. The impact of the Romans upon ancient British society was similarly subject to re-evaluation: see chapter 4 above.
105. John Bigland, *Beauties of England and Wales: or Original Delineations, Topographical, Historical and Descriptive, of Each County*, 18 vols (London, 1805–18), xvi, pp. 6–7.
106. Hearne (ed.), *Life of Aelfred the Great*, p. 8.
107. Bicknell, *Life of Alfred the Great*, p. xii.
108. Gough, *British Topography*, Bodleian Library, Gen. Top. 363, p. xxxiii.
109. British Library, Add. MS 36987, fol. 22, Henry Ellis to Richard Gough, no date. Ellis went on to become one of the leading antiquaries of his day, secretary to the Society of Antiquaries and a keeper of the British Museum. He eventually received a knighthood.

110. Thomas Fosbroke acknowledged communications from Henry Ellis on the lapses and defects in Gibson's edition of the Chronicle, *British Monachism: or Manners and Customs of the Monks and Nuns of England*, 2 vols (London, 1802), ii, p. 223.
111. Paul-Henri Mallet, *Northern Antiquities: or A Description of the Manners, Customs, Religion and Laws of the Ancient Danish and other Northern Nations; Including those of our own Saxon Ancestors*, 2 vols, trans. Thomas Percy (London, 1770); Beck, *Northern Antiquities*; E. H. Harvey Wood, 'Letters to an Antiquary: The Literary Correspondence of G. J. Thorkelin (1752–1829)', unpublished Ph.D. thesis, University of Edinburgh (1972).
112. Grimr Thorkelin had discovered the Beowulf manuscript whilst working at the British Museum in the 1780s and made a transcript, but this was not published until 1815 as *De Danorum rebus gestis secul. iii et iv, poema danicum dialecto anglosaxonica* (Copenhagen, 1815).
113. Sharon Turner, *A History of the Anglo-Saxons* (London, 1799); *A Vindication of the Genuineness of the Ancient British Poems or Aneurin, Taliesin, Llywarch Hen, and Merdhin, with Specimens of the Poems* (London, 1803); 'An Inquiry Concerning the Early Use of Rhime' and 'A Further Inquiry into the Early Use of Rhime', *Archaeologia*, 14 (1803), pp. 168–86, 187–204.
114. Samuel Pegge 'Of the Introduction, Progress, State, and Condition, of the Vine in Britain', *Archaeologia*, 1 (1770), pp. 319–32; Daines Barrington, 'Mr Pegge's Observations on the Growth of the Vine in England Considered and Answered', *Archaeologia*, 3 (1775), pp. 67–95. Barrington argued that the references to vines in Domesday Book actually referred to currant bushes.
115. See chapter 3; see also John Pinkerton 'Letters to the People of Great Britain on their Cultivation of their National History', *Gentleman's Magazine*, 58 (1788), pp. 284–86, 414. Pinkerton's call for a description of the Saxon court, an account of the private life of the Saxons and a history of the regal power of the Saxon crown, indicates the influence of Joseph Strutt's publications upon his thought.
116. John Conybeare, 'An Account of a Saxon Manuscript in the Cathedral Library at Exeter', *Archaeologia*, 17 (1814), pp. 180–97.
117. Robert Willan, 'A List of Ancient Words at Present Used in the Mountainous District of the West Riding of Yorkshire', *Archaeologia*, 17 (1814), p. 165.
118. Influential texts on Gothic origins included Robert Sheringham, *De Anglorum gentis origina disceptatio* (London, 1670); Francis Wise, *Some Enquiries Concerning the First Inhabitants, Language, Religion, Learning and Letters of Europe* (Oxford, 1758); Mallet, *Northern Antiquities*. For a discussion of the literature see Beck, *Northern Antiquities* and Kidd, *British Identities before Nationalism*, pp. 211–49 and Frank Edgar Harley, *Scandinavian Influences in the English Romantic Movement* (Cambridge, Massachusetts, 1903).
119. Philip Cluever, *Germania antique: libra tres* (Leiden, 1616) and *Introduction into Geography, both Ancient and Modern* (Oxford, 1657); Johann Georg Keysler, *Antiquitates selectae septentrionales et celticae* (Hanover, 1720); Simon Pelloutier,

Histoire des Celtes (Paris, 1740) reissued in 1771; Abbé Pezron, *L'Antiquité de la nation et la langue des Celtes* (1703) translated as *Antiquities of Nations* (London, 1706).

120. Margaret Clunies Ross, *The Norse Muse in Britain, 1750–1820* (Trieste, 1998), p. 41; Evan Evans's correspondence with Percy is published in Aneirin Lewis (ed.), *The Correspondence of Thomas Percy and Evan Evans* (Baton Rouge, Louisiana, 1957) pp. 90–91. Evan Evans was the author of *Some Specimens of the Poetry of the Antient Welsh Bards* (London, 1764). See chapter 3.
121. Mallet, *Northern Antiquities*, i, pp. xiii–xxi.
122. Thomas Pownall, 'An Account of a Ship Temple near Dundalk', *Collectanea de rebus hibernicis*, 6 vols (second edition, Dublin 1786–1804), ii, p. 201, used the word '*vikenger*'. It became '*vikingr*' in his *Antiquarian Romance* (London, 1795), pp. 42–77; John Pinkerton, *An Enquiry into the History of Scotland Preceding the Reign of Malcolm III, Including the Authentic History of that Period*, 2 vols (London, 1789), ii, p. 179 used 'vikingur'; Sharon Turner, *The History of the Anglo-Saxons*, 2 vols (2nd edn, London, 1807), i, pp. 205–8, ii, p. 116; George Chalmers, *Caledonia: or An Account Historical and Topographic of North Britain, from the Most Ancient to the Present Times*, 3 vols (London, 1810), ii, pp. 7, 213, and in John Lingard, *The Antiquities of the Anglo-Saxon Church*, 2 vols (Newcastle, 1806), i, pp. 224–28. Camden had used *wiccinga*, meaning pirates, to refer to the Danes, see for example the 1722 edition of *Britannia*, i, p. ccvi. See also Ethel Seaton, *Literary Relations of England and Scandinavia in the Seventeenth Century* (Oxford, 1935), p. 204.
123. Francis Wise, *Further Observations upon the White Horse and Other Antiquities in Berkshire* (Oxford, 1742), p. 52.
124. Shelton, *Wootton's Short View*, p. 11.
125. Wise, *Letter to Dr Mead*, p. 11.
126. The catalogue of Thoresby's Museum is listed in *Ducatus Leodiensis*, pp. 269–568. The Danish coin is described at p. 339.
127. Squire, *Enquiry into the Foundation of the English Constitution*, p. 231.
128. Hutchinson, *View of Northumberland*, i, pp. 2–3.
129. Turner, *Anglo-Saxons*, pp. 209, 224–28.
130. Ibid., p. 431.
131. John Milner, *The History Civil and Ecclesiastical and Survey of the Antiquities of Winchester*, 2 vols (2nd edn, Winchester, 1809), i, p. 57; Martin Dunsford, *Historical Memoirs of the Town and Parish of Tiverton in the County of Devon* (Exeter, 1790), p. 26. This prejudice goes back to the long standing tradition that William the Conqueror had triumphed because the English, corrupted by the Danes, were incapacitated by drunkenness. See Keith Thomas, 'The Perception of the Past in Early Modern England', *Creighton Trust Lecture* (1983), p. 16.
132. Strutt, *Compleat View of the Manners, Customs, Arms, Habits*, i, p. 71.
133. British Library, Add. MS 32325.
134. National Library of Scotland, Adv. MS 29.5.7, fol. 136, George Paton to Richard Gough, 23 June 1789. 'Due Respect', complained Paton, 'ought to be paid by

every one to their native Country, yet it should be moderated with a similar or proper regard for Antiquities etc that may occur to learned persons in a distant Country from their own.'

135. Thomas, 'Perceptions of the Past', pp. 5, 7; Adam Fox, *Oral and Literate Culture in England, 1500–1700* (Oxford, 2000), pp. 243–47; Daniel Woolf, 'Of Danes and Giants: Popular Beliefs about the Past in Early Modern England', *Dalhousie Review*, 71 (1996), pp. 166–209, and idem, *The Social Circulation of the Past: English Historical Culture, 1500–1730* (Oxford, 2003), pp. 343–49.
136. Sir Joseph Ayloffe included it as one of the first books the aspiring antiquary should read. Nichols (ed.), *Literary Anecdotes*, viii, pp. 486–87. For the seventeenth-century background see Seaton, *Literary Relations of England and Scandinavia*, pp. 157–65, 237–51 and Graham Parry, *The Trophies of Time: English Antiquarians of the Seventeenth Century* (Oxford, 1996); Jensen, *History of Scandinavian Archaeology*, pp. 18–26. See for example, Robert Plot's description of the Rollrich (sic) Stones in *The Natural History of Oxfordshire, Being an Essay towards the Natural History of England* (2nd edn, Oxford, 1705), pp. 344–50. There is also a brief overview in Harley, *Scandinavian Influences in the English Romantic Movement*, pp. 1–24.
137. Walter Charleton, *Chorea Gigantum: or Stone-Heng Restored to the Danes* (London, 1663). For the identification of Stonehenge as an ancient British work see chapter 3. Parry, *Trophies of Time*, pp. 285–86.
138. Douglas, *Nenia Britannica*, p. 178.
139. John Hutchins, *The History and Antiquities of the County of Dorset*, 2 vols (London, 1774), i, p. xx.
140. Samuel Gale, 'An Historical Dissertation on the Antient Danish Horn, Kept in the Cathedral Church of York', *Archaeologia*, 1 (1770), p. 187.
141. Society of Antiquaries, Minute Books, vii (typescript), pp. 157–58, 5 July 1753.
142. J. A. W. Bennett, 'The History of Old English and Old Norse Studies in England from the Time of Francis Junius till the End of the Eighteenth Century', unpublished D.Phil. thesis, University of Oxford (1938); Farley, *Scandinavian Influences in the English Romantic Movement*; Clunies Ross, *The Norse Muse in Britain.*
143. Lewis (ed.), *Correspondence of Horace Walpole*, x, p. 148, Walpole to George Montague, 19 February 1765. National Library of Scotland, Adv. MS 29.5.6, fol. 183, 9 September 1778.
144. Thomas Warton, *The History of English Poetry, from the Close of the Eleventh to the Commencement of the Eighteenth Century* (London, 1774), p. vi. Warton's view did not go uncontested and was notably challenged by Joseph Ritson, *Observations on the Three First Volumes of the History of English Poetry in a Familiar Letter to the Author* (London, 1782), which in turn provoked an extended correspondence in the pages of the *Gentleman's Magazine*, 53 (1783), pp. 42–47, 100–1, 281–84.
145. G. Thorkelin, 'Fragments of English and Irish History in the Ninth and Tenth Century Translated from the Original Icelandic', in J. Nichols (ed.), *Bibliotheca*

topographica britannica, 48 (London, 1788); Andrew Wawn, *The Vikings and the Victorians: Inventing the Old North in Nineteenth-Century Britain* (Bury St Edmunds, 2000), pp. 61–62.

146. Thomas Burgess, *An Essay on the Study of Antiquities* (London, 1781), p. 15.
147. Clunies Ross, *Norse Muse in Britain*, pp. 46–49.
148. Bennett, 'Old English and Old Norse', p. 283.
149. George Hickes had effectively demonstrated this in the *Thesaurus*; see also Wise, *Some Enquiries Concerning the First Inhabitants*, pp. 83–92.
150. Bennett, 'Old English and Old Norse Studies', pp. 294–300; Farley, *Scandinavian Influences in the English Romantic Movement*, pp. 4–7.
151. William Drake, 'A Letter to the Secretary, on the Origin of the English Language', and idem, 'Some Further Remarks on the Origin of the English Language', *Archaeologia*, 5 (1779), pp. 306–17, 379–89.
152. James Wallace, *An Account of the Islands of Orkney: To Which is Added an Essay Concerning the Thule of the Ancients* (London, 1700), pp. 68, 106–7; Sir Robert Sibbald, *History Ancient and Modern of Sheriffdoms* (Edinburgh, 1710), p. 13.
153. National Library of Scotland, Adv. MS 33.5.24, fol. 1, Alexander Pope, 'A Dissertation upon Pictish Buildings and Antiquities in Caithnes and Sutherland'.
154. Charles Cordiner, *Antiquities and Scenery of the North of Scotland in a Series of Letters to Thomas Pennant* (London, 1790), pp. 121–24.
155. George Low, *A Tour through the Islands of Orkney and Schetland: Containing Hints Relative to their Ancient, Modern and Natural History Collected in 1774* (Kirkwall, 1879).
156. Banks, who was not without antiquarian interests himself, brought back a collection of manuscripts and Icelandic texts which he later presented to the British Museum. On the importance of the Banks bequest see Peter C. Hogg, 'The Development of the Pre-1801 Scandinavian Printed Collections in the British Library', *British Library Journal*, 25 (2001 for 1999), pp. 147–51. On Pennant's relationship with Banks and the extent of Banks's antiquarian interests see John Gascoigne, *Joseph Banks and the English Enlightenment* (Cambridge, 1994) and Harold Carter, *Sir Joseph Banks* (London, 1988), pp. 33–48.
157. George Low referred to his attempts to record the poems spoken by an elderly Orkneyan inhabitant in the 'Norn tongue' in a letter to Thomas Percy, National Library of Scotland, Adv. MS 29.5.8, fol. 158, 29 August 1777.
158. Colin Kidd, 'Teutonist Ethnology and Scottish Nationalist Inhibition, 1780–1880', *Scottish History Review*, 74 (1995), pp. 45–68; *British Identities before Nationalism*, pp. 204–10.
159. Colin Kidd, *Subverting Scotland's Past: Scottish Whig Historians and the Creation of an Anglo-British Identity, c. 1689–1830* (Cambridge, 1993).
160. John Pinkerton, *An Enquiry into the History of Scotland*, 2 vols (London, 1789), i, p. 18. See also George Barry, *The History of the Orkney Islands* (London, 1805), p. 210.

161. John Pinkerton, *A Dissertation on the Origin and Progress of the Scythians or Goths: Being an Introduction to the Ancient and Modern History of Europe* (London, 1787), pp. vii, xiii.
162. John Pinkerton, 'Letters to the People of Great Britain on their Cultivation of their National History', *Gentleman's Magazine*, 58 (1788), pp. 414, 284–86.
163. Kidd, *Subverting Scotland's Past*, pp. 250–53.
164. John Callander's proposals for *Bibliotheca septentrionalis* (Edinburgh, 1778) bound in Bodleian Library, Gough Saxon Literature 79 (6).
165. Harvey Wood, 'Letters to an Antiquary', pp. 96–97; Colin Kidd, 'Race, Theology and Revival: Scots Philology and its Contexts in the Age of Pinkerton and Jamieson', *Scottish Studies Review*, 3 (2002), pp. 20–33.
166. Clare O'Halloran, 'Golden Ages and Barbarous Nations: Antiquarian Debate on the Celtic Past in Ireland and Scotland in the Eighteenth Century', unpublished Ph.D. thesis, University of Cambridge (1991); Jacqueline Hill, 'Popery and Protestantism, Civil and Religious Liberty: The Disputed Lessons of Irish History, 1690–1812', *Past and Present*, 118 (1988), pp. 95–129.
167. Edward Ledwich, *Antiquities of Ireland* (Dublin, 1790).
168. O'Halloran, 'Golden Ages and Barbarous Nations', pp. 119–31. Ledwich's earlier essays published in *Collectanea de rebus hibernicis* took up a less extreme position *vis-à-vis* Vallancey's oriental theories. The full-blown articulation of his thesis on Gothic origins came in *The Antiquities of Ireland* (Dublin, 1790).
169. See for example, Walter Harris, *The History and Antiquities of the City of Dublin from the Earliest Accounts* (Dublin, 1766), pp. 1–13; Charles Smith, *State of the County and City of Waterford: Being a Natural, Civil, Ecclesiastical, Historical and Topographical Description Thereof* (Dublin, 1756), p. 113; Sylvester O'Halloran by contrast challenged the 'absurdity' of supposing Irish towns to have been of Danish foundation, *An Introduction to the Antiquities of Ireland* (London, 1772), pp. 80–86.
170. Edward Ledwich, 'A Dissertation on the Round Towers in Ireland' *Collectanea de rebus hibernicis*, 6 vols (2nd edn, Dublin, 1786–1804), ii, pp. 119–43, suggested that they were originally belfries built by the Danes. Charles Vallancey, 'Some Remarks on the Round Towers of Ireland', ibid., pp. 194–96, argued that they were built for fire worship – a central element of the religion of the Orient. See also O'Halloran 'Golden Ages and Barbarous Nations', p. 128.
171. In particular, the interest in Norse poetry was not shared by the Irish antiquaries, who concentrated on the Gaelic language and literature.
172. James Ingram, *The Saxon Chronicle, With an English Translation and Notes, Critical and Explanatory* (London, 1823), pp. ii–iii.

Notes to Chapter 7: The Middle Ages

1. Early modern attitudes towards medieval church and society before the Reformation are discussed by Keith Thomas, 'The Perception of the Past in Early Modern England', *Creighton Trust Lecture* (1983), pp. 9–25.

2. D. C. Douglas, *English Scholars, 1660–1730* (London, 1939). For Rymer see pp. 285–301.
3. Hearne's edition of Robert of Gloucester published in 1724, for example, has been described as 'the first workmanlike edition of a Middle-English text'. See Anne Hudson, 'Robert of Gloucester and the Antiquaries, 1550–1800', *Notes and Queries*, 214 (1969), p. 441.
4. James Nasmith (1740–1808), was the librarian of Corpus Christi (Benet College), Cambridge, and completed a catalogue of the manuscripts in the Parker Library in 1777; his *Itineraria Symonis Simeonis et Willelmi de Worcestre, quibus accedit tractatus de metro* was published in 1778. Modern authorities describe it as 'remarkably good' given the state of local historical studies and medieval palaeography at the time. See John Harvey (ed.), *William Worcestre Itineraries* (Oxford, 1969), p. xxii. Nasmith also compiled the additions for the revised edition of Thomas Tanner's *Notitia Monastica* (London, 1787).
5. Douglas, *English Scholars*, pp. 354–71.
6. On the continuity of this strain of political thought in the eighteenth century see R. J. Smith, *The Gothic Bequest: Medieval Constitutions in British Thought, 1688–1863* (Cambridge, 1983); Reed Browning, *The Political and Constitutional Ideas of the Court Whigs* (Baton Rouge, Louisiana, 1982), pp. 117–44; J. G. A. Pocock, 'The Varieties of Whiggism from the Restoration to Reform', in idem, *Virtue, Commerce and History* (Cambridge, 1985), pp. 215–310; on the gradual displacement of ancient constitutionalism in political thought see J. W. Burrow, *A Liberal Descent: Victorian Historians and the English Past* (Cambridge, 1981), pp. 18–35; Mark Francis and John Morrow, 'After the Ancient Constitution: Political Theory and English Constitutional Writings, 1765–1832', *History of Political Thought*, 9 (1988), pp. 283–302.
7. Smith, *Gothic Bequest*, p. 91.
8. Douglas, *English Scholars*, p. 173.
9. Joan Evans, *A History of the Society of Antiquaries* (Oxford, 1956), p. 40 Thomas Hearne had also recommended the publication of Domesday Book: Thomas Hearne, *A Collection of Curious Discourses*, 2 vols (2nd edn, London, 1771), i, pp. lxii–lxiii.
10. Bodleian Library, MS Eng. Lett. c. 364, fol. 227, Sambrooke Russell to John Nichols, 13 August 1792.
11. Henry Penruddocke Wyndham, *Wiltshire Extracted From Domesday Book* (Salisbury, 1783), p. iii.
12. Sir Robert Atkyns, *The Ancient and Present State of Glostershire* (London, 1712), p. 7.
13. Society of Antiquaries, Minute Books, vii (typescript), pp. 394–95, 18 December 1755; Philip Carteret Webb, *A Short Account of Some Particulars Concerning Domesday Book* (London, 1756).
14. The debate over whether to publish by engraving or typeface is discussed by Maria Grazia Lolla, 'Monuments and Texts: Antiquarianism and the Beauty of Antiquity', *Art History*, 25 (2002), pp. 431–49.

15. HMSO, *Domesday Rebound* (London, 1954), p. 11.
16. Samuel Henshall and John Wilkinson, *Domesday: or An Actual Survey of South Britain by the Commissioners of William the Conqueror, Completed in the Year 1086* (London, 1799); Robert Kelham, *Domesday Book Illustrated* (London, 1788); Wyndham, *Wiltshire Extracted from Domesday Book*; Richard Warner, *Hampshire Extracted from Domesday Book* (London, 1789).
17. Henry Ellis agreed that with annotations and a glossary this it would be very acceptable to Nichols' readers. Bodleian Library, MS Top. Gen. 364, fol. 354, Henry Ellis to John Nichols, 14 September 1795.
18. See, for example, John Nichols, 'Dissertation Concerning Domesday Book', in idem, *The History and Antiquities of the County of Leicester*, 4 vols (1795–1815), i, pt 1, pp. xxxiii–xl.
19. These findings were not published, but were presented in papers to the Society of Antiquaries during the 1750s and 1760s.
20. His collections were a valuable resources for both Joseph Strutt and Sharon Turner in their work on Anglo-Saxon and Anglo-Norman history and antiquities.
21. Astle's collections passed to the marquis of Buckingham upon the payment of a nominal sum of £500 to the British Museum in 1804 and were housed in a room specially designed by Sir John Soane at Stowe. In 1849 the Stowe collections were sold privately to the earl of Ashburnham, and in 1883 were sold by his son to the British Museum for £45,000.
22. Thomas Astle, *The Origin and Progress of Writing* (London, 1784), pp. i–iv.
23. Kenneth Clark, *The Gothic Revival: An Essay in the History of Taste* (London, 1962); Michael McCarthy, *Origins of the Gothic Revival* (New Haven and London, 1987); Giles Worsley, 'The Origins of the Gothic Revival: A Reappraisal', *Transactions of the Royal Historical Society*, 6th series, 3 (1993), pp. 105–50.
24. Quoted by John Brewer, *Introduction to the Original Delineations, Topographical, Historical, and Descriptive, Intituled the Beauties of England and Wales* (London, 1818), p. 477.
25. Browne Willis, *An History of the Mitred Parliamentary Abbies and Conventual Churches*, 2 vols (London, 1718), i, p. 3.
26. Quoted by H. M. Colvin, 'Aubrey's *Chronologica Architectonica*', in John Summerson (ed.), *Concerning Architecture: Essays on Architectural Writers and Writing Presented to Nikolaus Pevsner* (London, 1968), p. 1.
27. See pp. 219–20.
28. Bodleian Library, MS Top. Cambs d. 6, fol. 2, Charles Lyttelton to James Bentham, 17 April 1758; reproduced in William Stevenson's 1812 edition of James Bentham, *The History and Antiquities of the Conventual Church of Ely*, p. 7.
29. Christopher Hildyard, *A List, or Catalogue of All the Mayors and Bayliffs, Lord Mayors and Sheriffs of the Most Ancient, Honourable, Noble and Loyall City of Yorke* (York, 1664), address to the reader; Thomas Gent, *History of York* (York, 1730), p. 53.

30. The comments in this paragraph are based upon Margaret Aston, 'English Ruins and English History: The Dissolution and the Sense of the Past', *Journal of the Warburg and Courtauld Institutes*, 36 (1973), pp. 231–55. See also Daniel Woolf, *The Social Circulation of Knowledge: English Historical Culture, 1500–1730* (Oxford, 2003), pp. 204–12.
31. Michael Hunter, *John Aubrey and the World of Learning* (London, 1975), p. 166.
32. Sir William Dugdale, *The Antiquities of Warwickshire* (London, 1656) quoted in Aston, 'England's Ruins', p. 252.
33. Graham Parry, *The Trophies of Time: English Antiquarians of the Seventeenth Century* (Oxford, 1995), pp. 234–38, and idem, 'Wenceslaus Hollar, the Antiquarians' Illustrator', *Ariel* (1972), pp. 42–52.
34. 'There are some, I hear, who take it ill that I have mention'd Monasteries and their Founders. I am sorry to hear it; but (with their leave) they are possibly such who are angry, and would have it forgotten, that our Ancestors were, and we are, Christians; since there are not anymore certain and glorious Monuments of their Christian Pity; nor were there any other Seminaries for the propagation of Religion and Learning; however, in a corrupt Age, Weeds might run up, which were necessary to be rooted out.' Camden, *Britannia*, ed. Gibson (1693), preface.
35. The world of non-juring, Jacobite antiquarianism in the early eighteenth century is described in detail by Theodor Harmsen, *Antiquarianism in the Augustan Age: Thomas Hearne, 1678–1735* (Bern, 2000). See also Paul Monod, *Jacobitism and the English People* (Cambridge, 1989), p. 287.
36. On Browne Willis see J. E. Jenkins, *The Dragon of Whaddon: A Life of Browne Willis* (High Wycombe, 1953).
37. Andrew Coltée Ducarel, 'Memoir of Browne Willis', in Nichols (ed.), *Literary Anecdotes*, vi, pp. 186–211.
38. Willis, *Mitred Parliamentary Abbies and Conventual Churches*, i, dedication to Archbishop Wake.
39. Browne Willis, *A Survey of the Cathedrals*, 3 vols (2nd edn, London, 1742), iii, p. 504.
40. Andrew Coltée Ducarel acknowledged the debt owed by ecclesiastical antiquarian studies to his research in 1760 in an address to the Society of Antiquaries: 'he was indeed, one of the first who placed our ecclesiastical history and antiquities upon a firm basis by grounding them upon records, and registers; which in the main are unexceptionable authorities'. Nichols (ed), *Literary Anecdotes*, vi, p. 187.
41. Thomas Gent, *The Life of Mr Thomas Gent* (London, 1832), p. 201, letter from Browne Willis to Thomas Gent, 18 January 1743.
42. Richard Rawlinson, *The History and Antiquities of the City and Cathedral Church of Hereford* (London, 1717); idem, *The History and Antiquities of the Cathedral Church of Salisbury, and the Abbey Church of Bath* (London, 1719); idem, *The History and Antiquities of the Cathedral Church of Rochester* (London, 1723).

43. British Library, Add. MS 34727 fol. 266, Richard Rawlinson to John Hare, 2 March 1715/16, quoted in R. J. Enright, 'Richard Rawlinson: Collector, Antiquary and Topographer', unpublished D.Phil. thesis, University of Oxford (1956), p. 63. Accounts of Hereford, Worcester, Lichfield and Rochester were published in 1717 and of Salisbury and Bath in 1719.
44. Richard Gough, *British Topography*, 2 vols (London, 1780), ii, pp. xvi–xvii.
45. James Storer, *History and Antiquities of the Cathedral Churches of Great Britain*, 4 vols (London, 1814); Richard Fenton, *A Historical Tour through Pembrokeshire* (London, 1810), p. 70, described the account compiled by a resident of St David's in response to Browne Willis's queries as still the best available. Willis's *Survey of St Asaph* was republished in 1801 with additions.
46. Thomas Staveley, *The History of the Churches in England: Wherein is Shewn, the Time, Means, and Manner of Founding, Buildings, and Endowing of Churches, both Cathedral and Rural, with their Furniture and Appendages* (London, 1712), pp. ii–iii, 151–52.
47. Staveley *History of the Churches*, p. 152.
48. Willis, *Survey of the Cathedrals*, p. vii.
49. Francis Peck, *Academica tertia anglicana* (London, 1727), pp. 52–53. Peck's comments were also republished as an appendix in the second edition of Staveley's *History of the Churches* (London, 1773). Peck had worked as an assistant for Browne Willis for some years after leaving Cambridge; the complementarity of their views was therefore only to be expected.
50. Robert Atkyns, *The Ancient and Present State of Glostershire* (London, 1712), preface.
51. Norfolk and Norwich Record Office, Rye MS 32, fol. 21, Thomas Tanner to Francis Blomefield, 4 December 1733. Tanner subsequently became bishop of St Asaph's.
52. William Stukeley, *Itinerarium curiosum* (London, 1724), p. 31. See also his 'Account of Lesnes Abbey', read 1753 and published in *Archaeologia*, 1 (1770), p. 53: 'This is one of those abbies that happened to become a prelude to the fatal dissolution, so terrible a stroke to our history and antiquities.'
53. British Library, Stowe MS 752, fol. 91, William Nourse to Charles Lyttelton, 19 October 1748.
54. British Library, Stowe MS 752, fol. 31v, Smart Lethieullier to Charles Lyttelton, 29 September 1749.
55. Christine Gerrard, *The Patriot Opposition to Walpole: Politics, Poetry and National Myth, 1725–42* (Oxford, 1994), pp. 101–23.
56. James Lee Milne, *Earls of Creation* (London, 1962), pp. 37–46; the folly was illustrated in Samuel Rudder, *A New History of Gloucestershire* (Cirencester, 1779), plate facing p. 356.
57. Such sentiments are quite explicit in the correspondence between Miller and his friends. See Lilian Dickins and Mary Stanton (ed.), *An Eighteenth-Century Correspondence: Letters to Sanderson Miller* (London, 1910).
58. Charles Lyttelton, 'Dissertation on the Antiquity of Brick Buildings in England,

Posterior to the Time of the Romans', *Archaeologia*, 1 (1770), p. 156. Andrew Coltée Ducarel's dedication to Lyttelton in *Anglo-Norman Antiquities* (London, 1767) suggests that Lyttelton first became interested in the difference between Saxon and Norman architecture around 1742; his earliest church notes extant date from December 1741 (Society of Antiquaries, MS 153). See also Thomas Cocke, 'Rediscovery of the Romanesque', in *English Romanesque Art, 1066–2000* (London, 1984), pp. 360–63.

59. See Hunter, *John Aubrey and the World of Learning*, pp. 181, 184, 206 and H. M. Colvin, 'Aubrey's *Chronologia Architectonica*', in Summerson (ed.), *Concerning Architecture*, pp. 1–12.
60. See in particular Bodleian Library, Ballard MSS 37, 42, 43.
61. British Library, Stowe MS 752, fol. 21. Lyttelton was making similar observations to Francis Drake, comparing the ornamentation around the Saxon arches with the the luxuriant fancies and grotesque ornaments in the margins of illuminated manuscripts. Bodleian Library, MS Eng. Misc. d. 188, fol. 5, Lyttelton to Drake, 16 September 1749. A similar argument was developed at greater length by the architect William Wilkins in 'An Essay towards a History of the Venta Icenorum of the Romans, and of Norwich Castle: With Remarks on the Architecture of the Anglo-Saxons and Normans', *Archaeologia*, 12 (1796), p. 174: 'It is well known that the dates of ancient MSS may frequently be ascertained by the forms of the letters only ... Thus, it seems likewise, that the respective dates of architecture are distinguishable by peculiar characters also.'
62. British Library, Stowe MS 752, fos 22, 39, Smart Lethieullier to Charles Lyttelton, 3 March 1747/8 and 14 July 1750.
63. See James Bentham, *The History and Antiquities of the Conventual Church of Ely* (Cambridge, 1771), pp. 15–17.
64. Society of Antiquaries MS 153, fol. i.
65. British Library, Stowe MS 752, fol. 76, Lethieullier to Lyttelton, 29 November 1752.
66. British Library, Stowe MS 752, fol. 52v, Lethieullier to Lyttelton, 7 May 1751.
67. Lyttelton, 'Dissertation on the Antiquity of Brick Buildings', pp. 140–48.
68. British Library, Stowe MS 752, fol. 130v, 13 March 1750/1, fol. 132, 26 March 1751, and fol. 121, 27 January 1749. Borlase promised to send him any building which would answer Lyttelton's character of the Saxon manner. See also Lyttleton's letters to George Ballard, Bodleian Library, MS Ballard 42, fol. 57.
69. Francis Drake, *Eboracum: or The History and Antiquities of the City of York, from its Original to the Present Time* (London, 1736), p. 475.
70. Nichols (ed.), *Literary Anecdotes*, v, p. 459, George North to Andrew Coltée Ducarel, October 1752.
71. Sarah Markham (ed.), *John Loveday of Caversham, 1711–89: The Life and Tours of an Eighteenth-Century Onlooker* (Salisbury, 1984), p. 301.
72. British Library, Stowe MS 752, fol. 94, Lethieullier to Lyttelton, 5 July 1754.
73. Cf. William Clarke's argument that the Goths and Vandals were less barbaric than often assumed, and had acquired elements of Roman civilisation such

as the coining of money. He described the Witenagemot as a variation upon the Roman Senate: *The Connexion of Roman, Saxon and English Coins Derived from Observations on Saxon Weights and Measures* (London, 1767), pp. 400–48.

74. British Library, Add. MS 37219, fol. 11, Ducarel to Morant, 10 May 1753. Ducarel's observations were published in A. C. Ducarel, *A Tour through Normandy, Described in a Letter to a Friend* (London, 1754), and in rather fuller detail in his *Anglo-Norman Antiquities Considered in a Tour through Part of Normandy* (London, 1767).
75. See for example, the analysis of Saxon and Norman tenurial and inheritance patterns by his brother, Lord Lyttelton, *History of the Life of King Henry the Second*, 4 vols (1767–71), ii, pp. 188–89; Smith, *The Gothic Bequest*, pp. 94–95.
76. Bodleian Library, MS Gough Top. Cambs d. 6, fol. 22, Lyttelton to Bentham, 3 April 1758.
77. British Library, Stowe MS 752, fol. 69, Lethieullier to Lyttelton, 15 July 1752.
78. Lyttelton bequeathed his collection to the Society of Antiquaries.
79. *Some Account of the Cathedral Church at Exeter: Illustrative of the Plans, Elevations and Sections of that Building* (London, 1797). Lyttelton's account of Exeter Cathedral has recently been discussed by Sam Smiles, 'Data, Documentation and Display in Eighteenth-Century Investigations of Exeter Cathedral', *Art History*, 4 (2002), pp. 500–19.
80. British Library, Add. MS 37219, fol. 33, Ducarel to Morant, 24 December 1754. Ducarel announced that the society was about to publish an engraving of St Augustines at Canterbury 'whereby a judgment may be formed of a truly Saxon building.' See plates 15 and 16 of *Vetusta monumenta*, ii. On plans to publish the Caedmon manuscript see previous chapter and Bodleian Library, MS Ballard 42, fol. 176v; Edward Rowe Mores, *A Dissertation upon English Typographical Founders and Founderies* (1778), ed. Harry Carter and Christopher Ricks, Oxford Bibliographical Society (1961).
81. Miller's clients included Sir Roger Newdigate, Lord Dacre of Belhouse and Louisa, countess of Pomfret; Miller also drew up plans for a Gothic Hagley Hall, the seat of Lyttelton's brother, Lord Lyttelton, but these were never realised. See McCarthy, *Origins of the Gothic Revival*, pp. 116–35; Miller was projecting a history of Gothic architecture in the 1750s. Smart Letheuillier referred to it on 21 September 1750, British Library, Stowe MS 752, fol. 45v. 'You give me great Pleasure in the Thoughts of Mr Millers being desired to write the History of Architecture in Great Brittain [sic]'. William Borlase referred to the plan in correspondence in 1754. See British Library, Stowe MS 752, fos 167, 174.
82. Stukeley, 'Account of Lesnes Abbey', p. 43.
83. William Warburton, *Notes to Pope's Moral Essays* (London, 1760). Warburton's correspondence with Stukeley was published in Nichols (ed.), *Illustrations of Literature*, ii, pp. 1–60.
84. Sir James Hall, *Essay on the Origins and Principles of Gothic Architecture* (Edinburgh, 1797). Hall argued that Gothic buildings were built to resemble wooden buildings; the arches were therefore the equivalent of the supporting

beams of a wooden house. The ornamentation, he suggested, originated in imitation of the sprouts which developed when willow poles were planted in the ground and put forth leaves, p. 20: 'As it would frequently happen, that the willow rods, thrust into the ground, would strike root and grow, the architect seems to have taken advantage of this circumstance, by representing them as decorated with buds and tufts of leaves, whenever he thought that such ornaments could introduced with good effect.' The fact that such ornaments in the finials and crockets more usually resembled 'cabbage' leaves rather than willows, was, he suggested, the practical response of the stonemason, in that willow leaves were too small to render satisfactorily. He put his theory to the test by building one such 'rustic edifice' and accompanied his thesis with illustrations engraved by Joseph Halfpenny.

85. Stephen Wren, *Parentalia: or Memoirs of the Family of Wren* (London, 1750).
86. John Frew and Carey Wallace, 'Thomas Pitt, Portugal, and the Gothic Cult of Batalha', *Burlington Magazine*, 128 (1986), pp. 582–84.
87. Bodleian Library, MS Gough Gen. Top. 44, fol. 79v, Richard Gough to Michael Tyson, 28 March 1772. (See also Nichols (ed.), *Literary Anecdotes*, viii, p. 588.) Gough wrote that he had just been reading a tour of Portugal made in 1760 with most accurate drawings and plans of the principal moorish and Gothic buildings and a comparison of the two styles of architecture. Gough later lent the manuscript to Tyson (fol. 143, 10 December 1772), telling him that he could keep it as long as he wished 'provided dirty [double underline] Antiquarians' paws are kept from him'. (Nichols directed that this line should not be printed.)
88. James Essex, 'Some Observations on Lincoln Cathedral', *Archaeologia*, 7 (1777), pp. 149–59.
89. John Whitaker, *The Ancient Cathedral of Cornwall Historically Surveyed*, 2 vols (London, 1804), i, p. 82.
90. Sir William Chambers, *Treatise on Civil Architecture* (London, 1759).
91. Richard Hurd, *Letters on Chivalry and Romance* (London, 1762), p. 223.
92. On Warton see J. M. Levine, 'Eighteenth-Century Historicism and the First Gothic Revival', in idem, *Humanism and History: Origins of Modern English Historiography* (Ithaca and London, 1987), pp. 190–213; on Gray see Marion Roberts, 'Thomas Gray's Contribution to the Study of Medieval Architecture', *Architectural History*, 36 (1993), pp. 49–68.
93. Warton's notebooks and itineraries are to be found in Bodleian Library, MS Dep. e. 287; British Library, Add. MS 11395 (notes made on travels during the 1780s); Winchester College MSS 107–12; Thomas Warton, *A Description of the City, College, and Cathedral of Winchester* (London, 1750), p. 108, distinguished between three styles representing three phases of construction in the cathedral: the Saxon, the simple Gothic, and the ornamental or improved Gothic. A second edition was published in 1760.
94. Gray's commonplace books are held at Pembroke College, Cambridge. His essay on Gothic architecture was first printed in 1814 as 'Architectura Gothica',

in Thomas Mathias (ed.), *The Works of Thomas Gray with Memoirs of his Life and Writings by William Mason: To which are Subjoined Extracts Philological, Poetical and Critical*, 2 vols (London, 1814), ii, pp. 98–103.

95. Gough, *Anecdotes of British Topography*, p. xx. The proposals are reproduced in McCarthy, *Origins of the Gothic Revival*, pp. 180–82. James Essex got hold of them and used them in his unpublished history of Gothic architecture, which was later deposited in the British Library by Thomas Kerrich. Muntz did not meet with the response he had hoped for – the price of three and a half guineas no doubt deterred many subscribers. He left the country to enter the service of the king of Spain and his treatise remained unpublished. In Horace Walpole's copy of Gough's *British Topography* at the Huntington Library, p. xxiv, where Gough refers to the proposed history, Walpole comments that 'Mr Munts was a Swiss Painter, & knew nothing of Gothic architecture but what he picked up by living two or three years at Strawberry Hill; and as he was entirely ignorant of our history, was very incapable of undertaking'.

96. Sir Peter Thompson (ed.), *The Fashion of Windows in Civil and Ecclesiastical Buildings, Before the Conquest* (London, 1766). William Huddesford of Trinity College, Oxford, and keeper of the Ashmolean wrote to Gough describing Aubrey's manuscript, and also mentioning the fact that he intended to 'give it to the publick' at some date; Huddesford does not appear to have been aware of the 1766 publication. Bodleian Library, MS Don. d. 88, fol. 333, William Huddesford to Richard Gough, 6 November 1769.

97. Gough, *Anecdotes of British Topography*, p. xx. Gough had been at Cambridge at Benet Hall at the time that Thomas Gray was developing his interests in Gothic architecture. Whether the two were acquainted at this stage is unclear. He was certainly aware that Gray had been making collections towards a history of Gothic architecture by the time of his death in 1771. 'When Gray's Videnda appear', he wrote to Tyson, 'I fear I shall seem to have seen nothing in Great Britain.' Bodleian Library, MS Gough Gen. Top. 44, fol. 39v, 25 November 1771. See also Nichols (ed.) *Literary Anecdotes*, viii, p. 571.

98. Gough, *British Topography*, i, p. xxiii; on Essex see Donald Steward, 'James Essex, an Eighteenth-Century Pioneer of Gothic Scholarship', *Architectural Review*, 108 (1950), pp. 317–21; Thomas Cocke, 'James Essex, Cathedral Restorer', *Architectural History*, 18 (1975), pp. 12–22; Thomas Cocke, *The Ingenious Mr Essex, Architect* (Cambridge, 1984), pp. 5, 36.

99. The majority of Gough's correspondence with Michael Tyson was published in Nichols (ed.), *Literary Anecdotes*, viii, pp. 567–672. The originals are in Bodleian Library, MS Gough Gen. Top. 44. Nichols printed most of the interesting content, but routine detail on prices of books or arrangements for delivering parcels were omitted, along with passages which reflected less flatteringly upon the correspondents. All references to Tyson's drinking problems, for example, were tactfully excised.

100. Bodleian Library, MS Gough Gen. Top. 44, fol. 429, Gough to Tyson, 11 December 1779. See also Nichols (ed.), *Literary Anecdotes*, viii, p. 657. The

journal of the tour which Essex undertook to Flanders with Michael Tyson in 1771 has been published *Journal of a Tour through Part of Flanders and France, in August 1771 by James Essex FSA*, ed. W. M. Fawcett, Cambridge Antiquarian Society (1888).

101. McCarthy, *Origins of the Gothic Revival*, p. 171. The manuscript is now British Library, Add. MS 6762.
102. British Library, Add. MS 5824, fos 52v, 62v, William Cole to Mr Allen of Tarporley, Cheshire, 1769.
103. Lyttelton, Bentham (and others) assumed that certain twelfth-century buildings, founded much earlier, were actually as old as their foundation charters, and therefore believed that these smaller and more ornate buildings preceded the larger Norman edifices. See Thomas Cocke, 'The "Old Conventual Church" at Ely: A False Trail in Romanesque Studies?', in *Art and Patronage in the English Romanesque*, Society of Antiquaries Occasional Papers, new series, 8 (1986), pp. 77–86.
104. Bentham, *History and Antiquities of the Cathedral Church of Ely*, p. 31.
105. Ibid., p. 41.
106. Marion Roberts, 'Thomas Gray's Contribution to the Study of Medieval Architecture', *Architectural History*, 36 (1993), p. 49, quoting William Mason, *The Poems of Mr Gray* (York, 1775), p. 339. Bentham's unacknowledged borrowings from Gray were the subject of an exchange in the pages of the *Gentleman's Magazine*, 53 (1783), p. 376; ibid., 54 (1784), p. 505. The allegations against Bentham were erroneously perpetuated by the article on Gothic architecture in Rees's *New Cyclopedia* (London, 1811). Bentham was said to be collecting materials for illustrating the 'Ancient Architecture of this Kingdom' at the time of his death.
107. J. Mordaunt Crook, *John Carter and the Mind of the Gothic Revival* (London, 1995), p. 4.
108. 'At length the opportunity is arrived to tear down this rag of prejudice, this scum of innovation, this word 'Gothic', which for a century past has branded with ignominy all our national works', *Gentleman's Magazine*, 71 (1801), p. 413.
109. J. M. Frew, 'An Aspect of the Gothic Revival in England, *c.* 1770–1815: The Antiquarian Influence with Special Reference to the Career of James Wyatt', unpublished D.Phil. thesis, University of Oxford, 2 vols (1976), i, pp. 90–97.
110. *Gentleman's Magazine* (1814), ii, p. 315, quoted in Mordaunt Crook, *John Carter*, p. 44.
111. William Gilpin, *Observations on the Mountains and Lakes of Cumberland and Westmoreland*, 2 vols (London, 1786), i, p. 15.
112. Quoted in Mordaunt Crook, *John Carter*, p. 8; Mark Girouard, *The Return of Camelot: Chivalry and the English Gentleman* (New Haven and London, 1987), p. 42; J. M. Frew, 'Gothic is English: John Carter and the Revival of the Gothic as England's National Style', *Art Bulletin*, 64 (1982), pp. 315–19.
113. Quoted in Mordaunt Crook, *John Carter*, p. 31.
114. Carter was not, of course, responsible for inventing this interpretation of the

middle ages. For manifestations of a similar view of a medieval golden age see Thomas, 'Perceptions of the Past'.

115. The issue of the preservation and restoration of medieval buildings is one which will be dealt with below.

116. 'There is very little doubt that the light and elegant style of building, whose principal and characteristic feature is the high pointed arch struck from two centres, was invented in this country: it is certain that it was here brought to its highest state of perfection.' *Some Account of the Cathedral Church of Durham: Illustrative of the Plans, Elevations, and Sections of that Building* (London, 1801), p. 3.

117. G. D. Whittington, *An Historical Survey of the Ecclesiastical Antiquities of France: With a View to Illustrate the Rise and Progress of Gothic Architecture in Europe* (London, 1809). Whittington had died in 1807 at the age of twenty-six and his survey was published posthumously under the auspices of the earl of Aberdeen, later president of the Society of Antiquaries. Aberdeen, whose own interests did not lie in this direction, prefaced the account with the curious comment that 'The subject is not in itself very generally interesting, nor from the accurate and detailed manner in which it is treated, can we reasonably expect that it should be rendered more popular' (pp. xiv–xv). John Carter's unremittingly hostile response appeared in the 'Architectural Innovation' essays in *Gentleman's Magazine*, 79 (1809), pp. 523–27, 627–30, 697–700. Carter's comments evoked a measured defence of Whittington (almost certainly written by Thomas Kerrich), pp. 1097–99.

118. *Gentleman's Magazine*, 79 (1809), pp. 698. Samuel Lysons wrote to Thomas Kerrich that 'Carter you see goes on writing with might and main against poor Whittington's work in the *Gentleman's Magazine*, and abusing every body for inaccuracy', Corpus Christi College, Cambridge, Parker Library, Kerrich MS 605, fol. 107, 22 September 1809.

119. Thomas Kerrich, 'Observations on the Gothic Buildings Abroad, Particularly those in Italy; and on Gothic Architecture in General', *Archaeologia*, 16 (1812), pp. 292–304. The papers were originally read on 11, 18 May and 1 June 1809.

120. Corpus Christi College, Cambridge, Parker Library, Kerrich MS 606, fol. 59, Francis Douce to Thomas Kerrich, 1 July 1809.

121. George Saunders, 'Observations on Gothic Architecture', *Archaeologia*, 17 (1714), pp. 1–29; Samuel Ware, 'Observations on Vaults', *Archaeologia*, 17 (1814), pp. 40–84.

122. Daniel and Samuel Lysons, *Magna Britannia: Being a Concise Topographical Account of the Several Counties of Great Britain*, 6 vols (London, 1806–19), ii, p. 51. Although it was projected to cover the entire country, Samuel Lysons died before the work was completed. The sixth volume, covering Devonshire, proved to be their last.

123. These qualities and their relationship to an English 'identity' are discussed by Paul Langford, *Englishness Identified: Manners and Character, 1650–1850* (Oxford, 2000).

124. Thomas Rickman, *An Attempt to Discriminate the Styles of English Architecture* (London, 1817), pp. 37–39.
125. Brewer, *Introduction to the Original Delineations*, pp. 442–76. Brewer suggested that the freemasons were responsible for spreading the use of the pointed arch in buildings through Europe; given that this was an international fraternity, the issue of national origins was irrelevant.
126. A. C. Pugin, *Specimens of Gothic Architecture* (London, 1821), p. 2.
127. *The History of Gothic and Saxon Architecture in England ... Compiled from the Works of James Bentham ... and Browne Willis* (London, 1798); *Essays on Gothic Architecture, by the Rev. T. W., the Rev. J. Bentham, Captain Grose and the Rev. J. Milner* (London, 1800).
128. *Quarterly Review*, iv (1809), p. 143, quoted in Simon Bradley, 'The Gothic Revival and the Church of England, 1790–1840', unpublished Ph.D. thesis, University of London (1996), p. 238.
129. *Essays on Gothic Architecture*, p. vi.
130. William Dickinson, *Antiquities Historical, Architectural, Chorographical and Itinerary in Nottinghamshire and the Adjacent Counties* (Newark, 1801), p. viii.
131. T. D. Fosbroke, *An Original History of the City of Gloucester* (London, 1819), p. 117.
132. These were Exeter, Durham, Gloucester, Bath and Wells, and St Albans.
133. Britton, *Autobiography*, ii, p. 2.
134. John Britton, *The Architectural Antiquities of Great Britain*, 5 vols (London, 1807–26), v, pp. ix–xiv. The literature was reviewed, pp. 31–102.
135. *The Architects' and Antiquaries' Club* (London, 1820).
136. Hall, *Essay on the Origin and Principles of Gothic Architecture.*
137. John Brewer, *Introduction to the Beauties of England and Wales* (London, 1818), p. 409.
138. Daines Barrington, 'Observations on Welsh Castles' *Archaeologia*, 1 (1770), pp. 301–14. Barrington argued (p. 306) that Edward I must have adopted the style of construction from the east which he had visited upon crusade: 'I suppose that this king had seen such castles in Asia; for I cannot hear on inquiry, that any of the same kind are to be found in other parts of Europe; nor does Poussin, or the other great painters of landscape, make use of them, though so very picturesque objects.'
139. Thomas Pennant, *A Tour in Wales*, 3 vols (London, 1778, 1781–83), iii, p. 311. Even here the actual description was perfunctory with the emphasis upon size and magnificence. His blind spot for Gothic architecture was not limited to the tour in Wales and is a characteristic of all his writings.
140. Sir Richard Colt Hoare, *The Itinerary of Archbishop Baldwin through Wales AD MCLXXXVIII by Giraldus de Barri: Translated into English and Illustrated with Views, Annotations, and a Life of Giraldus*, 2 vols (London, 1806).
141. Charles Norris, *Saint David's in a Series of Engravings, Illustrating the Different Ecclesiastical Edifices of that Ancient City* (London, 1811). Norris (1779–1858) was born in London and moved to Pembrokeshire c. 1800, living first near Milford Haven, and from 1810 outside Tenby.

142. Mervyn Archdall, *Monasticon Hibernicum: or An History of the Abbies, Priories, and Other Religious Houses in Ireland* (London, 1786), p. ix; Archdall used Pococke's tour, which included some few comments on architecture. See G. T. Stokes (ed.), *Bishop Pococke's Tour in Ireland in 1752* (Dublin and London, 1891).
143. Archdall's patron, William Burton Conyngham, had amassed a large collection of drawings of Irish antiquities from 'the time of the Druids to the Reformation' including plans of all the most remarkable castles and abbeys; many of these were used in Grose's *Antiquities of Ireland.* Nichols (ed.), *Illustrations of Literature*, vi, pp. 432–33. Nichols, p. 435, quoting the *European Magazine* (1794), referred to his collection of drawings of Irish churches, abbeys and castles as the most extensive in existence.
144. The emphasis in a publication such as R. Twiss, *A Tour in Ireland in 1775* (London, 1776) was on the simplicity of the Irish people and the picturesque qualities of the unspoilt scenery.
145. William Beauford, 'A Memoir Respecting the Antiquities of the Church of Killossy, in the County of Kildare; with some Conjectures on the Origin of Ancient Irish Churches', *Transactions of the Royal Irish Academy*, 3 (1790), pp. 75–85. Similarly, William Burton Conyngham's interest in the church at Batalha was aroused by the attempts of Irish antiquaries establish links with the Iberian peninsula. His patronage lay behind James Murphy's *Plans, Elevations, Sections and Views of the Church of Batalha in the Province of Estremadura in Portugal* (London, 1795). This church was, according to Murphy, 'one of the best specimens existing of the Gothic style', ibid., p. 2.
146. Sir Richard Colt Hoare, *Journal of a Tour in Ireland AD 1806* (London, 1807), pp. ii–iii.
147. Undated prospectus for John Brewer, *Beauties of Ireland: Being Original Delineations, Topographical, Historical and Biographical of Each County, Illustrated with Numerous Copper Plate Engravings, Representing Public Edifices; Castles; Parochial Churches, Eminent for Beauty or Antiquity of Architecture; Monuments, Ruins, Picturesque Scenery; Seats of the Nobility and Gentry*, Bodleian Library, MS Don. d. 87, fos 204, 214. The fact that Brewer's proposals were never realised offers further evidence for the lack of interest in Ireland of which he complained in the flier.
148. Francis Grose, *The Antiquities of Ireland*, 2 vols (London, 1791). Grose was assisted on this final project by his son, Daniel (c. 1766–1838). Daniel Grose's preparatory sketches for the volume recently came to light in 1989 and have been published: Daniel Grose, *The Antiquities of Ireland: A Supplement to Francis Grose*, ed. Roger Stalley (Dublin, 1991).
149. Grose, *Antiquities of Ireland*, i, unpaginated preface by Edward Ledwich.
150. Ledwich's essay 'Observations on Antient Churches', *Archaeologia*, 8 (1787), pp. 165–94, was based mainly on evidence from textual sources rather than observation of actual churches.
151. Ledwich writing in Grose, *Antiquities of Ireland*, p. xii. Sir Richard Colt Hoare

considered that Irish medieval architecture was greatly inferior to that of England, Scotland and Wales, *Tour in Ireland*, p. 217.

152. Joseph C. Walker, *Historical Memoirs of the Irish Bards* (London, 1786); Charlotte Brooke, *Reliques of Irish Poetry* (Dublin, 1789), pp. iii–v. Walter Harris, *The History and Antiquities of the City of Dublin* (Dublin, 1766) argued for a similar improvement in architecture of Dublin consequent upon the arrival of Danes and closer connections with the English during the sixteenth, seventeenth and eighteenth centuries, but his comments did not extend to any descriptions of the architectural antiquities in Dublin.
153. William Hutchinson, *A View of Northumberland with an Excursion to the Abbey of Mailross in Scotland*, 2 vols (Newcastle, 1776–78), i, pp. 282–87. Hutchinson's account was used by Grose in 1789 and thereafter found its way into all the subsequent derivative publications on Scottish antiquities.
154. Corpus Christi College, Cambridge, Parker Library, Kerrich MS 602, fol. 49, Edward Balme to Thomas Kerrich, 23 August 1813.
155. Gough, *British Topography*, ii, p. 553, quoting comments made in *Anecdotes of British Topography*, p. 618.
156. National Library of Scotland, Adv. MSS 34.1.10; 35.4.16–17 (manuscript collections of Richard Hay); Thomas Innes, *A Critical Essay on the Ancient Inhabitants of Scotland*, 2 vols (London, 1729); Robert Keith, *An Historical Catalogue of the Scottish Bishops Down to the Year 1688* (Edinburgh, 1755); Scottish antiquarian publications were reviewed by Gough, *British Topography*, ii, pp. 553–748. For modern interpretations see David Allan, *Virtue, Learning and the Scottish Enlightenment* (Edinburgh, 1993), pp. 46–48; Mark Goldie, 'The Scottish Catholic Enlightenment', *Journal of British Studies*, 30 (1991), pp. 20–62; Kidd, 'Antiquarianism, Religion and the Scottish Enlightenment', *Innes Review*, 46 (1995), pp. 139–54 and idem, *Subverting Scotland's Past*, pp. 77–79, 188–89.
157. Bodleian Library, MS Gough Gen. Top. 44, fol. 23, Gough to Tyson, 1 September 1771 or Nichols (ed.), *Literary Anecdotes*, viii, p. 568.
158. Gough, *Anecdotes of British Topography*, p. 618: 'we have as few subjects from the pencil or graver from the N. side of the Tweed as if the marches were still infested by marauders'. Twelve years later, he qualified the statement thus: 'till Mr Pennant with unremitting industry made his perambulation over this kingdom and its isles, we had as few ...', p. 554.
159. Adam Cardonnel, *Picturesque Antiquities of Scotland* (London, 1788); Charles Cordiner, *Remarkable Ruins, and Romantic Prospects of North Britain with Ancient Monuments and Singular Subjects of Natural History* (London, 1788) and *Antiquities and Scenery in the North of Scotland* (London, 1790).
160. National Library of Scotland, Adv. MS 29.5.6 (2), fol. 40.
161. National Library of Scotland, Adv. MS 29.3.14, fol. 76, earl of Buchan, anniversary address to the Scottish Society of Antiquaries, 15 November 1784.
162. Colin Kidd, *Subverting Scotland's Past: Scottish Whig Historians and the Creation of an Anglo-British Identity, c. 1689–1830* (Cambridge, 1993); James Anderson, *Sir Walter Scott and History* (Edinburgh, 1981).

163. Quoted by Stuart Piggott in 'The Origins of English County Archaeological Societies', in idem, *Ruins in a Landscape: Essays in Antiquarianism* (Edinburgh, 1976), p. 191.
164. British Library, Add. MS 23900, fol. 12v, Ducarel to Lethieullier, 24 October 1750.
165. *Vetusta monumenta*, ii, plates 39 and 40; Charles Lyttelton, 'Description of an Ancient Font at Bridekirk, in Cumberland', *Archaeologia*, 2 (1773), pp. 131–33; Samuel Pegge, 'Observations on an Antient Font at Burnham Deepdale in Norfolk', *Archaeologia*, 10 (1792), pp. 177–82; Richard Gough, 'Description of the Old Font of East Meon Hampshire, 1789; with some Observations on Fonts', *Archaeologia*, 10 (1792), pp. 183–207; Mr Holden, 'Description of the Reliefs on the Font at Thorpe Salvin in Yorkshire', *Archaeologia*, 12 (1796), pp. 207–8.
166. Bodleian Library, MS Eng. Misc. e. 122, fol. 84.
167. Reproductions of painted glass were becoming increasingly common in antiquarian publications. See, for example, John Carter, *Specimens of Ancient Sculpture and Painting now Remaining in this Kingdom from the Earliest Period to the Reign of Henry VIII*, 2 vols (London, 1780–86, 1787–94); the seven engravings of painted glass in William Fowler, *Twenty-one Engraving of the Principal Mosaic Pavements, and Six Engravings of Several Subjects in Stained Glass* (London, 1796–1828); engravings in Daniel Lysons, *The Environs of London: Being an Historical Account of the Towns, Villages and Hamlets within Twelve Miles of that Capital*, 4 vols (London, 1792); and Daniel and Samuel Lysons, *Magna Britannia*. Only one publication was devoted purely to the subject in this period: Philip Parsons, *The Monuments and Painted Glass of Upwards One Hundred Churches, Chiefly in the Eastern Part of Kent* (Canterbury, 1794).
168. Joseph Addison, *The Spectator*, ed. Donald F. Bond, 5 vols (Oxford, 1965), i, pp. 108–11: 'When I am in a serious Humour, I very often walk by my self in *Westminster* Abbey; where the Gloominess of the Place, and the Use to which it is applied, with the Solemnity of the Building, and the Condition of the People who lye in it, are apt to fill the Mind with a kind of Melancholy, or rather Thoughtfulness, that is not disagreeable.'
169. Smart Letheuillier, 'Mr Lethieullier's Observations on Sepulchral Monuments', *Archaeologia*, 2 (1773), pp. 291–300.
170. Gough, *British Topography*, i, pp. xxxvi, xlii.
171. Kenneth Garlick and Angus Macintyre (ed.), *The Diary of Joseph Farington*, 12 vols (New Haven and London, 1978–84), iv, p. 1290, 25 October 1799.
172. Gough, *Sepulchral Monuments*, i, p. 3.
173. C. A. Stothard, *The Monumental Effigies of Great Britain* (London, 1817), p. 5.
174. On the accuracy of Michael Tyson's draughtsmanship see Philip Lindley, 'The Imagery of the Octagon at Ely' and 'A Neglected King at Ely Cathedral', in idem, *Gothic to Renaissance: Essays on Sculpture in England* (London, 1995), pp. 113–46, 147–55.
175. John G. Dunbar (ed.), *Sir William Burrell's Northern Tour* (East Linton, 1997), p. 41.

176. Thomas Gent, *The Antient and Modern History of the Loyal Town of Rippon* (York, 1733), p. viii.

Notes to Chapter 8: Preservation

1. John Horsley, *Britannia Romana: or The Roman Antiquities of Britain* (London, 1732), p. 182.
2. British Library, Add. MS 5870, fol. 113. The incident was also described by Francis Grose, *The Olio* (London, 1792), pp. 176–77.
3. *Gentleman's Magazine*, 58 (1788), p. 689.
4. D. C. Douglas, *English Scholars, 1660–1730* (London, 1939), pp. 285–315. On Thomas Hearne see Theodore Harmsen, *Antiquarianism in the Augustan Age: Thomas Hearne, 1678–1735* (Bern, 2000).
5. Thomas Madox, *Formulare Anglicanum* (London, 1702), preface, sig. b.
6. R. J. Smith, *The Gothic Bequest: Medieval Institutions in British Thought, 1688–1863* (Cambridge, 1987), p. 91.
7. M. M. Condon and Elizabeth M. Hallam, 'Government Printing of the Public Records in the Eighteenth Century', *Journal of the Society of Archivists*, 7 (1984), pp. 359–73.
8. Copies were distributed to the members of the House of Lords, parliamentary officials and anyone in receipt of a warrant from the secretaries of state. Copies were also given for use in the State Paper Office, the Tower Record Office, Parliament Office at Dublin and the Advocates Library at Edinburgh. Hallam and Condon, 'Government Printing of the Public Records', p. 370.
9. Maria Grazia Lolla, 'Monuments and Texts: Antiquarianism and the Beauty of Antiquity', *Art History*, 25 (2002), pp. 438–44.
10. Edward Hasted, notably, did not include a facsimile transcription in his history of Kent, his reason being that 'none but those whose continued practice had gained a *technical* knowledge, in antient records, could have interpreted it, or even had read, and as such would have been of little use'. Edward Hasted, *The History and Topographical Survey of the County of Kent*, 12 vols (2nd edn, Canterbury, 1797–1801), i, p. ix.
11. Philip Carteret Webb, *A Short Account of Some Particulars Concerning Domesday Book, with a View to Promote its Being Published* (London, 1756), p. 8, quoting Thomas Hearne.
12. 'To Noblemen, Gentlemen of landed property, Clergymen, Lawyers and Jurymen, this Record will afford much pleasing and satisfactory Information; and the curious Customs enregistered in these volumes, will much elucidate the Common Law of the Land, the Manners of our Forefathers, the State of the Boroughs, Towns, and Villages, the Agriculture, Population and Commerce of the Kingdom', Samuel Henshall and John Wilkinson, *Domesday: or An Actual Survey of South Britain, by the Commissioners of William the Conqueror, Completed in the Year 1086* (London, 1799), p. iv.
13. British Library, Stowe MS 754, fol. 141, no date. Sir Joseph Ayloffe wrote to

Charles Lyttelton thanking him for his interest in securing the appointment on his behalf and that of Ducarel and Astle.

14. Astle's activities in this area are recorded in his correspondence with his clerk Lemon, and others in British Library, Add. MS 34711.
15. British Library, Add. MS 34711, fol. 78, Robert Lemon to Thomas Astle, 22 November 1778.
16. John Nichols, *The History and Antiquities of the County of Leicester*, 4 vols (London, 1795–1815), i, pt 1, p. xxxvi.
17. The first of six record commissions was established in 1800, charged with the regulating and providing for the better preservation of public records and the publication of calendars, indexes and manuscript editions. The Public Record Office Act of 1838, established the principle of a central repository for all records; its principal aim was to improve public access and its most immediate impact was to end the days of extortionate fees and restricted opening hours. Philippa Levine, *The Amateur and the Professional: Antiquarians, Historians and Archaeologists in Victorian England, 1838–1886* (Cambridge, 1986), pp. 101–34.
18. '… when the mere plodding drudge assumes the name, and pretence to the respectable character, of an Antiquary; whose ideas do not extend beyond pouring over some wretched black-lettered production of some illiterate monk, or transcribing a monumental inscription; who confines all knowledge and all taste within his own limited pale, who views with the same indiscriminating gaze of admiration every antient record, every ivied ruin; who has no standard to judge by, in appreciating the merit of buildings, pictures, and writings, but his own opinion or their remote antiquity; we cannot Mr Urban, but feel and lament the ridicule, the contempt and the disgrace, which he brings on the antiquarian profession'. *Gentleman's Magazine*, 55 (1785), p. 1066.
19. Françoise Choay, *The Invention of the Historic Monument*, trans. Lauren M. O'-Connell (Cambridge, 2001), pp. 29–38.
20. I. G. Brown, 'Gothicism, Ignorance and a Bad Taste': The Destruction of Arthur's O'on', *Antiquity*, 18 (1974), pp. 283–300.
21. See pp. 243–47 above.
22. Browne Willis, *A History of the Mitred Parliamentary Abbies and Conventual Churches*, 2 vols (London, 1718), i, p. 2. Similarly Theodor Harmsen draws attention to Thomas Hearne's attempts to reconstruct the physical form of the monastery at Glastonbury, *Antiquarianism in the Augustan Age*, p. 254.
23. F. C. Mather, 'Georgian Churchmanship Revisited: Some Variations in Anglican Public Worship, 1714–1830', *Journal of Ecclesiastical History*, 36 (1985), pp. 255–83.
24. These were published in *Parentalia* and in Francis Widmore, *An History of the Church of St Peter, Westminster* (London, 1751) and Francis Price, *A Series of Particular and Useful Observations, Made with Great Diligence and Care, Upon that Admirable Structure, the Cathedral-Church of Salisbury* (London, 1753).

25. *Some Account of the Cathedral Church at Exeter. Illustrative of the Plans, Elevations and Sections, of that Building* (London, 1797).
26. Bodleian Library, MS Eng. Misc. e. 122, fos 82–84.
27. Richard Gough, *Anecdotes of British Topography* (London, 1768), p. xxvi.
28. On Hereford see Gerald Aylmer and John Tiller (ed.), *Hereford Cathedral: A History* (London, 2000), pp. 241–85; on Lichfield see J. M. Frew, 'Cathedral Improvement: James Wyatt at Lichfield Cathedral, 1787–92', *Transactions of the South Staffordshire Archaeological and Historical Society*, 19 (1977–78), pp. 33–47.
29. J. Mordaunt Crook, *John Carter and the Mind of the Gothic Revival* (London, 1995), p. 35.
30. *Gentleman's Magazine*, 55 (1785), pp. 873–75. The response at pp. 1064–66 criticised the failure of the author to distinguish between what was merely old and what was beautiful and therefore worthy of preservation.
31. On the changes at Salisbury see Thomas Cocke and Peter Kidson, *Salisbury Cathedral: Perspectives in Architectural History* (London, 1993), pp. 24–46.
32. Lambeth Palace Library, MS 2215, fol. 128 (draft of a letter to the bishop of Salisbury published in the *General Evening Post*, 20–22 August 1789); see also articles by Gough on the same subject in *Monthly Review*, 31 (1789), p. 493 and *Gentleman's Magazine*, 59 (1789), pp. 874–5, 1194. Gough's criticisms were in turn challenged, pp. 1065–66 by William Dodsworth, the verger at Salisbury Cathedral and author of *A Guide to the Cathedral Church of Salisbury: With a Particular Account of the Late Great Improvements Made there Under the Direction of James Wyatt* (2nd edn, Salisbury, 1791). Carter's criticisms were published in the *Gentleman's Magazine* as part of his series 'Pursuits of Architectural Innovation', 73 (1803), pp. 515–17, 642–45, 735–37, 1020–23, 1122–24.
33. *Gentleman's Magazine*, 59 (1789), p. 1194–96. On Lichfield see Richard Gough writing as VIATOR in *Gentleman's Magazine*, 65 (1795), pp. 924–25, 1074–75; and John Carter, *Gentleman's* Magazine, 71 (1801), pp. 311–13; the alterations were defended by George Robinson, *Gentleman's Magazine*, 65 (1795), pp. 998–99.
34. In the event only the chapter house was completely dismantled; the roof of the Galilee chapel was removed, but no further destruction took place. Mordaunt Crook, *John Carter*, p. 35.
35. Carter was in fact an Anglican. Ibid., p. 58 incorrectly states that Gough was a Catholic. Gough's mother had come from a Dissenting family and Gough maintained connections with his mother's relatives, prompting William Cole to accuse him of Presbyterianism. British Library, Add. MS 5870, fol. 113; Add MS 5834, fol. 108; the character of Gough given in Nichols (ed.), *Literary Anecdotes*, vi, p. 272, described him as 'deeply impressed with a sense of the excellence and happiness of the English Constitution both in Church and State'.
36. The council minutes record that 'special care will be taken to avoid any Thing which can give offence or be considered as of a personal Nature, but the account will be confined to a strict statement of the present state of the Buildings described'. Society of Antiquaries, Council Minute Book, iii, 10 May 1799.

37. *Some Account of the Cathedral Church of Durham: Illustrative of the Plans, Elevations and Sections of that Building* (London, 1801), pp. 5, 8.
38. Thomas Cocke, 'The Architectural History of Ely Cathedral from 1540–1840', in *Medieval Art and Architecture at Ely Cathedral*, British Archaeological Association Conference Transactions for the Year 1976 (1979), pp. 71–77.
39. J. M. Frew, 'Richard Gough, James Wyatt and Late Eighteenth-Century Preservationism', *Journal of the Society of Architectural Historians*, 38 (1979), pp. 366–74.
40. Mordaunt Crook, *John Carter*, pp. 80–89, provides a complete check list of all these articles.
41. John Topham, *Some Account of the Collegiate Chapel of Saint Stephen, Westminster* (London, 1795).
42. Mordaunt Crook, *John Carter*, pp. 41–43.
43. In the early nineteenth century particular emphasis was placed upon the fact that many of these had been erected at public expense.
44. Joseph Addison, *The Spectator*, ed. Donald F. Bond, 5 vols (Oxford, 1965), i, pp. 108–11; Thomas Pennant, *Some Account of London* (2nd edn, London, 1791), p. 81: 'I shall quit these solemn scenes with the beautiful reflection of Mr Addison, made on the spot: and hope it may have the same weight with the reader, as it has on me, whenever I peruse the following piece of instructive eloquence.' Milton's lines from *Il Penseroso*, although not explicitly referring to Westminster Abbey, were quoted with equal frequency: 'But let my due feet never fail/To walk the studious cloister's pale,/ And love the high embowèd roof,/ With antick pillars massy proof,/ And storied windows richly dight,/Casting a dim religious light.'
45. Jean Marchand (ed.), *A Frenchman in England 1784: Being the Mélanges sur l'Angleterre of François de la Rochefoucauld*, trans. S. C. Roberts (London, 1995), p. 17.
46. Thomas Cocke and Donald Buttress, *900 Years: The Restorations of Westminster Abbey* (London, 1995), pp. 36–58.
47. John Dart, *Westmonsterium: or The History and Antiquities of the Abbey Church of St Peter's Westminster*, 2 vols (London, 1723); Francis Widmore, *An History of the Church of St Peter, Westminster, Commonly Called Westminster Abbey* (London, 1753).
48. *Gentleman's Magazine*, 71 (1801), pp. 328, 613.
49. J. P. Malcolm, *Londinium redivivum* (London, 1802), pp. 140, 209–11.
50. *Gentleman's Magazine*, 73 (1803), p. 511.
51. *Gentleman's Magazine*, 73 (1803), pp. 511, 1128–29; 74 (1804), pp. 738–40; 76 (1806), pp. 494–95; 77 (1807), pp. 1187–90; 80 (1810), p. 200; 81 (1811), pp. 204–6, 417–18, 430–31; 83 (1813), pp. 33–34, 235–36, 441–42
52. Cocke and Buttress, *The Restorations of Westminster Abbey*, p. 39.
53. *Commons Journals*, 62 (1807), p. 588.
54. Cocke and Buttress, *900 Years of Restoration*, pp. 57–59; J. M. Frew, '"The Destroyer" Vindicated? James Wyatt and the Restoration of Henry VII's

Chapel, Westminster Abbey', *Journal of the British Archaeological Association*, 134 (1981), pp. 100–6.

55. R. Ackermann, *The History of the Abbey Church of St Peter's Westminster, its Antiquities and Monuments*, 2 vols (London, 1812), i, p. xvi.
56. Linda Colley, *Britons: The Forging of a Nation, 1707–1837* (New Haven and London, 1992), pp. 195–236 and 'The Apotheosis of George III: Loyalty, Royalty and the British Nation, 1760–1820', *Past and Present*, 102 (1984), pp. 94–129.
57. *Gentleman's Magazine*, 66 (1806), pp. 817–18, 1027–29; 77 (1807), pp. 343–36, 297–98, 629–31, 710–11, 819–21, 1110–12; 68 (1808), p. 681; 69 (1809), pp. 220–22, 1113–15. The financial problems of the corporation which drove them to adopt this measure are analysed by E. J. Dawson, 'Finance and the Unreformed Borough: A Critical Appraisal of Corporate Finance 1660–1835, with Special Reference to the Boroughs of Nottingham, York and Boston', unpublished Ph.D. thesis, University of Hull (1978), pp. 584–85.
58. *Gentleman's Magazine*, 86 (1806), pp. 817–18.
59. Bristol Record Office, MS 0954/1. The cross was subsequently acquired by Henry Hoare of Stourhead, provoking further protests in the local press. See J. Latimer, *Annals of Bristol in the Eighteenth Century* (Bristol, 1893), pp. 186, 354.
60. British Library, Stowe MS 754, fol. 215, William Cowper to Charles Lyttelton, 20 June 1767.
61. John Throsby, *The History and Antiquities of the Ancient Town of Leicester* (Leicester, 1791), p. 364.
62. James Wallace, *A General and Descriptive History of the Ancient and Present State of the Town of Liverpool* (2nd edn, Liverpool, 1797), p. 47.
63. Sir Cuthbert Sharpe, *History of Hartlepool* (Durham, 1816), p. 130, describing improvements in 1808.
64. *Gentleman's Magazine*, 67 (1797), p. 638; John Milner, *A Dissertation on the Modern Style of Altering Antient Cathedrals, as Exemplified in the Cathedral of Salisbury* (London, 1798).
65. John Milner, *History of Winchester*, 2 vols (2nd edition, Winchester, 1811), ii, pp. 448–49.
66. *Gentleman's Magazine*, 76 (1806), p. 818.
67. C. Bruyn Andrews (ed.), *The Torrington Diaries*, 4 vols (London, 1970), ii, p. 111
68. *Gentleman's Magazine*, 74 (1804), p. 430; Mordaunt Crook, *John Carter*, p. 32 and *passim*.
69. Francis Grose, *Antiquities of England and Wales*, 4 vols (London, 1773–76), i, p. ii.
70. Colley, *Britons*, p. 173; Sir Richard Colt Hoare, *Journal of a Tour in Ireland, AD 1806* (London, 1807), p. v and idem, *Ancient History of South Wiltshire* (London, 1812).
71. See, for example, *Gentleman's Magazine*, 67 (1797), pt 2, pp. 927–28. Gough's second volume of *Sepulchral Monuments* similarly made the connection

between the preservation of domestic antiquities and the destruction which was taking place on the Continent, *Sepulchral Monuments*, ii, pp. 5–10.

72. Stebbing Shaw, *A Tour to the West of England* (London, 1789), p. 319.
73. *Antiquarian Repertory*, 4 (1775), p. 129.
74. William Gilpin, *Observations on the Mountains and Lakes of Cumberland Westmoreland*, 2 vols (London, 1786), ii, p. 188; Anne Janowitz, *England's Ruins: Poetic Purpose and the National Landscape* (Oxford, 1990), pp. 1–81.
75. *Antiquarian Repertory*, 9 (1776), p. 245.
76. William Gilpin, *Observations on the River Wye, and Several Parts of South Wales &c. Relative Chiefly to Picturesque Beauty: Made in the Summer of the Year 1770* (London, 1782), pp. 32–33.
77. Grose, *Antiquities of England and Wales.*
78. William Bray, *Sketch of a Tour* (London, 1777), p. 137.
79. See Thomas Girtin's 'Kirkstall Abbey, Yorkshire, from the South-East, after James Moore, Michael Angelo Rooker, 'Interior of the Abbot's Kitchen Glastonbury' or J. M. W. Turner, 'Transept of Ewenny Priory, Glamorganshire'.
80. John Carter, 'The Pursuits of Architectural Innovation', *Gentleman's Magazine*, 72 (1802), pt 2, p. 1115.
81. M. W. Thompson (ed.), *The Journeys of Sir Richard Colt Hoare through Wales and England, 1793–1810* (Stroud, 1983), pp. 98, 233.
82. Klindt Jensen, *A History of Scandinavian Archaeology* (London, 1975), p. 27. The preamble to a proclamation of 1666 deplored the apathy towards ancient monuments which allowed them to fall into decay or be destroyed and which ignored their value as testimony to posterity of the 'heroic achievements of the kings of Sweden and Gotland, their subjects, and other great men'. It forbad the destruction or damage of monuments (including castles, fortresses, dolmens, stones bearing runic inscriptions, tombs and ancestral barrows) whether situated upon Crown land or private property. Crown officials enforced the prohibition and priests were deputed to inspect all field monuments and send drawings of them to the king. The legislation was extended further in 1784 to cover artefacts such as coins, vessels and other artefacts.
83. Quoted in Evans, *History of the Society of Antiquaries*, p. 156. The Scottish antiquary George Chalmers was moved by the hardened barbarity of those who destroyed Gothic antiquities. In a letter to George Paton he suggested an 'act of the British Senate' was the only remedy to put an end to such 'folly, madness, impudence, sacrilege, pride, vanity, greediness'. There is no indication that Chalmers ever took this any further, and the overall hyperbolic tone of the letter must make one question how seriously he intended his suggestion to be taken. National Library of Scotland, Adv. MS 29.3.8, fol. 125, Chalmers to Paton, 20 October 1775.
84. See chapter 7 above.
85. Kenneth Garlick and Angus Macintyre (ed.), *The Diary of Joseph Farington*, 12 vols (New Haven and London, 1978–84), iii, p. 919, 9 November 1797; Carter penned a delayed response in the *Gentleman's Magazine*, 71 (1801), pp. 309–13.

86. The Society for the Protection of Ancient Buildings was not founded until 1877, and five years later saw the passage of the Ancient Monuments Protection Act 1882. Jane Fawcett (ed.), *Attitudes Towards Conservation: The Future of the Past, 1174–1974* (1976), p. 17 and Michael Hunter, 'The Preconditions of Preservation: A Historical Perspective', in D. Lowenthal and M. Binney (eds), *Our Past Before Us: Why Do We Save It?* (London, 1981), pp. 22–32; Michael Hunter, *Preserving the Past: the Rise of Heritage in Modern Britian* (Stroud, 1996), pp. 1–40.
87. Tim Clayton, *The English Print* (New Haven and London, 1997).
88. For a case study of the practice of grangerisation see Lucy Peltz, 'The Extra-Illustration of London: The Gendered Spaces and Practices of Antiquarianism in the Late Eighteenth Century', in Martin Myrone and Lucy Peltz (ed.), *Producing the Past: Aspects of Antiquarian Culture and Practice, 1700–1850* (Aldershot, 1999), pp. 115–34.
89. Graham Parry, 'Wenceslaus Hollar, the Antiquarians' Illustrator', *Ariel* (1972), pp. 42–52.
90. Quoted in John Farrant, *Sussex Depicted: Views and Descriptions, 1600–1800*, Sussex Record Society, 85 (Lewes, 2001), p. 82, from the prospectus for *Perspective Views of Remains of Antiquity* (London, 1737).
91. Browne Willis, *Survey of the Cathedrals of York, Durham, Carlisle, Chester, Man, Lichfield, Hereford, Worcester, Gloucester and Bristol*, 2 vols (London, 1727), i, p. 3.
92. Bodleian Library, MS Top. London c. 2, fol. 276.
93. Stukeley was closely acquainted with Samuel and Nathaniel Buck, and they provided some of the illustrations for *Itinerarium curiosum* and accompanied him on some of his tours. Like him they belonged to the Society of Antiquaries and the Gentleman's Society of Spalding. Gough gave Stukeley the credit for encouraging them to launch their perspective views of abbeys, religious foundations, castles and other remains of antiquity. Gough, *British Topography*, i, p. xli.
94. Stukeley made the survival of Waltham Cross a personal mission. In 1720 he was responsible for having two oak posts erected to prevent carriages running against it. In the 1750s he brought it to the attention of the Antiquaries again, as a particularly acute case of the 'too prevailing, if not general, Neglect of, and defacing antient monuments'. See Society of Antiquaries, Minute Books, viii (typescript), pp. 103–6, quotation at p. 105. He recorded that he had urged Lord Monson to erect a brick wall around it to protect it. See also Bodleian Library, MS Eng. Misc. e. 124, fol. 116. The society published engravings of the cross again in 1791 as part of a series illustrating all the Eleanor Crosses, drawn by Schnebbelie and engraved by Basire (*Vetusta monumenta*, iii, plates 16 and 17). A comparison of the two sets of images illustrates the changes which the antiquarian aesthetic underwent over the course of the century. Stukeley's image was divorced from its surrounding and focused upon illustrating the form and ornamentation of the cross, providing a cross-section

and view of the statues hidden from sight. By the 1790s the antiquarian aesthetic had shifted towards the picturesque and the cross was shown in all its decay, located in its vulnerable position on the edge of the road, with damaged statues, crumbling masonry, the protective fence broken down and iron bars holding the structure together. See also Lucy Peltz's discussion of some of these themes in 'Aestheticizing the Ancestral City: Antiquarianism, Topography and the Representation of London in the Long Eighteenth Century', in Dana Arnold (ed.), *The Metropolis and its Image: Constructing Identities for London, c. 1750–1950* (Oxford, 1999), pp. 6–28.

95. British Library, Stowe MS 754, fos 14–15, James Bentham to Charles Lyttelton, 17 April 1758.
96. Sir H. C. Englefield and J. Windham, *Report on the Proper Methods of Measuring and Drawing Antient Buildings* (London, 1792), bound in Richard Gough's copy of *Archaeologia*, 12 (1792), Bodleian Library.
97. Gough, *Anecdotes of British Topography*, p. xxviii.
98. Richard Gough, *Sepulchral Monuments in Great Britain, Applied to Illustrate the Families, Manners, Habits, and Arts, at the Different Periods from the Norman Conquest to the Seventeenth Century*, 2 vols (London 1786–1796), i, p. 4.
99. Society of Antiquaries, MS 891/1, fol. 68, Sir George Yonge to Hayman Rooke, 11 July, 1787.
100. British Library, Add. MS 29944 and Society of Antiquaries, MS 267.
101. On George Vertue see Martin Myrone, 'Graphic Antiquarianism in Eighteenth-Century Britain: The Career and Reputation of George Vertue (1684–1756)' in Myrone and Peltz (ed.), *Producing the Past*, pp. 37–56.
102. David Bindman, *Blake as an Artist* (Oxford, 1977), pp. 12–13.
103. J. T. Smith, *Antient Topography of London Embracing Specimens of Sacred, Public and Domestic Architecture from the Earliest Period to the Time of the Great Fire of 1666* (London, 1815), p. 2.
104. For a case study of the variation in the representation of Gothic buildings see Peltz, 'Aestheticizing the Ancestral City'.
105. *Gentleman's Magazine*, 73 (1803), p. 106.
106. Scipione Maffei, 'The Use of Inscriptions and Medals', in M. Langlet du Fresnoy, *A New Method of Studying History*, trans. Richard Rawlinson (London, 1728), p. 351.
107. D. N., *Gentleman's Magazine* (1788), pp. 689–9. The contributor has been identified by Joan Evans, *A History of the Society of Antiquaries* (Oxford, 1956), p. 191, as Richard Gough. There is, however, no evidence in the Nichols files of attributions of authorship to bear out this identification and Gough's customary signature was D.H. The criticisms which the author made of the Society of Antiquaries and the concerns raised are, however, in keeping with Gough's views expressed elsewhere. My thanks to Emily Lorraine de Montluzin of Virginia University for her assistance in my attempts to clarify this point.
108. Charles Norris, *Saint David's in a Series of Engravings, Illustrating the Different Ecclesiastical Edifices of that Ancient City* (London, 1811), p. i.

109. Choay, *Invention of the Historic Monument*, pp. 64, 70–71.
110. Britton, *Autobiography*, i, p. 138.
111. Colley, *Britons*, p. 176. Peter Mandler, *The Fall and Rise of the Stately Home* (New Haven and London, 1997), examines the association between the aristocracy and the creation of an idea of national heritage in the Victorian era, see especially pp. 21–106.

Notes to Chapter 9: Popularisation

1. Peter Mandler, 'In the Olden Time': Romantic History and English National Identity', in Laurence Brockliss and David Eastwood (ed.), *A Union of Multiple Identities: The British Isles, c. 1750–1850* (Manchester, 1997), pp. 78–92.
2. J. Hunter (ed.), *The Life of Mr Thomas Gent, Printer of York: Written by Himself* (London, 1832), pp. 184–203.
3. Thomas Gent, *The Antient and Modern History of the Loyal Town of Rippon* (York, 1733), p. xi.
4. Francis Howgrave, *An Essay on the Ancient and Present State of Stamford* (Stamford, 1726); Francis Peck, *Academica Tertia Anglicana: or The Antiquarian Annals of Stamford in Lincoln* (London, 1727); Nichols (ed.), *Literary Anecdotes*, viii, p. 573. This pattern continued through the century: Samuel Denne was approached by a local bookseller, Thomas Fisher, to write a history of Rochester; John Brand's *History and Antiquities of Newcastle*, was initiated by the bookseller Thomas Saint; and John Milner's history of Winchester was written at the request of an entrepreneurial local bookseller.
5. Daniel Woolf, *Reading History in Early Modern England* (Cambridge, 2000), p. 280.
6. Rosemary Sweet, *The Writing of Urban Histories in Eighteenth-Century England* (Oxford, 1997), p. 7.
7. John Cannon, 'Teaching in the Market Place, or 'Caesar adsum jam forte: Pompey aderat': the Retailing of Knowledge in Provincial England during the Eighteenth Century', in John Brewer and Roy Porter (ed.), *Consumption and the World of Goods* (London, 1994), pp. 335–77; R. M. Wiles, *Serial Publications in England before 1750* (Cambridge, 1957), emphasises that books upon history, antiquities and geography lent themselves best to this form of serialisation.
8. *Gentleman's Magazine*, 72 (1802), p. 719.
9. British Library, Stowe MS 752, fol. 179, William Borlase to Charles Lyttelton, 27 September 1756.
10. Sweet, *Writing of Urban Histories*, pp. 17, 29, 107–8.
11. E. Hargrove, *The History of the Castle and Town of Knaresborough* (Knaresborough, 1769), revised editions in 1775, 1782, 1789 and 1798.
12. Rosemary Sweet, 'History and Identity in Eighteenth-Century York', in Jane Rendall and Mark Hallett (ed.), *Eighteenth-Century York: Culture, Space and Society* (York, 2003).
13. Samuel Rudder, *The History of the Ancient Town of Cirencester* (Cirencester,

1780); idem, *The History and Antiquities of Gloucester* (Cirencester, 1781); see also Sweet, *Writing of Urban Histories*, pp. 16–18.

14. Bodleian Library, MS Top. gen. c. 8, fol. 66, Gough proposed to his co-editor, William Cuming, that they should published the account of Corfe Castle as a separate pamphlet as a vademecum for travellers. Proceeds from sales of the county history raised 100 guineas to send Miss Hutchins to India (where she married) and £260 for Mrs Hutchins. Ibid., fos 364–65.
15. Lionel Charlton, *The History of Whitby and Whitby Abbey* (Whitby, 1779).
16. William Hutton, *History of the Roman Wall* (London, 1802), pp. v, 325.
17. Hutton's account was not disregarded by other antiquaries. His detailed observations and measurements were used by the Northumberland antiquary John Hodgson, for example, in the account of the Roman Wall written for *The Beauties of England and Wales*, 18 vols (London, 1806–13), xii, pt 1, p. 3.
18. Hutton, *Roman Wall*, pp. 200, 295.
19. L. Jewitt (ed.), *The Life of William Hutton and the History of the Hutton Family: Edited from the Original Manuscripts* (London, 1872).
20. Pat Rogers, 'Defoe as a Plagiarist: Camden's *Britannia* and *A Tour thro' the Whole Island of Great Britain*', *Philological Quarterly*, 52 (1973), pp. 771–74; see also Katherine Turner, 'Defoe's *Tour*: The Changing Face of Things', *British Journal for Eighteenth-Century Studies*, 24 (2001), pp. 189–206. Daniel Defoe, *A Tour through the Whole Island of Great Britain*, ed. G. D. H. Cole, 2 vols (London, 1927), i, pp. 197–99; ii, pp. 491–92.
21. Daniel Defoe, *A Tour through the Whole Island of Great Britain* (London, 1778), p. 147.
22. Stebbing Shaw, *A Tour to the West of England in 1788* (London, 1789), p. 7.
23. George Lipscombe, *Journey into South Wales* (London, 1802), pp. xv–xviii.
24. David Morris, *Thomas Hearne and his Landscape* (London, 1989), p. 28.
25. On the subject of the picturesque see Malcolm Andrews, *The Search for the Picturesque: Landscape Aesthetics and Tourism in Britain, 1760–1800* (Aldershot, 1989); Christopher Hussey, *The Picturesque: Studies in a Point of View* (reprinted London, 1967); Ian Ousby, *The Englishman's England: Taste, Travel and the Rise of Tourism* (Cambridge, 1990); D. M. Solkin, *Richard Wilson and the Landscape of Reaction* (London, 1982).
26. Horace Walpole, *Anecdotes of Painting* (London, 1762), p. 107.
27. Bodleian Library, MS Gen. Top. 41, fol. 178, Edward Haistwell to Richard Gough, 24 June 1765.
28. Edward King, *Munimenta Antiqua: or Observations on Ancient Castles*, 4 vols (London, 1799), i, p. xv.
29. *Monthly Review*, 38 (1802), p. 269; Sam Smiles, 'Recording the Gothic: Art and Information', in *Artists and Visual Documentation in Britain, 1770–1830* (Aldershot, 2000), pp. 47–76.
30. The subscription lists are discussed in greater detail by Andrew Kennedy, 'Antiquity and Improvement in the National Landscape: The Bucks' Views of Antiquities 1726–42', *Art History*, 25 (2002), pp. 488–99.

31. John H. Farrant, 'The Travels and Travails of Francis Grose FSA', *Antiquaries Journal*, 75 (1995), pp. 365–80. Farrant compares Grose's price of 6d. with 1s. per plate for Paul Sandby's *Virtuosi's Museum* and 3s. for Hearne and Byrne's *Antiquities of Great Britain* (p. 369). Sandby himself claimed that most views comparable to his were priced at 2s. 6d. or even 5s. each: *The Virtuosi's Museum Containing Select Views, in England, Scotland and Ireland* (London, 1778), preface. Although Grose's publications may have appeared comparatively cheap, they were still beyond the means of a majority of the population, and by 1803 a four volume leather bound set of the *Antiquities of England and Wales* could cost as much as 8 guineas. Surrey History Centre, MS 85/1/46, diary of William Bray, 15 June 1803.
32. Francis Grose, *Antiquities of England and Wales*, 4 vols (London, 1772–76), i, p. ii.
33. Farrant, 'Travels and Travails', p. 374.
34. Anne Janowitz, *England's Ruins: Poetic Purpose and National Landscape* (Oxford, 1990).
35. Nichols (ed.), *Literary Anecdotes*, viii, p. 664.
36. John Milner in *Gentleman's Magazine*, 67 (1797), p. 638.
37. *Gentleman's Magazine*, 52 (1782), pp. 432, 480, 599; 53 (1783), pp. 138–39, 302–3, 375–76.
38. See pp. 260–66, 288–95.
39. Grose wrote to George Allan, 4 February 1776 'The Antiquarian Repertory goes on. You was misinformed as to my conducting it. I have given a number of drawings to Mr Godfrey, as I would to anybody else that wanted them, and gave him some pieces to help it on.' Nichols (ed.), *Literary Anecdotes*, viii, p. 695.
40. Hayman Rooke's correspondence with Godfrey in which he promises him a number of prints and other contributions is to be found in Society of Antiquaries, MS 891/1, fos 17–25.
41. Bodleian Library, MS Top. gen. c. 8, fos 364–65. Gough's opinion of the publication did not improve with the passage of time: he was far more critical of the *Antiquarian Repertory* in *British Topography*, i, p. xxxix, where he remarked that 'if more judiciously compiled, and the prints more accurately engraved, [it] is not without its share of merit. But the editor as he raises his price falls off in his execution.'
42. Bodleian Library, MS Gen. Top. 44, fos 437v–38, Michael Tyson to Richard Gough, 9 January 1780. Joseph Farington reported that Samuel Lysons had 'no high opinion' of Grose's antiquarian works: 'they are collated with very little trouble from 3 or 4 known works', Kenneth Garlick and Angus Macintyre (ed.), *The Diary of Joseph Farington*, 12 vols (New Haven and London, 1978–84), ii, p. 629.
43. *Antiquarian Repertory*, 1 (2nd edn, 1807), p. v.
44. A survey of illustrated topographical literature is provided by R. Russell, *Guide to British Topographical Prints* (London, 1979).

45. John Britton, *The Autobiography of John Britton*, 2 vols (London, 1850), i, pp. 257–58.
46. The classic exponent of this genre was John Trusler with, for example, *The Way to be Rich and Respectable* (London, 1775) or *The Principles of Politeness and of Knowing the World* (16th edn, London, 1800).
47. *Antiquarian Repertory*, 1 (1775), p. ii; *Historical Descriptions of New and Elegant Picturesque Views of the Antiquities of England and Wales* (London, 1785), p. i.
48. Britton, *Autobiography*, i, pp. 121–22. The assistance of subscribers and correspondents in furnishing materials was acknowledged in the prefatory passages to both series of volumes.
49. *The Antiquarian Itinerary, Comprising Specimens of Architecture, Monastic, Castellated, and Domestic: With Other Vestiges of Antiquity in Great Britain*, 10 vols (London, 1815), i, no pagination.
50. Rather more detail was offered in the letter press to the *History and Antiquities of the Cathedral Churches* and in particular the authors drew upon the descriptions (where possible) published by the Society of Antiquaries in the Cathedral series of engravings.
51. *The Antiquarian and Topographical Cabinet, Containing a Series of Elegant Views of the Most Interesting Objects of Curiosity in Great Britain*, 10 vols (London, 1807), i, no pagination.
52. The fact that Samuel Ireland was blackballed for membership from the Society of Antiquaries may be an indication of the regard in which his publications were held by the antiquarian community.
53. Britton, *Autobiography*, i, p. 136.
54. According to the biography the first five volumes (after which Britton and Brayley withdrew their services) had print runs of 500 royal octavo and 3000 small octavo. 2000 additional copies of the volume covering Middlesex were printed to accommodate additional demand from the London area. Britton, *Autobiography*, ii, pp. 53–56.
55. Bodleian Library, MS Don. d. 87, fol. 227.
56. The disagreements between Britton and Brayley and with Vernor and Hood are documented in correspondence in Bodleian Library, MS Don. d. 87, fos 176–236.
57. The best survey of John Britton's career to date is by J. Mordaunt Crook, 'John Britton and the Genesis of the Gothic Revival', in John Summerson (ed.), *Concerning Architecture: Essays on Architectural Writers and Writing Presented to Nikolaus Pevsner* (London, 1968), pp. 98–119. A substantial amount of information upon Britton's publishing career is to be found in his own *Autobiography of John Britton*, 2 vols (London, 1850). See also P. Ferriday, 'John Britton' *Architectural Review*, 77 (1957), pp. 367–69, and Richard Hatchwell, 'The Life and Work of John Britton (1771–1857)', *Wiltshire Archaeological and Natural History Magazine*, 85 (1992), pp. 101–13.
58. John Britton, *The Architectural Antiquities of Great Britain*, 5 vols (London,

1807–26). According to his autobiography it was the most successful of his many undertakings, earning him £1800 over the twenty one years which it took to produce, and for which he received £3266 as its joint owner. He prided himself that whereas most engravers offered only a half page or so of letter press to accompany their views, he provided at least a page and a half. Although Britton intended the series as a more specialist, antiquarian publication, attaching particular importance to the quality of the engravings, it was a fairly miscellaneous performance, with no geographical or chronological coherence to it. It never achieved the broad circulation of the *Beauties of England and Wales*, however – the largest sale of any volume in the series was 1300 copies. It was for the fifth and final volume to this series that Britton composed his historiographical review of the development of architectural antiquarian studies. See chapter 7.

59. See chapter 7. Smiles, 'Recording the Gothic: Art and Information' develops a similar argument.
60. Hearne and Byrne, *Antiquities of Great Britain.*
61. Society of Antiquaries, MS 267, fol. 137.
62. J. Partridge, *An Historical Account of the Town and Parish of Nantwich* (Shrewsbury, 1774), p. 22.
63. John Watson, *The History and Antiquities of the Parish of Halifax in Yorkshire* (London, 1775), pp. 357–58.
64. Anon, *The History and Antiquities of Winchester*, 2 vols (Winchester, 1773), ii, pp. 156–57.
65. 'The cathedral appears to be of one and the same style of building throughout, and no part older than King Edward the 1st's time, though some writers suppose the present fabrick was begun in King Stephen's time, but not a single arch, pillar, or window agrees with the mode which prevailed at that time. Indeed the lower part of the chapter-house walls, together with the door-way and columns at the entrance of the chapter-house I should pronounce of that age, or rather prior to King Stephen's reign, being true Saxon architecture.' William Barrett, *History and Antiquities of Bristol* (Bristol, 1789), pp. 286–87, 293, 573.
66. William Reader, *The History and Antiquities of the City of Coventry from the Earliest Authentic Period to the Present Time* (Coventry, 1810), p. 181.
67. Britton, *Autobiography*, i, p. 176. In later life he made a collection of Carter's papers and evidently saw himself as Carter's heir in the battle against innovation and the blind destruction of Gothic architecture.
68. John Blackner, *The History of Nottingham, Embracing its Antiquities, Trade and Manufacture, from the Earliest Authentic Period to the Present Period* (Nottingham, 1815), pp. 91–92.
69. See for example, Thomas Walford, *The Scientific Tourist through England, Wales and Scotland* (London, 1818).
70. James Moore, *A List of the Principal Castles and Monasteries in Great Britain* (London, 1798).

71. Mark Salber Phillips, *Society and Sentiment: Genres of Historical Writing in Britain, 1740–1820* (Princeton, 2000).
72. On nineteenth-century popular history writing and its debt to the eighteenth-century antiquarian traditions see Rosemary Mitchell, *Picturing the Past: English History in Text and Image, 1830–1870* (Oxford, 2000).
73. Joseph Strutt, *Horda Angel-Cynnan: or A Compleat View of the Manners, Customs, Arms, Habits etc of the Inhabitants of England from the Arrivals of the Saxons to the Present Time*, 3 vols (London, 1773–76); Brenda Lilian Hough, 'A Consideration of the Antiquarian and Literary Works of Joseph Strutt, with a Transcript of a Hitherto Inedited Manuscript Novel', unpublished Ph.D. thesis, University of London (1984), p. 156.
74. David Garrick is also known to have possessed a copy of *Dress and Habits*, see Hough, 'Joseph Strutt', p. 217.
75. Roy Strong, *And When Did You Last See Your Father?* (London 1978), pp. 50–52; Smiles, 'Recording the Gothic', pp. 51–52; Tim Clayton, *The English Print, 1688–1802* (New Haven and London, 1997), pp. 257–59.
76. Strutt, *Manners and Customs*, iii, p. 83.
77. Francis Grose, *Military Antiquities Respecting a History of the English Army, from the Conquest to the Present Time* (London, 1786) and *A Treatise on Ancient Armour and Weapons* (London, 1786).
78. Mark Girouard, *The Return of Camelot: Chivalry and the English Gentleman* (New Haven and London, 1981), pp. 19–23; Lionel Gossman, *Medievalism and the Ideologies of the Enlightenment: The World and Work of La Curne de Sainte-Palaye* (Baltimore, 1968).
79. Thomas Burgess, *An Essay on the Study of Antiquities* (Oxford, 1781), p. 16; Stebbing Shaw, *The History and Antiquities of Staffordshire*, 2 vols (London, 1798–1801), i, p. v.
80. Nichols (ed.), *Literary Anecdotes*, v, pp. 683–84; Hough, 'Joseph Strutt', pp. 277–85.
81. Quoted in Hough, 'Joseph Strutt', p. 284.
82. Gough in *Gentleman's Magazine*, 57 (1787), p. 425, reviewing William Rastall Dickenson's *History and Antiquities of the Town and Church of Southwell in the County of Nottingham* (London, 1787).
83. Sir Walter Scott, *Ivanhoe: A Historical Romance* (Edinburgh, 1998), pp. 5–12.
84. Henry Bourne, *Antiquitates Vulgares: or The Antiquities of the Common People* (Newcastle, 1725), pp. ix–xii. Bourne was also the author of a history of Newcastle, *The History of Newcastle upon Tyne: or the Ancient and Present State of that Town* (Newcastle, 1736). He was ordained by Edward Gibson (then bishop of Lincoln) and it is possible that he, like Morant (see pp. 54–55 below), saw this kind of antiquarian study as a means of gaining favour with his bishop. On Bourne see E. H. Adamson, 'Henry Bourne the Historian of Newcastle', *Archaeologia Aeliana*, 11 (1885), pp. 147–53, and Richard Welford, *Men of Mark 'twixt Tyne and Tweed*, 3 vols (London and Newcastle, 1895), i, pp. 353–57.
85. Peter Burke, *Popular Culture in Early Modern Europe* (London, 1978), pp. 1–25;

R. Bushaway, *By Rite: Custom, Ceremony and Community in England, 1700–1880* (London, 1982), pp. 1–20, 281.

86. John Brand, *Observations on Popular Antiquities* (Newcastle, 1777), p. 19.
87. Society of Antiquaries Minute Books, viii (typescript), p. 58, paper from William Stukeley on druidical customs, 28 April 1757; British Library, Stowe MS 754, fol. 120v, William Stukeley to Charles Lyttelton, 26 October 1749.
88. Richard Gough, *British Topography*, 2 vols (1780), i, p. xxxvii.
89. Collections for this second edition are in Bodleian Library, MS Eng. Misc. e. 242. Further editions were prepared in 1841 and 1870.
90. Joseph Strutt also contributed to this genre with substantial sections of *Horda Angel-Cynnan* devoted to 'sports and pastimes' and with *Glig-Gamena Angel Deod: Or The Sports and Pastimes of the People of England* (London, 1801).
91. Francis Grose, *A Provincial Glossary with a Collection of Local Proverbs and Popular Superstitions* (London, 1787), p. iii. See also Samuel Pegge, *Anecdotes of the English Language, Chiefly Regarding the Local Dialect of London and its Environs*, ed. J. Nichols (London, 1803).
92. Nostalgia was, of course, hardly a new element to antiquarianism. See, for example, Patrick Collinson, 'John Stow and Nostalgic Antiquarianism', in Julia Merritt (ed.), *Imagining Early Modern London: Perceptions and Portrayals of the City from Stow to Strype, 1598–1720* (Cambridge, 2001), pp. 27–51 and Daniel Woolf, *The Social Circulation of the Past: English Historical Culture, 1550–1730* (Oxford, 2003), pp. 56, 58–66.
93. Brand, *Popular Antiquities*, p. vi.
94. See for example William Barrett, *The History and Antiquities of the City of Bristol* (Bristol, 1789), p. 271. 'While the monasteries stood there was no act for their relief, so amply did those hospitable houses succour those in want, whereas in the next reign 39 Eliz no less than eleven bills were brought into parliament for that sole purpose, and how real a burden the poor tax has been since needs not to be mentioned.'
95. Antiquaries with non-juring sympathies such as Thomas Hearne or Abraham de la Pryme had always entertained a more sympathetic view of the monastic era; these views were very much in the minority in the early eighteenth century.
96. Hearne and Byrne, *Antiquities of Great Britain* (1786), nos 22 and 33. Given Hearne's reliance upon others for antiquarian information, the opinions expressed in *Antiquities of Great Britain* should not necessarily be attributed to Hearne himself.
97. Charlton, *History of Whitby*, p. 281.
98. Grose, *Provincial Glossary*, pp. iii, vii. Grose's image appears to be drawn directly from a passage in Bourne where he described how 'Nothing is commoner in *Country Places*, than for a whole Family in a *Winter's Evening*, to sit around the Fire, and tell Stories of Apparitions and Ghosts', except that in Bourne there was no sense of loss (*Antiquitates vulgares*, p. 7).
99. Bodleian Library, MS Eng. Misc. e. 242, fol. 6v.
100. Grose, *Antiquities of England and Wales*, i.

101. Mandler, 'In the Olden Time'; Mitchell, *Picturing the Past.*
102. Ritson was blackballed from membership of the Society of Antiquaries in 1789. Nichols (ed.), *Illustrations of Literature*, vii, p. 500, Michael Lort to Thomas Percy, 14 June 1789: 'Your old friend Ritson met with a repulse lately at our Antiquarian Society, a circumstance which I do not remember to have taken place in my memory.'
103. Joseph Ritson, 'Historical Introduction' to *Select Collection of English Song* (London, 1783). On Ritson see B. H. Bronson, *Joseph Ritson: Scholar at Arms* (Chicago, 1938); Marilyn Butler, 'Popular Antiquarianism', in Iain McCalman (ed.), *An Oxford Companion to the Romantic Age: British Culture, 1776–1832* (Oxford, 1999), pp. 328–38.
104. Joseph Ritson, *Observations on the First Three Volumes of English Poetry in a Familiar Letter to the Author* (London, 1782).
105. Walter Scott, *Minstrelsy of the Scottish Border*, 3 vols (Edinburgh, 1802–3), i, p. c.
106. Joseph Ritson, *Law Tracts. The Office of Constable; The Jurisdiction of the Court-Leet; A Digest of the Proceedings of the Court Leet of the Manor and Liberty of the Savoy* (London, 1794).
107. Blackner, *History of Nottingham*, p. 91 (my italics). On Blackner see J. C. Warren, 'The Life of John Blackner', *Transactions of the Thoroton Society*, 30 (1926), pp. 161–65.
108. William Hutton, *A History of Birmingham* (2nd edn, Birmingham, 1783), p. 29.
109. Martin Dunsford, *Historical Memoirs of the Town and Parish of Tiverton in the County of Devon* (Exeter, 1790), pp. 22, 24, 50, 60, 77. See also Sweet, *The Writing of Urban Histories*, pp. 173–84.
110. See chapter 6, pp. 196–97 above.

Notes to Chapter 10: Achievement

1. Sir Richard Colt Hoare, *The Ancient History of Wiltshire* (London, 1812), p. 7. 'WE SPEAK FROM FACTS NOT THEORY ... I shall describe to you what we have found; what we have seen; in short, I shall tell you a plain unvarnished tale, and draw from it such conclusions as shall appear not only reasonable, but even uncontradictable.'
2. On the emergence of archaeology from eighteenth-century traditions of antiquarianism see Philippa Levine, *The Amateur and the Professional: Antiquarians, Historians and Archaeologists in Victorian England, 1838–1886* (Cambridge, 1986). Levine argues that the terms historian, antiquary and archaeologist could be used to mean roughly the same thing in the early part of the nineteenth century. By the end of the century the words were being used much more specifically: 'historian' and 'archaeologist' denoted the trained professional, whilst the antiquarian was demoted to amateur status. Linda Ebbatson, 'Conditions of the Emergence and Existence of Archaeology in the Nineteenth Century: The Royal Archaeological Institute', unpublished Ph.D.

thesis, University of Durham (1999), p. 138, remarks that '*Antiquarian* was by far the most common synonym for *archaeologist.* In fact the former probably used more often and with less hesitation throughout the period from 1843–1913'.

3. John Horsley, *Britannia Romana: or The Roman Antiquities of Britain in Three Parts* (London, 1732), p. 178.
4. Samuel Lysons, *An Account of the Roman Antiquities Discovered at Woodchester* (London, 1797); Leicester Leicestershire and Rutland Record Office, DE 5463/38, fos 4–7, Sir Thomas Cave's copy of Samuel Carte's MS history of Leicester compiled between 1700 and 1740. On Carte see J. E. Bilson, *Leicester Memoirs* (Leicester, 1924), pp. 131–32.
5. Sharon Turner, *The History of the Anglo Saxons*, 2 vols (London, 1799–1806), i, p. 31, 'It will be more useful to select those few facts which may be gleaned from the writers of antiquity of this subject [the origins of the Saxons] and to state to the reader, rather what he may believe, than what he must reject'. James Douglas, *Nenia Britannica: or A Sepulchral History of Great Britain* (London, 1793), p. v, 'the work has been arranged under such heads, that the reader may frame his own conclusions, without any apprehension of being involved in the confusion of self opinionated theory'.
6. Francis Wise, *A Letter to Dr Mead Concerning Some Antiquities in Berkshire* (Oxford, 1753), p. 5.
7. Charles Clark quoted in the *Guardian*, 10 May 2003, p. 3.
8. See, for example, the exchange in the *Times Literary Supplement*, 13 March 2003.
9. Anon., *The Antiquities of Middlesex* (London, 1705), preface.
10. See most recently Roy Porter, *Enlightenment: Britain and the Creation of the Modern World* (London, 2000), and Jenny Uglow, *The Lunar Men* (London, 2002).

Index